STRATEGIC OPERATIONS MANAGEMENT

This revitalized new edition of *Strategic Operations Management* focuses on the four core themes of operations strategy, a vital topic for any company's objectives: strategy, innovation, services, and supply. Expertly authored by a team of Europe's top scholars in the field, the text is enhanced by the addition of new case examples, graphic images, learning objectives, discussion questions, and suggestions for further reading. In addition, the companion website offers a comprehensive set of web links and videos to augment the learning experience. This truly comprehensive volume underscores the differences between the core theories that underpin operations management.

Students taking MBA, MSc, and MBM classes on operations management, advanced operations management, and strategic operations management will find this textbook fulfils all their requirements whilst advanced undergraduate classes in these areas will also find the book an essential read.

Steve Brown is Professor of Management at the University of Exeter Business School, UK.

John Bessant currently holds the Chair in Innovation and Entrepreneurship at the University of Exeter Business School, UK.

Richard Lamming is Visiting Professor of Supply Chain Management at Manchester Business School, UK.

Companion website

A companion website accompanies this book at www.routledge.com/cw/brown and includes additional resources for both students and lecturers.

STRATEGIC OPERATIONS MANAGEMENT

Third edition

STEVE BROWN, JOHN BESSANT, AND RICHARD LAMMING

Routledge
Taylor & Francis Group

LONDON AND NEW YORK

First edition published in 2000 by Elsevier
Second edition published in 2005 by Elsevier

This edition published in 2013
by Routledge
2 Park Square, Milton Park, Abingdon, Oxon OX14 4RN

Simultaneously published in the USA and Canada
by Routledge
711 Third Avenue, New York, NY10017

Routledge is an imprint of the Taylor & Francis Group, an informa business

British Library Cataloguing in Publication Data
A catalogue record for this book is available from the British Library

Library of Congress Cataloging in Publication Data
Brown, Steve, 1957–.
  Strategic operations management/Steve Brown, John Bessant,
  Richard Lamming. – 3rd edition.
  pages cm
  1. Production management.   2. Strategic planning.   I. Bessant, J. R.
  II. Lamming, Richard.   III. Title.
  TS155.S838 2012
  658.4′012—dc23
  2012021719

ISBN: 978-0-415-58736-5 (hbk)
ISBN: 978-0-415-58737-2 (pbk)
ISBN: 978-0-203-07935-5 (ebk)

Typeset in Minion Pro and Futura
by Florence Production Ltd, Stoodleigh, Devon

Printed and bound by Ashford Colour Press Ltd, Gosport, Hampshire

CONTENTS

CONTENTS

ILLUSTRATIONS

FIGURES

TABLES

PREFACE

Operations management is perhaps the most misunderstood of all functions within a business. Harvard academic, Wickham Skinner, said it perfectly many years ago when he said 'manufacturing (operations) is perceived in the wrong way at the top, managed in the wrong way at the plant level, and taught in the wrong way in business schools.' We think he didn't go far enough because this misunderstanding also extends to how services are managed.

Although the business world has changed dramatically since Skinner made his statement in the 1980s, for those of us who have spent years researching in, consulting for, and teaching about organizations, the same problem persists. This misconception about operations management is one of the key reasons why we decided to write this book. The net result of not understanding the strategic importance of operations seems to be that well intentioned senior-level managers – including vice presidents and CEOs – sometimes make decisions that are almost *designed* to ruin their organizations' capabilities. We suggest that such senior-level managers are charged, among other things, with sourcing, accruing, and developing world-class operations capabilities that other organizations cannot copy – this is one of the very few ways to sustain competitive advantage today. Our view is very simple: organizations in manufacturing or service settings in private and public sectors are judged, ultimately, by what organizations actually do – or don't do – via their operations.

Our aim here is to show the *strategic* importance of operations management in a world that is more competitive and volatile than ever before. Simply put, operations management is about making the best possible use of limited resources and transforming a whole range of inputs into outputs – products and/or services – for customers, clients, and other important stakeholders.

The need to make the best possible use of resources comes at a time when globalization is the norm and operations take place within complex global networks. And it does so in a world where the concept of sustainability has become a core business requirement. We have tried to reflect this in the book, focusing not only on the core tools of operations management but also on these key themes around strategy, globalization, supply, services, innovation, and sustainability.

We have also tried to take a strongly practical perspective, bringing in a wide variety of case studies from around the globe and focusing (both in the book and on the accompanying website) on practical tools and techniques that can aid the strategic operations manager.

We hope that the book will be of help and interest to students and practitioners alike.

AUTHOR BIOGRAPHIES

Steve Brown is Professor of Management within the Business School at the University of Exeter. He joined Exeter in 2004 from the School of Management at University of Bath, where he had led the Operations Management Group. He has been involved in a number of funded research activities. He is a Visiting Professor to Baruch College, City University, New York and is also Visiting Professor at TiasNIMBAS in Holland, as well as Sussex and Southampton Universities in the UK. He is featured in *European Who's Who* publication. He is Editor-in-Chief for the *International Journal of Operations & Production Management*, which is the leading publication on operations management in Europe and in the top three in the world in the subject.

His management experience was gained in both the public and private sectors including large and SME organizations. He is actively involved in consulting in a range of organizations in the manufacturing and service sectors.

He has published numerous articles and is author of the books, *Strategic Manufacturing for Competitive Advantage – Transforming Operations from Shop Floor to Strategy* (1996); *Manufacturing the Future – Strategic Resonance for Enlightened Manufacturing* (2000); *Strategy, Operations and Tactics in Employee Development* (2005) with Juani Swart and Clare Mann; *The Business Marketing Course* (2002) with David Ford, Peter Naude, and Pierre Berthon; and *Operations Management – Policy, Practice and Performance Management* (2001) with Paul Cousins, Kate Blackmon, and Harvey Maylor.

Professor John Bessant, BSc., PhD. currently holds the Chair in Innovation and Entrepreneurship at the University of Exeter Business School. He previously worked at Imperial College, Cranfield, Brighton, and Sussex Universities. In 2003 he was awarded a Senior Fellowship with the Advanced Institute for Management Research and elected a Fellow of the British Academy of Management, and in 2006 became a Fellow of the Sunningdale Institute. Author of 15 books and many articles, he has acted as adviser to various national governments, international bodies including the United Nations, the World Bank and OECD and companies including Lego, Novo Nordisk, Mars, Toyota, UBS and Morgan Stanley.

See www.johnbessant.net for more information.

Richard Lamming has worked in, managed, researched, advised, and taught about purchasing, supplier relationships and supply chain management throughout his working life.

He began his career as an engineering apprentice with Jaguar Cars, Coventry, in 1970. He gained a Bachelors degree with Honours in Production Engineering at the University of Aston and earned his Doctorate at the Science Policy Research Unit (SPRU), University of Sussex, UK. From 1986 to 1990 he was a senior researcher on the International Motor Vehicle Program, based at Massachusetts Institute of Technology (US) and SPRU in the UK. This was the research programme that developed the concept of lean manufacturing. Professor Lamming published principles of lean supply in 1993. In 1990, he was appointed as the UK's first Professor of Purchasing and Supply Management in the School of Management at the University of Bath. He founded the *Centre for Research in Strategic Purchasing and Supply* (CRiSPS), with a personal focus on environmentally sound supply chains, lean supply, and innovation in supply relationships – themes he still pursues.

For eight years he was Director/Dean of two Business/Management schools in the UK (at the Universities of Southampton and Exeter) before returning full-time to his subject as a Visiting Professor at Manchester Business School in the UK. He now teaches MBA/master classes, presents keynotes around the world, and conducts research and publishing with a wide network of academics and practitioners.

SETTING THE SCENE

CHAPTER 1

INTRODUCTION TO OPERATIONS MANAGEMENT

LEARNING OBJECTIVES

The purpose of this chapter is to introduce you to the basic framework, scope, and management of activities involved in strategic operations management and to help you to:

- Understand some of the complexities in managing modern-day operations.
- Appreciate the strategic importance of operations management.

INTRODUCTION

In this chapter we will discuss some of the previous misconceptions that need to be corrected if an organization is to able to compete by using its operation's capabilities, and we look at the importance of linking both manufacturing and services together in order to provide the *total provision* or *offer*, of goods and services to the end customer.

In Chapter 2, we will develop some of these basics into the wider, *strategic* role and importance of operations management. One of the problems that organizations often have is in *not* seeing the *strategic* importance of their operations management capabilities. We will discuss why this is a problem and develop insights into the *strategic* role and importance of operations management.

THE WORLD OF OPERATIONS

We may not always be aware of this but operations take place around us, in various forms, all the time. Operations take place when we have a meal in a restaurant; when we have a 'service experience' – for example, when we are patients involved in a whole range of health care provisions; when we attend school and university; and when we see products being assembled. So, operations aren't just about production lines and high-value manufacturing. Operations take place in all kinds of settings – in manufacturing and services, and in the private and public sectors. Operations management is vitally important to any organization because, ultimately:

> **An organization is judged by how its operations perform and not what the organization says it is going to do!**

As customers we pay a great deal of attention to the capabilities of operations that organizations provide – or sometimes do not provide. As we shall see in Chapter 11, where we focus specifically on service operations, once we form an opinion of how an organization has performed its operations it is often difficult to change that opinion. So, managing operations is important – but what is operations management?

DEVELOPING A DEFINITION OF OPERATIONS MANAGEMENT

We offer the following as the basic definition of operations management:

> **Operations management is concerned with those activities that enable an organization (and not just one part of it) to transform a range of basic inputs (materials, energy, customers' requirements, information, skills, finance, etc.) into outputs for the end customer.**

We will see that operations is not really about a limited, specific function; rather, it is a company-wide and inter-firm activity embracing a number of different areas and utilizing these in order to satisfy customers and other important stakeholders. This is important because we must always bear in mind that operations do not take place in one, specifically confined, area of the organization. Rather, various forms of operations will take place simultaneously *across* the organization.

For example, in a manufacturing plant we might assume that operations take place merely at the point of production or assembly – but this limits what is actually taking place. In reality, a range of operations will have taken place, or will be taking place, in addition to the actual manufacture of the product. These operations include inventory management; supply and logistics; capacity and scheduling; quality control; management of process technology; managing human resources by ensuring that the right skills base is in place and is developed; as well as a range of operations related to information processing and office administration.

Similarly, in services the obvious point where we may think operations takes place is in the direct contact and interaction between the service provider and the recipient of the service. This point of contact is sometimes called the 'moment of truth'. However, behind the scenes (in services this is often called 'back office' operations) there will be a number of operations that would have needed to be put in place prior to this point of contact.

The organization uses different kinds of inputs: the transformational inputs (such as plant, buildings, machinery, and equipment), as well as less tangible but important inputs (such as learning, tacit knowledge, and experience) and transforms these into outputs.

A basic, organization-specific model of operations is shown in Figure 1.1.

As Hill (2004) explains:

> The operations task . . . concerns the transformation process that involves taking inputs and converting them into outputs together with the various support functions closely associated with this basic task
>
> (p. 5)

This basic model, which appears in similar forms in many management texts, can be expanded to identify main activities within operations as shown in Figure 1.2.

Although models like these are often used, we suggest that operations management in the modern era is more complex than this. The major issue is that operations management is not only an organization-wide issue, but also includes activities *across organizations*. Obviously, an important part of the transformation process will include purchasing goods and services from other organizations.

Such transformation processes can be applied to three main categories: materials, customers, and information. Material processing operations are typically associated with manufacturing; customer-processing operations with some sectors of the service industry; and information processing operations with other service sectors. In practice, most businesses rely on a combination of materials, customer, and information processing. In a factory, processing materials is obvious and can be easily observed. These transformations, (i.e. of parts into finished products) are not so obvious in many service operations. For example, banks, hospitals, social services, and universities transform inputs into outputs, and thus all carry out operations management. There may well be differing views as to what the outputs

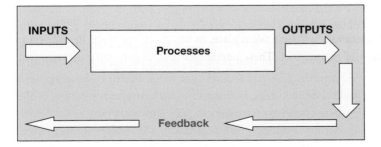

Figure 1.1 The basic operations system

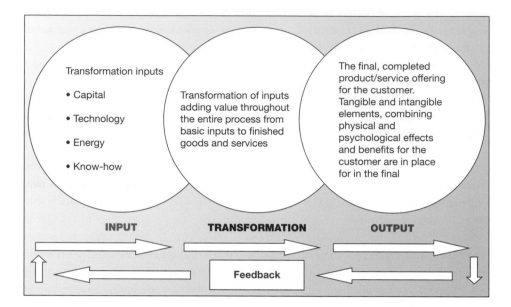

Figure 1.2 Factors within the input/output model of operations

are – and there may be several that are provided at the same time. For example, a university has a number of inputs (including staff expertise and experience, funding from the government, funding from students themselves or their sponsors, allocation of time, etc.) and these are then transformed by a number of operations (time spent in the classroom, scheduling students for particular courses, etc.) in order to provide outputs. The immediate output would be 'successful students' – those who have gained their intended qualifications. However, there would also be a number of, perhaps harder to identify, beneficiaries or recipients of these outputs – including potential employers and society in general.

Hill's (2004) definition of the task of operations management, which we cited above, is useful because it indicates the important link that operational activities have with a wider, organizational base. As we indicated earlier, it is important to view operations as a core organization-wide activity rather than the prerogative of one department only. It also demonstrates that operations management can be applied to a very wide range of human economic activity. There are significant sectors of an economy, both in terms of numbers employed and their contribution to gross national product, which engage in transformational processes that are more or less completely ignored in many operations management texts. These include tourism (tour operating, visitor attractions, and so on), the construction industry, medicine, the arts (theatres, cinemas, galleries), utilities (gas, water, electricity, sewerage) and the armed services. We shall, therefore, strive in this text to include as many sectors of the economy as possible, to illustrate operations management principles and practice.

In the modern era of operations management, organizations no longer see themselves as a stand-alone element in the above diagrams – the 'processes' – but will, instead see themselves as part of a wider, extended enterprise as shown on Figure 1.3. Here, there is a network of collaborative partners all of whom link together to form an extended enterprise within an industry. So the operations management model for current and future operations is no longer limited to an organization-specific arena. This means that the organization has to be willing to look outside of itself and to form strategic relationships with what were formerly viewed as competitive organizations.

The application of this model is further developed in both Chapter 3 on *supply management*, where the organization has to deal with collaborative (and not so collaborative) relationships with other organizations, and Chapter 4 on *innovation* (where collaboration has become increasingly important).

In the past, organizations tended to favour owning all activities within the supply chain from basic materials and inputs through to the end customer. In the relatively 'cash-rich' days of the 1970s, for example, there was a great deal of vertical integration taking place within large US and European corporations, whereby large manufacturing organizations sought to gain control and drive down costs by owning the supply chain. In service organizations too, there was a tendency for large companies to want to own the supply chain. This was evident in the UK, for example, when banks decided to buy forward into estate agencies in the housing market. As we shall see in Chapter 7, on *managing the transformation process*, the problem with this movement within complex supply chains and networks, is that organizations in both manufacturing and service operations will often be pulled in too many different and conflicting business directions. The chief difficulty for organizations that are intent on pursuing a vertical integration strategy, is that the organization moves into areas in which it

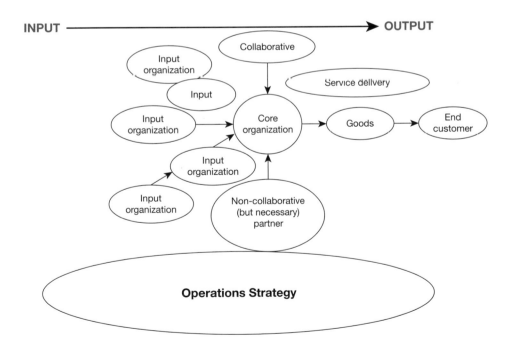

Figure 1.3 The operations infrastructure from basic inputs to end customer

may have little or no expertise. Once we realize that operations is no longer an organization-specific affair but is, instead, part of an extended supply chain involving collaboration with both vertical and horizontal partnerships, the strategic importance of operations begins to come into focus.

We have stated that operations management is important. Let's examine an example of how important operations management really can be, by looking at the following case on British Petroleum (BP).

CASE: BIG OIL TURNS ITS BACK ON BP

In an industry in which companies rarely criticize each other publicly, the Gulf disaster has touched off some unusual infighting. And beleaguered *BP* is the punching bag. Ever since the oil rig explosion in the Gulf, which has cost *BP* $3.5 billion and counting, rivals have been distancing themselves from the British oil giant. The latest flap: Two of *BP's* business partners in the stricken well, Anadarko Petroleum, based in The Woodlands, Tex., and MOEX Offshore, a unit of Japanese energy concern Mitsui Oil Exploration, have refused to help pay for cleanup costs. *BP* has asked Anadarko, which has a 25 percent stake in the well, to pay $272 million. Mitsui, a 10 percent owner in the well, has been asked to contribute $111 million.

On June 18, Anadarko Chief Executive Officer James T. Hackett caused a stir in a statement in which he said: 'The mounting evidence demonstrates that this tragedy was preventable and the direct result of *BP's* reckless decisions and actions.' Mitsui hasn't commented. *BP* thinks both Anadarko and Mitsui should pay their share. Both companies approved of 'certain key decisions relating to the well,' a *BP* spokesman said on July 13.

Another source of tension involves the future direction of offshore drilling regulations. The *BP* spill has fouled not only the waters and beaches of the Gulf but also one of the energy companies' most lucrative and fast-growing sources of oil and gas. After the Apr. 20 accident that triggered the spill and killed 11 people, the U.S. government halted drilling in water deeper than 500 feet, creating a huge hurdle for energy companies.

As a result, ExxonMobil and Royal Dutch Shell are now trying to persuade politicians and regulators that their practices are different from *BP's* – and that companies that operate safely should be allowed to keep drilling. ExxonMobil CEO Rex W. Tillerson said during congressional hearings on June 15: 'When you properly design wells . . . and focus on safe operations and risk management, tragic incidents like the one in the Gulf of Mexico today should not occur.'

Back in May, in a letter to the Minerals Management Service, which regulates drilling, Shell Oil U.S. President Marvin E. Odum listed a series of the company's drilling practices that differ from what has been reported about *BP's* well. Odum contended that around the world Shell uses safer well designs than the one that blew out on *BP* and incorporates extensive redundancy into its safety features, which should reduce the chances of a similar accident.

The American Energy Alliance, a Washington-based lobbying group financed by the energy industry, has launched a website called Save U.S. Energy Jobs, which offers interactive graphics illustrating the gaps between *BP* and other oil company industry practices. The AEA also calls the drilling moratorium 'The Second Gulf Disaster' because of its impact on jobs and U.S. energy security. 'We shouldn't lump the entire industry together,' says the group's president, Thomas J. Pyle.

More than a dozen oil services companies made a similar argument before a federal appeals court on July 9. The companies claim the blanket suspension fails to distinguish between companies that adhere to modern safety practices and *BP*. 'The industry leader is being treated the same way as the industry laggard,' says John Cooney, an attorney for Hornbeck Offshore Services.

The American public seems to be buying the industry line. Three-quarters of those surveyed in a Bloomberg National Poll published July 15 say that the spill was 'a freak accident' that shouldn't shut down deepwater drilling. 'People say *BP* must pay, but there's no sense of impending doom,' says J. Ann Selzer, president of pollster Selzer & Co.

Outraged as they may be with *BP*, rivals so far have done little to unwind the business partnerships that bind the industry. Because drilling and developing oil and gas fields costs billions, each project tends to be taken on by consortia rather than single companies. ExxonMobil, for instance, remains *BP's* partner in Thunder Horse, the largest producing platform in the Gulf of Mexico. Even Anadarko is committed to working with *BP* in Brazil, when *BP* completes the acquisition from Devon Energy of Brazilian properties in which Anadarko is a partner. Whatever the differences, it's still mostly business as usual.

Business Week, 19 July 2010, pp. 22–4

This case raises a number of important issues for operations management including all of the following key areas:

- *Ethical issues*: not surprisingly, when the disaster took place and oil began to spill into the sea, ethical issues became the real focus of media attention. We all watched in horror as oil poured out over vast areas of the sea, taking its toll on wildlife as well as on humans. Many innocent people lost their livelihoods through no fault of their own. Ethical factors have become increasingly important in operations management and we deal with this subject in Chapter 5.

- *Quality*: quality failure was clearly a problem here and quality is a core feature of any operations system. Many of us take quality for granted and assume that, somehow, it will automatically be in place. This case shows that quality demands an ongoing and relentless pursuit of improvements in many forms. Its failure can have dire and catastrophic consequences for communities as well as upon the collapse of large organizations. We will discuss the strategic importance of quality in Chapter 8.

- *Buyer–supplier relationships*: the problem of buyer–supplier relationships was clearly evident here with various stakeholders playing a 'blame game' for the responsibility for this disaster. As we shall see in Chapter 3, selecting, developing, and fully partnering with world-class suppliers becomes an essential and integral part of world-class practice in operations.

- *Project management*: building an oil platform comes under the general heading of project management. Many aspects of operations are treated as 'projects' with specific start and end dates, managed by the completion of various phases of programmed activities over planned time periods. We will develop the discussion on project management in Chapter 7 on the *transformation process*.

- *Capacity management*: in order for the development of the oil platform to have taken place, there would have been a great deal of analysis together with assurances over potential oil capacity. Geological surveys would have been undertaken and various feasibility exercises would have been in place to discuss the number of barrels of oil that could be produced on a daily basis. Typically, oil producers speak in terms of thousands of barrels of oil capacity per day.

All of the above factors in the BP case show that operations management includes important areas of responsibility and we need to explore these areas further.

KEY AREAS OF RESPONSIBILITY FOR OPERATIONS MANAGERS

There are many roles that fall under the responsibility of operations managers, as shown below.

AN INDICATION OF RESPONSIBILITIES FOR OPERATIONS MANAGERS

- Management of value;
- Capacity management;
- Location decisions – the range and locations of facilities;
- Process management – technology investment to support process and product developments;
- Managing technology;
- Human resources management;
- Formation of strategic buyer–supplier relationships as part of the organization's 'extended enterprise'; and
- The rate of new product or service introduction.

We shall deal with each of these in turn (the rate of new product or service introduction is discussed in depth in Chapter 4).

Management of value

Value added, in the most simplistic terms, means that the income or benefit derived from performing a particular operation is greater than the cost of doing so. All organizations, whether they are in the private or public sector, or in manufacturing or services, have operations within them. Increasingly, value-adding operations are important to both private and public sectors. In the 'credit crunch' era of the late 2000s many questions were being asked about real value-added activities in banking and other financial services. Value added becomes increasingly important in times of recession where the need to make the very best use of limited resources becomes paramount.

In private sectors, many industries and markets are so competitive that the organization cannot afford to be involved in non-value-adding activities. This is not simply down to costs but is also concerned with problems, which non-value-added activities might incur, such as slow delivery speed, poor delivery reliability, and (lack of) flexibility.

Traditionally, operations management has been very concerned with managing costs, but this important element of responsibility has changed recently to the management of value. Back in 1980, Harvard Professor Michael Porter suggested that organizations needed, ideally, to compete *either* on low cost *or* to provide differentiated products in order to be profitable and to avoid being 'stuck in the middle'. However, this is now seen as overly simplistic because an organization competing in today's volatile market requirements may have to offer both low-cost and differentiated features, together with ongoing innovation and rapid response and delivery times, merely to be able to compete at all in markets.

The implications for the operations manager are clear. In value-conscious markets, where margins are usually very slim – for example, in fast-food and other high-volume sectors – costs and prices must be carefully controlled. The ability to do so does not necessarily mean an automatic reduction in workforce numbers and other drastic measures. Instead, accumulated know-how, experience, appropriate use of technology, and better process quality through continuous improvement or *kaizen* will enable the organization to reduce costs (*kaizen* is discussed in Chapter 8). Such capabilities need to be developed and guarded over time (Barney 1991; Teece *et al.*, 1997).

Alternatively, where the organization is offering differentiated products then, according to Porter (1980), it may charge premium prices. This, though, does not mean that costs are ignored. In premium price market segments, the task for the operations manager is, amongst other things, to enable large margins to be obtained between premium price and actual costs. Such margins can be achieved by eliminating waste in all forms – the essence of *lean thinking* (Womack and Jones, 2003). As a result, a more holistic view of operations management is required, as Crainer (1998) suggests:

Companies must add value throughout every single process they are involved in and then translate this into better value for customers.

Capacity management

We touched on capacity in the BP case above, and capacity is another major factor for operations managers. Managing capacity is common to both manufacturing and service elements in ensuring the total provision of the right volume of goods and services to end customers. The operations manager needs to know the overall, company-wide capacity, as well as department-specific capacity inputs and outputs in-house. This will enable the operations manager to schedule without creating overload or 'bottlenecks' in certain areas (capacity is discussed in Chapter 10).

Location decisions

Location is an important consideration for operations managers and is linked to strategic capacity decisions – as well as supply management, which is explored in Chapter 3. Organizations will face important choices concerning location and this applies where there is a wish to expand in outlets both within the country of origin and also where expansion, via international/global efforts, is concerned. The Japanese car transplants, especially in the UK and North America, are an important example of such capacity expansion via strategic location decisions. A number of American service giants – including McDonalds – have been very aggressive in their growth strategies. These strategies have been realized by determining strategic locations for the business.

Process management

Managing processes that result in products or services is a major concern for operations managers. The operations manager has to understand the nature, specification, and assembly/delivery of the product or service. Over-design can cause major problems for organizations intending to innovate new products and services and will take up unnecessary time and capacity. As we shall see in Chapter 4, there has been an increased awareness within organizations to include operations managers in the early stages of new product development in both manufacturing and service sectors. For the operations manager, the range of products or services on offer has to be managed in order to satisfy the mix of volume and variety for customers. This is achieved by having appropriate process technology in place, which can deal with customer requirements of volume and variety.

Managing technology

Included in the tasks for operations managers is that of searching for, and purchasing, appropriate equipment. Investing and reinvesting in the appropriate equipment or technology, and maintaining it, are crucial decisions for operations managers. The temptation for some managers is *not* to invest, believing that such a risk is not necessary since the current machinery 'can cope' and 'has done well for us in the past'. In fact, this may be the correct decision if the useful life of the technology is shorter than the period over which the organization would need to recoup the investment – a situation that would hardly have seemed likely a decade ago. With product lives shortening in many product markets, the period between purchasing equipment and that equipment being made obsolete by newer technology is never certain. However, the approach of not investing could hardly be called strategic and may actually be shortsighted – often quickly depriving the organization of being able to compete in the long term against other organizations that have made more appropriate decisions. It is a question of maintaining secure access to the necessary technology. Being left with out-of-date technology, which has yet to be paid for, however, is a major liability for an organization and may even cause insolvency.

Human resources management

Human resources management is often a major concern for operations managers. Human resources and human know-how and capabilities are central to any resource-based view of strategy (Terziovski, 2010). Also, as the need for adherence to narrowly defined functional arrangements declines, managing human resources is no longer the prerogative of one department (Personnel, Human Resources, Management Development, and so on) but is, rather, an integral feature of any would-be world-class operations company.

Developing human resources is clearly evident in the following:

> **'Survival isn't just a matter of smart machines. Workers have to get smarter as well, and show a willingness to learn new technologies', says John A. McFarland, CEO of Baldor Electric Co., the largest maker of industrial electric motors in the U.S. A versatile corps of workers has helped Baldor ride out the manufacturing recession without a layoff.**
> 'The flexible factory', *Business Week*, 5 May 2003

It is important to note how Baldor's approach to managing human resources has had strategic benefits allowing them to compete successfully in spite of the recession in which the industry found itself. Human resources impact a number of areas of interest to the operations manager, including ideas for innovation (Chapter 4), quality improvements (Chapter 8), and process developments (Chapter 7) – all of which are dependent upon human resource know-how and inventiveness. Indeed, management of the supply chain (Chapter 3) is also very dependent upon the ability to form strategic partnerships throughout the supply chain, and this comes from human resource capability and not from technology or equipment.

The problem of ingrained cultures, unable to change because Human Resources have not been well managed is exemplified in the following:

> **On Jan. 21, 1988, a General Motors executive named Elmer Johnson wrote a brave and prophetic memo. Its main point was contained in this sentence: 'We have vastly underestimated how deeply ingrained are the organizational and cultural rigidities that hamper our ability to execute.'**
> *Wall Street Journal*, 'The Quagmire Ahead', 1 June 2009

A big problem for operations managers is that, often, senior level strategic decision makers will quickly downsize the workforce or divest areas of the enterprise that are closely linked to operations. This is sometimes done to satisfy short-term financial criteria, and as we shall see in the next chapter, such short-termism can be fatal when trying to develop world-class operations capabilities over time. The ease with which firms downsize the workforce – and, sometimes, the stupidity of such actions – was featured in Fortune:

> **Hay's new research shows that champion companies focus particularly on making sure employees feel engaged by their work. These firms are much more likely to have specified what employee engagement means, to measure it, to hold line managers . . . accountable for it, and to connect it to business objectives such as productivity, say, or efficiency. Companies that do those things are not only more admired but also much more profitable than others. . . . So why are many managers still clueless? Often they believe that Wall Street will massacre their stock if they don't thin the herd. Yet research by . . . the Bain consulting firm shows that this simply isn't true. Companies that whack employees as a means of cutting costs (rather than for strategic reasons such as a merger integration) lose more shareholder value over the course of the following year than companies that keep good workers. . . . Which brings us to a deeper lesson from the Most Admired: The industry leaders didn't launch their enlightened human capital philosophy when the recession hit; they'd followed it for years. Once a recession starts, it's too late. Champions know what their most valuable asset really is, and they give it the investment it deserves – through good times and bad.**
>
> *Fortune*, 22 March 2010, p. 82

Integration and buyer–supplier relationships

This brings us to the questions regarding the extent to which an organization owns and controls all the resources and operations needed to make the product or deliver the service. In some service organizations, affiliation through corporate franchise agreements with large-scale operators is a key element of their operational strategy. Affiliations such as franchising, sub-franchising, and contracting, are common in service organizations and are becoming more common in manufacturing. Firms in both sectors have tended to extend control over resources through forward, backward or horizontal integration (mergers and acquisitions). For example, for many years, firms in the brewing industry have forward integrated into distribution and retailing through licensed premises or pubs.

SUMMARIZING THE IMPORTANCE OF OPERATIONS

It becomes clear, therefore, that operations management is very wide in terms of the scope of responsibilities and will draw upon a range of functions within the organization and not be limited to a specific department. Understanding what operations management really is, is vital if the organization is to compete effectively. As we have noted, operations take place throughout the entire supply network in order to transform and complete the provision of goods and services to end customers. This means that operations managers have responsibilities both within their own organizations and in the relationship with suppliers and distributors within the supply chain. The extent to which operations managers become involved in activities in the entire supply chain depends on a number of factors including:

- *The nature of the industry*: in some industries (for example, automobiles, and market sectors within high-tech industries) two-way collaboration involving operations managers between two or more organizations is now commonplace. This is seen as a means to develop best practice and is often a central feature of innovation.

- *The reputation of the organization*: for example, because of its immense expertise, Toyota has often been involved in working with suppliers in developing skills and know-how within the supplier's plant. This enables know-how and expertise to become shared.

- *The size of the organization*: as we shall see in Chapter 3, in spite of the trend toward collaboration, some organizations will exercise their 'muscle' and influence on the supplying or distribution organization. The sheer size enables them to do so – this was a tactic used by General Motors in the early 1990s and, as we shall discover, this approach does not necessarily achieve long-term rewards for the larger organization.

The range of responsibilities that operations managers have within the plant or service itself is both profoundly important and wide in scope. Managing assets is an integral part of the operations manager's role. Hill (2004) observes that up to of 70 per cent of assets may fall under the responsibility of operations management. The greatest single cost in the transformation process within a manufacturing environment is usually in materials management. However, as we shall see in Chapters 3 and 9, this still remains a problem for many organizations, for two reasons. First, materials management becomes relegated to a tactical-clerical buying function, and is not seen in the strategic framework that it needs. Second, the organization will need to form excellent relationships with suppliers and such relationships are still difficult for organizations that are unable to form these strategic links.

OPERATIONS MANAGEMENT AND ADDED VALUE

Porter's (1985) value-chain model is a useful means of tracking the flow of movement from inputs to outputs as shown in Figure 1.4.

In explaining the value chain model, Porter (1985) states that:

Value is the amount buyers are willing to pay for what an organization provides them . . . creating value for buyers that exceeds the cost of doing so is the goal of any generic strategy. Value, instead of cost, must be used in analyzing competitive position.

(p. 38)

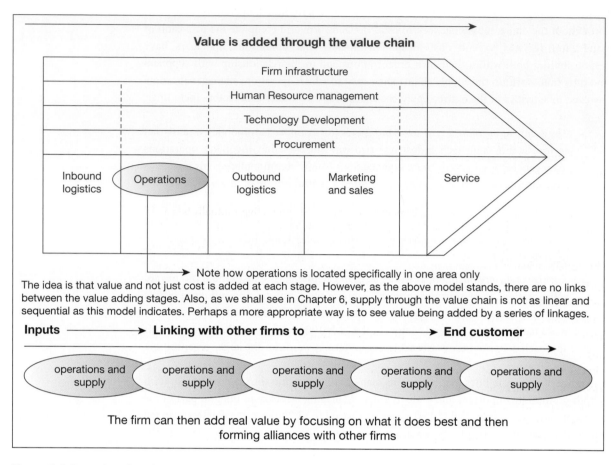

The idea is that value and not just cost is added at each stage. However, as the above model stands, there are no links between the value adding stages. Also, as we shall see in Chapter 6, supply through the value chain is not as linear and sequential as this model indicates. Perhaps a more appropriate way is to see value being added by a series of linkages.

The firm can then add real value by focusing on what it does best and then forming alliances with other firms

Figure 1.4 Porter's value chain.
Brown (1996)

As we shall see in the next chapter, part of the strategic task for the organization is to analyze those activities, which it does best, and to focus on these. But operations managers have to be careful: what operations excel in may not be what customers and markets require. For example, reducing costs may be a corporate goal but this may prove futile if the market requirements demand customization, delivery speed, innovation, and a range of other competitive factors instead. This means that senior-level managers, dealing with strategic issues, need first to understand and then to focus on the organization's core strengths and to use these capabilities to provide added value for the organization's customers. In doing so, the organization must then become dependent upon strategic partnerships with other organizations in order to provide value in those areas and activities that it has now sub-contracted.

The extent to which the organization will decide to be involved in all areas of this transformation process is a critical issue for organizations. As we shall see in the next chapter, operations management is very much linked to key strategic business decisions below.

THE KEY STRATEGIC DECISIONS WITHIN OPERATIONS MANAGEMENT

- What business is the firm really in?
- What does the firm do best (and so what)?
- Should it outsource some of its activities, and if so why, where, and how?
- How can opportunities become quickly exploited and how can the firm's capabilities help to ward off external threats from new and existing players?

We need to view operations management as part of a fluid, interactive, mutually beneficial series of relationships between raw materials and the end customer.

Many organizations encapsulate what business they are in through a mission statement. This usually states where a firm expects to be at some time in the future. However, from an operations perspective, it may be more useful to adopt what has been called the 'service concept' statement. This articulates both customers' perceptions of what the firm has to offer, and the firm's own view of its business proposition. It therefore incorporates more than a typical mission statement, providing all stakeholders in the business – notably customers, shareholders, and employees – with a mental map of what the firm offers, stated in terms of benefits and outcomes. Although called a 'service concept', it can apply equally to manufacturing. For example, Daewoo adopted an integrated approach to making and selling cars in the UK, through its own chain of salesrooms, with a sales force paid salaries rather than on commission.

Part of the problem facing the operations manager, therefore, has been determining where operations management really 'lines up' in the wider aspects of the organization in which they are operating. This is where strategy comes into play. Strategy is about 'how' the organization will conduct business.

Thus, not only is the organization concerned with transferring goods and services to end customers, it has to do so in a value-adding way.

OPERATIONS AND OUTSOURCING

A key decision facing senior-level managers is to determine how much of the organization's operations should be outsourced to other firms. This has become increasingly important in an era where, as we shall see, some firms have focused on services and outsourced all manufacturing operations. The issue with this is twofold:

- Once operations activities have been outsourced (and often divested) it is almost impossible to claim them back – often they are gone forever.
- The outsourcing firm has to be careful that it does not create competition by outsourcing to suppliers who then copy products and services and sell these themselves.

- However, outsourcing can have benefits but the outsourcing firm has to ensure that it can develop world-class buyer–supplier relations. An example of the codependence needed in outsourcing operations is exemplified in the following example.

> The 787, a midrange cruiser, is packed with technological firsts. . . . Equally remarkable is the way in which Boeing has structured its manufacturing process, bestowing unprecedented opportunities on small suppliers and ushering in a new era 'for the aerospace industry. Boeing says 70 per cent of the 787 has been outsourced; rival Airbus is relying on subcontractors for about 50 per cent of its A350 plane, now in development.
>
> 'How many small businesses does it take to build a jet?',
> *Fortune*, July/August 2007, 17(6), pp. 42–5

However, as we mentioned above, there are risks with outsourcing.

> The downside of getting the balance wrong, however, can be steep. Start with the danger of fostering new competitors. Motorola hired Taiwan's BenQ Corp. to design and manufacture millions of mobile phones. But then BenQ began selling phones last year in the prized China market under its own brand. That prompted Motorola to pull its contract. Another risk is that brand-name companies will lose the incentive to keep investing in new technology. 'It is a slippery slope,' says Boston Consulting Group Senior Vice-President Jim Andrew. 'If the innovation starts residing in the suppliers, you could incrementalize yourself to the point where there isn't much left.'
>
> 'Outsourcing innovation', *Business Week*, 21
> March 2005, p. 34

THE MANUFACTURING/SERVICE 'DIVIDE'

Throughout this text, one of our core messages is that manufacturing and service operations often combine to provide a complete offer to customers and other key stakeholders for the organization. We are not advocating that the tasks of managing service and manufacturing operations are identical. Clearly, there are differences. But both manufacturing and services are vital and, in contrast to the old-fashioned view of manufacturing *versus* services, it is clear that both depend on each other in modern economies. For example, if we look at the *Fortune* 500 (US firms), and the *Fortune* Global 500, it is important to bear in mind that the massive retail outlets (a service setting) are very dependent upon manufactured goods. But manufactured goods in turn depend on excellent service in retail outlets. This may seem obvious but often people will classify retail as a service industry, as if, somehow, it is an entity that is entirely independent from manufacturing.

The 60 largest global companies in 2011 listed in the *Fortune* 500 in terms of revenues are listed in Table 1.1.

Table 1.1 The Global 500 in 2011

Rank	Company	Revenues ($ millions)	Profits ($ millions)
1	Wal-Mart Stores	421,849	16,389
2	Royal Dutch Shell	378,152	20,127
3	Exxon Mobil	354,674	30,460
4	BP	308,928	–3,719
5	Sinopec Group	273,422	7,629
6	China National Petroleum	240,192	14,367
7	State Grid	226,294	4,556
8	Toyota Motor	221,760	4,766
9	Japan Post Holdings	203,958	4,891
10	Chevron	196,337	19,024
11	Total	186,055	14,001
12	ConocoPhillips	184,966	11,358
13	Volkswagen	168,041	9,053
14	AXA	162,236	3,641
15	Fannie Mae	153,825	–14,014
16	General Electric	151,628	11,644
17	ING Group	147,052	3,678
18	Glencore International	144,978	1,291
19	Berkshire Hathaway	136,185	12,967
20	General Motors	135,592	6,172
21	Bank of America Corp.	134,194	–2,238
22	Samsung Electronics	133,781	13,669
23	ENI	131,756	8,368
24	Daimler	129,481	5,957
25	Ford Motor	128,954	6,561
26	BNP Paribas	128,726	10,388
27	Allianz	127,379	6,693
28	Hewlett-Packard	126,033	8,761
29	E.ON	125,064	7,752
30	AT&T	124,629	19,864

continued . . .

Table 1.1 . . . *continued*

Rank	Company	Revenues ($ millions)	Profits ($ millions)
31	Nippon Telegraph & Telephone	120,316	5,950
32	Carrefour	120,297	574
33	Assicurazioni Generali	120,234	2,254
34	Petrobras	120,052	19,184
35	Gazprom	118,657	31,895
36	J.P. Morgan Chase & Co.	115,475	17,370
37	McKesson	112,084	1,202
38	GDF Suez	111,888	6,114
39	Citigroup	111,055	10,602
40	Hitachi	108,766	2,789
41	Verizon Communications	106,565	2,549
42	Nestlé	105,267	32,843
43	Crédit Agricole	105,003	1,673
44	American International Group	104,417	7,786
45	Honda Motor	104,342	6,236
46	HSBC Holdings	102,680	13,159
47	Siemens	102,657	5,268
48	Nissan Motor	102,430	3,727
49	Pemex	101,506	−3,758
50	Panasonic	101,491	864
51	Banco Santander	100,350	10,835
52	International Business Machines	99,870	14,833
53	Cardinal Health	98,602	642
54	Freddie Mac	98,368	−14,025
55	Hyundai Motor	97,408	4,708
56	Enel	97,185	5,814
57	CVS Caremark	96,413	3,427
58	JX Holdings	95,964	3,640
59	Lloyds Banking Group	95,682	−4,103
60	Hon Hai Precision Industry	95,191	2,450

Fortune (2011)

As can be seen from the above list there is a vast range of sectors and industries here and, when looking at the complete 500 listings, this broad spectrum of manufacturing and services in various forms becomes wider. The distinction between manufacturing and services is not quite as profound as often stated, for a number of reasons.

First, manufacturing and service operations often link together in providing a *total customer offering* within the supply chain. For example, the automobile industry is often seen as a purely manufacturing concern and much research has been undertaken on Japanese versus Western approaches to manufacturing (for example see Womack *et al.*, 1990; and Lamming, 1993). For the automotive customer, however, the service end of the overall supply chain may be, at key points of the transaction, equally important in the decision to purchase. Activities such as arranging finance, offering warranties and guarantees, together with general after-sales service are, often, critical.

In many cases, it does appear that the automobile manufacturers have made great strides in assembling cars but have yet to master leanness in their distribution chains; indeed, this is now the subject of important research and development, as the vehicle assemblers pursue the holy grail of the 'three day car' (i.e. a situation in which the customer can specify any car they want and have it within three days).

In the computer industry the customer is paying not only for the 'tangibles' (the hardware and software) – after-sales service is an important part of the overall offering and the assurance of help-lines for troubleshooting problems is also a key feature in the complete transaction. In that sense, therefore, we should not see operations in terms of manufacturing *versus* services but, rather, as combination of joint efforts throughout the entire supply chain as a means of providing customer satisfaction. Consequently, the issue of quality will depend not only on the performance of a car but also on the service quality provided at the point of sale to the customer. We illustrate this in Figure 1.5.

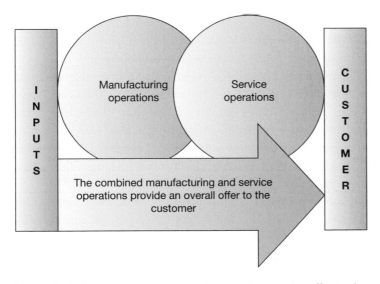

Figure 1.5 The manufacturing/service interface in the offer to the customer

THE EMERGENCE OF SERVITIZATION

What has happened in recent years is that what were formerly labelled 'manufacturing firms' have now taken on an array of service offerings to satisfy customers in order to remain competitive. In particular, there has been the emergence of *servitization* (Baines *et al.*, 2011), which we will now discuss, and return to in greater depth in Chapter 11.

In the last 20 years, many manufacturing firms have examined their offering to their customers and moved beyond their focus on production expertise to add a range of services. There are two main reasons for this. First, many manufacturing firms make little or no profits via their manufactured products alone and so they have to turn to services to provide a profitable offer. Second, customers increasingly buy an overall 'offer', which includes 'solutions' or other bundles of services that go beyond the purchase of the product itself.

Some firms have merged with others to offer servitization, while other manufacturing firms have formed alliances or developed relationships with service providers. There were indications of this some time ago with retailers who, although selling hard goods had, in addition, to provide assurances for customers as part of the purchase experience. Many retailers subcontracted out such services – with varying degrees of success and customer satisfaction.

In manufacturing firms operating in global markets, where much outsourcing and offshoring has taken place, the main driver for such strategies has been to reduce costs. As we shall see in Chapter 2 there are other equally pressing competitive requirements that need to be achieved, which are sometimes ignored by offshoring. Faced with such financial pressures, though, firms are increasingly seeking to become service providers to add value to their product offerings. The term, servitization, first appeared in 1988 in an article by Vandermerwe and Rada.

Neely (2009) analysed data from 10,000 manufacturers in 23 countries to examine the extent to which servitization was in place. He found that 30 per cent offered services in one form or another. About 22 per cent offered design services, 16 per cent systems and solutions, 12 per cent retail and distribution and 12 per cent maintenance and support.

Similarly, we have found many examples of manufacturing firms that now add servitization as part of their offering to customers. For example, DAF Trucks no longer merely manufactures trucks, although this remains its core business. In addition to this, DAF has created tracking devices to ensure 'green' processes are in place with its logistics; DAF has also become involved in training drivers, both within the firm and with other organizations, to help drivers become better at achieving better mileage usage which, again, factors into aspirations that many organizations have to be 'green'.

Similarly Xerox, the photocopier producer, responded to intense global competition from its rivals by offering a range of services including supply, maintenance, configuration, and user support. This transformation took some time to ensure that it could offer such a range of services but Xerox now competes against the likes of Hewlett-Packard, Kodak, and Canon by providing document-management and other consultancy services to a number of different sectors including energy, car producers, public libraries, airlines, and large retailers. Likewise IBM no longer thinks of itself as a computer manufacturer but as a firm providing 'business solutions'.

Another example of a manufacturer-turned-service-provider is UK aerospace group Rolls-Royce. Its sensor technology (a manufactured product) now ties in closely with service provisions to diagnose problems remotely long before the systems pose problems, thus offering a better service to airlines in terms of preventative maintenance, which goes to the whole issue of customer quality. Since 2006, over 55 per cent of Rolls-Royce's annual revenues have come from a range of services.

SKF of Sweden, the world's number one bearings maker, had excelled in manufacturing for many years. However, although rationalization and automation had dramatically cut costs the remaining thin margins threatened SKF's research and development – an area in which it needed to retain excellence in order to preserve SKF's leading technology and quality. The result of such competitive and financial pressures led to the creation of SKF Bearing Services that emerged not just to offer bearings, but 'trouble-free operations'. Today, SKF offers asset management condition monitoring and other services such as training and logistics, and such services have become an integral part of SKF's business portfolio.

THE 'PROBLEM' WITH MANUFACTURING

The simple reality is that the size and power of many manufacturing firms has declined across industries. For some firms servitization has been embraced because these firms were running out of strategic options and their manufacturing operations had nowhere to go. Although servitization has become increasingly important – and a requirement even for many market segments – wandering into services cannot be used simply to mask poor manufacturing operations. In addition, although we are not suggesting that manufacturing is 'better' than services, we must say that service exports have not managed to plug the gap between manufactured imports and exports in many countries, as is especially evident in the UK and US.

If we look at the automobile industry, for example, some telling information comes to light. We use this industry as a good example because of its importance – Peter Drucker, an eminent academic, rightly described the car industry as the 'Industry of Industries', referring to its immense size as well as its strategic importance for the economic wellbeing of individual countries. Indeed, if the car industry were a country it would be the sixth largest economy. Table 1.2 shows the main car producers in 2010.

As can be seen from Table 1.2, there is a considerable range of countries evident here, all trying to compete in what is already an oversaturated industry (it has been estimated that if all the plants in North America were to close there would still be excess capacity). However, this industrial landscape does not seem to have put off those countries that are listed in Table 1.3.

Clearly, globalization is now a major issue and the US and other Western economies are feeling the repercussions of such intense competition.

Table 1.2 Major car producers

Rank	GROUP	Total	CARS	LCV	HCV	HEAVY BUS
	Total	**60,499,159**	**51,075,480**	**7,817,520**	**1,305,755**	**300,404**
1	TOYOTA	7,234,439	6,148,794	927,206	154,361	4,078
2	G.M.	6,459,053	4,997,824	1,447,625	7,027	6,577
3	VOLKSWAGEN	6,067,208	5,902,583	154,874	7,471	2,280
4	FORD	4,685,394	2,952,026	1,681,151	52,217	
5	HYUNDAI	4,645,776	4,222,532	324,979		98,265
6	PSA	3,042,311	2,769,902	272,409		
7	HONDA	3,012,637	2,984,011	28,626		
8	NISSAN	2,744,562	2,381,260	304,502	58,800	
9	FIAT	2,460,222	1,958,021	397,889	72,291	32,021
10	SUZUKI	2,387,537	2,103,553	283,984		
11	RENAULT	2,296,009	2,044,106	251,903		
12	DAIMLER AG	1,447,953	1,055,169	158,325	183,153	51,306
13	CHANA AUTOMOBILE	1,425,777	1,425,777			
14	B.M.W.	1,258,417	1,258,417			
15	MAZDA	984,520	920,892	62,305	1,323	
16	CHRYSLER	959,070	211,160	744,210	3,700	
17	MITSUBISHI	802,463	715,773	83,319	3,371	
18	BEIJING AUTOMOTVIVE	684,534	684,534			
19	TATA	672,045	376,514	172,487	103,665	19,379
20	DONGFENG MOTOR	663,262	663,262			
21	FAW	650,275	650,275			
22	CHERY	508,567	508,567			
23	FUJI	491,352	440,229	51,123		
24	BYD	427,732	427,732			

#	Manufacturer	Total				
25	SAIC	347,598	347,598			
26	ANHUI JIANGHUAI	336,979	336,979			
27	GEELY	330,275	330,275			
28	ISUZU	316,335		18,839	295,449	2,047
29	BRILLIANCE	314,189	314,489			
30	AVTOVAZ	294,737	294,737			
31	GREAT WALL	226,560	226,650			
32	MAHINDRA	223,065	145,977	77,088		
33	SHANGDONG KAIMA	169,023	169,023			
34	PROTON	152,965	129,741	23,224		
35	CHINA NATIONAL	120,930		120,930		
36	VOLVO	105,873		10,032	85,036	10,805
37	CHONGQING LIFAN	104,434	104,434			
38	FUJIAN	103,171	103,171			
39	KUOZUI	93,303	88,801	2,624		1,878
40	SHANNXI AUTO	79,026		79,026		
41	PORSCHE	75,637	75,637			
42	ZIYANG NANJUN	72,470	72,470			
43	GAZ	69,591	2,161	44,816	12,988	9,626
44	NAVISTAR	65,364			51,544	13,820
45	GUANGZHOU AUTO	62,990	62,990			
46	PACCAR	58,918				58,918
47	CHENZHOU JI'AO	51,008	51,008			
48	QINGLING MOTOR	50,120	50,120			
49	HEBEI ZHONGXING	48,173	48,173			
50	ASHOK LEYLAND	47,694		1,101	28,183	18,410

International Organization of Motor Vehicle Manufacturers (2010)

Table 1.3 Manufacturers of cars by country

Country	Cars	Commercial vehicles	Total	Change (%)
Argentina	380,067	132,857	512,924	−14.1
Australia	188,158	39,125	227,283	−31.0
Austria	56,620	15,714	72,334	−52.2
Belgium	524,595	12,510	537,354	−25.8
Brazil	2,576,628	605,989	3,182,617	−1.0
Canada	822,267	668,365	1,490,632	−28.4
China	10,383,831	3,407,163	13,790,994	48.3
Czech Rep.	967,760	6,809	974,569	3.0
Egypt	60,249	32,090	92,339	−23.0
Finland	10,907	64	10,971	−38.7
France	1,819462	228,196	2,047,658	−20.3
Germany	4,964,523	245,334	5,209,857	−13.8
Hungary	180,500	2,040	182,540	−47.3
India	2,166,238	466,456	2,632,694	12.9
Indonesia	352,172	112,644	464,816	−22.6
Iran	1,359,520	35,901	1,395,421	9.5
Italy	661,100	182,139	843,239	−17.6
Japan	6,862,161	1,072,355	7,934,516	−31.5
Malaysia	447,002	42,267	489,269	−7.8
Mexico	942,876	618,176	1,561,052	−28.0
Netherlands	50,620	25,981	76,601	−42.2
Poland	819,000	65,133	884,133	−7.1
Portugal	101,680	24,335	126,015	−28.1
Romania	279,320	17,178	296,498	20.9
Russia	595,839	126,592	722,431	−59.6
Serbia	8,720	1,355	10,075	−13.4
Slovakia	461,340	0	461,340	−19.9
Slovenia	202,570	10,179	212,749	7.5
South Africa	222,981	150,942	373,923	−33.6
South Korea	3,158,417	354,509	3,512,926	−8.2

continued . . .

Table 1.3 ... *continued*

Country	Cars	Commercial vehicles	Total	Change (%)
Spain	1,812,688	357,390	2,170,078	−14.6
Sweden	128,738	27,600	156,338	−49.3
Taiwan	183,986	42,370	226,356	23.7
Thailand	313,442	685,936	999,378	−28.3
Turkey	510,931	358,674	869,605	−24.2
Ukraine	65,646	3,649	69,295	−83.6
UK	999,460	90,679	1,090,139	−33.9
USA	2,246,470	3,462,382	5,708,852	−34.3
Uzbekistan	110,200	7,700	117,900	−43.3
Supplementary	302,450	110,109	412,559	−22.4
Total	47,952,995	13,761,694	61,714,689	−12.8

International Organization of Motor Vehicle Manufacturers (2010)

> The US remained the world's biggest manufacturing nation by output last year, but is poised to relinquish this slot in 2011 to China – thus ending a 110-year run as the number one country in factory production. . . . Hal Sirkin, head of the global operations practice at Chicago-based Boston Consulting Group, said the US should not despair too much at the likelihood that it would lose the global crown in manufacturing to China. 'If you have a country with four times the population of the US and a tenth of the wages, it is fairly obvious they will pull ahead at some time in productive capabilities.'
>
> *Financial Times,* **20 June 2010**

In the UK manufacturing operations have not fared well in recent years as can be seen in Figure 1.6.

The impact that such declines have had upon manufacturing's contribution to the UK's GDP is evident in Figure 1.6. The perceived wisdom that a loss in manufacturing output is somehow compensated automatically by services is not valid. As we have noted, both sectors depend upon each other and they are not mutually exclusive, but weaknesses in the manufacturing base can have profound repercussions for the economic wealth of nations.

For example, although the US managed to improve its manufacturing base dramatically during the 1990s and now has many plants that can termed *world-class*, the damage to the economy is ongoing because the US still imports more manufactured products than it exports, and the difference is not met by the export of services. Warnings about the problems of neglecting manufacturing operations had been offered by a number of academics over a number of years – as Garvin (1992) describes:

All too often, top managers regard manufacturing as a necessary evil. In their eyes, it adds little to a company's competitive advantage. Manufacturing, after all, merely 'makes stuff'; its primary role is the transformation of parts and materials into finished products. To do so it follows the dictates of other departments.

(p. xiv)

Garvin (1992) argued that the definition of manufacturing has to be seen in a wider context and he quotes the Manufacturing Studies Board publication, *Toward a New Era in U.S. Manufacturing* in which it is stated:

Part of the problem of U.S. manufacturing is that a common definition of it has been too narrow. Manufacturing is not limited to the material transformation performed in the factory. It is a system encompassing design, engineering, purchasing, quality control, marketing, and customer service as well.

(p. xiv)

Former Harvard Professor, Wickham Skinner, whose contribution to our understanding of the role of operations within a strategic context has been seminal, perfectly captured the problem for the US and many European nations years ago when he stated:

Manufacturing is generally perceived in the wrong way at the top, managed in the wrong way at plant level, and taught in the wrong way in the business schools.

(Skinner, 1985, p55)

Index number (2006 = 100) seasonally adjusted

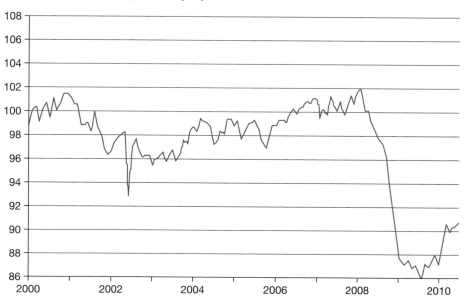

Figure 1.6
Index of manufacturing in the UK, 2000–2010

Office for National Statistics, 17 September 2010

Skinner's assessment is equally true today, and the dire consequence of this has been manifested in the massive decline of the manufacturing bases in many Western countries, notably in the US. This trade deficit – typically brought about by inadequate performance in a range of operations – has had some profound consequences, as *Industry Week* noted:

'We are losing jobs to low-wage nations like China, and when Congress finally wakes up, our manufacturing base will be eroded,' warns Zawacki, who also is chairman of the Precision Metal Association, a trade group of about 1,300 North American companies. Even as what he terms the 'Big Guys' take off for China and other low-wage countries, 'small and medium manufacturers, mostly suppliers, are trying to hang on without any support,' he claims. 'I am scared for my kids and future generations.' As a result of outsourcing production both in the U.S. and overseas, IBM Corp. is 'just a shadow of [its] former self in terms of manufacturing operations,' asserts Edward W. Davis, a professor at the University of Virginia's Darden Graduate School of Business Administration in Charlottesville. And a rule-of-thumb calculation suggests that the movement of manufacturing operations to China in 2002 cost the U.S. about 234,000 jobs.

(*Industry Week*, 2003)

The problem was made even clearer in the following:

U.S. manufacturing executives, in addition to their understandable concerns about a U.S. economic recovery from recession that has been agonizingly slow, are worried, among other things, about innovation, outsourcing, protecting proprietary tech- nologies, and perceived imbalances between the U.S. dollar and other currencies. . . . Manufacturing is at a crossroads. . . . We face fundamental changes, which if left unaddressed, could result in huge economic losses and the erosion of our industrial leadership.

(*Industry Week*, 2003)

Business Week provided further insights into job losses due to the decline in manufacturing:

Since the manufacturing sector tipped into recession in mid-2000, it has shed 2.1 million jobs, leaving fewer industrial workers in the U.S. than at any time since the early 1960s.

(*Business Week*, 2003)

More recently, in the *Harvard Business Review*, Pisano and Shih (2009, p. 114) stated:

As the United States strives to recover from the current economic crisis, it's going to discover an unpleasant fact: The competitiveness problem of the 1980s and early 1990s didn't really go away. It was just hidden during the bubble years behind a mirage of prosperity, and all the while the country's industrial base continued to erode. Now, the U.S. will finally have to take the problem seriously. Rebuilding its wealth-generating machine – that is, restoring the ability of enterprises to develop and manufacture high-technology products in America – is the only way the country can hope to pay down its enormous deficits and maintain, let alone raise, its citizens' standard of living.

In contrast, China has shown a remarkable increase in its balance of payments since 1986, as can be seen in Figure 1.7.

We are not suggesting that there is an easy solution to these problems. What we shall see in Chapter 2, though, is that often decisions to outsource, downsize, and abandon manufacturing activities within the firm are made by those who may know very little about operations. The strategic implication is clear: getting rid of manufacturing operations is relatively easy to do, getting them back is almost impossible. What needs to be done is for firms to see their operations in a strategic manner. This means accruing and developing capabilities over time in operations that other competitors simply cannot copy. This means going beyond the typical low-cost financial myopia to, instead, a longer strategic approach to managing operations. Part of this improvement has to do with being honest about the reasons behind the demise of operations, as *Industry Week* pointed out:

> Apparently, then, there can't possibly be any domestic reasons for why the U.S. manufacturing industry is losing jobs (you know, little things like declining customer service, poor product designs, broken supply chains, bloated inventories, or neglectful maintenance practices). And certainly there's not a chance in the world that the management of the U.S. trade unions has in any way failed the workers they profess to serve. Nope, it's gotta be the Chinese who are behind it all.
>
> (*Industry Week*, 2008)

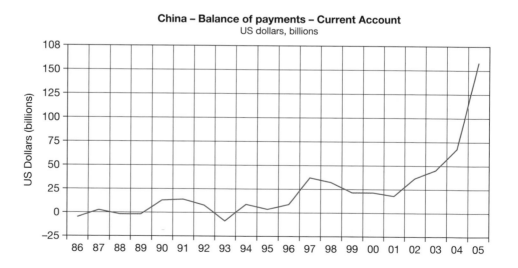

Figure 1.7
China's balance of payments, 1986–2005

Reuters Eco Wire

OPERATIONS MANAGEMENT AND MARKETS

The ability to enter and compete in both new and existing markets is very dependent upon operations capabilities. Of course, other areas are also vitally important – marketing, finance, and other major functions – and we are not seeking to 'score' operations over these other areas. However, we argue that operations management is about uniting these other areas and functions into a central core of capabilities for the organization. This is true in both manufacturing and service settings.

For example, Toyota's remarkable success, over decades, has been well documented and, with other Japanese and other world-class organizations, Toyota has been both aggressive and remarkably successful in their pursuit of targeted markets. For sure, major problems with Toyota's quality defects in 2010 called into question some of the myths about their success. However, we should be careful not to dismiss Toyota – and other companies that have world-class capabilities in operations – simply because of occasional, and often unbalanced, media attention when problems arise. We should bear in mind that in the early decades of the new millennium it is still Honda and, particularly, Toyota whose operations capabilities remain the criteria by which the rest of the automobile industry is judged.

How did Japanese and other world-class companies gain so much success against other competitors? The key means of doing so was described perfectly by Hayes and Pisano back in 1994 and is true today:

> Japanese companies began in the late 1970s to assault world markets in a number of industries with increasing ferocity. Their secret weapon turned out to be sheer manufacturing virtuosity. Most were producing products similar to those offered by Western companies and marketing them in similar ways. What made these products attractive was not only their cost but also their low incidence of defects, their reliability, and their durability.
>
> (Hayes and Pisano, 1994, pp. 80–1)

That is not to say that Japanese and other world-class organizations are internally-myopic and operations-driven and that they ignore customer requirements. We are certainly not advocating that a firm's strategy should be limited by its current operations capabilities. What we are saying is that world-class firms are able to out-perform other organizations and satisfy customer requirements by virtue of their remarkable operations capabilities, which are aligned to market requirements.

THE CRITICAL LINK WITH MARKETING

In the next chapter we discuss how operations management needs to be linked with customer requirements and how the aims of operations management include supporting the business in the marketplace, and enabling the organization to compete successfully against other players.

The task facing operations is perfectly summarized by Ridderstrale and Nordstrom (2000):

> Let us tell you what all customers want. Any customer, in any industry, in any market wants stuff that is both cheaper and better, and they want it yesterday.

(p. 157)

This is wonderful for us as customers, but the downside is that it presents a massive challenge to operations managers. In order for operations managers to achieve these customer requirements, operations needs to be closely allied to marketing and must have a good knowledge of customer requirements. By doing so, operations can help to shape future sales in existing markets as well as help to determine the viability of entering new markets. One of the most critical areas of responsibility, therefore, is in working closely with marketing. Capacity, quality, delivery capabilities, and costs are all within the realm of operations management. Discussing these traits becomes part of the overall information required by marketing, as shown in Figure 1.8.

In service industries the link between operations and marketing has always tended to be close. This is because service firms have always recognized that having the customer in the business itself provided them with ideal opportunities for sales and marketing efforts, such as upselling and promotions.

Thus far, in this chapter, we have provided insights into the strategic importance of operations and we shall develop this theme in Chapter 2. Before then, it is important to see how operations management has changed over time and we will now explore this.

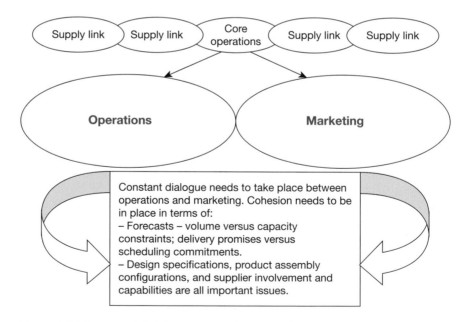

Figure 1.8 The critical link between marketing and operations

CHANGES TO OPERATIONS MANAGEMENT OVER TIME

Before we discuss the major points of strategy in the next chapter, it is important to note that the reason why strategy is vital is that the nature of most operations has undergone major changes over time, as shown in Figure 1.9.

We will discuss each of the key periods in operations and then in Chapter 2 we'll develop this further by explaining how these changes had profound importance to the way that strategy is both formulated and implemented within firms.

The craft era

The first major era is now referred to as 'craft' manufacturing, and service 'shop' delivery. This system was European in origin and linked to the way in which skills were developed: the apprentice–journeyman–master progression which led to the creation of guilds of skilled people who sought to control the supply of their speciality, and the consolidation of skills within a subsector of society (as, for example, skills were passed on from father to son).

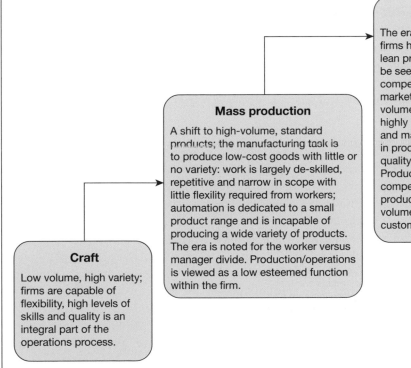

The current/future era

The era of mass customization, where firms have to be agile, flexible and lean producers and manufacturing has to be seen as strategic. The era of global competition in many markets; and these markets demand high variety and high volume at the same time; this calls for a highly motivated and flexible workforce and management is largely self-managed in production teams, responsible for quality and other competitive requirements. Production/operations is seen as a core competence and has to be capable of producing a wide range and different volumes of output as required by customers.

Mass production

A shift to high-volume, standard products; the manufacturing task is to produce low-cost goods with little or no variety: work is largely de-skilled, repetitive and narrow in scope with little flexibility required from workers; automation is dedicated to a small product range and is incapable of producing a wide variety of products. The era is noted for the worker versus manager divide. Production/operations is viewed as a low esteemed function within the firm.

Craft

Low volume, high variety; firms are capable of flexibility, high levels of skills and quality is an integral part of the operations process.

Time

Figure 1.9 The transition from craft to strategic operations

This was noted for low volume, high variety products, where workers tended to be highly skilled and quality was built into the very process of operations. It was also appropriate for largely national markets, supplied internally with minimal imports and exports.

Some craft manufacturing still remains today, in markets where exotic products and services can control demands through some unique feature or high level of desirability. For instance, some house building, furniture making, and clock and watch making are still carried out by skilled craftsmen/women working on a single or few items of output at a time. While the processes and techniques used by these craftsmen/women are highly inefficient, the unique quality of their products commands a premium price, as illustrated by the second-hand value of products such as a Daniels pocket watch or a Morgan car. In the case of Morgan, however, it is a mistake to conclude that the passenger car industry might still be able to employ craft production. Morgan is unashamedly part of a sector which is closer to specialist toys than that concerned with personal transportation. It is also the end of a very thin tail, other parts of which (AC, Aston Martin, Rolls-Royce, etc.) have already been absorbed by volume producers, keen to operate in exotic niches for purposes that are closer to corporate advertising than to income generation. In the clothing industry, one significant sector of the industry – haute couture – is based on the craft production approach.

In services, the craft era has also continued – perhaps even more so than in manufacturing. The slower pace of change within some services derives from the extent to which customer-processing operations can adopt new technologies and new systems. Only services that require little skill at the operating level (such as fast moving consumer goods or petrol retailing) or processing large amounts of information (such as financial services) are significantly different now from what they were like even 30 years ago. The core nature of many services such as hotels, schools, hospitals, hairdressers, vehicle repair, and transportation have changed very little, despite new technologies.

The mass production era

The second major era is known as mass production, although once again its principles were by no means restricted to manufacturing. This system grew in North America to accommodate three principal requirements of the developing giant: the need to export, the need to provide employment for a massive, largely unskilled workforce, and the need to establish itself as a world player, which meant infiltrating other regions with ideas clearly associated with the US.

In short, the Americans could not play by European rules, so they reinvented the game: innovating by destroying the competitive position of craft production. The system was massively successful and changed the working and buying practices of the world in the first three decades of the twentieth century. In order to sell the standardized products made by standardized operations practices, mass production had to standardize the market requirements too. Fortunately, the market was immature and would do what it was told to do. Thus, mass production reversed the paradigm of craft production: volume was high with little variety. The marketing ploy (and the resultant manufacturing strategy) was exemplified by Henry Ford's famous declaration, from now on, 'a customer can have a car painted any colour he likes, as long as it is black'. In mass production, workers were typically unskilled. This was the era owing much to the contribution of F.W. Taylor's *scientific management* whereby workers had very narrowly defined jobs involving repetitive tasks, and quality was left to 'quality experts' at the final stage of the overall process rather than being an integral part of operations at each step.

Taylor enabled firms, for the first time, to control costs, times, and resources, rather than rely on skilled craftsmen and women to decide what was appropriate. Coupled with the developments made in mechanization and employee coordination during the European industrial revolutions, Taylor's ideas provided to be an entirely different way of operating.

In 1926 *Encyclopaedia Britannica* asked Henry Ford to christen his system, and he called it mass production. He meant 'mass' in the sense of large volume production. Perhaps he did not see the other meaning of mass as 'heavy, cumbersome', which is what the system turned out to be (in terms of management systems and superstructure), once the market no longer bought what it was told.

These principles, originating in the 1920s, were slow to be adopted in services, but by the 1970s Ted Levitt from Harvard Business School was able to identify the 'industrialization' (Levitt, 1972) of service and the 'production-lining' (Levitt, 1976) of service. He cited fast food, the automatic teller machine (ATM) outside banks, and supermarket retailing as examples of this. Schmenner (1986) coined the phrase 'mass service' to exemplify this type of service operation. Some of the aspects of working life that are typical in this mass production context have been extended to life in general by Ritzer (1993), who refers to it as the McDonaldization of society.

The shift from 'craft' marketing to marketing in the mass production age is clearly demarcated by the publication of Levitt's (1960) article in the *Harvard Business Review* entitled 'Marketing myopia'. In mass production, customers bought what was supplied, while producers concentrated on keeping costs, and hence prices, down and focused on selling to customers through aggressive advertising and sales forces. As organizations were product-led, operations management was relatively straightforward. Mass-producing goods at the lowest cost meant minimizing component and product variety, large production runs, and scientific management. The success of Ford made this view highly persuasive. In 1909 the Model T automobiles were sold for US$950, but by 1916 following the introduction of the assembly line it had fallen to US$345, and three quarters of the cars on American roads were built by Ford (Bryson, 1994).

However, as Levitt (1960) pointed out, Ford was eventually outstripped by General Motors, who were not product-led but market-led. They gave customers what they wanted – choice, model updates, and a range of colours (not just black!).

The symbol of this age is the brand. Originally (in the craft era) the brand was a mark on the product, often a signature – for example, on a painting – or symbol, signifying its ownership or origin. But in mass production the brand took on far more significance. It became the means by which one product (or service) could differentiate itself from a competitor's product (or service). Procter & Gamble set up brand managers in 1931 to sell their different soap products. Later the brand also became a guarantee of product and service quality. Kemmons Wilson's motivation in 1952 to open the first Holiday Inn hotel was his own disappointment with the variable standards and sleaziness of the motels he stayed in whilst on a family holiday. The success of delivering a consistently standard level of service resulted in Wilson opening one hotel every two and half days in the mid-1950s.

The modern era

By the 1990s brands had come under threat. Markets became and remain highly fragmented, the proliferation of niches makes target marketing more difficult, product and service life-cycles are shortening, and product/service innovation is quicker than ever before, while increased customer sophistication has reduced the power of advertising.

The third era (the current and, for the foreseeable future at least, the likely scenario) is more difficult to name and has been called various things. The terms used to describe the current era include:

- *Mass customization* (Pine *et al.*, 1993): reflecting the need for volume combined with a recognition of customers' (or consumers') wishes.
- *Flexible specialization* (Piore and Sabel, 1984): related to the manufacturing strategy of firms (especially small firms) to focus on parts of the value-adding process and collaborate within networks to produce whole products.
- *Lean production* (Womack *et al.*, 1990): developed from the massively successful Toyota Production System, focusing on the removal of all forms of waste from a system (some of them difficult to see).
- *Agile* (Kidd, 1994): emphasizing the need for an organization to be able to switch frequently from one market-driven objective to another.
- *Strategic* (Brown, 1996; 2000; Hill, 2004): in which the need for the operations to be framed in a strategy is brought to the fore.

Whatever it is called, the paradigm for the current era addresses the need to combine high volume and variety, together with high levels of quality as the norm, and rapid, ongoing innovation in many markets. It is, as mass production was 100 years ago, an innovation that makes the system it replaces largely redundant.

As each era appeared, however, it did not entirely replace the former era. As we have seen, a few pockets of craft manufacturing still exist. Mass production is still apparent in chemical plants and refineries and other high volume/low variety environments. However, many are changing fundamentally as existing economies of scale are questioned: thus steel manufacture faces variety requirements and has to develop 'mini-mills' to lower economic batch sizes. The same is true for brewers and pharmaceutical companies.

FORCES THAT DRIVE CHANGE IN OPERATIONS MANAGEMENT

We now know that operations management has gone through three periods of change from craft, through mass production, to the present era. We know that different sectors of many economies have gone through these periods at different rates. In some, the transition has been incremental, in others spasmodic, usually in response to some new invention. We also know that in some industries there has been an almost complete transition from the old approach to the newest, whereas in others there remains a high proportion of craft manufacture or old-style service delivery. Why is this so? If we can understand these forces then we may be able to predict what changes are likely to occur in the future.

We would argue that the three key forces to date have been economic, social, and technological, or to put it more simply wealth, fashion, and invention. Wealth influences economic activity and hence operations management in two main ways. The aspiration to become wealthy provides a highly proactive workforce, while the attainment of wealth creates a growing market for all kinds of goods and services. When a significant proportion of a population is relatively poor, goods and services have to be provided at the lowest possible cost and consumers are prepared to accept standardization. The wealthy can afford customized products and indeed demonstrate their wealth by doing so. Furthermore, social and economic status is not demonstrated simply by ownership but by style, fashion, or 'quality'. For what the American economist Thorstein Veblen called 'conspicuous consumption' it is not enough to just have a television, but one must have a digital television; not enough to have a mobile phone, but the latest hi-tech version with a personalized key pad; not enough to own a car but important to have a 'special edition'.

Fundamentally, goods and services can be categorized as necessities or luxuries. Necessities are those goods and services which are *perceived* by people to be essential. These are normally food, drink, health products/services, housing, and so on. Making a product or delivering a service that is perceived as essential clearly has advantages as even during periods of shortage or economic downturn consumers will continue to purchase these items. What is deemed essential by the population of one country or by one group of people, however, may not be desired by another population or group.

But not only does 'fashion' vary between groups, it also varies over time within groups. Luxury products and services that were once fashionable become unfashionable. Up until the 1960s nearly everyone wore a hat (as evidenced by any black and white movie made and set in the 1940s or 1950s). This is no longer the case. It is claimed that the hat-making industry was sent into decline by President Kennedy – the first US president to walk to his inauguration in Washington in January without a hat, hence making hat-wearing unfashionable. Many industries operate in a context of uncertainty derived from the impact of changes in fashion – toys, clothing, shoe manufacture, entertainment, the media, fabric manufacturers, and so on.

Wealth and fashion are the powers that drive the forces of demand for goods and services, while invention enables or constrains supply. If costs are to be driven down then new ways of doing things are required. The mass assembly solution to lower costs created by Ford does not work for all industries. It may be highly effective in those industries that rely on the assembly of parts to produce finished goods, but there are many sectors, even in materials processing, that do not function in this way. It also does not work well in customer processing operations (although in Russia, some eye operations are carried out on patients who are placed on a conveyor belt that moves them from one specialist surgeon to another!).

As well as process redesign, invention can also create new machinery or equipment for use within the transformation process. The single most important recent invention in this respect is undoubtedly the microprocessor (in 1975), which has been integrated into machinery and control systems throughout the manufacturing and service sector, in order to increase speed and accuracy, reduce labour input, and so on.

Finally, invention also creates new types of products and services that have not existed before. This means that being the best at producing any product or delivering any service is not sufficient if the market for that output is replaced by demand for something different. This questions the wisdom of such phrases as 'best practice' and 'world class': expertise may only be temporary. There are many companies that were the world class or best practitioners who no longer exist because people stopped wanting their products or services and the associated skills became redundant.

THE ERA OF VOLATILE MARKETS AND INDUSTRIES

This analysis of the forces that drive change helps to explain the current situation. The current era has been called one of 'chaos' (Peters, 1987; Stacey, 1993). Creating and sustaining competitive advantage in either manufacturing or service firms is both complex and difficult, and a number of giant organizations have been humbled in recent times, apparently unable to do just that. Examples of giants in manufacturing and service sectors that suffered declines by the mid-1990s include Boeing, Caterpillar, Dayton-Hudson, Du Pont, Texas Instruments, Westinghouse, and Xerox.

In the early 1990s huge financial losses were incurred by giants such as Citicorp, America's biggest international bank – a loss of $457 million in 1991. General Motors suffered losses of $23.5 billion in 1992 and IBM had losses of $8.1 billion in 1993, having enjoyed profits of $6 billion in 1986. By the end of the 1990s IBM again reaped profits of around $8 billion per annum. Some of these giants have re-emerged since the 1990s into world-class organizations able to compete with the very best once again today. The ability to do so, though, has come from a fundamental reorganization of operations capabilities. We shall provide examples of this throughout the text, but we can say here that the likes of Xerox, IBM, and Caterpillar have all had to reinvent themselves by making their operations capabilities more strategic in nature – poised and ready to compete in volatile markets.

Such erratic performances have led to a number of observers doubting the validity and worth of being in the Fortune 500. This was exemplified by the management guru Peter Drucker declaring that 'The 'Fortune 500' is over' (*Fortune*, 1998). Volatility seems common to many firms who have appeared in the *Fortune* 500 – for example, between 1990 and 2011 over 70 per cent had disappeared from the *Fortune* 500. So, less than 30 per cent of what were once powerful US giants in 1990 still exist today – a truly shocking statistic.

The reasons for such 'turbulence' are complex but fundamentally go back to the three forces identified above – wealth, fashion and invention/innovation. Whereas in the past wealth was confined to a relatively small proportion of countries, it is now more widespread. This means that wealth creation, in the form of significant economic activity and market demand, are global. Such globalization creates complexity. Second, fashion becomes global through the worldwide media of cinema and television. When movie or sports stars are seen to frequent certain types of establishment, wear identified types of clothing or use certain types of product, consumers are influenced in their views and values. Paid product-placement in films is now a significant proportion of profit for some types of movie and most sports stars earn more from their affiliation with goods manufacturers than they do from their salaries or winnings. Thirdly, the pace of invention is increasing, as we shall see in Chapter 4. As Joseph Schumpeter (1942) correctly stated decades ago, new innovations offer 'creative destruction' of existing products and services. This destruction goes wider, though, and includes the demise of some organizations themselves.

All of the above demands that operations management is seen within a strategic context. This is necessary if organizations hope to compete in such volatile markets where speed, reliability, quality, inventory management, and a range of other operations capabilities have to be in place. We shall discuss reasons why this poses problems for some organizations – and we shall discuss examples of truly world-class capabilities in other organizations – in our next chapter.

SUMMARY

- The range of responsibilities that operations managers have within the plant or service itself is profound, important, and wide in scope.
- Operations management is concerned with those activities that enable an *organization* (and not one part of it only) to transform a range of basic inputs into outputs for the end customer.
- Operations management has a very wide in scope of responsibilities, will draw upon a range of functions within the organization, and will not be limited to a specific department.
- Operations management is concerned with uniting these other areas and functions into a central core of capabilities for the organization.
- Operations management is no longer limited to a narrow focus on organization-specific activity. In the modern era of operations management, organizations no longer see themselves as a stand-alone element in the overall 'process' but will, instead, see themselves as part of a wider, extended enterprise.
- Not only is the organization concerned with transferring goods and services to end customers, it has to do so in a value-added way. Value added, in the most simplistic terms, means that the income or benefit derived from performing a particular operation is greater than the cost of doing so. All organizations, whether they are in the private or public sector, or in manufacturing or services, have operations within them. Increasingly, value-added operations are important to both the private and public sectors.
- The link between operations and marketing is a critical one. Constant dialogue needs to take place in order to satisfy customer requirements. Expertise in one may be negated by failure in the other.
- Instead of seeing manufacturing *versus* services we need to see manufacturing alongside services in terms of understanding the range of interlinking activities, from basic inputs to end customer delivery.
- The distinction between manufacturing and services is not quite as profound as often stated, for a number of reasons. The key issue is more likely to be differences between materials, customers, or information-processing operations.

The central aim of this book is to deal with issues of operations management within a strategic context. In the next chapter we will look at how operations strategies can be devised and implemented. In the subsequent chapters we look at key strategic issues of the transformation process: innovation, inventory, supply, capacity, human resources, and development and growth.

KEY QUESTIONS

1. What are the major areas of responsibility for operations managers?
2. Why is it important to go beyond the organization-specific, input–processes–output model in modern-day operations management?
3. What challenges does servitization pose for modern day operations?
4. What global opportunities and challenges are there for organizations today?
5. What strategic questions do firms need to deal with when being involved in global operations?

ONLINE CONNECTION

Professor Simon Croom of the University of San Diego discusses operations and strategy within the supply chain with Nigel Slack, Professor of Operations at Warwick Business School: www.youtube.com/watch?v=ZRcDVm6G50Y

FURTHER READING

Brown, S., Squire, B. and Lewis, M. (2010) 'The impact of inclusive and fragmented operations strategy processes on operational performance', *International Journal of Production Research*, 48(14), 4179–98.

Pinheiro de Lima, E., Eduardo Gouvêa da Costa, S. and Reis de Faria, A. (2009) 'Taking operations strategy into practice: Developing a process for defining priorities and performance measures', *International Journal of Production Economics*, 12(1), 403–18.

Rosenzweig, Eve D., Laseter, T.M. and Roth, A.V. (2011) 'Through the service operations strategy looking glass: Influence of industrial sector, ownership, and service offerings on B2B e-marketplace failures', *Journal of Operations Management*, 29(1/2), 33–48.

Schniederjans, M. and Cao, Q. (2009) 'Alignment of operations strategy, information strategic orientation, and performance: An empirical study', *International Journal of Production Research*, 47(10), 2535–63.

REFERENCES

Baines, T., Lightfoot, H. and Smart, P. (2011) 'Servitization within manufacturing: Exploring the provision of advanced services and their impact on vertical integration'. *Journal of Manufacturing Technology Management*, 22(7), 947–54.

Barney, J.B. (1991) 'Firm resources and sustained competitive advantage', *Journal of Management*, 17, 99–120.

Brown, S. (1996) *Strategic Manufacturing for Competitive Advantage*, Hemel Hempstead: Prentice Hall.

Brown, S. (2000) *Manufacturing the Future: Strategic Resonance for Enlightened Manufacturing*, London: Financial Times Books.

Brown, S., Squire, B. and Lewis, M. (2010) 'The impact of inclusive and fragmented operations strategy processes on operational performance', *International Journal of Production Research*, 48(14), 4179–98.

Bryson, W. (1994) *Made in America*, London: Minerva.

Business Week (2003) 'The flexible factory', 5 May 2003.

Business Week (2005) 'Outsourcing innovation', 21 March 2005, p. 34.

Business Week (2010) 'Big oil turns its back on BP', 19 July 2010, pp. 22–4.

Crainer, S. (1998) *Thinkers that Changed the Management World*, London: Pitman.

Financial Times (2010) 'US manufacturing crown slips', 20 June 2010, p. 4.

Fortune (1998) 'Peter Drucker takes the long view: The original management guru shares his vision of the future with Fortune's Brent Schlender', 28 September 1998.

Fortune (2002) 'Fast food, slow service', 30 September 2002.

Fortune (2007) 'How many small businesses does it take to build a jet?', 17(6), 42–5.

Fortune (2010) 'American made . . . Chinese owned', 22 March 2010, p. 82.

Fortune (2011) 'The Global 500 in 2010', 25 July 2011, 164(2).

Garvin, D. (1992) *Operations Strategy, Text and Cases*, Eaglewood Cliffs, NJ: Prentice Hall.

Hayes, R. and Pisano, G. (1994) 'Beyond world-class: The new manufacturing strategy', *Harvard Business Review*, January/February, pp 77–86.

Hill, T. (2004) *Production/operations management*, Hemel Hempstead: Prentice Hall.

Industry Week (2003) 'Manufacturing's global future', 30 May 2003.

Industry Week (2008) 'Just in time: Heroes and villains', September 2008 (9), p. 60.

International Organization of Motor Vehicle Manufacturers (2010) *Manufacturers of Cars by Country*, July, Paris, France.

Johnston, R. and Clark, G. (2001) *Service Operations Management*, Hemel Hempstead: Prentice Hall.

Kidd, P. (1994) *Agile Manufacturing: Forging New Frontiers*, Reading, MA: Addison Wesley.

Lamming, R. (1993) *Beyond Partnership*, Hemel Hempstead: Prentice Hall.

Levitt, T. (1960) 'Marketing myopia', *Harvard Business Review*, July/August, pp. 35–56.

Levitt, T. (1972) 'The production-line approach to service', *Harvard Business Review* 50(5), 20–31.

Levitt, T. (1976) 'The industrialisation of service', *Harvard Business Review*, 54(5), 32–43.

Muhlemann, A., Oakland, J. and Lockyer, K. (1992) *Production and Operations Management*, London: Pitman.

Neely, A.D. (2009) 'Exploring the financial consequences of the servitization of manufacturing', *Operations Management Research*, 2(1), 103–18.

Normann, R. (2000) *Service management*, 3rd edition, New York: Wiley.

Peters, T. (1987) *Thriving On Chaos*, London: Pan Books/Macmillan.

Pine, B., Bart, V. and Boynton, A. (1993) 'Making mass customization work', *Harvard Business Review*, September/October, pp. 108–19.

Pinheiro de Lima, E., Eduardo Gouvêa da Costa, S. and Reis de Faria, A. (2009) 'Taking operations strategy into practice: Developing a process for defining priorities and performance measures', *International Journal of Production Economics*, 12(1), 403–18.

Piore, M. and Sabel, C. (1984) *The Second Industrial Divide: Possibilities For Prosperity*, New York: Basic Books.

Pisano, G.P. and Shih, W.C. (2009) 'Restoring American competitiveness', *Harvard Business Review*, 87(7/8) 114–25.

Porter, M. (1980) *Competitive Advantage*, New York: Free Press.

Porter, M. (1985) *Competitive Strategy*, New York: Free Press.

Prahalad, C.K. (2002) *Financial Times*, 13 December 2002, p. 14.

Ridderstrale, J. and Nordstrom K. (2000) *Funky Business*, London: FT Books.

Ritzer, G. (1993) *The McDonaldization of Society*, California: Pine Forge.

Rosenzweig, Eve D., Laseter, T.M. and Roth, A.V. (2011) 'Through the service operations strategy looking glass: Influence of industrial sector, ownership, and service offerings on B2B e-marketplace failures', *Journal of Operations Management*, 29(1/2), 33–48.

Samson, D. (1991) *Manufacturing and Operations Strategy*, Sydney, Australia: Prentice Hall.

Schmenner, R.W. (1986) 'How can services business survive and prosper?', *Sloan Management Review*, 27(3), 21–32.

Schniederjans, M. and Cao, Q. (2009) 'Alignment of operations strategy, information strategic orientation, and performance: An empirical study', *International Journal of Production Research*, 47(10), 2535–63.

Schumpeter, J. (1942) *Capitalism, Socialism and Democracy*, New York: Harper.

Skinner, W. (1985) *Manufacturing: The Formidable Competitive Weapon*, New York: Wiley and Sons.

Stacey, R. (1993) *Strategic Management and Organizational Dynamics*, London: Pitman.

Teece, D., Pisano, G. and Shuen, A. (1997) 'Dynamic capabilities and strategic management', *Strategic Management Journal*, 18(7), 509–33.

Terziovski, M. (2010) 'Innovation practice and its performance implications in small and medium enterprises (SMEs) in the manufacturing sector: A resource-based view', *Strategic Management Journal*, 31(8), 892–902.

Vandermerwe, S. and Rada, J. (1988) 'Servitization of business: Adding value by adding services', *European Management Journal*, 6, 314–24.

Wall Street Journal (2009) 'The quagmire ahead', 1 June 2009.

Womack, J., Jones, D. and Roos, D. (1990) *The Machine That Changed the World*, New York: Rawson Associates.

Womack, J. and Jones, D. (2003) *Lean Thinking: Banish Waste and Create Wealth in Your Corporation*, New York: Simon Shuster.

CHAPTER 2

STRATEGIC OPERATIONS MANAGEMENT

LEARNING OBJECTIVES

This chapter will enable you to:

- Understand why there is a need for all organizations to develop operations strategies.
- Gain insights into how operations strategy has developed over time.
- Provide indications of the process and content of strategy.
- Appreciate why some organizations struggle with devising and implementing operations strategies.
- Realize the vital role of operations strategy.
- Explore why many firms struggle with forming operations strategies.
- Understand the need for strategic resonance.

INTRODUCTION

In this chapter we will expand upon a number of key issues faced by operations managers in both manufacturing and service environments that we discussed in Chapter 1. We will develop the theme of how operations management must be seen in terms of *strategic* importance and discuss how strategies have to be in place if organizations want to be able to compete in the modern business world.

In Chapter 1 we looked at the major responsibilities that face operations managers. As we saw, these responsibilities are wide in scope and extremely important in themselves. It is important to bear in mind that operations managers have responsibilities that go beyond management of assets, costs, and human resources in the transformation process (as important as these managerial responsibilities are). In the current business environment, operations must be managed in a way that will enable the firm to compete successfully against ever increasing levels of competition from around the world. This means that managing operations takes on wholly different requirements to how it was performed in the past. In short, operations management becomes *strategic* operations management. The modern business world requires rapid and continuous innovation, and there is global competition in many industries and markets.

SOME KEY ISSUES

In their *Harvard Business Review* article, Collis and Rukstad, (2008, p. 82) state:

> It's a dirty little secret: Most executives cannot articulate the objective, scope, and advantage of their business in a simple statement. If they can't, neither can anyone else.

They then put forward the challenge:

> Can you summarize your company's strategy in 35 words or less? If so, would your colleagues put it the same way?

The authors of this text agree both with the assertion and the challenge above. In our management consulting experience and research we have found that most CEOs and other senior-level managers struggle either to articulate a strategy or, just as importantly, they fail to share and implement the strategy with all employees. It's made worse because many CEOs know very little about operations management. For example, if you were to speak to a senior-level manager within an organization, the likelihood is that, within a short period of time, you would be a having a conversation that included a number of management terms – *core competences*, *key performance indicators*, and *critical success factors*, among others. Ask the same manager about how operations and operations management line up within these terms and the likelihood is that he or she might be mystified or perplexed by the question. We'll explore the key reasons for this but we begin here by stating the following:

Operations processes and operations management are of strategic importance to an organization.

This is because the aspirations that modern-day organizations have to excel in *mass customization*, *lean production*, *agile manufacturing*, *customer-centric provision*, and so on, depend on their ability to actually *do* these things, and such capabilities reside within operations.

The problem with some organizations is that they simply do not have senior-level personnel in place who fully understand the potential that operations can have and, as a consequence, capabilities are often either not developed or, worse still, given up by firms by divesting plants and services within the organization (Brown and Blackmon, 2005; Brown *et al.*, 2007). However, where strategy is clearly defined and implemented the advantages can be enormous, as is evident in Case 2.1.

CASE 2.1: STRATEGY AT EDWARD JONES

Edward Jones, [is] a St. Louis–based brokerage firm . . . The fourth-largest brokerage in the United States, Jones has quadrupled its market share during the past two decades, has consistently outperformed its rivals in terms of ROI through bull and bear markets, and has been a fixture on Fortune's list of the top companies to work for. It's a safe bet that just about every one of its 37,000 employees could express the company's succinct strategy statement: Jones aims to 'grow to 17,000 financial advisers by 2012 [from about 10,000 today] by offering trusted and convenient face-to-face financial advice to conservative individual investors who delegate their financial decisions, through a national network of one-financial-adviser offices.'

Collis and Rukstad, (2008)

WHAT IS STRATEGY ANYWAY?

Strategy comes from the Greek word, *strategos*, which is used to mean 'a general' in a military setting and implies that the role includes facets of leadership, direction, and so on. The military connection is further exemplified in the book, *The Art of War*, which is a Chinese military treatise attributed to Sun Tzu, writing in the late sixth-century BCE. Thus the term 'strategy', as used in the 'business strategy', sense originated in military terminology. Some writers do not like this analogy (see Kay, 1993, for example) because strategy is not always about obliterating the competition.

We do not pretend that strategy is easy or straightforward. Strategy is clearly a complex issue (Whittington, 2001; Mintzberg *et al.*, 2000). For example, Chaharbaghi and Willis (1998) showed just how complex strategy is when they listed some of the, often contradictory, views as to what strategy really means (some of which are quite amusing as can be seen in the following box).

WHAT IS STRATEGY?: SOME AMUSING COMPLEXITIES

Strategy is:

- A bizarre game (Stacey, 1993);
- A plan, a master plan, a pattern, a position, a ploy, a perspective (Mintzberg, 1994; Wheelen and Hunger, 1992);
- An integrative blueprint (Hax, 1990);
- A way of thinking or state of mind (Dixit and Nalebuff, 1991; Ohmae, 1982);
- Innovation (Baden-Fuller and Pitt, 1996);
- A black art (Hax, 1990);

- Language (Goddard and Houlder, 1995); and
- A learning process (Senge, 1990).

Strategy is also considered to be about:

- Standardization (Douglas and Wind, 1987);
- Differentiation and cost leadership (Porter, 1985);
- Sticking to the knitting (Peters and Waterman, 1982);
- Fit and scope (Johnson and Scholes, 1997);
- Stretch and leverage (Hamel and Prahalad, 1994);
- Differentiating managerial tasks and asserting vital continuity (Hax, 1990);
- Exploiting leverage (Lele, 1992);
- Survival (Booth, 1993);
- Winning (Ellis and Williams, 1995);
- Global co-ordination (Prahalad and Doz, 1986);
- Dependence, independence, and interdependence (Bartlett and Ghoshal, 1987);
- Market coverage (Daems, 1990);
- Intent (Hamel and Prahalad, 1989);
- Developing core competencies (Prahalad and Hamel, 1990);
- Anticipating change (Peters and Waterman, 1982);
- Vision (Mintzberg, 1995);
- Responding to external opportunities and threats, establishing purpose and the economic and non-economic contribution made to stakeholders (Hax, 1990);
- Proconfiguring thinking (Pascale, 1984);
- Developing distinctive capabilities that add value (Kay, 1994);
- Parenting advantage and adding value (Goold and Campbell, 1991);
- Logical incrementalism (Quinn, 1978);
- Coping with competition (Porter, 1979);
- Implementation (Hrebiniak and Joyce, 1984);
- Time-based competitive advantage (Stalk, 1988);
- Capabilities-based competition (Stalk *et al.*, 1992);
- Outpacing (Gilbert and Strebel, 1989);
- Portfolio planning (Haspeslagh, 1982);
- Portfolio management, restructuring, transferring skills, and sharing activities (Porter, 1987);
- Structure (Chandler, 1962);

- Co-operation (Contractor and Lorange, 1988);
- Alliances (Reve, 1990);
- Collaboration (Hamel *et al.*, 1989);
- Confrontation (Cooper, 1995);
- Network positions (Johanson and Mattsson, 1992);
- Bringing order from chaos (Stacey, 1993);
- Choosing good firms (Baden-Fuller and Stopford, 1992); and
- Choosing good industries (Porter, 1980; 1990).

Strategy can also be:

- Generic (Porter, 1980);
- Deliberate or emergent (Mintzberg, 1994);
- Rational or incremental (Johnson, 1988);
- Prescriptive, descriptive, or configurational (Mintzberg and Ansoff, 1994); and
- Implicit or explicit (Mintzberg and Ansoff, 1994).

Adapted from Chaharbaghi and Willis, 1998

So, as we can see, strategy can be complicated. However, we suggest that there are common recurring themes that emerge, which are of use to managers.

STRATEGY IS . . .

- Concerned with meeting existing market needs as well as exploiting opportunities for potential market segments (Kim and Mauborgne, 2002; Nunes and Cespedes, 2003).
- About making the best use of resources, and to leverage these resources either alone or with partners (Wernerfelt, 1984; Barney, 1991; Dierickx, and Cool, 1989; Hines, 1994; Ireland *et al.*, 2002; Stump *et al.*, 2002). For example in China:

  Ogilvy China broadened its understanding of consumer needs by working with the Communist Youth League of China, an organization of 70 million people. The Indiana-based diesel engine maker Cummins faced a shortage of well-trained engineers in India, so it teamed up with Maharshi Karve Stree Shikshan Samstha – a 112-year-old women's educational institution in Pune – to create a new women's engineering college (Ghemawat and Hout, 2008).

- The ultimate responsibility of senior-level managers within the firm – although of course we recognize the vital of importance of a range of stakeholders in the process both within the firm and with eternal linkages to the enterprise (Hax and Majluf, 1991; Dougherty and Corse, 1995; Frambach *et al.*, 2003).
- About devising and implementing processes that will enable the enterprise to compete and, ideally, to create competitive advantage (Whittington, 2001; Hamilton *et al.*, 1998).
- Concerned with developing capabilities within the firm's operations that are superior to other competitors and which other competitors either cannot copy, or will find it extremely difficult, to copy (Teece *et al.*, 1997; Eisenhardt and Martin, 2000).

This last factor has important implications for new markets as shown in Case 2.2 regarding Procter and Gamble in China.

CASE STUDY

CASE 2.2: P&G CHINA

P&G China has been so successful because it can do things Chinese competitors can't yet do. It has the ability, for example, to send local product developers to global R&D facilities to work with experienced technical specialists on creating better segment-specific products for China. Consequently, P&G, which is already the overall (all segments combined) leader in China in nearly all of the 16 product categories it competes in, will most likely continue to increase its presence in the country's lower-tier segments, where local companies have always held an advantage.

Ghemawat and Hout (2008)

These indications of what strategy is about are important because they are all linked to operations management in various ways. That is a challenge in itself, but it is made more difficult because firms often do not organize themselves in a way that will allow them to make the best possible use of their operational capabilities. This is true of both manufacturing and service organizations. If anything the situation has been even worse in service organizations, which have lagged considerably behind the revolution in manufacturing practices that has taken place over the last 30 years. While there is now a well-established service management academic discipline in some business schools, and an emerging research agenda, this is a very recent phenomenon.

The very idea that operations should be seen as a 'strategic' factor is still a problem for some firms whose overall strategy may be governed by a few people at the top of the hierarchy of the firm who might know very little about production and operations management. As a result of this, the rationale behind, and the measurement of the success of, business decisions may be driven almost entirely by short-term financial criteria. As we noted in Chapter 1, such an approach may often rob the firm of vital investment to support and sustain key operations areas such as technology, plant modernization and ongoing training.

The use of management accounting tools and 'justification by numbers', although important, is not enough. For example, there simply is no formula to determine financial ratios or outcomes if the firm *doesn't* invest in these key areas. Ultimately, if the firm fails to invest – and, as we shall see in Chapter 7, the opposite extreme of 'throwing money at the problem' is not the answer either – then the net result is that the firm will fail to compete and will face decline.

The distortion brought about by lack of investment was perfectly captured by an American academic lamenting the situation in the USA:

THE INVESTMENT PROBLEM FOR OPERATIONS MANAGERS

'This focus on quarterly profits among the large, publicly held companies is deathly. If there is any hope on the horizon for this country it is in the privately held, medium-size companies,' he says. 'I see them with a willingness to take greater risks in investments that benefit the competitiveness of the company and don't just make the ROI look better in the short run. I see them with a better balance of outsourcing.'

'If I could change one thing about this country that I think would help improve manufacturing in the long run, it would be to pass a law to forbid the reporting of company profits on a quarterly basis. I think that the short-term focus on profits has done more to hurt manufacturing than probably any other thing.'

Quote from Professor Edward W. Davis in *Industry Week*
(2003) 'Waking Up To a New World',
June 2003, 252(6).

Businesses face increasing levels of competition which is becoming more global in nature in many industries. Coping with this competition demands that strategies are in place because being prepared and poised to act rarely, if ever, comes about by accident or 'just happens' by chance.

THE STRATEGY MISSION

As we noted in Chapter 1, firms will often articulate a mission linked to its strategy. This core mission does not have to be particularly lengthy, or wonderfully articulated when stated, but it does have to be meaningful. For example, Komatsu's vision of 'Maru-C' – to encircle

Caterpillar, Komatsu's major rival; and Coca-Cola's intention of being able to position a coke within 'arm's reach' of every consumer in the world; are entirely appropriate for their firms. The mission is dependent upon what the firm does via its operations capabilities. On occasions the core mission's intention may be a little more dramatic, as in Honda's case:

> When Honda was overtaken by Yamaha as Japan's number one motorbike manufacturer, the company responded by declaring 'Yamaha so tsubu su!' (We will crush, squash and slaughter Yamaha!).
>
> (Whittington, 2001, p. 69)

The ability to launch such an impressive amount of innovations in a short time came about by mobilizing a set of capabilities that had been developed over time by Honda. These operations capabilities were then able to be utilized in the market in order to ward off competitive advances. However, it is futile to assert a strategy if operations capabilities are not in place. One telling example of this problem was with Compaq in the PC industry back in the 1990s.

CASE: PROBLEMS WITH COMPAQ'S STRATEGY

Compaq's problems began in 1994 when its former CEO, Pfeiffer, announced that Compaq would make all its PCs on a 'build to order' basis by 1996. At the time of the 'build to order' statement from Pfeiffer, Compaq built less than 5 per cent of its machines to order. By the beginning of the new millennium, Compaq was way behind Dell in build-to-order capabilities and Dell had surpassed Compaq in desktop PC sales to US businesses for the first time. Perhaps more than any other single factor, it was the absence of customer-focused operations strategies that cost Compaq's former CEO, Pfeiffer, his job. Compaq's failure also led to the merger with Hewlett-Packard – and H-P has been the dominant partner in this merger.

The success of operations strategy has nothing to do with how long the planning process has taken; nor has it to do with how nicely or how wonderfully articulate the strategy is presented to the firm's employees – if indeed the strategy is articulated to employees at all. Rather, the success of operations strategy will be determined by the extent to which it focuses the efforts of operations into an integrated set of capabilities. These capabilities should, in turn, enable the firm to compete in the increasingly competitive environment common to many industries. It is not argued that manufacturing/operations managers should necessarily take the lead in business strategy, but that they should be an integral part of the strategic planning process. Without operations managers' capabilities, the best marketing and corporate plans have little chance of being achieved. The importance of being able to accomplish the strategic vision once it has been formed was highlighted by Fortune.

Not only do the majority of the world's most admired companies have a winning strategy – they're also able to carry it out. That's the conclusion of a follow-up study conducted by the Hay Group in the last quarter of 2003. The study found that a key difference between the most admired companies and others surveyed lies in execution. 'It's not a secret what needs to be done,' says A.G. Lafley, CEO of Procter & Gamble, which ranked No. 1 in the household and personal products industry and had the highest overall score of any of the 346 companies on this year's list. 'The challenge is to put the strategy, systems, and capabilities in place, and then drive deployment and execution.'

Fortune (2008) 'The Secrets of Execution',
8 March 2004, p. 42

THE 'HOW' OF STRATEGY

If the mission of the company is about stating *what* the firm is about, then strategy is about *how* the firm will achieve the mission. In Honda's case the mission (the 'what' element) was 'to crush, squash and slaughter Yamaha!' but the strategy (or the 'how' element) was by launching a large range of products at a dramatic rate in 18 months.

In essence, then, we can illustrate basic strategy in Figure 2.1.

However, in order to have a sense of what the organization can – and cannot – do, the senior-level strategists need to have a good understanding of operations capabilities. Of course, in a business world that is increasingly about forming networks, it is important that strategists do not limit themselves to operations that reside within the firm only. But any

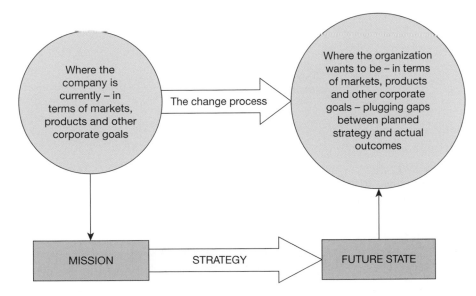

Figure 2.1 The basic strategy model

firm wishing to be involved in supply chains or networks has to 'bring something to the party' in terms of a range of capabilities that other firms within the same network either do not possess or do not intend to acquire.

It is important that we do not think of operations as a limiting factor in strategic formulation. Indeed, many companies have senior-level strategists who do understand the capabilities within the firm and can think in terms of how these capabilities can be targeted

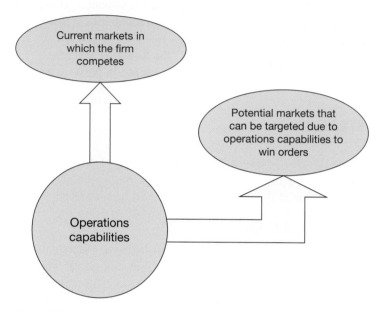

Figure 2.2 Using operations capabilities in strategy formulation

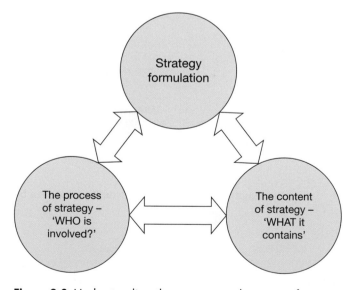

Figure 2.3 Understanding the process and content of strategy

to where the firm currently may not have a presence. For example, Sony is famous for exploiting its capabilities in miniaturization in a number of different markets. This 'reverse marketing' approach – using operations capabilities to target future markets – is part of the resource-based view of strategy, which we will discuss later. It is illustrated in Figure 2.2.

In order to understand strategy it is, perhaps, sensible to think of it in terms of both the process and content involved in the process. Figure 2.3 indicates the basic difference.

In reality, the process (the 'who') defines to a large extent the content (or the 'what') of strategy. For example, if the strategy is made by senior-level managers the scope of the content, typically, will be wider and more 'business focused' than if the process were left to functionally-focused managers. However, as we shall see, in order for strategy to be meaningful, the link between business and operations strategy is vital.

THE VITAL ROLE OF STRATEGY

Although there may not be absolute agreement on the definition of strategy, there are at least four characteristics that tend to distinguish *strategic* from *tactical* decisions.

1. The role of senior management

We can say that strategy *formulation* tends to be the prerogative of senior managers within the firm and that the final decisions regarding the direction of the firm will rest with these senior-level managers. However, other levels of the firm may also be involved in the development of strategic plans and these other levels will certainly be involved in their *implementation* (see Johnson and Scholes, 2008, for a good discussion on strategic formulation).

2. Creating competitive advantage

Strategic decisions are intended to create competitive advantage for the firm or, at the very least, to allow the firm to continue to compete in its chosen markets. However, it should fall under the realm of strategists within the firm to determine and exploit opportunities and, at the same time, to be aware of, and diffuse, potential threats from other players. So a feature of strategy is the need for awareness and vision outside of the firm, as Hamel and Prahalad (1994, p. 78) explain:

> To get to the future first, top management must either see opportunities not seen by other top teams or must be able to exploit opportunities, by virtue of preemptive and consistent capability-building, that other companies can't.

For some firms this will mean attacking and exploiting opportunities, where a major player has not paid attention or has believed a particular market segment to be insignificant. For example, GM has lost vast amounts of market share (it went from a high in the domestic market of 61 per cent in 1980 down to around 20 per cent in 2012) to the likes of Honda, Mazda, Toyota, Chrysler, and Ford, who either attacked or, indeed, *created* market segments neglected by GM. These neglected, or ignored segments included 4-wheel-drives, sub-compacts, turbos, and minivans.

On the other hand, ACCOR Hotels has come to dominate the hotel market in France by deliberately developing a strategy based on having a hotel brand for all market segments – Formula 1 and Urbis at the lower end of the market, Orbis and Novotel for the middle market, and Sofitel at the top end.

However, as we noted above, strategy does not necessarily concern itself with the destruction of other players but, if we expand the military application of strategy further, a firm may often develop alliances with other competitors rather than seek their destruction. These alliances may play a major factor in the success of the firm in specific areas, as we shall see in Chapter 4 on innovation and Chapter 3 on strategic partnerships in the supply chain. A key requirement for entry into these alliances, though, is in the operations capability that each firm can bring to a particular alliance.

3. The profound consequences of strategic decisions

A strategic decision can profoundly alter, and have major consequences for, the firm. Examples of such decisions might include massive financial investment (for example GM's $80 billion investment in technology); radical reconfigurations of entire business structures, (as happened with many US 'giants'); and radical downsizing within the enterprise (again exemplified by many US giants from the 1990s through to the present day). An operations strategy concerned with supply may lead to a reshaping of the organization, including outsourcing and insourcing operations, and configuring an internal supply chain, thus profoundly altering its nature.

When business strategy decisions turn out to be flawed the consequences can be profoundly damaging, as was the ill-fated merger between Chrysler and Daimler, which has led to Chrysler's demise.

CASE: PROBLEMS AT CHRYSLER

So it's come to this. Chrysler, inventor of the minivan (one of the best-selling ideas in automotive history), is starting to turn itself into a marketer and contract manufacturer of other people's cars. To plug gaping holes in its truck-heavy lineup, the U.S. automaker already plans to stick a Chrysler badge on a restyled Nissan Motors Versa subcompact. Now comes word that it is negotiating with the Japanese company to start selling a version of the Altima family sedan. Plus, to pick up the slack at its underutilized truck and minivan plants, Chrysler aims to become an assembler-for-hire for any maker that needs those vehicles. This plan did not spring from the brain of a car guy. It smells of the moneymen who are now deeply nested in Chrysler's operations. Cerberus Capital management paid $7.4 billion for 80 per cent of the company and, having underestimated the difficulty of turning it around, is looking to cut costs and conserve cash.

Business Week (2008) 'It's a strange detour for Chrysler', 25 August 2008, pp. 28–9.

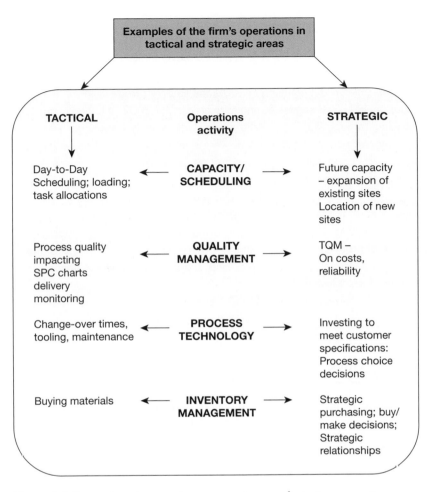

Figure 2.4 Tactical and strategic concerns in manufacturing operations

4. Long-term horizons

Strategic decisions can have long-term implications for the firm and hence the factor of time is an important one for strategists (Das, 1991; Itami and Numagami, 1992). It is important to note that strategic planning is not simply crystal-ball gazing into the far future; for strategy to be effective it also needs to have a sense of timing and urgency in its implementation.

There are a number of areas of operations which are simultaneously tactical and strategic in scope, and these are listed in Figure 2.4. The problem with many firms is that the perceived tactical concerns are seen to rest with Production/operations staff, whereas the strategic concerns do not.

THE FAILURE OF OPERATIONS STRATEGIES

For much of the past two decades, the stunning growth of the U.S. economy was widely hailed in academic, business, and government circles as evidence that America's competitiveness problem was as obsolete as leg warmers and Jazzercise. The data suggest otherwise. Beginning in 2000, the country's trade balance in high-technology products – historically a bastion of U.S. strength – began to decrease. By 2002, it turned negative for the first time and continued to decline through 2007. . . . What, then, was actually happening when it seemed things were going so well? Companies operating in the U.S. were steadily outsourcing development and manufacturing work to specialists abroad and cutting their spending on basic research. In making their decisions to outsource, executives were heeding the advice du jour of business gurus and Wall Street: Focus on your core competencies, off-load your low-value-added activities, and redeploy the savings to innovation, the true source of your competitive advantage. But in reality, the outsourcing has not stopped with low-value tasks like simple assembly or circuit-board stuffing. Sophisticated engineering and manufacturing capabilities that underpin innovation in a wide range of products have been rapidly leaving too. As a result, the U.S. has lost or is in the process of losing the knowledge, skilled people, and supplier infrastructure needed to manufacture many of the cutting-edge products it invented.

Pisano and Shih, (2009) 'Restoring american competitiveness',
Harvard Business Review, 87(7/8), 114–25

STRATEGIC FAILURES

Part of the issue for many firms is that their 'strategies' have not been strategies at all. The strategic decisions have not served to create long-term competitive advantage for the company but have often been driven by short-term myopia. When many of firms do this it can be problematic on a national scale, robbing a country of skills, knowledge, and the possibility of 'learning by doing' in operations. This was described very well by Pisano and Shih (2009) – see box above.

Not surprisingly this has had massive implications for the US trade deficit, as shown in Figure 2.5.

Many firms' strategic decisions in a range of industrial sectors now mean that manufacturing operations take place in China and not in the US or Europe:

China-based producers assemble most of the world's laptop and desktop computers, and nearly all of that work is done by Taiwanese-owned and managed factories – for instance, Hon Hai, Quanta, and Asustek. These engineering and manufacturing specialists are contracted by Dell, Hewlett-Packard, and other multinationals. Their business model is to do assembly and test work in China; build huge scale (Hon Hai is the biggest of these specialists, with global revenues of $51 billion and net earnings of $2.3 billion, and a Shenzhen campus that employs 270,000 people); and stick to a narrow value-add focus, adding less than 5% of the product's total cost. These specialists also manufacture cell phones and other electronic consumer goods.

Ghemawat and Hout (2008)

This has had a catastrophic impact on the US economy, which by 2012 had debts of more than $15 trillion with no solution in sight.

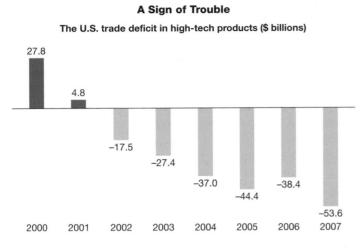

A Sign of Trouble

The U.S. trade deficit in high-tech products ($ billions)

Note: Sectors included are: biotechnology, life sciences, optoelectronics, information and communications, electronics, flexible manufacturing, advanced materials, aerospace, weapons, nuclear technology, and computer software.

Figure 2.5
The US trade deficit in high-tech products ($ billions)
Pisano and Shih (2009)

This gap between revenue and costs is shown in Figure 2.6:

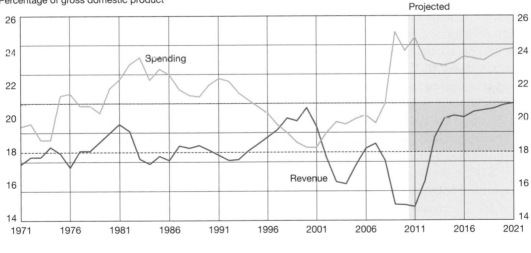

*1971 to 2010
Source: Congressional Budget Office

Figure 2.6 US budget gap, 1971–2021

However, at the very time when many Western firms are outsourcing to China, some Chinese firms are, ironically, setting up in the West as shown in Case 2.2.

CASE 2.2: AMERICAN MADE . . . CHINESE OWNED

Companies from China are spending billions to build factories in the U.S. – and creating new jobs for American workers.

About a mile past the Bountiful Blessings Church on the outskirts of Spartanburg, S.C., make a right turn. There, tucked into an industrial court behind a row of sapling cherry trees not much taller than I am, past a company that makes rubber stamps and another that stitches logos onto caps and bags, is a brand-new factory: the state-of-the-art American Yuncheng Gravure Cylinder plant. Due to open any day now, it will make cylinders used to print labels like the ones around plastic soda bottles. But unlike its neighbors in Spartanburg, Yuncheng is a Chinese company. It has come to South Carolina because by Chinese standards, America is darn cheap.

Yes, you read that right. The land Yuncheng purchased in Spartanburg, at $350,000 for 6.5 acres, cost one-fourth the price of land back in Shanghai or Dongguan, a gritty city near Hong Kong where the company already runs three plants. Electricity is cheaper too: Yuncheng pays up to 14¢ per kilowatt-hour in China at peak usage, and just 4¢ in South Carolina. And no brownouts either, a sporadic problem in China. It's true that American workers are much more expensive, of course, and the overall cost of making a widget in China remains lower, and perhaps always will.

But for hundreds of Chinese companies like Yuncheng, the U.S. has become a better, less expensive place to set up shop. It could be the biggest role reversal since, well . . . when Nixon went to China. 'The gap between manufacturing costs in the U.S. and China is shrinking,' explains John Ling, a naturalized American from China who runs the South Carolina Department of Commerce's business recruitment office in Shanghai. Ling recruited Yuncheng to Spartanburg, and others too: Chinese companies have invested $280 million and created more than 1,200 jobs in South Carolina alone.

Today some 33 American states, ports, and municipalities have sent representatives like Ling to China to lure jobs once lost to China back to the U.S. Besides affordable land and reliable power, states and cities are offering tax credits and other incentives to woo Chinese manufacturers. Beijing, meanwhile, which has mandated that Chinese companies globalize by expanding to key markets around the world, is chipping in by offering to finance up to 30 per cent of the initial investment costs, according to Chinese business sources.

The enticements are working. Chinese companies announced new direct investments in the U.S. of close to $5 billion in 2009 alone, according to New York City-based economic consultancy the Rhodium Group, which tallied the numbers for Fortune. That's well below Japanese investment in the U.S., which peaked at $148 billion in 1991, but a big jump from China's previous investments, which had been averaging around $500 million a year. Chinese firms last year acquired or announced they were starting more than 50 U.S. companies. And when China finally allows the value of its currency, the yuan, to appreciate – and it's just a question of when – Americans can expect to see Chinese projects, small today, really take off and have an impact on the U.S. economy. This could be a good thing for relations between the two countries. 'It will take many years to balance out the flow of U.S. investment into China,' says Dan Rosen, a principal at the Rhodium Group. But, he says, China's aggressive interest in U.S. investment suddenly gives Washington some leverage as it seeks to negotiate with Beijing on tariffs, trade issues, and economic policy.

None of that matters much in Spartanburg. Skilled workers at American Yuncheng will earn $25 to $30 an hour, line operators $10 to $12. That's a lot more than the $2 an hour that unskilled labor costs in China, but the company can qualify for a state payroll tax credit of $1,500 per worker (for any company creating more than 10 jobs). And by being closer to companies like Coca-Cola, Yuncheng can respond more quickly when they need new labels designed to show that a product has reduced its fat content or added more flavor. If business goes well, company president Li Wenchun expects to double the size of his operation, maybe in five to 10 years, and employ up to 120 Americans. 'I'd like it to be next month, but it depends on how fast we develop the market here,' he tells me through a Mandarin interpreter.

So far there's little sign of anti-Chinese sentiment among South Carolinians, who watched their state lose its cotton-based textile-manufacturing industry to low-cost countries like China. Fortune asked Sen. Jim DeMint, a Republican torchbearer for conservative causes, what he thinks of communists creating work in his home state. 'South Carolina is one of the best places in the world to do business, and that's why so many international companies are moving jobs into our state' is his only reply. . . .

Chinese companies see America as more than a manufacturing center. So far this year they have announced plans to build a wind-energy turbine plant and wind farm in Nevada that will create 1,000 American jobs; purchased the 400-employee Los Angeles Marriott Downtown out of foreclosure; and acquired a shuttered shopping center in Milwaukee, with plans to turn it into a mega-mall for 200 Chinese retailers. In some cases Chinese companies are resuscitating American outfits that had been left for dead. About 70 miles west of Spartanburg, near the Georgia border, past signs reading '24-hour fried chicken,' another Chinese company is hiring engineers – metallurgical and mechanical, some from nearby Clemson University. In June 2009, Top-Eastern Group, a tool manufacturer based in China's coastal city of Dalian, acquired a factory here along with three other facilities from Kennametal, one of America's largest machine-tool makers, after the U.S. company, based in Latrobe, Pa., reported a $137 million loss (citing a slowdown in industrial activity) in the quarter before the sale. . . .

And how do the employees feel about having a Chinese entrepreneur come to their rescue? 'Just because it's a Chinese owner, they don't really care,' says Scott Henderson, a 47-year-old manufacturing manager who had been furloughed one week a month along with his workers before Chee bought the factory. 'They're all happy to be working 40 hours a week.' They also have the opportunity for overtime, and a third, graveyard shift has been added to serve a nearly 40 per cent rise in orders. 'I feel great about it,' says Sam Marcengill, a 24-year-old technician at the plant. Last year he was laid off for six months before Chee's purchase gave him his job back. Now he's on overtime, 48 hours a week. 'The work's a lot more steady. It's better. Personally I'm a lot better off. It's a great thing.' . . .

Now the only way to know you're in a Chinese factory is by looking up at the large Chinese flag hanging from the rafters – alongside an American one, of course – and by the very Chinese motivational slogans on the walls: SPIRIT OF ENTREPRENEURSHIP – STRIVE FOR A CLEARLY DEFINED OBJECTIVE AND MAKE THE IMPOSSIBLE POSSIBLE WITHOUT AN EXCUSE reads the banner over the refrigerator testing line. And if you come in February, Sexton organizes a Chinese New Year party with food and outdoor firecrackers.

What is perhaps most startling about the Haier factory is that it is actually shipping goods back to China. Best known for its mini-fridges for dorm rooms and studio apartments, Haier's U.S. plant also

CASE STUDY

makes large units, good for supersized American McMansions but too large for a typical Chinese household. Now a growing number of wealthy people in China want to supersize too, so Haier has realized it can ship a small number, maybe 4,000 a year, of its highest-end refrigerators home and sell them for $2,600 apiece – more than China's average annual income of around $2,000. (Haier also ships U.S.-made refrigerators to India, Australia, Mexico, and Canada.) There aren't enough wealthy customers yet to make it worthwhile retooling any of the 29 Haier factories in China, but the nearby deepwater port in Charleston, S.C., makes export easy enough. 'There are folks in China who want high-end products,' says Haier America factory president Joseph Sexton. 'China is a much different place than people think.'

Fortune (2010) 'American made . . . Chinese owned', 24 May 2010, 161(7), 84–92.

FROM BUSINESS STRATEGIES TO OPERATIONS STRATEGY

There is no one, best way to formulate strategy, and the debate on whether strategy should be internal, resource-based on the one hand, or fully externally market-driven on the other, may be seen as one of mainly intellectual interest. In practice, many organizations will combine both internal and external considerations in the same way that they tend to innovate as a result of both 'push technology' (from internal developments) and 'pull demand' (from market requirements). These capabilities are not limited to operations only but they must include operations capabilities including quality, innovation, flexibility of volume and variety requirements, delivery speed, and reliability. While excellent marketing skills need to be in place within an organization, they are of little use if there are not world-class operations management capabilities (internal and external) also in place to support the marketing intentions of the organization. Every firm must be aware of external issues, including macro-economic factors, and social and technological changes. The PEST model ('political economic social and technical' elements) is a convenient – but hardly exhaustive – approach to scanning external issues. However, the firm must also pay great attention to internal capabilities and link these with opportunities and threats that may influence the firm. Brown *et al.*, (2001) offer a simple model of managing the process (see Figure 2.7).

In some firms, operations personnel will be involved from stage two onwards. However, some firms involve operations from stage four and for others, stage six (design operations systems) is where production/operations come into the process – a role which is to react to plans and strategies *already in place*. However, by that stage the original corporate aim could be 'out of line' with production/operations capability.

In the same way that there is no fixed way in the process of strategy, it is also best to see the *content* of strategy as a dynamic rather than fixed entity. However, we suggest that the content should include at least those items listed below:

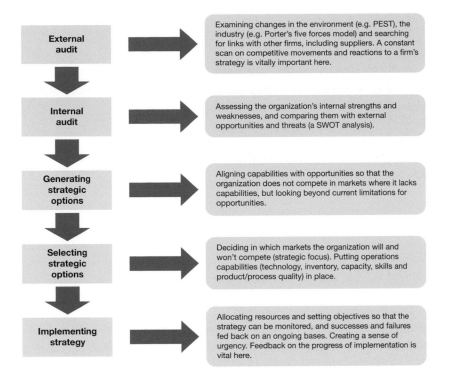

Figure 2.7
A simplified process
of strategy
Brown *et al.* (2001)

- *Process choice*: the selection of the right approach to producing goods or delivering service;

- *Innovation*: the adaptation or renewal of the organization's processes or outputs to ensure they adapt to changes in the external environment;

- *Supply chain management*: the external management of relationships with suppliers to ensure the effective and efficient supply of inputs;

- *Control of resources*: the internal management of inventories;

- *Production control*: the effective and efficient management of processes;

- *Work organization*: the management and organization of the workforce within the organization;

- *Customer satisfaction*: the management of quality.

If any of these imperatives are mismanaged the future of the organization is placed in jeopardy. It is for this reason that each of these has a chapter in this book devoted to it and the key approaches to managing the imperative are identified. Specifically, an operations strategy must include *at least* the following:

- Amounts of capacity required by the organization to achieve its aims.

- The range and locations of facilities.

- Technology investment to support process and product developments.

- Formation of strategic buyer–supplier relationships as part of the organization's 'extended enterprise'.

- The rate of new product or service introduction.

- Organizational structure – to reflect what the firm 'does best', often entailing outsourcing of other activities.

UNDERSTANDING MANUFACTURING AND OPERATIONS STRATEGY

Manufacturing strategy was the forerunner of the wider aspects of operations strategy. Manufacturing strategy was established as a core topic in operations management by the major contributions from US academics, including Skinner (1969; 1978; 1985), along with Hayes and Wheelwright (1984), as well as from the UK, particularly Hill (1995). Skinner (1969) had pointed out that not only was the manufacturing function being neglected as a strategic element of the planning process, but also that the linkage between manufacturing and strategic planning was elusive and ill-defined.

Over 40 years on since Skinner's seminal contribution, it has been estimated that over 250 conceptual and empirical papers on manufacturing strategy have been published in over 30 major journals (Dangayach and Deshmukh, 2001). The discussions on the role and purpose of manufacturing strategy have been broad and include many frameworks for identifying key manufacturing decisions. Although there are no absolute agreements about the role of manufacturing strategy – and it has even been questioned by one of the field's leading scholars, Kim Clark, if manufacturing strategy is passé (Clark, 1996) – most writers agree that its potential role can be both central and pivotal.

For operations strategy to be useful, it needs to have consistency among decisions that affect business-level strategy, competitive priorities, and manufacturing infrastructure (e.g., Skinner, 1969; Hayes and Wheelwright, 1984; Hill 2000). Much of the degree to which manufacturing strategy will be effective relies on the internal consistency of manufacturing strategy, manufacturing capabilities, marketing–manufacturing congruence, and their effects on manufacturing performance (Bozarth & Edwards, 1997).

There is some confusion in terms of both where, and when, operations strategy might appear within the overall strategic planning process of the firm. For example, it has been questioned whether operations strategy has been replaced by specific approaches such as *just-in-time* (JIT, which we discuss in Chapter 9) and *total quality management* (TQM, in Chapter 8). Mills *et al.* (1995, p. 17) summarize the perceived confusion concerning operations strategy as applied to manufacturing when they ask:

> What is a manufacturing strategy nowadays – is it world-class, lean production, JIT, cells or TQM? Is it none of them, some of them or all of them?

However, Hayes and Pisano (1994, p. 77) assert that manufacturing strategy is wider than this:

Simply improving manufacturing – by, for example, adopting JIT, TQM or some other three-letter acronym – is not a strategy for using manufacturing to achieve competitive advantage.

The same could equally be true of services. However, there has been less research into service strategy, although we will discuss its importance in this chapter as well as in Chapter 11 on *service operations*.

The perceived confusion with manufacturing strategy is discussed by Kim and Arnold (1996) who, similarly, conclude that managers often find it hard to distinguish between approaches such as JIT and other issues which might be included in manufacturing strategy. Some clarity of the process and content of strategy is provided by Hayes and Wheelwright (1984) who speak of four stages where manufacturing strategy (as part of operations strategy) can appear in, and contribute to, the firm's planning process:

- *Stage 1 – Internally neutral*: the role here is to ensure that manufacturing will not disrupt the intention of the firm and manufacturing's role is purely reactive to an already devised strategy.

- *Stage 2 – Externally neutral*: the role here is for manufacturing to look externally and to ensure that it is able to achieve parity with competitors.

- *Stage 3 – Internally supportive*: here manufacturing exists to support business strategy. Manufacturing capabilities are audited and the impact of a proposed business strategy upon manufacturing is considered.

- *Stage 4 – Externally supportive*: here manufacturing capabilities are central in determining the nature of business strategy and their involvement is much more proactive.

Although the model relates, essentially, to the formulation of manufacturing strategy, we suggest that the same model could be used for services and, in any event, should be seen within the wider view of operations strategy.

Hayes and Wheelwright's contribution is also important because it helps to explain what a manufacturing strategy should *contain* (1984, p. 30):

Manufacturing strategy consists of a sequence of decisions that, over time, enables a business unit to achieve a desired manufacturing structure, infrastructure and set of specific capabilities.

The scope of structural/infrastructure areas that can form part of operations strategy is wide-ranging and can include quality capabilities (including quality requirements that a plant might demand from its supplier base), manufacturing processes, investment requirements, skills audits, capacity requirements, inventory management throughout the supply chain and new product innovation. Manufacturing strategy is concerned with combining responsibility for resource management (internal factors) as well as achieving business (external) requirements:

> Manufacturing strategy is viewed as the effective use of manufacturing strengths as a competitive weapon for the achievement of business and corporate goals.
>
> (Swamidass and Newell, p. 1987)

Although applied to manufacturing, the above analysis is equally relevant to services. Hence we can refer to an 'operations strategy' applicable to any business organization.

KEY TASKS IN OPERATIONS STRATEGY

One of the key tasks for operations managers in developing strategy is that these managers are aware of competitive factors and, as a result, are able to put in place capabilities to deal with such competitive requirements. The link between these requirements and operations capabilities is shown in Table 2.1.

All of these capabilities depend, to a very large extent, on managing production/operations in a strategic manner. Forming an operations strategy, which links into, and forms part of, the overall business strategy, can also be a vital factor in uniting the organization. In spite of all of the chaos and turbulence in markets, a clear strategy can play an important part in the firm's success as, Hayes and Pisano (1994, p. 77) state:

> In today's turbulent competitive environment, a company more than ever needs a strategy that specifies the kind of competitive advantage that it is seeking in the marketplace and articulates how that advantage is to be achieved.

Table 2.1 The link between operations and competitive factors

Competitive factors	Operations task
Offer consistently low defect rates	Process quality
Offer dependable delivery	Delivery reliability
Provide high-performance products or amenities	Product quality
Offer fast deliveries	Delivery speed
Customize products and services to customer needs	Flexibility
Profit in price competitive markets	Low-cost production
Introduce new products quickly	Rapid innovation
Offer a broad product line	Flexibility
Make rapid volume changes	Flexibility
Make rapid product mix changes	Customization; flexibility
Make product easily available	Delivery speed/reliability (distribution)
Make rapid changes in design	Flexibility

Brown (1996)

The need for business and operations strategies to be linked is as crucial today as in Skinner's day. Strategy matters because without it firms' short-term decisions will conflict with their long-term goals (St John and Young, 1992). A firm must be poised and ready to meet future market opportunities as illustrated in Table 2.1 (Brown, 1996). If not, strategic successes are as likely to be due to chance as to plan, and thus cannot be reliably sustained or repeated. Operations play an important role in the overall performance of the business unit, as measured by market share, growth, and profits (see for example Ramanujam and Venkatraman, 1987).

Tunälv (1992) found that firms with a formulated operations strategy achieve higher business performance than firms without such a strategy, with respect to return on sales. Papke-Shields and Malhotra (2001) extended this research by explicitly testing the alignment between business and manufacturing strategies and firm performance. Sun and Hong (2002) examined the relationships between alignment, business performance, and manufacturing performance. They found that alignment has a positive, although not linear, relationship with four subjective measure of business performance. Joshi *et al.*, (2003) provided interesting insights into strategic alignment within the firm and operations performance. Brown *et al.*, (2010) found specific links between the contribution of manufacturing strategy involvement and alignment on the one hand and world-class manufacturing performance on the other.

So, operations capabilities – if properly utilized – can provide a 'competitive weapon' in the firm's strategic planning (Skinner, 1969). Operations strategy contributes substantially to business strategy as well as day-to-day operations management (Meredith and Vineyard, 1993), because the process, content, and implementation of operations strategy are the means by which operations resources are deployed to complement the business strategy. Operations strategy influences areas as diverse as:

- Selecting new process technologies (Honeycutt *et al.*, 1993; Beach *et al.*, 2000; Das and Joshi, 2007);
- Developing new products (Spring and Dalrymple, 2000); and
- Managing human resources (Youndt *et al.*, 1996; Paiva *et al.*, 2008).

Operations strategy should be aligned to the business unit's competitive environment through business-level strategy (Ward and Duray, 1995), which requires linking business and operations strategies.

Thus, the firm's external competitive environment affects the structure and infrastructure of operations and for performance (Pagell and Krause, 1999). Operations strategy should therefore be involved in strategy formulation and implementation at the business unit level.

Operations strategy must match operations capabilities with market requirements in three key areas, shown below (Brown and Blackmon, 2005):

- Operations strategy must support the goals of the strategic business unit (SBU) through being aligned with business-level competitive strategy (e.g. Skinner, 1969; Hayes and Wheelwright, 1984).

- Operations strategy must align with other functional-level strategies, particularly the marketing and human resources strategies of the SBU (e.g. Deane *et al.*, 1991; Berry *et al.*, 1995; Menda and Dilts, 1997);
- Operations strategy must lead to internal consistency within the operations function (e.g. Hill, 1995).

WHY ORGANIZATIONS STRUGGLE WITH FORMING OPERATIONS STRATEGIES

Companies are full of highly intelligent people but, often, they struggle with the notion of operations strategy. We suggest that the key for this is linked to the changes to operations management over time that we discussed in Chapter 1. Here we provide some insights into how the changes have had important impacts on the formulation of operations strategy.

Looking back . . .

Under Craft Production, the operations that an organization performed and the strategy that it pursued were very closely linked together. This is because, often, the persons running the business were those who had performed operations within the company. Also, craft organizations tended to be quite flat in terms of hierarchy and the 'distance' between strategic and operations realms was close. Many texts on operations management tend to focus merely on the changes of volume of production when they describe the developments from craft to mass production. However, this tells only a superficial part of what really took place in this shift.

The transition from craft, through mass production, to the current era, provides insight into the changing role of operations personnel within firms, and at least three major factors emerge. First, we can say that operations personnel were often absent from the most senior levels of the firm as enterprises became larger and more functionally organized (Lazonick, 1990; Chandler, 1992; Lazonick and West, 1995). While increasing importance has been placed on operations personnel in terms of their contribution to the firm's capabilities (see for example, Womack *et al.*, 1990; Kenney and Florida, 1993) this has not necessarily included involvement in terms of their seniority within the hierarchy of the firm, which is a telling indication of the operations management role in many Western plants.

Second, the role of operations managers often became that of a technical specialism rather than an involvement in the business of the firm. Often, Operations' contribution, in terms of its capability, is ignored until *after strategic plans have already been formulated* by an elite planning group whose understanding of the specifics of operations or service delivery may be very limited (Hayes and Wheelwright, 1984). The relegation of operations to a mere function, unrelated to the strategy process, is discussed by Lazonick (1990; 1991) and Prais (1981) in comparisons made between the UK and US on the one hand, and Japan and Germany on the other.

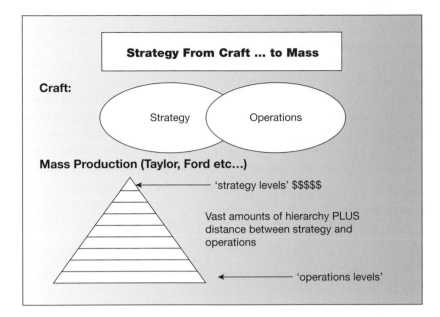

Figure 2.8 From craft to mass and the impact upon strategy

Third, strategy formulation and planning became the prerogative of senior managers and operations personnel were, typically, excluded from the process because of their position within the firm, so that operations strategies, where they did exist, were merely the means by which an already existing business strategy became translated into plant operations.

The case for a better, more integrated approach, involving all levels of the firm, was made by *The Economist*:

> **The trouble with many multinationals is that they are legacies of a very different era. Many grew up in the heyday of command-and-control management, when strategy was made by a tiny elite at the top, work was broken down into its simplest component parts and workers were monitored by layer upon layer of managers. But today fashion is so fickle and markets so quicksilver that decisions are best taken by front-line workers rather than by lethargic middle managers.**
> *Economist* (1995) 'Survey of multinationals:
> Who wants to be a giant?', 24 June 1995

THE PRESENT DAY PROBLEM

Many strategic decisions in firms are made by those who might know very little about operations and whose approach to strategy is, often, dictated by purely financial and short-term applications. Thus, even a decision that might have long-term implications – investment in process technology or a cut in the training budget, for example – is sometimes made as a quick-fix, cost-cutting device rather than as a means to enhance capability in a number of competitive areas, other than low-cost production. In consequence, firms will often place too much of an emphasis on the wrong things.

For example, 'productivity' and 'return on equity, or capital employed' (ROCE) ratios – often touted by corporate officials within the firm – can be easily distorted to appear better than they really are, and it is vital to 'get behind the numbers' and calculations to know what the figures actually mean. For example, the productivity ratio is derived by dividing a firm's outputs by its inputs. In the UK, whole areas of the manufacturing base declined between 1980 and 2000 but, during this period, Britain's productivity ratio was second only to Japan's – but for entirely different reasons. In Britain, inputs went down (sometimes in terms of whole industries) and the cost of this approach is best summarized by Hamel and Prahalad (1994, p. 9):

> Between 1969 and 1991, Britain's manufacturing output . . . went up by a scant 10% in real terms. Yet over this same period, the number of people employed in British operations . . . declined by 37% . . . during the early and mid 1980s . . . UK manufacturing productivity increased faster than any other major industrialized country except Japan . . . British companies were, in fact, surrendering global market share.

And the same sort of 'improvement' through productivity was also apparent in the US where, as Dertouzos *et al.*, (1989, p. 31) commented:

> There is a dark side to these developments, however. A significant fraction of the productivity gains in manufacturing were achieved by shutting down inefficient plants and by permanently laying off workers at others. Employment in U.S. operations industry declined by 10 percent between 1979 and 1986, and that loss of jobs accounted for about 36 percent of the recorded improvements in labor productivity.

Similarly, the ROCE ratio by itself says very little. Of course, it is important to know how the firm's money is being used and to assess if it could be better used elsewhere (which is one of the reasons behind the ROCE ratio) but if a firm wants to appear to have sound ROCE it can achieve this quite easily – simply by not investing in the plant or service over a period of time. Of course, the manufacturing plant or service operation will then be unable to compete against the world's best but, in terms of ROCE, the firm will 'look good'. There have to be better ways of determining success for the firm and one of the best ways for doing so lies in the role and contribution of operations strategy.

Part of the problem for both manufacturing and service settings are that senior level managers are often separate from front-line operations and customer interface. This is because the changes that took place from craft to mass production have not been addressed. Market requirements have changed remarkably since the development of mass production and, as we shall see, market requirements are now volatile. This demands that strategies are in place to deal with such volatility but, for many organizations, the gap between strategy and operations remains in place. This means that those developing strategy have little understanding of operations. This was perfectly summarized by Hemp (2002):

> It's easy for senior executives to hold forth about the importance of getting close to customers, anticipating their needs, exceeding their expectations. But how many of them have ever been out there on the front lines, experiencing firsthand what this actually feels like? What might they discover if they tried to find out – particularly at a company known for its obsessive commitment to customer service? Certainly, they would learn a lot from observing the operation at close range. But they would also glean useful insights from being part of the operation, from standing in the shoes and getting inside the heads of employees trying to satisfy demanding customers.

Hemp (2002) concluded that a key part of the strategy has to be ownership by the organization's employees:

> You don't demand that employees say, 'Certainly, my pleasure;' until it feels right to them. You don't mindlessly assume every guest wants to be pampered; some people just want to eat their dinners. . . . A recent study of hotel workers by researchers at Cornell's School of Hotel Administration found that, while job satisfaction plays a major role in employee retention, it isn't the key factor in a hotel's ability to provide excellent customer service. Rather, it is employees' emotional commitment – which is achieved in part through symbols and rituals that enhance employees' sense of identity with the company – that contributes most to superior performance . . . every company, even a two-year-old start-up, has traditions and even legends that can be tapped to help build employee commitment.

HOW OPERATIONS STRATEGY CAN CONTRIBUTE TO THE FIRM'S OVERALL STRATEGY

Operations strategy can be vitally important to achieving business goals and gaining competitive advantage in at least two ways. First, it can be central to the *implementation* of an already devised business strategy, which, as we have already noted, operations personnel may, or may not, have helped to formulate. In this approach, Operations' role is important in providing 'strategic fit' in focusing efforts and resources so that operations strategy is consistent with, and helps to support, the already devised business strategy (Hayes and Wheelwright, 1984; Miller and Roth, 1994).

Second, operations strategy can be used in a more proactive approach. Here, operational capabilities would be viewed as part of the core capabilities/competencies (Hamel and Prahalad, 1994) which can be exploited and used to create new opportunities and to target new areas. In this approach, Operations' contribution would be central to the *planning* stages of business strategy and is not restricted to the implementation of an already devised strategy.

This resource- and competence-based approach to strategy has become an important feature in the literature on strategy (see for example Stalk *et al.*, 1992; Collis and Montgomery, 1995). This approach equates with stage four of Hayes and Wheelwright's (1984) model, discussed earlier, whereby Operations' role is central in *creating* strategies to gain competitive advantage. This approach places profound importance on the link between operational and business strategies in terms of the consistency, and ongoing pursuit, of the firm's objectives.

Organization-specific capabilities, although very important, also need to be seen within a wider context of sets of capabilities that reside within what are, often, complex networks (Buhman *et al.*, 2005; Boyer *et al.*, 2005; 2006; Kouvelis *et al.*, 2006; Holcomb and Hitt, 2007; Rudberg and West, 2008). The context of an organization within networks becomes part of what is termed *extended resource-based theory* (Arya and Lin, 2007). For example, Wilk and

1 Corporate objectives	2 Marketing strategy	3 How do you qualify and win orders in the market place?	Operations strategy	
			4 Process choice	5 Infrastructure
Growth	Product/service	Price	Choice of various processes	Function support
Survival	Market and segments	Quality conformance	Trade-offs embodied in the process choice	Operations planning and control systems
Profit	Range	Delivery		Quality assurance and control
Return on investment	Mix	• speed	Process positioning	
	Volumes	• reliability	Capacity:	Systems engineering
Other financial measures	Standardization versus customization	Demand increases	• size	Clerical procedures
		Colour range	• timing	Payment systems
	Level of innovation	Product/service range	• location	Work structuring
	Leader versus follower alternatives	Design leadership	Role of inventory in the process configuration	Organizational structure
		Technical support		
		Brand awareness		
		New products and services – time to market		

Figure 2.9 The Hill framework

Hill (2000); Hill and Hill (2009)

Fensterseifer (2003) suggest that competitiveness is dependent upon not only individual resources and capabilities, but also on those shared within supply chains, or clusters of firms within supply chains or networks, and we shall discuss this in Chapter 3 on *supply* and Chapter 9 on *managing inventory*.

Such operations strategies can offer much to mainstream strategy, particularly resource-based approaches. For example, Corbett and Van Wassenhove (1994) and Gagnon (1999) view operations strategy as having a key role in the competence-based approaches to strategy and one that can nullify any notions of competitive tradeoffs in strategy formulation. This is endorsed by Beach *et al.*, (2000) and D'Souza and Williams (2000) in their respective discussions on the role of strategy in enhancing capabilities in flexibility. Similar claims for the importance of operations strategy have been made in relation to mass customization (Spring and Dalrymple, 2000). A key element of accruing capabilities in flexibility comes from the utilization of process technology where, again, the role of operations strategy can be pivotal (Kathuria and Partovi, 2000).

An important contribution on operations strategy came from Hill (2000). Hill talks about the need to have a fluid process that links corporate, marketing, and operations strategies into a unified process, as illustrated in Figure 2.9.

As can be seen, the links between corporate, marketing, and operations strategies is made very clear and the need for dialogue between them is vital. There is no doubt that this model provides excellent insight into the process of strategy. However, as important as this model is, its focus is based on strategy within the firm. It is also important that the firm looks outside itself and sees how it lines up within what are increasingly complex networks. We will develop the process when we look at strategic resonance later in the chapter. For now, a note on order-winning and order-qualifying criteria is pertinent here.

ORDER-WINNING AND ORDER-QUALIFYING CRITERIA

A powerful means of linking operations capability with market requirements is presented by Hill (1995; 2005) when he discusses the need to understand order-winning and order-qualifying criteria. Order winners are those factors that win orders in the marketplace over competitors; order-qualifying criteria are those factors that the firm needs to be able to achieve in order to compete *at all* in the marketplace. Without these capabilities the firm will lose orders – in fact, order qualifiers may become order losers for the firm.

Order-qualifying criteria must not therefore be viewed as less important than order-winning criteria because failure to achieve these will cause the firm to decline. In high-tech industries, an order qualifier must include up-to-date technology – without this the firm cannot hope to compete and will decline. However, a range of order-winning criteria come into play: low cost is an obvious one but delivery requirements are important too; in addition, the ability to configure to customer requirements (due to mass customization) is also important. Likewise, when John Martin transformed Taco Bell into a fast-food giant, he discovered that offering Mexican food was only an order-qualifying factor. Customers' order-winning criteria were found to be what was termed FACT (fast, accurate, clean, timely).

This approach – distinguishing between order-qualifying and order-winning criteria – provides a useful insight, but it is important to note the following caveats. First, order-qualifying and order-winning criteria may change over time – once a firm has undertaken an audit of these criteria it must be prepared to adapt as the criteria themselves change. In other words, the assessment of order-winning/qualifying criteria has to be an ongoing, dynamic process.

Second, the link between the order-winning/qualifying criteria and the process choices that Terry Hill made has been questioned (and we highlight the problem with this in Chapter 7). The concern is that the firm may make similar products under one choice of process but that these might be targeted at more than one market segment and there may be conflicting and differing requirements in these segments for the same product made under one type of process.

Third, consumers will not necessarily distinguish between order-qualifying and order-winning criteria and may, instead, look at the overall value or package being offered. For example, in buying a personal computer the customer may have rough guides or indications of price and basic specifications but will adjust both of these as the overall package offering becomes clearer.

Fourth, the organization must be prepared and able to improve all areas of operations management simultaneously. Again, this is very noticeable in high-tech markets where up-to-date technology, rapid innovation of new products, high quality levels, and low cost have to be achieved simultaneously.

SERVICE OPERATIONS

Much of the literature pertaining to the process and content of operations strategy has direct relevance to service strategy too. Although we devote an entire chapter to services (Chapter 11) a discussion on the specifics of service operations strategy is relevant here too. Similar to operations firms, service organizations have to consider capacity management, which we discuss in Chapter 10. This is true for new emerging economies, like India, as exemplified in Case 2.3.

Operations strategy is vital for service firms in terms of the strategic positioning of the offer to customers. For example, Singapore Airlines is noted for service excellence 'in an industry whose service standards are tumbling' Heracleous and Wirtz (2010). As well as providing excellent service it is also one of the industry's cost leaders. This goes against the grain for some schools of strategy:

SIA's success in executing a dual strategy of differentiation and cost leadership is unusual. Indeed, management experts, such as Michael Porter, argue that it's impossible to do so for a sustained period since dual strategies entail contradictory investments and organizational processes. Yet SIA, and a few other emerging-economy companies, view the dualities as opposites that form part of a whole. SIA executes its dual strategy by managing four paradoxes: Achieving service excellence cost-effectively, fostering centralized and decentralized innovation, being a technology leader and follower, and

CASE 2.3: ADDING SERVICE AND OPERATIONS CAPACITY IN INDIA

Titan Industries Ltd (TITN.BO), India's top watch and jewellery retailer, plans to add 80 to 100 retail stores . . . and up watch operations capacity by 3 million units annually on robust demand, a top official said. 'Expansion will go hand in hand with retail sales. We expect to grow topline by about 25 percent (next year) and in accordance with that we will open retail stores,' Titan Managing Director Bhaskar Bhat told Reuters on Wednesday 3 February.

Titan, which has 518 retails stores now, sells watches under a range of brands including the premium Titan and the economy brand Sonata. It has two jewellery retail chains – Tanishq and Goldplus. Titan may add between 80 to 100 retail stores next fiscal though the exact number was not finalised, Bhat said. The stores added would fall under different brands such as World of Titan, Tanishq, GoldPlus, Fastrack and Titan Eye+. 'A large part of store expansion will be done through the franchise route and hence would not require funding,' he said. 'The firm has spent most of its targeted capex of 700 million rupees for the current fiscal but had not yet finalised an amount for the next fiscal,' he said.

It is spending about 100 million rupees on setting up a new watch assembly facility in the northern state of Uttarakhand to keep up with the uptick in consumer demand. Bhat said the plant would have a operations capacity of 3 million watches annually and would help increase capacity to 18 million units per annum. 'It is expected to become operational in the next 3–4 months,' he said.

Titan, which also makes accessories such as eyewear, had last week reported a surge in quarterly profits and sales beating analysts expectations due to robust growth in both its jewellery and watch businesses. Sales in its jewellery business rose nearly 34 percent in the quarter ending Dec. 31, while revenues from the watch business grew 25 percent, indicating a turnaround in consumer sentiment. Its overall sales rose over 30 percent.

Bhat said jewellery business volume was expected to rise between 3 to 5 percent in Jan–March, despite higher gold prices. Titan had seen jewellery volumes grow 4 percent on year in the quarter to Dec. 31.

Titan has not changed prices of its watches and does not have any immediate plans for a revision. 'Jewellery . . . depends on the price of gold and gold has been higher by about 25 percent this year,' Bhat said. Bhat also said the company would continue to see robust growth in the coming quarters though it may not match that of the December quarter as the period included the favorable impact of festive season sales.

Reuters (2010) 'Titan to add retail stores, watch capacity', 3 February 2010.

CASE STUDY

---

using standardization to achieve personalization. The results speak for themselves: SIA has delivered healthy financial returns; it has never had an annual loss; and except for the initial capitalization, the Asian airline has funded its growth itself while paying dividends every year.

Heracleous and Wirtz (2010)

We need to remember: such capabilities do not come about by chance but are realized by the vision, implementation, and execution of strategy. As Prajogo and McDermott (2008)

Reaping the Rewards of a Dual Strategy

SIA has consistently maintained above-average profit margins, demonstrating that in an unforgiving industry it pays to have more than one source of competitive advantage.

Sources: IATA Financial Forecast, March 2010; Singapore Airlines Annual Report 2008–2009, 10-Year Statistical Record

Figure 2.10
Success at Singapore Airlines

Heracleous and Wirtz (2010)

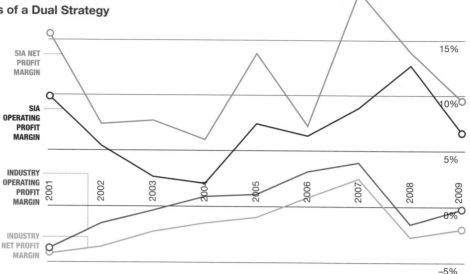

found when examining the relationships between operations strategies and operations activities in service context – high-performing service firms have stronger relationships between their operations strategies and operations activities than low-performing firms.

In the Singapore Airlines case, the rewards for pursuing such a strategy are evident in Figure 2.10.

Sometimes successful service operations depend upon the 'harder' tangible elements of the overall offering to customers. We touched on the importance of servitization in Chapter 1 and we will do so again in Chapter 11. This strategy is one of the few ways in which traditional 'manufacturing' players can create profits themselves; and they do so by providing value-added service to the firm's customers:

> Service is becoming 'super service' as machine tool builders and other production equipment vendors innovate a new competitive model. No longer a tired after-sales routine, service is now the strategy that builds and establishes reputations, sells the product and creates new business potential for vendor and customer alike. The customer lesson: Leverage the service strategy of your suppliers.
>
> (*Industry Week,* 2006)

Ignoring the crucial importance of service to the total offer to customer can be fatal, as described in Case 2.4.

For some service firms, the strategy is to provide what are termed 'integrated solutions'. As defined by Brax and Jonsson (2009, p. 541), integrated solutions are:

> a bundle of physical products, services, and information, seamlessly combined to provide more value than the parts alone, that addresses customer's needs in relation to specific

CASE 2.4: AKIMBO AND THE PROBLEM WITH ITS SERVICE OFFERING

Here's A Cautionary Tale: In 2004, when online video provider Akimbo decided to combine a set-top box with a movie-downloading service, it seemed like the perfect offering. The product and service were inextricably linked – one was worthless without the other. Sales of the DVR would drive a steady revenue stream from subscription fees, and customers wanting the convenience of downloading videos would have to invest in the hardware. But the company stumbled when it priced the less-valued component of the bundle, the set-top box, at a high $199, without understanding that the real profit potential was in the downloading service. Things went awry when the company charged users for its movie service. The shows were not top quality, and customers resented having to pay for them on top of what they'd already paid for the high-priced box. The offering failed, and the company went out of business in 2008.

Shankar *et al.*, (2009)

function or task in their business system; it is long-term oriented, integrates the provider as part of the customer's business system, and aims at optimizing the total cost for the customer.

For example, Intel has developed a number of mobile communication and computing offerings in the emerging field of health-care information technology and competes in this field through the concept of integrated service. The development of this concept and its components (e.g. electronic medical records solutions; mobile point-of-care solutions enabling access to patient information at the bedside, in labs, and in operating theatres; and secure patient infrastructure solutions) has been accomplished through collaborative projects with research hospitals and clinics in North America and Europe.

There are different forms of customer integration and co-creation, as shown in Table 2.2.

SERVICE OPERATIONS: THE SERVICE PROFIT CHAIN

Service operations thinking may be said to have originated with the publication of Sasser, Olsen and Wyckof's book on the subject in 1976. One reason why strategic operations may be so important derives from a long-term research programme into successful businesses by a group of Harvard academics. In 1997 Heskett, Sasser and Schlesinger published their book *Service Profit Chain* which 'simply stated ... maintains that there are direct and strong relationships between profit, growth, customer loyalty, customer satisfaction, the value of goods and services delivered to customers, and employee capability, satisfaction loyalty, and productivity'. Their model is illustrated in Figure 2.11. Although their work has focused on service firms, as they themselves state they believe this may apply to goods as well as services.

Fundamental to the service profit chain is the idea that in order to achieve profits and growth for the firm, an operations strategy must be in place. In their terms, this strategy

Table 2.2 Modes of service innovation activity: key aspects of co-creation

Characteristics	Mode of Service Co-Creation		
	Client-Driven	Provider-Driven	Balanced
Company Cases	MySAP, MySQL, NowPublic	Apple iTunes, Dell, Google, Microsoft, Nokia	Intel, McAfee, Skype, TVU Networks
Competitive Superiority	Value propositions are typically directed toward known clients and their explicit needs through client-driven market pull	Technology push in innovation-oriented development of services targets prospective clients	Ambidextrous innovation activity combines both market and technology orientation in service co-development
	Customer-centric innovation activity serves existing needs optimally through well-defined market-oriented solutions	The provider-driven development activity may create new innovative services that would not otherwise exist	Strategic congruence based on mutual interests enhances current and future value co-creation
Relational Complexity	Strong focus on immediate clients' needs forms a bias in collaborative relationships and reduces service reproducibility	The provider-driven innovation activity poses challenges concerning clients' willingness to commit to the service provider's priorities	Relational client-provider collaboration manifests enthusiasm for win-win situations in service co-creation
	Client is sensitive to providers' reluctance to invest in the client-driven innovation, which may affect the service relationship commitment	Pursuing clients to adapt service innovations leads to economic and social burdens, causing friction in relationships	Highly complex and sometimes contradictory interests in partnership-oriented relationships pose challenges for collective value creation
Operational Priority	Clients lead service co-development activity and challenge providers to adapt their capabilities to meet clients' wants and needs	The service provider is proactive in exploring new service opportunities for the future	Efficient service co-design requires the utilization and adaptation of both the service provider's and client's capabilities
	Efficient service co-creation depends on client's ability to exploit provider's resources	The service provider is wiling to accept business risks related to breaking the traditional frames of conducting business	Services are integrated to both the client's needs and the provider's offering portfolio
Cognitive Exigency	Humility and responsiveness to client's conditions epitomize the activity of service providers	Service providers need courage to prioritize future opportunities over current needs	The desire to cooperate and commit to common goals is a key requirement for both service providers and clients
	Client's confidence in demanding service and externalizing their requirements drives the innovation activity	Clients need to be content with the partial fulfilment of current needs	Collective innovation activity requires openness and trust in collaboration

Möller et al. (2008)

The Links in the Service-Profit Chain

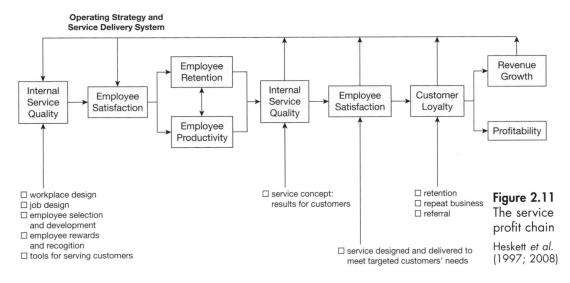

Figure 2.11
The service profit chain

Heskett *et al.*
(1997; 2008)

identifies where the most effort will be placed, how quality and cost will be controlled, and how performance will be measured against the competition. Derived from this is a so-called 'service delivery system', which is the specific combination of facilities, layout, equipment, procedures, technology, and employees needed to achieve this strategy. Heskett *et al.* argue that the highly successful firms they have studied, such as Southwest Airlines and Wal-Mart, have achieved their success through the development and implementation of an operations strategy. Wal-Mart's strategy is linked to its value proposition.

CASE: WAL-MART'S VALUE PROPOSITION

Wal-Mart's value proposition can be summed up as 'everyday low prices for a broad range of goods that are always in stock in convenient geographic locations.' It is those aspects of the customer experience that the company overdelivers relative to competitors. Underperformance on other dimensions, such as ambience and sales help, is a strategic choice that generates cost savings, which fuel the company's price advantage.

Collis and Rukstad (2008)

A key element of Heskett *et al.*'s (1997; 2008) research findings is evidence to suggest three strong links in successful firms. First there is a link between employee satisfaction and capability. Put simply, happy employees are more productive and consistently deliver better quality. For example, in Taco Bell, the Mexican-style restaurant chain, it was found that the outlets with the highest rates of staff retention (a major indicator of employee satisfaction) consistently outperformed those with high staff turnover. These differences were great – on average high staff retention outlets had double the sales and 55 per cent higher profits than the worst ones. Similar links have also been reported in the financial services sector (Zornitsky, 1995).

Not only did employee satisfaction lead to better firm performance, but related to this is a clear link between employee and customer satisfaction. Heskett *et al.* have found this in Chick-Fil-A, Bank of Ireland, MCI, Swedbank, and AT&T Travel. Indeed, this view has been adopted as a fundamental business philosophy in some firms. For instance, J.W. Marriott Senior is often quoted as saying 'It takes happy employees to make happy customers'. The third strong link is perhaps not surprising – it is between customer satisfaction and growth/profits. Heskett *et al.* report that Banc One found that in all its operating divisions, there was a direct relationship between profitability and loyal customers; whilst Waste Management reported 65 per cent more profitability in divisions with the highest levels of customer satisfaction. Heskett *et al.* (2008) endorse the importance of employee involvement:

> A growing number of companies that includes Banc One, Intuit, Southwest Airlines, ServiceMaster, USAA, Taco Bell, and MCI know that when they make employees and customers paramount, a radical shift occurs in the way they manage and measure success. The new economics of service requires innovative measurement techniques. These techniques calibrate the impact of employee satisfaction, loyalty, and productivity on the value of products and services delivered so that managers can build customer satisfaction and loyalty and assess the corresponding impact on profitability and growth. In fact, the lifetime value of a loyal customer can be astronomical, especially when referrals are added to the economics of customer retention and repeat purchases of related products. For example, the lifetime revenue stream from a loyal pizza eater can be $8,000, a Cadillac owner $332,000, and a corporate purchaser of commercial aircraft literally billions of dollars.

Southwest Airlines' performance against its rivals is very impressive as can be seen in Figure 2.12.

The service profit chain concept therefore makes a strong argument in support of strategic operations management. It also suggests that how a firm measures its strategic performance may need to be considered. Heskett *et al.* are enthusiastic advocates of the balanced scorecard approach and, again, Wal-Mart is a good example of this in Figure 2.13.

STRATEGIC RESONANCE

Although much of the literature in both operations management and mainstream strategy has been useful, there are specific problems, which include the following:

- Operations literature (and sometimes practice) sees the need to 'make the case' for strategy, but there is not a great deal of cross-over to strategy mainstream.

How Southwest Compares with Its Competitors

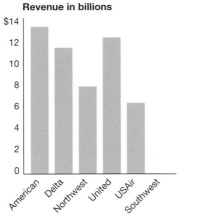

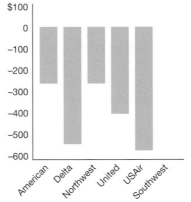

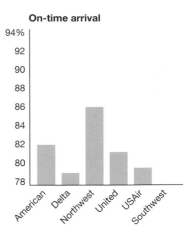

Figure 2.12 Southwest outperforms its rivals

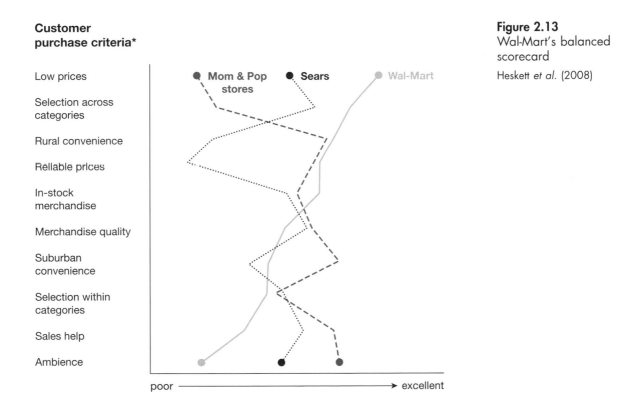

**Customer
purchase criteria***

Low prices

Selection across
categories

Rural convenience

Reliable prices

In-stock
merchandise

Merchandise quality

Suburban
convenience

Selection within
categories

Sales help

Ambience

poor ——————————————▶ excellent

Delivery on criteria

* in approximate order
 of importance to Wal-Mart's
 target customer group

Figure 2.13
Wal-Mart's balanced
scorecard

Heskett *et al.* (2008)

- Mainstream strategy will use terms like core competences, key success factors, and so on without necessarily linking these with operations management.
- There is often a conflict between *resource-based* and *market-led* views of strategy.

As important as operations capabilities are it is important that we do not excel in the wrong things. Verdin and Williamson (1994, p. 10) warn about this when they state that:

> Basing strategy on existing resources, looking inwards, risks building a company that achieves excellence in providing products and services that nobody wants . . . market-based strategy, with stretching visions and missions, can reinforce and complement competence or capability-based competition. And that successful strategy comes from matching competencies to the market.

A solution to the conundrum comes with the notion of *strategic resonance*. Brown (2000, p. 6) has previously defined strategic resonance as:

> an ongoing, dynamic, strategic process whereby customer requirements and organizational capabilities are in harmony and resonate. Strategic resonance is more than strategic fit – a term which has often been used (rightly in the past) to describe the 'fit' between the firms' capabilities and the market that it serves. Strategic resonance goes beyond that. Strategic fit may be likened to a jigsaw where all parts fit together. This is a useful view but it can have [. . .] a very static feel to it. In strategic fit it is as if once the 'bits' are in place, the strategic planning is done.

By contrast, strategic resonance is a dynamic, organic process, which is about ensuring continuous linkages and harmonization between:

- The market and the firm's operations capabilities.
- The firm's strategy and its operations capabilities.
- All functions and all levels within the firm.

Firms need to find and exploit their strategic resonance – between markets and the firm; within the firm itself; and between senior level strategists and plant-level, operations capabilities. The concept of strategic resonance is illustrated in Figure 2.14.

In essence strategic resonance is concerned with managing two sets of capabilities that need to be in place simultaneously. These are:

1. Within the firm's functions so that there is cohesion and strategic alignment within them; and
2. Between the firm's capabilities and the market segments in which the firm wishes to compete.

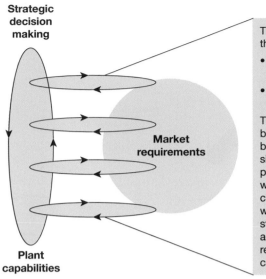

Strategic decision making

Market requirements

Plant capabilities

The essence of strategic resonance is that ongoing linkages are made between:

- Strategic decisions and operations capabilities
- The firm's strategy and market requirements

This ensures that there is no conflict between market-driven and resource-based strategies. Instead, they operate simultaneously and resonate. This prevents the firm being excellent in the wrong things; it also prevents the firm chasing after business and markets in which it cannot hope to compete. The strategy process is ongoing and changing, adapting to ensure that customer requirements and organizational-wide capabilities continue to resonate.

Figure 2.14 Strategic resonance
Brown (2000, p. 6)

Strategic resonance is also about ensuring that the firm will develop and protect those capabilities that can be used to exploit market opportunities. As we have indicated, such capabilities do not come about by chance. A model of how strategic resonance ties in with resource-based and market-led views of strategy is illustrated in Figure 2.15.

The appreciation of the strategic resonance concept, and the recognition of it as a real issue that should concern firms, is important because the current competitive environment is increasingly characterized by rapid technological changes in new and existing products, brought about, in part at least, by enhanced levels of competition.

Strategic resonance could be seen perhaps as an element within the broader concept defined by Teece *et al.* (1997) of *dynamic capability*. However, the contribution of strategic resonance lies in understanding the current problems within the domain of strategic-level processes that need to be rectified so that capabilities can be developed over time and employed as needed in order to create, or respond to, market opportunities. Strategic resonance addresses both the process and content of strategy in three ways:

1. It is a dynamic process whereby senior-level strategists communicate with operations personnel so that there is awareness about the capabilities (and incapabilities) that reside within the firms operations.

2. It is a dynamic process that ensures resonance between the firm and its existing customers.

3. It is a dynamic process that utilizes capabilities to search for new markets segments.

Figure 2.15
Strategic resonance versus resource-based and market-led strategies

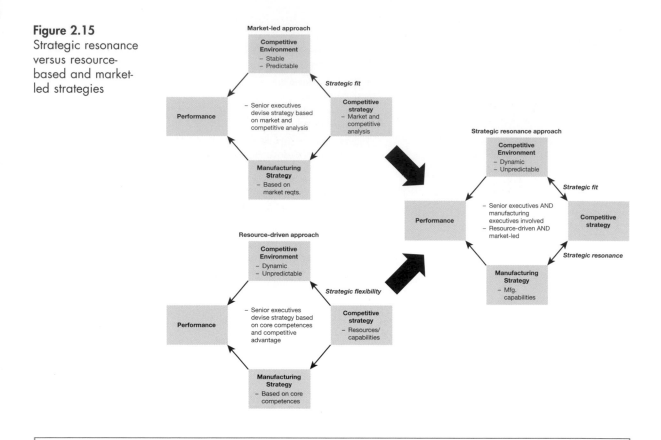

CASE: CREATING AND SUSTAINING STRATEGIC RESONANCE

Michael Dell is an example of a Chief Executive Officer who has a profound knowledge of operations and may also be seen, simultaneously, as a Chief Operating Officer. There aren't too many cases where the CEO really does understand operations (Brown, 2000). Dell understands market requirements and how to utilize operations capabilities to meet these needs. Speed of response is now a critically important feature of the PC industry. Dell is more focused than any of its competitors offering customized PCs – but Dell remain fully committed to speedy operations and delivering inexpensive, top-quality PCs.

COMPETITIVE PROFILING IN OPERATIONS STRATEGY

Part of the external audit that an organization undertakes is in benchmarking against 'best practice' of competitors in the same industry or by looking outside the industry to see if learning can be gained from other industries. For example, large computer firms will not always benchmark against each other in areas of services. Instead, they will often look to 'best service' companies as good criteria for service performance. For example, the NHS in the UK has used benchmarking with transport companies, including airlines. Of course, on the surface they are in entirely different businesses – but they do share a key process in common: moving people within the service.

However, it is important not only to benchmark against other organizations but also to question if a particular capability that the organization might have provided any competitive advantage or value. In other words, the organization needs to avoid being good at the wrong things. For example, an organization may become obsessed with its own technology – the problem of technophilia (Bessant, 1993) – and forget that other key factors such as delivery speed and cost are paramount for its customers. The benchmarking process is illustrated in Figure 2.16.

When undertaking benchmarking as part of the company's strategic formulation, there are two key questions that need to be addressed:

1. Are the organization's capabilities superior to competitors?
2. Do the weaker areas cause major disadvantages?

This analysis is important because without it a firm can excel in the wrong things. An alternative approach from the service literature (Johnston and Clark, 2001) is to profile process based around the extent to which they are 'commodity' or 'capability' driven. 'Commodity processes' are essentially those that lead to high volume but limited-variety outputs. Whereas 'capability processes' lead to relatively low volume but a high variety of outputs. These two types of process have characteristics against which a specific process may be profiled, as in Figure 2.17.

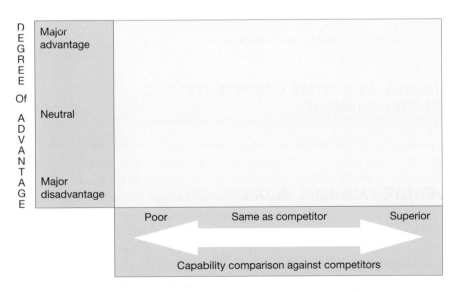

Figure 2.16 Using benchmarking of operations capabilities to determine competitive advantage

Figure 2.17
Profiling within
service operations

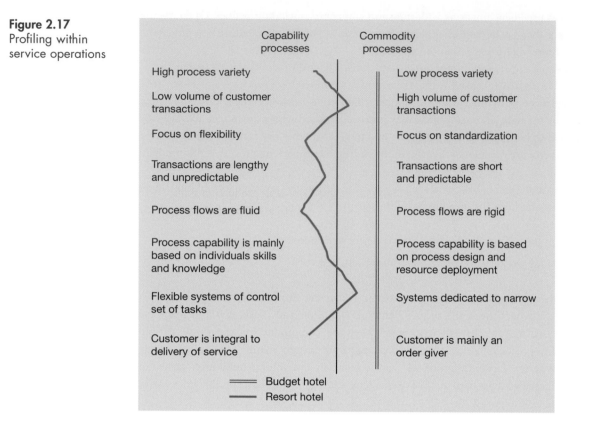

Profiling has links to 'benchmarking', which is an import feature of operations strategy – but it has caveats and we shall discuss these in Chapter 8.

OPERATIONS AS A 'CORE COMPETENCE' AND 'DISTINCTIVE CAPABILITY'

Some organizations view the abilities of their operations as a 'core competence' (Hamel and Prahalad, 1990; 1994) and a 'distinctive capability' (Kay, 1993). These two terms are quite similar because both emphasize the need to focus on, and build upon, those capabilities that the organization has which might provide competitive advantage. The firm needs to have a bundle of skills in place which will enable them to create leverage, or at least to be able to compete at all, against competitors. Such skills can have an important input in planning strategy. The role of internal resource-based strategies was developed in the 1990s (Prahalad and Hamel, 1990; Stalk *et al.*, 1992; Hayes and Pisano, 1994) and there has been considerable debate on the possible conflict between internal, resource-based strategies versus external, market-driven strategies.

Hamel and Prahalad (1994) define core competence as 'a bundle of skills and technologies rather than a single discrete skill or technology. As an example, Motorola's competence in fast cycle time production . . . rests on a broad range of underlying skills' (p. 202) and a core competence is also 'a tapestry, woven from the threads of distinct skills and technologies' (p. 214).

Hamel and Prahalad's key points about the nature of core competencies are vital for any discussion on operations strategy. First, core competencies can provide a competitive advantage based around operations capability:

> a core competence should be difficult for competitors to imitate. And it *will* be difficult if it is a complex harmonization of individual technologies and production skills.
>
> (Hamel and Prahalad, 1990, p. 80)

Second, the cultivation of these skills is a major challenge for, and increasingly a requirement of, CEOs who will:

> be judged on their ability to identify, cultivate, and exploit core competencies.
>
> (p. 91)

If such CEOs know and appreciate little of operations capabilities then, clearly, there will be problems.

Third, core competencies have to be part of the organizational learning of the firm and, again, this impacts on operations:

> Core competencies are the collective learning in the organization, especially how to coordinate diverse production skills and integrate multiple streams of technologies.
>
> (p. 90)

Fourth, core competencies in operations capability enable the firm to be agile, able to exploit these capabilities in a number of different industry applications. Exploiting internal capabilities does not mean that strategy is, therefore, fixed and rigid. Indeed, Hayes and Pisano (1994) talk of the need for strategic flexibility. Similarly, Corsten and Will (1994) warn against inflexibility brought about by a fixed adherence to a particular strategy and Beach *et al.* (1995) suggest that the ability of organizations to adapt to their changing environment is a corporate requirement. Such ideas are echoed by Gerwin (1993) and Gupta (1993).

THE CURRENT ERA AND ITS IMPACT ON THE NEED FOR FLEXIBILITY AND AGILITY

We now work in very volatile business environments. This volatility manifests itself in many ways, including the nature of employment.

> The U.S. Department of Labor estimates that today's learner will have 10–14
> jobs . . . By the age of 38. According to the U.S. Department of Labor . . . 1 out
> of 4 workers today is working for a company they have been employed by for
> less than one year.
>
> More than 1 out of 2 are working for a company they have worked for less
> than five years.
>
> **US Department of Labor (2007)**

This turbulence impacts upon operations, of course. Basically, operations managers have to make sure that they have strategies in place to deal with such rapid change. The need for such change and agility in operations was first highlighted by Skinner (cited in Wallace, 1989):

> 'On Monday, they want low cost. On Tuesday, they want high quality. On Wednesday, they want no backorders. On Thursday, they want low inventories. On Friday, they want maximum overhead absorption, so we have to work the weekend'.

We mentioned earlier how the current era in operations and service demands that both variety and high volume must be achieved. The problem for the modern operations manager, therefore, is that the requirements of cost, quality, no backorders or service queues, low inventories, and so on (provided in the above quote by Skinner) are all needed simultaneously. This is good for customers who may demand such requirements but it poses major potential headaches for operations managers who are charged with the responsibility of having to deliver all of these requirements simultaneously.

This is a very different scenario from that of mass production or mass service to which we alluded earlier. Skinner's (1969; 1978) initial solution was to speak in terms of 'focused' factories – and he spoke of the need to have a tradeoff between cost, quality, delivery, and flexibility. This may have 'solved' the problem in the former *mass-production* era (1970s), and Skinner's suggestion was certainly a means of dealing with the perceived confusion in running a plant but, as Schonberger stated in 2001 – by which time the current era of mass customization was in place – the tradeoff solution was not a solution after all:

> World class strategies require chucking the (trade-off) notion. The right strategy has no optimum, only continual improvement in all things.
>
> (p. 21)

The 1980s saw the apotheosis of strategic thinking with the publication of Michael Porter's *Competitive Strategy* in 1980 and *Competitive Advantage* in 1985. In the former Porter identified five competitive forces – suppliers, customers, substitutes, new entrants, and rivalry. In the latter he identified three generic strategies that could be applied to all industries – lowest-cost production, differentiated production, and focused production. The implications of this type of strategic thinking for operations management were to reinforce the scientific approach of shop floor Taylorism and continue the emphasis on planning. Inherent in this thinking, especially in Porter's generic strategies, is also the concept that cost and quality are a tradeoff. In the current competitive arena, cost, speed, quality, and other features are not tradeoffs, but are, instead, combined in unique ways to meet strategic goals. Firms that are frequently cited as reinventing the rules of the game in their sectors are CNN, Federal Express, Body Shop, First Direct, and IKEA.

We will discuss agility and mass customization in Chapter 7, but we mention them here because having an operations strategy is an important feature of agility. This is because such capabilities do not 'happen by chance' but have to be intentional and planned.

AGILE OR LEAN?

We will discuss agility and leanness in other chapters but a note is pertinent here. Modern managers are perhaps ill served by terminology, often shortened to just initials, and there is often contempt for those who seek to capture the essence of an idea in a 'buzzword'. The adjectives 'agile' and 'lean' were perhaps used by their progenitors to avoid this problem. However, some observers have felt that the two are in conflict, and thus devalued. Since we are using these and other terms in this book, it is perhaps necessary to discuss them briefly here.

Simply put, leanness is taken as the state of an operation (in the extended sense: internal and external) when unnecessary resources have been eliminated, so that it may function as close to perfection as possible. Waste is identified in terms of materials, time, labour, rework, poor design, and so forth (some observers use the Japanese term 'muda' for this, identifying seven different types). Agility is seen as the nature of an operations system which enables it to change quickly, refocusing on new challenges. Clearly, to be agile a system needs to be lean – but not denuded of resources that enable the change to take place. The approach to operations strategy which results in leanness and agility is thus seen as normal, for our purposes.

As we have mentioned before, the problems and requirements facing the firm include:

- Rapid change and volatility in many markets;
- Emergence of globalization in many firms;
- Increased national as well as international competition; and
- Agility and flexibility.

Having operations strategies in place becomes an important feature in dealing with these requirements. The ability to deal with them has to be planned and executed because these capabilities will not 'just happen'. The firm has to be equipped and strategies have to be in place to ensure that the firm can compete against other players. This is where strategy comes into play, and in the following sections we look at: the nature and importance of strategy; how strategy is formulated; competitive profiling; and the debate on whether strategy is developed by exploiting the firm's capabilities or if it is down to reacting to requirements.

The need for agility and flexibility comes as a result of the operations capabilities of one or more players competing within particular industries. For example, in the computer industry firms dealt in different ways with the shift to *mass customization* and *agility* in their operations.

The ability to be agile can be a powerful competitive weapon for the firm and, as Roth (1996, p. 30) states:

> The ability to rapidly alter the production of diverse products can provide manufacturers with a distinct competitive advantage. Companies adopting flexible operations technology rather than conventional operations technology can react more quickly to market changes, provide certain economies, enhance customer satisfaction and increase profitability. Research shows the adoption and use of technological bases determines an organisation's future level of competitiveness. Corporate strategy based on flexible operations technology enables firms to be better positioned in the battles that lie ahead in the global arena.

In services, technology (especially computer technology) has radically altered many of the transformation processes associated with service provision. This applies especially to back-of-house activities – for example cheque processing in banks, reservations in hotels, and inventory management in retail stores.

The other 'revolution' in services might be seen as the opposite of a 'high technology' – the significant growth of self-service. Many people have seen, and continue to see, this as a lowering of quality standards as a means of reducing costs. Significant savings in labour cost may be achieved if the customer does things previously done by a service worker. In effect, this is perceived as a tradeoff, similar to that described by Skinner. But increasingly it is being understood that quality is enhanced if customers participate in their own service. For instance, diners who serves themselves from a restaurant salad bar enjoy a product individually customized to their personal tastes, appetite, and value perception. From its humble origins in self-service cafeterias, this concept has developed to the notion of 'value constellations' as suggested by Normann and Ramirez (1993), in which the customer's role is explicitly adding value to an already high-quality product – for example in self-assembly furniture as sold by IKEA.

Modern service firms, like their operations counterparts, are now extending mass service into mass customization by adding value into low-cost services. In many respects this means allowing consumers to select from a range of service alternatives, each at a different price. It is now common in the US for petrol filling stations to have two rows of pumps, one self-service and the other attended. Petrol is typically a few cents per gallon more expensive if the attendant serves it. Supermarket consumers of the future will be faced with a range of alternatives including: compiling your own shopping list or letting the supermarket do it for you; emailing your list to the supermarket, dropping it off at the supermarket or carrying it around the supermarket with you; filling your own trolley or paying someone to do it for you; putting your items through the checkout or billing yourself on a hand-held machine on the trolley.

The ability of some service firms to customize is based on the impact that computerizing their systems has had. Service firms know a great deal about the purchase behaviour of their customers. 'Data-mining', or the analysis of this customer information, enables service providers such as banks, retailers, hoteliers, and restauranteurs to predict very accurately the needs of the customer, sometimes even before the customer is aware of these needs for themselves.

However, all of these requirements for customization, agility, leanness, and so on, have derived from greater levels of competition. The ability to achieve these aspirations will owe much to operations capabilities – and the strategies devised to accrue and utilize such capabilities for customers.

SUMMARY

- In addition to the huge managerial responsibility of managing key assets, costs, and human resources, the contribution of production and operations management is vital because it can provide a number of competitive opportunities for the firm.

- Strategies must be in place if the organization is to compete in a business world which is now chaotic, requiring rapid and continuous innovation, and open to global competition in many industries and markets.

- In Japanese and other world-class companies, the contribution of operations management to business planning is central. This involvement helps to guide the firm by matching its core capabilities with market requirements.

- There have been major transitions from craft-production to mass-production through to the current era of *mass customization, agility, leanness* and *strategic manufacturing*. Each of these has represented a major, world-wide innovation, with implications for strategy formulation and profoundly changing the way people work. In each case, the new paradigm has made the previous one largely, but not totally, redundant.

- Operations strategy is vital as part of the wider business strategy, in integrating and combining major competitive requirements including cost, delivery speed, delivery reliability, flexibility, and customer-specific configurations.

- Having an operations strategy is important because the ability to be *agile*, *lean*, and flexible does not come about by chance – such states are achieved by enabling the organization to be poised to achieve such requirements. Operations strategy becomes the means by which capabilities become realized.

KEY QUESTIONS

1. What are the links between *operations strategy* and *business strategy*?
2. What are the problems that might be faced in formulating an operations strategy?
3. Why have operations and business strategies become separated in some firms over time?
4. Why is operations strategy vitally important in modern day operations management?
5. Discuss the Hill model and the Brown and Blackmon Resonance approach to forming operations strategy. Choose any industry and apply these models to them.

SUGGESTED READINGS

Brown, S. and Blackmon, K. (2005) 'Aligning manufacturing strategy and business-level competitive strategy in new competitive environments: The case for strategic resonance', *Journal of Management Studies*, 42(4), 793–815.

Economist (2008) 'High seas, high prices', 9 August 2008, 387(8592), 50–3.

Fortune (2006) 'Manufacturing Matters', 6 March 2006, 153(4), 12.

Hayes, R. and Pisano, G. (1994) 'Beyond world-class: The new manufacturing strategy', *Harvard Business Review*, 72(1), 77–87.

Hayes, R. and Upton, D. (1998) 'Operations based strategies', *California Management Review*, 40(4), 8–25.

Industry Week (2006) 'Manufacturing's most influential thinkers and doers', March 2006, p. 2.

Pisano, G. and Shih, W. (2009) 'Restoring American competitiveness', *Harvard Business Review*, 87(7/8), 114–25.

Shah, R. and Ward, P.T. (2003) 'Lean manufacturing: Context, practice bundles, and performance', *Journal of Operations Management*, 21, 129–49.

Weeks, M.R. and Feeny, D.F. (2008) 'Outsourcing: From cost management to innovation and business value', California Management Review, 50(4), 127–46.

REFERENCES

Arya, B. and Lin, Z. (2007) 'Understanding collaboration outcomes from an extended resource-based view perspective: The roles of organizational characteristics, partner attributes, and network structures', *Journal of Management*, 33(5), 697–723.

Baden-Fuller, C. and Pitt, M. (1996) *Strategic Innovation: An International Casebook on Strategic Management*, London: Routledge.

Baden-Fuller, C. and Stopford, J. (1992) *Re-juvenating the Mature Business: The Competitive Challenge*, London: Routledge.

Barney, J.B. (1991) 'Firm resources and sustained competitive advantage', *Journal of management*, 17, 99–120.

Bartlett, C. and Ghoshal, S. (1987) 'Managing across borders', in B. De Wit and R. Meyer, (eds), *Strategy: Process, Content and Context*, New York: West Publishing, pp. 521–9.

Beach, R., Muhlemann, A.P., Paterson, A., Price, D. and Sharp, J. (1995) 'A process for developing manufacturing management information systems to support strategic change', in D. Stockton and C. Wainwright, (eds) *Advances in Manufacturing Technology, IX*, London: Taylor and Francis, pp. 646–50.

Beach, R., Muhlemann, A.P., Price, D.H.R., Paterson, A. and Sharp, J.A. (2000) 'Manufacturing operations and strategic flexibility: Survey and cases', *International Journal of Operations and Production Management*, 20(1), 13–27.

Berry, W.L., Hill, T.J. and Klompmaker, J.E. (1995) 'Customer-driven operations', *International Journal of Operations and Production Management*, 15(3), 4–16.

Bessant, J. (1993) 'The lessons of failure: Learning to manage new manufacturing technology', *International Journal of Technology Management*, Special Issue on Manufacturing Technology, 8(2/3/4), 197–215.

Booth, S.A. (1993) *Crisis Management Strategy: Competition and Change in Modern Enterprises*, London: Routledge.

Boyer, K. and Frohlich, M.T. (2006) 'Analysis of effects of operational execution on repeat purchasing for heterogeneous customer segments', *Production and Operations Management*, 15(2) 229–42.

Boyer, K., Hult, G. and Tomas, M. (2005) 'Extending the supply chain: Integrating operations and marketing in the online grocery industry', *Journal of Operations Management*, 23(6), 642–61.

Bozarth, C. and Edwards, S. (1997) 'The impact of market requirements focus and operations characteristics focus on plant', *Journal of Operations Management*, 15(3), 162–80.

Brax, S. and Jonsson, K. (2009) 'Developing integrated solution offerings for remote diagnostics', *International Journal of Operations and Production Management*, 29(5), 539–60.

Brown, S. (1996) *Strategic Manufacturing for Competitive Advantage*, Hemel Hempstead: Prentice Hall.

Brown, S. (2000) *Manufacturing the Future: Strategic Resonance for Resonant Manufacturing*, London: Financial Times/Pearson Books.

Brown, S. and Blackmon, K. (2005) 'Linking manufacturing strategy to the strategy mainstream: The case for strategic resonance', *Journal of Management Studies*, 42(4), 793–815.

Brown, S., Blackmon, K., Cousins, P. and Maylor, H. (2001) *Operations Management: Policy, Practice and Performance management*, Oxford: Butterworth Heinemann.

Brown, S., Blackmon, K. and Squire, B. (2007) 'The contribution of manufacturing strategy involvement and alignment to world class manufacturing performance', *International Journal of Operations and Production Management*, 27(3), 282–302.

Brown, S., Squire, B. and Lewis, M. (2010) 'The impact of inclusive and fragmented operations strategies on operations performance', *International Journal of Production Research*, 48(14), 4179–98.

Buhman, C., Kekre, T. and Singhal, J. (2005) 'Interdisciplinary and interorganizational research: Establishing the science of enterprise networks', Production *and* Operations Management, 14(4), 493–513.

Business Week (2008) 25 August 2008, pp. 28–29.

Chaharbaghi, C. and Willis, R. (1998) 'Strategy: The missing link between continuous revolution and constant evolution', *International Journal of Operations and Production Management*, 18(9/10), 1017–27.

Chandler, A. (1992) 'Corporate strategy, structure and control methods in the United States during the 20th century', *Industrial and Corporate Change*, 1(2), 263–84.

Chandler, A.D. (1962) *Strategy and Structure: Chapters in the History of the American Industrial Enterprise*, Boston, MA: MIT.

Clark, K. (1996) 'Competing through operations and the new operations paradigm: Is operations strategy passé?', *Production and Operations Management*, 5(1), 42–58.

Collis, D. and Montgomery, C. (1995) 'Competing on resources: Strategy in the 1990s', *Harvard Business Review*, 73(4), 118–28.

Collis, D.J. and Rukstad, M.G. (2008) 'Can you say what your strategy is?', *Harvard Business Review*, 86(4), 82–90.

Contractor, F. and Lorange, P. (1988) *Cooperative Strategies in International Business*, Boston, MA: Lexington Books.

Cooper, R. (1995), *When Lean Enterprises Collide: Competing through Confrontation*, Boston, MA: Harvard Business School Press.

Corbett, C. and Van Wassenhove, L. (1994) 'Trade-offs? What trade-offs? Competence and competitiveness in manufacturing strategy', *California Management Review*, 35(4), 107–20.

Corsten, H. and Will, T. (1994) 'Simultaneously supporting generic competitive strategies by production management', *Technovation*, 14(2), 111–20.

Daems, H. (1990) 'The strategic implications of Europe 1992', *Long Range Planning*, 23(3), 41–8.

Dangayach, G.S. and Deshmukh, S.G. (2001) 'Manufacturing strategy: Literature review and some issues', *International Journal of Operations and Production Management*, 21(7), 884–932.

Das, S.R. and Joshi, M.P. (2007) 'Process innovativeness in technology services organizations: Roles of differentiation strategy, operational autonomy and risk-taking propensity', *Journal of Operations Management*, 25(3), 643–60.

Das, T.K. (1991) 'Time: The hidden dimension in strategic planning', *Long Range Planning*, 24(3), 49–57.

Deane, R.H., McDougall, P.P., and Gargeya, V.B. (1991) 'Manufacturing and marketing interdependence in the new venture firm: An empirical study', *Journal of Operations Management*, 10(3), 329–43.

Dertouzos, M., Lester, R. and Solow, R. (1989) *Made In America*, Cambridge, MA: MIT Press.

Dierickx, I. and Cool, K. (1989) 'Asset stock accumulation and sustainability of competitive advantage', *Management Science*, 35, 1504–11.

Dixit, A.K. and Nalebuff, B.J. (1991) *Thinking Strategically: The Competitive Edge in Business, Politics, and Everyday Life*, London: Norton and Company.

Dougherty, D. and Corse, S.M. (1995) 'When it comes to product innovation, what is so bad about bureaucracy?', *Journal of High Technology Management Research*, 6, 55–76.

Douglas, S. and Wind, Y. (1987) 'The myth of globalisation', in B. De Wit and R. Meyer (eds), *Strategy: Process, Content and Context*, New York: West Publishing, pp. 495–505.

D'Souza, D.E. and Williams, F.P. (2000) 'Toward a taxonomy of operations flexibility dimensions', *Journal of Operations Management*, 18, 577–93.

Economist (1995) 'Survey of multinationals: Who wants to be a giant?', 24 June 1995.

Economist (2008) 'High seas, high prices', 9 August 2008, 387(8592), 50–3.

Eisenhardt, K.M. and Martin, J.A. (2000) 'Dynamic capabilities: What are they?', *Strategic Management Journal*, 21(10/11), 1105–22.

Ellis, J. and Williams, D. (1995) *International Business Strategy*, London: Pitman Publishing.

Fortune (2004) 'The secrets of execution', 8 March 2004, 149(4), 42.

Fortune (2006) 'Manufacturing matters', 6 March 2006, 153(4), 26–7.

Fortune (2010) 'American made. . .Chinese owned', 24 May 2010, 161(7), 84–92.

Frambach, R.T., Prabhu, J. and Verhallen, T.M.M. (2003) 'The influence of business strategy on new product activity: The role of market orientation', *International Journal of Research in Marketing*, 20(4), 377–97.

Gagnon, S. (1999) 'Resource based competition and the new operation strategy', *International Journal of Operations and Production Management*, 19(2), 125–38.

Gerwin, D. (1993) 'Manufacturing flexibility: A strategic perspective', *Management Science*, 39(4), 395–408.

Ghemawat, P. and Hout, T. (2008) 'Tomorrow's global giants', *Harvard Business Review*, 86(11), 80–8.

Gilbert, X. and Strebel, P. (1989) 'From innovation to outpacing', *Business Quarterly*, 54(1), 19–22.

Goddard, J. and Houlder, D. (1995) 'Beyond magic: Conjectures on the nature of strategy in the late 1990s', *Business Strategy Review*, 6(1), 81–107.

Goold, M. and Campbell, A. (1991) 'From corporate strategy to parenting advantage', *Long Range Planning*, 24(1), 115–17.

Gupta, D. (1993) 'On measurement and valuation of manufacturing flexibility', *International Journal of Production Research*, 31(12), 2947–58.

Hamel, G., Doz, Y. and Prahalad, C.K. (1989) 'Collaborate with your competitors – and win', *Harvard Business Review*, January/February, 133–45.

Hamel, G. and Prahalad, C.K. (1989) 'Strategic intent', *Harvard Business Review*, May/June, 63–76.

Hamel, G. and Prahalad, C. (1990) 'Strategy as stretch and leverage', *Harvard Business Review*, 71(2), 75–84.

Hamel, G. and Prahalad, C. (1994) *Competing for the Future*, Cambridge, MA: Harvard Business School Press.

Hamilton, R.D. III, Eskin E., Max P. and Michaels M.P. (1998) 'Assessing competitors: The gap between strategic intent and core capability', *Long Range Planning*, 31(3), 406–17.

Haspeslagh, P. (1982) 'Portfolio planning: Uses and limits', *Harvard Business Review*, January/February, 58–73.

Hax, A. (1990) 'Redefining the concept of strategy', in B. De Wit and R. Meyer (eds), *Strategy: Process, Content and Context*, New York: West Publishing, pp. 8–12.

Hax, A. and Majluf, N. (1991) *The Strategy Concept and Process*, Eaglewood Cliffs, NJ: Prentice Hall.

Hayes, R. and Pisano, G. (1994) 'Beyond world-class: The new manufacturing strategy', *Harvard Business Review*, 72(1), 77–86.

Hayes, R. and Upton, D. (1998) 'Operations based strategies', *California Management Review*, 40(4), 8–25.

Hayes, R. and Wheelwright, S. (1984) *Restoring Our Competitive Edge*, New York: Wiley & Sons.

Hemp, P. (2002) 'My week at the Ritz as a room-service waiter', *Harvard Business Review*, 80(6), 50–9.

Heracleous, L. and Wirtz, J. (2010) 'Singapore Airlines' balancing act', *Harvard Business Review*, 88(7/8), 145–9.

Heskett, J., Sasser, E. and Schlesinger, L. (1997) *Service Profit Chain*, New York: Free Press.

Heskett, J.L., Jones, T.O., Loveman, G.W., Earl Sasser, Jr. W. and Schlesinger L.A. (2008) 'Putting the service–profit chain to work', *Harvard Business Review*, 86(7/8), 118–29.

Hill, T. (1995) *Manufacturing Strategy*, Basingstoke: Macmillan.

Hill, T. (2000) *Manufacturing Strategy*, Basingstoke: Macmillan.

Hill, T. (2005) *Operations Management*, 2nd edition, Basingstoke: Macmillan.

Hill, T. and Hill, A. (2009) *Manufacturing Strategy: Text and Cases*, 3rd revised edition, Basingstoke: Palgrave Macmillan.

Hines, P. (1994) *Creating World Class Suppliers: Unlocking Mutual Competitive Advantage*, London: Pitman.

Holcomb, T. and Hitt, M. (2007) 'Toward a model of strategic outsourcing', *Journal of Operations Management*, 25(2), 464–81.

Honeycutt, E.D., Siguaw, J.A. and Harper, S.C. (1993) 'The impact of flexible operations on competitive strategy', *Industrial Management*, 35(6), 2–15.

Hrebiniak, L. and Joyce, W. (1984) *Implementing Strategies*, London: Macmillan College Publishing.

Industry Week (2003) 'Waking Up To a New World', June 2003, 252(6), 22–5.

Industry Week (2006) 'Winning with service', 1 April 2006, 255(4), 30–47.

Ireland, R., Hitt, M.A. and Vaidyanath, D. (2002) 'Alliance management as a source of competitive advantage', *Journal of Management*, 28(3), 413–46.

Itami, H. and Numagami, T. (1992) 'Dynamic interaction between strategy and technology', *Strategic Management Journal*, 13, 119–35.

Johanson, J. and Mattsson, L. (1992) 'Network positions and strategic action', in B. Axelsson and G. Easton (eds), *Industrial Networks: A New View of Reality*, London: Routledge.

Johnson, G. (1988) 'Rethinking incrementalism', in B. De Wit and R. Meyer (eds), *Strategy: Process, Content and Context*, New York: West Publishing, pp. 61–9.

Johnson, G. and Scholes, K. (2008) *Exploring Corporate Strategy*, 8th edition, Hemel Hempstead: Prentice Hall.

Johnston, R. and Clark, G. (2001) *Service Operations Management*, London: Financial Times.

Joshi, M.P, Kathuria, R. and Porth, S.J. (2003) 'Alignment of strategic priorities and performance: An integration of operations and strategic management performance', *Journal of Operations Management*, 21(3), 353–69.

Kathuria, R. and Partovi, F.Y. (2000) 'Aligning workforce, management practices with competitive priorities and process technology: A conceptual examination', *The Journal of High Technology Management Research*, 11(2), 215–34.

Kay, J. (1993) *Foundations of Corporate Success*, Oxford: Oxford University Press.

Kenney, M. and Florida, R. (1993) *Beyond Mass Production*, New York: Oxford University Press.

Kim, J. and Arnold, P. (1996) 'Operationalizing manufacturing strategy: An exploratory study of constructs and linkages', *International Journal of Operations and Production Management*, 16(12), 45–73.

Kim, W C. and Mauborgne, R. (2002) 'Charting your company's future', *Harvard Business Review*, 80(6), 76–83.

Kouvelis, P., Chambers, C. and Wang, H. (2006) 'Supply chain management research and production and operations management: Review, trends, and opportunities', *Production and Operations Management*, 15(3) 449–69.

Lazonick, W. (1990) *Competitive Advantage on the Shopfloor*, Cambridge MA: Harvard University Press.

Lazonick, W. (1991) *Business Organization and the Myth of the Market Economy*, Cambridge, MA: Harvard University Press.

Lazonick, W. and West, J. (1995) 'Organizational integration and competitive advantage: Explaining strategy and performance in american industry', *Industrial and Corporate Change*, 4(1), 229–69.

Lele, M. (1992) 'Selecting strategies that exploit leverage', in B. De Wit and R. Meyer (eds), *Strategy: Process, Content and Context*, New York: West Publishing, pp. 381–90.

Menda, R. and Dilts, D. (1997) 'The operations strategy formulation process: Linking multifunctional viewpoints', *Journal of Operations Management*, 15, 223–41.

Meredith, J. and Vineyard, M. (1993) 'A longitudinal study of the role of operations technology in business strategy', *International Journal of Operations and Production Management*, 13(12), 4–25.

Miller, J. and Roth, A. (1994) 'Taxonomy of manufacturing strategies', *Management Science*, 40(3), 285–304.

Mills, J.F., Neely, A., Platts, K. and Gregory, M. (1995) 'A framework for the design of manufacturing strategy processes: Toward a contingency approach', *International Journal of Operations and Production Management*, 15(4), 17–49.

Mintzberg, H. (1994) *The Rise and Fall of Strategic Planning*, London: Prentice-Hall.

Mintzberg, H. (1995) 'The entrepreneurial organisation', in H. Mintzberg, B. Quinn and S. Ghoshal (eds), *The Strategy Process*, London: Prentice-Hall, pp. 588–97.

Mintzberg, H. and Ansoff, I. (1994) 'A discussion on strategy paradigms', in B. De Wit and R. Meyer (eds), *Strategy: Process, Content and Context*, New York: West Publishing, pp. 69–84.

Mintzberg, H., Ahlstrand, B. and Lamprel, J. (2000) *Strategy Safari: A Guided Tour Through the Wilds of Strategic management*, London: Financial Times Books.

Möller, K. Rajala, R. and Westerlund, M. (2008) 'Service innovation myopia? A new recipe for client-provider value creation', *California Management Review*, 50(3), 31–48.

Normann, R. and Ramirez, R. (1993) 'From value chain to value constellation: Designing interactive strategy', *Harvard Business Review*, 71(4), 65–78.

Nunes, P.F. and Cespedes, F.V (2003) 'The customer has escaped', *Harvard Business Review*, 81(11), 96–105.

Ohmae, K. (1982) *The Mind of the Strategist*, London: McGraw-Hill.

Pagell, M. and Krause, D.R. (1999) 'A multiple-method study of environmental uncertainty and operations flexibility', *Journal of Operations Management*, 17, 307–25.

Paiva, E., Roth, A.V. and Fensterseifer, J. (2008) 'Organizational knowledge and the manufacturing strategy process: A resource-based view analysis', *Journal of Operations Management*, 26(1), 115–32.

Papke-Shields, K. and Malhotra, M. (2001) 'Assessing the impact of the manufacturing/operations executive's role on business performance through strategic alignment', *Journal of Operations Management*, 19(1) 5–22.

Pascale, R.T. (1984) 'Perspectives on strategy: The real story behind Honda's success', *California Management Review*, 26(3), 47–72.

Peters, T. and Waterman, R. (1982) *In Search of Excellence: Lessons from America's Best-run Companies*, New York: Harper & Row.

Pisano, G. and Shih, W. (2009) 'Restoring American competitiveness', *Harvard Business Review*, 87(7/8), 114–25.

Porter, M. (1979) 'How competitive forces shape strategy', *Harvard Business Review*, March/April, 137–45.

Porter, M. (1980) *Competitive Strategy: Techniques for Analyzing Industries and Competitors*, New York: Free Press.

Porter, M. (1985) *Competitive Advantage: Creating and Sustaining Superior Performance*, New York: Free Press.

Porter, M. (1987) 'From competitive advantage to corporate strategy', *Harvard Business Review*, May/June, 43–59.

Porter, M. (1990) *The Competitive Advantage of Nations*, London: Macmillan.

Prahalad, C.K. and Doz, Y. (1986) *The Multinational Mission: Balancing Local Demands and Global Vision*, Boston, MA: The Free Press.

Prahalad, C.K. and Hamel, G. (1990) 'The core competence of the corporation', *Harvard Business Review*, May/June, 79–91.

Prais, S. (1981) *Productivity and Industrial Structure: A Statistical Study of Manufacturing in Britain, Germany and the US*, Cambridge: Cambridge University Press.

Prajogo, D.M. and McDermott, D. (2008) 'The relationships between operations strategies and operations activities in service context', *International Journal of Service Industry Management*, 19(4), 506–20.

Quinn, J. (1978) 'Strategic change: Logical incrementalism', *Sloan Management Review*, 1(2), 7–21.

Ramanujam, V. and Venkatraman, N. (1987) 'Planning system characteristics and planning effectiveness', *Strategic Management Journal*, 8(5), 453–68.

Reuters (2010) 'Titan to add retail stores, watch capacity', 3 Feb 2010.

Reve, T. (1990) 'The firm as a nexus of internal and external contracts', in M. Aoki and O.E. Williamson (eds), *The Firm as a Nexus of Treaties*, London: Sage Publications.

Roth, A.V. (1996) 'Achieving strategic agility through economics of knowledge', *Strategy and Leadership*, 24(2), 30–7.

Rudberg M. and West B. (2008) 'Global operations strategy: Coordinating manufacturing networks', *Omega*, 36(1), 91–106.

Sasser, W.E., Olsen, R.P. and Wyckoff, D.D. (1976) *The Management of Service Operations*, Boston, MA: Allyn and Bacon.

Schmenner, R.W. (1986) 'How can services business survive and prosper?', *Sloan Management Review*, 27(3), 21–32.

Schonberger, R. (2001) *Building a Chain of Customers*, London: Hutchinson Business Books.

Senge, P.M. (1990) *The Fifth Discipline*, London: Century Business.

Shah, R. and Ward, P.T. (2003) 'Lean manufacturing: Context, practice bundles, and performance', *Journal of Operations Management*, 21, 129–49.

Shankar, V., Berry, L and. Dotzel, T. (2009) 'A practical guide to combining products and services', *Harvard Business Review*, 87(11), 94–9.

Skinner, W. (1969) 'Manufacturing: The missing link in corporate strategy', *Harvard Business Review*, 47(3), 136–45.

Skinner, W., (1978) *Manufacturing in the Corporate Strategy*, New York: Wiley.

Skinner, W. (1985), *Manufacturing, The Formidable Competitive Weapon*, New York: Wiley & Sons.

Spring, M. and Dalrymple, J.F. (2000) 'Product customisation and operations strategy', *International Journal of Operations and Production Management*, 20(4) 23–36.

St John, C.H. and Young, S.T. (1992) 'An exploratory study of patterns of priorities and trade-offs among operations managers'' *Production and Operations Management*, 1(2), 133–50.

Stacey, R. (1993) *Strategic Management and Organizational Dynamics*, London: Pitman.

Stalk, G. (1988) 'Time: The next source of competitive advantage', *Harvard Business Review*, July/August, 41–51.

Stalk, G., Evans, P. and Shulman, L. (1992) 'Competing on capabilities: The new rules of corporate strategy', *Harvard Business Review*, 70(2), 57–69.

Stump, R., Athaide, G. and Ashwin, W J. (2002) 'Managing seller–buyer new product development relationships for customized products: A contingency model based on transaction cost analysis and empirical test', *Journal of Product Innovation Management*, 19(6), 439–54.

Sun, H. and Hong, C. (2002) 'The alignment between manufacturing and business strategies: Its influence on business performance', *Technovation*, 22(4) 699–705.

Swamidass, P. and Newell, W. (1987) 'Manufacturing strategy, environmental uncertainty, and performance: A path analytical model', *Management Science*, 33(3), 509–34.

Teece, D., Pisano, G. and Shuen, A. (1997) 'Dynamic capabilities and strategic management', *Strategic Management Journal*, 18(7), 509–33.

Tunalv, C. (1992) 'Manufacturing strategy: Plans and business performance', *International Journal of Operations and Production Management*, 12(3), 4–24.

US Department of Labor (2007) 'Number of jobs held, labor market activity, and earnings growth among the youngest baby boomers: Results from a longitudinal survey', *News: United States Department of Labor*, 25 Aug 2006, Bureau of Labor Statistics.

Verdin, P. and Williamson, P. (1994) 'Successful strategy: Stargazing or self-examination?', *European Management Journal*, 12(1), 10–19.

Wallace, T. (1989) *The Manufacturing Strategy Report*, No.4, June, Cincinnati, OH: T.F.Wallace Inc.

Ward, P.T. and Duray, R. (1995) 'Business environment, operations strategy, and performance', *Journal of Operations Management*, 13, 99–115.

Weeks, M.R. and Feeny, D.F. (2008) 'Outsourcing: From cost management to innovation and business value', *California Management Review*, 50(4), 127–46.

Wernerfelt, B. (1984) 'A resource-based view of the firm', *Strategic Management Journal*, 5(4), 171–180.

Wheelen, T. and Hunger, D. (1992) *Strategic Management and Business Policy*, Reading, MA: Addison-Wesley Publishing.

Whittington, R. (2001) *What is Strategy – and Does it Matter?* London: Routledge.

Wilk, E.O. and Fensterseifer, J.E. (2003) 'Use of resource-based view in industrial cluster strategic analysis', *International Journal of Operations and Production Management*, 23(9), 995–1010.

Womack, J., Jones, D. and Roos, D. (1990) *The Machine That Changed the World*, New York: Rawson Associates.

Youndt, M.A., Snell, S.A., Dean, J.W. Jr. and Lepak, D.P. (1996) 'Human resource management, operations strategy, and firm performance', *Academy of Management Journal*, 39(4): 836–65.

Zornitsky, J.J. (1995) 'Making effective human resource management a hard business issue', *Compensation and Benefits Management*, Winter, 16–24.

THE BIG PICTURE OF STRATEGIC OPERATIONS

CHAPTER 3

SUPPLY MANAGEMENT

LEARNING OBJECTIVES

- Understand what supply management is and how it has changed over time, in concept and practice.
- Gain insights into the strategic importance of supply within operations.
- Understand how supply management is undertaken in practice and develop a critical perspective on some approaches.
- Appreciate concepts such as lean supply, agility and the management of supply chain relationships.

DEFINITION AND DEVELOPMENT

Ten years ago we started this chapter by remarking 'It is perhaps necessary to explain at the outset why we have dedicated a whole chapter to the subject of supply management, and what we mean by the term'. In the intervening period the importance of developing expertise in supply 'chain' management has become accepted in every part of business and the subject is now amongst the most popular research topics in the area. It is also of crucial importance in global operations, including in the pursuit of sustainability (see Chapter 5).

Development of the idea

The practice of buying and selling is one of the oldest 'professions' in the world. In the remains of cities within Mesopotamia (modern-day Iraq) archaeologists have found records of transactions that took place 6,000 years ago, bearing a chilling resemblance to today's purchase orders and materials schedules. Down through the ages, markets, merchants, cultivated demand, and international transportation have been the livelihood and drivers of societies, cities, and warfare. What has changed recently is the scope of concern that the purchaser and seller must have for supply, in order to ensure that their organizations survive and prosper. The copper traders in ancient Ur (once a port but now far inland, near the modern Iraqi city of Nasiriyah) may have paid the merchants from Dilmun (Bahrain) for minerals from Makan (Oman) and considered they were doing business over great distances. Today, the same distance takes a couple of hours by air and traders in the modern equivalent of each of these countries are dealing by internet and mobile, wireless telephony with collaborators, customers, and competitors in every part of the globe. (Meanwhile, the price of copper doubled between 2009 and 2011).

Thus, managing the provision of the resources necessary to conduct the operations of the organization – a function variously called purchasing, procurement, buying, and materials management (it doesn't really matter which term we use) – is now increasingly a matter of competing for scarce commodities which may differentiate the product or service in the eyes of the customer or consumer. As we shall see in Chapter 5, this links supply management with sustainable development in a very profound way. It is a short, simple step to connect such activity with the operations strategy for an organization.

There have, of course, always been supply chains. If you follow the exploits of any military campaign, from Alexander the Great (356–323 BCE) to modern conflicts, you will find that many of the successes and failures can be attributed as much to good or bad supply management as to strategy in battle. As Napoleon said, (although it may have originated from Frederic the Great) 'An army marches on its stomach'.

In the trading world there are also many historic examples of supply chains changing society; nations have gone to extreme lengths – frequently including warfare – to bring precious commodities, such as metals, jewels, spices, and human labour, home from afar. (Sadly, though, the myth of Marco Polo bringing noodles from China to Italy and thereby inventing spaghetti is not true.)

For business (and therefore for Operations Management) the current importance of supply chains can be linked to the rise of international *mass production* in the early part of the twentieth century (see Chapter 1). As North American manufacturers began to assemble products, most notably automobiles, in several, geographically distant, locations, they created 'networked' organizations. This made it necessary to transport materials and components from suppliers to assembly plants, to arrive in time, in the right quantities, to the right specification, at the right cost, and in the right place. We know that many supply chains (admittedly for relatively simple products by today's standards) were well managed 100 years ago: the much celebrated *just in time* systems, observed in Japan in the 1980s, were in evidence over half a century before, for example, in Ford's assembly plants in the UK.

It is, perhaps, primarily the complexity of modern market demands for products and services, fired by technological developments and relentless marketing, that makes it vital to study supply chains in everyday business, and it turns out that the theoretical models provided by economics do not help us much in practice. We shall not dwell on this but it is important to reflect on the neoclassical economic paradigm that has driven much of business policy making for the last 100 years, in this context. Put simply, this normative paradigm assumes that markets work; in theory, every buyer has perfect knowledge of every seller and vice versa. All that is necessary is for the price of the item to be reduced to its marginal cost (the minimum at which a supplier can afford to sell it) and then an exchange will take place. Another feature of this theory is that there are no business costs associated with transactions (buying and selling) as the market mechanism will lead to their minimization or eradication.

For the supply strategist, the important issue here is that the neoclassical economist would argue that working relationships between companies buying and selling in the market (collaborative or otherwise) are simply market failures – they just should not be there in theory. The problem is, of course, that they are certainly there in practice. This anomaly was dealt with first in a seminal economics article by the British economist Ronald Coase in 1936 (at the age of 26 – his Nobel prize came over 50 years later), who pointed out that there were flaws in the theory of the firm. This was developed by the American academic Oliver Williamson (a student of Coase) in a 1975 book that launched the concept of *transaction cost economics*. Williamson focused on 'dyadic' relationships (i.e. between two organizations) rather than chains or networks. His influential ideas have been debated and developed for over three decades. We need not explore this too much here but we should recognize that theory has caught up with practice and that we now have a broad range of useful concepts to employ in understanding what happens in supply chain relationships (we'll look at the practical aspects of this later).

The concept of *supply chain management* originated as a management consultancy concept in the early 1980s and immediately caught the imagination of theorists and practitioners alike (first explained by Houlihan in 1987). It had its roots in the field of *industrial dynamics* (now *system dynamics*), beginning with the ground-breaking post-World War II work of Jay Forrester (1958: credited by Houlihan, and an article well worth reading) and his analysis of the exaggerations in demand, traced back in a supply chain from end user through manufacturers and component suppliers to raw materials. This has become known as the *Forrester effect*, and also the *bull-whip effect*, in logistics. This is embodied in the famous 'beer game' – a simulation exercise (developed at MIT in the 1960s) that is well worth experiencing.

Logistics is the visible, physical part of supply management – the warehouses, ships, aircraft, trains, and trucks that contain or carry goods and materials, and the information systems that accompany and support them. We shall not deal much with this side of supply in this book; it is the management of the operation, which includes the supply chain relationships, individually and collectively, that we are interested in. It is important to recognize, however, that concepts such as *lean* and *agile* have very different implications if one is speaking of logistics (focused largely on where inventory is held, and explored largely by Marketing researchers) rather than strategic supply management, where they have much the same implications.

The 'chain' metaphor is simplistic: things do not happen in straight, linear lines or chains in practice. The reality is much more complicated. Supply strategy is about making sense of a muddle – a disorganized group of organizations and intermediaries, put in tension by differing commercial motives, intellectual property, national cultures, and so on – and then making it work the way you want it to. The first step is to recognize that it is a network, not a chain, and that even this is simplifying the muddle into something with which we can deal. The practical version of this is often termed a *supply base* – suggesting a 'solid' foundation of suppliers upon which an operation relies, presumably organized, coordinated or structured in some way. This realization has been widespread, but such is the strength of the chain metaphor (it finds a very strong resonance in the human psyche, in many languages, perhaps linked to concepts such as the food chain, chain reaction or chain of command) that it has survived 30 years.

So, when someone refers to a supply chain, they do not mean a simple linear chain but a messy, complex system that can be reduced at least to a network. Choi *et al.* (2001) provide an interesting and useful discussion of this point, using a concept of *complex adaptive systems* first proposed by Pfeffer in 1997. Their conclusion is that greater levels of shared working norms, procedures, and language among firms in a supply network will increase the 'operational fit' between the firms, i.e. improve the supply chain relationships. We'll explore this a little further later on. For now, the difference between the consultants' simplicity and the complex reality is shown in Figure 3.1.

It is usual to refer to 'upstream' and 'downstream' firms in the supply chain but also quite common to find the two terms used incorrectly. Clearly they are terms that relate to a reference (or focal) firm. Suppliers are said to be upstream while distributors and customers are downstream. Think of a stream flowing from a mountain spring down to the sea and you will get the picture.

There are many different types of supply network and many attempts have been made to classify them (see, for example, Harland, 1996; Lamming, *et al.*, 2000; and Christopher *et al.*, 2006). Management practice has sometimes struggled to deal with this problem, developing models for controlling supply chains based upon the assumption that one organization can intervene in the business activities of another. We shall examine this vexed

Supply chains are typically represented as simple linear systems

In practice, they are usually a muddle which supply managers have to try to deal with on a daily basis. The symbols represent complexity, unknowns, and wasteful or non-commercial factors

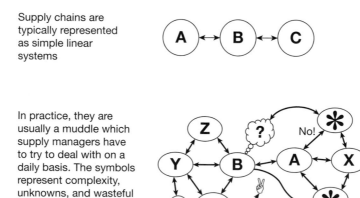

Figure 3.1 The supply chain metaphor: the simplicity may be inappropriate

subject later. The process of forming a strategy for the operational concerns of the organization outside its boundaries of ownership and physical presence cannot rely upon a concept of remote control, however; some better theory is required that managers can employ and this is where supply management comes in.

Research over a period of 30 years by a group of academics from around the world, known collectively as the *Industrial Marketing and Purchasing* group, has concluded that it is not possible to manage networks – instead, it is suggested, organizations may only seek to manage *within* them (their work is brought together well in Håkansson *et al.* 2009). So far, research in the area has not disproved this position and in discussing supply strategy as a part of, or within, operations strategy we shall retain the assumption. Forming supply strategy as an accompaniment to operations strategy begins with managing the relationships between the organization and the other organizations with which it deals directly. As a result of this 'relationship management', influence may be exerted on the activities of organizations elsewhere in the network that are involved in delivering the goods and services that form the focus of the supply strategy. Some of the strong *keiretsu* hierarchical groups formed in Japan during the twentieth century do appear to be controlled by their principal firms, although research in 1999 showed that this had changed profoundly as Japan weathered ten years of recession and the impacts of global operations (see Lamming, 2000). In supply management terms, the *keiretsu* groups are hierarchies, not networks.

This is a natural approach for a strategist: to form a plan for one's own activities and then try to influence others (either directly or indirectly) so that it may be complemented and therefore successful. It isn't a chain, and you can't manage it: but 'supply chain management' is the term which has become common parlance around the world – for managers, academics, management consultants, and politicians. We shall use it here, but we'll focus on supply management (i.e. the management of the goods and services that the organization chooses to obtain from outside, rather than some assumed ability to manage suppliers or networks). In particular, we are interested in *supplier relationship management* – the management of supply relationships between two organizations (including the activities which one might term 'purchasing' and 'selling') for the purposes of improving supply management.

We shall begin by exploring the nature of supply chains and supply bases and then explore essential factors for developing a supply strategy. Briefly put, these are: a policy on supply positioning, with a strategy to implement it; an internal strategy on the location of the purchasing and supply process within the organization; and a set of techniques for managing relationships between organizations – the essence of supply.

The nature of supply chains and supply bases – strategic supply and focused operations

Supply management has always played a role in how an organization is defined and organized. In the early twentieth century, in developing his famous Model T, Henry Ford planned to make everything himself, in his River Rouge plant near Detroit. He actually managed it for a while, even making his own glass and tyres as well as engines, bodies, chassis, and electrics

– a very broad range of manufacturing technologies and skills. This was total *vertical integration* – from top to bottom, the manufacturing was envisaged and structured as a single controlled and owned entity.

As the business grew, however, Ford could not remain the best at everything and had to find other, specialist manufacturers to do some of the work, to supply some of the components for his cars. This was a *disintegration* strategy and it accelerated through the late twentieth century. As we shall see in Chapter 4, this thinking is akin to the concept of 'open innovation' captured in the expression by Bill Joy, co-founder of Sun Microsystems:

'Not all the smart guys work for us.'

By 1980, Ford's own manufacturing (more correctly, *assembly*, but including component divisions) accounted for about 87 per cent of the cost of the car; the figure is now about 40 per cent. (Ford formed much of its component manufacturing business into a new company – Visteon – in 1997 and spun it off from the parent corporation in 2000. General Motors followed a similar strategy, forming Delphi. Whereas Visteon blossomed, Delphi went into liquidation in 2005 and its assets were sold. It is now called DPH Holdings Corp.) Despite the different fortunes, it is easy to see how supply management can become more important, in value terms, to a manufacturer than manufacturing.

IBM provides a similar case. In the past, the giant computer systems firm produced the silicon, software, and hard-drives for its computers. This approach was replaced by *outsourcing* strategies: literally, finding outside sources (suppliers) from which materials, components, and services could be purchased instead of being made 'in-house'. Initially (in the 1980s), this meant discontinuing manufacturing and letting others do it instead. In IBM's case, however, the strategy changed the company as it exited the small hardware business entirely to focus on business systems and services. Nowadays, a new, product-based enterprise would typically begin, not by planning how to manufacture it themselves, but by choosing a firm to make it for them – complete vertical disintegration. If the selected manufacturers are in a distant, low-labour-cost country such as China or India, the enterprise will have to develop expertise in supply management (rather than manufacturing) to ensure timely delivery of its product, at the right quality and price levels, to the markets.

For large-scale organizations, and for SMEs, operations management relies on a strategic balance: what to do yourself and what to have done for you by others and the importance of supply management reflects the decisions made. This is, of course, the classic 'make or buy?' decision. In deciding on this, the operations strategist is defining the *focus* of the organization (as we saw in Chapter 1: see Figure 1.5). Focus may be very specific and can have a profound importance for the firm. An organization can focus in a number of ways including:

- Choosing the customer groups and market segments which it serves.
- Adopting a particular type of manufacturing process – as we saw in Chapter 1 the choice of process or technology determines to a large degree what the firm can and cannot do.

- Focusing the plant into a number of different but specific allocated areas. These 'cells' of production or service units can be focused by customer, process, geographic region, product or service.
- Outsourcing areas of the business in which they are not competitive in an international market.
- Concentrating on specific activities within the supply chain and forming strategic buyer–supplier relationships to carry out others, thus developing a supply chain network or supply base.

The last two points clearly relate directly to management of supply.

In developing supply management, therefore, focus determines what the organization will *not* do itself and must therefore obtain from its supply network; the choice forms part of its operations strategy and can be transformational. For example, focus within the supply network played a key part when, in 1991, Hewlett-Packard (H-P) decided to enter the PC market. H-P did this with great intensity and was one of the top four PC producers by 1997. Later, H-P decided to move away from being a manufacturer to being an assembler of products. This shift in focus placed even greater emphasis on the need for excellent supplier relations throughout the supply chain, especially with those suppliers on whom H-P greatly depended. It also freed the firm from needing to make expensive investments in manufacturing plant and technology. Subsequently, H-P realized that it would be better placed if it outsourced the assembly of finished units. When H-P merged with its competitor, Compaq, in 2001, consolidation of its supply chains and outsourcing strategies was key to its success. H-P went on later in the decade to acquire more IT companies, including smartphone producer Palm Inc., digital electronics manufacturer 3com, and IT company EDS. Elsewhere, and less happily, a planned merger of Volvo and Renault in the 1993 was abandoned at a late stage largely because the two parties could apparently not agree on how to achieve this consolidation. Whirlpool and Maytag did rather better in 2005: see Case 3.1.

Today, the impact of strategies such as this, which have been followed by all the well-known computer companies, has led to a major shake-up in the industry so that now the majority of laptop computers are manufactured by just a handful of companies, operating internationally but manufacturing almost solely in East Asia. The equipment produced in this way is then labelled, or 'badged', for marketing by the big global brands.

In economic terms, when an organization focuses its operations it means it must analyse specific aspects of the process of production, or provision of a service, to see where it can really add value at competitive cost and still make money for its shareholders. For activities where this is not possible, the work may be outsourced. Responsibility is given to suppliers (e.g. for running parts of a service, manufacturing components or a whole product, or management of further input resources, such as supplies of raw materials). As we have seen, such a strategy may change the entire nature of a business, and thus the suppliers inevitably become much more significant strategic players in the process. In the 1990s an entirely new sector arose in this context – *contract manufacturers* – with firms such as Flextronics (founded

CASE 3.1: WHIRLPOOL AND MAYTAG SUPPLY CHAIN MERGER

Any time two large manufacturers merge, one of the many areas that has to be looked at is the supply chain. On one hand, the merger represents an opportunity to address inefficiencies in the system. Yet when this aspect of the business has been left unexamined and unchanged for a long time, the reworking of it can be costly and tedious. And doing so is demanded just when the company has various other pressing matters to deal with, such as integrating the workforce and cutting costs.

Fortunately for appliance maker Whirlpool, when it acquired Maytag in 2005 it had already started taking a good hard look at its supply chain. According to Brian Hancock, the company's vice-president in charge of supply chain, the company recognized that its system was out-of-date. 'Whirlpool had realized that it had focused on product and brand as a way to go after the marketplace. But as the marketplace had changed, supply chain had been something that we had neglected as a company,' says Hancock.

A new consumer mindset was at the root of what Whirlpool saw as a big shift in the appliance industry. Instead of mulling over the purchase of say, a new washer and dryer over a long period of time, as had traditionally been the way in which people shopped for major appliances, Hancock says a majority of customers had begun to act more quickly, buying new machines because the old ones broke down and had to be replaced or even treating them as somewhat discretionary purchases. 'The supply chain needed to be able to get that appliance to [the consumer] within 48 hours,' he says.

Whirlpool decided that to meet this quicker demand it would pare back the bulky inventories it formerly delivered to retail partners, consolidate its own warehouses into fewer, larger regional distribution centers, and optimize its technology for faster and more reliable shipment tracking. Hancock terms this last, crucial component 'schedule actualization' – knowing the whereabouts of products 'literally to the day, to make sure [retail partners] know exactly what's coming off that line.' This just-in-time approach to finished goods inventory became critical because people buy appliances with the expectation that the store will be able to deliver them in just a couple of days. And being able to meet consumer expectations is critical for the retailers.

Whirlpool's $2.7 billion acquisition of appliance rival Maytag, announced nine months after the new supply chain strategy was put into place, drastically changed the plan's scope. 'The complexity was just complicated by a factor of two, because the two companies were about the same size,' says Hancock. 'The buildings that we both had needed to be consolidated, the technologies that we had needed to be optimized and consolidated, and . . . the cash flow was probably about 200 to 300 million [dollars] out of whack from what we wanted it to be.'

Still, Whirlpool's new campaign to streamline its supply chain helped managers make decisive moves in the integration of the two huge manufacturers. By 2009, Whirlpool had closed some 100 facilities and completed construction on 10 regional distribution centers. Eventually, it will have eliminated about $60 million in operating costs from its supply chain.

Hancock only regrets one hiccup in the process: moving too slowly on permits for the new constructions. 'The process in some of these larger cities for a facility that's maybe a million or 2 million square feet can take a long time, so I would [have gotten] that started as quickly as possible,' he says.

Douglas MacMillan, Interactive Case Study, *Business Week*
24 October 2008, www.businessweek.com/managing/
content/oct2008/ca20081024_801808.htm

CASE STUDY

in 1969 but flourishing in the 1990s), Celestica (spun-out from IBM at this time), and Foxconn in China (see Chapter 12) all rising to prominence.

Focusing the operations may even mean that the firm becomes (or starts as) a *virtual* organization, employing very few people but achieving business goals associated with a much larger enterprise. For example, TopsyTail, a small Texan company, sold $100 million worth of its hair-styling equipment during the mid 1990s although it had virtually no permanent employees of its own. Subcontractors handled almost all of the organization's activities: design, manufacturing, and marketing. The Italian motorcycle manufacturer Aprilia, became successful by sourcing all the components for its bikes and scooters from suppliers in the region around its home in Mestre, near Venice, trading on its excellent design skills and simply assembling to order, managing its supplies accordingly. Its own organization is small, representing the hub of a network that forms a virtual organization. This appears to be an increasingly popular organizational strategy. It raises the question: is outsourcing simply a form of supply management (including buyer–supplier relationship management) or something more structurally strategic?

Supply and outsourcing

As we have seen, focusing may mean a firm divests itself of assets that had been developed during a period of diversification: a clear decision to exit a specific technology and buy whatever is needed from more proficient suppliers who have themselves focused on that technology. Outsourcing, however, is more often associated with a strategic decision to configure operations partly inside and partly outside the firm. Again this decision is made on the basis of which organization is best suited to add value as lowest cost and most sustainable quality, thereby arriving at the optimum degree of integration. Sometimes a firm will refer to its supply chain as 'integrated' but this is confusing; in the normal terminology, integrated means 'owned'. As we saw above, the move to outsourced production as a norm has changed the manufacturing industry and brought about the emergence of powerful new players whose names do not appear on the product in the shops.

In the US, such outsourcing has seen a remarkable growth in small manufacturing enterprises, such that by the mid 1990s companies with fewer than 100 employees comprised some 85 per cent of the US's 370,000 manufacturing firms (OECD, 1996). In addition, a sector of very large contract manufacturers has arisen (we shall discuss this later). Service industries soon followed manufacturing – for example, with the development of call-centres (for sales enquiries and customer service) sited offshore. These typically entail moving operations from the US or the UK to countries such as India or Malaysia, where international English is spoken.

In 2002, a report on 'offshoring' by the Forrester research group in the US estimates that 3.3 million white-collar American jobs (500,000 of them in IT) will have shifted offshore to countries such as India by 2015. Stephen Roach, the chief economist at Morgan Stanley, describes the opportunity represented by outsourcing as a 'new and powerful global labour arbitrage' that has led to an accelerating transfer of high-wage jobs to India and elsewhere. While the dominant trend has been US/UK to India (where 23 per cent of people speak

English) there are also cases of Japan offshoring to north east China (where Japanese is spoken), from Russia to Eastern Europe, and from Switzerland to the Czech Republic. In addition to the low costs of labour in such countries, the logic of offshoring is boosted by the fall in the cost of international phone calls and rise in internet connectivity. Such activities have not always been successful or popular with consumers: see Case 3.2.

During the 1990s in the UK, local councils were required to go out to tender for many of their public services, in a campaign to reduce costs (the assumption being that employing people to provide them was too expensive). This led to services such as street cleaning, maintenance, security, care of the elderly, and even such practices as planning authorities, being outsourced to private-sector organizations, many from outside the UK. The local council employees were transferred to the successful bidder, with only some of their employment rights protected by the TUPE legislation, (see www.cipd.co.uk/hr-resources/factsheets/transfer-of-undertakings-tupe.aspx) and many found themselves working for foreign firms.

CASE 3.2: UK FIRMS DECIDE IT'S TIME TO HANG UP ON INDIAN CALL CENTRES

In July 2011 Santander added its name to a growing list of British companies dumping their Indian call centres and bringing customer service operations back to the UK. With immediate effect, all of Santander UK's 1.5 million monthly customer service calls were to be answered in the UK, the company said.

Britain's third-largest bank created 500 jobs in Glasgow, Leicester and Liverpool to absorb the calls that would have gone to Bangalore and Pune, taking the group's total UK contact centre staff to 2,500. The move was a straightforward response to demand, according to Santander UK chief executive Ana Botin, who was struggling to improve the bank's customer service performance after it was rated third worst in the country in 2010.

'Our customers tell us they prefer our call centres to be in the UK and not offshore,' Ms Botin said yesterday. 'We have listened to the feedback and have acted by re-establishing our call centres back here.'

The trend for shifting customer service operations to India started in the 1990s, with call centre-intensive companies lured by the promise of costs slashed by as much as 40 per cent. The public was suspicious from the start. Despite repeated assurances from the industry that the homegrown call centre sector was growing fast enough to easily offset the small percentage of jobs shifting abroad, there was a widespread sense of inequity as household names from National Rail Enquiries to Prudential laid off staff to move operations abroad.

More pertinent still, as Ms Botin's comments noted, was the impact on customer satisfaction levels. Indian call centre operators went to sometimes absurd lengths, with agents taking English names, swotting up on local weather conditions and even watching episodes of EastEnders. But complaints soared as the frustrations of language problems became lodged in the public consciousness. By 2010 the guarantee that calls would be answered in the UK became a selling point in advertising campaigns for organisations, such as Royal Bank of Scotland (which had never moved its call centres overseas).

CASE STUDY

While other major global banks including Barclays and HSBC maintained both onshore and offshore call centres, Santander was far from alone in bringing operations back onshore. United Utilities, BT and Powergen had also cut back. In June 2011, the UK telecommunications company, New Call Telecom, announced plans to shift its Mumbai call centre back to Lancashire.

But experts warned that predictions of the demise of the unpopular offshore contact centre were premature. 'We are not seeing the end of the Indian call centre,' Stephen Whitehouse, at PricewaterhouseCoopers, said, 'but thanks to retailers like Tesco and John Lewis, the expectation on day-to-day service has been significantly raised, and customers do want to speak to someone within their country that can resolve their enquiry at the point of call.'

There were also pressing financial factors. Companies wowed by the potential cost reductions of moving offshore had soon found the expense of managing far-flung operations eating into their savings. Costs were also rising as India's economy continued to rocket, with attrition rates of up to 35 per cent amongst call centre staff and wages set to balloon by 12 per cent in 2012. New Call Telecom was explicit that its decision to re-locate to Burnley came down to price. Claudia Hathway, the editor of Call Centre Focus, said: 'Despite the rhetoric of listening to what customers want, rising costs are the true reason for companies coming back onshore.'

There had also been major changes in the nature of customer service operations themselves. As self-service via the internet took off, the need for large-scale telephone help lines diminished, and calls that were made, tended to be more demanding.

Added to this was the rise of so-called 'multi-channel' strategies – giving customers the options of contacting the company using anything from email to webchat to automated voice services – complicating the picture further. While customer service on the telephone might be best done from the UK, other elements could still be run effectively from elsewhere.

Abridged from *The Independent*, 9 July 2011

At the national level, outsourcing of information systems in central UK government departments was conducted apparently without any clear policy or sharing of information. This resulted, by the mid-1990s, in contracts for over three quarters of the central government's information systems being placed with one, North American, company, a worrying fact that only became apparent later, causing much dismay. Outsourcing in the public sector, now very much the norm, clearly has significant social factors and risks, just as in the private sector.

In the USA, where similar developments have been under way, some cases have elicited a strong negative reaction. For example, in November 2002, the state government in Indiana withdrew from a $15m contract with the American subsidiary of a leading Indian IT outsourcing firm. The reason given by Governor Joe Kernan was that the contract did not fit with Indiana's 'vision' of providing better opportunities to local companies and workers.

So although the decision to outsource has become a popular one for supply strategists it can cause unrest and strategic problems if it is poorly designed or managed (and there is evidence to show that this has often been the case) or political issues are not well handled. But simply divesting part of what was previously an owned asset is only one part of the puzzle. For such outsourcing to be successful, strategic buyer–supplier relationships need to be in place, as we shall see.

MANAGING SUPPLY: THE OBJECTIVE

As we have seen, the major proportion of the value offered by a firm to its customers is often actually derived not from doing things itself but from adding further value to components it has 'bought-out'. This is sometimes referred to as the 'purchasing ratio'. In a fast-food outlet, for example, the cost of the components of the meals is typically around 30 per cent of the cost of the meal itself (the restaurant is thus adding 70 per cent of the value). The cost of component parts of an aeroplane often add up to over 80 per cent of the total cost: the aircraft assembler is adding less than a fifth of the value for all its assembly labour, management, design, sales effort, and administration. Many manufacturers of consumer durable products have a purchasing ratio of over 70 per cent. In arriving at this figure it is important to make it clear whether the denominator is the product (or service) cost or the sale price – potentially very different figures. If we use product cost and represent it as a pie chart, a typical manufactured product might appear as shown in Figure 3.2.

In both cases, efforts to reduce the size of the pie – and thus the cost of the item – clearly need to concentrate on all three factors, but with differing expectations. In the first chart, typical of manufacturing in the 1990s, a 10 per cent reduction in labour costs would result in a 1 per cent reduction in overall cost; 10 per cent off overhead costs would lead to a 4 per cent reduction. A similar reduction in material (bought-out) costs would reduce the overall pie by 5 per cent – a significant saving. This simple point leads to the conclusion that control of material costs has always been more important than savings on labour costs or overheads in such a cost structure. As Purchasing people like to point out, such savings go directly to the bottom line for the company and improve profits in a way that increased sales could rarely achieve. In the second chart, which might be the situation after significant outsourcing, a 10 per cent reduction in the purchased cost of materials would give an 8 per cent cost reduction for the firm.

It is worth noting the transient nature of low labour costs, in the context of lower prices for outsourced manufacturing operations – as mentioned in Case 3.2. Social change happens very quickly; people naturally expect increasing benefits and rewards as their standards of living improve. By 2010, the labour cost in the east coast region of China – the first to benefit from offshored manufacturing contracts – was double that in the inner and western regions of the country, after barely a decade of such activity.

In China, the logic of exploiting low labour costs may be expected to push such contracts west, resulting in the problems and costs of disruption and social problems in the east. 2010 saw the first significant recent strikes in China as workers protested against working conditions and rates of pay, including the horrific suicide protests at Foxconn, a supplier of Apple's newly launched iPad. In the light of global outrage, workers at Foxconn secured a 70 per cent pay rise (thereby significantly reducing the logic underpinning their employment). In the same year, Honda's four Chinese assembly plants were stopped by a strike at Honda Lock

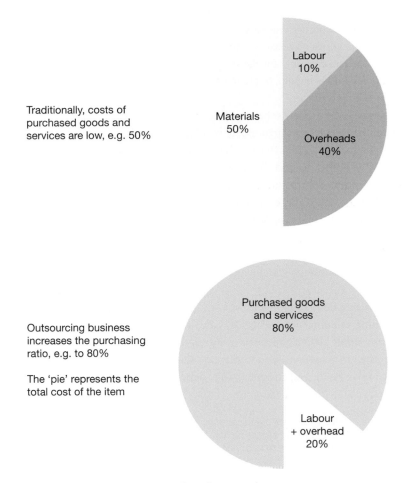

Traditionally, costs of
purchased goods and
services are low, e.g. 50%

Labour
10%

Materials
50%

Overheads
40%

Outsourcing business
increases the purchasing
ratio, e.g. to 80%

The 'pie' represents the
total cost of the item

Purchased goods
and services
80%

Labour
+ overhead
20%

Figure 3.2 Unit costs: internal and external

(Guangdong). Workers eventually returned to work hoping to achieve an increase of 24 per
cent that had been agreed at another Honda supplier.

Issues such as health and safety, paid holiday allowance, and elimination of unfair
conditions may be expected to erode low labour costs, wherever they arise: the social changes
that the world's developing economies are being required to achieve in a few decades took
centuries to achieve in the West. We shall explore this further in Chapter 12.

Adding value for the end customer

In practice, as we saw in Chapter 1, material costs result from a series (or chain) of events
– this has similarities with the supply chain concept. This means we can apply a value-
addition perspective to the supply chain analysis, always remembering that the actual system

is a muddle, not a simple chain. Reducing material costs as part of supply management is thus not simply a matter of attacking the immediately obvious target – for example, negotiating down the price paid for the goods or services – but a more complex task of analysing the build-up of value (what the end customer for the supply chain would pay for that part of the process if this connection could be made), in the light of the costs and time involved for the organization in producing the value.

As we saw in Chapter 1, the materials that are to be bought are actually part of a service provided by the supplier: materials surrounded by delivery, presentation, treatment, innovation, aftercare, and so on. It follows that one is not simply buying a product but paying for a service. This must be borne in mind when considering the value being acquired. It is also a major part of price negotiation, as the amount that should be paid for the costs of the added value (design, materials handling, component sourcing, etc.) is often disputed.

Figure 3.3 shows how firms (in a simplified representation of a product's supply chain) might be viewed in the context of progressive value addition (note that the end customer is a part of this process and can be required to add value for which they pay: for example, the total value of 'flat pack' furniture eventually includes the value which the owner adds by constructing it).

The 'stripped-down' simplicity employed in Figure 3.3, which we have used to make the single point about adding value in relationships, should not make us forget the muddled complexity of the entire supply system addressed by an organization, as we saw earlier. The purpose is to show how an increase in value added at any stage of the process might lead to an increase in eventual value for the end customer, while a reduction in time taken to process

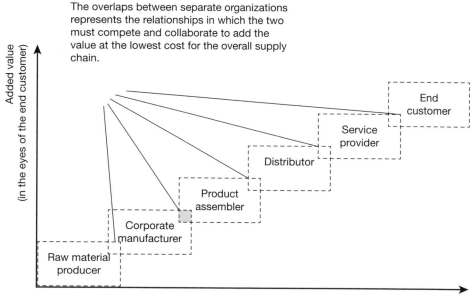

Figure 3.3 Build up of value and cost in the supply chain, as a product-creation process

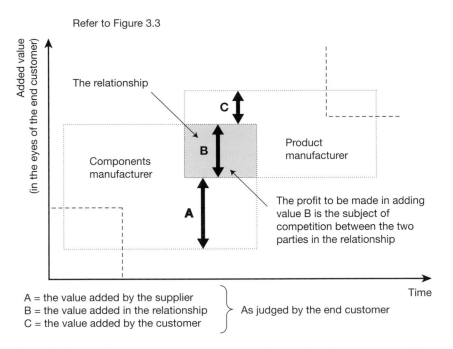

Refer to Figure 3.3

A = the value added by the supplier
B = the value added in the relationship } As judged by the end customer
C = the value added by the customer

Figure 3.4 Representation of a customer–supplier relationship as a part of the value-adding process

the product, and thus cost, may be reduced at any point. Since either of these should increase the likelihood of the product succeeding in the marketplace, either should be to the benefit of all parties in the supply chain. In addition to this, each organization in the chain is naturally concerned with the financial gain it makes from adding value in the process – in effect, the value it receives itself on behalf of its shareholders. Each organization must thus have a supply strategy in order to operate within the chain, and in order for the chain itself to operate competitively.

The firms in the chain thus have two concerns – for the overall competitiveness of the chain and for their own prosperity within it. Since they derive their income from the value they add (i.e. how much the immediate customer will be prepared to pay for it above what it costs them to produce, but viewed within the context of what the next customer, or the end customer, will pay), each firm may be expected with the others to add more of the total value. It follows that the customer and supplier at each stage in the chain are actually competing inside the relationship for the profit that they could make from value-adding work within it: they are competitors as well as collaborators. Where the boxes in Figure 3.3 overlap there lies a space for this competition – the value should be great, the time or cost small. The overlap is shown in more detail in Figure 3.4.

This leads to a set of dynamic partnerships in the chain which, if it works efficiently in market terms, should lead to individual and mutual prosperity.

So much for the concept: how does it work in practice? Each organization is driven by its owners – shareholders in the case of a limited company, taxpayers (via their representatives) in the case of, say, a government department or the armed forces. In either case, the responsibility of the directors and managers in the organization is to their stakeholders: their shareholders, employees, customers, and members of the community affected by the activities of the organization. The dominant force here has traditionally been the first one: the owners. Recently, the stakeholder concept has been extended to include suppliers to the organization, as the actions of the organization may have an adverse effect upon the suppliers in the short term and on the supply chain (and thus the organization itself) in the long term. This domination has led managers to be concerned principally (often exclusively) with their own organization – especially in the case of a limited company, where shareholders are most directly aware of the results of any strategy. As we shall see in Chapter 5, the stakeholder view has increased importance when we consider the organization within the imperatives of sustainable development and the threats of scarce resources.

STRUCTURING THE SUPPLY BASE

As the supply strategist contemplates the desired nature of supply relationships, one natural factor will be the interplay between them and the strategic position of each supplier relative to others (e.g. important vs. minor, high-tech vs. low tech, long term vs. temporary, new vs. about to exit). It is also necessary for the supply strategist to understand how each supplier sees them as a customer, along much the same lines. This leads to the need to consider structure and the idea of the supply base.

Observers of Japanese industrial structures of the late twentieth century coined the term 'first-tier' to describe the powerful, large firms that supplied directly to the household name, or branded, manufacturers of cars, consumer durables, and capital equipment that were such an important part of Japan's revival in the post-war period. The structure of supply 'base' – a sort of pyramid of firms upon which the final product assembler sat – was a feature of the historical Japanese social structure and key to the formation of the giant groups (known as *zaibatsu* in the first half of the twentieth century, and *keiretsu* in the second half). As Nishiguchi (1986) pointed out, these supply structures should not be seen as separate 'mountains' but as a sort of *alpine* structure – a great base of manufacturing companies, from which peaks (the well-known product assemblers) emerge (the point being that components from any of the firms in the sub-structure might end up in a product of any of the 'peak' organizations).

In Japan, the tiers were clearly marked (and well documented). Elsewhere, they do not really exist, simply because the historical development of firms has been more autonomous, international, multicultural, and random. The image of tiers is so strong, however, that there has been a tendency to call suppliers 'first-tier' and 'second-tier' without a logical basis, even though it has become standard practice. A tier, after all, is a very specific feature of a structure; it has a hierarchical position. In this case, the first is above the second, since the referencing is done from the top (i.e. the customer firm), but it could easily be the reverse in a different situation – for example, the first tier of a multi-level wedding cake is at the bottom, and lateral links can exist to other items in the same tier, such as seats in a stadium or theatre arranged in connected, integrated rows.

The danger of casually referring to organizations in the supply chain, base, or network as 'first-tier' (or second-tier, and so on) is that the expectations thus created may bear no actual resemblance to the activity that will be addressed by the organization in question, since the lateral links, which may be essential for the expected activity, do not exist. Thus, a vehicle assembler may require a major supplier to buy components from other suppliers, and construct and deliver complete 'systems' (e.g. an entire engine cooling system, consisting of the radiator, hoses, brackets, sensors, etc., ready to fit into the car). The systems supplier might be called 'first-tier' but have little linking-up with other suppliers with whom their supply of systems must be interfaced or integrated. Much electronics design within consumer (e.g. mobile phones) and industrial (e.g. network base-stations) products lends itself to modular manufacture in this way, strengthening the idea of key suppliers keeping close to the assembler and taking responsibility for coordinating other, perhaps less significant, suppliers. It is now common to hear supply strategists speak of 'tier-half', referring to suppliers to whom so much responsibility (e.g. for design and production) has been given that they must be seen as not entirely separate from the customer. This rather odd terminology fits well with the concept that a relationship as close as this is actually an overlap between the two organizations, rather than a bridged gap.

During the 1980s, some Western supply strategists began to realize that they had, in general, too many suppliers. It was quite common for an organization, of any size, to have more suppliers than employees. A practice emerged for reducing the number of suppliers

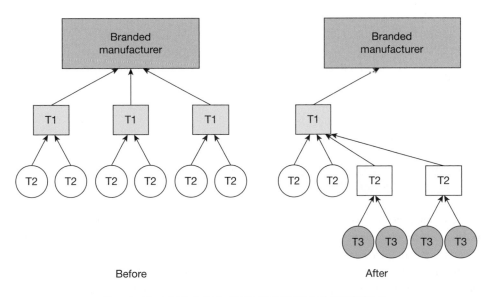

Before

After

Tier structure before and after rationalization of supply base

Figure 3.5 Tiers in supply bases, showing flaws in some approaches to supply base rationalization

with whom the organization dealt on a regular basis, in order to focus the cost of dealing with them onto a smaller number who would therefore benefit from the customer's attention. This was fashionably termed 'supply base rationalization'.

In fact, it seldom appears rational in practice – a commonly observed problem being the one illustrated in Figure 3.5. In the second diagram (post-rationalization) there are in fact just as many suppliers involved in the supply base, despite the number of direct suppliers being reduced by two thirds. Moreover, the ex-first-tier suppliers, now called second-tier by the 'branded manufacturer' (assembler) are likely to be demoralized, and possibly dissatisfied with supplying to the remaining first-tier supplier (who might have been a competitor previously). In many cases, the producer will stipulate that the first-tier supplier must purchase from specific ex-first-tier suppliers, for political reasons, leaving the remaining first-tier organization in a commercial trap. The supply strategist must avoid this situation and devise some more rational approach if this practice is to produce genuine benefits. There have, of course, been many examples of organizations genuinely reducing the number of suppliers with whom they work, usually by addressing a 'tail' of less significant contracts. An example is shown in Case 3.3.

CASE STUDY

CASE 3.3: SONY SUPPLY BASE RATIONALIZATION, 2009

In April 2009, Sony's Executive Deputy President Yutaka Nakagawa decided to drastically overhaul the company's supply chain for its digital cameras, videogame machines and liquid-crystal-display TVs. His aim was to halve the number of parts and materials suppliers over two years, and cut purchasing costs by 20% in the first half of this period. The technology giant had about 2,500 suppliers and planned to reduce that number to 1,200 by March 2011.

Sony officials informed companies in its supply chain in May 2009. The news was a mixed bag for suppliers: bad for those that were dropped, good for those that could expect to see a jump in orders.

By buying bigger volumes of parts from each supplier, Sony expected to lower its costs, ultimately shaving 500 billion Yen (US$ 5.2 billion) off the 2.5 trillion Yen (US$ 26.3 billion) that Sony spent on parts in the fiscal year 2008–09. The savings were in addition to the $3.1 billion Sony expected to save by selling off factories and reducing other fixed costs.

Abridged from *Business Week*, 21 May 2009. See also Sony's Procurement page at: www.sony.net/SonyInfo/procurementinfo/index.html

---

The *supply network* concept removes the hierarchical nature of the supply base and also reduces rigidity (suppliers' roles may change as they take more or less responsibility, become more or less important, etc.) The Japanese supply bases of the late twentieth century were clearly managed, technically making them hierarchies. It may be that by retaining the idea of first-tier suppliers (and so on) customers limit the potential dynamism in their supply bases that might be enabled by recognizing the non-hierarchical, non-managed network.

With the nature of relationships and the structure of the supply chain firmly in focus, the supply manager can begin to build a strategy.

ESSENTIAL FACTORS IN DEVELOPING A SUPPLY STRATEGY

Setting up a supply strategy

As we noted earlier, in forming a supply strategy there are four requirements. The first two may be considered together:

- A *policy* on how the organization is to engage with its external activities, accompanied by a *strategy* for implementing it;
- An *internal strategy* for the role that the purchasing process (and thus the functions associated with it) should play; and
- A *set of specific approaches* to managing supply relationships.

Supply policy and strategy

The purpose of a policy is to clarify an organization's position on a specific matter – a clear statement of its stance on an issue or an expression of its values and norms. In this case, the matter is supply management, so it is a *supply policy*. For example, the directors of an organization may decide that the nature of their business means that they must be very competitive in supply chain management (i.e. in terms of controlling the value-adding process) rather than collaborative.

A supply policy such as this might be appropriate where the resources needed for the business (including skills, materials, information, locations, equipment, and finance) are scarce and the number of suppliers or subcontractors with whom one might work is high. In this case, simply getting hold of, or controlling, what Cox (1997) called the 'critical assets' in the supply chain, might be enough to ensure success for the organization. The fact that this might cause one or two other firms in the chain to suffer a fatal difficulty, causing them to exit, might not matter in economic terms. In other circumstances, the resources needed might be more widely available, and the number of firms with whom one might work small. In this case, the policy might be to act in collaboration, since success might only come from differentiating the product or service through innovation and creative development, in which the organization and its suppliers would need to work together. Collaboration might also be the policy when resources are scarce and the organization needs to keep close to a specific supplier ('supply partner') to ensure sustained supplies.

Some organizations make their supply policies public and they can be found on their websites. In some cases they address specifics (e.g. sustainability) or use different terminology (e.g. 'philosophy'). Some also focus on expectations they place upon suppliers rather than committing themselves: we shall explore this later. Here are a few interesting examples:

- Magnox North (UK), www.magnoxnorthsites.com/suppliers/supply-chain-policy
- Apple (US), www.apple.com/supplierresponsibility/

- Doves Farm (UK), www.dovesfarm.co.uk/global-policies/supply-chain-policy/
- Sony (Japan), www.sony.net/SonyInfo/procurementinfo/activities/index.html
- Siemens (Germany), https://w9.siemens.com/cms/supply-chain-management/en/supply-chain/Pages/supply-chain.aspx
- REXAM (UK), www.rexam.com/files/pdf/policies/supplychain.pdf

As industries tend to become more concentrated (i.e. mergers and acquisitions are frequent, leading to a small number of powerful firms) managing the costs of global operations makes aligning oneself with the right supplier an increasingly important strategic factor. In the aerospace industry, for example, there are three manufacturers of engines for large passenger jets: Rolls-Royce, General Electric, and Pratt and Whitney. For aircraft manufacturers, the supply of engines is a vital area, but it would make no sense for, say, Boeing to acquire General Electric's engines business, since the latter requires non-Boeing business to support its research and development and production activities.

Such a strategy should not be seen as a soft position for the supplier, however: for several years now, in the large engines business of the aircraft industry, a supplier has had to commit to achieving a specified annual 'cost-out' (typically 7 per cent per annum) just to retain its position in the supply base. If this is not accepted or achieved, the customer may be expected to bring in another company that can do so and the supplier might reduce in importance in the supply network as a result – possibly in contrast to their marketing strategy.

The supply policy might also include meddling with the resources issue – to create scarcity, and thus influence the degree of competitiveness or collaboration in the chain. This is a central theme of Cox's (1997) approach and one that he suggests is universally applicable. It naturally includes acquisition, so that one might become the owner of assets required by a competitor, and thus hold the whip hand.

An example of this was Apple's acquisition of Texas-based semi-conductor manufacturer Intrinsity Inc., in April 2010. The supplier had developed the 1 gHz 'Hummingbird A8' processor in partnership with Apple's aggressive competitor Samsung in 2009. Apple is famous for secrecy (it had made similar acquisitions before) but it is believed the Hummingbird A8 processor was crucial to the success of the iPad.

Other commentators argue that there are cases in which the immediately apparent benefits of controlling all the assets may lead to longer-term dysfunction in the supply markets as players upon whom the organization must rely (for activities that may not be appropriate for it to conduct itself) are starved and exit the field. This might mean that the meddling organization is left to buy the products and services from a reduced number of suppliers (who will feel little sympathy with it, possibly as they are from a distant country) or make the items for itself. The investments necessary for the latter may not be possible, or sensible, for the organization and it is thus left with an inappropriate portfolio of activities to manage – buying from an oligopoly. This may not be a problem for Apple (whose supply chain management was awarded 'best in the world' status in 2010 (see www.supplymanagement.com, 7 June 2010)), but clearly few customer firms enjoy the same positional strength.

So, this policy can only be put into practice, through a strategy, if the organization is in a competitive situation and has the ability to acquire and shed activities and businesses strategically. If this is not the case, the potential for strategic supply may be limited.

Other factors may enter the policy making process, such as ethical and environmental issues, social considerations, and the nature or position of the organization, including the constraints on its freedom of action. This will entail a series of tradeoffs, such as the commercial benefits of sourcing in low labour-cost countries versus issues such as child labour or employee conditions, which may form a part of the reasons behind those low labour-costs.

Once policy is set, an overall strategy for supply requirements may be formed. This will include matters such as 'make or buy', supplier location, and tactical or strategic alliances. The first of these may entail sub-contracting or outsourcing. This is clearly fundamental to the organization's sustainable success and is not usually left to supply managers (e.g. purchasing directors) who clearly have a vested interest (i.e. a preference for the 'buy' option.) It is also, almost always, a political decision, possibly implying issues such as job losses and retention or loss of strategic competences, and is thus treated as a matter for the Board.

The mass-production approach to this was neatly summed up by Henry Ford: 'If you need a machine and you do not buy it, you will eventually find that you have paid for it but do not have it.' With the long product lives and forcefully controlled consumer markets of mass production in early twentieth-century North America, the logic of this statement was powerful and remains so wherever such market conditions persist. As the commercial lives of products and process technologies have shortened, however, with the opening of markets and the need to recognize the 'voice of the customer', and as the specialization and sophistication of production equipment has increased, so the wisdom of buying 'the machine' has become less simple.

Put briefly, it may be a choice between, on the one hand, operating without a critical resource by buying-in the service (thereby risking paying too much for the service and losing competitiveness, or even having to do without it) and on the other hand, being caught with a sunk-cost investment in a technology that is no longer commercially valuable (and thus paying off the investment long after it has ceased to provide the necessary revenue). The former problem (which would be avoided by developing the resource 'in-house') may lead to a cost penalty and loss of sales, while the latter (which could be avoided by outsourcing) might lead to a cash flow crisis and insolvency, or other problems such as poor quality, uncertain performance etc.

In fact, either could prove fatal. Once again, the answer might be to meddle in the supply market, suppressing technologies that appear (e.g. by buying them – like Apple buying Intrinsity) in order to increase the period of 'economic rent' – and thus recouping the investment. The extreme form of this would be monopoly, in which case, the organization's concerns would be reduced – at least temporarily. However, the rate of technological change in many sectors has made monopoly a difficult – even unfeasible – concept to rely on. Examples such as Microsoft (no longer a monopoly) are very rare, and basing a supply strategy purely on such a case would have limited practical use. Even the very powerful Apple has little prospect of being a monopoly – perhaps a factor that keeps it so innovative.

Sourcing strategy

Much has been written on ways of deciding where and how to procure products and services. These are usually linked to the nature of the purchase, not the supplier, in the context of the buying organization's technical, operational, or commercial requirements and market situation. The most well respected and widely adopted modern approach was published in the *Harvard Business Review* as long ago as 1983, by the Slovenian management thinker Peter Kraljic, a senior member of the strategic consultancy McKinsey. Despite being 30 years old, Kraljic's sourcing matrix still evidently provides the conceptual basis for many purchasing strategies – sometimes in the original form, sometimes modified (often without credit given to its creator). The original article is definitely worth reading, and the basic matrix is shown in Figure 3.6.

Kraljic's argument is that for any item, the risk of being caught without it (and thus, for example, stopping the production line, or failing to fill an order) may be high or low. Kraljic calls this *risk of exposure*. The cost to the organization (of the procured item) may also be dichotomized into high and low. Cost may include many factors in addition to purchase price – for example the costs of acquiring, storing, insuring, and maintaining the item.

Combining these two factors enables the supply strategist to decide on what approach should be taken to managing the item. Those in the top right-hand box might be treated as strategically important and thus managed through close collaboration with the supplier, while those in the bottom left might be dealt with via, say, automated buying and stock control.

Taking its origins clearly from such ideas as the well known Pareto '80–20' effect (which observes, in this context, that 80 per cent of expenditure on goods and services supplied

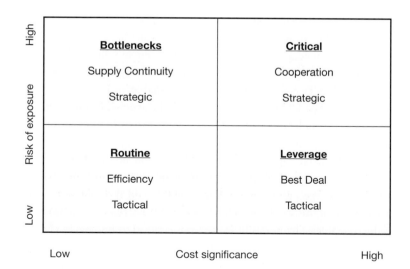

Figure 3.6 Kraljic's sourcing matrix
Kraljic (1983)

to the organization will probably be accounted for by 20 per cent of the suppliers from whom these things are bought), Kraljic's matrix has for many years encouraged supply managers in many sectors to consider more than the immediate aspects of their sourcing decisions – reflecting the title of his HBR paper: 'Purchasing Must Become Supply Management'.

Its simplicity is appealing to supply strategists, and many modern strategies consist of little more than this diagram (almost always with different wording, as the analysis has been customized to a specific organization's situation.) Anyone wishing to be taken seriously as a professional purchaser must be able to recognize and use this tool – as a basic skill. As with all 'two-by-two' analysis methods, the tool is open to criticism for over simplification – there are many other variables involved in sourcing. There has also been recent discussion over the appropriateness of the boxes: for example, an item that is low in cost and has little risk of exposure attached to it may still be a vital part without which the organization cannot function – the traditional 'halfpenny's worth of tar which [by its absence] spoiled the ship'.

During the 1990s, as supply strategists realized that collaborative approaches would be necessary where straightforward customer power did not provide what they wanted, sourcing strategies often focused on types of relationship (and thereby types of supplier). This often resulted in categories ranging from 'strategic partner' to 'standard supplier' (or some such euphemism), often in four gradations. Such strategies would usually assign resources to the different types of relationship, perhaps linked to the returns expected. As we shall see later, these were based on mass-production thinking, including the notion that the customer's view of the situation was the only important one, which is hardly an approach that could expect to bring the best from a supply base. (For example, as we saw in Figure 3.5, a third-tier supplier is only third-tier when viewed from the point of view of the branded manufacturer.)

A popular marketing and logistics perspective on supply strategy begins with addressing the problem of the volatile nature of market demand. A number of such authors (i.e. those that take a marketing or logistics channel perspective, for example Fisher, 1997; Christopher and Towill, 2001) propose the idea of *agile* supply, which denotes the ability to respond rapidly to unpredictable changes in demand or supply. Supply strategy thus becomes an attempt to reduce the risk embedded in the supply chain.

Christopher and Peck (2004) identify two ingredients necessary for agility in logistics as *visibility* and *velocity*. The first of these they define as the ability to 'see' from one end of the pipeline to the other. Visibility implies a clear view of upstream and downstream inventories, demand and supply conditions, and production and purchasing schedules. The achievement of supply chain visibility is based upon close collaboration with customers and suppliers as well as internal integration within the business. Collaborative planning with customers is seen as being important in enabling visibility of demand. Supply chain velocity is defined as distance over time. Reducing the end-to-end time, the interval between the focal firm placing orders and when it delivers to its customers, would increase velocity (Christopher and Peck, 2004).

INTERNAL STRATEGY FOR THE ROLE OF THE PURCHASING PROCESS

Having chosen and developed a strategy for supply and a way of understanding the management of sourcing decisions, the supply strategist must decide how purchasing is conducted within the organization. This has two parts – location and process.

LOCATING PURCHASING AND SUPPLY MANAGEMENT IN THE ORGANIZATION

Location – where purchasing actually takes place – depends upon the way in which the organization is structured. In a general sense, the organization may be set up to run with functional departments, each of which contains career specialists who are both the operational competence of the organization and also its 'eyes and ears' in that specialism (i.e. they ensure that the organization's competence in their area is up to date). These vertical, functional pillars within the organization (sometimes called 'silos', after the agricultural storage device in which materials such as animal foodstuffs are delivered into the top of an upright cylinder, and drawn off as needed from the bottom, fed by gravity) form its structure. Between and across them (i.e. 'horizontally' from one functional area to another) flow the processes of the organization – product development and order fulfilment being two basic activities – much as we saw in Chapter 1.

Over the last few decades, many firms have removed their functional silos and organized themselves along process lines, supporting the 'horizontal' flows with the necessary functional expertise at appropriate points. The operational manifestation of this is *cross-functional teams*, in which experts with a variety of functional and commercial skills are put together (often 'co-located' in one office) to take responsibility for a specific process – such as bringing a new product to market on time.

Thus, *Purchasing*,[1] as the traditional home of responsibility for supply management, may be located as a separate functional department, with processes passing into and out of it (in which case the management role is to ensure that the interfaces with other departments do not delay communications or add cost to the process) or as part of a cross-functional team within a process-orientated organization, where there are no clear 'departments'. There are, of course, many examples of hybrid arrangements. Either way, the organization will need an internal strategy for the way in which the purchasing process takes place, which will influence the way in which it is organized.

A well-known and practised strategy for this was developed by Reck and Long in 1988. Like the Kraljic model, this useful approach has survived all the way from the 1980s, developed many times in theory but still well respected and used in practice. Naturally, it has been criticized and it is worth searching the literature on purchasing strategy as well as reading the original article (some suggestions are included at the end of this chapter). The

---

1   When referring to the department, Purchasing is capitalized.

Reck and Long model describes a four stage, dynamic, hierarchical framework with which managers may compare themselves as they develop Purchasing's role and position in the supply management of the organization. At all times, of course, this needs to be conducted in light of the policy and strategy discussed above. The model is shown in Table 3.1.

The Reck and Long model enables the supply strategist to define the role of both the purchasing process and the function (i.e. the department). It may be used first to identify the present situation and then to define the appropriate position. Moving from one to the other then becomes a project of change.

Other writers – and many management consultants – have constructed similar, multi-level, models for explaining the ways in which purchasing may be positioned to ensure the best use is made of the expertise, and that the best 'fit' with corporate purposes is maintained. Naturally, supply strategy must be made to fit with higher-level direction in the company and thus the Reck and Long model is used in the context of corporate strategy. Reviews of Purchasing and Supply strategy include Ellram and Carr (1994) and Frohlich and Westbrook (2001); research on the concept is reported in Harland *et al.* (1999) and González-Benito (2010). Meanwhile, a simple glimpse at the Internet will produce a plethora of supply strategy offerings from management consultancies – from snake-oil salesmen to global experts.

Two developments have fundamentally affected the way in which purchasing is positioned as part of the supply process: successive waves of new information and communications technologies (ICT), and the massive global expansion of business organizations and markets. The two are, of course, related. ICT has made possible practices such as electronic purchasing (i.e. paperless and instant), sharing scheduling information with suppliers via access to the organization's intranet (leading to the removal of the need to schedule deliveries and requiring the supplier to monitor stock levels of their products within the organization's stores and replenish them as necessary) and almost unlimited communication and information exchange through intranet technologies and the internet.

So-called 'e-procurement', emerging in the 1990s and burgeoning in the following decade, often combines structures such as Kraljic's model with fast and extensive communications, to encourage people within organizations to purchase their own requirements, using electronic catalogues that maintain a corporate knowledge of 'best buys'. This approach

Table 3.1 Reck and Long's model for developing the role of purchasing

Stage	Definition
Passive	No strategic definition: primarily reacts to requests from other functions
Independent	Adopts latest purchasing techniques and practices, but strategic direction is independent from the organization's competitive strategy
Supportive	Supports the organization's competitive strategy by adopting purchasing techniques that strengthen its competitive position
Integrative	Purchasing strategy is fully integrated with the organization's competitive strategy and constitutes part of an integrated effort among functional peers to formulate and implement a strategic plan

Reck and Long (1988)

is now widely used for purchasing everything from business travel to electronic components for product assembly. It can take the purchasing activity away from the specialist and into the hands of the first line-manager, or even lower-level operatives.

The purchase may be made with a corporate credit card, so that the budget holder can monitor expenditure against the plan, and be accountable for it. This 'atomization' of purchasing responsibility has the benefit of leaving the specialists free to concentrate on strategic matters (including setting up the framework agreements for the supply of the items covered) and relationship management for strategic items. The potential problem is that control of expenditure will be lost. Despite the rigour of budget management, the individuals given the freedom to purchase their requirements may not adhere to corporate guidelines in practice (so called 'maverick buying': see below). If the individual is a line manager who needs replenishment of production components, there may only be one or two specified sources that can be used (controlled by the information system). If the item required is a laptop computer, however, there may be dozens – the proliferation of suppliers of such items, accessed through catalogues, is precisely the type of uncontrolled activity that results in administrative congestion within an organization.

The technicalities are endless but the principle is clear. Giving responsibility for sourcing to non-specialists throughout the organization requires discipline and support but can lead to a downsizing in formal (centralized) Purchasing departments, thus actually saving the organization money.

The last decade has seen the widespread adoption of *on-line auctions*, in which suppliers bid for business in a live, on-screen event, run by the customer or their agent. On-line auctions (once called 'reverse' auctions, because the prices are driven downwards in the bidding) are now commonplace, either within Internet exchanges or simply as tools within the sourcing process. Much of the initial concern for suppliers' interests has abated and such methods are seen simply as the way in which sourcing will be done in future (as often seen, electronic communication replaces paper). In practice, however, the online auction only replaces part of the sourcing process – it is still important in many cases for purchasers and prospective suppliers to discuss details of the contract personally. This may be a complication where the customer has chosen to run the online auction worldwide. (See Hawkins *et al.*, 2009.)

The globalization of operations and markets leads to further challenges for positioning supply management. The customer for a manufactured product expects it to operate efficiently in any country and to be compatible with other items that may have been made in a different part of the world. The same expectations of consistency exist for international hotel chains, courier services, and airlines. In global manufacturing, the production system costs (which include supply of materials and components) for an item made in, say, Latin America, need to be as close as possible to those in, say, South Korea, in order for location decisions to made on the simplest basis possible (wage level, subsidies, logistics, etc.).

To address this need, global operators have developed global purchasing and supply practices – dealing with other global players on a worldwide level. One way of managing this is to the assign responsibility for technical expertise in a particular product or commodity area to a specific geographical office, for example the global head of purchasing for a computer manufacturer might say 'Our purchasing expertise in DRAMs (dynamic random access memory chips, used for the main memory in laptop and workstation computers, games consoles, and so on) is located in Shanghai: anyone who needs to purchase DRAMs has only to speak to Shanghai in order to get the best deal from our global supply partners' (of course, 'speaking' is done via intranet). In this case, Shanghai might be called the 'lead buyer' for DRAMs.

An alternative way of addressing this supply management need is to set up *commodity councils* – working groups with members drawn from all operating divisions around the world that are in constant touch with each other, meeting in person occasionally as well as via intranet and telephone or telepresence (video conferencing). These originated in IBM and have been widely adopted, especially in the US and in public procurement. See, for example:

- www-03.ibm.com/procurement/proweb.nsf/contentdocsbytitle/United+States~ Commodity+councils)
- www.wrcoc-aic.org/Archive/RS/RS08/RS08–24.pdf
- www.nj.gov/agriculture/divisions/md/news/commcouncils.html

In practice, the commodity council becomes the organization's knowledge base and develops expertise and 'good deals' in purchasing and supply. The advantage over the 'lead buyer' approach is that the expertise is spread around the divisions and may grow from a multiplicity of inputs and perspectives, rather than the narrowly focused efforts of one group. People who work in commodity councils often see their colleagues as those they communicate with globally, even though they may work thousands of miles apart and never actually meet.

For some years, large companies have been operating so-called *international procurement offices* or 'IPO's, typically in Asia, in order to make the most of opportunities for sourcing there. This is clearly a strategy driven by geography and development trajectories. The IPO may be very much more than a channel for sourcing, however, as shown by the Motorola example in Case 3.4.

CASE 3.4: MOTOROLA MAKES BIG SUPPLY CHAIN INVESTMENT IN SINGAPORE

CASE STUDY

Between 2006 and 2008 Motorola spent US$60 million in Singapore, to centralize and streamline global supply chain operations. The company's chairman and CEO, Ed Zander, said the new investment, in what he called Motorola's 'control tower' would allow Motorola to manage supply chain management activities across its businesses including mobile devices, networks and connected home products.

When the scheme was launched in 2006, Motorola was managing more than US$10 billion worth of activities each year in supply chain operations, such as manufacturing and distribution. Stu Reed, Motorola's executive vice president of integrated supply chain, said prior to the new Singapore investment, the company ran disparate supply chain operations around the world 'This is the first time that we are driving centralization. There was no "control tower" of supply chain activities before [this],' he said.

The investment was spent on manpower as well as research and development in manufacturing technology. Motorola planned to work with local academia to enhance manufacturing processes and to hire some 200 professionals in Singapore to support its supply chain operations.

Zander said the company realized several years ago that it needed world-class supply chain capabilities to stay competitive. 'Your cost structure, quality of manufacturing and the way you compete in the next decade is through your supply chain,' he noted.

Asked how much cost saving Motorola was expecting to reap from centralized supply chain management, Zander said: 'It's not about saving money ... it's about faster time to market and improving [product] quality. The best-run companies usually have the best supply chain.' Reed noted that enhancing supply chain operations could typically rein in 'double-digit' productivity growth and allow a company to respond faster to changing product cycles by 30 to 40 percent.

Zander said Motorola's cellphone product cycles usually ranged from six to nine months. The company operates in multiple geographies, with some products shipped exclusively for certain markets such as China and India. Operating in such a complex and fast-changing environment means Motorola needs to bolster its supply chain operations for future success, he said.

Abridged from *Business Week*, 6 June 2006

We now have the basis for a supply strategy in place:

- A policy on how we perceive our supply market and how we prefer to operate within it;
- A strategy for implementing this policy;
- A way of planning sourcing activities, categorizing items in the light of their significance to the organization;
- An internal strategy for the management of supply – including how the organization's purchasing expertise is positioned and the process managed; and
- A way of dealing with the needs of global supply, including sharing expertise between regional offices and ensuring information systems support purchasing decisions.

All that remains is to do the purchasing and supply management.

THE PROCESS OF PURCHASING AND SUPPLY MANAGEMENT

The nature of the purchasing and supply process includes responding to demands for products and services from within the organization by providing the necessary resources as required.

This involves knowledge, competence, and action. The identification of the services and products that the organization requires, and preferences regarding their sources, may stem from any of three directions.

The first is the user of the product or service (sometimes called the 'internal customer'). Clearly, a designer of a product will be concerned about the parts that fit within it and will keep a close eye on the possible sources of supply. Similarly, budget holders who want items of capital equipment will have clear ideas of the models they would like to get. The manager of a hotel within a global group will know which laundry service works best for him/her; the catering manager at a company restaurant will be aware of the best place to buy fresh vegetables and wish to maintain good relationships with local suppliers. The supervisor responsible for a piece of process equipment may have preferences for the type, brand, or supplier of maintenance items, based on long experience, and may not be interested in trying a new, cheaper alternative.

The risk here is that the budget holder may not be in touch with the commercial consequences of specifying a particular supplier for the parts or perhaps not be up to date with market developments. The same may apply to the purchase of capital equipment (it is less likely that the problem would arise for the hotelier or catering manager, who may be expected to be very much in touch with the immediate commercial consequences of their sourcing decisions). However, the user is the traditional origin of the requirement (the 'requisition') for a purchased item and will often go beyond identifying the generic resource, suggesting, or even specifying, the supplier of the item with whom Purchasing should place the contract for supply.

The commercial problems of this should be obvious: the supplier will know that the Buyer has no choice but to buy the item from them and will negotiate accordingly – with considerable power. It is not surprising, therefore, that it is the goal of every sales representative to have their component or product specified by the designer of a product or the user of the item, before Purchasing becomes involved. The potential problem may be addressed strategically by deciding that Purchasing should be involved early, perhaps advising the designer on potential suppliers that might be considered.

The strategic supply manager is thus the second source of knowledge for sourcing an item and must develop and maintain knowledge of the supply market as good as that concerning the sales market which would be expected of a marketing manager. If this is done, the supply manager becomes a genuine influence in the decisions about what resources to use in the organization's business.

The name given to sourcing of items outside contracts set up by Purchasing with agreed suppliers is 'maverick buying'. (Maverick is the term given by herdsmen to an unbranded calf that is separated from its mother; more recently the term has developed to mean someone who takes and independent stand on something.) The problem with maverick buying is that, while the person buying the item may get a good deal (mobile phones were a prime example of this, early on), the contract details attached to the purchase may commit the maverick buyer's company to costly or difficult conditions. Another form of an individual enforcing a personal preference might be called 'prima donna purchasing' (see Case 3.5).

CASE 3.5 PRIMA DONNA PURCHASING

In the mid 1990s, a UK NHS hospital decided to rationalize its purchasing of rubber gloves, used by surgeons during surgery, as part of its review of purchasing practices and a cost-saving exercise. The rationalized range included several types and all the necessary sizes. Surgeons were asked by Purchasing to keep their requests for the supply of gloves within this range.

On senior consultant demanded a different, more expensive, type of glove. When he was asked to change to one of the types provided in the interests of cost control his response was 'I use the gloves that I prefer. Do you want the patient to die?'

Abridged case from the Author's research

The third origin of ideas for sources for purchased items comes from outside the organization: the supply base. Suppliers of services and products to an organization are often able to use their expertise, developed from working with a variety of customers, to the benefit of that organization. Managing this resource must be done with care since the organization must retain its own strategic choice rather than become dependent upon suppliers for it resource management. Others within the organization may suspect the supply manager's introduction of a supplier's idea into, say, a design discussion (especially if it conflicts with the preference of the designer), and tension in the internal relationships between functional specialists and Purchasing is apparent in practice in almost any case of integrating external and internal resource management. The designer may not be skilled in negotiation techniques and this can lead to problems for the buying company: see Case 3.6. Nevertheless, if the full strategic advantages of a properly managed supply process are to be realized, the ideas and expertise of the supply base must be tapped.

CASE 3.6 INVOLVING THE DESIGNER IN NEGOTIATIONS WITH THE SUPPLIER

In the UK division of a global computer producer, a Buyer was conducting a negotiation with a supplier of complex technical components. The team included the designer from the customer firm, an engineer. At one point, in a discussion about problem solving, the engineer said to the supplier 'You know, you are the only people we can get this stuff from'. The Buyer's heart sank!

Abridged case from the Author's research

Despite the fact that this third source of ideas is well recognized, it appears that most training of Buyers still concentrates on telling the supplier what to do and then developing sophisticated ways of managing the problems that result from this rather arrogant posture.

This is often called 'managing the supplier'. Suppliers, meanwhile, work with lots of customers and will naturally know their own business (service or product) well: if the customer tries to manage them, they are likely to defend themselves against the cost and strategic implications of the customer's demands, setting up a traditional relationship battlefield.

In mass production this was the general *modus operandi*: a battle of wits in which the supplier (who would be assumed to be 'in league' with other suppliers, through trade associations and other mechanisms) would build-in costs to the transaction to pay for the difficulties the customer caused through operational arrogance. In post-mass production days (see Chapter 1), where end customers, or consumers, demand what they want rather than accept what providers offer, the costs of this battlefield may be punitive for the supply chain. Listening to suppliers has become an accepted activity for some purchasers. Even the companies that invented the old way, 100 years before, now seek a new way. The demise of mass production thinking in other parts of the organization means that some better ways of working are required in purchasing and supply, starting with recognizing and managing supply relationships.

TECHNIQUES FOR MANAGING RELATIONSHIPS

Organizations see their supplier relationships very differently, depending on their position in the marketplace. An interesting contrast was provided by two policies set up by very different organizations as the financial troubles of 2008 hit the UK. See Case 3.7.

CASE STUDY

CASE 3.7 DIFFERING APPROACHES TO RELATIONSHIPS

In December 2009, the huge UK retailer Tesco changed its payment terms from 30 days to 60 days from 1st December (six weeks notice) for all non-food suppliers to 'free-up millions of pounds as it enters the all-important Christmas trading season'. With the money that it did not pay to suppliers, Tesco revamped its finance division into *Tesco Bank,* to sell retail loans to customers. In other words, Tesco used its suppliers as a source of free lending, to sell the money on, at interest, to customers. In October 2010, Tesco had 30.8 per cent of the UK grocery market and posted a 12 per cent increase in half year profits.
Financial Times, 24 October 2008

At the same time, Devon County Council realized that the looming recession would hit its suppliers hard and could even cause business failures. Its response was to improve payment terms from the 'industry standard' of 30 days, down to 20 days, thus helping suppliers with their cash-flow problems.

SUPPLIER RELATIONSHIP MANAGEMENT

In the next part of this chapter we shall look at the ways in which supply managers approach supply chain relationships (i.e. with suppliers of materials, components, and services to the organization), and explore some ways in which these may need to be developed in order to ensure the supply chain is effective. This is known as *supplier relationship management*, or SRM. (Note the resemblance to *customer relationship management*, or CRM, which is a core feature of industrial marketing approaches – so called Business to Business or B2B. See Ford *et al.* 2011.)

In doing so, we shall examine the principles of 'lean supply' – the supply management activity necessary to provide a lean supply chain within a lean production system. We shall not concern ourselves with semantic differences between 'lean', 'agile', and 'mass customization' for these purposes – in the supply chain context, especially in relationships and beyond basic logistics, there is no significant difference. The focus is on developing relationships to ensure that strategic supply functions perfectly. In order to be able to change quickly to address market conditions (i.e. to be agile), the relationship needs to have been relieved of the non-value-adding activities installed in it by mass production thinking (i.e. to be lean).

The three aspects of SRM that we shall use in exploring the move from mass production thinking to lean supply are: how performance in the supply chain is assessed; how development is approached and conducted; and how information and knowledge are shared within the supply chain.

In each case we shall consider the 'traditional' approach, which has developed over a century of mass production and may in some cases be characterized by wasteful (non-value-adding) or counter-productive practices. The surprising point here is that some of the well-established and professionalized practices may be identified in this category when viewed critically. Then we shall explore principles of lean supply in practice, countering the mass-production approaches (as manufacturers and service organizations have been doing for two decades now, since the publication of the seminal work *The Machine that Changed the World*, Womack *et al.*, 1990) by removal of wasteful activities.

Assumptions and presumptions in supply relationship management

It was Gordon Selfridge, the very successful American retailer who coined the phrase 'The customer is always right' while working with his mentor, Marshall Field in Chicago in 1880. (He also thought up 'Only xx shopping days until Christmas!') The same phrase was coined, in French, by Cesar Ritz in Paris in 1908. This phrase, and the mindset behind it, appears to have set up a fatally flawed assumption on the part of supply strategists – that of infallibility.

In fact, the phrase is a trick – a sales device to soften up a customer and make them buy. The more relaxed and gullible the customer, the more likely a sale. When an industrial purchaser starts to believe this they will manage supply relationships on that basis – assume that everything that goes wrong is the suppliers fault and devise ways of blaming them for it and then telling them what to do. Of course, this makes purchasing fun but it also builds in costs for the supplier which they must include to cover the activities necessary to retaliate. It also builds in costs for the customer (i.e. to police the relationship), but these are usually dismissed as necessary parts of managing the supply relationship (and they generate the fun). As we can see, much of the activity in traditional, mass production supply relationships adds cost but not value; blaming is a good example of this.

When someone is blamed they have three possible reactions:

- To *capitulate*: agree that it is their fault;
- To *negate*: suggest that it is no one's fault; or
- To *retaliate*: to accuse the blamer.

In business, neither of the first two is sustainable: no one wants to deal with someone who repeatedly admits that they have made a mistake or tries to suggest that 'stuff happens'. The only sustainable strategy is: when blamed, the immediate response is always to retaliate. A supplier is rarely in a position to be able to blame a customer directly and must therefore 'get their own back' in more subtle ways. Normally, this is by charging a *risk premium* – a component of the price that will fund the work the supplier must do in putting up with the blaming. Naturally it is not possible to determine the size of this – no company would admit to including it. However, the costs of dealing with being blamed are such that were the risk premium to be left out, the supplier would probably cease to make a profit.

We shall see that mass production approaches are based heavily and perhaps fatally upon this misunderstanding of Selfridge's aphorism (i.e. that the customer is never wrong) and that this can lead to wasteful practices and reduced value in the relationships.

Customer or something else?

We have become so accustomed to referring to the organization that buys the goods or services as 'the customer' that we overlook the true meaning of the term, and especially its limits. A reflection on this might reveal the expectations we might reasonably have in relationships and, importantly for our purposes, the roles that organizations play within them. There are three common terms that we could employ:

- The customer. This is an organization that customarily buys something from the supplier; they 'give their custom'; it is their custom to buy, and so on. However, their responsibility is limited to decent behaviour: to be clear on what they want, to honour the commitment to buy once made, and to pay according to the agreed terms. Beyond this, if anything falls short of expectation, the supplier may be expected to provide remedy or reparation.
- The consumer. This is a term associated with mass production, which for the first time separated the end-user of the product from its manufacturer. For the producer of the goods, the end user is just a statistic and should have no contact with the producer. Thus a producer of cornflakes needs to know about market information –

trends, preference, etc. – to plan its product portfolio and output schedules, but never wants to have a personal complaint from any one consumer. The same is true for a service such as insurance or Internet provision, which is why such businesses employ agents to keep the consumer at bay. One of the problems that lead to dissatisfaction with 'help lines' in call centres (see Case 3.2) is that the end user assumes the facility is there to provide 'customer service' and that they themselves are customers. In fact they are consumers and the call centre is actually there to protect the provider from their individual complaints.

- The client. This term is generally reserved for provision of services that are considered 'professional': the architect, the lawyer, the dentist, (and, perhaps, the sex worker). In fact, the basis for the expression is that the receiver of services shares responsibility for a successful outcome. The dentist cannot provide oral hygiene if the client does not clean their teeth regularly. The lawyer cannot provide a successful outcome unless the client tells them the truth, and so on. As we saw in Chapter 1, the industrial supply of products is actually a service – the product itself is surrounded by other value-adding factors, such as design, transportation, after-sales service, calibration, and so on. In a strategic relationship, the status of the organization buying the goods or services is actually closer to 'client' than 'customer': they share responsibility for the successful outcome of the interaction. The idea that the customer is always right cannot therefore be applied to industrial supply in which long-term or strategic relationships are sought, and SRM practices that are based upon it will inevitably reduce the effectiveness of the relationship.

Despite this reflection, for our purposes here, the term 'customer' will be retained as the concept of client status in this context is new and might cause confusion. It is important to bear the issue in mind, however, perhaps in the development of more 'responsible' industrial customers.

SRM AND PERFORMANCE ASSESSMENT

Measurement of performance is an important part of strategy. This requires prior identification of the criteria for success, disciplined monitoring of performance against the criteria and their component parts, and careful interpretation of results. In the field of supply management, this process has become established over three decades and is typified by schemes that are generally known as 'supplier (or vendor) assessment'.

The principle of supplier assessment is that the customer sets up an articulation of its expectations and requirements, monitors the supplier's performance against them, and then converts the results into an assessment of the supplier's performance, complemented in some cases by suggested paths towards improvements. Note that throughout this reasoning it is assumed that the supplier should be blamed for anything that goes wrong in the supply of goods or services.

Supplier assessment began in the 1960s, tracing its origins to the quality management movement that grew from the work of Walter Shewhart in North America in the 1930s (see Chapter 8). The development of quality management in Japan following World War II was supported by American consultants such as Deming and Juran, itself leading to a renaissance of concern for quality in the West. Part of this concern focused upon the quality of incoming goods and materials. In the defence (aerospace) and automotive industries, schemes began to appear for, typically, 'supplier quality assurance'. These schemes generally employed some statistical analysis of data concerning performance criteria set by the customer – 'hoops' through which the supplier had to 'jump'.

The focus on product quality was gradually replaced (on both sides of the Atlantic and in the other areas of the industrialized world that took their steer from the US and Europe) by a focus on service and on appropriate management approaches in the supplier organizations. Thus, schemes emerged with complex algorithms for calculating the supplier's performance, often accompanied by annual award ceremonies with all manner of celebrations, the customer, in a superior fashion, usually deigning to anoint a 'supplier of the year'.

Interestingly, Japanese manufacturers did not develop such schemes in the way those in the West did. Instead, it appeared, they had embedded the ideas learned from the American visionaries into the manufacturing processes. Quality concerns were included in any discussion about manufacturing (much less so in service businesses, such as Japanese banks, which were notoriously poor quality, eventually helping to cause the ten years recession in Japan which started in 1993).

When the Japanese firms began to set up operations in the West and to buy from Western suppliers they found it necessary, in addition to inculcating their 'philosophies', to create such schemes. Work by automotive firms, including Nissan and Honda, developed a scheme assessing quality, cost, delivery, development and management (QCDDM) in their suppliers. Such schemes were one-way, top-down processes, but then they were dealing, in effect, with developing countries (see the later section on *supplier development*). This caught the imagination of Western manufacturing and is still widely found in the slightly truncated version QCDM, with D standing variously for development, design or delivery.

In the 1980s, some companies began to institute schemes which involved two-way assessment: the customer would tell the supplier how well or poorly they were performing and seek the supplier's view of them as a customer, in return. Sadly, suppliers would naturally tend to be complimentary, fearing retribution from the customer for a criticism, and the resultant good feedback from suppliers would encourage organizations to refer to themselves, rather naïvely, as 'preferred customers'. This was clearly not a genuinely valuable process. Some schemes were clearly sincere, however, although in the case of B&Q's bold project 'QUEST' in the mid 1990s, supply market conditions subsequently led to major changes. See Case 3.8.

Supplier/vendor assessment has a basic flaw: responsibility for the performance of the supply activity, and thus the blame for anything other than perfect performance (e.g. less than 100 per cent on-time in-full deliveries) cannot simply be laid at the door of the supplier. The manner in which the customer (and not just its Purchasing department) conducts itself in the transaction is also heavily influential on the smooth running, or otherwise, of supply

CASE 3.8 THE EFFECT OF SUPPLY MARKET CONDITIONS ON ASSESSMENT POLICIES

In 1995, the leading UK DIY retailer, B&Q, introduced a supplier assessment scheme called QUEST. While it was supplier-focused, it was remarkable in that the first of ten categories of assessment rated the supplier on their critical feedback on how B&Q performed as a customer. The retailer made it clear it wanted real criticism – suggestions for how it could improve (and if the supplier provided none they were awarded no points).

In subsequent years, however, the growth of the supply market in developing economies altered B&Q's focus of attention to one of supplier development (see below) and the retailer had to guide nascent suppliers in basic things such as good factory management, workers' rights, and use of child labour. QUEST was replaced by the B&Q Operational Standards for Supply Chains (see www.diy.com/diy/jsp/aboutbandq/social_responsibility/BQ_OPERA.PDF).

B&Q had not lost the wish to receive critical feedback from suppliers, but the reality of their supply network meant that their 'top-down' guidance to suppliers was now necessary to ensure product quality (and sustainability) and was also of genuine value to firms in developing economies seeking to supply to UK retailers.

and the related costs. Put simply, responsibility for a successful outcome of the contract is shared (not necessarily equally) by customer (client) and supplier. Any performance assessment scheme needs to reflect this rather than focusing on 'half of the postcard'.

So, supplier/vendor assessment, born at a time when the cracks in the mass-production paradigm were beginning to show, results not in the improvements in supply that are expected (and may indeed be shown and measured by proud customers) but in a systemic corruption of the process, as suppliers learn how to deal with dozens of different customers' assessment schemes, managing by guile to avert the commercial disaster that full compliance with all of them would almost certainly precipitate.

The principle of supplier assessment is logical but limited. There are many different types of scheme in operation and it is clear that, in some cases, the suppliers are actually helped by them. However, the area of assessment is thus one in which supply strategists need to employ their imagination and creativity. If it is not worthwhile to measure the individual performance of the supplier (which results, almost always, in a game of blame and defence) nor even that of the two separate parties (customer and supplier – again, this becomes a game of 'blame and counter blame', if, indeed, it ever moves beyond the 'blame and pleasantry' model) then some other focus must be found for the performance measurement that is a critical part of strategic management.

Beyond the one-way use of assessment by proficient firms with suppliers in developing countries, supplier/vendor assessment has no place in strategic supply management. And yet this example of mass-production thinking remains (see Hald and Elleraard, 2011; Field and Meile, 2008).

How might a radically innovative lean approach deal with this: how can wasteful practices be destroyed and replaced? The answer lies in considering the whole picture – the relationship.

Assessing relationships is not a new idea, but in this context it can be said to have to have emerged as part of the lean supply work (as *relationship assessment*) at the end of the 1980s (Lamming, 1993, pp. 252–3). At the same time, and separately, the *Relationship Positioning Tool*, was being developed by academics at Glasgow Business School (Macbeth and Ferguson, 1994) using a facilitator between the two parties to provide the rationale in assessment and a common framework for assessment. The performance of each organization is mapped independently (by the consultant/facilitator) and then a comparison and discussion takes place to identify ways forward.

A further development of this is to manage the unique relationship that is shared by the two parties as an entity itself. That is to say, the overlap of operational value-adding between one stage in the chain and the next (as shown in Figure 3.4) is seen as a jointly owned activity with 'fuzzy' responsibility instead of a simple, clear division, at least for operational purposes. The legal difficulties with this may be small or great, depending upon the situation. In the early 1990s the expression 'partnership' became popular within this context, with organizations professing mutual interest embodied in the relationship of partners.

This served them well in terms of awareness of shared responsibility but raised potential problems, especially when things went wrong. In the UK, under the 1891 Partnership Act, any two parties acting as if they are partners become jointly responsible for one another's liabilities (as partnerships in, say, the legal profession do). Two companies acting this way may therefore incur unwanted liabilities – even if they do not actually call their relationship a partnership, or even claim that it is not (the interpretation is left to the courts). In the US, a major legal battle was caused by the use of the term by a major electronics manufacturer in its supply chain management and the term was subsequently not favoured in North America. It may be that the only way around this is actually to form a third party – a joint venture company – and when the stakes are high this is precisely what some firms have done.

Assuming that the customer and supplier do not need to go to quite these lengths, it is reasonable to view the joint operation of organizing supply as a shared responsibility, and measuring its performance becomes a mutual interest. Since the activity of either party in the relationship (customer or supplier) might affect the performance, there is clearly no point in one of them simply blaming the other (other than as a tactical ploy in the 'competition' part of the relationship). Instead, the two can jointly assess the relationship and take appropriate action to reduce the difficulties it is experiencing, thereby improving the efficiency and cost effectiveness of the value-adding process.

This technique was pioneered at researchers at the University of Bath, in the form of the *Relationship Assessment Process* (*RAP*), (see Figure 3.7) and subsequently, in the UK aerospace industry, as the *Relationship Evaluation Process* (See Case 3.9). In the early years of the new century, the field of management consultancy in purchasing and supply began to abound with relationship assessment models (perhaps a good example of practice, via consultancy, lagging academic research by about ten years).

The Relationship

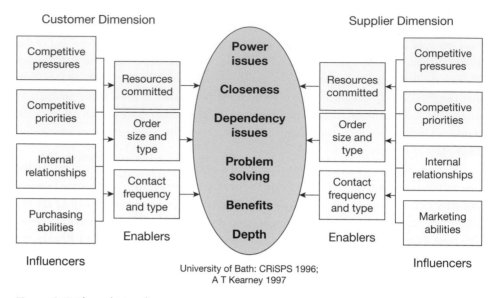

Customer Dimension   Supplier Dimension

University of Bath: CRiSPS 1996;
A T Kearney 1997

Figure 3.7 The relationship assessment process

Lamming *et al.* (1996)

CASE 3.9: RELATIONSHIP ASSESSMENT AS A SECTOR STRATEGY IN THE AEROSPACE INDUSTRY

When the Berlin wall came down in 1989 the world rejoiced. For the European aerospace industry, however, it was followed by a slump in orders as 'peace broke out'. In the UK the civil aerospace development was intrinsically linked with that of military aircraft: the passenger aircraft business would suffer as much as that in warplanes.

The Society of British Aircraft Companies (SBAC) decided that a sector-wide national strategy was needed to maintain the industry's competitiveness through this period – until military business picked up again. The approach was based upon improving supply chain relationships. SBAC built an initiative called *Supply Chain Relationships in Aerospace* (SCRIA). This contained a great deal of common sense and straight talking about relationships with customers and suppliers in the industry committed to real change.

Companies in this industry were well aware of the lean manufacturing principles (which had been developed in the automotive industry in the previous decade) and were already implementing them. Key players in SBAC were also aware of the work underway in lean supply and knew about the University of Bath *Relationship Assessment Process* model (*RAP*). Academics from Bath were asked to develop a version of *RAP* for SCRIA. This became the SCRIA *RET: Relationship Evaluation Tool*. This was a disruptive innovation – requiring the rejection of traditional, mass production, supplier/vendor assessment as the sole approach to performance assessment in critical issues. It embodied the principles of leanness in relationship management and enabled problem-solving through attention to specific improvements, such as a relationship's facets, or characteristics, that were managed jointly by customers and suppliers.

As the century ended, the lull in military aerospace business abated. SBAC was inspired, however, by the impact and value of sector-wide transformational initiatives and wished to continue the idea. The Lean Aerospace programme had brought major benefits to the sector and this was combined with SCRIA into '21st Century Supply Chains or SC21'. The radical innovation of relationship assessment, developed from academic research, was carried forward into SC21 and remains in use, as part of lean supply, as the *Relationship Management Matrix*, ten years after its inception.

In this century, *Supplier Relationship Management* has become popular and models for it are now regularly provided by consultants. Meanwhile, an interesting review and development of the *RAP* idea was published in 2008 (see Johnsen *et al.*, 2008).

SRM AND DEVELOPMENT

The development of supplier assessment over three decades reveals perhaps the most acute misappropriation of Selfridges's famous declaration. The extension of this suggestion to commercial and industrial supply has left a legacy of techniques in which the customer assumes the role of infallible despot, while the suppliers become wily and resourceful, living on their wits and tricks. As we saw above, activity on both sides of this conflict adds cost. Just as supplier assessment needs a fresh look and new approach for post-mass-production supply strategy, so its close cousin, *supplier development*, is also ripe for new perspectives.

The notion that customers should blame suppliers for all shortcomings in the supply process led not only to the one-way assessment mentality but also to the idea that customers might tell suppliers how to run their businesses (apparently assuming that the latter did not know how to do it for themselves) under the banner of 'supplier development'. This clearly harks back to early mass production, where an innovative and visionary manufacturer such as the young Henry Ford would be understandably concerned about the abilities of his new suppliers, accustomed as they were to an earlier paradigm with slower deliveries and time to apply craftsmanship. Such suppliers could not be classed as 'strategic partners' in modern terms and it was natural for an industrial customer to take the lead. There were, however, several high-quality component manufacturers in the early twentieth-century US (for example, Bosch) so the technique of supplier development must have had its early detractors (Bosch was actually more established than Ford in the US at that time).

In more recent times, growing in popularity on the back of supplier assessment in the 1980s, this approach meant that by the mid-1990s many customers were seeking to 'develop' their suppliers in industries far from the origins of the approach (once again, aerospace and automotive). While even in this period some logic may be seen in, say, a global electronics company telling a small components manufacturer how do adopt statistical process control, the rationale for an airline telling its bakery supplier how to make its bread rolls (rather than just specifying the type and quality of the rolls) is difficult to see. The latter example is real, however, and illustrates how far a fashionable management idea can drift from its relevant basis.

Supplier development is actually a 'developing countries' strategy – used when an organization from a developed country wants to set up supply lines in a new, foreign venture, as we saw in the case of B&Q refocusing its supplier assessment programme in this way (Case 3.8). This also applies in the case of redeveloping economies and was evident in the strategies of the Americans entering Europe in the early twentieth century and Japan in the 1940s, and the Japanese entering the US and the UK in the 1980s. The UK television industry at the time was in ruins and the arrival of three of the top Japanese manufacturers in South Wales, an area replete with labour recently made redundant by the closure of coal mines and the scaling down of steel production, resulted in fundamental regeneration of industrial wealth (coupled, as it was, with a similar development in the automotive industry in the region).

The technique of supplier development consists of the customer providing an indication of what is to be achieved, in terms of performance characteristics and attributes, often packaged into a campaign – identified by a catchy title or acronym. This is usually integrated with a supplier assessment scheme (with all its potential flaws, as discussed above). The customer may opt for a generic scheme, such as the ISO 9000 series, considering that accreditation of the supplier's systems would be sufficient guarantee of performance.

There are two commonly employed approaches to supplier development: they have been called 'cascade' and 'intervention' (Lamming, 1996). Twenty-five years on, the techniques are still very much in regular use (see Figure 3.8). In the first case, on the left, the customer organization develops a new concept that it would like to have adopted throughout its supply chain, formulates it in some way (often with the help of consultants) and cascades it 'downwards' to its direct, or first-tier, suppliers. It is either implicitly or explicitly expected that the direct suppliers will cascade the idea on further downwards to their own suppliers (the supposed 'third-tier'). The mechanisms for doing this vary, but are seldom more than documentation and presentation (sometimes given at the annual award ceremony for 'supplier of the year', as part of the supplier assessment programme). Suppliers encounter, and accommodate, many of these schemes and have to develop a strategy that enables them to survive in the messy and sometimes contradictory combination of them all. Suppliers may be expected to develop expertise in dealing with such complexity, appearing to comply with all while in fact approximating each to a common operating model.

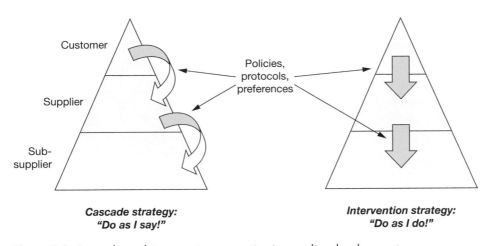

Figure 3.8 Cascade and intervention strategies in supplier development
Lamming (1996)

The second strategy has the same basis as the first: good ideas stem from the customer and are passed on down to the suppliers. However, in this case the customer 'intervenes' in the business of the supplier, actually working at the operating level to help the supplier to develop specific skills. In this case, the customer is clearly making a real investment in the process, and this is likely to be more respected by the supplier as a valuable contribution (rather than simply issuing edicts *ex cathedra*). From the customer's point of view it may actually be possible to make ideas 'stick' by working alongside the supplier's personnel in implementation.

The risk with an intervention strategy is that suppliers may simply become dependent upon the customer for new ideas, and follow like sheep, never offering developmental ideas or innovations. The customer gets nothing from this, other than compliance, and therefore learns little from the practice. The strategy should be used with care, therefore, and for a limited period only. This path was followed by the Japanese vehicle assemblers on coming to the UK and the US: the intervention was for a limited period, following which the supplier was expected to develop their own competences (although the customer still brought new challenges and initiatives), to ensure that suppliers were aware of the pressures in the end markets that had to be transmitted all the way back along the supply chain.

In the course of time, one might expect the advanced supply strategist to construct a way of capturing the learning available from the interaction with suppliers, so that the customer and not just the supplier sought to develop. This might be a two-way, 'vertical' activity or perhaps, recognizing the complexity of the actual situation, a case of network development, where any player might learn from, and help to develop, any other. If the explicit objective of such an initiative is not simply to exact efficiencies from the supplier (mass production thinking) but to innovate, perhaps disruptively, to destroy non-value-adding activities and explore different ways of doing things, at the same time removing waste, then this would be a lean approach.

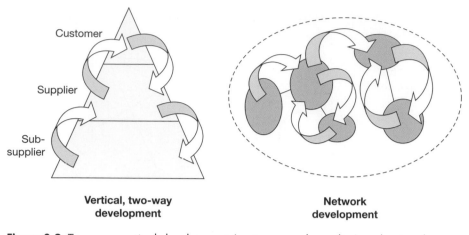

Figure 3.9 Two-way vertical development (customer and supplier) and network development

Lamming (1996)

This approach was common in mid-twentieth-century Japan where manufacturers commonly brought suppliers together into supplier associations (the Japanese word is *kyoryokukai*). In this approach, the customer sets up a series of meetings between suppliers that it wants to form into a development group – the objective being to improve the overall situation in supply for the customer's products (with consequent benefits for all in the supply chain). These meetings may take place on neutral territory, and it may be necessary for the customer to be absent, at least after an initial 'bonding' has taken place. Supplier associations remain a central feature of the Japanese system and have been adopted in the West successfully in several industries, the first European example being set up by Canon in France in the early 1990s.

This idea, which is illustrated in Figure 3.9, is still not the norm in practice although one good early example was provided by the *Supply Network Innovation Programme* developed in the UK nuclear industry in the early twenty-first century (see Case 3.10).

Supply development naturally employs other ideas in addition to relationship management, such as the early involvement of suppliers in the development of new products, and discussion of future plans. For a discussion on this see Cousins *et al.* (2007, p. 216).

Whichever ways the development of skills, knowledge, learning, and techniques are fitted into a supply strategy, it is important not to lose sight of the degree to which the customer, as well as the supplier, should seek to develop and improve in all aspects of its activity in the relationship. Not to do so represents a waste of resources – a failure to exploit lean principles for the business. It is a question of retaining strategic autonomy in both the supplier and the customer, recognizing the fundamental competition that exists between the supply chain 'partners', and managing the limitations to both so that each exploits the business opportunity to the level necessary to ensure their continued, combined activity.

CASE 3.10: SUPPLY DEVELOPMENT IN THE UK NUCLEAR INDUSTRY

At the turn of the century, the UK nuclear industry was going through a major reorganization, partly as the result of privatization policies in the 1990s and partly as most of society realized, perhaps unwillingly, that nuclear power had to play a part in future energy production and so redevelopment was necessary.

The major corporation, British Nuclear Fuels plc (BNFL), had been reorganized as part of this and prepared for privatization. A great deal of concentration went into its supply chain. At the time, it was an international business employing 23,000 people in 16 countries. Its activities covered the entire nuclear energy cycle, from reactor design and fuel manufacture, generating electricity in nuclear power stations to spent fuel recycling and decommissioning and cleaning up redundant nuclear facilities. The company had a large supply base, providing materials and services, many of a highly specialized high-technology nature.

In 1998, BNFL decided to develop a 'supplier of the year award' scheme, to reward outstanding suppliers for their achievements over the past year, on an annual basis. This was seen as a normal approach to supply management, underway in many industries, but before they embarked upon it BNFL purchasing strategists did some deep thinking.

They brainstormed, workshopped, consulted widely and talked to their suppliers. They realized that to go down this route would simply be following an old-fashioned idea – treating the performance as the responsibility of the supplier alone whereas, in fact, it reflected on the customer as well. Rather than development being something that should be done *to* suppliers, they realized that *they* should develop too, as part of the process.

Leaving what they saw as an outdated, mass-production idea behind, BNFL began to work on a radical, lean idea. The supply network, they reasoned, could develop in many ways, using good relationships between BNFL and suppliers (singly and in groups) as the means for delivering mutual benefits and removing noise from the supply network.

They designed and implemented a new scheme – the Supply Network Innovation Programme, (SNIP). Within this programme, project teams would form, consisting of people from BNFL and a supplier (in practice this sometimes became two or three suppliers at once – a mini-network). Each team would be set up on the basis of an identified development project that would provide benefits and learning for BNFL and the supplier. Where investment was required (people's time, etc.) a cost–benefit analysis would be drawn up to show the business logic for both parties – and identify the criteria for success (in fact, this became the norm).

The projects would be intended to run for about nine months, at which point their success would be assessed. (In practice, many projects have continued well beyond this period, delivering joint benefits for several years.) The most impressive projects would then be presented to an annual celebration event, attended by a broad range of suppliers and funded by BNFL, at which those involved in the projects (the BNFL people as well as those from the supplier) would be given mementos of the celebration – such as small, specially commissioned sculptures – not awards but symbols of the team's success. The intrinsic reward to suppliers and BNFL of being celebrated for their achievements, in front of 200 representatives of many industry organizations, was significant.

The scheme was a resounding success, resulting in major financial benefits for BNFL and its suppliers. Many of the projects (some 30 celebrated between 1999 and 2003) provided significant cost savings for BNFL and increased business or improved terms for the supplier. When most of the company was transferred to the private sector, with its major divisions being sold as successful separate businesses, the SNIP concept survived as a feature of purchasing strategy. There was a legacy of success stories, many genuinely innovative in their approach to *supply* – rather than *supplier* – development.

SNIP was an example of lean supply at work: mutual benefits through *network development*, an organization leaving behind the flawed mantra of 'the customer is always right' and removing the noise or waste in the system that had built up as a result of mass-production attitudes to performance measurement.

SRM and information sharing: open-book negotiation

The practice of a customer requiring a supplier to reveal all sorts of sensitive costing and pricing information in its bids for business, in the interests of joint competitive position, has been popular for many years. The principle is that, if the supplier shows the customer how the costs are structured for a particular product or service (including, sometimes, their profit margins) the customer will be able to help the supplier to reduce costs, and thus prices. Sometimes this is dressed up as part of a joint effort, amid claims that the customer's own product or service might become more competitive in the marketplace, thus ensuring the supplier's business too. The suppliers are rarely fooled by this of course and recognize a negotiation tactic when they see one.

The principle of open-book negotiation comes straight from mass-production thinking: it is basically sound in theory but in practice it appears to be flawed. The supplier must manage resources to meet corporate objectives – generally a matter of shareholder value and return on capital employed. To do so, it has to manage risk and reward. Business is all about taking risks (i.e. making investments) and then ensuring that the reward is sufficient to justify having done so. When two parties compete, one will try to ensure that the other does not receive adequate reward for the risk and suffers accordingly. If they are collaborating, however, it is in the interests of both that they each receive appropriate reward. For truly strategic operations to be conducted, therefore, each party must be free to decide its own rate of return.

In the supply chain, the organizations are both competing and collaborating. Thus they must ensure that each makes appropriate reward but there will be constant tension over who actually takes what risk and how the rewards (which are clearly jointly generated as each party is dependent upon the other) are shared.

A supply strategy that requires one side of a supply relationship (the supplier) to take a risk while the other (the customer) does not, with the latter seeking to articulate, sometimes in heroic terms, what the reward should (or might) be for the former, appears unlikely to succeed in the long term. When a customer stipulates to a supplier, therefore, that private information must be revealed (i.e. the supplier must take a very great risk) and also what the reward should be (i.e. the supplier is not supposed to make a strategic determination of the vital risk–reward business balance) it is inevitable that the supplier will take the only sensible business action and resort to cheating (what is described in transaction-cost economics, as self-seeking guile). This may be expected to include cost information being distorted and misrepresented, incomplete, and arcane. The customer, believing that they have extracted valuable information, perhaps borne up by its army of cost analysts and process engineers, will act accordingly, and may only find after some time that they are not deriving the value from the transaction that they expected (for example, the failure of some European automotive manufacturers to make profits after a decade of such – publicly declared – initiatives may be related to this).

The only solution to this is to manage the risk in some way, so that it makes economic sense for the supplier to share information. If the customer takes a risk, as well as requiring the supplier to do so, there may be a chance of genuine information and knowledge emerging. Thus, for a worthwhile supply strategy, exchange of sensitive information must be two-way – the customer must share information as well as demand it. Such 'transparency' may result in focused activity towards real improvements, but it will often require a great deal of confidence on the part of the supplier that the customer has really taken a risk. Since this approach might result in genuine removal of the wasteful nonsense encouraged by one-way open-book negotiation, it qualifies as a lean supply technique.

Research on this has developed the management technique of 'value transparency' – a concept that profoundly challenges established thinking. This was trialled in firms in the UK and US – for an explanation, see Lamming *et al.* (2006). It is not currently a common-place practice, however. It is apparently too great a threat to established ways in practice (and to those who have invested personal credibility in them) and is actually considered impossible in some instances. It is, perhaps, an area in which the supply strategist who is able to recognize the drawbacks of applying mass production to modern operations must explore and innovate.

Policy and strategy

Equipped with a policy, supply strategy, internal strategy for the purchasing and supply process, and set of techniques for managing relationships, the supply strategist can make a significant contribution to operations strategy – in both financial and technical terms. The structure of the organization may change fundamentally as a result, perhaps leading to more dissipated, atomized or decentralized activity, in which case the activity of supply management becomes even more important.

This may challenge or even threaten some traditional approaches to strategy and organizational analysis. When it is stripped of its mass production baggage, however, supply management can employ a lean, clear logic and pragmatism that cannot be ignored for long.

CASE 3.11: A CASE OF FACING THE COMPLEX PROBLEMS OF MANAGING SUPPLY*

In order to illustrate the differences between lean supply and intervention strategy in supply chain management, we may consider the case of a Spanish manufacturer, identified here as 'Nunca'. This company is located in north east Spain and manufactures a high technology, high complexity consumer product to which its clients add finishing touches (only a few features, in some cases) before selling the product as their own, to be marketed through distributors to end customers.

Nunca's unit cost for the product includes approximately 70 per cent bought-in components and materials. In addition to these, Nunca often receives materials 'free-issue' from its clients.

The Nunca name is well known – especially for design. Many of the items of equipment that they make for their client are actually Nunca designs, and the consumers who buy them appreciate this. The famous Nunca insignia is displayed on the product in addition to that of the client.

Nunca's clients are all skilled in manufacturing processes similar to those conducted by Nunca, but are accustomed to working in high volumes. Nunca, on the other hand, has chosen to specialize in making high profile, niche products (or equipment that constitutes a large part of the finished product) for its clients to market. The components that are issued free of charge to Nunca are generally those the client purchases for use on a high-volume product, which are also fitted to the low volume, niche model made by Nunca.

In the late 1990s, a very large French client 'Choux' that had been dealing with Nunca for many years began to treat the Spanish firm as 'a partner'. Although the equipment that Nunca made constituted almost the total value of Choux's product, in some cases, (i.e. the 'package' that Choux sells to consumers is basically the Nunca product with the Choux badge added), the relationship had been one of master–servant, with Nunca allowed to make only minor decisions in sourcing components. This was a very limited expectation for Choux to exhibit in respect of a 'first-tier' supplier.

As part of its supplier development programme, Choux started to intervene in Nunca's supply operation. Nunca had its own supplier accreditation (vendor assessment) scheme, but Choux insisted on visiting the second-tier suppliers itself. Nunca understood lean production and supply but Choux did not take them seriously when Nunca's management team explained its plans for implementing the latter. It was true, however, that Nunca had sometimes experienced problems in maintaining the required levels of manufacturing quality or timeliness.

This was an intervention strategy which may only be considered as part of a collaborative approach if it is conducted in a co-operative manner. In this case, however, the visits to second-tier suppliers were characterized by Choux's representatives insisting on activities being done in the way they stipulated, often embarrassing Nunca in front of its suppliers.

Nunca could not refuse Choux's proposals, even though it could often see a better way to solve a particular problem. It also needed to develop its relationships with suppliers but found Choux's intervention disruptive in this respect.

Finally, Choux exhibited nationalist tendencies, often refusing to condone Nunca's choice of supplier (not just the Spanish ones), requiring instead that a French firm was awarded the business – especially one from which Choux already bought. If Nunca persisted and did manage to gain agreement for one of its partner suppliers to supply a component in preference to Choux's choice, it knew that the French were 'just waiting for something to go wrong – to say "I told you so".'

Choux was using an intervention strategy in this case. As a result, it was unable to develop lean supply, since the potential contribution of Nunca was not valued. It could not afford to lose Nunca in the short term, however. Nunca's strategy was to develop lean production in its own operation and to demonstrate to the client – and others – that it was capable of running its own lean supply base, perhaps with co-operative, rather than dictatorial, intervention from the client.

In the end, it took several visits by the most senior managers in Nunca (including the Chairman and CEO) to Paris to convince Choux that their supply management was counterproductive. As a result, Choux altered the words of its contracts to allow more scope for Nunca to contribute to technology and logistical matters. By that time, however, Nunca had begun to court a new set of clients (non-European) who valued the company's contribution more highly.

* This describes an actual case in the French and Italian automotive industry, mid 1990s. What occurred is still common practice. As it is critical of the customer's behaviour, the organizations involved are disguised.

SUMMARY

- The strategic management of supply is a critical part of managing the operations of an organization. As corporations become more global and the trend towards outsourcing increases, it may even represent the most critical part.
- The supply process is not a chain – it is a network, or even a 'muddle'. It is not possible to manage it in a straightforward manner; it may be possible to manage *within* it, pursuing strategies for one's own activities which influence rather than control the activities of others.
- The term 'supply chain management' is in common parlance and may be used as an approximation to the actual situation, as a point of departure. In fact, *supplier relationship management* offers a more realistic focus for managing the process of supply.
- The organizations within a supply chain are both competitors and collaborators. Their operations are interdependent but they must also compete for the available value adding business from which profit may be made.
- The structuring of supply 'bases' may include assumptions and expectations that are not backed up in practice. Simply calling a supplier 'first-tier' may not bring the benefits expected of a structure supply base, such as that observed in post-war Japan.
- In order to develop a supply strategy, it is necessary to have a policy regarding how the organization should behave in the supply chain, a strategy to implement that policy, an internal strategy for the positioning of the purchasing and supply

process, and a set of techniques for managing relationships within the supply chain.

- The organization buying the goods or services may not be a customer, but more correctly a client. This means they may have joint responsibility for the successful outcome of the interaction and should concentrate on their own performance improvements within the relationship, as well as those of the supplier.

- Some currently available and practised techniques for supplier relationship management are based upon mass-production thinking and may not be appropriate for the post-mass-production era. Innovative techniques that form parts of lean supply – the removal of noise or waste from the supply relationship and process – can provide alternatives to such outdated approaches, especially those based on the mass production idea that the customer is always right.

KEY QUESTIONS

1. What are the challenges facing operations managers in obtaining competitive advantage from proficiency in supply management? Use examples from a heavy manufacturing industry, a light manufacturing industry, a service-sector organization using materials and a service organization with almost no materials.

2. Give examples of ways in which organizations might achieve differentiation in their own sale market by managing supply in new ways.

3. What factors in their own market position might influence an organization's approach to managing supplier relationships?

4. Trace the influence of Henry Ford to today's supply relationships: what techniques may be attributed to his ideas of mass production and in what ways are they now being questioned in the light of lean thinking?

5. In what ways are customers and suppliers competitors and collaborators? How would this apply if one of them has a monopoly?

FURTHER READING

Cousins, P.D., Lamming, R.C., Lawson, B. and Squire B. (2007) *Strategic Supply Management: Concepts and Practice*, London UK: FT Prentice Hall.

CPO Agenda Magazine www.cpoagenda.com

Evangelista, P., McKinnon, A., Sweeney, R. and Esposito, E. (eds) (2011) *Supply Chain Innovation for Competing in Highly Dynamic Markets: Challenges and Solutions*, Hershey, PA: IGI Global.

IFPSM E-zine, www.ifpsm.org

The Lean Enterprise Academy, www.leanuk.org

The Lean Institute, www.lean.org

Procurement Leaders, www.procurementleadrs.com

Van Weele, A.J. (2010) *Purchasing and Supply Chain Management*, 5th Edition, London: Cenage Learning.

The following journals are the main source of up-to-date literature in this area:

- *Journal of Purchasing and Supply Management*
- *Journal of Supply Chain Management*
- *International Journal of Operations and Production Management*
- *Journal of Operations Management*
- *Supply Chain Management: an International Journal*
- *Industrial Marketing Management*
- *Production Planning and Control*

REFERENCES

Caniëls, M.C.J. and Gelderman, C.J. (2005) 'Purchasing strategies in the Kraljic matrix: A power and dependence perspective', *Journal of Purchasing and Supply Management*, 11(2–3), 141–155.

Choi, T.Y., Dooley, K.J., Ruanglusanathan, M. (2001) 'Supply networks and complex adaptive systems: Control versus emergence', *Journal of Operations Management*, 9, 351–66.

Christopher, M. and Peck, H. (2004) 'Building the Resilient Supply Chain', *International Journal of Logistics Management*, 15(2), 1.

Christopher, M., Peck, H., and Towill, D. (2006) 'A taxonomy for selecting global supply chain strategies', *International Journal of Logistics Management*, 17(2), 277–87.

Christopher, M. and Towill, D. (2001) 'An integrated model for the design of agile supply chains', *International Journal of Physical Distribution and Logistics Management*, 31(4), 235–46.

Cousins, P.D., Lamming, R.C., Lawson, B. and Squire, B. (2007) *Strategic Supply Management: Concepts and Practice*, London UK: FT Prentice Hall.

Cox, A.W. (1997) 'Relational competence and strategic procurement management: Towards an entrepreneurial and contractual theory of the firm', *European Journal of Purchasing and Supply Management*, 2(1), 57–70.

Ellram, L.M. and Carr, A. (1994) 'Strategic purchasing: A history and review of literature', *Journal of Supply Chain Management*, 30(2), 9–19.

Field, J.M. and Meile, L.C. (2008) 'Supplier relations and supply chain performance in financial services processes', *International Journal of Operations and Production Management*, 28(2), 185–206.

Fisher, M. (1997) 'What is the right supply chain for your product?', *Harvard Business Review*, March/April.

Ford, D., Gadde, L-E., Håkansson, H., Snehota, I. (2011) *Managing Business Relationships*, 3rd edition, Chichester: Wiley.

Forrester, J.W. (1958) 'Industrial dynamics: A major breakthrough for decision makers', *Harvard Business Review*, 36(4), 37–66.

Frohlich, M.T. and Westbrook, R. (2001) 'Arcs of integration: An international study of supply chain strategies', *Journal of Operations Management*, 19(2), 185–200.

González-Benito, J. (2010) 'Supply strategy and business performance: An analysis based on the relative importance assigned to generic competitive objectives', *International Journal of Operations and Production Management*, 30(8), 774–97.

Håkansson, H., Ford, I.D., Gadde, L.-E., Snehota, I. and Waluszewski, A. (2009) *Business in Networks*, Chichester: Wiley.

Hald, K.S., and Ellegaard, C. (2011) 'Supplier evaluation processes: The shaping and reshaping of supplier performance', *International Journal of Operations and Production Management*, 31(8), 888–910.

Harland, C. (1996), 'Supply chain management: Relationships, chains and networks', *British Journal of Management*, 7(March), 63–80.

Harland, C.M., Lamming, R.C. and Cousins, P.D. (1999) 'Developing the concept of supply strategy', *International Journal of Operations and Production Management*, 19(7), 650–673.

Hawkins, T.V., Randall, W.S. and Wittmann, C.M. (2009) 'An empirical examination of reverse auction appropriateness in B2B source selection', *Journal of Supply Chain Management*, 45(4), 55–71.

Houlihan, J.B. (1987) 'International supply chain management', *International Journal of Physical Distribution and Logistics Management*, 17(2), 51–66.

Johnsen, T.E. (2011) 'Supply network delegation and intervention strategies during supplier involvement in new product development', *International Journal of Operations & Production Management*, 31(6) 688–708.

Johnsen, T.E., Johnsen, R. and Lamming, R.C. (2008) 'Supply relationship evaluation: The relationship assessment process and beyond', *European Management Journal*, 26(4), 274–87.

Kidd, P. (1994) *Agile Manufacturing: Forging New Frontiers*, Reading: Addison Wesley.

Kraljic, P. (1983) 'Purchasing must become supply management', *Harvard Business Review*, (March/April) 61(5), 109–17.

Lamming, R.C. (1993) *Beyond Partnership: Strategies for Innovation and Lean Supply*, Prentice Hall, London.

Lamming, R.C. (1996) 'Squaring lean supply with supply chain management', *International Journal of Operations and Production Management*, 16(2), 183–93.

Lamming, R.C. (2000) 'Japanese supply chain relationships in recession', *Long Range Planning*, 33(6), 757–78.

Lamming, R.C., Cousins, P.D. and Notman, D.M. (1996) 'Beyond vendor assessment: The relationship assessment process', *European Journal of Purchasing and Supply Management*, 2(4), 173–81.

Lamming, R.C., Johnsen, T., Harland, C.M. and Zheng, J. (2000) 'An initial classification for supply networks', *International Journal of Operations and Production Management*, 20(5/6), 675–91.

Lamming, R.C., Caldwell, N.D. and Phillips, W.E. (2006) 'A conceptual model of value transparency in supply', *European Management Journal*, 24(2/3), 206–13.

Macbeth, D.K. and Ferguson, N. (1994) *Partnership Sourcing: An Integrated Supply Chain Approach*, London: Pitman.

Nishiguchi, T. (1986) 'Competing systems of automotive components supply: An examination of Japanese 'clustered control' and the 'Alps structure', *First Policy Forum, International Motor Vehicle Program*, Cambridge MA: Massachusetts Institute of Technology.

Nollet, J., Ponce, S. and Campbell, M. (2005) 'About "strategy" and "strategies" in supply management', *Journal of Purchasing and Supply Management*, 11(2/3), 129–140.

OECD (1996) *SMEs: Employment Innovation and Growth. The Washington Workshop Organization for Economic Cooperation and Development*. See http://www.oecd.org/dataoecd/10/60/2090756.pdf

Pfeffer, J. (1997) *New Directions for Organization Theory*, New York: Oxford University Press.

Reck, R.F. and Long B.G. (1988) 'Purchasing: A competitive weapon', *International Journal of Purchasing and Materials Management*, (Fall), 2–8.

Williamson, O.E. (1975) *Markets and Hierarchies*, New York: Free Press.

Williamson, O.E. and Masten, S.E. (eds) (1999) *The Economics of Transaction Costs*, Cheltenham: Edward Elgar.

Womack, J., Jones, D. and Roos, D. (1990) *The Machine that Changed the World*, New York: Free Press.

CHAPTER 4

INNOVATION

> ## LEARNING OBJECTIVES
>
> By the end of this chapter you will:
>
> - Understand the strategic importance of innovation.
> - Recognize the core process of innovation.
> - Realize that operations management can play a central and pivotal role in the innovation process.
> - Appreciate how operations 'lines up' within the innovation process.

THE INNOVATION IMPERATIVE

> *It is not the strongest of the species that survives, nor the most intelligent that survives.*
> *It is the one that is the most adaptable to change.*
>
> *Charles Darwin*

This chapter looks at the theme of innovation – why it matters, what it involves, and how it can be organized and managed effectively. Any organization might get lucky once – but to deliver a continuing stream of new products and services and regular improvement and replacement of operating processes requires a more systematic approach. Innovation is the core business process associated with *renewing* what the organization does and what it offers to the world – and as such is a key area of focus for strategic operations management.

Darwin's views do not simply refer to biological organisms – they are a pretty useful guide to understanding the dynamics of business evolution. Organizations need to innovate

– to change what they offer and how they produce that offering – to survive. History is very clear on this point: survival is not compulsory but those enterprises which do survive and grow do so because they are capable of regular and focused change. And change is a two-edged sword – for those established organizations a failure to move with the times can threaten their continued existence, but for the entrepreneur seeking to enter or even create a market innovation represents a golden opportunity.

Innovation is certainly linked to economic growth – not for nothing did Karl Marx label it 'the locomotive of growth' in capitalist society. As the economist William Baumol pointed out 'virtually all of the economic growth that has occurred since the eighteenth century is ultimately attributable to innovation', and various studies highlight this correlation across the world (Baumol, 2002).

As Table 4.1 shows, innovation can contribute strategic advantage in many ways – not just in a business marketplace, but also in the wider social context where the 'competition' may be in dealing with social needs like literacy, healthcare or food security.

Table 4.1 Strategic advantages through innovation

Mechanism	Strategic advantage	Examples
Novelty in product or service offering	Offering something no one else can	Introducing the first ... Walkman, fountain pen, camera, dishwasher, telephone bank, on-line retailer, etc... to the world
Novelty in process	Offering it in ways others cannot match – faster, lower cost, more customized, etc.	Pilkington's float glass process, Bessemer's steel process, Internet banking, online bookselling, etc.
Complexity	Offering something which others find it difficult to master	Rolls Royce and aircraft engines – only a handful of competitors can master the complex machining and metallurgy involved
Legal protection of intellectual property	Offering something which others cannot do unless they pay a licence or other fee	Blockbuster drugs like Zantac, Prozac, Viagra, etc.
Add/extend range of competitive factors	Move basis of competition – e.g. from price of product or service to multiple factors: price, quality, choice, etc.	Car manufacturing, where the competitive agenda has systematically moved from price to quality, to flexibility and choice, to shorter times between launch of new models, and so on – each time not trading these off against each other but offering them all
Timing	First-mover advantage – being first can be worth significant market share in new product or service fields	Amazon.com, Yahoo – others can follow, but the advantage 'sticks' to the early movers
	Fast follower advantage – sometimes being first means you encounter many	Personal digital assistants (PDAs) and smart phones which have captured a huge

continued . . .

Table 4.1 . . . *continued*

Mechanism	Strategic advantage	Examples
	unexpected teething problems, and it makes better sense to watch someone else make the early mistakes and move fast into a follow-up product	and growing share of the market. In fact the concept and design was articulated in Apple's ill-fated Newton product some five years before Palm launched its successful Pilot range – but problems with software and especially handwriting recognition meant it flopped. By contrast Apple's success with the iPod as an mp3 player came because they were quite late into the market and could learn and include key features into their dominant design
Robust/platform design	Offering something which provides the platform on which other variations and generations can be built	Sony's original 'Walkman' architecture which has spawned several generations of personal audio equipment – through minidisk, CD, DVD, MP3, iPod

Boeing 737 – over 50 years old, the design is still being adapted and configured to suit different users – one of the most successful aircraft in the world in terms of sales

Intel and AMD with different variants of their microprocessor families |
| Rewriting the rules | Offering something which represents a completely new product or process concept – a different way of doing things – and makes the old ones redundant | Typewriters vs. computer word processing, ice vs. refrigerators, electric vs. gas or oil lamps |
| Reconfiguring the parts of the process | Rethinking the way in which bits of the system work together – e.g. building more effective networks, outsourcing and coordination of a virtual company, etc. | Zara, Benetton in clothing, Dell in computers, Toyota in its supply chain management |
| Transferring across different application contexts | Recombining established elements for different markets | Rapid changeover techniques from manufacturing used in low-cost airlines to facilitate fast turnaround times at airports

Polycarbonate wheels transferred from application market like rolling luggage into children's toys – lightweight micro-scooters |
| Others? | Innovation is all about finding new ways to do things and to obtain strategic advantage – so there will be room for new ways of gaining and retaining advantage | Peer-to-peer file sharing, social networking platforms, networked networks |

Tidd and Bessant (2009)

Of course, not all innovation is about creating commercial value. Public services like healthcare, education, and social security may not generate profits but they do affect the quality of life for millions of people. Bright ideas which are well implemented can lead to valued new services and the efficient delivery of existing ones – at a time when pressure on national purse strings is becoming ever tighter. New ideas – whether wind-up radios in Tanzania or micro-credit financing schemes in Bangladesh – have the potential to change the quality of life and the availability of opportunity for people in some of the poorest regions of the world. There is plenty of scope for innovation and entrepreneurship – and at the limit we are talking here about real matters of life and death.

The video interview with Suzana Moreira gives a good example of social innovation.

For example, in healthcare there have been major improvements in efficiencies around key targets such as waiting times. Hospitals like the Leicester Royal Infirmary in the UK or the Karolinska Hospital in Stockholm, Sweden, have managed to make radical improvements in the speed, quality, and effectiveness of their care services – such as cutting waiting lists for elective surgery by 75 per cent and cancellations by 80 per cent – through innovation.

On the website there are case studies of public sector innovations in fields like patient care and safety.

CASE 4.1: THE ARAVIND EYE CARE SYSTEM

CASE STUDY

The Aravind Eye Care System has become the largest eye care facility in the world with its headquarters in Madurai, India. Its doctors perform over 200,000 cataract operations – and with such experience have developed state-of-the-art techniques to match their excellent facilities. Yet the cost of these operations runs from US$50 to US$300, with over 60 per cent of patients being treated for free. Despite only 40 per cent of patients being paying customers, the company is highly profitable and the average cost per operation (across free and paying patients) at US$25 is the envy of most hospitals around the world.

One of the key building blocks in developing the Aravind system has been transferring the ideas of another industry concerned with low costs, and high and consistent quality provision – the hamburger business pioneered by Ray Croc and underpinning McDonalds. By applying the same process innovation approaches to standardisation, workflow, and tailoring tasks to skills, he created a system which not only delivered high quality but was also reproducible. The model has diffused widely – there are now five hospitals within Tamil Nadu offering nearly 4,000 beds, the majority of which are free.

It has moved beyond cataract surgery to education, lens manufacturing, research and development, and other linked activities around the theme of improving sight and access to treatment.

In making this vision come alive Dr Venkataswamy – Aravind's founder – has not only demonstrated considerable entrepreneurial flair, he has created a template which others, including health providers in the advanced industrial economies, are now looking at very closely.

For more on this case, see the full study on the website.

IT'S A MOVING TARGET

While there are growth opportunities in innovation there are also challenges to those who attempt to stand still in the face of a turbulent and changing environment. It's a disturbing thought – but the majority of companies have a lifespan significantly less than that of a human being. Even the largest firms can show worrying signs of vulnerability – for example, companies like Digital Equipment and Wang Laboratories dominated the computer industry of the 1970s yet have disappeared, whilst giants like IBM had to radically change themselves to avoid a similar fate. For the smaller firm, the mortality statistics are even more worrying.

Sometimes it's individual firms which face the problem, sometimes it is whole sectors. For example, the UK used to be known as 'the workshop of the world' – but one by one many of its proud manufacturing industries – for example, machine tools, motorcycles, and shipbuilding – faded away, and leadership in these fields moved elsewhere around the world, an indication of how fragile competitive advantage can be. What goes up can come down just as fast.

Happily it is not all doom and gloom – there are also plenty of stories of new firms and new industries emerging to replace those that die. Within the past 15 years some major new corporations have appeared on the global scene and dominate their industries – for example, Amazon in online retailing, eBay in e-auctions, Skype in voice-over-Internet telecoms and Google in everything from search engines, through advertising to mobile telephones. And there are other examples of *renaissance* – dusty old brands or niche market players moving to centre stage through changes in what they offer and how they offer it. For example, Apple moving to overtake Microsoft as the largest IT firm on the back of a rebirth fuelled by online music and then communications. Or Nokia – once a sprawling conglomerate based on paper and forest products and now a key player in the global mobile communications market. Arie de Geus, (for many years the planning director for Shell and responsible for helping that company navigate the turbulent waters of the oil business), cites the example of the Stora company in Sweden which was founded in the twelfth century as a timber cutting and processing operation but which is still thriving today – albeit in the very different areas of food processing and electronics (de Geus, 1996).

In 2001 an influential report from the American Bar Association was presented to the annual conference of a key economic sector laying down the innovation challenge in clear terms:

> we are at the brink of change of an unprecedented and exponential kind and magnitude . . . We must be willing and able to discard old paradigms and engender and embrace manifest change. . . . These required changes include implementing new customer-centric processes and products, cutting costs and improving service through the application of IT and business process re-engineering and putting in place systems and a culture for sustainable innovation.

Another study from Codexx Consultants, in 2006, reviewed the capability of firms within this sector to deal with innovation and highlighted problems such as:

- No culture of innovation.
- No strategy for where to focus innovation efforts.
- Innovation is seen to conflict with fee paying work and is thus not always valued.
- A formal innovation process does not exist.
- Project management skills are very limited.

At first sight these seem to be typical of statements made regularly about the importance of innovation in a manufacturing economy and the difficulties individual firms – particularly the smaller and less experienced – face in trying to manage the process. But these are in fact *service* sector examples – the first report was to the US Bar Association, the second the result of a survey of 40 professional law firms in the UK trying to prepare for the big changes likely to arise as a result of the Clementi (2004) review into deregulation.

Competitive advantage undoubtedly can come from innovation in services. Citibank was the first bank to offer an automated telling machinery (ATM) service and developed a strong market position as a technology leader on the back of this process innovation, whilst Bank of America is literally a textbook case of service innovation via experimentation with new technologies and organizational arrangements across its branch network. Benetton is one of the world's most successful retailers, largely due to its sophisticated IT-led production network, which it innovated over a ten-year period, and the same model has been used to great effect by the Spanish firm Zara. Southwest Airlines achieved an enviable position as the most effective airline in the USA despite being much smaller than its rivals – its success was due to process innovation in areas such as reducing airport turnaround times. This model has subsequently become the template for a whole new generation of low-cost airlines whose efforts have revolutionized the once cosy world of air travel.

The innovation imperative has always been there – but it is becoming increasingly important across the global board, and in public as well as private sector. Think about an old, established industry like printing – for centuries the pace of change was relatively slow. As the eminent management writer, Peter Drucker comments:

My ancestors were printers in Amsterdam from 1510 or so until 1750 . . . *and during that entire time they didn't have to learn anything new.*

(1985, italics added)

Contrast that 250-year stable pattern with changes in the printing industry over the past 25 years. Right up until the late 1980s we had an industry which was based on very physical technologies and a network of specialist suppliers who contributed their particular parts of the complex puzzle of publishing. For example, copy – words or pictures – would be generated by

---

CASE: BUSINESS SUCCESS THROUGH REWRITING THE RULES OF THE GAME

There are plenty of examples of firms which have made an impact in established sectors through doing something differently – either in what they offer or how they produce that offering. For example:

- Amazon.com revolutionized the world of publishing and bookselling through the early adoption of the Internet as a mechanism for advertising, ordering, and distributing books. So successful has the project been that now almost all the major booksellers have added Internet operations to their existing physical bookshops.

- The Body Shop broke new ground in the well-established cosmetics and toiletries field of retailing by a strategy based on environmentally friendly products and a strong commitment to international development aid. Again, their success caused other players in the field to alter their own behaviour and to produce products and redesign packaging and retailing operations to match.

- Dell Computers have redefined the computer as a consumer product, taking advantage of several technological and social changes. They offer not only a rapid delivery and low price but also customization – each machine is built to an individual customer specification. Achieving this is done through a mixture of careful modular design and the management of an extended web of outsourced capabilities – in manufacturing, distribution, service, etc. The result is a highly successful mass customizing company which operates from a tiny core – a true virtual business.

- Easyjet, Ryanair, Air Berlin and a host of other airlines have innovated in services with their low cost scheduled flights – and in doing so have revolutionized the air travel industry. Learning lessons originally developed by Southwest Airlines in the USA, they began with an innovation in market positioning (opening up air travel to non-fliers) and then developed a stream of product and process innovations to enable their low cost model to work.

a specialist journalist or photographer. He/she would then pass this on to various editors who would check, make choices about design and layout, etc. Next would come typesetting where the physical materials for printing would be made – hot metal would be cast into letters and grouped into blocks to form words and sentences within special frames. Pictures and other items would be transferred on to printing plates. The type frames or printing plates would then be fixed to presses, these would be inked and some test runs made. And finally the printed version would appear – and be passed on to someone else to distribute and publish it.

Such a method might still be recognizable to Messrs. Caxton and Gutenberg – the fifteenth-century pioneers of the printing industry. But it is a fair bet that they would not have a clue about the way in which publishing operates today, with its emphasis on information technology. Now the process has changed such that a single person could undertake the whole set of operations – create text on a word processor, design and lay it out on a page formatting program, integrate images with text, and when satisfied print to either physical media or – increasingly – publish it worldwide in electronic form.

CASE STUDY

CASE 4.2: REINVENTING THE TEXTILE INDUSTRY

Despite a global shift in textile and clothing manufacture towards developing countries the Spanish company, Inditex (through its retail outlets under various names including Zara) have pioneered a highly flexible, fast turnaround clothing operation with over 2,000 outlets in 52 countries. It was founded by Ajaccio Ortega Goanna who set up a small operation in the west of Spain in La Coruna – a region not previously noted for textile production – and the first store opened there in 1975. Central to the Inditex philosophy is close linkage between design, manufacture, and retailing, and their network of stores constantly feeds back information about trends which are used to generate new designs. They also experiment with new ideas directly on the public, trying samples of cloth or design and quickly getting back indications of what is going to catch on. Despite their global orientation, most manufacturing is still done in Spain, and they have managed to reduce the turn-around time between a trigger signal for an innovation and responding to it to around 15 days.

A more detailed description of the Zara/Inditex story appears on the website.

KEEPING PACE WITH A CHANGING ENVIRONMENT

Table 4.2 gives some idea of the massive and accelerating shifts in context which are driving the pace of innovation – and making it more of an imperative than ever.

Of course, not all firms recognize the need to change; for some there appears to be security in size or in previous technological success. Take the case of IBM – a giant firm which can justly claim to have laid the foundations of the IT industry, and one which came to dominate the architecture of hardware and software and the ways in which computers were marketed. The trouble is that such core strength can sometimes become an obstacle to

Table 4.2 Changing context for innovation management

Context change	Indicative examples
Acceleration of knowledge production	OECD estimates that $750bn is spent each year (public and private sector) in creating new knowledge – and hence extending the frontier along which 'breakthrough' technological developments may happen
Global distribution of knowledge production	Knowledge production is increasingly involving new players especially in emerging market fields like the BRIC nations (Brazil, Russia, India, China) – so the need for search routines to cover a much wider search space increases
Market fragmentation	Globalization has massively increased the range of markets and segments – putting pressure on search routines to cover much more territory, often far from 'traditional' experiences – such as the 'bottom of the pyramid' conditions in many emerging markets (Prahalad 2006) or 'the long tail' (Anderson 2006)
Market virtualization	Increasing use of internet as marketing channel means different approaches need to be developed. At the same time emergence of large-scale social networks in cyberspace pose challenges in market research approaches – for example, Facebook currently has over 700 million subscribers, making it the third largest 'country' in the world in terms of population!
Rise of active users	Although user-active innovation is not a new concept there has been an acceleration in the ways in which this is now taking place (Von Hippel 2005) In sectors like media the line between consumers and creators is increasingly blurred – for example, YouTube has around 100 million videos viewed each day but also has over 70,000 new videos uploaded every day from its user base.
Development of technological and social infrastructure	Increasing linkages enabled by information and communications technologies around the internet and broadband have enabled and reinforced alternative social networking possibilities. At the same time the increasing availability of simulation and prototyping tools have reduced the separation between users and producers (Schrage 2000; Gann 2004)

Bessant and Venables (2008)

seeing the need for change – as proved to be the case when, in the early 1990s the company moved slowly to counter the threat of networking technologies, and nearly lost the business in the process. In 1993 IBM lost nearly $8bn and global lay-offs of employees ran close to 100,000. Its subsequent return to good health under a new chief executive, ex-consultant Lou Gerstner, is reflected in his public message to his employees in 1993:

> Basically, you need to change the way you think and act, every hour of every day for the rest of your IBM career. If you are comfortable with tradition and procedure, you will likely find all this difficult, if not impossible, to accomplish.

Changing core strengths is often a problem for large companies – the case of General Motors is another example, where the challenge of 'lean production' was ignored for many years. Building on *core competence* is importance but it is also important to remember how easily this can turn into *core rigidity* as Dorothy Leonard-Barton calls it (Leonard-Barton, 1995).

CASE 4.3: FROZEN IN TIME

Sometimes the pace of change appears slow and the old responses seem to work well. It appears, to those within the industry, that they understand the rules of the game and that they have a good grasp of the relevant technological developments likely to change things. But what can sometimes happen here is that change comes along from outside the industry – and by the time the main players inside have reacted it is often too late. For example, in the late ninteenth century there was a thriving industry in New England based upon the harvesting and distribution of ice. In its heyday it was possible for ice harvesters to ship hundreds of tons of ice around the world on voyages that lasted as long as six months – and still have over half the cargo available for sale. By the late 1870s the 14 major firms in the Boston area of the US were cutting around 700,000 tons per year and employing several thousand people.

The industry made use of a variety of novel techniques for cutting, insulating, and transporting ice around the world. But the industry was completely overthrown by the new developments which followed from Linde's invention of refrigeration and the growth of the modern cold-storage industry. The problem – as James Utterback of MIT points out in his book studying a number of industries – is that the existing players often fail to respond fast enough to the new signals coming from outside their industry. Yet three quarters of the industry changing innovations that he examined originated from outside the industry itself (Utterback, 1994).

For smaller enterprises, the luxury of enough resources to weather a crisis may not be available – failure to change can destroy the business. Yet by their nature these organizations are often very preoccupied with day-to-day crisis management, the 'firefighting' of keeping going, that they miss important shifts in their external environment. Just like IBM, but for different reasons, they can quickly become isolated, insulated from the ability to pick up on signals of threatening change, until it is too late to do anything about it.

So innovation is not a luxury or an optional extra – it is essential to an organization's survival. But simply changing things for their own sake is not necessarily the answer. The problem with innovation is that it is uncertain – by its nature, it involves risks and there are no guarantees of success. This makes its *management* a primary strategic task for the enterprise.

The case study of Marshalls on the website gives a good illustration of how businesses can survive and grow through constant innovation even if their technological and market environment over a 100 year period has been turbulent and difficult.

LEARNING TO MANAGE INNOVATION

Innovation isn't accidental – it's the product of human ingenuity and creativity deployed to create value. It lies at the heart of what organizations do to renew themselves in terms of what they offer and how they create and deliver that offering. For this reason it is of central concern to strategic operations managers, whose role is coordinating the development and deployment of capabilities which make innovation happen.

So what have we learned about the successful management of innovation? We can distil the main findings of innovation research over the past 80 years (see Ernst, 2002; Adams,

CASE STUDY

2006; Tidd and Bessant, 2009, for a much fuller account of this). The good news is that there is evidence that innovation can be managed – it isn't simply gambling! Research regularly highlights key practices that help and whose absence is associated with failure – so there is a basic recipe book on which to draw. But that doesn't take away the challenge for strategic operations managers – rather, it puts the spotlight firmly on them since the real challenge is not to find the general recipe book but to actually create – and continue to create – different dishes from it.

Take the case of 3M – a company whose commitment to innovation is such that it bases its branding on themes like 'Innovation – working for you'. 3M see strategic advantage in their being able to come up with a regular stream of product innovation, so much so that they have a policy that 50 per cent of sales should come from products invented during the past three years. In practice this means that they are betting on their ability to bring new ideas to market not once or twice but consistently and across a range which now numbers around 60,000 products worldwide. Underpinning this is a particular set of firm-specific capabilities which 3M have learned, adapted, and developed over time – and which seem to work more often than they fail. There are some problems, and the occasional disaster, but the company's track record on innovations (from sandpaper, through Scotch tape, overhead projection film, magnetic tape and discs, to the 'post-it' notes) strongly supports their particular ways of doing things.

The website has a detailed case study of 3M and an analysis of how it has developed its own particular approaches to managing innovation.

It's not just 3M. Smart organizations of many different shapes and sizes share the common characteristic that they reflect on and actively try and manage and improve their innovation systems and processes. For example Toyota (Toyota Way), H-P, Apple, Procter and Gamble (Connect and Develop) and Google (Nine points) are all organizations which have actively reflected upon and codified their particular approach to making innovation happen.

The particular bundle of structures, policies, procedures, and techniques which define the 'way we manage innovation' in a particular firm can be called its 'innovation capability'. For example, in Hewlett-Packard researchers are encouraged to spend up to 10 per cent of time on their own pet projects, and have 24-hour access to laboratories and equipment. The company tries to keep divisions small to focus team efforts. In the pharmaceutical company Merck, researchers are given time and resources to pursue high-risk, high-payoff products, whilst in Johnson and Johnson the principle of 'freedom to fail' is a core corporate value. General Electric lays particular stress on jointly developing products with customers – for example, this approach helped developed the first thermoplastic body panels for cars through joint work with BMW.

One important feature about firm-specific behaviour of this kind is that it can't be copied easily – it has to be learned the hard way, through experience, trial and error. Many firms have tried, for example, to emulate 3M's famous 15 per cent rule – a policy which encourages experimentation and curiosity by allowing staff to 'play around' with ideas and hunches for up to 15 per cent of their working time. This helps create 'space' in which innovative ideas can flourish within 3M – but it doesn't necessarily transplant to other companies. Instead they need to develop their own particular way of making some 'space' (Augsdorfer, 1996).

But the good news is that although these and other firms learn to play the game in their own particular style, the underlying model which they use is the same. And it starts with a recognition that innovation is not like the cartoons, where a light bulb flashes above someone's head and the rest is easy. Instead it is a *process* with particular stages and activities – familiar territory for strategic operations management.

Innovation is the successful exploitation of new ideas
UK Department of Trade and Industry (2004)

The word itself comes from the Latin – *innovare*, meaning to create something new or to change. We can take more elaborate definitions – for example, Chris Freeman, one of the key writers on the topic saw it as

Industrial innovation includes the technical, design, manufacturing, management and commercial activities involved in the marketing of a new (or improved) product or the first commercial use of a new (or improved) process or equipment.

(Freeman and Soete, 1997)

Whether we are talking about a physical product or a service offering, the key point is that innovation is a process.

INNOVATION AS A PROCESS

If someone asked you 'when did you last use your Spengler?' they might well be greeted by a quizzical look. But if they asked you when you last used your 'Hoover' – the answer would be fairly easy. Yet it was not Mr Hoover who invented the vacuum cleaner in the late nineteenth century but one J. Murray Spengler. Hoover's genius lay in taking that idea and making it into a commercial reality. In similar vein the father of the modern sewing machine was not Mr Singer, whose name jumps to mind and is emblazoned on millions of machines all around the world. It was Elias Howe who invented the machine in 1846, but Isaac Singer who brought it to technical and commercial fruition. We need to recognize that ideas are important but they are not the same as innovation – there is much more to be done to realize the potential commercial or social value in an idea than simply having it.

Perhaps the godfather of successful innovators in terms of turning ideas into reality was Thomas Edison who during his life registered over 1,000 patents. Products for which his organization was responsible include the light bulb, 35 mm cinema film, and even the electric chair. Many of the inventions for which he is famous were not in fact invented by him – the electric light bulb for example – but were developed and polished technically and their markets opened up by Edison and his team.

More than anyone else, Edison understood that *invention* is not enough – simply having a good idea is not going to lead to its widespread adoption and use. Much has to be done – as Edison is reputed to have said, 'it's 1 per cent inspiration and 99 per cent perspiration!' – to make ideas into successful reality. His skill in doing this created a business empire worth, in today's prices, around $21.6 billion. He put to good use an understanding of the interactive nature of innovation, realizing that both technology push (which he systematized in one of the world's first organized R&D laboratories) and demand pull need to be mobilized.

Take the light bulb for example. To bring that to fruition required enormous technical development on both the product and the process to produce it at the right cost and quality, and it required the creation and development of a market into which it could be sold. But Edison also recognized that although the electric light bulb was a good idea it had little practical relevance in a world in which there was no power-point to plug it in. Consequently his team set about building up an entire electricity generation and distribution infrastructure, including designing lamp stands, switches, and wiring. In 1882 he switched on the power from the first electric power generation plant in Manhattan and was able to light up 800 bulbs in the area. In the years that followed he built over 300 plants all over the world.

In other words, invention is just the first step along an extended process of translating ideas into reality, and it is of central concern in operations management. Innovation is a process – a sequence of activities which lead to an outcome. In the organization it is a core process concerned with renewal – creating and recreating the future. Figure 4.1 gives an illustration of this in simple form and the model is discussed more fully in Tidd and Bessant (2009).

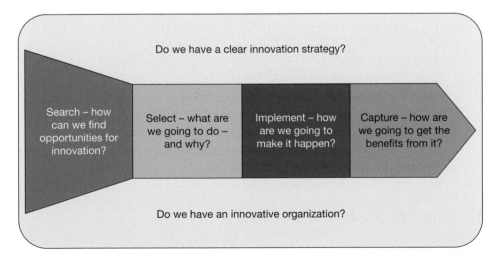

Figure 4.1 Simple model of the innovation process

It involves:

- *Search*: scanning the environment (internal and external) to find signals which could trigger change. These might be the results of formal R&D work, insights from listening to customers about their needs, good ideas which we have seen a competitor introduce, changes in direction which government regulation forces on us, or even bright ideas which occur in the shower. The important thing is to ensure that we search widely and actively to pick up the signals for change.

- *Selection*: deciding (on the basis of a strategic view of how the enterprise can best develop) which of these signals to respond to.

- *Implementing* the project, including making sure we can obtain the resources to enable the response and managing through the inevitable uncertainty which creating or doing something new will involve.

- *Capturing value*: making sure the new thing we offer gets taken up by the market and diffuses widely, or the new process we introduce becomes one which people 'buy into', or our world-changing social innovation really does do that. And we get a return – financial or social – on our investment of time, money, energy, and resources. The other hugely valuable element in this stage is the chance to *learn* how to do it better next time, to accumulate and build capacity to manage innovation more effectively in the future.

Of course, this process doesn't take place in a vacuum – it is subject to a range of internal and external influences which shape what is possible and what actually emerges. In particular, innovation requires:

- Clear strategic leadership and direction, plus the commitment of resources to make this happen. Innovation is about taking risks, about going into new and sometimes completely unexplored spaces. No organization has resources to waste in scattergun fashion – innovation needs a strategy.

- An innovative organization in which the structure and climate enables people to deploy their creativity and share their knowledge to bring about change.

- Proactive links across boundaries inside the organization and to the many external agencies who can play a part in the innovation process – suppliers, customers, sources of finance, skilled resources, and knowledge, etc. Twenty-first century innovation is a global game where connections and the ability to find, form, and deploy creative relationships is of the essence.

VARIATIONS ON A THEME

Whatever their size or sector, all organizations are trying to find ways of managing this process of creation and renewal. There is no 'right' answer, but each needs to aim for the most appropriate solution for its particular circumstances. For example, those firms concerned with large, science-based activities – such as pharmaceuticals or electronics – will tend to develop solutions to the problem of managing innovation which include formal R&D inside and outside the firm, patent protection and searching, internationalization, etc. By contrast a small engineering subcontractor might develop very different solutions which aim at creating a capacity to respond very quickly. Firms in the retail sector may not invest much in formal R&D but they are likely to stress scanning the environment to pick up new consumer trends, and to place heavy emphasis on marketing. Heavy engineering firms involved in products like power plant are likely to be design intensive, and critically dependent on project management and systems integration aspects of the implementation phase. Consumer goods producers may be more concerned with rapid product development and launch, often with variants and repositioning of basic product concepts.

By the same token deciding to install a new piece of process technology also follows this pattern. Signals about needs – in this case internal ones, such as problems with the current equipment – and new technological means, are processed and provide an input to developing a strategic concept. This then requires identifying an existing option, or inventing a new one which must then be developed to such a point that it can be implemented (i.e. launched) by users within the enterprise – effectively a group of internal customers. The principles of needing to understand their needs and to prepare the marketplace for effective launch will apply just as much as in the case of product innovation.

Services involve a similar process of search (albeit with a much stronger demand-side emphasis), experiment and prototyping (which may extend the 'laboratory' concept to pilots and trials with potential end-users) and a gradual scaling up of commitment and activity leading to launch. Service businesses may not have a formal R&D department but they do undertake this kind of activity in order to deliver a stream of innovations. Importantly the knowledge sets with which they work involve a much higher level of user insight and experience.

The model also applies in what can be termed 'complex product systems'. These are typically the kind of product/system which brings together many different elements into an integrated whole, often involving different firms, long timescales and high levels of technological risk. Examples might be major construction projects, or developing and rolling out a new telecoms network. Although such projects may appear very different to the core innovation process associated with, for example, producing a new soap powder for the mass market, the underlying process is still one requiring a careful understanding of user needs, and then the meeting of those needs. There are differences in the intensity each key stage – for example, the involvement of users throughout the development process, and the close integration of different perspectives, will be of particular importance – but the overall map of the process is the same.

As we have already seen, innovation is also not simply a matter for commercial organizations. Public sector innovation is critically important – but how to organize and manage it will vary widely. Not least, public services involve a three-way tradeoff between risk and reward (the typical balance in commercial innovation) and *reliability* – for many services like health, welfare, and education the possibility of failure is simply not acceptable.

And social enterprises also need to organize and manage the process of innovation – but their models will often need to develop extensive networks and connections in order to secure support and resources and to sustain and scale their operations.

 The video interview with Simon Tucker of the Young Foundation gives some examples of social innovation.

MODELS OF THE INNOVATION PROCESS

We need to look more closely at how we think about how the process takes place – not least because our mental models tend to shape how we approach organizing and managing innovation in practice. At the extreme it is clear that one such model might be the cartoon representation of innovation simply involving 'light bulb' moments or Archimedes-type flashes of inspiration. If that is all we think there is to innovation then we will pay attention to and support activities which generate many ideas – but we will probably fail at innovation because we haven't considered the downstream development of those ideas, or the issues involved in successfully launching and diffusing them.

Table 4.3 gives some examples of what happens if our mental models of how the process happens are limited.

Early models of how to organize and manage innovation were simplistic linear affairs and mainly about physical products and processes – the typical 'technology push' or 'demand pull' stereotypes. These days we recognize that it is much more a matter of 'horses for courses' – we need different and flexible models which involve the interplay of many different actors creating and diffusing different kinds of innovation.

Table 4.4 gives an overview of some of the different ways in which innovation can be organized, depending on the context.

INNOVATION STRATEGY: WHAT DO WE CHANGE AND WHY?

So far we've looked at the 'What?' question of innovation – what we have to do to manage the process effectively. But we should also consider the 'How?' and 'Why?' questions – *how* is innovation going to take our organization forward? We could change many things – the product or service offering, the processes which underpin our operations, the markets we deliver into, even the very way we think about and frame the business. And we can make these changes in incremental steps or radical leaps. The one thing we can be certain of is that trying to do everything will probably get us nowhere – we need a strategic approach.

In this next section we will look at the different types of innovation which we might work with and how we might pull them together into a coherent innovation strategy for the organization.

Table 4.3 Problems of partial views of innovation

If innovation is only seen as . . .	. . . the result can be
Strong R&D capability	Technology which fails to meet user needs and may not be accepted – 'the better mousetrap which nobody wants'
The province of specialists in white coats in the R&D laboratory	Lack of involvement of others, and a lack of key knowledge and experience input from other perspectives
Meeting customer needs	Lack of technical progression, leading to inability to gain competitive edge
Technology advances	Producing products which the market does not want or designing processes which do not meet the needs of the user and which are opposed
The province only of large firms	Weak small firms with too high a dependence on large customers
Only about 'breakthrough' changes	Neglect of the potential of incremental innovation. Also an inability to secure and reinforce the gains from radical change because the incremental performance ratchet is not working well
Only associated with key individuals	Failure to utilize the creativity of the remainder of employees, and to secure their inputs and perspectives to improve innovation
Only internally generated	The 'not invented here' effect, where good ideas from outside are resisted or rejected
Only externally generated	Innovation becomes simply a matter of filling a shopping list of needs from outside and there is little internal learning or development of technological competence
Only about products	Service organizations don't see themselves as needing to innovate

Tidd and Bessant (2009)

Incremental or radical?

Whilst we might associate innovation with big dramatic leaps forward, the reality is that most of the time it is actually about doing what we already do a little better. Most of the time change is gradual, moving incrementally forward with a sequence of little, cumulative improvements. For example, although the invention of the electric light bulb was a dramatic breakthrough, it was a constant stream of small improvements in the design of the bulb and

Table 4.4 Different ways of organizing innovation

Model	What is it?	Where to use it	How to support it
R&D led	Ideas are developed by specialists, refined, developed and launched	Useful for scientific and technology based products, but should not be used in areas that require high discretion	Currently has the strongest support Build connections with companies with strong track records of technical innovation
High involvement	All employees engaged in process of incremental problem solving	Suited to developing incremental process innovations in areas requiring high degree of uniformity and little employee discretion	Focus on maximizing level of discretion of employees within bounds of their role and provide space, reward and recognition for developing and adopting ideas
Network	Ideas developed, adapted and adopted through networks	Particularly important in areas where high levels of discretion are necessary	Ensure networks are properly resourced and supported
Radical/discontinuous	Group is given the license to think the unthinkable and develop ideas on the edges or apart from the mainstream	Suited to developing radically different services or ways of doing things	Requires an autonomous unit with license to 'think the unthinkable,' a multi-disciplinary team and 'godparents' within mainstream system
Entrepreneur driven	Ideas developed on a small scale inside or outside an organization	Potentially taps into the rich vein of social entrepreneurship in and around the public sector Space and support should be continuously present	Supporting and working with intermediary or brokering organizations who provide entrepreneurs with 'wrap-a-round' support Provide space, reward and recognition for innovation
Recombinant	Idea adapted and adopted from one setting into another	Organizations should continually be open to ideas from outside, whether in their sector or beyond	Mechanisms to bridge between different worlds (e.g. innovation scouts) and translators to adapt innovations Porous organization with learning culture
User led	Users innovate themselves through co-production with professionals or using voice or choice	Customer insight important in all models Co-production or choice particularly appropriate for relational services tackling wicked issues	Can be supported by platform innovations (e.g. personal budgets) or enabling and encouraging frontline workers to co-produce solutions with users

in the process for manufacturing it that led to a fall in price of over 80 per cent between 1880 and 1896 (Bright, 1949). As a result the innovation was able to diffuse widely and supplant gas or oil lighting as the dominant form of domestic illumination.

Making this distinction between 'incremental' and 'radical' innovation is important because the ways in which we might organize and manage processes to support the two are likely to be different. It is helpful to think about innovation in terms of a spectrum with incremental 'do better' at one end. At the other end of the spectrum we have innovations that are major changes, often representing significant shifts in what we offer or how we create it. At the limit there is 'discontinuous' change where innovation involves a jump to something completely different and rewrites the rules of the game.

CASE 4.4: SEEING NEW SOLUTIONS

The glass window business has been around for at least 600 years and is – since most houses, offices, hotels and shops have plenty of windows – a very profitable business to be in. But for most of those 600 years the basic process for making window glass hasn't changed. Glass is made in approximately flat sheets which are then ground down to a state where they are flat enough for people to see through them. The ways in which the grinding takes place have improved – what used to be a labour-intensive process became increasingly mechanized and even automated, and the tools and abrasives became progressively more sophisticated and effective. But underneath the same core process of grinding down to flatness was going on.

Then in 1952 Alastair Pilkington working in the UK firm of the same name began working on a process which revolutionized glass making for the next 50 years. He got the idea whilst washing up when he noticed that the fat and grease from the plates floated on the top of the water – and he began thinking about producing glass in such a way that it could be cast to float on the surface of some other liquid and then allowed to set. If this could be accomplished it might be possible to create a perfectly flat surface without the need for grinding and polishing.

Five years, millions of pounds and over 100,000 tonnes of scrapped glass later the company achieved a working pilot plant and a further two years on began selling glass made by the float glass process. The process' advantages included around 80 per cent labour and 50 per cent energy savings plus those which came because of the lack of need for abrasives, grinding equipment, etc. Factories could be made smaller and the overall time to produce glass dramatically cut. So successful was the process that it became – and still is – the dominant method for making flat glass around the world.

The website has case examples of innovation patterns in the lighting and the music industries where the interplay of incremental and occasional radical change can be seen.

CASE STUDY

A good example of radical process innovation is that of the automobile. When Henry Ford and his team of engineers began looking at the motor car in the late nineteenth century, the process was essentially one of craft manufacture. Skilled men working in small groups would more or less hand build a car, fashioning components one by one on general purpose machines where the key to what was produced lay in the operator's head and hands. The cars took weeks to build and each was slightly different – very much as a hand-made suit is built up and shaped to an individual client. Not surprisingly, this process was expensive and slow.

It was not without change – there was a continuous stream of minor incremental improvements in the ways in which craft production operated (for example, in the materials used or the machinery involved). But the shift which Ford and his team introduced was fundamental – a radical jump from craft production to an early version of what we now term 'mass production'. The combination of new organizational practices (based on Taylor's 'scientific management' ideas) and standardization of product and process elements, meant that huge increases in productivity were possible – for example, an 800 per cent jump in productivity in engine building between 1912 (craft) and 1913 (early mass production) (Womack *et al.*, 1991).

This model did not stop with the car industry – it became the dominant approach for much of the manufacturing sector and spread out to services like banking and insurance. Another key aspect of innovation is the continuing nature of change – and so 'mass production' models themselves gave way to other innovations – for example 'lean thinking' and 'mass customization'.

Similar patterns can be found in services. For example, there were many incremental retailing innovations but the development of self-service shopping – the supermarket model – revolutionized first the US industry and later the retail sector around the world because of the massive shifts in productivity which it made possible.

There are several case studies of innovations on the website, including the Model T Ford, and a detailed review of contemporary innovation in retailing, looking at how Tesco is changing itself in order to enter the US market.

These examples are mainly about 'process innovation' – changes in the way in which we create and deliver our offerings. But we can see other examples in the field of products – for example, the telephone. This moved through a phase of radical innovation when it was first invented and then stabilized into a pattern of incremental improvements – both in terms of the external styling and shape and the internal electromechanical functioning. Throughout its life there have been long periods of such incremental development, punctuated by surges of radical change – for example, the move to electronic mechanisms, to mobile communications, and now to 'smart' phones which involve the convergence of computing and communications.

In recent years major impacts have been felt across information-intensive sectors like banking and insurance as a result of the impact of information and communications technology development. Until the bursting of the 'dotcom bubble' there were dire predictions about the fate of many other industries with an information handling component – for example, travel, media, retailing, etc. – but the impact on these has varied widely (Evans and Wurster, 2000).

Of course, many customer-processing operations have experienced much less innovative turbulence. A range of sectors continue to use processes and offer outputs that have changed relatively little – hotels, cinemas, hairdressers, schools, etc. But a closer look at these highlights the role which incremental innovation plays – in improving efficiencies, in differentiating services, in building customer loyalty, etc.

The website has a video case study of a fish-and-chip shop – not a place one would instantly associate with innovation! But the video shows how much innovation space is available and the ways in which competitive advantage can be developed and sustained through innovation in such a business.

The line between incremental and radical innovation is hard to fix – not least because novelty is in the eye of the beholder. For some firms an innovation may be a simple and logical next step in an incremental process of improvement. But for others it may represent a major shift.

Innovation is often confined to the level of the firm, but there are occasions where it influences and shapes a whole sector – as in the case of the glass industry. Other examples of such radical change include the shift in steel-making technology enabled by the Bessemer process, or in chemicals by the continuous Solvay process replacing the batch-wise Leblanc for the manufacture of soda ash and other key alkali products. And periodically something comes along which has an impact across sectors and affects whole societies – for example, the advent of steam power in the first industrial revolution, or the current 'revolution' that the convergence of computing, communications, and electronics has brought about.

Component or system level?

We also need to think about innovation as often being like Russian dolls – we can change things at the level of components or we can change a whole system. For example, we can put a faster transistor on a microchip on a circuit board for the graphics display in a computer. Or we can change the way several boards are put together into the computer to give it particular capabilities – a games box, an e-book, a media PC. Or we can link the computers into a network to drive a small business or office. Or we can link the networks to others into the Internet. There's scope for innovation at each level – but changes in the higher level systems often have implications for those lower down. For example, if cars – as a complex assembly – were suddenly designed to be made out of plastic instead of metal, it would still leave scope for car assemblers but would pose some sleepless nights for producers of metal components.

This distinction – between what we can call 'component level' and 'system level' innovation – is important to build into our map of different types of innovation. Figure 4.2 gives an overview.

Figure 4.2
Types of innovation
Tidd and Bessant (2009)

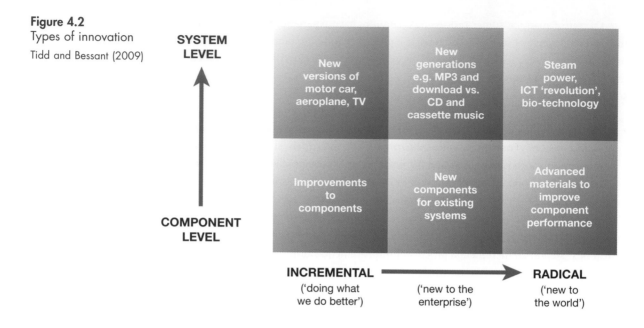

MANAGING DIFFERENT INNOVATION TYPES

Why is it important to think about the different types of innovation? Put simply, they need different ways of managing. An incremental change in process in a familiar context is not a high risk action and can probably be managed in day-to-day fashion – for example, as part of a shop-floor daily 'review and improve' activity. Equally, a radical new product being launched in a new market will require care and attention to manage the risks and resource flows – and will probably form the basis of a special project team's work. At the limit, radical change in product, process, and context may offer the chance to change the rules of the business game – but it will need very careful and focused management. For successful strategic operations management of the innovation process we need a portfolio approach and in the following section we'll look at a systematic model for exploring and populating the innovation space for an organization – what changes could it make?

EXPLORING INNOVATION SPACE

Change – as we have seen – can happen in many different ways and it is helpful to think of a kind of 'innovation compass' which maps these out. We can identify four key directions:

1. *Product innovation*: changes in the things (products/services) which an organization offers.

2. *Process innovation*: changes in the ways in which they are created and delivered.

3. *Position innovation*: changes in the context in which the products/services are introduced.

4. *Paradigm innovation*: changes in the underlying mental models which frame what the organization does.

Figure 4.3 shows how these '4Ps' provide the framework for a map of the innovation space available to any organization.

A new design of car, a new insurance package for accident-prone babies, and a new home entertainment system, would all be examples of product innovation. And change in the manufacturing methods and equipment used to produce the car or the home entertainment system, or in the office procedures and sequencing in the insurance case, would be examples of process innovation.

Sometimes the dividing line is somewhat blurred – for example, a new jet-powered sea ferry is both a product and a process innovation. Services represent a particular case of this where the product and process aspects often merge – for example, is a new holiday package a product or process change?

Innovation can also take place by repositioning the perception of an established product or process in a particular user context. For example Haagen Dazs were able to give a new and profitable lease of life to an old-established product (ice cream) made with well-known

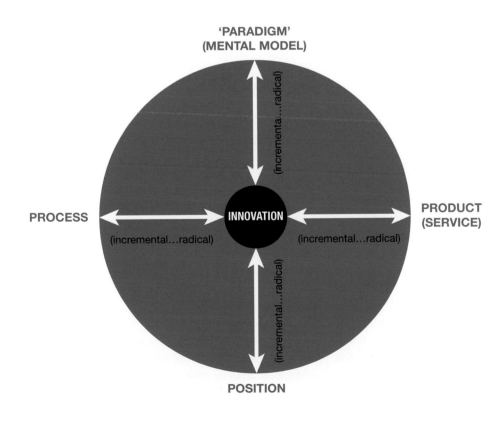

Figure 4.3
The 4Ps of innovation space
Tidd and Bessant (2009)

processes. Their strategy was to target a different market segment and to reposition their product as a sensual pleasure to be enjoyed by adults – essentially telling an 'ice cream for grown ups' story. This is, of course, the strategy which low-cost airlines used to open up new space and challenge the established players in that industry, and it is what Nintendo did with the Wii – a simple (by comparison with the X-Box and Playstation) computer gaming device which opened up the games market to families.

CASE 4.5: GRAMEEN BANK AND THE DEVELOPMENT OF 'MICROFINANCE'

A good example of innovation in position is the development of 'micro-finance' pioneered by the Grameen Bank project. One of the biggest problems facing people living below the poverty line is the difficulty of getting access to banking and financial services. As a result they are often dependent on moneylenders and other unofficial sources – and are often charged at exorbitant rates if they do borrow. This makes it hard to save and invest – and puts a major barrier in the way of breaking out of this spiral through starting new entrepreneurial ventures. Awareness Of this problem, led Muhammad Yunus, Head of the Rural Economics Program at the University of Chittagong, to launch a project to examine the possibility of designing a credit delivery system to provide banking services targeted at the rural poor. In 1976 the Grameen Bank Project (Grameen means 'rural' or 'village' in the Bangla language) was established, aiming to:

- Extend banking facilities to the poor;
- Eliminate the exploitation of the poor by money lenders;
- Create opportunities for self-employment for unemployed people in rural Bangladesh;
- Offer the disadvantaged an organizational format which they can understand and manage by themselves; and
- Reverse the age-old vicious circle of 'low income, low saving and low investment', into virtuous circle of 'low income, injection of credit, investment, more income, more savings, more investment, more income'.

The original project was set up in Jobra (a village adjacent to Chittagong University) and some neighbouring villages and ran from 1976 to 1979. The core concept was of 'micro-finance' – enabling people (and a major success was with women) to take tiny loans to start and grow tiny businesses. With the sponsorship of the central bank of the country and support of the nationalized commercial banks, the project was extended to Tangail district (a district north of Dhaka, the capital city of Bangladesh) in 1979. Its further success there led to the model being extended to several other districts in the country and in 1983 it became an independent bank as a result of government legislation. Today Grameen Bank is owned by the rural poor whom it serves. Borrowers of the Bank own 90 per cent of its shares, while the remaining 10 per cent is owned by the government. It now serves over 5 million clients, and has enabled 10,000 families to escape the poverty trap every month.

Grameen Bank have moved into other areas where the same model applies – for example, Grameen Phone is one of the largest mobile telephone operators in Asia but bases its model on providing communication access to the poorest members of society through innovative pricing models.

CASE STUDY

Sometimes opportunities for innovation emerge when we reframe the way we look at something. As have seen, Henry Ford fundamentally changed the face of transportation not because he invented the motor car (he was a comparative latecomer to the new industry) nor because he developed the manufacturing process to put one together (as a craft-based specialist industry car-making had been established for around 20 years). His contribution was to change the underlying model from one which offered a handmade specialist product to a few wealthy customers to one which offered a car for Everyman at a price they could afford. The ensuing shift from craft to mass production was nothing short of a revolution in the way cars (and later countless other products and services) were created and delivered.

Recent examples of 'paradigm' innovation – changes in mental models – include the provision of online insurance and other financial services, and the repositioning of drinks like coffee and fruit juice as premium 'designer' products. Concerns about global warming and the sustainability of key resources like energy and materials are, arguably, setting the stage for some significant paradigm innovations across many sectors as firms struggle to redefine themselves and their offerings to match these major social issues.

Table 4.5 offers some examples of innovations mapped on to this 4P model.

The website has some case studies where you can see this approach being used to think about strategic direction for innovation.

BUILDING INNOVATION MANAGEMENT CAPABILITY

It would be wonderful if the solution to the innovation management problem involved one or two simple actions – for example, 'spend more money on R&D' or 'increase your market research budget'. Unfortunately extensive research on the innovation process tells us otherwise – it's less about being really good at one instrument than trying to conduct a huge orchestra and get everyone to play in time, bringing their particular skills and creativity to the process but also making sure they stay on the same page of the score – or (sometimes) that they are playing the same piece of music! Innovation researchers Keith Goffin and Rick Mitchell use the metaphor of the pentathlon in athletics – a sport where being good at one discipline is not enough – you need to master many different skills (Goffin and Mitchell, 2005).

No organization is born with a perfect capability for managing innovation. Startup entrepreneurs may be lucky and succeed first time, but even those who do would reflect on things they might have managed better. And businesses which grow beyond their first successful innovation do so by learning – through a mixture of trial and error, luck and judgment, reflection and accident, how to do it better. We can think of this process as an evolutionary one, learning and building capability over time and moving through a number of stages in maturity.

So, for example, an organization with no clear innovation strategy, with limited technological resources and no plans for acquiring more, with weak project management, with poor external links and with a rigid and unsupportive organization, would be unlikely to succeed in innovation. By contrast, one which was focused on clear strategic goals, had

Table 4.5 Some examples of innovations mapped on to the 4Ps model

Innovation type	Incremental – do what we do but better	Radical – do something different
Product – what we offer the world	– Windows 7 replacing Vista replacing XP – essentially improving on existing software idea – VW EOS replacing the Golf – essentially improving on established car design – Improved performance incandescent light bulbs	– New to the world software – for example the first speech recognition program – Toyota Prius – bringing a new concept – hybrid engines – LED-based lighting, using completely different and more energy efficient principles
Process – how we create and deliver that offering	– Improved fixed-line telephone services – Extended range of stockbroking services – Improved auction house operations – Improved factory operations – efficiency through upgraded equipment – Improved range of banking services delivered at branch banks	– Skype and other VOIP systems – Online share trading – eBay – Toyota Production System and other 'lean' approaches – Mobile banking in Kenya and the Philippines – using phones as an alternative to banking systems
Position – where we target that offering and the story we tell about it	– Haagen Dazs changing the target market for ice cream from children to consenting adults – Low-cost airlines – University of Phoenix and others, building large education businesses via online approaches to reach different markets – Dell and others segmenting and customizing computer configuration for individual users – Banking services targeted at key segments – students, retired people, etc.	– Addressing underserved markets – for example the Tata Nano which targets the huge but relatively poor Indian market using the low-cost airline model – target cost is 1 lakh (around US$3000) – 'Bottom of the pyramid' approaches using a similar principle – Aravind eye care, Cemex construction products – One laptop per child project – the US$100 universal computer – Microfinance – Grameen Bank opening up credit for the very poor
Paradigm – how we frame what we do	– Bausch and Lomb – moved from 'eye wear' to 'eye care' as their business model, effectively letting go of the old business of spectacles, sunglasses (Raybans) and contact lenses all of which were becoming commodity businesses. Instead they moved into newer high-tech fields such as laser surgery equipment, specialist optical devices and research in artificial eyesight – IBM moving from being a machine maker to a service and solution company – selling off its computer making and building up its consultancy and service side – VT moving from being a shipbuilder with roots in Victorian times to a service and facilities management business	– Grameen Bank and other microfinance models – rethinking the assumptions about credit and the poor – iTunes platform – a complete system of personalized entertainment – Rolls Royce – from high-quality aero engines to becoming a service company offering 'power by the hour' – Cirque de Soleil – redefining the circus experience

Tidd and Bessant (2009)

developed long-term links to support technological development, had a clear project management process which was well supported by senior management and which operated in an innovative organizational climate would have a better chance of success.

Let's return to our model of the process and remind ourselves of the overall process model. In essence successful innovation management is about asking questions around how well we have established this and how we continue to review and develop it. Based on the model in Figure 4.1, any organization needs to ask itself questions in five key areas:

- Do we have effective enabling mechanisms for the innovation process – to search, to select, to implement and to capture?
- Do we have a clear innovation strategy and is it communicated and deployed effectively?
- Do we have an innovative organization, one which provides a supportive climate for innovation?
- Do we build and manage rich external linkages to enable 'open innovation'?
- Do we capture learning to help us develop improved innovation management capability?

On the website there is a self-assessment audit framework to help explore these questions and identify where an organization is strong and where it might look to develop its capabilities further.

INNOVATING INNOVATION MANAGEMENT: DYNAMIC CAPABILITY

Having a model framework setting out the basic patterns of behaviour associated with successful innovation management is of enormous value – and there is good evidence that organizations can and do learn and build innovation management capability. But in a constantly changing environment that capability may not be enough – faced with moving targets along several dimensions (markets, technologies, sources of competition, regulatory rules of the game) we have to be able to adapt and change our framework. This process of constant modification and development of our innovation capability – adding new elements, reinforcing existing ones, and sometimes letting go of older and no longer appropriate ones – is the essence of what is called *dynamic capability* (Teece *et al.*, 1992).

Key questions to keep asking are:

- What do we need to do more of, to strengthen?
- What do we need to do less of, or stop?
- What new routines do we need to develop?

The risk of not continuing to ask questions is that we may find old recipes which worked in the past are no longer appropriate – and at the limit we fail to survive and grow through innovation. The earlier examples, when we were considering the 'innovation imperative' are reminders that no organization can guarantee it will last forever – it needs to change and keep changing. Some of the most disturbing research has been done in recent years on the problem of 'discontinuous innovation' – what happens when the rules of the game are suddenly changed by new technologies, changing markets or other dramatic shifts in the innovation landscape? The evidence here is that established firms and organizations are often in difficulties, but also that many of them are not blindly resistant to change – rather they try and apply their old recipes (which served them well in the past), but discover these no longer work.

On the website there are examples of 'discontinuous innovation' and some of the tools which organizations use to give themselves early warning of emerging threats and opportunities, together with an audit tool to assess capability in this area.

WORKING AT THE FRONTIER: EMERGING CHALLENGES IN MANAGING INNOVATION

In this chapter we have explored the main themes around innovation and why it is a survival and growth imperative. We need to change and keep changing – but how we do that is an important question, focusing our attention on some key strategic operations management activities. In this final section we'll look briefly into the future and try and get a sense of some of the major new areas for developing further our innovation management capability at the frontier.

Two major research projects have been trying to develop alternative pictures of how innovation will work in the future in terms of challenges and solutions – and how we might approach managing them. How will we search, what opportunities (and threats) might emerge, and what changes might we need to make to take advantage of them.

In the first, Anna Trifilova and Bettina von Stamm have pulled together a book and website drawing on the insights of nearly 400 innovation researchers from around 60 countries to paint a picture of the different ways in which 'the future of innovation' can be seen (www.thefutureofinnovation.org).

The second is a European Union funded programme – INFU (Innovation Futures for Europe) with multiple partners aiming at developing scenarios for the future of innovation. They present a variety of different scenarios and invite further elaboration and addition through an interactive website (www.innovation-futures.org).

Try visiting both websites and exploring the range of alternative futures being presented. How might you elaborate further on these search directions? What threats – and more importantly, opportunities – might be found in them?

Three themes are worth mentioning here – knowledge competition, open collective innovation, and sustainability.

Knowledge competition

First, we need to recognize that innovation is always a race in which front-runners are constantly being chased and caught. Finding something which confers sustainable and protectable competitive advantage is a key challenge – and we have come to realize that in a global economy this is not an easy task. In particular advantages of location, of access to cheap labour or raw materials, is often not sustainable, because globalization means that others can move somewhere with similar or better factor endowments. Even technology is not a good solution – having a machine with powerful and clever capabilities is not really an edge since anyone else with deep enough pockets can also buy such a machine or, if the underlying technology is protected, they can reverse engineer or even steal the ideas.

For these reasons we are beginning to think of competitive advantage as lying fundamentally in knowledge – in what we know about that we can deploy in new products or processes. This places emphasis on the aspects of innovation to do with acquiring, capturing, and managing the knowledge bases of the firm as the key task (Teece, 1997). Thinking in this way brings a new perspective to the task of managing innovation – we need to recognize that innovation is essentially a knowledge creating and deploying process (Leonard-Barton, 1992). Developing the capacity to learn becomes central to strategic operations management.

The key message here for strategic operations management is to ensure that the ways in which the organization carries out its various tasks are tuned to capturing and using knowledge. And much of this comes through learning by doing, trying things out, and capturing useful lessons from that experience for next time. The good news is that we know a lot about how to do this – as we'll see, strategic operations management is very much about learning and optimizing the systems which enable the organization to operate. For example, in Chapters 6 and 8 we will look at the ways in which employee involvement in continuous incremental improvement can build a rich knowledge base that contributes to competitive advantage. Toyota may not be the most glamorous car maker, but for the past 40 years it has been the most productive. This edge comes mainly from its ability to mobilize and manage the ideas and creativity of its huge workforce and to channel them into building a rich knowledge base.

On the website there are several cases which explore the growing role played by high involvement in supporting the innovation activity of manufacturing, service, and public sector organizations.

In Chapter 3 we saw how managing supply and logistics networks develops ways of accessing and using knowledge drawn from a rich network of collaborating players – one that can be used to deliver a stream of product, service, and process improvements. Organizations like Zara, Benetton, Dell, and Toyota owe much of their continuing competitive advantage to their abilities to mobilize and manage external knowledge through networks.

Open collective innovation

Innovation has always been a multiplayer game, one which involves weaving together many different strands of what could be termed 'knowledge spaghetti' to create something new. So building rich and extensive linkages with potential sources of innovation has always been important – for example studies in the UK in the 1950s identified one key differentiator between successful and less successful innovating firms as the degree to which they were 'cosmopolitan' as opposed to 'parochial' in their approach towards sources of innovation (Carter and Williams, 1957).

US professor Henry Chesbrough coined the term 'open innovation' to describe the challenge facing even large organizations in keeping track of and accessing external knowledge rather than relying on internally generated ideas (Chesbrough, 2003). Put simply, open innovation involves the recognition that 'not all the smart guys work for us'.

These days it's not simply new R&D knowledge about science and technology that is exploding – there are similar shifts on the market demand side, and in the interests of users in greater customization and even participation in innovation. What this means is a significant acceleration in the opening up of the innovation search game in a number of converging areas, and as more players become relevant so the challenge for strategic operations management increases.

Part of this challenge lies in making effective linkages with the outside world, and it is here that some of the core skills and tools around managing extended networks for supply and distribution have a clear role to play. IBM carries out a regular survey of chief executives about the ways in which major corporations build and sustain competitiveness. Significantly, one of the key themes to develop over the past five years has been the use of cooperative networks as a source of advantage – these days it is about learning to manage systems.

One of the early users of the 'open innovation' model was Procter and Gamble, whose Chief Executive set the ambitious target for the business of sourcing 50 per cent of its innovations form outside – a big shift for a company which had traditionally done everything itself. On the website there is a case study of 'Connect and Develop' – their name for their open innovation programme – and Roy Sandbach, a senior manager within the business explains in a podcast some of the challenges which this posed for them.

Another aspect of this challenge lies in the concept of 'user-led innovation'. As Eric von Hippel of MIT has shown over many years, the idea that users are simply passive consumers of new products and services is too simplistic (Von Hippel, 2005). Most users have views, opinions, ideas, and reactions to those innovations, and a significant proportion are prepared to put their frustration, inspiration or desire for something different into action and create their own products. Often these are simple sketches or crude prototypes but they can be picked up by manufacturing and service organizations, polished, and developed to the point where they are offered to the wider marketplace.

This pattern is clear in many studies of innovation and in some sectors – like medical devices – the role of specialist user innovators is of key strategic importance. But the emergence of powerful communication technologies which enable the active cooperation of user communities in co-creation and diffusion of innovations has accelerated the trend. Organizations now need to look hard at the potential contribution of users as active co-creators of innovation, a trend reflected in much of the work on 'mass customization' (Pine, 1993).

Once again, there is both a challenge for strategic operations management and an opportunity to build on strengths. Lessons learned about close customer linkages – especially in service operations – mean that there is already a proven set of tools and techniques on which to draw. And much of the work on the 'servitization' of manufacturing (see Chapter 2) suggests the need to spread this service perspective into co-creation with users as they become active partners in long-term service-based relationships.

On the website there are several cases – especially Lego and Threadless.com – which highlight the growing role of users as co-creators in the innovation process. The podcast interview about Anaesthetic Medical Systems illustrates the principle of user-led innovation, and there are also links to some videos produced by Eric von Hippel, one of the founding figures in this field of innovation management research.

Sustainability

The final area in which there are significant future challenges for the strategic operations manager in managing the innovation process lies in the concept of sustainability. One of the implicit problems in innovation is that it assumes anything is possible, that there is always something new in product or process. The trouble with this view is that it ignores the fact that we live on a planet with finite resources, many of which are not renewable. Increasingly there is public concern about changes which appear to have negative effects on the world we live in or on quality of life – not just for ourselves but throughout the value chain, from raw material to finished product. People like new designs in furniture, for example, but are no longer so interested when they find that such innovative products are made by destroying a non-renewable teak forest in Indonesia.

On the website is a video interview with Melissa Clark-Reynolds, founder of Minimonos, an online game to help raise awareness of sustainability issues amongst children.

Thinking about more sustainable products and forms of consumption is becoming increasingly important and is affecting many aspects of operations management. The challenge in the context of innovation is to harness the creativity within the organization to find product and process ideas which contribute to sustainability whilst also preserving and developing business opportunities.

The website has a case example of Philips and how this major corporation is restructuring its innovation process to make sustainability a core feature in its future products and services, and in its internal processes.

Related to this is the question of innovations to provide goods and services for the 4 to 5 billion people currently living at the 'bottom of the pyramid' in economic terms – earning less than US$2 per day. Much work is now going on at the innovation frontier to create radically different solutions to meet the needs of this group, and there is a major question about whether ideas developed in this laboratory – for example, around low-cost health care or transportation – may eventually diffuse back to 'mainstream' economies.

There are several case examples of 'bottom of the pyramid' innovations on the website, including the Aravind Eye Clinics and Grameen Bank, and there is also a podcast interview with Girish Prabhu of Shristi Labs, an Indian organization specializing in developing such solutions.

SUMMARY

- Innovation is not a luxury but an imperative – it is essential for survival and growth.
- Although the process is uncertain, it is not a lottery – evidence shows that it can be managed to competitive advantage.
- The key to this lies in recognizing that it is a *process* like any other in organizational life, the difference being that this process is concerned with renewing the things an organization offers and the ways in which it creates and delivers them. Managing the process is thus of central concern in strategic operations management.
- Operations management plays a central and pivotal role in the development process within innovation.

KEY QUESTIONS

1. 'Invention is not enough' was the response given by a major designer/manufacturer when asked about the secrets of successful innovation. What other factors need to be managed to ensure a good idea makes it through to successful implementation?
2. We have only scratched the surface of the topic of innovation in this chapter and have presented a general model of how the process works. What factors (for example, sector, type of product, etc.) might shape the ways in which a particular firm needs to go about the process? How might they affect its management?

3. Introducing process innovation – change in 'the way we do things around here' – can be thought of in the same way as trying to launch a new product in the commercial marketplace. What similarities and differences might there be between the two, and what messages emerge for the successful management of both?

4. 'Innovation is a survival imperative, not a luxury.' Thinking of an organization with which you are familiar, think about whether this statement applies – and if it does, what kinds of innovation can you trace in its history? What triggered them, and what difference did they make?

5. In this chapter we have positioned innovation as a core process in the business, concerned with renewing what the organization offers and the ways in which it does so. This process operates in parallel with those concerned with the present-day operations – managing supply through to satisfying customers. Inevitably there will be points of conflict between managing today and building for the future. Where do you think these 'flashpoints' might emerge, and how would you deal with them as an operations manager?

FURTHER READING

Bason, C. (2011) *Leading Public Sector Innovation*, London: Policy Press.

Bessant, J.R. and Tidd J. (2011) *Innovation and Entrepreneurship*, Chichester: Wiley.

Chesbrough, H. (2003) *Open Innovation: The New Imperative for Creating and Profiting from Technology*, Boston, MA: Harvard Business School Press.

Chesbrough, H. (2011) *Open Services Innovation*, San Francisco, CA: Jossey Bass.

Christensen, C., Anthony, S. and Roth, E. (2007) *Seeing What's Next*, Boston, MA: Harvard Business School Press.

Freeman, C. and Soete L. (1997) *The Economics of Industrial Innovation*, Cambridge, MA: MIT Press.

Kelley, T., Littman, J. and Peters, T. (2001) *The Art of Innovation: Lessons in Creativity from Ideo, America's Leading Design Firm*, New York: Currency.

Prahalad, C.K. (2006) *The Fortune at the Bottom of the Pyramid*, New Jersey: Wharton School Publishing.

Tidd, J. and Bessant J. (2009) *Managing Innovation: Integrating Technological, Market and Organizational Change*, Chichester: John Wiley and Sons.

Verganti, R. (2009) *Design Driven Innovation*, Boston, MA: Harvard Business School Press.

Von Hippel, E. (2005) *The Democratization of Innovation*, Cambridge, MA: MIT Press.

REFERENCES

Adams, R. (2006) 'Innovation management measurement: A review', *International Journal of Management Reviews*, 8(1), 21–47.

American Bar Association (2001) *Annual Report*, Chicago, IL: American Bar Association.

Augsdorfer, P. (1996) *Forbidden Fruit*, Aldershot: Avebury.

Bason, C. (2011) *Leading Public Sector Innovation*, London: Policy Press.

Baumol, W. (2002) *The Free-Market Innovation Machine: Analyzing the Growth Miracle of Capitalism*, Princeton, NJ: Princeton University Press.

Bessant, J.R., Richards, S. and Hughes, T. (2010) *Beyond Light Bulbs and Pipelines: Leading and Nurturing Innovation in the Public Sector.* Sunningdale: Sunningdale Institute, National School of Government.

Bessant, J.R. and Tidd J. (2011) *Innovation and Entrepreneurship*, Chichester: Wiley.

Bright, A. (1949) *The Electric Lamp Industry: Technological Change and Economic Development from 1800 to 1947*, New York: Macmillan.

Carter, C. and Williams, B. (1957) *Industry and Technical Progress.* Oxford: Oxford University Press.

Chesbrough, H. (2003) *Open Innovation: The New Imperative for Creating and Profiting from Technology.* Boston, MA: Harvard Business School Press.

Chesbrough, H. (2011) *Open Services Innovation*, San Francisco, CA: Jossey Bass.

Christensen, C., Anthony, S. and Roth, E. (2007) *Seeing What's Next*, Boston, MA: Harvard Business School Press.

Clementi, D. (2004) *Report of the Review of the Regulatory Framework for Legal Services in England and Wales*, London: Department of Business, Economics and Regulatory Reform.

Codexx Consultants (2006) 'Process innovation in legal services', London.

Drucker, P. (1985) *Innovation and entrepreneurship*, New York: Harper and Row.

de Geus, A. (1996) *The Living Company*, Boston, MA: Harvard Business School Press.

Ernst, H. (2002) 'Success factors of new product development: A review of the empirical literature', *International Journal of Management Reviews*, 4(1), 1–40.

Evans, P. and Wurster, T. (2000) *Blown to Bits: How the New Economics of Information Transforms Strategy*, Cambridge, MA: Harvard Business School Press.

Freeman, C. and Soete, L. (1997) *The Economics of Industrial Innovation*, 3rd edition, Cambridge, MA: MIT Press.

Goffin, K. and Mitchell, R. (2005) *Innovation Management*, London: Pearson.

Kelley, T., Littman, J. and Peters, T. (2001) *The Art of Innovation: Lessons in Creativity from Ideo, America's Leading Design Firm*, New York: Currency.

Leonard-Barton, D. (1992) 'Core capabilities and core rigidities: A paradox in new product development', *Strategic Management Journal*, 13, 111–25.

Leonard-Barton, D. (1995) *Wellsprings of Knowledge: Building and Sustaining the Sources of Innovation*, Boston, MA: Harvard Business School Press.

Goffin, K. and Mitchell, R. (2005) 'Is Europe losing its innovative edge', *European Business Forum*, Issue 22, Autumn, pp. 17–18.

Pine, B. J. (1993) *Mass Customisation: The New Frontier in Business Competition*, Cambridge, MA: Harvard University Press.

Prahalad, C.K. (2006) *The Fortune at the Bottom of the Pyramid*, New Jersey: Wharton School Publishing.

Teece, D., Pisano, G. and Shuen, A. (1992) *Dynamic Capabilities and Strategic Management*, Berkley, CA: University of Berkeley.

Teece, D., Pisano, G. and Shuen, A. (1997) 'Dynamic capabilities and strategic management', *Strategic Management Journal*, 18(7), 509–33.

Tidd, J. and Bessant, J. (2009) *Managing Innovation: Integrating Technological, Market and Organizational Change*, 4th edition, Chichester: John Wiley.

Utterback, J. (1994) *Mastering the dynamics of innovation*, Boston, MA: Harvard Business School Press.

Verganti, R. (2009) *Design Driven Innovation.* Boston, MA: Harvard Business School Press.

Von Hippel, E. (2005). *The Democratization of Innovation*, Cambridge, MA: MIT Press.

Womack, J., Jones, D.and Roos, D. (1991) *The Machine that Changed the World*, New York: Rawson Associates.

CHAPTER 5

SUSTAINABILITY

> ## LEARNING OBJECTIVES
>
> The purpose of this chapter is to introduce you to the basic framework, scope, and management of activities involved in strategic operations management and to help you to:
>
> - Understand why sustainability is a competitiveness issue.
> - Gain insights into how it may be brought into day-to-day decision making in operations.
> - Gain some specific knowledge of topics and access an extensive wealth of resources on the subject via the internet.
> - Perhaps formulate your own personal approach to the subject, in concept or practice, as an operations strategist.

So much has been written and argued about sustainability (also called corporate social responsibility, sustainable development, and so on) in the last three decades that it is normal to accept it as a well recognized factor in strategic decision making, in design, in energy generation, in logistics, and in operations management. Its meaning, and perhaps its implications, remain poorly understood at the detailed operating level and are perhaps obscured by passionate arguments on whether or not the human race is responsible for global warming, or climate change, which is now clearly evident (whatever is causing it).

In the early chapters of this book we noted that the current business environment means that operations must be managed in a way that will enable the firm to compete against extensive and increasing levels of competition from around the world. Sustainability is very much part of this increased competition. At present it is open to interpretation, but as its implications become clearer, and perhaps some consensus is reached, it is likely to become more central in strategic competition between business organizations. It will always have its detractors, who are perhaps biased by political or commercial interests.

In this chapter we shall explore the ways in which operations strategists need to incorporate knowledge of sustainability in their decision making and other activities – as a business issue. You might find some of this knowledge rather exotic but that is the nature of the concept. It requires a combination of business thinking, science, politics, history, and human behaviour, wrapped up in implications for operations management. We shall explore concepts such as resource scarcity and endangered materials, carbon trading and life-cycle assessment, and revisit leanness and *muda*. We shall take a critical look at ideas such as corporate social responsibility and grapple with the combined effect of population growth and levels of consumption.

It is important to emphasize at the outset that this will be a very practical view of sustainability – we are not concerned here with the moral health of the human race, nor 'saving the planet'. When viewed at its broadest level, sustainability includes issues of ethics, fairness, equity, security, and many other global-level concerns. These and many other profound debates are naturally of the greatest importance for the twenty-first century, but they are to be dealt with in other places. To prepare the operations strategist, however, it is important to consider the impacts of the decisions they may have to make through this broad 'lens'. Some of the findings may be surprising.

A DEFINITION: THE 'TRIPLE BOTTOM LINE'

The term 'sustainability' was defined by the UN's Brundtland Commission in 1987, as 'development that meets the needs of the present without compromising the ability of future generations to meet their own needs'. A year later, Sir John Elkington formed the think tank, 'Sustainability' in the UK. In 1994, he coined the term 'triple bottom line of 21st century business' (Elkington, 1997). It is usually represented as a Venn diagram with three overlapping circles. They are labelled 'economic', 'environment', and 'social'. In some later versions these are replaced by other terms – Elkington himself developed a version labelled 'profit', 'planet', and 'people'. The three single overlaps sometimes have labels, e.g. 'bearable', 'equitable', and 'viable' but the triple overlap at the centre is always 'sustainability' or 'sustainable development'. For his part, Elkington famously did not trademark it and indeed ensured that 'no one could protect it' (Elkington, 2004): see Figure 5.1.

The point of the triple bottom line is to remind strategic decision makers that all three aspects need to be taken into account in order to develop sustainably: simply focusing on one (as business organizations often do) or two, is not enough and will simply build up problems that will emerge later. In other words, ignoring part of this triple bottom line leads to unsustainable activity. Until now, the business strategist may have recognized this but felt that there was time to make money from such activity and get out before the problems took effect. One purpose of this chapter is to show that this may no longer be an option for operations strategists.

Figure 5.1 An example of the 'triple bottom line'. See the video at: www. howtodothings.com/video/john-elkingtons-triple-bottom-line

THE PROSPECTS: 2010–2050 – NOT SURPRISING BUT PERHAPS ALARMING

Two things are undeniable: in the last 50 years the human population of the Earth has more than doubled: from 3.1 billion in 1961 to 6.8 billion. Secondly, each of us in the developed – and developing – world (West and East) is using up a great deal more in terms of raw materials than we were in 1961. Some of these materials cannot be replaced. Others can, but only over time. The combination of these two facts leads us to the challenge for operations strategy.

The rate of population growth naturally varies from region to region and this is expected to continue. Reasons for this include such things as birth control (or lack of it), fertility rates, and social, political or religious regimes (see below). We are not concerned primarily with such things; it is simply the practical impacts and their implications that we need to understand. Data on population from the UN Development Programme are shown in Table 5.1 and Figure 5.2, and they tally with other forecasts. Note that about 90 per cent of the increased population in the coming decades will be born in what might now be called 'have-not' countries.

Population growth is not new, of course, but it has naturally not occurred on this scale before (see Figure 5.3). In debates about its effects, it is usually not long before someone will mention Robert Malthus (1766–1834), a British economist who argued that the human race would gradually become unable to feed itself, as population would expand exponentially while food production would increase only arithmetically. It is worthwhile considering his ideas here, in our current practical context.

Malthus was angered by contemporary theologians who preached that mankind was immortal as a species, or race, on earth with the concomitant notion that all technological

Table 5.1 Population growth forecast, 2010–2050 (billions)

	Year	
Region	2010	2050
Africa	1.00	2.00
Asia	4.10	5.20
Europe	0.73	0.69
USA/Canada	0.35	0.48
Latin America	0.58	0.73
World	**6.76**	**9.10**

UNDP (2010)

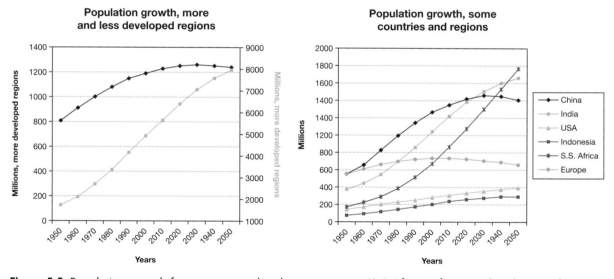

Figure 5.2 Population growth forecasts – graphical representation (S.S. Africa refers to Sub-Saharan Africa)
United Nations Population Division (2006)

progress and growth were good and without threats to human existence and prosperity. In short: God would find a way. He was writing early in the industrial revolution, before its impacts were fully realized, so it could be argued that the methods of production that developed soon afterwards reduced the value of his argument against this credo. Indeed, farming in the early twentieth century was seeing annual increases of 10 per cent in productivity and has continued to extract more and more from each hectare of land ever since. More recently, for example, it has become possible to grow a tree (at least for pulp and paper industry) in just seven years, rather than the 30 or so traditionally allowed.

However, Malthus's solution, far from seeking increased outputs through innovation, was to avoid supporting the poor – effectively to let them perish through famine and disease. This was widely ridiculed even in 1798; today it would be unthinkable, although some of the disasters in Africa exhibit some of the characteristics (see Diamond, 2005, Ch. 10, for the terrible story of Rwanda). Despite regional atrocities, the present situation – with anomalies such as: 1 billion people are illiterate; only 700 million people have no access to a mobile phone signal but 1.3 billion have no access to clean water; and two thirds of the world's population live on less than $2 a day– is generally seen as a shared, global problem. Malthus also had a very narrow, Western (or even British) focus. For example, he wrote at one point that 'The state of the poor in China would not be improved by an increase in wealth from manufactures.' He also opposed free trade, which would put him at odds with most modern thinking. So, we can't look to Malthus for an answer.

Meanwhile, there are still many people who believe that God will find a way to solve the economic problems caused by humans. For example, when Texas Governor Rick Perry organized a seven-hour 'prayer and fasting' event in Houston in August 2011, 30,000 people turned up and prayed fervently to ask God to provide a way out of the US's massive economic recession. On that day, Standard and Poor's reduced the US credit rating from AAA to AA+, the country's sovereign debt stood at around US$14 trillion, over a quarter of it owed to foreign creditors (including China at US$1.4 trillion, and Japan at US$900 billion), and its trade deficit was US$700 billion (the deficit with China being US$350 billion).

Ironically, Malthus, a clergyman, opposed birth control, an exacerbation of the population problem caused by social pressures and religious and political regimes which remains to this day. In centrally-planned, Communist China, the family-planning policy which limits each

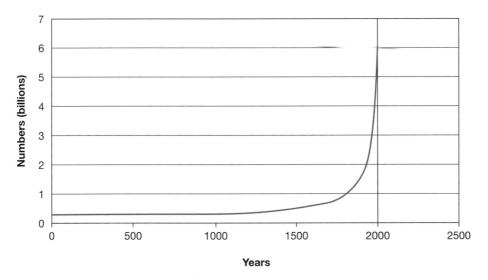

Figure 5.3 Population growth in the past

United Nations Population Division, *The World at Six Billion*, www.population-growth-migration.info/population.html

urban married couple to just one child has been in force since 1978, at a time when the population of China had almost doubled in less than four decades (563 million in 1950 to more than 1 billion in the early 1980s). The policy is said to affect just over a third of the population. Leaving aside any discussion of the moral or social implications of such a policy, it is clear that this policy has helped China to control population growth, reportedly preventing 250 million births over this period. The population is now 1.34 billion and it is expected to be about the same in 2040. India, meanwhile, will grow from 1.15 billion now to 1.52 billion by 2040. In the same period, Africa is expected to double from 1 billion to 2 billion.

Political initiatives are not only used to restrict population growth. In Malaysia, a government-backed scheme to develop and favour the indigenous Bumiputra population (Islamic with Malay ethnic origins), called the New Economic Policy (1971), included an attempt to address the imbalance that existed, with the Malaysian 'Straits' Chinese then representing 45 per cent of the population (and a very much higher majority proportion of economic ownership). At the time, the population was around 10 million (1960). By 2010, the population was 28 million, with Bumiputra representing 60.3 per cent and the Chinese 22.9 per cent.

Little wonder, then, that the twenty-first century is generally recognized as the century of Asia (see Sachs, 2008, p. 3).

All this might be good news for operations strategists – a massive increase in the numbers of consumers and sources of supply. For three decades the West has lived with the immediate but welcome challenges or opportunities of such unregulated growth: how best to transfer manufacturing and service operations from Europe to Asia ('offshoring') to exploit low wages in developing countries and cheap global transportation, to feed the demands of the growing and increasingly affluent Western (and latterly, Eastern) populations. The challenge that now has to be faced is rather different, however. Less welcome and much more complicated, it originates in the propensity of people to consume.

Something that Malthus could never have foreseen (although he does come tantalizingly close to it once or twice) is the fact that the resources of the earth are not only finite (we have just the one planet) but have actually been steadily depleted by the human lifestyle that has emerged over the twentieth century. Once a certain level of consumption is exceeded (i.e. the balanced or sustainable level), we start eating into the capital (the Earth) in addition to harvesting its renewable outputs. In supply chain terms, our sole supplier of raw materials is not only being asked to provide more than 100 per cent (and by only one of its customers – we are not the only species), it is also seeing its capacity disappear.

How can we measure this to express it as something operations strategists can understand and deal with? Fortunately, there are data on it, tracking the trends. One source is freely available and, while one should always get more than one view on something this important, it is robust enough to explore here.

The Living Planet Report (LPR), issued by the World-Wide Fund for Nature (WWF) every two years, tracks the levels of consumption of the human race and the impacts upon our sole supplier of physical resources: the Earth (see http://panda.org/downloads/lpr2010. pdf). Two principal factors are of importance to operations strategists in planning their processes, supplies, and outputs. These are the level of resources available (for Earth, this is called 'bio capacity') and the amount each person consumes (including how it is obtained and disposed of).

The first of these is not difficult to understand. The LPR expresses it as an area of the Earth's surface that each person uses up each year as a result of everything they consume (eat, drink, wear, drive, use to warm or illuminate themselves, play with, live in, or use in everyday life). The measure includes generating the item and disposing of it. It then compares this, globally and nationally, with the Earth's usable land area and fisheries (about 13.6 billion hectares.) The LPR estimates that, on average, consumption has more than quadrupled between 1961 and 2001, from 0.5 hectares per person (about 60 per cent of a football pitch) to 2.3 hectares (more than three football pitches). Note that the land may be anywhere on the Earth's surface, depending on the geographical location of the available source of the material. This leads to the use of the term *global hectare* or 'gha'.

It is not difficult to see the logic in this: in 1961 there were few, or no, central heating and air conditioning systems, computers, automatic washing machines and tumble driers, dishwashers, multi-car households, colour televisions, personal electronics, mobile phones, holidays and business trips involving extensive flying, motorways, plastic packaging, and factors in general over-consumption, such as junk food (in supermarkets or fast food outlets), direct marketing and avaricious youth cultures. There were fewer cars, none of the absurd use of fashionable but wasteful four-wheel-drive vehicles for domestic purposes, and less exotic diets. On a global level, there were far fewer conurbations consuming energy and materials: the massive expansion in the Middle East, South East Asia and Western developments such as East London and Berlin had yet to begin.

Again, an increase in consumption is *prima facie* good news for operations strategists – just think of all those customers for products and services and suppliers of materials and components!

But if we combine the population growth and the consumption growth, the positive aspect of such increases reveals the problem: the 'supply' of 13.6 billion gha is fixed (we have just the one planet, even though innovation may allow us to exploit its resources more efficiently, reaching new sources of oil, metals, minerals, etc. and perhaps emitting less CO_2 in the process). The demands upon it have increased (1961–2001) from 3.1 billion × 0.5 gha to 6.2 billion × 2.3 gha (WWF, 2010). In other words, in 2001, the demand of the human race on the planet equated to 14.26 billion global hectares of resources (materials, energy, food, etc.) – more than the planet's capacity. By 2010, the LPR reveals that the human race was drawing resources from the planet at the rate of 1.5 'Earths' on average, with countries such as Europe and North America living at three or five times higher than this (note that the urban regeneration that partly fuels this consumption started several decades earlier in the US than elsewhere). This means that the Earth would need 1.5 years to replace the resources used in one year by the human race.

One way to think about this is to imagine having capital in the bank – say £1,000,000 – and living entirely off the interest (say £50,000 a year at 5 per cent). If your lifestyle means you actually spend, say, £75,000 a year, you have to start spending your capital. Gradually your capital lessens and thus generates less interest; so, you spend more of your capital and eventually have nothing left. Of course, long before you ran out of money, you would go into a depressed, perhaps desperate state. If the Earth's resources are the capital (13.6 hectares of land and fisheries) and its available resources are interest, then we are currently spending 50 per cent more than the income generated by the interest – 150 per cent of our interest. In fact, in Europe, the figure is typically 300 per cent. So, if your income is £50,000 p.a. but your lifestyle costs £75,000 p.a. to maintain, and you want to keep your home, you have to change your lifestyle. Figure 5.4 shows how our global home capital is being depleted while our global lifestyle expenditure increases.

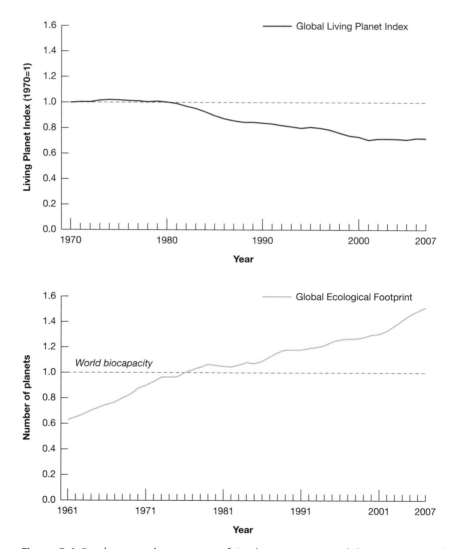

Figure 5.4 Depletion in the capacity of Earth's resources and the increase in global demand. Also, see the video: www.ted.com/talks/lang/eng/jason_clay_how_big_brands_can_save_biodiversity.html

WWF (2010)

Here are some interesting observations made by the WWF in relation to this. They all have relevance for business:

- The average US citizen consumes 43 times each year as much as the average African.
- The average European cat has a larger environmental footprint in its lifetime than the average citizen of Chad.
- Income, and thus expenditure, in developing countries is expected to grow by 500 per cent between 2010 and 2050.
- To supply this, we would have to triple production of goods and services and at the same time reduce use of resources by 33 per cent on today's rate of consumption.
- The Earth's 6.9 billion consumers speak 7,000 languages (350 of them 'major' languages) and fewer than 1 per cent of Chinese speak English.

What implications would a rational business person take from this, in business terms? Perhaps the first two bullet points would suggest that European cat food and accessories looks like a good business? Or, let's try to supply as much as possible to the US (ignoring the fact that the US is living well beyond its means and frequently at risk of not being able to pay its bills). The third point might make us turn our attention East and South, but the last two points might blow our rationale.

Think what would happen if the African nations, as they increase from 1 billion to 2 billion, increased their consumption by five times, largely financed by China, a scenario not hard to imagine. It would still be nowhere near the current North American lifestyle (bullet point one) but the demands on the planet would overwhelm the systems of production (point four). The problem emerges as one of resources – especially getting hold of them in the first place in the face of massively increased competition. We also know that wealth is not evenly spread in such development; very often, a few get very rich indeed while the masses remain in poverty.

So, what can operations strategists do about all this? Is it possible to operate differently in order to run a sustainable 'one planet' business? Can innovation increase the effective biocapacity of the planet by providing solutions that produce more for less? The science itself may be difficult to incorporate but the principle is clear: use a great deal less in your operations (and waste less) but also recognize that your sources of supply may give you less as resources get scarce, and your customers (who may increase massively in number) may individually want to buy less as they start to work in a similar manner – a very different picture from the last 50 years of 'conspicuous consumption' and unsustainable growth.

We shall explore this in three parts: our inputs (supply chain management); our processes (manufacturing and services); and our outputs (products and services, byproducts, and unintended consequences). First, though, we shall deal with some general issues and principles that impact on each part of this.

GENERAL THEMES

Corporate social responsibility

CSR, as it is widely known, has been a hot topic of conversation for three decades during which time it has frequently been under attack from all sides. For the business analyst, for example, the suggestion that a reputation for being 'responsible' could add anything to a company's market value was sometimes greeted with derision. Meanwhile environmentalists often saw it as a cynical nod towards their agenda. The expression was coined at the same time as 'stakeholder', another term that has often caused controversy.

Gradually the concept has gained acceptance, with companies including CSR in their annual reports and even their advertising campaigns. Companies such as Nespresso have made great play of their Sustainable Coffee Network, (see www.nespresso.com/ecolaboration) while other organizations have been formed especially to address the SCR agenda – notably Fairtrade (www.fairtrade.org.uk/). Meanwhile, supermarkets stress the ethical and environmentally sound provenance of their produce, with varying degrees of accuracy. And a whole industry of auditing claims has built up, sometimes with *causes celebres* to reveal: see Case 5.1.

CASE STUDY

CASE 5.1: TOP TUNA BRAND DROPS ENVIRONMENTAL CLAIM

In January 2011, Princes, one of Britain's biggest tuna brands, agreed to drop an environmental claim from its tins following an investigation by Greenpeace. The environmental group had complained to the UK Office of Fair Trading that Princes' labelling was misleading the public, and dubbed its tuna 'the tin full of sin.' Princes said it would immediately ditch labelling that claimed that its fishing methods protected the environment and marine life, and would instead refer shoppers to an environmental statement on its website.

In a survey, Greenpeace had ranked Princes, then supplying one third of the UK's tinned tuna, bottom of eight branded and supermarket own-brand tunas for sustainability. John West, another big tuna company, was ranked second bottom.

Both companies were heavily reliant on 'purse seining,' a fishing method which scoops up and kills all marine life congregating under fixed rafts known as fish aggregating devices (FADS) including sharks and turtles; see www.greenpeace.org.uk/blog/oceans/purse-seining-when-fishing-methods-go-bad-20100518. Despite this, Princes had been stating on its labels: 'Princes is fully committed to fishing methods which protect the marine environment and marine life.' Greenpeace researchers and Hugh Fearnley-Whittingstall, the TV chef who led the 2011 *Fishfight* campaign (www.fishfight.net/), questioned that claim.

Ahead of a national television programme fronted by Fearnley-Whittingstall, a Princes spokeswoman told *The Independent*: 'We were going to commit to remove our label anyway and we have brought that forward a little.' The new label will read: 'To view our seafood sustainability statement, visit princes.co.uk.'

At the same time, Britain's biggest supermarket, Tesco, announced that it was abandoning purse seining and would move to the more sustainable pole and line method by 2012. Tesco said: 'We've been moving in this direction for some time – just recently we increased the proportion of pole-and-line to 25 per cent of our own brand canned tuna as a step towards our goal.' Greenpeace had been intending to rank Tesco last in its table but, following its change of heart, ranked it fourth, behind Sainsbury's, Marks & Spencer and Waitrose which already sold only pole and line caught tuna. (Some months later, Fearnely-Whittingstall, long a thorn in Tesco's side, publicly praised the supermarket's efforts to become more sustainable on their fish range.)

Joss Garman, campaigner for Greenpeace, said: 'This climb down is an admission that Princes have been caught red handed. Thousands of sharks, turtles and possibly even dolphins are being caught in Princes tuna nets, and all when they could use other greener fishing methods like Sainsbury's already do.' (Note that Dr David Gibson, of the UK National Marine Aquarium in Plymouth, estimates that the global population of sharks has been reduced by 90 per cent over the past 15 to 20 years.)

The Independent (Martin Hickman), Wednesday, 12 January 2011

The UN has issued *Principles for Responsible Investment* (www.unpri.org) and there is a draft international standard for Social Responsibility: ISO 26000, issued in May 2010 (www.iso.org/iso/social_responsibility). Interestingly, the draft standard includes some very clear assurances that ISO 26000 is not intended for certification purposes (as ISO 9000 and 14000 were), perhaps reflecting just how complex and non-standardized approaches to CSR (or just 'SR') are perceived.

For some time, the suggestion has been made by observers that the term CSR should be replaced by 'sustainable development'. In the last few years, academics, led by Michael Porter and Mark Kramer, have gone further, developing an alternative concept of 'creating shared value' or CSV, presenting it as a direct replacement for CSR (see Porter and Kramer, 2007; 2011). This concept, and its explanation, has a 'business' and 'strategy' feel to it, possibly making it appealing to managers and policy makers.

The operations strategist will probably be operating within a CSR policy drawn up by the organization, with some well defined codes of practice, working in combination with other constraints (such as health and safety procedures). To an extent, then, CSR is something that must be taken into account within operations in a regulatory manner. Inevitably, some existing practices will fall foul of CSR principles and so the regulation may be seen as an unwelcome constraint. As we shall see below, however, it is quite possible for the operations manager to affect the organization's sustainability through innovation and different thinking.

Life-cycle assessment/analysis

LCA, as it is known, is a technique for framing decision making about the process (and sub-processes) associated with a product or service from the point of its creation to the point of its end. The Royal Society of Chemists defines it as:

a tool that can be used to assess the environmental impacts of a product, process or service from design to disposal i.e. across its entire lifecycle, a so called cradle to grave approach. The impacts on the environment may be beneficial or adverse. These impacts are sometimes referred to as the 'environmental footprint' of a product or service. LCA involves the collection and evaluation of quantitative data on the inputs and outputs of material, energy and waste flows associated with a product over its entire life cycle so that the environmental impacts can be determined.

(See http://www.rsc.org/images/LCA_20100215_
tcm18-97943.pdf)

The ardent environmentalist would take issue with the RSC over the phrase 'cradle to grave', preferring 'cradle to cradle' to remind us that materials should always be recycled (see McDonough and Braungart, 2009). The idea is well established, however: at each stage of its life, a product or service impacts the environment in some way. An assessment at each stage of the life cycle should show where impacts – environmental or ethical – can be lessened (the link with CSR is clear). The history of LCA includes much learned debate and occasionally heated argument, and there is little agreement on how to measure impact (much as there is no agreement on how to measure the temperature of the Earth).

For the operations manager, the process-oriented thinking idea behind LCA may hold an appeal, for analysing both internal activities and investigating up and down the supply chain. Advice from the parent organization should be sought on preferences for the corporate LCA approach (which should exist and should be easily available) rather than 'going it alone'. One key realization is that some products cause more environmental damage (and are thus unsustainable) in their production than in their use. We shall explore this later.

Externalities

In addressing the sustainability agenda it is important to consider unintended consequences of operations strategies. Economists call these 'externalities' – things you think you can safely ignore in planning your business. For example, some years back, lung cancer due to smoking would have been an externality for restaurant owners; now it is a constraint and very much an operational issue. Before 2010, BP thought that the risk of not quite meeting regulation could be considered an externality (i.e. the risk of a fine, probably easily accommodated, if found out), and learned an expensive lesson, in the Gulf of Mexico disaster, as a result: it was not an externality. There is currently little or no control of the pollution caused by sea transportation although there is an increasing recognition that it is a major cause of acidification of the oceans: an externality under consideration? (See, for an introduction, www.stateoftheocean.org/ipso-2011-workshop-summary.cfm.)

Imagine what would happen to supply chains and global sourcing if the real costs of sea transport were increased to reflect the damage done by shipping. In several countries in the world, governments are being asked to avoid cutting down rainforests because of the disastrous effects this would have on the climate in neighbouring countries. As we shall see below, one-planet issues do not observe national boundaries.

Clearly there is a need for innovation in operations that deliver products and services – to enable us to sustain our business. A reduction in local impact is one thing (use less, recycle more, etc.) but the impacts of operations are clearly global and so the scope of decision making has to include factors far afield. For example, during the 1990s the citizens of Los Angeles cleaned up the smog that had famously choked them for years. LA was clear and bright. Now it is suffering again from choking pollution. But it is not of its own making, or its own solution: it is estimated that at least 25 per cent of the pollution is borne across the Pacific on trade winds from China. For the Chinese this is an externality, but for how long? So, we are talking about open, or shared innovation. China's carbon emissions almost doubled between 1997 and 2005, with the share attributable to exports rising from 12 per cent in 1987, to 21 per cent in 2002 and 30 per cent by 2005 (Weber and Matthews, 2008).

Endangered elements

Most of us are familiar with resource depletion through overconsumption, although in the West we do not often feel the effect. To start with a simple example, let's consider the fish that we eat. We have already considered some of the ethical issues (in Case 5.1), and the charts in Figure 5.5 illustrate another aspect of overconsumption. The research from which these charts originate measures the amount of fish (by ton) found per square kilometre. The headline is that 50 per cent of wild fisheries in the North Atlantic are now fully exploited; 25 per cent are over-exploited; and 75 per cent face commercial extinction. Can this be addressed through fish farming? Perhaps, but this marine agribusiness has its own problems.

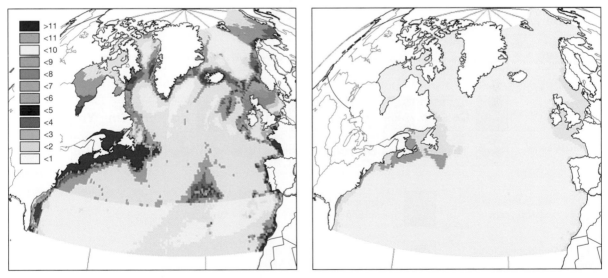

Year: 1900   Year: 2000

Figure 5.5 Biomass of table fish in North Atlantic fisheries (tons per km²)

Christensen *et al.* (2003)

It is important to emphasize that data such as these present a managerial choice: should an operations strategist consider changing what they do and if so when? Consider the forecasts shown in Figure 5.6 about endangered elements. We may accept that for our grandchildren the tiger will be as dead as the dodo is for us – and that we can do little about it; there are 3,000 in the wild today compared with 100,000 in 1900, and 5,000 in captivity. But, what if supplies of materials common today were to be exhausted?

Mike Pitts, a British research chemist working on sustainability in Government-funded research, estimates that at present rates of consumption, limited availability of lithium is a future risk to supply, and that zinc is at serious threat in the next 100 years. Does this matter to business? What are the implications of 'business as usual?' At present, perhaps all that can be done is to collect intelligence and make informed decisions: the timescale, or your horizon, is up to you.

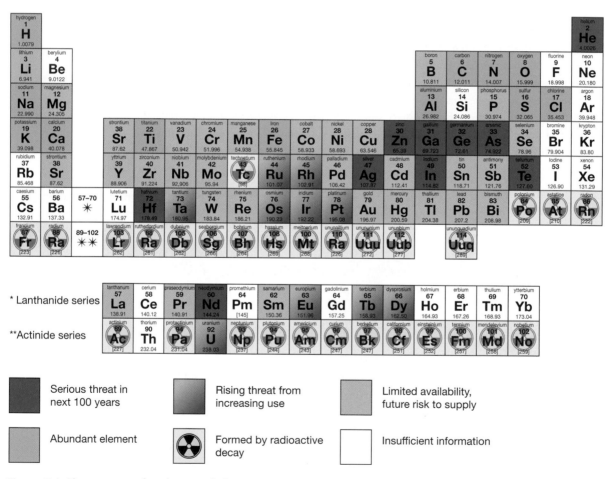

Figure 5.6 The concept of endangered elements

M Pitts, Sustainability Manager Chemistry Innovation KTN, UK Technology Strategy Board, www.chemistryinnovation.co.uk/roadmap/sustainable/roadmap.asp?previd=425&id=426

A worrying example of this is the case of the rare earth substances neodymium (Nd) and dysprosium (Dy). Both are used in the production of high-performance magnets (such as those used in medical scanners and high-quality earphones) and hybrid vehicles (see Case 5.4). Both are mainly found in China, whose policy is believed to entail restricting exports and retaining the materials for domestic production only. There are other sources for neodymium (Brazil, USA, India, and Australia) while 99 per cent of dysprosium comes from China (further sources exist in problematic countries such as Burma), but estimates based upon current manufacturing forecasts suggest that demand for these substances will significantly exceed supply by 2014. By this time, the large automobile manufacturers plan to be making large numbers of hybrid vehicles.

Carbon

It is now widely judged that by far the greatest constraint on the Earth's biocapacity (its ability to provide resources) is the growth of carbon emissions (so-called 'anthropogenic greenhouse gases' or GHGs), and this is why there has been so much attention to this subject. A great deal of regulation and legislation is now in place, or on the way, that will affect decision making for operations managers. We'll consider these below, as they apply to processes (and, in fact the whole business).

Most people are now familiar with the concept of a 'carbon footprint' – an assessment of the GHG impact of a product or an operation. It is now fairly easy to calculate this and there is a plethora of organizations, all with excellent websites, that can help. Most are selling a commercial service and so it is not appropriate to give references here, but it is well worth exploring the website of the publicly funded research project: http://www.ccalc.org.uk/. The carbon trust, a government funded not-for-profit organization, is also worth investigating (www.carbontrust.co.uk), and Mike Berners-Lee's book *How Bad are Bananas?* (2010) come highly recommended.

There are well-publicized international developments under way in carbon management, about which the operations manager should be aware, but which don't really warrant taking up space here. The Internet will quickly bring you many reports, papers, and definitions, so what follows is a brief guide.

It is worth starting with the Kyoto Protocol (http://unfccc.int/kyoto_protocol/items/2830.php) and the Intergovernmental Panel on Climate Change (IPCC: see www.ipcc.ch/), because this is where concepts such as international emissions reduction targets originate. Most are at the level of governments and countries although some have implications for operations.

Amidst the schemes for carbon reduction and carbon trading, for example (both easy to explore and well worthwhile), it is important to understand the concept of carbon leakage – an operations issue. Under the Kyoto protocol and international trade rules, countries' emissions are based on production levels rather than consumption. For some Western countries more than 30 per cent of consumption-based emissions are imported and hence not accounted for, whilst for China 22.5 per cent of its emissions are generated in the production of goods for consumers elsewhere (Davis and Caldeira, 2010) That is why this is called 'carbon leakage' – carbon emissions slip through the measurement net and this can

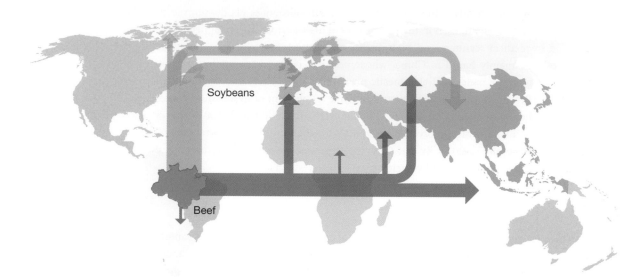

Soybeans	Embodied Carbon (TgCO$_2$e)	% of Total	Beef	Embodied Carbon (TgCO$_2$e)	% of Total
Asia	31.0	12.1	Afria	7.3	3.0
EU	80.3	31.2	EU	29.6	12.3
Rest of World	17.2	6.7	E. Europe	29.9	12.5
Brazil	128.4	50.0	Mideast	18.8	7.8
			Rest of World	34.5	14.4
			Brazil	120.0	50.0

Figure 5.7 Cumulative carbon emission liability (1990–2006) for countries importing soybeans and beef from the Amazon

Zaks *et al.* (2009)

introduce significant inequalities on countries' rights to carbon allowances (Andrew and Forgie 2008; Zaks *et al.* 2009), as well as leading to perverse results such as the reduction of domestic pollution at the expense of foreign producers.

So, if a company sited production in China it may well end up being charged heavily for the carbon emissions (as China passed on penalties to foreign producers) even though the products would end up being used in, say, the UK. In the past this might have been seen as legitimate strategy – hiding the problem until caught – but the scene is changing. The case of soybeans and beef, produced in Brazil and imported by other countries, is shown in Figure 5.7. As Zaks *et al.* (2009) point out, the total carbon emissions liability of importing countries for these products become the liability assigned to Brazil.

INPUTS: THE SUPPLY CHAIN

The issue of carbon leakage brings us nicely to focus on sustainability in supply chains. We saw in Chapter 3 how customers in supply chains (purchasers) like to assume the mantle of controller (supply chain manager) all too readily and may create counterproductive conditions as a result. It appears that the same thing may happen in the context of sustainability. We shall look at the idea of accredited practices later but it is worth bearing in mind that the quality and environmental management standards (ISO 9001 and ISO 14001) include the concept of supplier management. For information on such standards, see www.bsi-emea.com/Standards_Schemes/index.xalter.

So, a first move by supply chain managers in seeking sustainability might typically be to demand that all suppliers to gain ISO 14001 accreditation for the operations that provide the materials and products that are to be supplied. A similar stipulation might be made on ethical issues such as child labour, following, say, the UN's International Labour Organization advice and code (www.ilo.org/global/topics/child-labour/lang–en/index.htm).

Such quite reasonable demands make use of standard systems but it is also quite usual for the customer to add a few requirements of their own. Once this takes place, the customer places themselves in the position of presumed authority and all the potential dangers we saw in Chapter 3 may be expected. Work by Baden *et al.* (2009; 2011) showed that SME suppliers contracting with larger customers who stipulated specific levels of environmental performance often unknowingly set targets lower than the levels that the supplier could achieve. The suppliers saw this as a 'ceiling' effect, meaning that they would only achieve the level requested, even though, left to their own devices, they could have provided much better environmental standards.

Work by Kibbeling *et al.* (2010) showed further that while encouragement by customers for suppliers to be innovative can often yield positive results, the same may not be true for environmental performance.

As with all technological development (see Chapter 3), a more appropriate way of dealing with suppliers may be to work in collaborative mode so that the supplier brings ideas for better performance into the relationship. Many large organizations now do this – a really good example is provided by the Philips Supplier Sustainability Involvement Program, shown in Case 5.2. It covers all the basics, from policy to detailed practice (although some of the concepts covered in Chapter 3 might be considered in this context).

Schemes such as that at Philips may enable supply chain managers to ensure that they are working with sustainability aware suppliers. There remains the choice of sourcing geography. Bearing in mind the LCA principle, and the case of motor cars (see Case 5.4, below), we know that the sustainability of a sourcing arrangement requires us to look at the process that creates the product or service as well as the transportation that brings it to our door. Doing this may blow away certain myths – such as the one surrounding local sourcing.

Food miles

In the mid-1990s, the UK retailer Waitrose caused a stir when it was revealed that beef advertised as 'local' in many of its shops may well have been reared locally but had been shipped to and from a single abattoir in the north of England for slaughter. Intuition told people that this must be very wasteful in terms of transportation. The concept of 'food miles'

CASE 5.2: THE PHILIPS SUPPLIER SUSTAINABILITY INVOLVEMENT PROGRAM

The Philips Supplier Sustainability Involvement Program is built on five pillars: setting out our requirements; building understanding and agreement; monitoring identified risk suppliers through audits using the EICC checklist; working with suppliers to resolve issues quickly; and engaging stakeholders.

The company explains it in detail

In line with Philips' General Business Principles, we are a responsible partner in society, acting with integrity towards our suppliers. Similarly, we award business to suppliers and partners who act legally and ethically, and who are committed to fairness and integrity towards their stakeholders. We introduced our One Philips approach to supplier sustainability in 2003. Given the importance of this sustainability in the supply chain, this topic is now a routine agenda item at our monthly business review meetings, including continuous monitoring of corrective action implementation.

What we expect from our supplier

As a baseline to build a sustainable business relationship with our supplier, we require our suppliers to conform to The Philips Sustainability Code for Suppliers, which consists of two parts: The Royal Philips Electronics Supplier Sustainability Declaration and The Royal Philips Electronics List of Regulated Substances and obligations as set by REACH.

Supplier Sustainability Declaration

Our Supplier Sustainability Declaration sets out the standards and behaviour we require of our suppliers to improve conditions for workers. The Supplier Sustainability Declaration specifies everything from child labour avoidance and work-hour limits to safe working conditions.

Child labour policy

We also specify our expectations of Supplier in incidents of child labour. In our Child Labor Policy suppliers are expected to follow the three H's approach as set out in the ILO guide for employers on child labour:

- a stop to underage **H**iring

- removing children from tasks where the risks from **H**azards are high
- reducing **H**ours to the legal level

How we work with suppliers to foster sustainability

Industry collaboration

We endorsed the Electronic Industry Code of Conduct (EICC) in 2006 and joined its implementation Steering Committee. Working with EICC member companies to develop standardized tools and processes, which allows for increased efficiency, productivity and simplicity for our suppliers and ourselves.

We have also independently supplemented the code with an additional requirement on freedom of association. This supplement is in response to comments from various stakeholder groups. It aims to ensure that constructive dialogue between employers and workers at our suppliers can take place.

Standards

All suppliers with an annual spend of over €1000 must sign and adhere to the Supplier Sustainability Declaration. This constitutes an integral part of our purchase agreements, purchase orders and terms and conditions.

Training and capacity building

We know that awareness and engagement are critical for building a sustainable electronics industry and recognize our responsibility in helping create them.

Our training sessions, Supplier Day events and briefings aim to build knowledge and commitment among our suppliers. We also participate in the EICC capacity-building program.

We encourage our suppliers to analyze gaps and areas for improvement by completing the ICT Supplier Self-Assessment Questionnaire for each site that manufactures products for Philips.

Audit approach

To help us determine our criteria for supplier sustainability audits, we identified risk countries based on independent sources and also determined a threshold on spend. Philips conducts onsite sustainability audits to gain a representative picture of the supplier's overall sustainability performance and compliance with the EICC.

The audits are conducted by a Philips in-house auditor or an EICC-certified auditing body. They are carried out using the Philips Supply Sustainability Audit

CASE STUDY

CASE STUDY

Tool and cover the entire site, not just the production lines set up exclusively for Philips products.

Issue resolution

If non-conformances are identified during an audit, Philips expects the supplier to take the initiative to resolve the issues involved. Philips will work with the supplier to define a Corrective Action Plan, specifying the required steps, milestones and responsibilities, and to trace and track progress of the plan.

Supplier ratings and sourcing decisions

We are committed to awarding business to suppliers who conform to our standards of sustainability and performance. To do this, we will periodically audit suppliers against these standards, rating them for performance and improvement.

We communicate these results in our management reviews with suppliers. The results are also incorporated in our overall supplier rating system which helps us decide which suppliers to use.

became popular. However, a great deal of research has now shown that the transportation component in food production is often actually a minor source of carbon or energy use: production may be much more significant. So, by running one abattoir well, and routing all British beef through it, Waitrose was using less energy than if it had several such facilities around the country.

Research in the US in 2008 showed that while much of the food consumed by Americans travelled very large distances, the production stage typically accounted for 83 per cent of the GHG emissions associated with the product, and the transportation just 11 per cent. The researchers then pointed out that as red meat is about 150 per cent more GHG-intensive than chicken or fish, a dietary shift would be a more effective way of reducing the impact of food than a 'buy local' campaign (see Weber and Matthews, 2008).

The report in Case 5.3 puts the case against food miles very clearly.

Examples of what is wrong with the food miles idea are plentiful. A study by Schlich and Fleissner (2005) concluded that New Zealand lamb bought in a German supermarket used less energy per kilogram than locally reared lamb, and also that German apple juice, consumed in Germany, used more energy than orange juice imported from Brazil. Studies such as this try to cover all effects but it is still important to set them in the greater context. As we saw above, the energy used in intercontinental shipping may be accounted for but it is estimated elsewhere that as much as 50 per cent of the CO_2 released by burning fossil fuels is absorbed by the oceans. As this happens, the ocean becomes more acidic; plankton die, then fish, and so on (www.stateoftheocean.org/ipso-2011-workshop-summary.cfm).

CASE 5.3: HOW GREEN ARE YOUR BEANS?

Consider that supermarket stalwart: green beans from Kenya. These are air-freighted to stores to allow consumers to buy fresh beans when British varieties are out of season. Each packet has a little sticker with the image of a plane on it to indicate that carbon dioxide from aviation fuel was emitted in bringing them to this country. And that, surely, is bad, campaigners argue. Rising levels of carbon dioxide are trapping more and more sunlight and inexorably heating the planet, after all.

But a warning that beans have been air-freighted does not mean we should automatically switch to British varieties if we want to help the climate. Beans in Kenya are produced in a highly environmentally-friendly manner. 'Beans there are grown using manual labour – nothing is mechanised,' says Professor Gareth Edwards-Jones of Bangor University, an expert on African agriculture. 'They don't use tractors, they use cow muck as fertiliser; and they have low-tech irrigation systems in Kenya. They also provide employment to many people in the developing world. So you have to weigh that against the air miles used to get them to the supermarket.'

When you do that – and incorporate these different factors – you make the counter-intuitive discovery that air-transported green beans from Kenya could actually account for the emission of less carbon dioxide than British beans. The latter are grown in fields on which oil-based fertilisers have been sprayed and which are ploughed by tractors that burn diesel. In the words of Gareth Thomas, Minister for Trade and Development, speaking at a Department for International Development air-freight seminar: 'Driving 6.5 miles to buy your shopping emits more carbon than flying a pack of Kenyan green beans to the UK.'

The Observer, 23 March 2008

In time, it may be expected that sea transport will make better use of technologies old and new (including solar power and fuel cells, sails, and kites). For some fascinating examples, see:

- www.turanor.eu/index.php?id=1&L=1,
- www.dnv.com/searchresult/index.asp?query=Shipping
- www.skysails.info/index.php?id=472&L=2

For now, though, Schlich and Fleissner's conclusion makes the point simply for operations strategists: 'The efficiency and logistics of the production and the operations determine the specific energy turnover.'

So we should turn to operations management for our focus for improving sustainable, lower carbon activity.

PROCESSES: IN THE OPERATION

In the 1980s, manufacturing industry, followed by the service sector, adopted an international standard – the ISO 9000 series (now 9001) – for quality assurance, including activities within the supply chain (see Chapter 8). This grew out of Defence Standards in the US and the UK, coupled with British Standard 5750 and some other European systems (notably DIN in Germany). As the awareness of environmental management grew, this standard gave rise to a further scheme, ISO 14000 series (formally BS7750), designed to instil 'best practice' – again including supply chain management, in an environmental management context. ISO 14000/01 was a success and is still very well respected. As with ISO 9000/01, the environmental standard is focused on how a product or service is produced rather than on the product itself. ISO 19011 is a combined scheme for an organization that wishes to be accredited for both standards at once.

An innovative response for sustainability: lean thinking

The approach to operations that developed in Japan in the second half of the twentieth century caught the imagination of managers and observers in the West and led to a prolonged period of study and learning about how to undo some of the problems caused by adherence to mass production (i.e. supply-led thinking) in a world that had moved on, to be led by markets (demand-led). The approach was identified by the term *just in time*, and the adoption in the West of Japanese terms such as, *muda, muri, kaizen, kanban, heijunka, poka yoka*, and was often likened to the particular manufacturing strategy known as the Toyota Production System. It was necessary only to read Schonberger's seminal 1982 book, *Japanese Manufacturing Techniques: Nine Hidden Lessons in Simplicity*, to understand all this, perhaps complemented by Monden's *Toyota Production System* (2011).

The theme running through all this was the removal of waste, in all its forms. This became known as *muda*, although as Schonberger reported there were several other terms used in Japan for various kinds of waste. Taichi Ohno, Chief Engineer at Toyota, developed his famous list of seven types of waste and production engineers worldwide began to learn. These will be referred to within the discussion on just-in-time in Chapter 9, but they are applicable here in our discussion on sustainability and are shown in Table 5.2.

All these types of waste may be portrayed in the context of competition, for example as indicated in Table 5.2 for *unnecessary transportation*. For *inventory* the same is true: if your competitor can hold less stock than you without failing to supply what is demanded, they will have lower costs and a more sustainable business. This contextualizing can be done for each type of waste.

In the West, in about the same period as Ohno's work, another great, innovative engineer was thinking similarly but in terms of design, not manufacturing. Colin Chapman, founder and chairman of Lotus Cars, was the first to use the term 'lean' in its modern meaning, to describe the design (for a racing car) that had no waste. He knew that weight, not lack of power, was the enemy of a racing car. Chapman famously said: 'To add speed, add lightness'. His lean thinking led Lotus to win the Formula 1 world championship six times between

Table 5.2 Linking Ohno's seven wastes with sustainability issues

Ohno's waste	Sustainability issue
Overproduction: making more than you can sell or use immediately	Scrapping unsold products is waste in itself, as is all the use of resources involved in producing them. The same is true for a service that is set up but not wanted by anyone. Holding finished products consumes resources and may not be sustainable
Unnecessary transportation: wasted energy in relocation (for example, your downstream delivery logistics is all waste if your competitor builds a manufacturing plant on your customer's doorstep!)	Clearly an issue – but remember that logistics impacts may be overshadowed by inefficiency or unsustainable practices in production (Case 5.3). Logistics activity is a consumer of resources; operating excessive or inappropriate amounts of transportation is thus unsustainable
Inventory: strictly speaking, any inventory is waste. For some businesses, however, it may be argued (usually by Marketing) that some stock has to be kept to satisfy demands quickly and be agile. Stock on the shelf in a shop may help to sell the product. The challenge is: how little can be held without failing to satisfy, or stimulate, demand?	Inventory requires resources to acquire, store, move and dispose of: having more than the minimum may be unsustainable
Motion: human effort that does not add value is waste	Human labour is a resource; it may be in plentiful supply but appropriately trained and equipped labour takes quality resources to maintain it. Making work too demanding, or unnecessarily complicated, in labour terms, may be unsustainable
Defects: wasted effort embodied in something that cannot be sold or used, or needs rework	A special case of scrappage (see above). The product may not be thrown away but the rework is a waste of resources
Over-processing: doing more work on something than is required by the customer	Similar to the issue with *Motion* – see above – but expressed in downstream market terms
Waiting: paying for something that is not happening!	Perhaps not itself a sustainability issue but the waste of labour capacity – a consumer of resources – may be unsustainable

1963 and 1973, and changed the sport forever. Fifteen years later it would lead to a revolution in operations management.

The major research that developed the concepts of *lean manufacturing, design, and supply* at MIT in the 1980s effectively combined the two threads: Ohno and Chapman (basically the same thinking), delivering the lessons in a way that has influenced operations and business more broadly for the past two decades. Lean emerged not as a way of improving efficiency (as is often mistakenly averred) but as creative destruction – radical innovation. This echoed both the words of Colin Chapman in rethinking the racing car and the vision of Taichi Ohno in destroying the top-down control precepts of mass production.

As we have seen, sustainability – and the search for 'one-planet' operations – will require radical innovation to address the growth in consumption and the depletion of nature's resources. At the operations level, this challenge can be addressed by understanding lean thinking as fundamental to innovation and the fanatical removal of *muda*. If waste is defined as the unnecessary use of resources (materials, energy, space, wealth, etc.) then sustainability is the reverse: the appropriate use of such things.

It appears, therefore, that sustainable, one-planet operations and processes should be approached from a lean perspective – using continuous improvement techniques (or '*kaizen*').

Returning to some of Ohno's wastes, we can explore them in a sustainability context:

Overproduction

If more products are made than are wanted, perhaps in one specific region of the world, then in global terms they are waste. One of the world's chronic – and often also acute – problems in this context is that of food distribution. For example, research in the US by the Department of Agriculture in 1997 revealed that Americans throw away 27 per cent of the food they purchase – about 500g every day per person. The US Environmental Protection Agency estimated that Americans generate about 30 million tons of food waste per year. In the UK, recent research showed a similar picture: a third of food, around 7 million tonnes, is thrown away each year, including 4 million apples, 1.2 million sausages and 2.8 million tomatoes. The cost to the UK is estimated at £10.2 billion a year (when production, storage, and transportation are taken into account) and the waste accounts for 5 per cent of the UK's GHG emissions (see Stuart, 2009). In Sweden, parents with young children throw away about a quarter of the food they buy (see Gustavsson *et al.*, 2011). The use of energy, human abilities, and materials to produce things that are simply thrown away may still make money for the owners of the production process in the short term but it is clearly not sustainable business – nor ethical – in the light of finite resources (see also www.foodethicscouncil.org/topic/Waste).

Unnecessary transportation

This is clearly an unsustainable waste of energy and thus, often, non-renewable fuel. However, the whole picture must be borne in mind (see the section on *food miles*, above). Many interesting projects exist and are worth considering, including the innovations at sea noted above, and on land, such as that in Richmond council (see www.theecologist.org/how_to_make_a_difference/transport/375428/councils_using_chip_fat_as_fuel_and_road_filler.html).

Inventory

Products that are made and then not used immediately may become obsolete, damaged or simply dumped, having consumed resources in their production, packaging, transportation, and storage. Much of the food waste discussed above comes into this category. Once again, the firm that made and sold the products may not care in the short term that their customer is not gaining any value from their purchase, especially as they have probably been paid for it, but this is clearly not sustainable business.

Over-processing

Doing more work on something than is required by the customer is clearly wasteful and unsustainable in the long term. It may be less costly to standardize according to a single specification that some customers want (e.g. to include functions on a remote control unit than most customers will never want to use) than to customize. From a resources perspective, however, it is clear that the energy and materials used up in non-value-adding activity cannot be sustained.

The techniques associated with lean production (including in service operations) have been well developed over the last two decades and we do not need to rehearse them here. Many case studies have been published and are freely available (see, for example, www.lean.org and www.leanuk.org – organizations run by the lead researchers on the original International Motor Vehicle Program at MIT between 1986 and 1990 – James Womack and Daniel Jones). Perhaps the answer to the rather facile and clichéd question 'What comes after lean?' is 'sustainable.'

As we noted above, some products create more environmental damage in their production than in use. Perhaps the best know example of this, currently under the public microscope, is the motor car. See Case 5.4.

Design of products

This is not strictly an operations area but the role that operations can take in redesigning products and services is well recognized (from 'design-for-manufacture', to employees' suggestions schemes). A good response to the concern that a type of material is endangered – as we saw above – is to design it out of the product. The same would be true for a process.

Without doubt one of the villains of the piece is the well-known concept of 'planned obsolescence'. This means that manufacturers want the consumer to use the product just long enough to like it, but then for it to fail and need replacement – preferably with another of that manufacturer's products. Making it more expensive to repair a product than to replace it is a direct cause of waste; products are thrown away needlessly, when some modest reworking might render them perfectly usable. Sometimes this is justified in the cause of technology (e.g. having to replace a complete headlight unit rather than just a bulb, because the light can be more efficient as a sealed unit); elsewhere the design can mean it would take several hours to repair, when a new (improved specification) product would cost less than the labour.

'Product churn' – the marketing ploy of bringing out new versions of a product at intervals that encourage people to throw away (or perhaps recycle) their existing product and buy a new one – may benefit the manufacturer (and the upstream supply chain and downstream channel) but it is surely a major issue in sustainability (for example, leading to the idea of replacing one's mobile phone every year – a disaster for endangered elements). The idea of keeping cars for longer (see Case 5.4) would make sustainability sense but inevitably lead to economic crises in automotive manufacturing industries (see Guiltinan, 2009).

Clearly, planned obsolescence and product churn are the children of that other great twentieth-century villain: conspicuous consumption (in studying this vexatious subject, it is

CASE 5.4: CO_2 EMISSIONS FROM THE PRODUCTION AND USE OF MOTOR CARS

Motor vehicles are generally seen as a challenge for nations wanting to develop sustainable personal transport. But where should efforts be focused in an attempt to reduce their environmental impacts?

We are now able to measure (or at least, get a good estimate for) the emissions from the manufacture of a car. Manufacturers publish these data and they are checked and authenticated in several ways. The usual expression used for the emissions is 'CO_2e' or 'carbon dioxide equivalent' (since several other gases are emitted, causing just as much harm, but chemists can calculate a total volume – normally expressed in terms of weight – for the mixture).

For example, a summary of the emissions created by the production of three popular European passenger cars shows:

- Citroen C1, basic specification: 6 tonnes CO_2e
- Ford Mondeo, medium specification: 17 tonnes CO_2e
- Land Rover Discovery, top of the range: 35 tonnes CO_2e

Manufacturers also publish figures for the emissions caused by using (i.e. driving) the car. A 2 litre, petrol, Ford Mondeo, for example, is quoted as generating 184 grams of CO_2e per kilometre. Using these numbers we can calculate that the CO_2e generated by driving a medium specification Ford Mondeo is the same after about 92,390 km (57,282 miles) as that emitted in its manufacture: i.e. 17 tonnes from each source.

At this point in the car's life, our attempts to reduce environmental damage from its creation and use, in the interests of sustainability, should be concerned as much with manufacture as with driving of the car. (Incidentally, 17 tonnes of CO_2e is the same as the emissions created by three years consumption of electricity and gas in the typical UK home.) So, if the Mondeo owner drives 7,133 miles per year (2006: latest UK average quoted in figures from government statistics) and keeps the car for eight years, half the total emissions for the car would still be due to its original manufacture (while most of the public attention is typically focused on use). If however, the Mondeo owner replaced the car after, say, four years, the car's manufacture would account for 75 per cent of total impact up to that point.

The proportions of environmental impact from manufacture and driving clearly depend on how long the car is used for: its 'lifetime'. If the lifetime of the car was, say, 185,000 km/114,700 miles, then clearly the proportion of CO_2e from manufacture would have dropped to a third (i.e. 66 per cent from use), and so on.

The sustainability argument in this context might be that we should all keep all products (not just cars) for much longer than we typically do, even though this would hurt manufacturers who like us to buy a new one as frequently as possible (e.g. a new mobile phone each year). Figures on the average lifetime of a car are difficult to establish. One approach is to take the nationally published figures for miles travelled by car, total number of vehicles on the road, and vehicle sales (figures that are generally available although the last one may vary between estimates). This provides lifetime mileage averages of 160,000 miles for the US; UK, 125,000; France, 115,000; Rest of Europe, 105,000; and Japan, 70,000.

If we take a car that emitted 200 g CO_2e/km in use and 20 tonnes CO_2e in manufacture (a higher specification Mondeo, perhaps) then the 50/50 point would be reached at 100,000 km. To reduce the impact of manufacture to, say, 20 per cent the car would have to 'live' for 400,000 km/228,000 miles (by which time it would have emitted 80 tonnes of CO_2e, to add to the 20 tonnes in making it).

Plenty of examples exist for cars being able to survive this long if well maintained but none of the estimated averages noted come close to this lifetime. (Incidentally, the 'real-world' consumptions are generally thought to be at least 15 per cent higher than the advertised figures as they are generated in laboratory conditions, without wind, on 'rolling roads', etc.; this would increase the usage proportion.) Meanwhile, emissions from use are constantly being reduced (for an interesting example, see www.volkswagen.co.uk/technology/efficiency-and-bluemotion-technologies).

Figures for manufacture must be carefully considered, too. Hybrid vehicles are becoming popular due their low petrol consumption but they are clearly more complex in production, having, effectively, two drive trains. Making the petrol-engine Citroen C1 creates 6 tonnes CO_2e (contrasting with the Mondeo's 17 tonnes) and the car emits 104 g/km. This is the same emissions as quoted for the hybrid Toyota Prius. Meanwhile, Toyota are secretive about the manufacturing emissions for the Prius, but in October 2010 the company publicly confirmed the Automotive News figures that showed the model was 'worse than class average across all five emissions categories' in this respect. Industry analysts have been bemused by Toyota's subsequent activities, which have included planting trees and even developing new strains of nitrogen oxide-absorbing flowers to counteract the above-average emission of CO_2e in production of Prius. Meanwhile, as we saw earlier, hybrid vehicle manufacture currently relies on rare earth supplies (neodymium and dysprosium) that are likely to be unavailable within a few years (actually, or practically).

An electric car (such as the Nissan Leaf), will produce zero emissions in use but there is no reason why its manufacture should be assumed to be less

CASE STUDY

environmentally hazardous. It is also dependent on rare earths and, of course, there is the matter of producing the electricity, and the infrastructure, to charge its batteries.

Of course there are many other factors such as recycling the car at the end of its life (Toyota claims claim 85 per cent for Prius), second-hand markets, consumables such as tyres, brakes, oil, etc., and wear-and-tear on roads and bridges. And of course, CO_2e emissions are only one bad thing about petrol – its extraction is damaging too.

As analysts Mike Berners-Lee and Duncan Clark observe: 'Interestingly, the input–output analysis suggests that the gas and electricity used by the auto industry itself, including all the component manufacturers as well as the assembly plant, accounts for less than 12% of the total emissions from its manufacture. The rest is spread across everything from metal extraction (33%), rubber manufacture (3%) and the manufacture of tools and machines (5%) through to business travel and stationery for car company employees. The upshot is that – despite common claims to contrary – the embodied emissions of a car typically rival the exhaust pipe emissions over its entire lifetime. Indeed, for each mile driven, the emissions from the manufacture of a top-of-the-range Land Rover Discovery that ends up being scrapped after 100,000 miles may be as much as *four times* higher than the tailpipe emissions of a Citroen C1.'

Abridged from *The Guardian* 23 October 2010, and various other sources. See also Berners-Lee, 2010

worth starting with Thorstein Veblen's original 1902 book and working forwards). Meanwhile, there are many good examples of sustainable design, including reduced use of materials, substitution of scarce materials with others, refurbishing, recycling, and so on (see Kinokuni *et al.*, 2010).

Energy usage

Lastly we should mention the need for operations to be aware of measures that relate energy usage to sustainability. There are too many to include here but perhaps the best known is the carbon footprint (see above). Other routes to reducing energy usage are generally common sense: designing working space to use natural light, getting rid of air-conditioning (in favour of 'peak-lopping' which only cools the air once it passes a peak level – typically 23°C, which occurs on only a few days per year), and so on. Different forms of energy generation also need to be considered: there are some that may be available at a company level (e.g. wood-chip or biomass boilers) as well as the nationally provided utilities.

It is clear that energy costs are set to increase inexorably and so energy savings are synonymous with cost savings for all businesses. Cost saving is a part of operations management as well as sustainability and so the connection is an easy one to see.

OUTPUTS: PRODUCTS AND SERVICES

Much of the discussion on downstream supply chain sustainability will be common with that on the upstream side: the myth of food miles, the evil of planned obsolescence, the need for LCA thinking to identify where the focus of attention should lie, and, of course, lean thinking. For services, the delivery is simultaneous with the creation, by definition, and the discussion above on processes will be relevant.

Taking a broader view, however, we should consider the role the organization has in influencing the sustainable activity of the customer.

Reverse logistics

This is the simple idea of unwanted products or byproducts (such as packaging) flowing in the reverse direction to those initially delivered: recycling. This has become an industrial sector of its own, including 'remanufacturing', the return of unsold goods, recycling for disassembly and reclaim of materials, and a vibrant consultancy subsector. Alongside the practice, an extensive literature has arisen and management concepts developed (see Chan *et al.*, 2010; Dowlatshahi, 2010; and Ramírez, 2011). There is even a Reverse Logistics Association, which is worth exploring: www.reverselogisticstrends.com/reverse-logistics.php.

Choice editing

It was recognized many years ago that consumers cannot be expected to make choices in their purchases that are dependent upon sustainability issues. Thus, a hard-pressed shopper in a supermarket, on a limited budget, could not be expected to eschew the 'two chickens for £5' offer, or the summer shirt for £3, even though the conditions under which the chicken was reared or the person making the shirt was employed might be suspect. Similarly, someone buying a fridge-freezer could not be expected to pay, say, 10 per cent more for a model with lower energy use. When the system for rating the energy usage of white goods was introduced in the early 1990s, it was possible to buy something in, say, grade E (see Figure 5.8).

You could not buy the refrigerator indicated in Figure 5.8 today – white good sellers will not stock anything below B and indeed most now boast 'AA'. The same is true across the board. Retailers are editing the choice of their consumers, either because no-one would buy the E-grade appliance any more or because this has simply become a sustainability driven market. There has been perhaps inevitable questioning of some of the authenticity of the labelling (similar to the cases in Case 5.1) but it has become generally accepted.

For the tight domestic budget in food shopping, however, it is not as simple. Only some supermarkets sell Fairtrade bananas, for example, and elsewhere they are cheaper, selling in large volumes.

In conclusion, we can see that sustainability connects minute, perhaps overlooked, aspects of operations management (e.g. tiny details of a production process in a factory, or

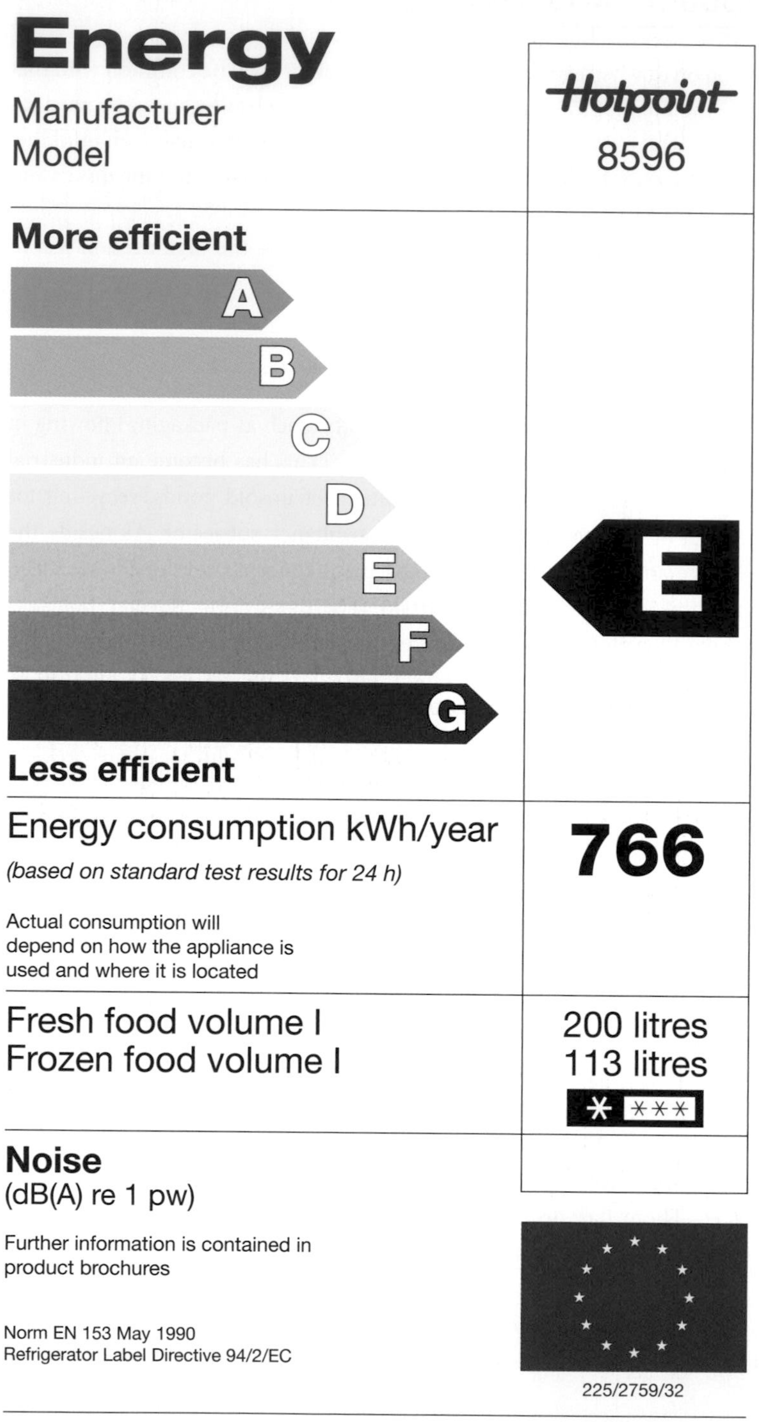

Energy

Manufacturer
Model

Hotpoint

8596

More efficient

A

B

C

D

E

F

G

E

Less efficient

Energy consumption kWh/year	766

(based on standard test results for 24 h)

Actual consumption will
depend on how the appliance is
used and where it is located

| Fresh food volume l | 200 litres |
| Frozen food volume l | 113 litres |

* ***

Noise
(dB(A) re 1 pw)

Further information is contained in
product brochures

Norm EN 153 May 1990
Refrigerator Label Directive 94/2/EC

225/2759/32

Figure 5.8 The beginnings of awareness, before 'choice selection'

of the design of packaging for a small product) with the most massive and profound (depletion of the Earth's resources and disappearance of elements). The connection has always been there, but in the past only massive factors have been noticed (the London smog of the nineteenth century, or perhaps the demise of the Easter Islanders: see Case 5.5). It is now more evident due to the growth of populations and living standards around the world. In the past, the only way we have known to improve living standards is now apparently unsustainable, and operations strategists have to be part of the solution, using innovation and lean thinking to remove waste and create sustainable development.

CASE 5.5: EASTER ISLAND

Easter Island (or Rapa Nui) is one of the world's great archaeological sites, and also one of the most remote. The hardy Polynesians who found Rapa Nui came prepared to stay. They brought tools and food, and plants and animals to begin a new life. Although small it had a forest of large palms and other trees, and volcanic craters held drinking water. Obsidian was available for tools and weapons. Lapilli tuff – the perfect material for making statues – was abundant.

The islanders, once settled, gradually spread across the island, occupying nearly all the available areas. In order to plant their crops, they resorted to slash and burn agriculture to remove the forest cover. Eventually this caused topsoil to erode during storms and, over time, the productivity of the land declined.

They built houses and shrines, and carved enormous statues (called *moai*). The statues were carved by master craftsmen, highly honoured for their skills.

As statue making increased, the supplies of timber and rope gradually became scarce. The lack of trees meant that canoes could no longer be built, restricting offshore fishing. Without canoes, they could not set off for another island. The Rapanui found themselves trapped in a degrading environment.

The size of the population at its peak is controversial; some put it as high as 7,000; others suggest a higher number. Whatever the population, when combined with environmental deterioration, it was more than this small island could sustain.

Adapted from *The Easter Island Foundation*, www.islandheritage.org

* * *

As we try to imagine the decline of Easter's civilization, we ask ourselves, 'Why didn't they look around, realize what they were doing, and stop before it was too late? What were they thinking when they cut down the last palm tree?'

Gradually trees became fewer, smaller, and less important. By the time the last fruit-bearing adult palm tree was cut, palms had long since ceased to be of economic significance. That left only smaller and smaller palm saplings to clear each year, along with other bushes and treelets. No one would have noticed the felling of the last small palm.

Jared Diamond, *Discover Magazine*, August 1995.
See also Diamond (2005), especially Chapter 2

CASE STUDY

SUMMARY

- The combination of population growth and increasing standards of living are leading to a situation in which established ways of producing products and services cannot be sustained at a global level.
- While the connections between this and climate change may be the subject of debate, it is clear that wasting resources is a part of the problem and this is very much an operations strategy issue.
- There are concepts associated with this, which operations strategists need to know about – some quite exotic. Together, they provide a basis for decision making; only the individual strategist can decide on the timing.
- Some concepts are general and apply across the board. Others are especially relevant to specific parts of operations: supply chain, processes, delivery of outputs.

KEY QUESTIONS

1. What are the priorities for operations strategists in gathering information about sustainability?
2. How might you work best with other organizations (e.g. suppliers) to bring about improvements in sustainable operations?
3. Over the next five years, how will the geography of your operations strategy change and what will influence it?
4. How might sustainability fit with lean approaches?
5. How might sustainability fit with innovation?

FURTHER READING

This is an extremely complex and politically charged issue. The student is advised to read as widely as possible before forming views.

Berners-Lee, M. (2010) *How Bad are Bananas: The Carbon Footprint of Everything*, London: Profile Books.

The British Geological Survey www.bgs.ac.uk (especially www.bgs.ac.uk/mineralsuk/statistics/riskList.html)

Diamond, J. (2005) *Collapse: How Societies Choose to Fail or Survive*, London: Penguin.

Malthus, T.R. (1993) *An Essay on the Principle of Population* (1798), Oxford: Oxford World Classics.

Stuart, T. (2009) *Waste: Uncovering the Global Food Scandal*, London: Penguin.

REFERENCES

Andrew, R. and Forgie, V. (2008) 'A three-perspective view of greenhouse gas emission responsibilities in New Zealand', *Ecological Economics*, 68(1–2), 194–204.

Baden, D.A., Harwood, I.A., and Woodward, D.G. (2009) 'The effect of buyer pressure on suppliers in SMEs to demonstrate CSR: An added incentive or counter productive?', *European Management Journal*, 27(6), 429–41.

Baden, D., Harwood, I. and Woodward, D. (2011) 'The effect of procurement policies on downstream corporate social responsibility activity: Content-analytic insights into the views and actions of SME owner/managers', *International Small Business Journal*, 29(3), 259–77.

Berners-Lee, M. (2010) *How Bad are Bananas: The Carbon Footprint of Everything*, London: Profile Books.

Brundtland, G.H. (1987) *Our Common Future, Report of the World Commission on Environment and Development, World Commission on Environment and Development, 1987*. Published as an Annex to UN General Assembly document A/42/427 *Development and International Co-operation: Environment August 2, 1987* and subsequently by Oxford University Press.

Chan, H.K., Yin, S. and Chan, F.T.S. (2010) 'Implementing just-in-time philosophy to reverse logistics systems: A review', *International Journal of Production Research*, 48(21), 6293–313.

Christensen *et al.* (2003) *Millennium Ecosystem Assessment*, Washington, DC: World Resources Institute.

Davis, S. J. and Caldeira, K. (2010) 'Consumption-based accounting of CO2 emissions', *PNAS*, 8 March 2010, www.pnas.org/content/early/2010/02/23/0906974107.full.pdf+html

Diamond, J. (2005) *Collapse: How Societies Choose to Fail or Survive*, London: Penguin.

Dowlatshahi, S. (2010) 'A cost–benefit analysis for the design and implementation of reverse logistics systems: Case studies approach', *International Journal of Production Research*, 48(5), 1361–80.

Elkington, J. (1997) *Cannibals with Forks: The Triple Bottom Line of 21st Century Business*, London: Capstone.

Elkington, J. (2004) 'Enter the Triple Bottom Line', in Henriques, A. and Richardson, J. (eds) *The Triple Bottom Line, Does it All Add Up? Assessing the Sustainability of Business and CSR*, London: Earthscan.

Guiltinan, J. (2009) 'Creative destruction and destructive creations: Environment ethics and planned obsolescence', *Journal of Business Ethics*, 89(1), 19–28.

Gustavsson, J., Cederberg, C., Sonesson, U., van Otterdijk, R. and Meybeck, A. (2011) *Global Food Losses and Food Waste: Extent, Causes and Prevention*, Rome: Food and Agriculture Organisation of the United Nations, www.fao.org/fileadmin/user_upload/ags/publications/GFL_web.pdf

Kibbeling, M.I., Van der Bij, H., Van Weele, A.J. and Di Benedetto, A.C. (2010) 'CSR orientation as a guiding principle for innovativeness: A supply chain perspective', *Conference Proceedings*, 19th IPSERA Conference, Lappeenranta, Finland, 17–19 May 2010, pp. 250–69.

Kinokuni, H., Ohkawa, T. and Okamura, M. (2010) '"Planned antiobsolescence" occurs when consumers engage in maintenance', *International Journal of Industrial Organisation*, 28(5), 441–50.

Malthus, T.R. (1993) *An Essay on the Principle of Population* (1798), Oxford: Oxford World Classics.

McDonough, W. and Braungart, M. (2009) *Cradle to Cradle: Remaking the Way We Make Things*, London: Vintage Books.

Monden, Y. (2011) *Toyota Production System: An Integrated Approach to Just-in-time*, 4th Edition, New York: Productivity Press.

Porter, M.E. and Kramer, M.R. (2007) 'Strategy and society: The link between competitive advantage and corporate social responsibility', *Harvard Business Review*, 84(12), 78–92.

Porter, M.E. and Kramer, M.R. (2011) 'The big idea: Creating shared value', *Harvard Business Review*, 92(1). See also interview at http://hbr.org/2011/01/the-big-idea-creating-shared-value/ar/1.

Ramírez, A.M., Morales, V.J.G. and Bendito, V.V.F. (2011) 'The influence of environment and green logistics towards good corporate practices in Europe', *Economics and Management*, 16, 589–96.

Sachs, J.D. (2008) *Common Wealth: Economics for a Crowded Planet*, London: Penguin.

Schlich, E.H and Fleissner, U. (2005) 'The ecology of scale: Assessment of regional energy turnover and comparison with global food', *International Journal of Life Cycle Analysis*, 10(3), 219–23.

Schonberger, R.J. (1982) *Japanese Manufacturing Techniques: Nine Hidden Lessons in Simplicity*, New York: Macmillan.

Stuart, T. (2009) *Waste: Uncovering the Global Food Scandal*, London: Penguin.

United Nations Population Division (2006) *World Population Prospects: 2006 Revision*, www.population-growth-migration.info/population.html

Veblen, T. (1902) *The Theory of the Leisure Class: An Economic Study of Institutions*, New York: Macmillan.

Weber, C.L. and Matthews, H.S. (2008) 'Food-miles and the relative climate impacts of food choices in the United States', *Environmental Science and Technology*, 42(10), 3508–13.

WWF (2010) *Living Planet Report 2012: Biodiversity, Biocapacity and Development*, Gland, Switzerland: WWF International, www.panda.org.

Zaks, D.P.M., Barford, C.C., Ramankutty, N. and Foley, J.A. (2009) 'Producer and consumer responsibility for greenhouse emissions from agricultural production: A perspective from the Brazilian Amazon', *Environmental Research Letters*, 4(4), 1–12.

CHAPTER 6

HUMAN RESOURCES AND STRATEGIC OPERATIONS MANAGEMENT

LEARNING OBJECTIVES

By the end of this chapter you will:

- Understand the key role which people play in operations.
- Recognize the challenges to SOM in mobilizing employee engagement.
- Develop awareness of the major elements in high performance work systems.
- Appreciate the ways in which SOMs can influence the development of such systems through:
    - Creating appropriate structures.
    - Fostering learning and development.
    - Communicating a clear sense of shared purpose.
    - Developing high involvement work systems.

INTRODUCTION

People matter. This apparently obvious statement underpins one of the key lessons which strategic operations management has learned over the years. Think about any aspect of operations in a public or private sector organization – and imagine the influence people have on its success or failure. We may have sophisticated computer-based systems for managing the stocks and flows of materials and activities across our organizations – but they depend on individual operators putting in the right data at the right time. 'Lean' thinking has revolutionized productivity in all sorts of settings, much of it coming through using the ideas and experience of the people closest to operational tasks developing ways of doing them better. But this doesn't happen by accident – it all depends on them being trained, feeling empowered, and actually motivated to contribute their ideas.

Service quality and the customer experience is all about a relationship between the customer and the person or people creating and delivering the experience. People on the front line are at the sharp end, the contact point which can make or break the best efforts of service designers. Whether it is bar staff in a club, call centre operators in banking, or sales assistants in a shop, the success (or otherwise) of the transaction depends on their interface with a customer. Over time this can build – or destroy – the reputation of even the largest and best established business: the human factor is central to effective service delivery.

As we will see in Chapter 8: reliable, consistent, and safe operations in any organization ranging from out-patient management to offshore oil exploration comes down in the end to human beings and how far they are engaged, enabled, and willing to take responsibility for quality.

Of course it doesn't always work – there are many examples of problems whose roots lie in the ways in which human resources are managed. The recent BP Deepwater Horizon disaster appears to have been due to management placing undue pressure on staff to compromise on safety standards and procedures. China's glowing reputation as a manufacturing powerhouse has been tarnished somewhat by a spate of suicides seemingly triggered by unacceptably high pressures placed on workers in some of the factories. And growing concern about working conditions in some factories in emerging economies have led major retailers to rethink their sourcing policies.

All of this raises a challenge for strategic operations management. Whilst there is undoubted potential in the staff of any organization, unlocking it – for example, in systematic high involvement in problem-solving around the quality question – is not easy. Fashions abound – for team working, for empowerment, for knowledge and learning workers – but implementing these themes requires fundamental changes in the way people think and behave within the organization. Obtaining commitment and 'buy-in' to new ways of working requires a skilful combination of leadership, communication, and motivation, coupled with appropriate designs for new work organization.

Simple recipes are not enough – for example, 'empowerment' sounds good but allowing people the freedom to decide what they do and how they do it may be somewhat dangerous when applied in the context of complex systems or safety-critical operations. 'Team-working' requires more than just throwing a group of individuals together; effective teams are the result of careful selection, training, and experience. 'Employee involvement' in problem solving (sometimes called *kaizen* or continuous improvement) requires a supporting and enabling system and a long-term commitment to establishing this as the 'way we do things around here'.

So what have we learned – and what can we do – to help create the conditions within which the 'human factor' can be mobilized in positive ways? One central theme in this

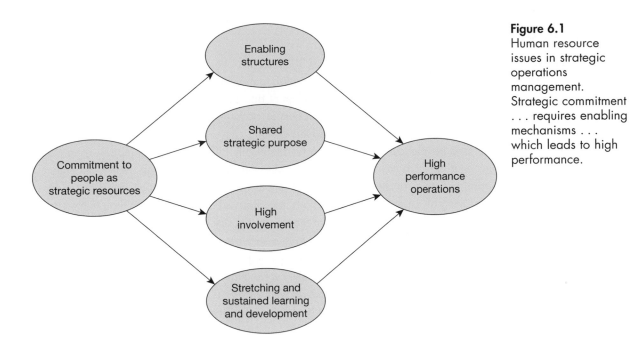

Figure 6.1
Human resource issues in strategic operations management. Strategic commitment . . . requires enabling mechanisms . . . which leads to high performance.

chapter is that it is not enough to pass the responsibility over to the 'human resources' department as the specialists in the area. In the past looking after people-related issues may have been the province of specialists – in personnel and industrial relations – working on basic issues of recruitment, reward, working conditions, etc. But in recent years it has become a critical concern for operations management.

If people are such an important asset then a key task will be the 'developmental' side of human resource management – for example, the need to train and equip people to make a contribution to the operational competencies of the organization. But highly-trained and flexible human resources need to be integrated with the mainstream operations – and one of the key skills in strategic operations management is going to be learning how to motivate and direct such resources.

So what should a strategic operations manager think about in designing and operating such high-performance workplaces? Research suggests that we can group the key factors into a simple model (see Figure 6.1) and we will look in more detail at each of these areas during the rest of the chapter.

WHY DO PEOPLE MATTER IN OPERATIONS MANAGEMENT?

Before we look in detail at the 'How?' question, it's worth reminding ourselves of the ways in which people – human resources – can make a strategic difference to operations (see Case 6.1 on Southwest Airlines).

CASE 6.1: FLYING HIGH

One of the significant business revolutions in the past 30 years has been the phenomenal growth in low-cost air travel. The old game, dominated by a well-established market and a few key players, has been transformed by the entry of new players with very different approaches. It is now highly competitive, driven forward by a steady stream of service and process innovations and opening up airline travel to millions who might never before have contemplated this option.

Underpinning the idea of safe low-cost flying is a fundamentally different business model – and one which requires continuing high productivity growth. Achieving this depends to a high degree on human resource practices and in particular the engagement of employees in delivering high levels of service and continuously improving all aspects of the operations. Nowhere is this clearer to see than in the case of Southwest Airlines – perhaps the 'grandfather' of the whole industry.

Established in 1971, the business did not start out from a very promising position. They did not have specially designed aircraft but used industry standard equipment. They lacked access to major international reservation systems, and for many years they were unable to fly in and out of their primary regional airport – Dallas-Fort Worth – so had to make do with smaller local airports. Their chosen market segment was not in a small niche but in the mainstream business of trying to sell a commodity product – low price, no frills air travel.

Yet Southwest has consistently achieved significantly better productivity than the industry average, more passengers per employee and more seat miles per employee. One of its most significant achievements was to slash the turnaround time at airports, getting its planes back in the air faster than others: around 80 per cent of its flights are turned around in only 15 minutes against an industry average of around 30 minutes. All of this is not at a cost to service quality – SWA is one of the only airlines to have achieved the industry's 'triple' crown (fewest lost bags, fewest passenger complaints, best on-time performance in the same month) – and it has been able to repeat this feat regularly.

Significantly, much of their success comes not through specialized equipment or automation but through high involvement innovation practices. The company makes a strong commitment to employees – for example, they have never laid anyone off despite difficult times – and they invest heavily in training and teambuilding. This commitment showed through in the period immediately after the September 11 terrorist attacks in New York which crippled the airline industry. Despite federal government emergency support of around $15bn most airlines struggled to regain operating profitability. To help reduce losses the major players cut the number of flights by 20 per cent and laid off 16 per cent of their workforces. The exception was Southwest, which maintained its staffing levels as a deliberate commitment to maintaining the strong culture which they had spent decades building. As co-founder and Chairman Herbert Kelleher pointed out, 'Nothing kills your company's culture like layoffs. Nobody has ever been furloughed [at Southwest], and that is unprecedented in the airline industry. It's been a huge strength of ours.'

Perhaps not surprisingly, Southwest has an enviable reputation as a desirable place to work. *Fortune* magazine regularly lists it in their survey of the '100 Best Companies to Work for in America' and many commentators link its undoubtedly strong financial and productivity performance with its ability to build and sustain relationships characterized by shared goals.

Southwest is not an exception, though it is the front-runner in the airline industry. But in many other sectors a similar pattern can be found. The long-running success story of General Electric owes much to its 'Workout' programme originally instituted by Jack Welch, which harnessed the initiative and ideas of its huge workforce. Toyota has managed to remain the world's most productive carmaker year on year through a high degree of involvement of its workforce in continuous improvement – *kaizen*. And 3M's survival and strength over a hundred years of operation owes much to the strong cultural foundations laid down by one of its early CEOs, William McKnight. His views are well summarized in the following quote:

> As our business grows, it becomes increasingly necessary to delegate responsibility and to encourage men and women to exercise their initiative. This requires considerable tolerance. Those men and women, to whom we delegate authority and responsibility, if they are good people, are going to want to do their jobs in their own way.
>
> Mistakes will be made. But if a person is essentially right, the mistakes he or she makes are not as serious in the long run as the mistakes management will make if it undertakes to tell those in authority exactly how they must do their jobs.
>
> Management that is destructively critical when mistakes are made kills initiative. It's essential that we have many people with initiative if we are to continue to grow.
>
> (Gundling, 2000)

These are not isolated examples – many other studies point to the same important message. For example, research on the global automobile industry in the 1980s showed that the significant performance differences between the best plants in the world (almost entirely Japanese operated at that time) and the rest were not explained by differences in areas like automation – indeed, in many cases non-Japanese plants had higher levels of automation and use of robots. They arose in large measure through the way work was organized and in the approach taken to human resources (Womack, Jones and Roos, 1991).

The reality is that from a position in which people were seen simply as factors of production, as 'hands' to work in factories and offices, we have moved to a recognition of the enormous potential contribution that human resources can offer. Whether in systematic and widespread problem-solving, in the flexibility of team working or in the emerging role of 'knowledge workers', the distinctive capabilities of human beings is now being recognized. In the 'resource-based' view of strategy, organizations are encouraged to identify and build upon their core competencies. What is now clear is that a major (but still often under-utilized) resource is the people involved in the organization – the 'human resources'.

There is compelling evidence going back several decades about the benefits of strategic human resource management, seeing people as part of the solution rather than as the problem (Datta *et al.*, 2003). For example, in work on US companies Jeffrey Pfeffer noted the strong correlation between pro-active people management practices and the performance of firms in a variety of sectors (Pfeffer, 1998), a finding supported by Way in his survey of smaller businesses (Way, 2002). In regular surveys of high performing UK firms the same pattern of 'competitiveness through partnerships with people' regularly emerges (CIPD, 2001). As a major review study commented:

more than 30 studies carried out in the UK and US since the early 1990s leave no room to doubt that there is a correlation between people management and business performance, that the relationship is positive, and that it is cumulative: the more and the more effective the practices, the better the result.

(Caulkin, 2001)

Behind this is a recognition of the need to shift focus from seeing people as part of the problem to recognizing that they are a key part of the solution. For example, a report for the UK Chartered Institute of Personnel and Development collected evidence to support the contention that in the twenty-first century 'Tayloristic task management gives way to knowledge management; the latter seeking to be cost-efficient by developing an organization's people assets, unlike the former which views labour as a cost to be minimized' (CIPD, 2001).

Nick Bloom's UK work (later replicated in many other countries) points to the considerable impact of 'management practices' on productivity, highlighting those which deal with human resource management and employee involvement in innovation (Bloom and Van Reenen, 2006). US studies present similar findings (Pfeffer, 2007). The long-running UK Workplace Employee Relations Survey regularly polls the views of managers and employees and has repeatedly shown the importance of 'high performance work systems' – essentially configurations of HR practices which underpin high levels of motivation and innovation, and lead to high productivity (Brown et al., 2009).

As we saw in Chapter 2, there is a strong link between employee satisfaction and quality and productivity (Heskett et al., 2008). Figures for Taco Bell suggest that outlets with the highest rates of staff retention (a major indicator of employee satisfaction) consistently outperformed those with high staff turnover. On average high staff retention outlets had double the sales and 55 per cent higher profits than the worst ones. Similar links have also been reported in the financial services sector (Zornitsky, 1995).

Importantly, not only did employee satisfaction lead to better firm performance but also to improved customer satisfaction. Heskett et al. (2008) found this pattern in Chick-Fil-A, Bank of Ireland, MCI, Swedbank, and AT&T Travel. And this link translates into profitable growth – again Heskett et al. (2008) report that Banc One found that in all its operating divisions there was a direct relationship between profitability and loyal customers, whilst Waste Management reported 65 per cent more profitability in divisions with the highest levels of customer satisfaction.

In these and other cases the evidence is clear – competitive advantage is coming not through scale of operations, or special market position, or the deployment of major new technologies, but rather from what these organizations do with their people. Team working, employee involvement, decentralization of many decisions, training, flexibility – all of these become meshed into a pattern of behaving – 'the way we do things around here' which we call the company culture. Although it could be seen as 'soft' and intangible, the evidence is clear that possessing such a culture is as powerful a strategic resource as a major patent or an advantageous location. But such cultures don't emerge by accident – they must be built and maintained.

On the website there is an interview with Patrick McLaughlin, Managing Director of Cerulean, who talks about his approach to strategic HR management and the benefits which come from engaging workforce ideas, enthusiasm and creativity. The video interviews with Hugh Chapman, Operations Director of Veeder Root, and with Emma Taylor of Denso, give a similar picture of what can be achieved through developing high performance employee involvement.

There is another compelling reason for paying attention to the human resource dimension in strategic operations management – if we don't, there is a high risk that our sophisticated technologies won't work.

Since the earliest days we have needed to work together to accomplish all but the simplest task – whether it is foraging for food, hunting, constructing houses or developing productive farming, we have learned that it makes sense to cooperate. And pretty soon 'technology' emerged as a way of helping with this.

We think today of 'technology' as machinery, equipment, gadgets – something physical which enables us to achieve incredibly complex tasks. But the origin of the word – and the concept – is much simpler. Coming from the Greek 'techne' – to do, to fashion – technology is about tools and the ways we *use* them. It is equipment, yes, but it is also the skills with which we can deploy it and the ways in which we organize work around it. Simple tools like hammers and chisels can enable us to construct basic structures in wood or stone – but they can also help us build a cathedral which towers above a city for centuries as a symbol of human civilization.

Technology has evolved alongside our ability to organize far more complex tasks. So, for example, we moved from simple village level making of clothes and construction to manufacturing through more sophisticated organizational models linked to more powerful tools. The Industrial Revolution enabled massive rises in productivity and access to a huge range of goods which were previously the province of a wealthy few. Henry Ford's Model T factories created a car for Everyman at a price every man could afford – through this same combination of tools and organization.

A key trend in the development of technology has been to embody the skills and motive power which people contributed into the equipment itself. Early stages involved mechanization – replacing the physical labour with machinery. But the accelerating trend over the past two centuries has been towards automation – embedding human intelligence and decision-making into the control and operation of equipment. Computers and robots are the latest in a long line of technologies which have been substituting the hands and heads of human beings.

We can see this in the world of agriculture, which used to occupy the vast majority of people in early societies. Such employment began to decline sharply with the Agricultural Revolution as mechanization enabled the release of a workforce to move to cities and enter the growing number of factories. And these days computer-controlled tractors operating with GPS guidance and laser direction can plough a straighter furrow than even the most skilled ploughman – and do so on farms whose fields are measured in kilometres. The result is that very few people remain employed in this sector – although it is more productive than ever.

Similarly, manufacturing has moved from a labour-intensive activity to one increasingly dominated by sophisticated machinery and controls. It happened first in those sectors where the scale, complexity, and speed required moving beyond human intervention – in chemicals, oil refining, steel making. But it has spread to all manner of other making tasks so that once again overall manufacturing employment has declined.

And we are now beginning to see the same pattern in services – especially in those 'back office' operations where information is processed and data handled. While the customer interface may remain dependent on 'the human touch' much of the remaining activity can be – and has been – automated. Think about the revolution that the Internet has brought about in areas a diverse as stock market trading, holiday booking or retailing and it becomes clear that the trend towards replacing people with automated systems is gathering pace.

The Taiwanese manufacturer Foxconn produces a wide range of devices under contract for major brands in the elctronics industry, including the iPhone for Apple and products for others such as Sony, Nokia, Dell, and Hewlett-Packard. It has much of its production in China, employing around one million workers, but has faced criticism in recent years for its employment standards and practices. In July 2011 it announced it was investing in a huge robotics programme to replace many of these workers with one million robots (up from its current 10,000) over the next three years.

The trouble is that it becomes easy to be seduced by the potential of such technology into thinking that the trajectory has only one destination – full automation. Driverless transportation, workerless factories, self-service delivery of all manner of needs – this is the stuff of regular science fiction. Across the board the attractions are obvious – improve productivity by reducing and removing the need for human intervention.

But there are also limits to how far simply replacing people can take us – as a long-running set of studies demonstrate (Kaplinsky, Hertog and Coriat, 1995; Ettlie, 1999; Parasuraman and Wickens, 2008). Experience has shown that we still need people in those situations, and that over-reliance on the equipment end of technology can have disastrous consequences.

People matter – though the skills and experience required of them may change to reflect a shifting balance. Activities which required human intervention – like direct operation or handling – become substituted with automated machinery – but with that comes a growing demand for programming, maintenance, and supervisory skills. The automatic tractors ploughing the fields of Queensland or Ohio now need highly skilled mechanics able to support them across a range of disciplines, from mechanical engineering to software and hardware diagnosis and repair. Robots may be faster, more dexterous and able to work 24-hour shifts without a break – but they need similar support from design through to maintenance. Pilots now spend much of their time watching a bewildering array of automated controls in the cockpit of their airliners, but when an unexpected crisis emerges – like a bird strike over the Hudson River – it is their skills, judgment, and experience that is deployed to resolve it safely.

The implications for strategic operations management are clear – if we are to get the best out of our increasingly expensive and extensive investments in advanced technologies, then we also need to invest in training, organizing, and managing the people whose experience and skills support them.

TAKING PEOPLE OUT OF THE EQUATION . . .

One of the difficult questions to answer in thinking about the evolution of operations management is how the potential contribution of people has become marginalized. Clearly this is not the product of a conspiracy on the part of operations managers, but rather an unfortunate by-product of centuries of trying to make operations more efficient and effective. To understand what has happened we need to take a brief look at the history of operations management.

Managing agricultural production was the dominant challenge for all countries until comparatively recently. And while the forms of management were often less than enlightened (including a sizeable element of slavery) there was a clear relationship between what people did and what they produced. The vast majority of work was as direct labour rather than involved in indirect activity, and the challenges faced were relatively simple tasks. Where specialized skills were needed – craftsmen working as wheelwrights, as blacksmiths, as masons, carpenters, etc. – there was the Guild system to regulate and professionalize. Here strong emphasis was placed on a learning process, from apprenticeship, through journeyman, to master craftsman, and this process established clear standards of performance and what might be termed 'professional' values. Again there was a close link between what a craftsman produced and the man himself and this gave rise to a strong sense of pride in quality.

The Industrial Revolution changed all of this. The gradual drift towards the cities and the increasing use of machinery led to a rethink about how operations were managed. Its origins can be traced back to Adam Smith and his famous observations of the pin-making process, which marked the emergence of the concept of the division of labour. By breaking up the task into smaller, specialized tasks performed by a skilled worker or special machine, productivity could be maximized. During the next 100 years or so considerable emphasis was placed on trying to extend this further, by splitting tasks up and then mechanizing the resulting smaller tasks wherever possible to eliminate variation and enhance overall managerial control.

The resulting model saw people increasingly involved as only one of several 'factors of production' – and in a rapidly mechanizing world, often in a marginal 'machine minding' role. At the same time the need to coordinate different operations in the emerging factories led to a rise in indirect activity and a separation between doing and thinking/deciding. This process accelerated with the increasing demand for manufactured goods throughout the nineteenth century, and much work was done to devise ways of producing high volumes in reproducible quality and at low prices.

This 'American system' stressed the notion of the 'mechanization of work'. As Jaikumar puts it:

whereas the English system saw in work the combination of skill in machinists and versatility in machines, the American system introduced to mechanisms the modern scientific principles of reductionism and reproducibility. It examined the processes involved in the manufacture of a product, broke them up into sequences of simple operations, and mechanized the simple operations by constraining the motions of a cutting tool with jigs and fixtures. Verification of performance through the use of simple gauges insured reproducibility. Each operation could now be studied and optimized.

(Jaikumar, 1988)

That the convergent blueprint for this kind of manufacturing has come to be known as 'Fordism' reflects the enormous influence of Henry Ford in the way in which he (and his gifted team of engineers) developed and systematized such approaches. His model for the manufacture of cars was based on a number of innovations which reduced the need for skilled labour, mechanized much of the assembly process, integrated preparation and manufacturing operations for both components and finished product and systematized the entire process. As Joe Tidd points out, the basic elements of the Ford system were already largely in existence; the key was in *synthesizing* them into a new system (Tidd, 1989).

For example, the idea of flow production lines for motor cars was first used in the Olds Motor Works in 1902, while Leland's Cadillac design of 1906 won an award for the innovation of using interchangeable, standardized parts. The challenge of high-volume, low-cost production of the Model T led Ford engineers to extend the application of these ideas to new extremes – involving heavy investment in highly specialized machine tools and handling systems, and extending the division and separation of labour to provide workers whose main tasks were feeding the machines. The dramatic impact of this pattern on productivity can be seen in the case of the first assembly line, installed in 1913 for flywheel assembly, where the assembly time fell from 20 man minutes to five. By 1914 three lines were being used in the chassis department to reduce assembly time from around 12 hours to less than two.

This approach extended beyond the actual assembly operations to embrace raw material supply (such as steelmaking) and transport and distribution. At its height a factory operating on this principle was able to turn out high volumes (8,000 cars per day) with short lead times – for example, as a consequence of the smooth flow which could be achieved it took only 81 hours to produce a finished car from raw iron ore – and this included 48 hours for the raw materials to be transported from the mine to the factory. In the heyday of the integrated plants such as at River Rouge, productivity, quality, inventory, and other measures of manufacturing performance were at levels which would still be the envy even of the best organized Japanese plants today.

The list in the box below highlights some of the key features of this blueprint for manufacturing, typified in the car plants of Henry Ford but applied to many other industries throughout the 1920s and beyond.

Faced with the challenge of a widely differing workforce, many of whom lacked manufacturing skills and in a lot of cases spoke poor English as a second language, Ford and his engineers used scientific management principles to develop an alternative approach to making cars. From a highly variable activity with low productivity and variable quality the 'mass production' system changed car manufacturing dramatically.

CASE: CHARACTERISTICS OF THE FORD/TAYLOR SYSTEM FOR MANUFACTURING, CIRCA 1920

- Standardization of products and components, of manufacturing process equipment, of tasks in the manufacturing process, and of control over the process.

- Time and work study, to identify the optimum conditions for carrying out a particular operation and job analysis, to break up the task into small, highly controllable and reproducible steps.

- Specialization of functions and tasks within all areas of operation. Once job analysis and work-study information was available, it became possible to decide which activities were central to a particular task and train an operator to perform those smoothly and efficiently. Those activities which detracted from this smooth performance were separated out and became, in turn, the task of another worker. So, for example, in a machine shop the activities of obtaining materials and tools, or maintenance of machines, or of progressing the part to the next stage in manufacture, or quality control and inspection, were all outside the core task of actually operating the machine to cut metal. Thus there was considerable narrowing and routinization of individual tasks and an extension of the division of labour. One other consequence was that training for such narrow tasks became simple and reproducible and thus new workers could quickly be brought on stream and slotted into new areas as and when needed.

- Uniform output rates and systemization of the entire manufacturing process. The best example of this is probably the assembly line for motor cars, where the speed of the line determined all activity.

- Payment and incentive schemes based on results – on output, on productivity, etc.

- Elimination of worker discretion and passing of control to specialists.

- Concentration of control of work into the hands of management within a bureaucratic hierarchy with extensive reliance on rules and procedures – doing things by the book.

There is a more detailed description of the Ford system on the website, and links to some video materials.

There is little doubt that this was a 'better' way of making cars – at least in terms of the overall production figures (although the question of whether the conditions under which manufacturing took place is perhaps more open to question). But the trap it set was to help embed the powerful beliefs that this was something which only specialists could be involved in designing and refining. Henry Ford is reputed to have once complained 'how come when I want a pair of hands I get a human being as well?'

The justification for this separation of hand and brain was that a well-designed system should not be interfered with through the introduction of unnecessary variation. A consequence – easy to see with hindsight but less so in the context of what were significant improvements in productivity and quality – was that many early mass-production factories came to resemble giant machines staffed by an army of human robots. The images in Charlie Chaplin's famous film *Modern Times* provide a picture of this kind of workplace.

The paradox which this raises is simple to express but hard to understand. Organizations need creativity and active learning in order to survive in a hostile environment. In today's turbulent times, with challenges coming from all directions – uncertainty in competing in a global market, uncertainty in political and social stability, technological frontiers being pushed back at a dizzying pace – the one certainty is that we need all the creativity and learning capacity that we can get. So why put so much effort into eliminating people when they are so good at contributing this?

. . . AND PUTTING THEM BACK IN AGAIN

There were, of course, other models which saw a different role for people in the operations of industrial and service businesses. Even in the early days of mass production, research work was going on to try and understand how people could work more productively in an industrial rather than a craft environment. In particular, a whole series of experiments at the Hawthorne plant of the Western Electric Company led to the emergence of what has come to be termed the 'human relations' school of management – an approach which tries to reintegrate people into work processes rather than marginalizing them (Lewin, 1947).

Another significant development was the recognition of the value of teamworking in improving both productivity and flexibility. Work in the UK, for example, looked at the problems of mechanization and automation in the coal industry. The aim was to improve productivity through the use of a new process for cutting coal, but early experience with the machinery was disappointing. Researchers from the Tavistock Institute highlighted the fact that the new system and equipment broke up what had been productive teams under the old system – and by working on both the social and technical systems simultaneously they produced a model for effective teamworking with new technology. Such 'socio-technical systems design' provided a strong influence on the development of capital-intensive industries such as petrochemicals, and for experiments in the car industry (for example at Volvo's Kalmar plant in the 1960s) (Miller and Rice, 1967).

Although these more human-centred approaches were visible, the dominant form of thinking and organizing continued to reflect the principles of Ford, Taylor, and their followers. It was not until the 1970s that serious cracks began to appear in this view – essentially reflecting the problems of such systems in meeting the changing demands of fragmenting markets and shifting patterns of demand. In particular, meeting the growing demand for high performance in non-price-factor areas – quality, flexibility, variety, speed – became increasingly difficult with systems geared around assumptions of stable, unlimited demand, and a market in which price was the key competitive factor. The position was exacerbated

CASE: THE EMERGENCE OF THE 'SOCIO-TECHNICAL' APPROACH TO WORK DESIGN

In the late 1940s the UK National Coal Board began introducing a new technology to raise productivity in coal mines. This 'long wall' system involved cutting two parallel horizontal shafts and then cutting coal across a long face between them using advanced machinery. Whilst the system offered significant potential advantages over the traditional model in which teams of miners worked with picks and shovels, there were concerns about realizing them in practice.

Working with researchers from the Tavistock Institute for Social Research, an alternative approach was developed which reorganized the labour process around this new system. Instead of each miner being responsible for a separate task workers were organized in relatively autonomous groups that rotated tasks and shifts among themselves with a minimum of supervision. The resulting productivity improvements were accompanied by higher worker satisfaction and an engagement in the continuous improvement of the overall system (Trist and Bamforth, 1951).

This model of co-development of the social and technical systems, with the involvement of workers in the design and implementation of technology, became known as the 'socio-technical systems' approach and laid the foundations for what has become common practice in the successful implementation of new technologies in a wide range of sectors. For example, experiments at the Volvo car plant in Kalmar during the 1970s and at their Uddevalla plant in the 1980s were deliberate attempts to replace the highly mechanistic mass production models typical of the industry with a different approach based on teamwork and small-group autonomy. This was partly in response to an acute labour shortage – people simply didn't want to work in factories which were seen as unpleasant and dehumanized. In many ways these experiments, replicated in many countries, anticipated the teamworking and cellular production approaches which are a major feature of modern 'lean' systems.

by the growth in global competition – it became increasingly clear that those enterprises which did not adapt to offer price and non-price advantages would be overtaken by those who did.

The inherent inflexibility in the 'mass production' approach was reflected particularly in the ways in which people were involved only as replaceable cogs in a large machine-like organization. As Piore and Sabel argued:

Mass production offered those industries in which it was developed and applied enormous gains in productivity – gains that increased in step with the growth of these industries. Progress along these technological trajectories brought higher profits, higher wages, lower consumer prices and a whole range of new products. But these gains had a price. Mass production required large investments in highly specialised equipment and narrowly trained workers. In the language of manufacturing, these resources were 'dedicated'; suited to the manufacture of a particular product – often, in fact, to make just one model. Mass production was therefore profitable only with markets that were large enough to absorb an enormous output of a single, standardised commodity, and stable enough to keep the resources involved in the production of the commodity continuously employed.

(1982, p. 113)

As demand began to fragment, so organizations began looking for ways of delivering some element of customization – something which 'bespoke' businesses had practised for many years. But making to order requires a very different approach to organization and management – it depends on human skills and their flexible deployment – and for this reason is often associated with small, specialized businesses. One solution to this growing trend towards 'mass customization' was to make use of powerful new technologies which allowed a degree of programmability – in design and manufacture – and hence enabled more flexible operation. But these required the same flexibility and skills of the workforce involved in their operations – once again pushing back on the somewhat mechanistic model of Henry Ford and followers.

PRODUCTIVITY THROUGH PEOPLE: LEARNING FROM 'LEAN'

Whilst many Western manufacturers experienced the growing problems of productivity, quality, and flexibility during the 1970s, it became clear that elsewhere – and particularly in Japan – the same story was not true. Manufacturing businesses there seemed able to manage the process of delivering customer value through speed, flexibility, quality, and with high productivity. Inevitably, attention focussed on how these gains were being achieved, and it became clear that a fundamentally different model of organizing manufacturing had been evolving in the post-war period.

Early attempts to emulate the Japanese experience often failed. For example, the widespread adoption of quality circles in the late 1970s often led to short-term gains and then gradual disillusionment and abandonment of the schemes later (Lillrank and Kano, 1990; Dale, 1995). In large measure this can be attributed to a mistaken belief in there being a single transferable solution to the problem of quality which Western firms had to try and acquire. The reality was, of course, that the 'Japanese' model involved a completely different philosophy of organizing and managing production.

This became increasingly clear as Western firms began to explore other dimensions of Japanese practice – for example, their approach to production scheduling, to inventory control, to flow, to maintenance and to flexibility (Schonberger, 1982). The emergent model was one in which people were treated as a key part of the solution to the problems of production – and as a problem-finding and -solving resource for dealing with new ones. In order to mobilize this potential it was necessary to invest in training, and the more widely this was done the more flexibly people could be used across a manufacturing facility. Having trained staff with the capability of finding and solving problems, it made sense to pass the responsibility for much of the operational decision making to them, so workers became involved in quality, in maintenance, in production scheduling, and smoothing, etc. And in order to maximize the flexibility associated with the devolution of decision making new forms of work organization, especially based around teamworking, made sense.

As we saw in Chapter 2, there is nothing peculiarly Japanese in any of these concepts – rather, they simply represent a reintegration of tasks and responsibilities which had been systematically fragmented and separated off by the traditions of the factory system in the nineteenth century and by Ford/Taylor-style mass production in the twentieth century. Nonetheless, the gap which had opened up was significant, and was highlighted in particular by a series of studies of the world automobile industry in the late 1980s.

From detailed studies of the productivity of car assembly plants around the world, it became clear that Japanese operated plants were significantly better performers across a range of dimensions. Efforts to identify the source of these significant advantages revealed that the major differences lay not in higher levels of capital investment or more modern equipment, but in the ways in which production was organized and managed.

> Our findings were eye-opening. The Japanese plants require one-half the effort of the American luxury-car plants, half the effort of the best European plant, a quarter of the effort of the average European plant, and one-sixth the effort of the worst European luxury car producer. At the same time, the Japanese plant greatly exceeds the quality level of all plants except one in Europe – and this European plant required four times the effort of the Japanese plant to assemble a comparable product.
>
> (Womack *et al.*, 1991)

Studies in other sectors confirmed this pattern. For example, Schroeder and Robinson (2004) reported that Japanese firms received around 37.4 ideas per employee, coming from around 80 per cent of the workforce and with nearly 90 per cent of these being implemented (Schroeder and Robinson, 2004). Comparative figures for US firms suggested 0.12 ideas per worker, with participation rates of less than 10 per cent and implementation rates of around 30 per cent. Similar studies in Europe highlight both the potential of employee involvement but also the relatively low diffusion of such practices (Boer *et al.*, 1999; Bessant, 2003).

The idea that people can contribute to innovation through suggesting and implementing their ideas isn't new. Attempts to utilize this approach in a formal way can be traced back to the eighteenth century, when the eighth shogun Yoshimune Tokugawa introduced the suggestion box in Japan. In 1871 Denny's shipyard in Dumbarton, Scotland, employed a programme of incentives to encourage suggestions about productivity-improving techniques – they sought to draw out 'any change by which work is rendered either superior in quality or more economical in cost' (Schroeder and Robinson, 1993). In 1894 the National Cash Register (NCR) company made considerable efforts to mobilize the 'hundred-headed brain' which their staff represented, whilst the Lincoln Electric Company started implementing an 'incentive management system' in 1915. NCR's ideas, especially around suggestion schemes, found their way back to Japan where the textile firm of Kanebuchi Boseki introduced them in 1905.

But although a simple principle it was neglected in most Western organizations until the last part of the twentieth century. In Japan, on the other hand, it thrived and became a powerful engine for innovation. Firms like Kawasaki Heavy Engineering (reporting an average of nearly seven million suggestions per year, equivalent to nearly ten per worker per week), Nissan (six million/three per worker per week), Toshiba (four million) and Matsushita (also with four million) testify to the importance placed on the approach. Joseph Juran, one of the pioneers of the quality movement in the US and Japan, pointed out the significance of 'the gold in the mine', suggesting that each worker in a factory could potentially contribute a valuable and continuing stream of improvements – provided they were enabled to do so.

Company level studies support this view. Ideas UK is an independent body which offers advice and guidance to firms wishing to establish and sustain employee involvement programmes. It grew out of the UK Suggestion Schemes Association and offers an opportunity for firms to learn about and share experiences with high involvement approaches. Its 2009 annual survey of around 160 organizational members highlighted cost savings of over £100 million with the average implemented idea being worth £1,400, giving a return on investment of around five to one. Participation rates across the workforce are around 28 per cent.

Specific examples include the Siemens Standard Drives (SSD) suggestion scheme, which generates ideas that save the company about £750,000 a year. The electrical engineering giant receives about 4,000 ideas per year, of which approximately 75 per cent are implemented. Pharmaceutical company Pfizer's scheme generates savings of around £250,000, and the Chessington World of Adventures' ideas scheme saves around £50,000. Much depends on firm size, of course – for example the BMW Mini plant managed savings of close to £10 million at its plant in Cowley which they attribute to employee involvement.

Similar data can be found in other countries – for example, a study conducted by the Employee Involvement Association in the US suggested that companies can expect to save close to £200 annually per employee by implementing a suggestion system. Ideas America report that around 6,000 schemes are operating. In Germany, specific company savings reported by Zentrums Ideenmanagement include (2010 figures) Deutsche Post DHL (€220 million), Siemens (€189 million), and Volkswagen (€94 million). Importantly, the benefits are not confined to large firms – amongst the SMEs were Takata Petri (€6.3 million), Herbier Antriebstechnik (€3.1 million), and Mitsubishi Polyester Film (€1.8 million). In a survey of 164 German and Austrian firms, representing 1.5 million workers, they found around 20 per cent (326,000) workers involved and contributing just under 1 million ideas (955,701). Of these two thirds (621,109) were implemented, producing savings of €1.086 billion. The investment needed to generate these was around €109 million, giving an impressive rate of return. Table 6.1 summarizes some key numbers.

Another major survey involving over 1,000 organizations in a total of seven countries provides a useful map of the take-up and experience with high involvement innovation in manufacturing. Overall around 80 per cent of organizations were aware of the concept and its relevance, but its actual implementation, particularly in more developed forms, involved around half of the firms (Boer *et al.*, 1999). The average number of years which firms had been working with high-involvement innovation on a systematic basis was 3.8, supporting the view that this is not a 'quick fix' but something to be undertaken as a major strategic

Table 6.1 High involvement innovation in German and Austrian companies

Key characteristic	Statistics
Ideas/100 workers	62
Participation rate	21%
Implementation rate (of ideas)	69%
Savings per worker (€)	622
Investment per worker (€)	69
Investment to realize each implemented idea (€)	175
Savings per implemented idea (€)	1,540
Ideas per worker per year	Ranges from average of 6 to as high as 21

Zentrums Ideenmanagement

commitment. Indeed, those firms that were classified as 'CI innovators' – operating well-developed high-involvement systems – had been working on this development for an average of nearly seven years. Similar patterns can be found in individual case studies explored in greater detail elsewhere (Gallagher and Austin, 1997).

To this impressive list should be added numerous examples from the public sector where employee engagement schemes have been increasingly used to improve productivity and draw out innovative approaches to public service delivery (Bason, 2011).

On the website there is an interview with Emma Taylor who is responsible to enabling employee involvement in continuous improvement within a subsidiary of the giant automotive components company, Denso.

AGILITY AND PRODUCTIVITY THROUGH PEOPLE

This extended look at history highlights several key points.

Things change

No model is appropriate for every circumstance. The craft system would not have been sufficient to cope with the explosive demands of expanding markets in the twentieth century – something like mass production had to emerge. In similar fashion, mass production is no longer an appropriate model for the twenty-first century (although we must be careful not to throw the baby out with the bathwater – there are many features which are still very relevant under certain contingencies).

People are a key part of the equation

Human beings are resources which can be mobilized in different ways. With hindsight, it is easy to be critical of the Ford/Taylor models – but we should also remember that they represented very effective solutions for their time. To get the kind of productivity which Ford's early plants achieved from unskilled and often illiterate workers, and to do so at consistent levels of quality, suggests that many ideas from that period had relevance. They diffused widely across both manufacturing and service sectors, becoming the norm in industries as diverse as baking and banking, fast food and floor coverings.

 The Aravind Eye Clinics case on the website shows how the model retains its power as a source of dramatic productivity improvement, especially applied in services like health care.

But the weakness in the model lay in its marginalizing of those characteristics of human beings which make them so useful in uncertain conditions – creativity, problem-solving, flexibility in team-working, etc. In an environment characterized by uncertainty we need to find models of organizing which maximize the opportunities to deploy these characteristics.

Good solutions to the operations management challenge are not country-specific

Solutions can be adapted and spread widely. Much is often made of the Japanese 'miracle' which gave birth to the 'lean revolution' – but although the conditions for the emergence of a new model were present in post-war Japan, the underlying principles are of much wider relevance. Just as mass production evolved in the factories of the US but then diffused widely, so those of lean production (and beyond) began life in Japan but have come to dominate the operations management agenda across the world.

Good solutions are not sector-specific

Solutions diffuse widely. Much of the preceding discussion has been about manufacturing – because this is where the changes first took place and where we can see most clearly the relationship between people and the tasks they do. But the same pattern has been going on in the service sector – for example, McDonalds' very sophisticated model for fast-food production and service replicates across 185,000 outlets, a model with which Henry Ford would feel quite comfortable.

People provide flexibility

At a time when 'agility' and 'customization' are increasingly in demand in manufacturing and service operations, human resources become central to delivering flexibility. Automation is a powerful resource, but even the most advanced systems lack the flexibility and adaptability which human interaction can provide.

CURRENT 'GOOD PRACTICE' IN STRATEGIC HUMAN RESOURCE MANAGEMENT

As we saw earlier, research studies exploring the links between strategic human resource management practices and organizational performance have several themes in common. Firstly, there is a clear link between investment in these practices and downstream performance. Whether we are looking at case studies of individual enterprises or industry-wide studies there is a high degree of correlation of such investment with important factors like reduced labour turnover or absenteeism, higher productivity, more contribution to problem-solving innovation, etc.

Secondly, these studies are not saying that a single practice will change things overnight. Rather, success comes through a systematic and integrated approach carried through over a sustained period of time. Changing the way an organization behaves is a matter of consistent reinforcement and the establishment of a different set of values.

Thirdly, there is consistency across the research about the dimensions of good practice – what should a strategic operations manager think about in designing and operating such high-performance workplaces? We can group the key factors into a simple model (see Figure 6.1) which provides an overview of the challenges for strategic operations management in this field.

Under each of the headings in Table 6.2 are a number of factors highlighting key elements, each of which will be explored in more detail in the following sections.

Table 6.2 Key elements in human resource management in strategic operations

Area	Key elements
Commitment to people as strategic resources	Employment security Choosing the right people Valuing and rewarding them Sending the right signals
Shared strategic purpose	Strategic leadership Shared planning processes Policy deployment Information sharing Employee engagement and ownership
Enabling structures	Appropriate organization design Job and work organization design Devolved decision making Supportive communications
Stretching and sustained learning and development	Commitment to training and development Embedding a learning cycle Measurement Continuous improvement culture
Shared involvement	Teamworking Cross-boundary working Participation and involvement mechanisms Stakeholder focus and involvement

COMMITMENT TO PEOPLE AS STRATEGIC RESOURCES

At the heart of 'high performance' organizations (like Southwest, Google, Toyota, or Aravind) lies a belief in the importance and potential contribution which employees can make. From this a series of practices follow which reinforce the message and enable sometimes extraordinary efforts from ordinary people. These include:

Employment security

One of the basic human needs is for security, and in an uncertain world providing some measure of employment security is a powerful way of signalling the value placed on human resources. Of course, this is not something which can be guaranteed and there is a risk of 'feather-bedding' employees – but providing some form of contract which shares the risks and the benefits is strongly correlated with success.

For example, one of the most consistently successful US firms is Lincoln Electric who operate on this basis:

> Our guarantee of employment states that no employee with 3 years or more of service will be laid off for lack of work . . . this policy does not protect any employee who fails to perform his or her job properly, it does emphasise that management is responsible for maintaining a level of business that will keep every employee working productively. The institution of guaranteed employment sprang from our belief that fear is an ineffective motivator . . . relief from anxiety frees people to do their best work.
>
> (Cited in Pfeffer, 1998)

The converse of this is also true – if people feel their efforts are likely to have a negative impact on their employment security, they will not make them. So introducing programmes which engage employees in improvement activities that raise productivity will only work if there is some form of reassurance that these employees are not improving themselves out of a job.

Recruit the right people

If people are going to play a key role in delivering ideas, energy, enthusiasm, and engagement then it is worth making sure they have these capabilities and are keen to use them in the organization. Similarly, making sure they are comfortable with its values and direction are going to be important in hooking up these capabilities to delivering on the strategy. And since so much depends on teamworking, making sure they can work well in teams, playing a role both as an individual with particular skills but also as a member of the group, contributing to shared problem-solving. For all of these reasons, high-performance organizations spend a lot on trying to ensure they recruit the 'right' people at the outset, using sophisticated tools like psychometrics and assessment centres as well as straightforward interviews and application forms.

Reward systems

Motivating people through incentives. The traditional view concentrated on simple reward systems, often linking wages to output in systems like piece work. But improved understanding of what motivates people, and the need for performance across a broad range of factors like quality, flexibility, and speed, has led to the emergence of new approaches. These include payment for acquiring skills, for effective teamworking, and for participation in problem finding and solving. Perhaps more important is the recognition that non-financial rewards are an important part of the package (Brown *et al.*, 2009).

Sending the right signals

Although there is some evidence that paying high wages is associated with improved performance, of greater significance is the reduction of wage and status differentials. A key issue – recently highlighted by increasing concerns about the 'bonus culture' in banking and financial services – is the extent to which employees perceive that the place in which they work in is a 'fair' one. Are there symbols – for example, separate and hierarchically arranged facilities like office space, canteens, car parking, etc. – which imply that some people are worth more than others? Or do they convey some sense of all being on the same team – for example, using shared facilities, company uniforms, and other symbols can help reduce this sense of status difference. In the end the task is one of building a shared set of values which bind people in the organization together and enable them to participate in its development.

SHARED STRATEGIC PURPOSE

Successful organizations do not happen by accident – they have a clear and well thought-out sense of direction, and can mobilize support for their strategic goals. Whilst charismatic leaders can and do make a difference, it is not sufficient to rely upon this phenomenon. Instead, high performance organizations need ways of building a sense of shared purpose.

This can be accomplished in a number of ways, not least through participation in the planning process itself. A growing number of firms make use of workshops and other mechanisms to gain input and discussion of strategic issues, while many others take pains to ensure the ideas are communicated throughout the organization – for example, via team briefings, newsletters, videos, etc. Others make use of the appraisal process to provide a mechanism for involvement in strategic planning and particularly for aligning the goals of the individual to those of the organization.

A key issue here is what is sometimes called 'policy deployment' – essentially a process of connecting the high-level strategic goals of the business with specific tasks and targets with which individuals and groups can engage. This requires two key enablers – the creation of a clear and coherent strategy for the business and its deployment through a cascade process which builds understanding and ownership of the goals and sub-goals.

This is a characteristic feature of many Japanese *kaizen* systems and may help explain why there is such a strong 'track record' of strategic gains through continuous improvement

(CI). In such plants overall business strategy is broken down into focused three-year mid-term plans, and typically the plan is given a slogan or motto to help identify it. This forms the basis of banners and other illustrations, but its real effect is to provide a backdrop against which efforts over the next three years can be focused. The MTP is specified not just in vague terms, but with specific and measurable objectives – often described as pillars. These are, in turn, decomposed into manageable projects which have clear targets and measurable achievement milestones, and it is to these that CI is systematically applied (Bessant, 2003).

> **On the website there are some detailed case studies of policy deployment in action in a number of companies. There is also a video of a UK company, Veeder-Root, in which the Managing Director Hugh Chapman explains how policy deployment and *kaizen* operate in his business. Finally, there is a detailed interview with another Managing Director, Patrick McLaughlin, about his approach to engaging workforce involvement in productivity improvements in his company, Cerulean.**

Policy deployment of this kind requires suitable tools and techniques and examples include *hoshin* planning, how–why charts, 'bowling charts', and briefing groups. (Some of these approaches are discussed in more detail in Chapter 8.)

Another way in which shared purpose can be developed is through involving employees as key stake- or share-holders. By the same token, reward systems which emphasize some element of gain-sharing – bonus schemes linked to stretching strategic targets which reflect high levels of active involvement – provide powerful mechanisms for ensuring commitment to a common purpose.

Linked to this is the need for shared understanding about what is happening and where the organization is going. Information-sharing and effective communication systems, which operate in two-way mode, are critical to building shared purpose. As one manager put it, 'if you're trying to create a high trust organisation . . . an organisation where people are all-for-one and one-for-all, you can't have secrets!' (John Mackey, CEO of Whole Foods markets, cited in Pfeffer and Veiga, 1999).

ENABLING STRUCTURES: THE LIMITS TO CHAOS

It's very easy to jump from seeing the importance of people as autonomous creative individuals to a model for organizing which has very little organization in it. 'Let it happen' might seem an attractive slogan, but the reality is that simply letting people loose may not contribute to the wider purpose of the organization (even if it is fun for the participants).

Central to this is the idea of structure – and here it is important to be clear that the prescription is not simply flat and loose. Whilst there are significant limitations to the kind of hierarchical design which characterized organizations in Henry Ford's day, simply substituting a new 'one-size-fits-all' model may be the wrong thing to do.

What we have learned over decades of research on organizational structures is that the choice is contingent on factors such as size, technology, the environment the firm works in, and what it is trying to do (strategy). There are some cases where it makes a great deal of sense to devolve decision making to the self-managed team on the shop floor, looking after a self-contained cell – for example, in a highly uncertain customer-focused business where each order is a special project. But that model may not be the best idea where we are trying to coordinate the activities of many different people in the production of a complex product or assembly. For example, empowering people working on the drug manufacture and packing lines in a pharmaceutical business to use their own judgement and come up with their own solutions may not be the safest or most reliable way to run things.

In general, organizational structures are influenced by the nature of the tasks to be performed within the organization. In essence, the less programmed and more uncertain the tasks, the greater the need for flexibility around the structuring of relationships. For example, activities like production, order processing, purchasing, etc. are characterized by decision making which is subject to little variation. (Indeed in some cases these decisions can be automated through employing particular decision rules embodied in computer systems, etc.) But others require judgement and insight and vary considerably from day-to-day, including those decisions associated with innovation. Activities of this kind are unlikely to lend themselves to routine, structured, and formalized relationships, but instead require flexibility and extensive interaction.

Valuable insights into this issue came originally from the work done in the late 1950s by researchers Burns and Stalker, who outlined the characteristics of what they termed 'organic' and 'mechanistic' organizations (Burns and Stalker, 1961). Organic forms are suited to conditions of rapid change whilst mechanistic forms are appropriate to stable conditions. The relevance of this model can be seen in an increasing number of cases where organizations have restructured to become less mechanistic.

For example, firms like General Electric in the US underwent a painful but ultimately successful transformation, moving away from a rigid and mechanistic structure to a looser and decentralized form. Other examples of radical changes in structure include the Brazilian white-goods firm Semco and the Danish hearing-aid company Oticon (Semler, 1993).

Guidewire is a software startup, seeking to supply mainstream insurers with back-end systems for claims and administration. The firm is unique in that they reorganize every single month. Using a process called Scrum, and organized into Sprint Teams, every month starts with a prioritization of all the things the company could do, and a selection from the top of the list. Every month ends with a review of what was accomplished, and a review of the process. Both are fed into the project reprioritization process, which starts anew again the next month. Guidewire has been remarkably successful with this model, and by 2007 is serving nearly 40 of the top insurers in the US with more than 350 employees. The question is how long the firm can continue to use their unique and agile organizational model, or whether they should consider other options.

Another important strand in thinking about organization design is the relationship between different external environments and organizational form. Once again, the evidence suggests that the higher the uncertainty and complexity in the environment, the greater the need for flexible structures and processes to deal with it. In part this explains why some fast-growing sectors – for example, electronics or biotechnology – are often associated with more organic organizational forms, whereas mature industries often involve more mechanistic arrangements.

An important contribution to our understanding of organizational design came in studies originated by Joan Woodward, associated with the nature of the industrial processes being carried out (Woodward, 1965). These studies suggested that organizational structures varied between industries – those with a relatively high degree of discretion (such as small batch manufacturing) tended to have more decentralized and organic forms, whereas more hierarchical and heavily structured forms prevailed in those involving mass production. Significantly, the process industries, although also capital intensive, allowed a higher level of discretion.

Many other factors have an influence on the structuring of organizations. These include size, age, and company strategy. What became a long-running debate on what determined organization structure began to resolve itself into a 'contingency' model in the 1970s (Child, 1980). The basic idea here is that there is no single 'best' structure, but that successful organizations tend to be those which develop the most suitable 'fit' between structure and operating contingencies. So if we were trying to replicate the operations of a company like McDonald's, so that it offered the same products and standards of service in thousands of locations around the world, it would make sense to structure it in a mechanistic and highly controlled form. But if we were trying to develop new drugs or respond to a rapidly-changing 'fashion' market we would need a more flexible and loose structure.

Table 6.3 gives some examples of the different structural options available in the design of organizations.

STRETCHING AND SUSTAINING LEARNING AND DEVELOPMENT

One lesson which emerges consistently when looking at high-performance organizations is their commitment to training and development. If a firm is to make the best use of new equipment or to produce products and services with novelty in design, quality, or performance then it needs to recognize that this depends to a large extent on the knowledge and skills of those involved. (It is worth reminding ourselves that the Japanese 'quality miracle' described in Chapter 8 was rooted in a strong and consistent investment in training and development of the workforce.)

Training and development has two contributions to make: first, of course, it equips people with the necessary skills and capabilities for understanding and operating equipment or processes; second, it also has considerable potential as a motivator – people value the experience of acquiring new skills and abilities, and also feel valued as part of the organization.

Similarly, if we want people to take on more responsibility and demonstrate more initiative – so-called 'empowerment' exercises – then training and development provides an important aid to the process. And if we are concerned with harnessing creativity and encouraging experimentation then we need to recognize that this depends on people having the necessary skills and confidence to deploy them.

A third key point concerns the use of training and development activities to develop flexibility and adaptability. As we saw in Chapter 4, survival and growth depends on continuously changing what we offer the world and the ways in which we create and deliver it – innovation. This isn't going to happen by accident – what we need is a 'learning organization', able to adapt and change to keep pace with a turbulent environment. Such an organization is 'skilled at creating, acquiring, and transferring knowledge, and at modifying its behavior to reflect new knowledge and insights' (Garvin, 1993).

Of course, organizations don't learn, it is the people within them who do; what we need to look for are those behaviour patterns the organization develops to enable the learning process, and in particular the ways in which individual and shared learning can be mobilized. Any 'learning organization' will require the continual discovery and sharing of new knowledge – in other words, a continuing and shared learning process. Putting this in place requires that employees understand *how* to learn, and an increasing number of organizations have recognized that this is not an automatic process. Consequently, they have designed and implemented training programmes designed less to equip employees with skills than to engender the habit of learning. Examples include firms offering access to courses in foreign languages, hobby-skills, and other activities unrelated to work but with the twin aims of motivating staff and getting them back into the habit of learning.

Garvin (1993, p. 147) suggests the following mechanisms as being important within learning organizations:

- Training and development of staff;
- Development of a formal learning process based on a problem-solving cycle (for example the 'Deming wheel');
- Monitoring and measurement;
- Documentation;
- Experiment;
- Display;
- Challenge existing practices;
- Use of different perspectives; and
- Reflection – learning from the past.

Learning in all of the ways cited above is a feature of 'world-class' businesses across many different sectors. They learn quickly and effectively, not only from their own successes but also from mistakes and failures – and they utilize the intellectual capability from their trained workforces to rectify the situation. Such learning then manifests itself in competitive areas

Table 6.3 Mintzberg's structural archetypes

Organization archetype	Key features	Innovation implications
Simple structure	Centralized organic type – centrally controlled but can respond quickly to changes in the environment. Usually small and often directly controlled by one person. Designed and controlled in the mind of the individual with whom decision-making authority rests. Strengths are speed of response and clarity of purpose. Weaknesses are the vulnerability to individual misjudgment or prejudice and resource limits on growth.	Small start-ups in high technology – 'garage businesses' are often simple structures. Strengths are in energy, enthusiasm and entrepreneurial flair – simple structure innovating firms are often highly creative. Weaknesses are in long-term stability and growth, and over-dependence on key people who may not always be moving in the right business direction.
Machine bureaucracy	Centralized mechanistic organization, controlled centrally by systems. A structure designed like a complex machine with people seen as cogs in the machine. Design stresses the function of the whole and specialization of the parts to the point where they are easily and quickly interchangeable. Their success comes from developing effective systems which simplify tasks and routinize behaviour. Strengths of such systems are the ability to handle complex integrated processes like vehicle assembly. Weaknesses are the potential for alienation of individuals and the build-up of rigidities in inflexible systems.	Machine bureaucracies depend on specialists for innovation, and this is channelled into the overall design of the system. Examples include fast food (McDonald's), mass production (Ford) and large-scale retailing (Tesco), in each of which there is considerable innovation, but concentrated on specialists and impacting at the system level. Strengths of machine bureaucracies are their stability and their focus of technical skills on designing the systems for complex tasks. Weaknesses are their rigidities and inflexibility in the face of rapid change, and the limits on innovation arising from non-specialists.
Divisionalized form	Decentralized organic form designed to adapt to local environmental challenges. Typically associated with larger organizations, this model involves specialization into semi-independent units. Examples would be strategic business units or operating divisions. Strengths of such a form are the ability to attack particular niches (regional, market, product, etc.) whilst drawing on central support. Weaknesses are the internal frictions between divisions and the centre.	Innovation here often follows a 'core and periphery' model in which R&D of interest to the whole organization, or of a generic nature is carried out in central facilities whilst more applied and specific work is carried out within the divisions. Strengths of this model include the ability to concentrate on developing competency in specific niches and to mobilize and share knowledge gained across the rest of the organization. Weaknesses include the 'centrifugal pull' away from central R&D towards applied local efforts and the friction and competition between divisions which inhibits sharing of knowledge.

Professional bureaucracy	Decentralized mechanistic form, with power located with individuals but co-ordination vic standards. This kind of organization is characterized by relatively high levels of professional skills, and is typified by specialist teams in consultancies, hospitals or legal firms. Control is largely achieved through consensus on standards ('professionalism') and individuals possess a high degree of autonomy. Strengths of such an organization include high levels of professional skill and the ability to bring teams together.	This kind of structure typifies design and innovation consulting activity within and outside organizations. The formal R&D, IT or engineering groups would be good examples of this, where technical and specialist excellence is valued. Strengths of this model are in technical ability and professional standards. Weaknesses include difficulty of managing individuals with high autonomy and knowledge power.
Adhocracy	Project type of organization designed to deal with instability and complexity. Adhocracies are not always long-lived, but offer a high degree cf flexibility. Team-based, with high levels of individual skill but also ability to work together. Internal rules and structure are minimal and subordinate to getting the job done. Strengths of the model are its ability to cope with high levels of uncertainly and its creativity. Weaknesses include the inability to work together effectively due to unresolved conflicts, and a lack of control due to lack of formal structures or standards.	This is the form most commonly associated with innovative project teams – for example, in new product development or major process change. The NASA project organization was one of the most effective adhocracies in the programme to land a man on the moon; significantly the organization changed its structure almost once a year during the 10-year programme, to ensure it was able to respond to the changing and uncertain nature of the project. Strengths of adhocracies are the high levels of creativity and flexibility – the 'skunk works' model advocated in the literature. Weaknesses include lack of control and over-commitment to the project at the expense of the wider organization.
Mission-oriented	Emergent model associated with shared common values. This kind of organization is held together by members sharing a common and often altruistic purpose – for example in voluntary and charity organizations. Strengths are high commitment and the ability of individuals to take initiatives without reference to others because of shared views about the overall goal. Weaknesses include lack of control and formal sanctions.	Mission-driven innovation can be highly successful, but requires energy and a clearly articulated sense of purpose. Aspects of total quality management and other value-driven organizational principles are associated with such organizations, with a quest for continuous improvement driven from within rather than in response to external stimulus. Strengths lie in the clear sense of common purpose and the empowerment of individuals to take initiatives in that direction. Weaknesses lie in over-dependence on key visionaries to provide clear purpose, and lack of 'buy-in' to the corporate mission.

Tidd and Bessant, (2009)

such as lower cost, enhanced delivery speed and reliability, higher levels of process quality, and speedier new-product development.

Of course, the paradox is that organizations need to stop what they are doing long enough to reflect on how they might do it better, and this 'breathing space' is often difficult to come by. Significantly, many successful organizations make formal allowance for space in which new ideas can take shape, in which reflection on operations and how to improve them might be carried out.

For example, 3M is famous for its '15 per cent' policy which allows employees to explore and experiment for a proportion of their time, effectively giving them 'permission' to think and innovate in directions not necessarily specified in their formal project or task allocations. This could result in lost productivity – but 3M's view is that it is also a regular source of breakthrough ideas for products and services which keep the business growing (Gundling, 2000). In similar fashion, Google expects its engineers to spend a proportion of their time on personal and experimental projects as a deliberate attempt to develop and preserve a high-involvement innovation culture (Iyer and Davenport, 2008).

Any 'learning organization' will require the continual discovery and sharing of new knowledge – in other words, a continuing and shared learning process. Putting this in place requires that employees understand *how* to learn, and an increasing number of organizations have recognized that this is not an automatic process. Consequently, they have designed and implemented training programmes designed less to equip employees with skills than to engender the habit of learning.

As we will see in Chapter 8, engaging employee involvement in continuous improvement is a key challenge in strategic operations management. Putting such systems in place and maintaining them provides the 'engine' for learning which can be linked to strategic targets for improvement and development.

SHARED INVOLVEMENT: THE IMPORTANCE OF TEAMS

Although there is scope for individual activity, one of the main advantages in working in organizations is to benefit from the team effect, whereby the benefits of working together outweigh those of the same number of people working alone. But simply throwing a group of people together does not make a team; the whole can only become greater than the sum of its parts if careful attention is paid to design and operation, and to training the skills for effective teamworking.

Teams have become a fashionable concept as organizations recognize the value in the flexibility and problem-solving capability which they can offer. Research has consistently shown that teams are both more fluent (the number of ideas which they generate) and more flexible (the number of different ideas they generate) than individuals in problem-solving tasks, and this attribute makes them a very suitable vehicle for dealing with the uncertainties of the current environment. At the same time the psychological pressure to conform means that teams become a powerful way of articulating and reinforcing patterns of behaviour – a culture – within an organization. Building effective routines for organizational activities can often be best achieved through the development and support of team norms.

Much research has been carried out to try and understand how teams work and how they might be developed (Neal *et al.*, 2005). Two strong conclusions emerge: first, as with the design of organizations, the design and working of a team depends on what it is trying to do and the context in which it works; second, high-performance teams, for whatever purpose, do not emerge by accident – they have to be built and sustained. They result from a combination of selection and investment in teambuilding, allied to clear guidance on their roles and tasks, and a concentration on managing group process as well as task aspects. For example, work by researchers in the US on a variety of engineering companies aimed at identifying key drivers and barriers to effective performance found that effective teambuilding is a critical determinant of project success (Thamhain and Wilemon, 1987). Other studies highlight components of building and managing the internal team and also its interfaces with the rest of the organization (Jassawalla and Sashittal, 1999; Dufrene and Lehman, 2010).

Summarizing such studies on effective team working highlights the importance of:

- Clearly defined tasks and objectives;
- Effective team leadership;
- Good balance of team roles and match to individual behavioural style;
- Effective conflict resolution mechanisms within the group; and
- Continuing liaison with external organization.

These findings about teamwork are not new – but they are remarkably stable. We shouldn't be surprised since, whilst business environments and organizations may shift dramatically, the fundamental psychological bases of relationships and behaviour are much less volatile. People tend to behave in ways we have learnt a great deal about – and we can make use of this to help in strategic operations management.

For example, extensive work on 'group dynamics' in the 1950s and 1960s found that there is a pattern to the way in which teams emerge. Teams typically go through four stages of development, popularly known as 'forming, storming, norming and performing' (Tuckman and Jensen, 1977). In practice they are put together, and then go through phases of resolving internal differences and conflicts around leadership, objectives, etc. Emerging from this process is a commitment to shared values and norms governing the way the team will work, and it is only after this stage that teams can move on to the effective performance of their task (Dufrene and Lehman, 2010).

Obviously, a key influence on team performance will be the mix of people involved – in terms of personality type and behavioural style. There has to be good matching between the role requirements of the group and the behavioural preferences of the individuals involved. Again, this has been the subject of extensive work, and one of the most useful models derives from the classic research carried out by Meredith Belbin in the UK (2004). In this model of team behaviour he classifies people into a number of preferred role types – for example, 'the plant' (someone who is a source of new ideas), 'the resource investigator', 'the shaper', and the 'completer/finisher'. Research has shown that the most effective teams are those with diversity in background, ability, and behavioural style. In one noted experiment highly talented but similar people in what he terms 'Apollo' teams consistently performed less well than mixed, average groups.

Teambuilding is not the only aspect affecting performance. Other influential factors include:

- Team size;
- Team structure;
- Team process – the way in which meetings are organized and decisions taken;
- Team leadership; and
- Team environment/organizational context.

Teams are increasingly being seen as a mechanism for bridging boundaries within the organization – and indeed, in dealing with inter-organizational issues. Cross-functional teams can bring together the different knowledge sets needed for tasks such as product development or process improvement – but they also represent a forum in which often deep-rooted differences in perspectives can be resolved. But, as we indicated above, building such teams is a major strategic task – they will not happen by accident, and they will require additional efforts to ensure that the implicit conflicts of values and beliefs are resolved effectively.

Teams also provide a powerful enabling mechanism for achieving the kind of decentralized and agile operating structure which many organizations aspire to. As a substitute for hierarchical control, self-managed teams working within a defined area of autonomy can be very effective. However, although there is considerable current emphasis on team working, we should remember that teams are not always the answer. In particular, there are dangers in putting nominal teams together where unresolved conflicts, personality clashes, lack of effective group processes, and other factors can diminish their effectiveness (Maginn, 2003).

CHANGE MANAGEMENT AND ORGANIZATIONAL DEVELOPMENT

The preceding discussion has focussed on the elements which we have learned are important in building and sustaining a high-performance organization. But change is central to organizational life – whether in the form of new procedures, new technologies, new structures or new locations. And this makes change *management* – the planned and effective introduction of those new systems, structures or procedures – one of the big challenges, and likely to become even more so in an environment where organizations need to reinvent themselves on a continuous basis.

One of the fundamental flaws in the Ford/Taylor model was the assumption that it represented the 'one best way' – that it was possible to design something which represented the 'perfect' manufacturing system. It was undoubtedly effective in terms of productivity (rises of 300 per cent in the first year of operation vs. craft production for example) and in its impact on costs (when competitors entered Ford was able to drop and continue to drop his prices to remain competitive). It was also attractive as an employment option – despite the hard conditions and the high labour turnover people flocked to work in his plants because of the high wages being paid. The problem for Ford was that the world doesn't remain static and if you have invested heavily in 'one best way' then it is a costly business to change.

Arguably, Ford's plants represented the most efficient response to the market environment of its time. But that environment changed rapidly during the 1920s, so that what had begun as a winning formula for manufacturing began gradually to represent a major obstacle to change. Production of the Model T began in 1909 and for 15 years or so it was the market leader. Despite falling margins the company managed to exploit its blueprint for factory technology and organization to ensure continuing profits (Abernathy, 1977). But by the mid-1920s growing competition (particularly from General Motors with its strategy of product differentiation) was shifting away from trying to offer the customer low-cost personal transportation and towards other design features – such as the closed body – and Ford was increasingly forced to add features to the Model T. Eventually it was clear that a new model was needed and production of the Model T stopped in 1927.

Changing over to the new Model A was a massive undertaking and involved crippling investments of time and money, since the blueprint for the highly integrated and productive Ford factories was only designed to make one model well. During the year it took to change over, Ford lost $200 million and was forced to lay off thousands of workers – 60,000 in Detroit alone. 15,000 machine tools were scrapped and a further 25,000 had to be rebuilt – and even though the Model A eventually became competitive, Ford lost its market leadership to General Motors.

These days we face a much more uncertain environment in which the only certainty is change itself. So the response cannot be 'one best way' because even if it were possible to find it, tomorrow's conditions would make it out of date. For this reason we need to build in a capability for planned organizational change – what is often termed 'organizational development' (OD) (Sullivan, 2010).

OD has a long history, but the key message is clear – people are not comfortable with change. We know that when major structural or organizational changes are introduced people often resist for a variety of reasons, not all of which are rational or clearly articulated (Smith and Tranfield, 1990). And even when the organizational structure stays constant but a new working method or technology is introduced – for example a new IT system – there will be concerns and worries about what the new system means for skills, working relationships, and even employment security.

Research suggests that a key element of this anxiety is the sense that the innovation will require abilities or skills which the individual does not possess, or pose challenges which are not fully understood. So training and development – not only in the narrow sense of 'know-how' but also a component of education around the strategic rationale for the change (the 'know-why') – can provide a powerful lubricant for oiling the wheels of such innovation programmes.

The list in the box below gives some typical – and understandable – reasons for resisting change, and reminds us of the challenge in designing effective change programmes.

WHY DON'T PEOPLE LIKE CHANGE?

- They don't see the point, or the need.
- They feel powerless to express any views – it's being done to them whether they like it or not.
- They are scared that it will need them to do things they don't feel capable of.
- They are scared it will cost them their jobs or change their jobs to something less pleasant.
- They are worried about losing their power or the control they have over what they do.
- They are sure there's a better way than the one you are proposing.
- They don't see what's in it for them.
- They feel overloaded with what they already have to do and lack resources for anything new.

'Change management is simple – either change the people or change the people!' (attributed to Hewlett-Packard).

This prescription might appear superficially to offer a solution to the change management problem. But simply getting rid of the people who won't participate isn't a very good option and it ducks the real issue, which is trying to find ways of getting them and keeping them on board. It also involves the risk of losing their skills, experience, and knowledge. Change management is about understanding that uncertainty and discomfort about change is a natural thing, understanding the typical sources of that uncertainty, and then doing something active to try and deal with these concerns.

Amongst key guidelines for effective implementation of change are:

- *Establish a clear strategy* at top level (a process which will itself involve considerable challenge and conflict in order to get real agreement and commitment to a common set of goals): once this has been done, the next stage is to communicate this shared vision to the rest of the organization – essentially this will involve a cascade process down through the organization during which opportunities are set up for others to challenge and take 'ownership' of the same shared vision.

- *Communication*: this is probably the single most effective key to successful implementation but requires a major effort if it is to succeed. It must be active, not passive, open (rather than allowing information to flow on a 'need-to-know' basis), timely (in advance of change – the informal communication network will disseminate this information anyway and a slow formal system will undermine credibility), and above all, two-way in operation. Unless there are channels through which people can express their responses and ideas and voice their concerns then no amount of top down communication will succeed in generating commitment.

- *Early involvement*: managers often resist the idea of participation since it appears to add considerably to the time taken to reach a decision or to get something done. But there are two important benefits to allowing participation and allowing it to take place as early as possible in the change process. The first is that without it – even if attempts have been made to consult or to inform – people will not develop a sense of 'ownership' of the project or commitment to it – and may express their lack of involvement later in various forms of resistance. And the second is that involvement and encouragement of participation can make significant improvements in the overall project design. As we have seen in this chapter, one of the keys to high-performance organizations is the effective mobilization of the creativity of all the staff in the company in solving problems of product and process design. Although this may add somewhat to the time and costs of early stages of the project, improvements and problem-solving here is much cheaper and cost-effective than later in the project's life.

- *Create an open climate*: in which the individual anxieties and concerns can be expressed and the ideas and knowledge held within the organization can be used to positive effect. Once again, this involves generating a sense of 'ownership' of the project and commitment to the shared goals of the whole organization – rather than a 'them and us' climate.

- *Set clear targets*: with major change programmes it is especially important to set clear targets for which people can aim. People need feedback about their performance and the establishment of clear milestones and goals is an important way of providing this. In addition, one of the key features in successful organizational development is to create a climate of continuous improvement in which the achievement of one goal is rewarded but is also accompanied by the setting of the next.

- *Invest in training*: traditionally training is seen as a necessary evil, a cost which must be borne in order that people will be able to push the correct buttons to work a particular new piece of equipment. Successful organizational change depends on viewing training far more as an *investment* in developing not only specific skills but also in creating an alternative type of organization – one which understands why changes are happening and one which is capable of managing some of the behavioural processes involved in change.

LOOKING FORWARD

As we have seen, the issues confronting strategic operations management change over time – and we need to update and change our approaches to dealing with them. That's particularly the case with the role of human resources and organizing for high performance. The twentieth century marked the shift from labour intensity to capital intensity, with people and manual work being gradually substituted by mechanization and automation. In the twenty-first century the shift is likely to be equally dramatic – and increasingly focused on the question of *knowledge* as a source of competitive advantage. Simply possessing assets or technology or access to raw materials or cheap labour is no longer sufficient – in a global business economy these advantages can be matched (Teece, 1998).

The key differentiator will be *knowledge* – and particularly the firm-specific knowledge which an organization can accumulate and protect. As we saw in Chapter 4, we are now in a world of 'open innovation' where even the largest and best-resourced companies recognize that 'not all the smart guys work for us'. So emphasis is shifting from knowledge creation to knowledge flow and trading, making connections between organizations, across the globe and, increasingly, via virtual networks. With so much knowledge flying around it becomes critical for organizations to understand and manage what they know and can trade with.

This may be in the form of codified knowledge – in patents or copyrighted materials – but much is likely to be in the form of knowledge embedded in the minds and behaviour patterns of the people working in the organization (Tidd and Bessant, 2009). The potential of such resources is considerable – from the tacit knowledge possessed by research scientists and engineers through to the day-to-day hands-on knowledge about how to get the best out of processes and machinery which shop-floor employees possess (Nonaka *et al.*, 2003). Capturing and sharing such knowledge – and creating new knowledge through experimentation and experience – is perhaps the key task in developing a competitive edge in organizations.

An important part of this is the ability to mobilize the problem-finding and problem-solving capacity of the workforce, and in Chapter 8 we look in some detail at approaches towards building such 'high-involvement innovation' cultures. They are undoubtedly associated with successful performance, but they are also not something that can be built overnight. Instead they require sustained commitment and support for long-term changes in the behaviour of the organization and the underpinning structures and procedures that support it.

Procter and Gamble's successes with 'connect and develop' owe much to their mobilizing rich linkages between people who know things within their giant global operations and increasingly outside it. They use communities of practice – Internet-enabled 'clubs' where people with different knowledge sets can converge around core themes, and they deploy a small army of innovation 'scouts' who are licensed to act as prospectors, brokers, and gatekeepers for knowledge to flow across the organization's boundaries. Intranet technology links around 10,000 people in an internal 'ideas market' while sites like Innocentive.com extend the principle outside the firm and enable a world of new collaborative possibilities.

3M – another firm with a strong innovation pedigree dating back over a century – similarly put much of their success down to making and managing connections. Larry Wendling, Vice President for Corporate Research, talks of

> 3M's 'secret weapon' – the rich formal and informal networking which links the thousands of R&D and market-facing people across the organization. Their long history of breakthrough innovations – from masking tape, through Scotchgard, Scotch tape, and magnetic recording tape to Post-Its and their myriad derivatives – arise primarily out of people making connections.

With the rise in the service economy comes a greater reliance on human resources to deliver, especially at the critical customer interface. Even where services can be automated – for example, in banking and insurance operations – the need for some form of human interaction is still a key factor in determining competitiveness. Consumer reluctance to work only with automated systems, and the need for a human problem-solving capability for the non-standard and exceptional issues which arise, means that there will continue to be a role for people in even these service businesses. In many others it is the perceived quality of service – expressed through interactions with customers as well as 'back office' efficient processes – which make the competitive difference.

Munich Airport, for example, is regularly rated as the most innovative airport in Europe and one of the leading innovators worldwide. As a strategic innovator, it has a clear innovation strategy, dedicated innovation budget, impressive history of innovation successes, and an impressive pipeline of future innovations. It also explicitly engages employees across intra-organizational boundaries in focused innovation initiatives. As part of the Germany-wide project 'Open-I: Open Innovation within the Firm' (www.open-i.eu), for example, the airport ran focused innovation projects with employees that traditionally had no responsibility for innovation activities. On the topic of hassle-free parking, for instance, ideas were collected, discussed, and further developed into a set of well-defined business plans for innovation investments. The process was run online and offline with the support of the 'Open-I Tool', an online community platform with distributed whiteboard facility, and dedicated open innovation process support for employees across the boundaries of business units, roles, and responsibilities.

In similar fashion, the mobile phone operator Orange (part of the France Telecom group) has been running an employee involvement programme called 'idee-cliq' for the past three years. It estimates that around 30,00 employees use the website every day and the ideas they have generated have saved around €1bn.

There is a video interview with David Simoes-Brown of 100% Open where he talks about this and other examples on the website.

It's not just an issue for commercial organizations – public services and not-for-profit organizations face the same challenges. In an environment where the resources available to tackle major social issues like education, healthcare or law and order are limited but where the demand is rising inexorably, the need for constant innovation is clear. Mobilizing knowledge across the organization, and learning to learn from and trade with others becomes a key challenge.

CASE 6.2: SOUTHAMPTON COMMUNITY HEALTHCARE

The district nurse development team at Southampton Community Healthcare is made up of six team members who provide hands-on care to some 176 housebound patients, mainly elderly, but also those requiring palliative care and those who have long-term chronic disease. Since initiating a team-based improvement programme the team has gone from one that was demoralized and unproductive to one that it is motivated both internally and across the whole organization. So successful was the implementation that it has now been adopted by other services in the organization to help improve quality care and drive up productivity.

> With the support of managers, The Productive Community Services programme helped us to work out a plan of action by questioning the processes, identifying what the problem was and then deciding what we needed to do to improve things. It helped us to unlock the jargon, understand what direction we wanted to head in and learn more about the information we were collecting.
> UK National Health Service Institute website, www.institute.nhs.uk

So, once again, the key resource which operations managers will need to work with is the human one – particularly in terms of its flexibility, problem solving, and creative capabilities. Operations can and will be significantly improved through the use of technology to automated and streamlined processes for the creation and delivery of products and services. But dealing with the exceptions and managing the customer interfaces will continue to depend on human resources, and their success will be linked to the level of training and capabilities of those people.

If strategic HRM is going to play such a significant role in the future, how will it be handled and what needs to be done? In parallel with the developments outlined in this chapter, we have seen the task of enabling the involvement of people changing. In the Ford/Taylor model the issue was one of hiring, firing, and managing contractual and other employment issues on a formal maintenance basis. The response was to create a specialist function of personnel management with capabilities in industrial relations, employment law and contracts, payment systems, etc.

With the growing recognition of the potential contribution of human resources came a need to think about the development of people as assets – much as equipment needs retooling. Thus the role shifted from employment to development with an increase in the scope of training and the use of more creative forms of motivation (including non-financial methods) and appraisal systems linked to career development. Recognition of the need for changing the shape and operation of the organization to enable people to contribute more meant that organizational development also came into the picture. The resulting – present-day – model of HRM is thus much more developmental in nature and addresses the individual and the organization in a long-term fashion.

The next step in the process may see an increasing the shift of responsibility for this broad set of HRM activities to operations managers. As we have argued throughout this chapter, strategic development and deployment of this set of resources may be the most important task facing operations management in the future, and whilst professional expertise can provide valuable help in the design and implementation of relevant structures and processes, an increasing share of the responsibility for HRM may be integrated into the day-to-day and future-planning role of strategic operations management.

What do strategic operations managers need to look for in the future? Essentially, their role will increasingly be to facilitate and coordinate the activities of a highly involved and committed workforce – and this will depend on constructing and maintaining the kind of conditions outlined in this chapter. The challenge is to enable more self-direction and autonomy within clear and bounded limits – the laboratory for learning rather than the factory or office. Agility comes through being able to respond and be proactive, but above al from fast learning. In an environment where we do not know what is coming, only that the challenges themselves will be new and need new responses, enabling this agility will be key.

CASE 6.3: HUMAN RESOURCES AND STRATEGIC OPERATIONS AT XYZ SYSTEMS

At first sight XYZ Systems does not appear to be anyone's idea of a 'world class' manufacturing outfit. Set in a small town in the Midlands with a predominantly agricultural industry, XYZ employs around 30 people producing gauges and other measuring devices for the forecourts of filling stations. Their products are used to monitor and measure levels and other parameters in the big fuels tanks underneath the stations, and on the tankers which deliver to them. Despite their small size (although they are part of a larger but decentralized group) XYZ have managed to command around 80 per cent of the European market. Their processes are competitive against even large manufacturers, their delivery and service level the envy of the industry. They have a fistful of awards for their quality and yet manage to do this across a wide range of products, some dating back 30 years, which still need service and repair. They use technologies from complex electronics and remote sensing right down to the basics – they still make a wooden measuring stick, for example.

Their success can be gauged from profitability figures but also from the many awards which they receive and continue to receive as one of the best factories in the UK.

Yet if you go through the doors of XYZ you would have to look hard for the physical evidence of how they achieved this enviable position. This is not a highly automated business – it would not be appropriate. Nor is it laid out in modern facilities; instead they have clearly made much of their existing environment and organized it and themselves to best effect.

Where does the difference lie? Fundamentally in the approach taken with the workforce. This is an organization where training matters – investment is well above the average and everyone receives 40 hours per year, not only in their own particular skills area but across a wide range of tasks and skills. One consequence of this is that the workforce are very flexible, having been trained to carry out most of the operations, they can quickly move to where they are most needed. The payment system encourages such cooperation and teamworking, with its simple structure and emphasis on payment for skill, quality, and teamworking. The strategic targets are clear and simple, and are discussed with everyone before

CASE STUDY

CASE STUDY

being broken down into a series of small manageable improvement projects in a process of policy deployment. All around the works there are copies of the 'bowling chart' which sets out simply – like a tenpin bowling scoresheet – the tasks to be worked on as improvement projects and how they could contribute to the overall strategic aims of the business. And if they achieve or exceed those strategic targets, then everyone gains thorough a profit sharing and employee ownership scheme.

Being a small firm there is little in the way of hierarchy, but the sense of teamworking is heightened by active leadership and encouragement to discuss and explore issues together, and it doesn't hurt that the Operations Director practices a form of MBWA – management by walking about!

Perhaps the real secret lies in the way in which people feel enabled to find and solve problems, often experimenting with different solutions and frequently failing – but at least learning and sharing that information for others to build on. Walking round the factory it is clear that this place isn't standing still – whilst major investment in new machines is not an everyday thing, little improvement projects – *kaizens* as they call them – are everywhere. More significant is the fact that the Operations Director is often surprised by what he finds people doing – it is clear that he has not got a detailed idea of which projects people are working on and what they are doing. But if you ask him if this worries him the answer is clear – and challenging:

> No, it doesn't bother me that I don't know in detail what's going on. They all know the strategy, they all have a clear idea of what we have to do [via the 'bowling charts']. They've all been trained, they know how to run improvement projects and they work as a team. And I trust them.

SUMMARY

- This chapter has reviewed the ways in which strategic development and deployment of human resources can make a significant impact on an organization's performance.

- In crude terms we have moved a long way from the position at the beginning of the twentieth century where people were seen as part of the problem, something to be eliminated or at worst kept on the sidelines because they were a source of unwanted variation in the operation of carefully designed manufacturing systems.

- Today's view is very different, seeing the contribution of people's flexibility and problem-solving capability as critical resources in dealing with a world characterized by uncertainty – and in which business systems and organizations have to change on a continuing basis. And it is likely that the future will bring increasing emphasis on the ability of organizations to learn, to remember and to deploy their collective knowledge more effectively – again a process which depends critically on the people within them.

- Strategic operations managers can influence the development of such systems through:

- Creating appropriate structures;
- Fostering learning and development;
- Communicating a clear sense of shared purpose; and
- Developing high-involvement work systems.

- Putting people at the centre of the stage rather than on the sidelines requires new approaches to their organization and management, and this chapter has tried to highlight the key areas in which such management needs to take place. These are big challenges for the strategic operations manager: not only does he/she have to create and implement new structures and procedures to enable and support more active participation in the development and improvement of the business – they also have to play a key role in the process of helping the organization 'unlearn' some of the beliefs and accompanying practices which pushed people to the side of the stage.

KEY QUESTIONS

1. It is commonplace to hear managers and chairmen of companies say that 'people are our biggest asset' – but often this is nothing more than words. In what ways can people make a difference to the way a business operates – and how can this potential be realized?

2. How and why has human resource management moved from a simple concern with recruitment and reward to a more strategic role in the business? In what ways is people management becoming a central concern for strategic operations managers – and in what ways can they enable human resources to make a strategically important contribution to the business?

3. In the 1980s there was great enthusiasm for the 'lights out' factory – a totally automated operation in which almost no people would be required. 30 years later, why do you think this idea has fallen from favour, and why are advanced organizations in many sectors now seeing people as a key resource in their businesses?

4. 'The beauty of it is that with every pair of hands you get a free brain!' This quote from a manager highlights the potential of employee involvement, but the fact remains that most organizations still do not manage to engage their workforce on a systematic and sustained basis. What are the main barriers to doing so – and how would you, as a SOM, try and increase active employee involvement in continuous improvement of the business?

5. Many pictures of the future stress themes such as 'the learning organization' or 'the knowledge-based business'. Such visions are likely to depend on human resources and achieving them poses challenges for how such resources are recruited developed and managed. How can SOMs contribute to the design and operation of such organizations?

FURTHER READING

Belbin, M. (2010) *Team Roles at Work*, London: Butterworth-Heinemann.

Bessant, J. (2003) *High Involvement Innovation*, Chichester: John Wiley and Sons.

Katzenbach, J. and Smith, D. (2005) *The Wisdom of Teams: Creating the High Performance Organization*, Boston, MA: Harvard Business School Press.

Kotter, J. (1996) *Leading Change*, Boston, MA: Harvard Business School Press.

Marchington, M. and Wilkinson, A. (2008) *Human Resource Management at Work: People Management and Development*, London: Chartered Institute of Personnel and Development.

Philips, J. (2003) *Return on Investment in Training and Performance Improvement Programs (Improving Human Performance)*, London: Butterworth-Heinemann.

Schein, E. (2010) *Organizational Culture and Leadership*, San Francisco, CA: Jossey Bass.

Schroeder, A. and Robinson, D. (2004) *Ideas Are Free: How the Idea Revolution Is Liberating People and Transforming Organizations*, New York: Berrett Koehler.

REFERENCES

Abernathy, W. (1977) *The Productivity Dilemma: Roadblock to Innovation in the Automobile Industry*, Baltimore, MD: Johns Hopkins University Press.

Bason, C. (2011) *Leading Public Sector Innovation*, London: Policy Press.

Belbin, M. (2004) *Management Teams: Why they Succeed or Fail*, London: Butterworth-Heinemann.

Belbin, M. (2010) *Team Roles at Work*, London: Butterworth-Heinemann.

Bessant, J. (2003) *High Involvement Innovation*, Chichester: John Wiley and Sons.

Bessant, J., Smith, S., Tranfield, D., Levy, P. and Ley, C. (1993) 'Organization design for factory 2000', *Academy of Management Executive*, 2(2), 95–125.

Bloom, N. and Van Reenen, J. (2006) *Measuring and Explaining Management Practices Across Firms and Countries* (p. CEP Discussion Paper No 716), London: London School of Economics.

Boer, H., Berger, A., Chapman, R. and Gertsen, F. (1999) *CI changes: From Suggestion Box to the Learning Organisation*, Aldershot: Ashgate.

Brown, W., Bryson, A., Forth, J. and Whitfield, K. (2009) *The Evolution of the Modern Workplace*, Cambridge: Cambridge University Press.

Burns, T. and Stalker, G. (1961) *The Management of Innovation*, London: Tavistock.

Caulkin, S. (2001) *Performance Through People*, London: Chartered Institute of Personnel and Development.

Child, J. (1980) *Organisations*, London: Harper and Row.

Christensen, C. and Raynor, M. (2003) *The Innovator's Solution: Creating and Sustaining Successful Growth*, Boston, MA: Harvard Business School Press.

CIPD (2001) *Raising UK Productivity: Why People Management Matters*, London: Chartered Institute of Personnel and Development.

Dale, B. (1995) *Managing Quality*, 2nd edition, London: Prentice Hall.

Datta, D.K., Guthrie, J.P. and Wright, P.M. (2003) 'HRM and firm productivity: Does industry matter?', *CAHRS Working Paper 3–2*, Ithaca, NY: Cornell University, School of Industrial and Labor Relations, Center for Advanced Human Resource Studies.

DTI (1997) *Competitiveness Through Partnerships with People*, London: Department of Trade and Industry.

Dufrene, C.M. and Lehman, D.D. (2010) *Building High Performance Teams*, London: Michael Trotter.

Ettlie, J. (1999) *Managing innovation*, New York: Wiley.

Gallagher, M. and Austin, S. (1997) *Continuous Improvement Casebook*, London: Kogan Page.

Garvin, D. (1993) 'Building a learning organisation', *Harvard Business Review*, July/August, pp. 78–91.

Gundling, E. (2000) *The 3M way to innovation: Balancing people and profit*, New York: Kodansha International.

Heskett, J.L., Jones, T.O., Loveman, G.W. Sasser, Jr., W.E. and Schlesinger, L.A. (2008) 'Putting the service-profit chain to work', *Harvard Business Review*, March/April, 164–74.

Iyer, B. and Davenport, T. (2008) 'Reverse engineering Google's innovation machine', *Harvard Business Review*, 83(3), 102–111.

Jaikumar, R. (1988) *From Filing and Fitting to Flexible Manufacturing*, Cambridge, MA: Harvard Business School.

Jassawalla, A.R. and Sashittal, H.C. (1999) 'Building collaborative cross-functional new product teams', *Academy of Management Executive*, 13(4), 50–63.

Kaplinsky, R., Hertog, F. and Coriat, B. (1995) *Europe's Next Step*, London: Frank Cass.

Katzenbach, J. and Smith, D. (2005) *The Wisdom of Teams: Creating the High Performance Organization*, Boston, MA: Harvard Business School Press.

Kotter, J. (1996) *Leading Change*, Boston, MA: Harvard Business School Press.

Lewin, K. (1947) 'Frontiers in group dynamics: Concept, method and reality in the social sciences', *Human Relations* 1(1), 5–41.

Lillrank, P. and Kano, N. (1990) *Continuous Improvement; Quality Control Circles in Japanese Industry*, Ann Arbor: University of Michigan Press.

Maginn, M. (2003) *Making Teams Work*, New York: McGraw Hill.

Marchington, M. and Wilkinson, A. (2008) *Human Resource Management at Work: People Management and Development*, London: Chartered Institute of Personnel and Development.

Miller, E. and Rice, A. (1967) *Systems of Organisation*, London: Tavistock.

Neal, A., West, M.A. and Patterson, (2005) 'Do organizational climate and competitive strategy moderate the relationship between human resource management and productivity?', *Journal of Management*, 31(4), 492–512.

Nonaka, I., Keigo, S. and Ahmed, M. (2003) 'Continuous innovation: The power of tacit knowledge', in L. Shavinina (ed.) *International Handbook on Innovation*, New York: Elsevier.

Parasuraman, R. and Wickens, C.D. (2008) 'Humans: Still vital after all these years of automation', *Human Factors*, 50, 511–20.

Pfeffer, J. (1998) *The Human Equation: Building Profits by Putting People First*, Boston, MA: Harvard Business School Press.

Pfeffer, J. (2007) 'Human resources from an organizational behavior perspective: Some paradoxes explained', *Journal of Economic Perspectives*, 21(4), 115–34.

Pfeffer, J. and Veiga, J. (1999) 'Putting people first for organizational success', *Academy of Management Executive*, 13(2), 37–48.

Philips, J. (2003) *Return on Investment in Training and Performance Improvement Programs (Improving Human Performance)*, London: Butterworth-Heinemann.

Piore, M. and Sabel, C. (1982) *The Second Industrial Divide*, New York: Basic Books.

Schein, E. (2010) *Organizational Culture and Leadership*, San Francisco, CA: Jossey Bass.

Schonberger, R. (1982) *Japanese Manufacturing Techniques: Nine Hidden Lessons in Simplicity*, New York: Free Press.

Schroeder, A. and Robinson, D. (2004) *Ideas are Free: How the Idea Revolution is Liberating People and Transforming Organizations*, New York: Berrett Koehler.

Schroeder, M. and Robinson, A. (1993) 'Training, continuous improvement and human relations: The US TWI programs and Japanese management style', *California Management Review*, 35(2).

Semler, R. (1993) *Maverick*, London: Century Books.

Smith, S. and Tranfield, D. (1990) *Managing Change*, Kempston: IFS Publications.

Sullivan, R. (2010) *Practising organizational development: A guide for leading change*, San Francisco, CA: Jossey-Bass.

Teece, D. (1998) 'Capturing value from knowledge assets: The new economy, markets for know-how, and intangible assets', *California Management Review*, 40(3), 55–79.

Thamhain, H. and Wilemon, D. (1987) 'Building high performance engineering project teams', *IEEE Transcations on Engineering Management*, 34(3), 130–37.

Tidd, J. (1989) *Flexible Automation*, London: Frances Pinter.

Tidd, J. and Bessant, J. (2009) *Managing Innovation: Integrating Technological, Market and Organizational Change*, 4th edition, Chichester: John Wiley.

Trist, E. and Bamforth, K. (1951) 'Some social and psychological consequences of the longwall method of coal getting', *Human Relations*, 4, 3–38.

Tuckman, B. and Jensen, N. (1977) 'Stages of small group development revisited', *Group and Organizational Studies*, 2, 419–27.

Way, S.A. (2002) 'High performance work systems and intermediate indicators of firm performance within the US small business sector', *Journal of Management*, 28(6), 765–85.

Womack, J., Jones, D. and Roos, D. (1991) *The Machine that Changed the World*, New York: Rawson Associates.

Woodward, J. (1965) *Industrial Organisation: Theory and Practice*, Oxford: Oxford University Press.

Zornitsky, J. (1995) 'Making effective human resource management a hard business issue', *Compensation and Benefits Management*, Winter, 16–24.

Part 3

MANAGING STRATEGIC OPERATIONS WITHIN ORGANIZATIONS

CHAPTER 7

MANAGING THE TRANSFORMATION PROCESS

LEARNING OBJECTIVES

The purpose of this chapter is for you to:

- Understand the strategic significance of layout and process choice which, together, form the core of the transformation process.

- Comprehend the strategic importance of layouts and process choice – these provide massive clues about what the organization can, and cannot, do.

- Realize that 'throwing money' at technology is not the answer, although appropriate investment in technology is a necessary requirement.

- Appreciate how process choice will help guide the organization, including how to avoid being pulled into market segments in which it cannot compete.

INTRODUCTION

The physical layout and the transformation process that an organization employs are critical factors for strategic operations management. This is because:

> Both the layout and, more specifically, the process transformation process (or *process choice* as it is sometimes called), provide massive clues about what the organization can do, as well as what it cannot do.

The above statement is important because sometimes an organization will be attracted to market opportunities, but this attraction will prove to be futile because the appropriate layout and process choices are not in place. Alternatively, organizations can become 'stuck' with existing processes which, although of use and relevant in the past, may not be appropriate for today's competitive environments. This was captured by Huckman (2009, p. 91):

> It's a classic problem: Your business succeeds by building operational strengths that allow it to develop and deliver products or services better than anyone else. Then, over the years, as the business naturally broadens for opportunistic or defensive reasons, it loses its edge: Core strengths atrophy, efficiency or quality suffers, and you become vulnerable to cherry picking by sharper rivals.

Industry is littered with examples where companies, with good intentions, failed to achieve their strategic mission due to a lack of understanding of the strategic importance of layouts and the transformation process. For example, a famous operations management case on this issue is the attempt by Babcock and Wilcox, a former *Fortune* 500 company – to enter the nuclear energy industry (Hill, 2000). This attempt was a disaster because the required change of transformation – from 'line' to 'job' processes – was not undertaken by Babcock and Wilcox. Like many organizations, they continued to do what they knew – the fatal 'the way we do things round here' mindset – which kills innovation and change initiatives within organizations.

As we saw in Chapter 1, there have been three major eras in manufacturing: craft, mass production, and the current era. This current era has been called a number of things, including *flexible specialization*, *mass customization*, *agile manufacturing* and *lean production*. These terms attempt to describe the simultaneous requirements of volume and variety that have placed enormous responsibility upon operations management. This is because the current era, with rapid change, fickle and dynamic global markets, constant innovation, and immense demands of flexibility, requires processes that enable the firm to meet customer demands accurately (i.e. without relying on compromise). The key issue in addressing this situation is that, within the current turbulence in sales and supply markets, it is inappropriate to use methods and processes that were previously adopted under mass production (which enjoyed a totally different, far less volatile market). This is particularly relevant in the use of technology in the transformation process. The nature of the new market requirements demands operations management capabilities that can deliver flexibility – this comes from an array of operating possibilities under the heading of 'flexible' manufacturing and customized service.

Process technology is a key part of innovation, as we saw in Chapter 4. However, innovation is not restricted to the launch of new products (as vitally important as this is). It includes acquiring and managing new process technology. Investment in process or product technology, *per se*, is not enough, however. An important part of the innovation process is in ensuring that there is sufficient and suitable *human* capacity – know-how and learning – in place to accompany and complement the investment in new process technology: this is the interface between technology management and operations management.

Process and product technology are often twin themes in the innovation process. This is because process technology must be in place to support new product innovations. Without this capability, new product developments will fail. New technology may also have an important influence on the wider issue of the firm's overall capacity. Capacity should not be seen just in terms of volume but also in the *variety* of products that the firm can provide. This capability – to produce a variety of products – is an important feature of the overall output of the firm.

Managing technology is a complex task because technology is uncertain and dynamic, and must be integrated with other areas, such as human skills and capabilities, cultural aspects (working practices), and financial protocols. Process choice – which is the means by which technology transforms inputs into products within the plant – is always a *major* strategic decision. This is because no amount of reactive, tactical measures can be expected to compensate retrospectively for inappropriate investment in processes which do not match the market requirements in which the firm or plant is competing. Decisions have to be based on current and future market demands and counter technical or engineering indulgence or idiosyncrasy within an influential group within the firm. One of the major considerations in selecting process technology is in the amount and nature of investment necessary – the financial factor, which we shall now discuss.

THE FINANCIAL FACTOR IN PROCESS AUTOMATION AND TECHNOLOGY

The state of markets for most products and services means that investment in technology is seldom a question of choice of whether or not to invest; the only choices often relate only to the *type* and *how much* for process technology investment. Many industrial sectors have seen the demise of firms that suffered from lack of investment over time – firms which became casualties of aggressive competitors that *were* prepared to invest in process technology. In some cases, this lack of investment has accounted for the demise of whole industrial sectors – including the British car manufacturers of the past and elements of ship-building throughout Europe and in the US. These industries represent a range of transformational types which fall under the title of process choice: the lack of investment has been apparent in high-volume, high-tech sectors as well as in sectors producing low-volume products.

There are two, equally dangerous, positions which can be taken when it comes to investment in process technology. Both may seem unrealistic to the newcomer to operations management, but evidence of both is depressingly common. The first is not to invest at all; the second is to 'throw money' at technology in the hope that, somehow, this very act will ensure success for the firm. If a firm does not invest, it may be expected to grow increasingly incapable of competing against other players in its market. The temptation not to invest – management indolence – is one of *the* easiest financial traps to fall into. In the short term, the plant may survive as if no mistake has been made. More alarmingly, the firm's return on net assets – RONA: one of the most misleading of all accounting ratios if used in isolation – will appear to improve! In the longer term, however, the plant or service will undoubtedly become uncompetitive and, typically, face closure. In global manufacturing, where politics are never far beneath the surface, this strategy may be used – with stealth – to justify withdrawal from a foreign plant when conditions in the home country favour retrenchment.

Justifying investment will always be a difficult matter, relying as much on management intuition as scientific analysis: there are no calculations that can state with certainty that a specific investment will yield a specified return. In other words, we cannot say that 'x amounts' of investment equals 'y values of return' within a specific period of time. But we must always bear in mind that the greatest cost will arise from *not* investing. This may mean that justifying an investment is seen as a 'leap of faith' to some degree – beyond the scope of straightforward accountancy techniques. Large sums may be involved and there is often a significant period between the time of investment and the benefits that might be attained. These benefits, such as improved speed and accuracy of delivery, greater flexibility, and enhanced quality, might not have an impact on the 'bottom line' for some time after the operational capabilities have been developed.

Financial ratios do not always provide solutions in these cases. Various attempts have been made to justify accounting criteria, including the payback period (Monohan and Smunt, 1984; Willis and Sullivan, 1984); break-even analysis (Starr and Biloski, 1984) and net present value (NPV) (Hutchison and Holland, 1982; Kulatilaka, 1984). However, the problem with these accounting measures is that there is a static and fixed 'feel' to them. For example, 'payback' criteria ignore any returns that might be forthcoming *beyond* the payback period. In addition, NPV – a ratio which is often used to evaluate investment – assumes that factors such as market share, price, labour costs, and the firm's competitive position in the market will remain constant over time. In practice, all of these factors may be expected to change. To allow for this scientifically, investment analysts would need to use parametric estimating – a complex technique only used at present for the largest, most long-term investments (such as governments' investments in major weapons systems, ships, and so on). More importantly, these operational factors may be expected to degenerate if the company retains outdated production methods, preventing it from competing on key competitive bases such as cost, delivery speed and reliability, and new product innovation.

In the past, the justification for investment was that it should result in a reduction in the numbers of people employed, thus reducing labour costs. This apparently ignores the point that labour costs are typically a small proportion of product cost. There are two traditional reasons for this – the first so surprising that it is difficult to believe. Since overhead costs were traditionally recouped on the basis of a labour hour charge (e.g. overheads might be costed to a product at, say, 300 per cent of labour costs) it was hoped that a reduction in labour would result in a reduction in overhead costs. This absurdity was actually prevalent in industry in the past revealing, perhaps, the degree to which a formulaic approach to management can result in myopia.

Just as important – especially in the justification for the vast amounts of expenditure, which took place in a number of US plants on robots in the 1980s and 1990s – was the argument that technological hardware does not incur the imponderable costs associated with human employees: machines do not go on strike, have unions or pay deals, nor bring any of the other annoyances that can cause managers and directors of plants major headaches when managing human resources. Justification for investment clearly has to go beyond simply replacing labour costs to the principle of competitive advantage in other areas such as product quality, delivery speed, and delivery reliability. In addition, a major issue that has emerged is that human capability is a very necessary complementary asset to the technological hardware in flexible manufacturing systems: it appears the most complex computer control will usually benefit from a 'human break' in its control loops at some stage.

The question of how much to invest in technology is made more difficult in many Western manufacturing firms, because there is no technological or manufacturing presence among senior managers involved in business strategy decisions, whose input might help in guiding the extent and appropriateness of technological investment decisions (Brown and Blackmon, 2005). The consequence of this in some cases is that there have been massive amounts of investment in technology that have resulted in no benefit for the firm.

For example, one of General Motors' most automated plants is in Hamtramck, Michigan. On 21 April 2010 GM announced it was going to invest $121 million dollars into the Hamtramck factory to ensure GM could keep up with the demand for the next generation Chevrolet Malibu. However, in spite of the level of automation in place, this plant, for a long time, was known for having lower productivity and poorer quality performance than GM's more labour-intensive plant at Fremont, California – the NUMMI project (New United Motor Manufacturing Industry) – a joint venture between GM and Toyota in an old GM plant, which ended, sadly, in 2010.

Keller (1993, p. 169) provides insight into the inappropriate investment at General Motors:

> While Smith provided the money for automation and supported it completely, he clearly didn't understand it. . . . With its 260 gleaming new robots for welding, assembling, and painting cars; its fifty automated guided vehicles to deliver parts to the assembly line; and a complement of cameras and computers to monitor, inspect, and control the process, the plant put stars in Smith's eyes. He believed it held the promise of a new era of efficiency and quality and would eventually become a model for all assembly plants. What it became was a nightmare of inefficiency, producing poor-quality vehicles despite the heroic efforts of workers to correct mistakes before they were shipped to dealers.

Between 1980 and 1995, GM is reputed to have spent $80 billion on manufacturing automation (at a time when the giant corporation's annual turnover was around $100 billion). This massive investment did not bring significant benefits to GM, however. In the early 1980s, GM enjoyed a domestic market share of around 60 per cent; by the end of the 1990s this had fallen to around 30 per cent and had diminished further to around 22 per cent by 2012.

What had happened was that GM's rivals – particularly the Japanese – invested in the *right technology* for the *right reasons*. The new Japanese car transplants in the US employed lean, flexible manufacturing techniques – a mix of human and technological capacity, which was to take the North American vehicle producers almost a decade to understand.

One of the reasons behind GM's investment disaster was that the decision to invest included wanting to reduce the workforce significantly. It did just that – in a six-year period – from 876,000 in 1986 to around 750,000 in 1992 (Brown, 1996). With the benefit of hindsight, we can see that GM's problem during this period was the lack of importance given to process technology as a *complementary* feature to the skills and inventiveness of humans, rather than a wholesale replacement for them. GM learned this lesson from Toyota in the NUMMI joint-venture project and later implemented it at the Saturn plant in Springhill TN.

Clearly, technology *can* replace human labour: this has been a concern since the early nineteenth century, when the British 'Luddites' destroyed the looms and 'spinning jennies' that threatened their livelihood in the industrial revolution. Computers have also been seen as a threat. For example, in the late 1940s Norbert Weiner, a pioneer of computing, forecast that this new technology would destroy enough jobs to make the depression of the 1930s appear tame by comparison. The case is not clear, however, as shown by this comment in *The Economist* back in 1995:

> Are such fears justified? In one way, yes. Millions of jobs have indeed been destroyed by technology. A decade ago, the words you are now reading would have reached you from two sets of hands: those of a journalist and those of a typesetter. Thanks to computers, the typesetter no longer has a job. . . . Although the typesetter no longer has that job, he may well have a different one. John Kennedy put it well in the 1960s: 'If men have the talent to invent new machines that put men out of work, they have the talent to put those men back to work.' That is as true now as it was then, and earlier.
>
> (*Economist*, 1995, p. 36)

Investment in technology can provide benefits for the firm and its workforce, principally by ensuring continued operation for a plant. The firm can gain from consistent process quality and quicker changeovers (set-up) which will result in greater flexibility. Robots can free humans from tiresome, repetitive, and monotonous tasks, allowing them to do more creative activities.

With specific regard to manufacturing technology, the 'Economist manufacturing technology survey' (*Economist*, 1994a) noted that:

> robots have not displaced men and women . . . despite the fact that their advent gave rise to yet another wave of speculation about the workerless factory. They have a role in manufacturing and have been used well in Japan. . . . The Japanese have understood that, if work is designed properly for robots, they will do it well – but they are not able to replace people at jobs that have evolved to need a human's innate ability to fit the world and ideas and intentions to that of deeds and objects.
>
> (pp. 8–9)

It is clear, then, that the justification for technological investment must go beyond cost reductions from reduced numbers in the workforce. Instead, it must follow on from an awareness of, and the desire to satisfy, market requirements.

Investment decisions are critical and must be made with the aim of equipping the firm or the plant to be more competitive in the market. Furthermore, wrong process choice decisions may severely reduce the company's capability to satisfy customer demands in particular markets. Process choice and technology are both vital because key competitive factors for customers including cost, delivery speed, and flexibility, can be enhanced by their combination. If appropriate investment is made in technology and process choice, the resultant capacity and capability should become a central part of the firm's competitive weaponry.

LAYOUT AND PROCESS CHOICE

As we noted earlier, we know there have been three eras of manufacturing: craft, mass production, and the current era. All three have direct relevance to the nature of the transformation process and process choice. They are also relevant to types of facilities layout to be understood: we start with this factor before linking layout to process choice. The basic types of layout are:

1. Fixed position;
2. Process layout;
3. A hybrid of process and product layouts, based around cells; and
4. Product layout.

We will explore each of these in turn.

Fixed position

A fixed layout is used where a product may be heavy, bulky or fragile and in this approach operators come to the product itself. The product is completed 'on site' and is not moved during completion. The product is housed around a particular, focused area. Examples of this are shown in Figure 7.1:

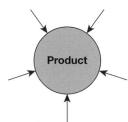

Operators perform process on the 'fixed' product. There may be more than one operation performed on the product at the same time. Each operation adds to the product until it is completed.

Examples:
In manufacturing, fixed layouts are used in ship-building, fabrication of aeroplanes and various forms of construction. In services, a dentist will be an example where the person remains 'fixed' or in place for the duration of the 'operation'.

Figure 7.1 Fixed position layouts

Process layout

In a process layout, a plant or service location has specific activities or machinery grouped together. In manufacturing this allows a range or variety of products to be made. The machines are not laid out in a particular, sequential process. Therefore, the product does not move in a specified sequence but will go to a machine centre as and when required for the particular product. The great advantage of process-oriented layouts is the flexibility in both equipment and labour assignments that they bring. The breakdown of a particular machine will not halt an entire process and work can therefore be transferred to other machines in the department. This type of layout is ideal for manufacturing parts in small batches – or job lots – and for producing a wide range of parts in different sizes and forms. Examples are shown in Figure 7.2.

The layout of the Arnold Palmer Hospital in the US has clearly embraced a process approach. This is a clever design because the layout has a core hub and this feeds various functions and departments, as shown in Figure 7.3.

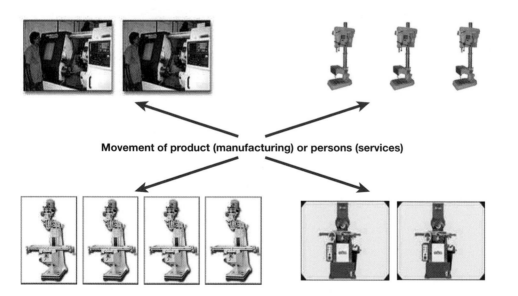

Movement of product (manufacturing) or persons (services)

'Random' movement takes place as products are moved according to process requirements. There is no 'flow' as such – each product will have its particular process requirements and will move to each machine group as and when required.

Examples:

In manufacturing, this layout is commonly used in job-shop environments where craft-type manufacture continues to this day. Examples would include low-volume furniture, haute couture clothing, and jewellery. In services, examples would include types of catering which are laid out enabling a person to move to an area as required; hospitals are also laid out like this – unless they are dedicated to one process only (such as an eye operation). Patients move around departments and wards as necessary. Hairdressing is another service example where areas such as washing, drying, and cutting are put in place to complete a range of different styles. A department store (retailing) is also arranged on this basis.

Figure 7.2 Process layout in a functional approach

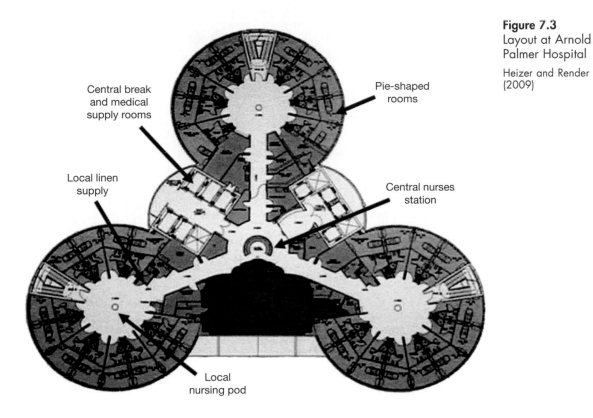

Figure 7.3
Layout at Arnold
Palmer Hospital

Heizer and Render
(2009)

Central break
and medical
supply rooms

Pie-shaped
rooms

Local linen
supply

Central nurses
station

Local
nursing pod

CASE: THE BENEFITS OF A 'CORE HUB' LAYOUT

Instead of the traditional 'racetrack' design (long hallways with a central nursing station on each floor), when the Arnold Palmer Hospital added the new building a circular 'pod' system was designed. The whole idea was to cut down the walking time of the hospital's most precious scarce resource: nurses. The average nurse (about 45 years old) was hiking 2.7 miles a day up and down the hallways to the central station.

The layout design process lasted over a year. Over 1,000 meetings of doctors, nurses, and patients turned into drawings and then into 'test' layouts. The hospital rented a warehouse a mile away and created full-sized mockups of every type of room. When we toured, we were encouraged to comment on every aspect of the layout, from placement of electrical outlets, to pictures on the walls, to Murphy beds for guests, to bathrooms.

The result was a roundish building with central nursing pods for each cluster of 34 rooms . . . What a change in walking time for nurses: a 20% drop with the new layout!

http://heizerrenderom.wordpress.com/2011/02/13/
video-tip-layout-of-the-new-arnold-palmer-hospital/

A video tour of the hospital is available here: www.orlandohealth.com/arnoldpalmerhospital/TakeaTour/
TakeaTour.aspx?pid=6312

Figure 7.4
Process layout in a
product family cell

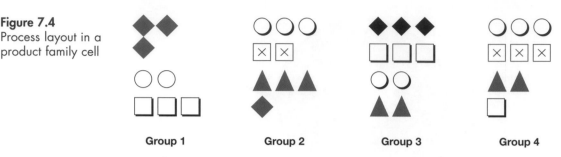

Examples:

This clustering/cell approach is common in high-tech manufacturing environments. This enables high volume and some variety to be achieved simultaneously. The same type of approach has been adopted in high-volume, batch type services such as call centres in finance-related sectors where calls are routed through to specific, focused areas.

The hybrid process/product layout

With the above approach, the machines or points of activity (for example operating theatres, or sections in a department store) are not dedicated to a particular product family (customer) but are available for a range of products. Another approach, shown in Figure 7.4, is to group machines or activities together around a focused, product family cell.

In manufacturing, machines or activities are grouped together in a way that best supports the manufacture of a particular family of products, or to provide a cluster of similar services. The variety of products or services around a particular group or 'cell' may be quite large but the essential nature of the product will remain similar and will, therefore, warrant a cell of its own, distinct from other, product family cells.

Product layout

In a product layout, machines are dedicated to a particular product – or a very similar small range of products – and each stage of manufacture is distinct from the next as shown in Figure 7.5:

The sequence of operations id designed in a linear, logical succession, where one activity in the line is dependent upon the preceding activity having taken place.

Examples:

In manufacturing this is common in car manufacture and other high-volume applications. In services it has been used to some degree in high-volume 'standard' provisions, especially where there is a tangible element in the overall offering: e.g. fast-food delivery in-house.

Figure 7.5 Product layout

Assembly line surgery

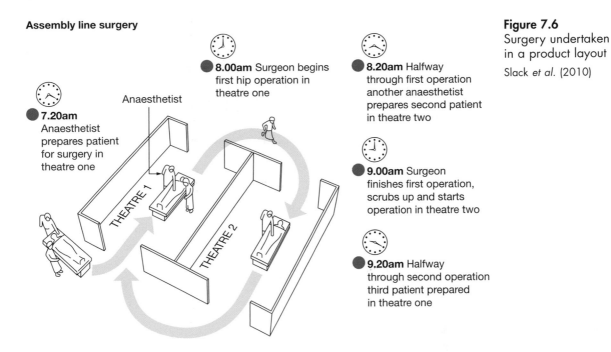

7.20am Anaesthetist prepares patient for surgery in theatre one

Anaesthetist

8.00am Surgeon begins first hip operation in theatre one

8.20am Halfway through first operation another anaesthetist prepares second patient in theatre two

9.00am Surgeon finishes first operation, scrubs up and starts operation in theatre two

9.20am Halfway through second operation third patient prepared in theatre one

Figure 7.6
Surgery undertaken in a product layout
Slack *et al.* (2010)

Each of the stations in Figure 7.5 is laid out in an operational sequence specific to the manufacture of a particular product or the provision of a repetitious service offering. This kind of layout has been used in some surgical procedures, as can be seen in the Figure 7.6.

Thus, physical layout provides some important insights into what an organization can, and cannot do. These become more evident when we understand the wider aspect of Process Choice:

PROCESS CHOICE

As we shall see, process choice will provide essential, major clues about how a firm competes and what it can – *and cannot* – do. The five types are:

1. Project;
2. Job;
3. Batch;
4. Line; and
5. Continuous Process.

The basic distinction between the five types of process choice is illustrated in Figure 7.7 and each type is discussed subsequently.

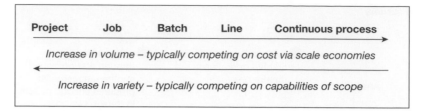

Figure 7.7 The key distinction of volume and variety outputs from process choice

As we shall see, the choice of the transformation process choice actually dictates, to a large extent, what the company 'sells' in terms of its capabilities and how it can compete. There may be more than one process type being used within the same company but there will usually be a dominant 'core' process which is best suited to support the company in the market. We need to be clear about the nature of each transformation process.

Project processes

In 'project' manufacturing environments, the nature of the products is often large-scale and complex. The designs of the products undertaken in project manufacturing are, essentially, unique by virtue of their not being repeated in exactly the same way. The distinguishing feature between 'project' and 'job' manufacture is that, during the process of completion, the product in project manufacture tends to be 'fixed'. Scheduling of projects tends to be undertaken in a 'phased-completion' programme, where each phase of completion will be distinct and separate from other subsequent, or parallel, stages. At the simplest level of management, tools such as Gantt charts will be used. Alternatively, more complicated programmes such as 'project network planning' will be employed.

> In manufacturing, projects include civil engineering of various types, aerospace, and some major high-tech projects – flight simulator manufacture would tend to fall into this category, for example. Projects tend to be 'one-offs' where repetition in terms of the product being exactly the same is unlikely. Construction in all forms – bridge manufacture, tunnel construction, and ship-building – is a common application of project process choice.
>
> In manufacturing environments, this ties the process choice (project) with the fixed type of layout. In services, all types of consulting would fall into this category. The relationship, expectations, and outcomes with each client should be seen as 'unique'. Each session with a client should be seen as unique. This means that the project process links to Schmenner's 'professional services' category which we discuss later in the chapter (see Figure 7.5).

Job processes

In manufacturing, job processes are used for 'one-off' or very small order requirements, similar to project manufacture. However, the difference is that the product can often be moved during manufacture. Perceived uniqueness is often a key factor for job manufacture. The volume is very small and, as with project manufacture, the products tend to be a 'one-off' in terms of design; it is very unlikely that they will be repeated in the short term and, therefore, investment in dedicated technology for a particular product is unlikely. Investment in automation is for general-purpose process technology rather than product-specific investment. Many different products are run throughout the plant and materials handling has to be modified and adjusted to suit many different products and types. Detailed planning will evolve around sequencing requirements for each product, capacities for each work centre, and order priorities. Because of this, scheduling is relatively complicated in comparison to repetitive 'line' manufacture.

> In manufacture, job processes are linked to traditional craft manufacture. Making special haute-couture clothing is a clear example. Job processes are common in the following:
>
> 1. Making prototypes of new products – even if the end volume is likely to be high for the product, it makes sense to produce a 'one-off' or very low volume, which lends itself to job manufacture.
> 2. Making unique products such as machines, tools, and fixtures to make other products. The process choice (job) is linked to the process layout.
>
> In services, a job process is linked to the 'service shop' in Schmenner's matrix. Car repairs and many hospital service activities are job processes.

Batch processes

As volume begins to increase, either in terms of individual products (i.e. total volume), or in the manufacture of similar 'types' or 'families' of products (i.e. greater number of products in any one group or family) the process will develop into 'batch' manufacture. The difficulty in batch manufacturing is that competitive focus can often become blurred – management attention becomes fixed upon optimizing the batch conditions to the detriment of customer service.

The batch process is, therefore, often difficult to manage: the key is to map the range of products in terms of either 'job' or 'line' characteristics. Batch production may be arranged either in terms of the similarity of finished *products* or by common *process* groupings. As a starting point, each product has to be determined by its volume – focused 'cells' of manufacture will then be arranged so that low and high volumes can be separated.

Automation, especially for lower volumes of batch manufacturing, tends to be general purpose rather than dedicated to a particular product whose volume does not demand product-specific investment in automation. Scheduling is often complicated and has to be completely reviewed on a regular basis – this applies to new products, to 'one-offs', and to higher volume, standard products: all of these types will need to be scheduled.

In batch production, operators have to be able to perform a number of functions. This is clearly also true for 'job' type processes, but in batch processes this flexibility is crucial as it allows operators to move to various workstations, as and when required. Where automation is being used, set-up time need to be short, the ideal set up time being that necessary to accommodate run lengths of just one unit, switching over to other models and volumes as required.

Batch is the most common form of process in engineering and the most difficult to manage. Only by determining the volumes of each product and dividing these into low- and high-volume sections can a company hope to be focused and, in turn, customer driven.

Typical examples of the batch process in manufacture would be in plastic moulding production – these would be distinguished by determining those products that need much labour input (hand laminating in glass reinforced plastic, for example) and high volume 'standard' products where considerable automation would be appropriate.

Other examples include bread making, where batches of similar types are produced. In general, batch processes link to process layout, although high-volume batches will tend to have a type of line (product) layout, depending upon how often the product is reproduced.

In services, 'batching a process' has become common in routing procedures for call-centres. The response message to many telephone call centres is: 'press "1" for this service; press "2" for that service' and so on. If the service centre adds the message: 'press "0" for all other enquiries', this puts the service provision back into a job-type service. This will equate either with a mass service or a service shop in Schmenner's matrix depending on the extent of customization involved with the customer.

Line processes

A 'line' process becomes more appropriate as the volume of a particular product increases, leading to greater standardization than in low batch volumes. Each stage of manufacture will be distinct from the next, and value and cost are added at each stage of manufacture until the product is completed. The line is dedicated to a particular product (with possible variations of models) and introducing new products that are significantly different from the former product is difficult or even impossible to realize on an existing line manufacturing process. Individual operation process times should be short in order to satisfy delivery expectations. Competitive advantages may be gained from simplification in production planning and control and the tasks themselves should also be simplified for each workstation (both these features were fundamental to the development of the just-in-time processes in Japan in the 1950s).

In line production, there should only be very small amounts of work in process: where it does exist, it represents a poorly balanced line loading and is seen as a signal for necessary improvement. Work in process is counted as an asset by traditional accounting systems, but is actually a liability to the company as it represents unsellable materials: unmanaged, this can ruin cash-flow and stifle quick response to market requirements. Workstations should be located as closely as possible to each other to minimize materials handling between them. Materials flow and control is critical and stock-outs have to be avoided.

High volume, 'standard' products – such as particular models of cars, TVs, hi-fi, VCRs and computers – lend themselves to line processes, often arranged in a U-shape. The process choice (line) ties it to the product type of layout. In services, a sequential, line-type process can be put in place where there is high standardization of the service offering. This equates to Schmenner's service factory quadrant. Where there is a high tangible element within the offering – for example in fast foods – the back-room facilities will resemble a factory and the mode of delivery will go through specific stages. In less tangible elements, the service may resemble a line process in that there may be, for example, set procedures to adopt for a particular type of service process. For example, in dealing with high volume, 'standard' applications – such as a mortgage – there will often be set sequences of events.

Since much of the discussion on automation – which appears later in the chapter – is based on developments around line processes, it is necessary for us to discuss some of the disadvantages of line processes here. The disadvantages to line manufacture include the following:

1. There can often be a lack of process flexibility, and introducing new products on existing technology can be difficult. This is alleviated to some degree by similar subcomponents which become included in the design for new products and which then allow the new product to be made on existing lines.

2. As standardization and volumes both increase, relative to 'batch' and 'job' manufacturing processes, investment in technology also increases. Special, product-specific technology is used and this often involves vast amounts of firm-specific investments: (for example GM's $80 billion investment in automation in the 1980s). Each workstation is dependent upon the next – consequently, the speed of the line is determined by the lowest capacity of a particular work centre; moreover, in 'standard' lines, if one set of machines is not operating, the whole line can come to a stop, thus preventing any production.

We often associate line layouts with Henry Ford but there is now evidence that a British engineer, Woollard, helped to pioneer production lines independent of Henry Ford's influence. Moreover, some of the terminology he used would be appropriate for modern-day lean production:

The ideal arrangement for flow production should resemble a watershed; the river being the main assembly track, fed by tributaries in the shape of sub-assembly lines which, in turn, would be supplied by streams representing the machine lines fed by brooks typifying the material conveyors. Each part should flow continuously forward. There should be few bends, no eddies, no dams, no storms, no freezing should impede the inevitable flow to estuarine waters – the dealers – and ultimately to the sea – the customers.

(Woollard, 1954, p. 48)

Emiliani and Seymour (2011, p. 67) provide further important context when they state:

Henry Ford is often cited by Toyota managers and others as a principal source of influence for the development of the Toyota Production System (TPS), also known as lean production. . . . This attribution, however, may have been more out of respect, admiration, and desire for future business relationships rather than actual direct influence on production methods because the scale of Ford's operations was much too large to be of use to Toyota executives. In addition, acknowledgement of Ford may have had to do more with his overall business and management philosophy . . . there is never any mention of the British automaker Morris Motors Ltd or the pioneering work of Frank G. Woollard as possible influences on Toyota Motor Corporation, particularly in its formative years (1933–1950). This is important because Woollard achieved flow in the mid-1920s using what we today recognize as distinctive characteristics of Toyota's production system: work cells, part families, standardized work, just in time, supermarkets, autonomation (jidoka), takt/cycle time, quick change-over, multi-skilled workers, arranging the equipment in the sequence in which value is added, etc.

In addition, Woollard understood the idea and practice of continuous improvement in a flow environment, saying that the need for modifications to the flow line 'should cause no anxiety, but rather should be a matter for rejoicing [. . .] the virtue of flow production lies in the fact that it brings all inconsistencies into the light of day and so provides the opportunity for correcting them,' and '[the] high visibility conferred on the company's activities by flow production will lead to unceasing and continuous improvement'.

Continuous processes

This is used when a process can (or must) run all day for each day of the year, on a continuous basis. The volume of the product is typically very high and the process is dedicated to making only one product. Huge investment in dedicated plant is often required. Much automation tends to be evident and labour input is one of 'policing' rather than being highly skilled as an integral input to the overall process.

In manufacturing, a chemical refining plant, a blast furnace or steel works, and very high-volume food processing are all examples where a continuous process

would be in place. In services, strictly speaking, there is no real equivalent. For example, even though technology might be in place to allow financial transactions to take place on a 24-hour basis, the amounts being transferred from one account to another would vary: it is not a case of one transaction being conducted many thousands of times.

MATRICES USED IN SERVICES

Examples of services in process choice were provided above. One of the major challenges in managing service operations is to understand the nature of the service provision. This challenge is helped by using a 'mapping process' focusing on a range of factors. In each factor the key issue is the degree of interaction between the service provider and the customer:

- Is the labour intensity: high or low?
- Is the degree of contact with the customer: high or low?
- Is the interaction: high or low?
- Is the degree of customization: choice, fixed or adaptation?
- Is the nature of the act: tangible or intangible?
- Is the recipient of the act: people or things?

These questions help us to define the very nature of the service provision and prevent us from thinking that all services are similar. A number of matrices provide additional insights into how to map the nature of the service.

In the service literature, a useful taxonomy has been proposed by Schmenner (1986) who identified that service could be categorized, using their degree of labour intensity and level of customization, into four types called: service shop, service factory, mass service, and professional service. This is shown in Figure 7.8.

The Schmenner matrix links the extent of customization with the level of labour input in the transformation process. As Schmenner observes, however, a service, although essentially rooted within a particular quadrant, may wander into other quadrants, consciously or otherwise. For example, a therapist may 'batch' the same types of questions when dealing with a number of patients. The reason for doing so may well be well intentioned: namely to 'speed up' the healing process. However, in doing so the therapist is moving from the 'professional service' quadrant into other areas and may even mimic elements of the 'service factory'.

The Schmenner matrix is of further use because not only does it help to map the actual nature of the service, it also provides indications of the challenges that managers will face as a result of being positioned within a particular service type. This is shown in Figure 7.9.

There are other important matrices that have been provided, notably by Lovelock (1983). One of these examines whether the nature of the service offer is tangible or intangible and

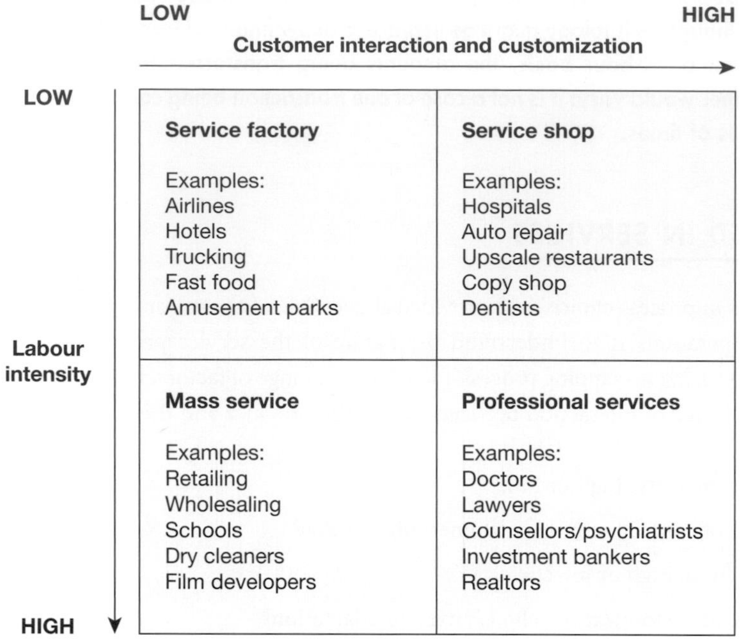

Figure 7.8 within the image:

	LOW ← Customer interaction and customization → HIGH	
LOW **Labour intensity** **HIGH**	**Service factory** Examples: Airlines Hotels Trucking Fast food Amusement parks	**Service shop** Examples: Hospitals Auto repair Upscale restaurants Copy shop Dentists
	Mass service Examples: Retailing Wholesaling Schools Dry cleaners Film developers	**Professional services** Examples: Doctors Lawyers Counsellors/psychiatrists Investment bankers Realtors

Figure 7.8 Schmenner's service matrix
Schmenner (1986)

then contrasts this against who or what is the recipient – whether the recipient is a person or an object. This is shown in Figure 7.10.

This helps us to understand the diverse nature of services, including the issue that, in some cases, customers must be physically present to receive services – where they are directed at their bodies or minds – but *need not be present* to receive other services directed at goods or intangible assets. This will have a major impact on service design, especially the design of service facilities.

Further insight is offered by Lovelock when he states how important it is to see the dimensions of 'who does what' against the number of sites involved in the service transfer. This is shown in Figure 7.11.

SUMMARIZING THE LINKS BETWEEN PROCESS CHOICE AND LAYOUT

As we have noted, there are clear links between the basic choice of process and type of layout. We can summarize this in Figure 7.12.

It is important to note that operations and industries are not forever tied to one type of process or one type of layout. In the early 1970s, Ted Levitt (1972) discussed the notion of production-lining service or service 'industrialization'. He illustrated this concept by

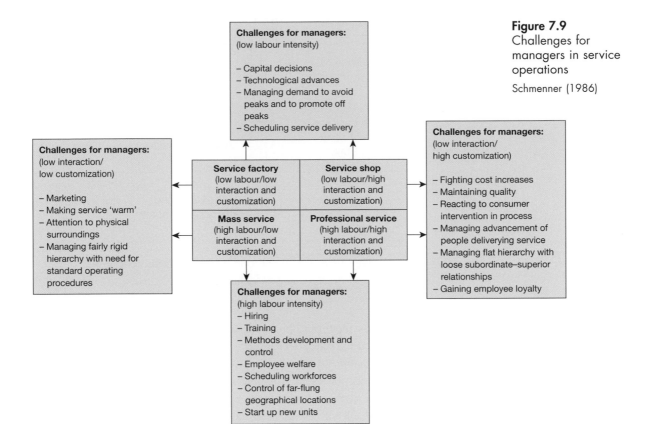

Figure 7.9
Challenges for managers in service operations

Schmenner (1986)

Challenges for managers:
(low labour intensity)

– Capital decisions
– Technological advances
– Managing demand to avoid peaks and to promote off peaks
– Scheduling service delivery

Challenges for managers:
(low interaction/
low customization)

– Marketing
– Making service 'warm'
– Attention to physical surroundings
– Managing fairly rigid hierarchy with need for standard operating procedures

Service factory
(low labour/low interaction and customization)

Service shop
(low labour/high interaction and customization)

Mass service
(high labour/low interaction and customization)

Professional service
(high labour/high interaction and customization)

Challenges for managers:
(low interaction/
high customization)

– Fighting cost increases
– Maintaining quality
– Reacting to consumer intervention in process
– Managing advancement of people deliverying service
– Managing flat hierarchy with loose subordinate–superior relationships
– Gaining employee loyalty

Challenges for managers:
(high labour intensity)
– Hiring
– Training
– Methods development and control
– Employee welfare
– Scheduling workforces
– Control of far-flung geographical locations
– Start up new units

Figure 7.10
Further mapping in service operations – the degree of tangibility and the nature of the recipient in the service

Lovelock (1983)

WHO OR WHAT IS THE DIRECT RECIPIENT OF THE SERVICE?

NATURE OF SERVICE

	PEOPLE	THINGS
TANGIBLE	**Services directed at people's bodies** health care beauty salons exercise clinics restaurants haircuts	**Services directed at goods** freight transport industrial repair and maintenance laundry landscaping
INTANGIBLE	**Services directed at people's minds** education broadcasting information services theatre museums	**Services directed at intangible assets** banking legal services accounting securities insurance

	Single site	**Multiple site**
Customer goes to the service organization →	Theatre Hairdressing	Bus service Fast food chain
Service organization comes to the customer →	Lawn care service Pest control Taxi	Mail delivery AA/RAC service
Customer and organization interact at arms length →	Credit card company	Broadcasting Telephone company

Figure 7.11 Understanding 'who does what' and the role of sites in services

discussing the concept of fast food. The innovation that lay behind the success and tremendous growth of this industry was the way in which the production and service of a hot meal was conceived and designed. Before fast food, meals were produced to order, once the customer had made their choice from the menu. This meant the restaurant could offer variety, as production only started once the order had been placed. Variety required a process layout and restaurants were (and still are) job shops. In the case of fast food, the meal is produced *before* the customer enters the restaurant. It is cooked, and wrapped ready for sale on a shelf – all the server has to do is assemble the order when the customer comes to the counter. This makes the service time considerably faster than in a conventional restaurant.

Since the hot meal (in McDonald's case the hamburger) has a short shelf life of approximately seven minutes, in order to avoid waste the restaurant needs a high volume of customers in order to ensure the stock is sold quickly. To achieve high volume the product needs to be relatively low priced and easy to eat anywhere. But also to avoid the production of unsold stock, the menu needs to be reduced down to as few items as possible. Hence a fast-food menu typically has a very small number of raw material items that can be processed in a variety of ways to produce a range of products – regular hamburger, cheeseburger, bacon and cheeseburger, etc. By increasing volume and decreasing variety, the fast food 'restaurant' was no longer a job shop, but a line operation based on a product layout – hence Levitt's notion of production-lining service.

However, in some industries, layout is not a matter of choice. This often applies in those operations in which the customer interacts with the service provider. The classic example of this is a hotel. Hotel rooms are cleaned in batches, each worker being allocated ten to 15 rooms to service. Ideally they should be organized on a process or product basis, but in reality they have a fixed position. The same is true of theme parks. The layout is fixed, although customers using the rides are processed in batches.

It is also the case that some operations do not involve one process type, nor have one layout. This is most obviously the case in those service operations which have a back and front office, such as a bank, or a front-of-house and back-of-house, such as a restaurant. In these operations it may be that customers are processed in one, typically as a job shop, while the materials and information processing that occurs to support the front office may be batch or even line production.

In such operations, in the past, it was typically the case that the back of house operation and front of house operation were of the same process type. However, many operations have now 'decoupled' the two parts of the operation so that a *choice* can be made over the best process to use. For instance, banks continue to process customers in their branches based on job-shop principles and process layout. However, in their back office the administration has been production-lined by setting up one large data processing facility to support a very large number of branches.

Once it is possible to decouple one part of the operation from another, it then becomes possible to consider outsourcing a part of the operation. For instance, large hotels engage in two types of food and beverage operation. They have restaurants, which are job shops, and banqueting, which is batch production. In some hotels, in recognition of this, there are two kitchens, one for the restaurant and one for the banqueting suites, although this results in inefficiencies due to duplication of equipment and staff. Where there is only one production kitchen, equipment and work activities design to cope with one operation often find it difficult to cope with the other – typically banquet service interrupts and slows down restaurant service. Partly for this reason, many hotels now outsource the production of banquet meals to specialist cook-chill suppliers. They also outsource because the supplier

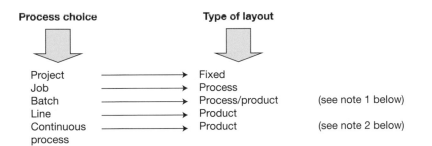

Process choice   **Type of layout**

Project ————————→ Fixed
Job ————————————→ Process
Batch ——————————→ Process/product   (see note 1 below)
Line ———————————→ Product
Continuous ————————→ Product   (see note 2 below)
process

Notes:
1. The link between Batch and the type of layout would depend upon volume and variety – in low volume/high variety Batch, Process layouts would be used; in high volume/low variety Batch, Product layouts would be appropriate.
2. Continuous process differs from line due to the fact that a line process can be stopped at a particular stage and the product will be at that stage of production; in Continuous process, stopping the process is an exception and is very costly (e.g. shutting down a blast furnace).

Figure 7.12 The link between process choice and layout

can supply the meals at a lower unit cost than they themselves are able to do. This is because the supplier has a process and layout that enables lower-cost production and economies of scale.

THE STRATEGIC IMPORTANCE OF PROCESS CHOICE

As we noted earlier, the type of process choice determines to a large extent what the firm can and cannot do. This provides major clues to the actual nature of the business that the firm is in. This shown in Figure 7.13.

One of the dangers for firms in both manufacturing and service settings is that there may be a mismatch between the type of process being used and the expectations of the customer. In services, for example, we have noted how the nature of professional services (around a job-type setting) would mean that one would expect high customization as well as high labour input. However, the danger is that, for example, lawyers, doctors, and other professionals might begin to batch the service process so that the customization becomes compromised in the name of gaining economies of scale or effort. This would have dangerous consequences – a clinical psychologist, for example, might batch certain questions together in order to speed up the therapy process but in doing so miss the deeper issues that would be expected in a one-to-one consultant/patient relationship.

Clearly, managing the process transformation is an enormously important challenge for operations managers in both service and manufacturing settings. Success does not come about purely by having the right technology. Other skills and tacit knowledge also come into play. We illustrate this using the example of Taco Bell, in Case 7.1.

PROCESS CHOICE AND COMPETITIVE FACTORS

As we saw in Chapter 2, Hill (2000) makes the very useful distinction between 'order-qualifying' and 'order-winning' criteria for a firm. Briefly put, order-qualifying criteria are those factors that a company needs in order to compete *at all* and order-winning criteria are those factors that a company needs to achieve in order to *win* in the market place. Hill suggests that order-qualifying and winning criteria can be mapped onto process choice as shown in Figure 7.14.

This framework can be a powerful tool for the company in 'mapping' how the process choice ties it to competitive factors. It is critically important to rank, or weight, the importance of these criteria in any specific case. It is important that firms do not see order-qualifiers as inferior because, as Hill argues, these can lose orders. A firm cannot simply 'skip over' order-qualifying criteria. For example, a PC producer, recognizing that price is an order-winner cannot skip over order-qualifying criteria of up-to-date technology, delivery and so on in order to reduce prices still further.

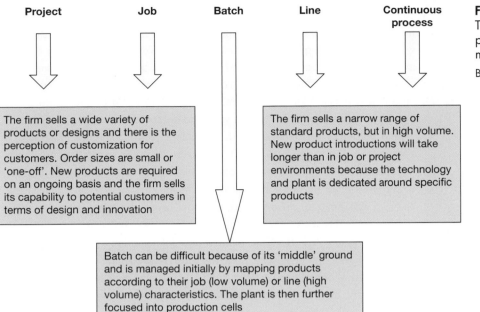

Figure 7.13
The link between process choice and marketing strategy
Brown (1996)

The firm sells a wide variety of products or designs and there is the perception of customization for customers. Order sizes are small or 'one-off'. New products are required on an ongoing basis and the firm sells its capability to potential customers in terms of design and innovation

The firm sells a narrow range of standard products, but in high volume. New product introductions will take longer than in job or project environments because the technology and plant is dedicated around specific products

Batch can be difficult because of its 'middle' ground and is managed initially by mapping products according to their job (low volume) or line (high volume) characteristics. The plant is then further focused into production cells

---

CASE 7.1: TACO BELL

CASE STUDY

In 1999 three out of every four Mexican fast-food meals purchased in the United States were made by one company – Taco Bell. However, this market dominance may never have come about unless the company had not transformed its operations throughout the 1980s.

In the early 1980s, Taco Bell was typical of its kind. It was essentially a job shop operation. Nearly all food production was carried out onsite – foodstuffs were prepared from their raw state, food items such as ground beef for tacos was cooked for a period of several hours in vats, guacamole and other sauces were made up, and beans were washed, cleaned, and cooked. Once these items were ready for sale, they were then assembled in response to a customer order. This meant that wait time at the cash register was 105 seconds on average, and even slower during peak periods.

This type of operation lead to a number of management challenges. Staff had to be scheduled and organized in shifts so that they mainly prepared food items and cleaned the units during slack periods, whilst they assembled orders and served customers during busy times. It was estimated that the restaurant manager spent an hour each day working on this crew schedule in order to match labour supply as closely as possible to potential demand, and thereby meet the company's labour cost targets. Food cost control was also a priority, which meant that a great deal of time and effort went into to ensuring that no menu item was prepared in too small or too large a quantity. But the complexity of this operation lead to quite wide variations in food quality, both within single units and between units in the chain. This was not helped by inconsistency in the quality of raw materials, which were mainly sourced locally.

The emphasis on in-house food production meant that that the ratio of kitchen to dining space was 70:30. Moreover, the main assembly line where food items were made to order ran parallel to the service counter, so that employees on the line were facing away from the customers. At that time, Taco Bell did not have a drive-through window, even though 50 per cent of competitors' sales were from this source.

Beginning in 1983, the CEO of Taco Bell, John Martin, made a number of major changes to the physical layout. The food assembly line was reconfigured to have two shorter lines at right angles to service counter. This improved product flow and improved customers' perception of the operation. The introduction of electronic point-of-sale not only improved order taking and cash handling, but also provided improved data on which food forecasting could be made. Other changes included adding new menu items, increasing the average size of new units from 1,600 square feet up to 2,000 square feet, adding drive-through windows, and upgrading the decor and uniforms of staff.

However, external pressures meant that Martin also had to adopt a new operations process. By the mid-1980s the US fast food market had matured and competition was fierce. Previously performance was judged on growth, which could be achieved by opening new units. In the mature marketplace, market share became much more significant. Labour shortages also meant an increase in labour costs, up by 18 per cent for the industry, but by 50 per cent for Taco Bell due to its relatively larger, skilled workforce. Whereas chains with burger or chicken concepts could offset this increase by taking advantage of falling food costs, Taco Bell's food costs remained at around 30 per cent of sales. So by 1989, Taco Bell was a relatively small player in the market being squeezed by rising costs.

In a series of initiatives, the operation was transformed. K-minus was a project which turned the kitchen into just a heating and assembly unit. Nearly all food preparation (the chopping, slicing, and mixing of vegetables and meat) and cooking was eliminated. Beef, chicken and beans arrived in pre-cooked bags, lettuce was pre-shredded, hard tortillas pre-fried, and guacamole delivered in cartridges. This changed the ratio of back-of-house to front-of-house to 30:70, reduced staffing levels in each unit, and increased the operational capacity of each unit. The SOS (speed of service) initiative was designed to respond to market research that showed customers wanted their food fast. Recipes were adapted and a heated staging area developed so that 60 per cent of the menu items, representing over 80 per cent of sales by volume, were pre-wrapped ready for sale. This reduced customer waiting time to 30 seconds, and increased peak hour capacity by over 50 per cent. Finally TACO (total automation of company operations) was an IT project designed to computerize in-store operations and network each unit to headquarters. TACO provided each manager with daily reports on 46 key performance measures, assisted with production and labour scheduling, and aided inventory control. This reduced the time restaurant managers spent on paperwork by up to 16 hours a week.

These process changes and the investment in technology were also accompanied by changes in human resource management. The restaurant manager's job was now very different from what it had been due to K-minus, SOS, and TACO. Taco Bell recognized that managers should now focus much more on front-of-house and on the customer. The management structure within each unit was therefore changed along with job descriptions and remuneration packages. Much more pay was performance related, so that top managers could earn $80,000 a year, a huge increase on previous salary scales. Selection criteria for new restaurant managers were also adapted to reflect the new style operation.

Between 1988 and 1994 Taco Bell doubled its sales and tripled its profits. Despite this competition remained tough. With the right processes in place, Martin could now look to other ways in which to improve operational performance. So in the mid 1990s the focus switched from technology to human resources, with the growth of team-managed units and the development of the learning organization within Taco Bell.

	Project	Job	Batch	Line	Continuous process
Order-winning criteria	Delivery quality design capability	Delivery quality design capability	⇔	Price	Price
Qualifying criteria	Price	Price	⇔	Delivery quality design capability	Delivery quality design capability

Note: There are many more order-winning and qualifying criteria than listed – the above list is indicative only. Also, it is important to weight the criteria for specific applications or industries.

Figure 7.14 Linking process choice and order-qualifying/order-winning criteria

CONCERNS WITH THE MAPPING PROCESS

Although the mapping process can be useful, there are some problems with it. An excellent critique on this is given by Spring and Boaden (1997). In addition, we would add that it is important not to be too rigid with the use of this framework, for the following reasons:

- A firm may produce the same type of product for two markets under one process choice. The particular needs of each market may differ even though the process choice is the same. For example, one of the authors acted as a management consultant for a firm producing flight simulator units. The two markets are commercial and military and the requirements for the two are entirely different in terms of cost, delivery reliability, and added features, even though each simulator product would be made under a project-process choice. However, under the process choice mapping model we would expect the competitive requirements to be the same because they share the same the same process choice. But this is not the case.

- In many environments, order-qualifying and order-winning criteria are often very linked to the point where they become almost indistinguishable. For example, in the UK's public sector, price has become less of an order-qualifier by itself and has been subsumed into a wider set of criteria concerned with perceived overall value where low cost alone does not secure entry into the market. Hence hospitals will not award contracts on price alone – perceived value and reputation of the supplier are key requirements. Similarly, the 'lowest cost contract award' in public sector activities such as road building and maintenance no longer view cost as a stand-alone factor. Rather, price is viewed as part of overall perceived value and is one of many important factors on the competitive menu.

- Hill rightly warns that what were once order-winning criteria may, over time, become order-qualifying. This may be especially so where competitors copy the technology or the firm loses control of the differentiating feature. This is where using weightings or scoring the criteria over time is very important.

- One of the key questions in this model is: 'How do products win orders in the market?' Therein lies another problem – products do not win orders; firms do, and they do so in a number of ways, including intangible but powerful factors such as reputation, perceived overall value for money, and other subjective but important elements to the buying decision.

- The majority of manufacturing in the West is made under batch production and the model does not seem to accommodate this 'middle' path too well.

The model is still important and can clarify what are often difficult strategic decisions, but perhaps a better approach would be to add pre-qualifying criteria, as shown in Figure 7.15.

We suggest the concept of pre-qualifying criteria is an important one in many market segments. For example, in a project environment a potential supplier will not even be

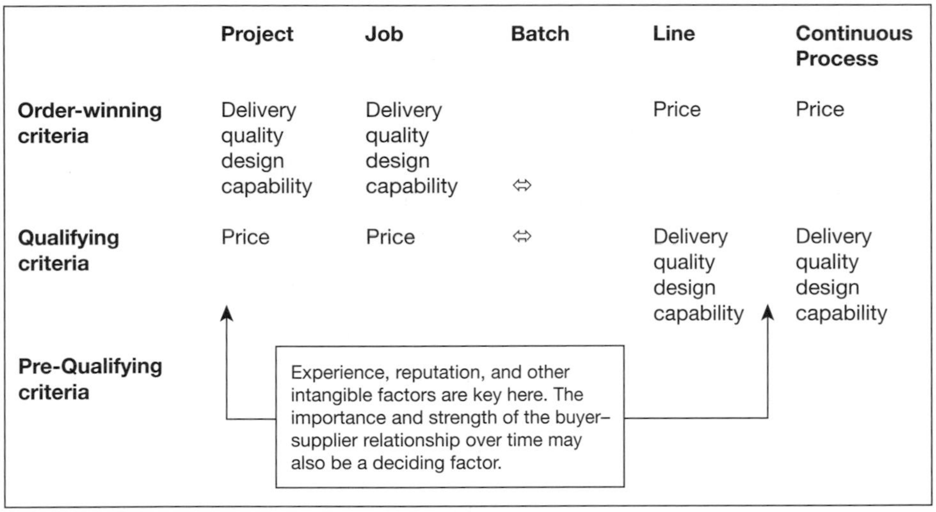

	Project	Job	Batch	Line	Continuous Process
Order-winning criteria	Delivery quality design capability	Delivery quality design capability	⇔	Price	Price
Qualifying criteria	Price	Price	⇔	Delivery quality design capability	Delivery quality design capability
Pre-Qualifying criteria		Experience, reputation, and other intangible factors are key here. The importance and strength of the buyer–supplier relationship over time may also be a deciding factor.			

Figure 7.15 The importance of pre-qualifying criteria

permitted to bid for a project unless they are known to possess pre-qualifying criteria. This may include something obvious such as ISO certification (the most popular being ISO 9000). However, it may revolve around less tangible factors such as perceived experience, know-how, and reputation. The annoying thing for firms is that these traits can take a considerable time to accrue, but can then be lost with a single incident such as a product recall.

THE IMPACT OF MANUFACTURING ERAS ON PROCESS CHOICE

Thus far we have linked process choice to types of layout and then indicated how each process choice links to the others. We can take this one stage further by mapping the previous and current eras of manufacturing on to types of process choice as shown in Figure 7.16.

The 'traditional' line process, which mass-produced one product in high volume, clearly fails to meet the requirement of variety. This then changes the demands on operations as summarized in Figure 7.17.

THE EMERGENCE OF MASS CUSTOMIZATION

Mass customization is not a specific type of process type but it depends fundamentally upon the transformation process. Davis (1987) coined the term mass customization and stated:

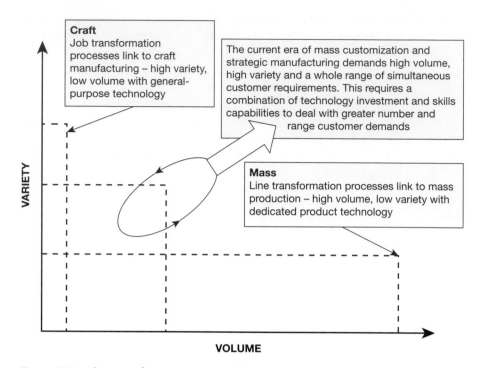

Figure 7.16 The manufacturing eras and their impact on process choice

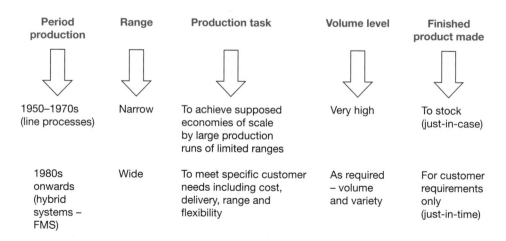

Figure 7.17 The changing task of manufacturing management

mass customization of markets means that the same large number of customers can be reached as in mass markets of the industrial economy, and simultaneously they can be treated individually as in customized markets of pre-industrial economies.

(Davis, 1987, p.169).

In essence this present era of mass customization, combines the best of the craft era, where products were individualized but at high cost, with the best of mass production, where products were affordable but highly standardized (Fralix, 2001).

Mass customization firms comprise a diverse range of products and services and cannot be identified as a homogeneous group. Lampel and Mintzberg (1996) illustrate the range of offers from 'pure standardization' to 'pure customization' in Figure 7.18.

Customer involvement in the operations process is argued to be one of the defining characteristics of mass customization.

Mass customization overcomes what has typically been seen as a trade-off between volume and variety. It achieves this in a number of ways, such as flexible manufacturing and agile production, which we discuss below. MacCarthey *et al.* (2003) suggest that there are actually five basic ways in which mass customization can be achieved, derived from how six key operations processes are configured. The six key processes are:

1. Product development and design;

2. Product validation or manufacturing engineering (translates product design into a bill of materials and set of manufacturing processes);

3. Order taking and co-ordination;

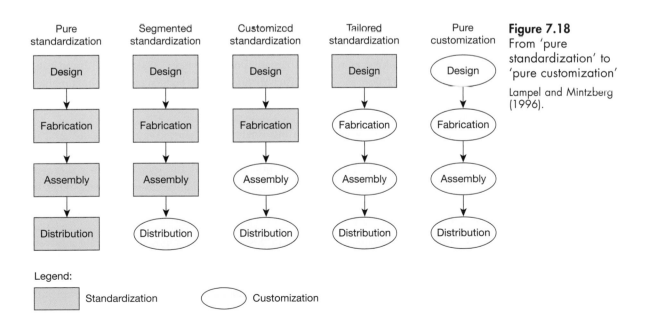

Figure 7.18
From 'pure standardization' to 'pure customization'

Lampel and Mintzberg (1996).

4. Order fulfilment management (schedules activities within the operation);

5. Order fulfilment realization (manages actual production and delivery); and

6. Post order processes (such as technical assistance, warranties, and maintenance).

As we have seen already, job shops make to order, and line production tends to make to stock. Within some of the six processes outlined above, firms also have a choice. Thus product development and design can be carried out before any orders are taken or in response to orders. Likewise, product validation can be established in advance or modified in relation to orders. Finally, order fulfilment realization capability can be fixed or modifiable. Hence 12 different combinations of these are theoretically feasible, although some are mutually exclusive. For instance, if the product range is designed prior to orders being taken, it is not necessary to have modifiable product validation or to have flexible order fulfilment realization.

Pine (1992) argues that mass production created economies of scale, whilst mass customization is based on economies of scope. So far the approaches discussed above, such as JIT, achieve the efficiencies of mass production (volume), whilst accommodating a wide product range. But Pine (1992) goes on to suggest that 'the best method for achieving mass customization is by creating modular components that can be configured into a wide variety of end products and services'. Such standardization of parts not only reduces production costs and increases customizable output, it also reduces new product development time and accommodates short life-cycles.

Take-home pizza delivery has used this approach for years. The typical menu offers a range of standard pizzas using specific ingredients, but these can be customized by the consumer who can request any one or more of these ingredients to be added to any one of the standard pizzas. So from a range of say ten pizzas and less than a hundred ingredients, literally thousands of different pizzas can be produced. Other examples of this approach include house paint mixed to the customer's specification at point-of-sale, Black and Decker power tools, Wendy's hamburger chain, Lutron Electronics lighting equipment, and Komatsu heavy equipment.

Pine (1992), building on work by Abernathy and Utterbuck (1978) and Ulrich and Tung (1991), outlines six kinds of modularity. They are not mutually exclusive and may be combined within one operation. The six forms are:

- *Component-sharing modularity*: this refers to the same component being used in multiple products, thereby reducing inventory costs and simplifying production. Forte Posthouse Hotels have recently redesigned the menus in their different restaurant concepts, so that the product range continues to offer a wide range of dishes, but the number of ingredients needed to make these has been reduced from over 4,000 to around 1,000.

- *Component-swapping modularity*: in this instance, as opposed to different products sharing the same components (as above), the same products have different components in order to customize them or differentiate them from each other. The classic example of this is Swatch, who produce a range of standard watches, but with a wide range of colours and faces.

- *Cut-to-fit modularity*: this modularity is based around the ability to adapt or vary a component to individual needs and wants, within preset or practical limits. Pine (1992) exemplifies this through Custom Cut Technologies, who make clothing to fit; National Bicycle Industrial Co., who can produce over 11 million variations on 18 models; and Peerless Saw, who use lasers to vary the dimensions of any saw.

- *Mix modularity*: this modularity is based on the concept of a recipe, so that components when mixed together become something different. This can be applied to paints, fertilizers, restaurant menu items, breakfast cereals, and any other process in which ingredients are mixed.

- *Bus modularity*: this is based around the concept of a standard structure to which different components can be added. The obvious example of this is the lighting track to which different light fittings can be attached. The term 'bus' derives from the electronics industry, which uses this as the base from which computers and other electronic devices are built up. This type of modularity allows variations in the type, number and location of modules that can plug into the product.

- *Sectional modularity*: this type of modularity is based on different types of components fitting together in any number of possible ways through the use of standard interfaces. Lego building blocks are the classic example of this. While this achieves the greatest degree of variety and customization, it is the most difficult to achieve. Few products are as simple as Lego blocks (or as precisely dimensioned: total interchangeability requires very high precision manufacturing of the basic 'building blocks'), but examples include Bally Engineered Structures (who use a standard panel to produce many different forms of refrigeration unit); Agfa Corporation's system for handling all forms and sizes of information; and American Express (who capture each transaction so that they may offer personalized products and services to match the buying needs and buying power of their customers).

Gilmore and Pine (1997) mention 'four faces of customisation': collaborative (designers working closely with customers); adaptive (where standard products are changed by customers during use); cosmetic (where packaging of standard products is unique for each customer); and transparent (where products are modified to specific individual needs). By contrast, Lampel and Mintzberg (1996) discuss a continuum of various mass customization strategies including different configurations of processes (from standard to customized), product (from commodities to unique), and the nature of the customer transaction process (from generic to personalized).

Da Silveira *et al.* (2001) provide a useful summary of perceived requirements for mass customization. These are:

1. Customer demand for variety and customization must exist;
2. Market conditions must be appropriate;
3. The value chain should be ready;
4. Technology must be available;

5. Products should be customizable; and

6. Knowledge must be shared.

Undoubtedly, mass customization presents firms with a number of challenges. Zipkin (2001) categorizes three types of challenge:

1. *Elicitation*: the requirement of an elaborate system for eliciting customers needs and wants. Zipkin (2001) argues that capturing customer input into the production process can prove difficult.

CASE 7.2: MASS CUSTOMIZATION

At a factory in Wichita, Kansas, run by the Cessna aircraft company, a gleaming new Citation Excel executive jet rolls off the production line roughly every three days.

While they may look almost identical, virtually every aircraft, which sell for an average of about Dollars 10m and are assembled from about 30,000 parts, is different depending on the requirements of the customer.

The production line at Cessna – which is part of the Textron industrial conglomerate – is a good example of the trend in much of industry towards mass customization.

This term was introduced in the early 1990s to describe how manufacturers can satisfy customer demand for product variants by introducing them into traditional factories.

But they don't sacrifice manufacturing efficiencies, the absence of which can push up costs and make the company uncompetitive. According to a seminal paper* in the *Harvard Business Review* in 1993, mass customization requires a dynamic and flexible organization.

The authors say 'the combination of how and when they (different production units) make a product or provide a service is constantly changing in response to what each customer wants and needs'.

Since this paper was written, more manufacturers have realized they need to introduce variation into production as a way of keeping customers happy – but without returning to employing craftsmen to fashion items in single batches and at astronomic cost.

Cessna has introduced principles of lean manufacturing to speed up production and worker efficiency, while at the same time allowing for a large degree of product variation.

Last year Cessna made 81 Excel aircraft, one of the company's best-selling models.

This is a five-fold improvement on 1998, since when the number of direct assembly workers has risen two-and-a-half times. In other words, worker productivity over this period has doubled.

Behind the improvement has been a number of changes to the processes on the assembly line involving extra worker training and a re-classification of the 1,000 or so individual assembly jobs that it takes to fit the parts together on an individual aircraft.

The result is that production variation is catered for by substituting different parts and sub-assembly routines within a mass-production environment. According to Garry Hay, Cessna's chief executive, the company's ability to provide a high level of customization without overly pushing up costs is a key factor

CASE STUDY

behind the company's good profits record and its likely increase in sales from Dollars 2.8bn last year to Dollars 3.1bn this year.

This is in spite of a cooling of the world economic climate.

Also keen on mass customisation is FAG Kugelfischer, a German manufacturer with sales last year of Euros 2.2bn and which is Europe's second biggest maker of rolling bearings (devices essential to virtually all kinds of rotary motion) after SKF of Sweden.

Uwe Loos, FAG's chief executive, suggests that how well the company can move in the direction of customised bearings that suit individual tastes will be a key determinant of future earnings growth.

Mr Loos says: 'In the bearings industry globally, 70 per cent of the sales come from standard bearings and just 30 per cent from special or customised bearings.

'At FAG, the ratio is closer to the other way round – 30 per cent standard and 70 per cent specials – and I want to move the ratio even further, to about 20:80, in the next few years.'

A reason for this goal is that, frequently, the profit margins on special, custom-made bearings are higher than for conventional standard bearings – a factor of their higher price.

While the bearings churned out in their hundreds of thousands for car wheels might sell for tens of dollars, a high-tech bearing for a jet engine might cost Dollars 15,000.

The interest in mass customization can be seen in FAG's main German ball-bearings plant in Schweinfurt, near Wurzburg. Here 270 people work using a high level of automated plant to turn out some 13,000 bearings a day, weighing 25 tonnes.

While the casual observer might imagine the bearings were nearly all the same, in fact each day's output can be divided into 50–60 types.

The main components for each bearing – the inner and outer rings, balls and cage to hold the balls in place – are shipped in the correct quantities and dimensions to separate units or cells charged with manufacturing individual product types.

As much of the detailed assembly (such as inserting balls inside a pair of inner and outer rings) is left to machinery, it is important to make the machines easy to re-program to increase their flexibility.

That, in turn, allows smaller production runs and a greater degree of product variance without unacceptable increases in costs.

Jens Krohn, FAG manager in charge of the ball-bearings plant, says: 'Increasingly we are trying to reduce the set-up times for the assembly machines, so we can change production more easily in tune with the demands of the market.

'The goal is to reduce set-up times by 10 per cent a year. In some cases, we can alter machinery (to make different kinds of products) in about 15 minutes when a few years ago it might have taken two to three hours.'

This kind of change allows it to be more cost effective to make products in relatively small batches, while it used to be uneconomic to do so.

*Making Mass Customization Work by Joseph Pine, Bart Victor and Andrew Boynton, Harvard Business Review, September-October 1993.

Financial Times (2002) 'Mass customisation: Make every one different', 21 May 2002.

2. *Process flexibility*: the requirement of highly flexible production technology. Zipkin (2001) argues that developing such technologies can be expensive and also time-consuming.

3. *Logistics*: the requirement of a strong direct-to-customer logistics system. Zipkin (2001) argues that processing and tracking individual customer orders through the supply chain presents a variety of challenges.

Mass customization has also been adopted in service settings, with impressive results.

Seeking a competitive edge in the battle for tourist dollars, the Maine Office of Tourism decided to mail a free personalized travel planner to anyone who visited its website and volunteered information about his or her travel plans. The variable elements included photos of attractions the traveller said they intended to visit, a calendar listing events taking place during the time of their stay, a custom letter, and a document featuring the regions and activities in which they expressed interest. The package was printed on demand and included a feedback card that offered respondents the chance to win a shopping spree at L.L.Bean, one of the state's most famous retailers.

Mailing the personalized package cost approximately 15 per cent more than mailing the standard info package, but the results clearly outweighed the costs. According to Xerox 1:1 Lab, which piloted the project, 24.1 per cent more people responded to the personalized package, with over 50 per cent of those responding providing feedback, and 73 per cent indicating that the guide was helpful.

Let's Get Personal: Mass Customization in Travel Marketing, 21 March 2010, http://sparksheet. com/let per centE2 per cent80 per cent99s-get-personal-mass-customization-in-travel-marketing/

FLEXIBLE MANUFACTURING

Flexible manufacturing is an element of mass customization and the move towards flexible manufacturing was one of the major competitive advantages of Japanese car manufacturing subsequently appearing in Western manufacturing. Segments of the car market are fragmenting as customer demands and expectations force firms to provide a wide variety of models. So whereas, at one time, a large producer could have produced 1 million of one model over its product lifetime, by the year 2000 it was rare to exceed 250,000 of a particular model. In consequence, processes that are structured around old-fashioned ideas of economies of scale and inflexible line processes must change to more 'customer driven' processes, including 'flexible manufacturing systems' (FMS). We should not be overly critical of past approaches around line processes; they were state of the art 100 years ago and simply no longer serve the current market requirements. Line processes (mass production) *was* entirely appropriate for past market requirements. As *Industry Week* points out:

> In the early days of the automotive industry, Henry Ford reportedly was able to produce a Model T Ford in less than 56 hours – from the conversion of iron ore into steel and through final assembly operations.

However, things have changed dramatically since then:

> But when a manufacturing organization bases its competitive strategy on offering customers greater product variety, that elevates the level of product and process complexity considerably . . . Supporting an endless flow of new products can trigger a chain of effects inside the organization that can burden it to the breaking point.
>
> (*Industry Week*, 1998)

This is not to say that flexible production leads to a proliferation of complexity in terms of products: the trick is to offer the market 'apparent variety' while reducing it in real terms at the point of operation. This is evident in a reduction in the amount of genuine variation of products offered by manufacturing plants.

This does not mean that there is a return to mass manufacturing with its narrow, dedicated lines. Instead, production has focused on developments around the 'batch' area – creating solutions in which FMS and 'group technology' are employed. FMS and group technology are different approaches, or 'step changes' – not just modifications of 'traditional' batch manufacture. They are major changes whereby both variety and volume may be achieved. The mass-production system has had to change to suit a volatile, changing environment with new competitors coming from all over the globe. Where mass production's process 'strategy' emphasized efficiency in production, modern world-class manufacturing firms emphasize product quality, differentiation, and any other factor perceived to be important for customers.

The advantages that FMS can provide go beyond the flexibility of the hardware. The real advantage comes with the plant-specific know-how and enhanced skills that accompany FMS. Consequently, investment in technologies such as computer-integrated manufacture (CIM) and advanced manufacturing technology (AMT) is seen as *strategically* important because it can provide competitive options for the firm:

> In most cases, AMT investments are irreversible because they are highly specialized, durable, and dependent on the firm's specific operating routines, information flows and knowledge surrounding both product design and process technology. However, the strategic options allowed by AMT help the firm recoup its investment. . . . The fragmentation of markets, the development of new market segments or niches, as well as faster design . . . all contribute to the need for strategic flexibility. Thus, flexible manufacturing technologies provide a strategic real option . . . in which high levels of

economies of scope and a 'design for response' capability position the firm to enter a broader range of different markets at its own discretion.

(Lei *et al.*, 1996, p. 503)

This learning effect is shown in Motorola's AMT investments in the flexible manufacture of components for cellular telephones which are now being used for other electronic component applications. This is typical of the sort of strategic opportunities that technology investment can present to the firm. As a result, AMT investments can enable the firm to provide a range of products or components based on group technology or shared design characteristics. This in turn provides strategic options based on economies of scope, rather than economies of scale.

Moreover, investment in FMS and other advanced manufacturing technologies provides strategic scope for the firm:

Flexible manufacturers are in a rather interesting position in the marketplace. When non-flexible manufacturing firms are asked, 'What business are you in?' they list the products they produce. When flexible manufacturers are asked the same question, they respond, 'Whatever business you want us to be in!' In a rapidly changing marketplace, the ability to almost instantly change what the firm can offer its customers can be a formidable competitive weapon'

(Honeycutt *et al.*, 1993, p. 7)

This has to be treated with some caution: it is clearly not realistic for a firm to claim that it is *any* business that *any* customer wants. Toyota might be able to produce many variations around a single platform but the auto giant could not respond to a customer who asked for, say, an aeroplane or a ship, because Toyota's technology remains focused on car production. So the term 'flexible' has to be seen within product-specific boundaries. (At a corporate group level, however, some technology transfer may enable sister divisions to excel at different products or services. The Toyota group, for example, has a division that makes pre-fabricated houses; Mitsubishi makes aircraft as well as cars; and almost every large firm provides some sort of financial services.)

FMS allows the firm to compete on *economies of scope* rather than economies of scale. Because technologies are more flexible, allowing numerous product variations to be made, the overall volume achieved can be almost as great as manufacturing large volumes of standardized products. This means that the basis of competition moves from a strategy of low-priced, commodity products, to an emphasis on low-cost special options and customized products.

This profoundly changes the rules of the game. As we saw in Chapter 2, Porter (1980) had stated in *Competitive Strategy* that in order to be profitable, firms were faced with two options: *either* low cost *or* differentiation. This reflected industrial economic theory at the time, but now firms have to compete on both fronts – amongst a range of other customer requirements. Due to the nature of competition, what were once differentiated features, able to provide sustained competitive advantage (for some time at least), have become the 'level playing field' (basic expectation) in many markets. This is because technology is often easy to copy. The computer industry exemplifies this. For years, Apple was able to charge premium prices for its 'differentiated' products. Once others emulated the technology, however, price became critical and the differentiating software became available on all PCs. So neither low cost nor differentiation is sufficient by itself. Instead, a range of new competitive requirements including speed, flexibility, and customization, have emerged as the key competitive drivers. Flexibility has become a central capability of world-class manufacturers.

The actual arrangement of production cells provides insight into how manufacturing becomes flexible. Flexible manufacturing systems are typically arranged in small, U-shaped cells as illustrated in Figure 7.19. The reasons for this shape include:

- Reduction of space;

- Shorter work flow paths; and

- Increased teamwork and better communication and motivation brought about by seeing a completed product in the cell.

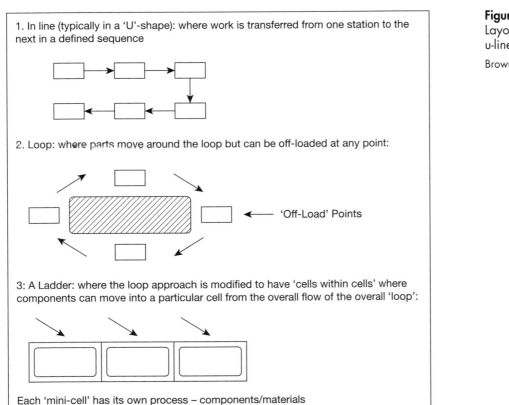

Figure 7.19
Layout of a typical u-line or cell

Brown (1996)

1. In line (typically in a 'U'-shape): where work is transferred from one station to the next in a defined sequence

2. Loop: where parts move around the loop but can be off-loaded at any point:

'Off-Load' Points

3: A Ladder: where the loop approach is modified to have 'cells within cells' where components can move into a particular cell from the overall flow of the overall 'loop':

Each 'mini-cell' has its own process – components/materials move into each cell as required

Workers are arranged into teams to operate the cells. A single cell can manufacture, inspect, and package finished products or components. Every cell is responsible for the quality of its products and each worker will normally be able to perform a range of tasks. Once again, process choice is the key insight in cell arrangements: under line processes, introducing variety, or changing the product, meant stopping the entire assembly line. Such breakdowns and shortages are very costly overheads for mass-producers, intent on low-cost production. To compensate for this, they have to carry large stocks of parts and spares, 'just-in-case'.

We shall discuss the critical importance of just-in-time – which is linked to cell manufacturing – in Chapter 9, but we can say here that stocks of partly finished products also tend to be high under traditional line processes. Components that have undergone part of the production process often sit idle, waiting for the next stage. This is a major source of waste. Large amounts of inventories, some sitting in large warehouses, are a feature of mass production. By contrast, flexible manufacturing, via U-shape cells, and low inventory levels go hand in hand.

> **Walk inside Autoliv's 350,000-square-foot facility today, and you feel like you've stepped inside a clock. You can almost hear the ticking. Eighty-eight compact, U-shaped production cells have replaced assembly lines on the main floor. Each consists of a group of workstations staffed by a handful of employees. A screw is tightened, the finished piece scanned and registered in inventory, and then it's handed off to the next associate, who tags it and drops it into a box to be picked up and shipped. There are cells for driver airbags, passenger airbags, and side-curtain airbags, whose sales have grown 50% annually during the past three years.**
>
> *Fortune* (2004) 'Elite factories', 6 September 2004

AGILE PRODUCTION

Like mass customization, agile production is not a particular process choice but it is wholly dependant upon the transformation process for agility to become a reality within the offer to customers. It is clear that we are in an era that has evolved from mass production offerings – 'any colour of car as long as it is black' – to that of customer-centric offerings, as indicated in by Ridderstrale and Nordstrom (2000) in Chapter 1: 'Let us tell you what all customers want. Any customer, in any industry, in any market wants stuff that is both cheaper and better, and they want it yesterday.' This comes under the umbrella of mass customization and agile production. There is some confusion about both of these terms, as Brown and Bessant (2003, p. 708) explain:

> there seems to be no firm agreement as to the definitions for, and major differences between, the paradigms of *mass customisation* and *agile manufacturing*. For example,

Feitzinger and Lee (1997) in their discussion on *mass customisation* also include 'Agile Supply Networks' as a necessary factor. In addition, Da Silveira *et al* (2001) mention *agile manufacturing* as a feature within their summary on the literature on *mass customisation*. We suggest that although it might be important to understand both we add that *agile manufacturing* and *mass customisation* are not mutually exclusive paradigms. Instead, we argue that *mass customisation* is best viewed as a powerful example of a firm's ability to be *agile*.

Bessant *et al.* (2001, p. 31) offer the following definition of *agility*:

Agility in manufacturing involves being able to respond quickly and effectively to the current configuration of market demand, and also to be proactive in developing and retaining markets in the face of extensive competitive forces.

Gunasekaran and Yusuf (2002, p. 1357) add:

Agile manufacturing can be said to be a relatively new, post-mass-production concept for the creation and distribution of goods and services. It is the ability to thrive in a competitive environment of continuous and unanticipated change and to respond quickly to rapidly changing markets driven by customer-based valuing of products and services. . . . It includes rapid product realization, highly flexible manufacturing, and distributed enterprise integration . . . technology alone does not make an agile enterprise. Companies should find the right combination of strategies, culture, business practices, and technology that are necessary to make it agile, taking into account the market characteristics.

Bessant *et al.* (2001, p. 727) offer an emerging model of *agile manufacturing capabilities*, consisting of four, key, interlinked parameters. The four major dimensions of the reference model are:

- *Agile strategy*: involving the processes for understanding the firm's situation within its sector, committing to *agile* strategy, aligning it to a fast-moving market, and communicating and deploying it effectively.
- *Agile processes*: the provision of the actual facilities and processes to allow agile functioning of the organization.
- *Agile linkages*: intensively working with and learning from others outside the company, especially customers and suppliers.
- *Agile people*: developing a flexible and multi-skilled workforce, creating a culture that allows initiative, creativity, and supportiveness to thrive throughout the organization.

Figure 7.20 shows the reference model for agile manufacturing practices.

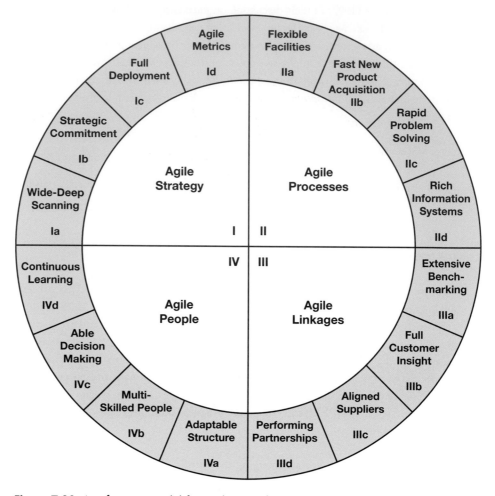

Figure 7.20 A reference model for agile manufacturing practices

Bessant *et al.* (2001)

Further insights are provided by understanding the configurations and dimensions of agility and some of the theoretical underpinnings. Figure 7.21 shows the dimensions of agility.

Of course, there is considerable overlap between mass customization and agile practices, and one will feed the other. It is best, therefore, not to see these paradigms as conflicting and competing approaches to 'best practice' but rather as complementary sets of skills and abilities that need to be in place for today's highly competitive and demanding conditions.

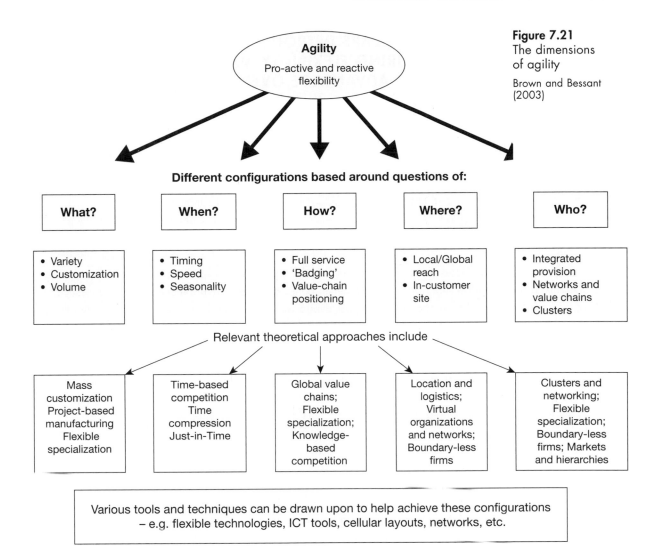

Figure 7.21
The dimensions
of agility

Brown and Bessant
(2003)

PUTTING IT ALL TOGETHER

There are no hidden secrets to running successful transformation processes in either manufacturing or service settings. There are, of course, many companies that will fall into the trap of purchasing 'instant solutions' via the latest technological offerings. However, these can, at best, mask what are fundamental mistakes in understanding the basics of the transformation processes within organizations. The following, although focused on manufacturing plants, has much that can be applied to service settings as well.

CASE 7.3: HOW NISSAN LAPS DETROIT – ITS MANUFACTURING FLEXIBILITY MAKES FOR A HUGE ADVANTAGE OVER THE BIG THREE

Jonathan Gates slaps a wide slab of tan-colored, hard foam rubber on his workbench. He fastens a numbered tag in one corner and some black foam insulation at the edges. As soon as he puts a number on the piece of foam, which will become the top of a dashboard for a Nissan Quest minivan, the vehicle has an identity. All of the parts for a big chunk of the minivan's interior, decked out with the customer's choice of colors, fabrics, and options, will come together in the next 42 minutes.

Gates and his co-workers fill a crucial role at Nissan Motor Co.'s new Canton (Miss.) assembly plant: Almost everything a driver touches inside a new Quest, Titan pickup, or Armada sport-utility vehicle is put together in a single module, starting at Gates's workbench. `This is the most important job,' he says. And yet, amazingly, Gates doesn't even work for Nissan. He works for Lextron/Visteon Automotive Systems, a parts supplier that also builds the center console between the front seats and a subassembly of the car's front end. The finished modules pass over a wall to be bolted into a car or truck body rolling down the assembly line. Lextron/Visteon does the work faster than Nissan could and pays $3 an hour less than the carmaker pays assembly workers. Nissan is using a similar strategy for its vehicle frames, seats, electrical systems, and completed doors.

It's a level of efficiency that Detroit auto makers are only beginning to attempt. Along with other features in Nissan's eight-month-old, $1.4 billion factory, the wholesale integration of outside suppliers is another reason why General Motors, Ford, and Chrysler are still playing catch-up with Japanese car manufacturers. The Big Three have made great strides in productivity in recent years: General Motors Corp.'s best plants now actually beat Toyota's factories. But overall, every time Detroit gets close, the competition seems to get a little better. `The Japanese are continually improving,' says Michael Robinet, vice-president of CSM Worldwide, an industry consultant.

Nissan has been the best example of that in North America for years. The Canton plant was designed with the same flexibility, shop-floor smarts, and management-dominated work rules that made Nissan's 20-year-old plant in Smyrna, Tenn., the most productive factory in North America year after year, according to Harbour & Associates. The Smyrna plant builds a car in just under 16 labor hours – 6 fewer than the average Honda or Toyota plant, 8 fewer than GM, and 10 fewer than Ford. Its profit per vehicle of $2,069 is the best in North America.

The Canton plant, which opened in May, will almost certainly top that. Nissan's secret? Sure, its plants use cheaper, nonunion labor. Besides lower wages, the Smyrna workers get about $3 an hour less in benefits than Big Three assemblers represented by the United Auto Workers. But there's more to it. Outsourcing offers huge savings, whereas the Big Three must negotiate the outsourcing of subassembly work with the union. And Nissan's plants are far more flexible in adjusting to market twists and turns. Canton can send a minivan, pickup truck, and sport-utility vehicle down the same assembly line, one after the other, without interruption.

MANEUVERING ROOM

The payoff: Nissan plans to build an impressive five different models in the Canton plant. And, like Toyota and Honda, Nissan will have more financial room to maneuver as it pushes aggressively into segments like pickups and SUVs. That is already putting pressure on Detroit's few remaining areas of dominance. When it launched the new Titan pickup this November, Nissan set the price at $22,000, undercutting the Ford F-150 by at least $2,000 while still maintaining a healthy profit margin.

At first glance, a Nissan factory does not look much different than one you would see in Detroit or St. Louis. But talk to the workers, and it soon becomes clear how relentlessly the company squeezes mere seconds out of the assembly process. 'There's no silver bullet,' says Emil E. Hassan, Nissan's senior vice-president of *manufacturing*. 'It's really just following up every day with improvements.'

On the Smyrna passenger-car line, for instance, a worker stands on a moving platform, called a lineside limo, that inches along the body of an Xterra SUV. The limo carries all the tools and parts he needs. The assembler grabs a seat belt from a bin next to him, bolts it in, then moves along and installs the rear struts – all without having to make what used to be a 20-foot walk back and forth, three times per car. Nissan started installing lineside limos 13 years ago at the suggestion of a line worker; GM and other auto makers also use these limos, but not as extensively. 'We don't have to do a lot of walking,' says Smyrna Vice-President of *Manufacturing* Gregory Daniels.

Still, there are some big differences between domestic and foreign plants in the U.S. The United Auto Workers is slowly allowing more outsourcing. But the UAW wants to outsource work only to union-friendly suppliers. And even then it has to be negotiated. Nissan, meanwhile, has free rein to outsource jobs. Two of Smyrna's vehicles – the Maxima and Altima sedans – were engineered to be built using modules built by suppliers. Every vehicle built in Canton was designed that way. All together, buying modules saves 15% to 30% on the total cost of that section of the car, according to the Center for Automotive Research (CAR) in Ann Arbor, Mich. And the Big Three? GM is the most 'modular' of the domestic manufacturers, but only a few of its plants have been designed to build cars using many big modules.

MAKING HEADWAY

One of the biggest advantages the Japanese have is that they can keep their plants busy pretty much no matter how the market shifts. In Nissan's case, if demand for the Titan surges it could cut production of, say, slower-moving Altima sedans. That means its workers are rarely idle and the company doesn't need rebates to keep its plants busy. This flexibility means that Nissan, Toyota, and Honda all run their plants at 100% capacity or higher, once overtime is figured in. GM, Ford, and Chrysler, on the other hand, use about 85 per cent. 'The key to making money in this *business* is running plants at 100% capacity,' says Sean McAlinden, chief economist with CAR.

Toyota is probably the most flexible auto maker in North America, according to Prudential Securities Inc., with five of its seven North American assembly lines building more than one vehicle. When Canton starts building the Altima, three of Nissan's four lines will be fully flexible. What that means on the factory floor is that Canton's body shop can weld any of four vehicles – two SUVs, a pickup, and a minivan – on the same line. Robotic arms can be quickly programmed to weld in the spots needed for different vehicles.

Detroit is slowly making headway. Prudential says half of GM's 35 North American assembly lines can make multiple vehicles. GM's two-year-old Cadillac pant in Lansing, Mich., will make three luxury vehicles: the CTS and STS sedans and SRX SUV. It has also been designed to get some large, preassembled modules from suppliers. GM is using the Cadillac plant as a model for upgrading other plants. `We're getting much more flexible,' says Gary L. Cowger, president of GM North America.

But it's much easier to design a new factory to be flexible from the ground up than to refurbish those built 30 or more years ago. And with so much excess capacity, the Big Three have no room to build new plants. Even if they could match the Japanese in productivity, they would have to account for the costs of laid-off workers, whose contracts entitle them to 75 per cent of their pay.

By contrast, Nissan runs a tight ship and works its employees harder. During the UAW's failed attempt to organize Smyrna in 2001, workers told the union that line speeds were too fast and people were getting injured, says Bob King, the UAW's vice-president of organizing. The union says that in 2001, Nissan reported 31 injuries per 1,000 workers – twice the average at Big Three plants – according to logs reported to the Occupational Safety & Health Administration.

SQUEAKS AND RATTLES

Nissan does not dispute the OSHA figures, but it denies its assembly lines are any less safe than Detroit's. Although the company won't release current numbers, executives do say that they have taken steps to reduce injuries. For instance, the company has workers do four different jobs during a typical eight-hour shift, to try to cut down on repetitive-motion injuries. Nissan claims that injury rates have fallen 60 per cent in the past two years.

As for the finished product, the real test is still to come for Nissan. The company has yet to prove that the popularity of its Altima and G35 Infiniti sedans can carry over to minivans, big pickups, and big SUVs. The company's quality rating is below average, and critics say the Quest has squeaks and rattles that need to be worked out at the factory. Trucks are Detroit's last bastion of dominance, and it will fight to maintain an edge. But at least in terms of efficiency, each new Nissan is rolling off the line with a huge headstart.

A Second Wave of Efficiency

Here's how Nissan pushes its productivity edge at auto factories in Canton, Miss., and Smyrna, Tenn.:

BODY SHOP Nissan can weld bodies for different cars and trucks using the same machines. Computer-controlled robots quickly change weld points to adjust.

PAINT SHOP Nissan's plants have highly automated processes to paint all kinds of vehicles one after the other, with no downtime for reconfiguration.

OUTSOURCING Nissan uses lower-wage suppliers to build the frame, dashboard, and seats. They are shipped right to the assembly line.

A MOVING STAGE Assembly workers can stand on a `lineside limousine,' which moves them, their tools, and parts along with the car. That eliminates having to walk back and forth to the parts bins and tool racks.

ELBOW GREASE Nissan works its staff hard. Critics say injury rates are high, though Nissan counters that it has been making ergonomic improvements.

Table 7.1

Best plants	Hours per vehicle*	Product
Nissan, Smyrna, Tenn.	15.7	Altima, Maxima
Gm, Oshawa, Ont. 1	16.4	Chevrolet Monte Carlo, Impala
Gm, Oshawa, Ont. 2	17.1	Buick Century, Regal
Worst plants	Hours per vehicle*	Product
Ford, Wixom, Mich.	44.2	Lincoln Town Car, Ls, Ford Thunderbird
Chrysler, St. Louis North	33.8	Dodge Ram Pickup
Gm/Suzuki, Ingersoll, Ont.	29.9	Suzuki Vitara, Chevrolet Tracker

* Average labor hours spent on vehicles made in 2002

Playing Catch-Up on the Factory Floor

General Motors has made great strides in efficiency, but Nissan still operates the most efficient auto plant in North America.

Business Week (2003) 'Playing catch-Up on the factory floor', December 2003, pp. 58–61.

CASE STUDY

SUMMARY

- Layout and process choice are of major strategic importance to manufacturing and services operations. The options to choose from are also essentially similar – it's not an infinite variety but a small number of options and switching between one to the other is by no means cost free, so there is an important strategic objective to align the transformation process with market requirements and to understand the implications of changing.
- The five basic types of process choice are: *project, job, batch, line,* and *continuous process.*
- The basic types of layout are: *fixed, process, hybrid* (cell) and *product.*
- There are links between the layout (the physicality of operations) and process choice (the transformation).
- A process choice will indicate what a firm *can* and *cannot* do. Process choice may significantly influence what the company sells and what it is able to offer.
- Increasingly, because of the need to satisfy volume and variety requirements, production technology is centred on the middle of the continuum between volume and variety.

- Process technology is not a quick-fix solution and investment must be made alongside skills and capabilities. Any investment has to be made to support the company in its chosen market and should not be at the whim of a particular technical specialist but should be a holistic decision for the company.

- Vast amounts of investment have been made in some plants with little competitive advantage being gained as a result. However, when appropriate investment is made it should allow the firm to operate at world-class levels, provided that it is used to meet the needs of the markets in which the firm is competing.

- Process technology is a requirement in order to meet the demands of markets. In order to meet these needs, technology can be used for rapid changeover and set up times, volume and variety mixes, delivery speed and reliability requirements, and for ensuring process quality. However, technology must not be seen as a replacement for human resource capability.

- Investment in technology is a strategic decision. Investment must be made to enable the firm to support the markets in which the firm is competing.

KEY QUESTIONS

1. Describe how types of layout are often linked to process choice.
2. What clues does process choice provide concerning how a company competes?
3. Why is investment in process technology often a difficult decision to make?
4. Describe the differences between order-winning, order-qualifying, and pre-qualifying criteria.
5. Why have agile production and mass customization emerged as important strategic issues for operations management?

WEB LINKS

The innovative layout at Arnold Palmer Hospital: www.orlandohealth.com/arnoldpalmerhospital/TakeaTour/TakeaTour.aspx?pid=6312

A description of how mass customization is taking place within travel: http://sparksheet.com/let per centE2 per cent80 per cent99s-get-personal-mass-customization-in-travel-marketing/

FURTHER READING

Berman, B. (2002) 'Should your firm adopt a mass customization strategy?', *Business Horizons*, July/August, 45(4), 51–60.

Holweg, M. and Pil, F. (2001) 'Successful build to order strategies: Start with the customer', *Sloan Management Review*, Fall, 43(1), 74–83.

Huckman R.S. (2009) 'Are you having trouble keeping your operations focused?', *Harvard Business Review*, 87(9), 90–5.

REFERENCES

Abernathy, W.J. and Utterbuck, J.M. (1978) 'Patterns of Industrial Automation', *Technology Review* 80(7) 40–7.

Berman, B. (2002) 'Should your firm adopt a mass customization strategy?', *Business Horizons*, July/August, 45(4), 51–60.

Bessant, J., Brown, S., Francis, D. and Meredith, S. (2001) 'Developing manufacturing agility in SMEs', *International Journal of Technology Management*, 22(1–3), 28–55.

Brown, S. (1996) *Strategic Manufacturing for Competitive Advantage*, Hemel Hempstead: Prentice Hall.

Brown, S. and Bessant, J. (2003) 'The strategy-capabilities link in mass customization', *International Journal of Operations and Production Management*, 23(7), 707–30.

Brown, S. and Blackmon, K. (2005) 'Linking manufacturing strategy to the strategy mainstream: The case for strategic resonance', *Journal of Management Studies*, 42(4), 793–815.

Business Week (2003) 'Playing catch-Up on the factory floor', December 2003, see www.businessweek.com/stories/2003–12–21/graphic-playing-catch-up-on-the-factory-floor

Da Silveira, G., Borenstein, D. and Fogliatto, F.S. (2001) 'Mass customization: Literature review and research directions', *International Journal of Production Economics*, 72, 1–13.

Davis, S. (1987) *Future Perfect*, Reading, MA: Addison-Wesley Publishing.

Economist (1994) 'Economist manufacturing technology survey', 333(6804), 38–45.

Economist (1995) 'Technology and unemployment: A world without jobs?' 334(7901), 23–5.

Emiliani, M.L. and Seymour, P.J. (2011) 'Frank George Woollard: Forgotten pioneer of flow production', *International Journal of Management History*, 17(1), 66–87.

Feitzinger, E. and Lee, H.L. (1997) 'Mass customization at Hewlett Packard: The power of postponement', *Harvard Business Review*, 75(1), 116–21.

Financial Times (2002) 'Mass customisation: Make every one different', 21 May 2002.

Forbes (1995) 'Custom-made. (PCs made to order)', 6 November 1995.

Fortune (2004) 'Elite factories', 6 September, 2004.

Fralix, M. (2001) 'From mass production to mass customization', *Journal of Textile and Apparel, Technology and Management*, 1(2), 1–7.

Gilmore, J.H. and Pine, J. (1997) 'Beyond goods and services', *Strategy and Leadership*, 25(3), 10–18.

Gunasekaran, A. and Yusuf, Y. (2002) 'Agile manufacturing: A taxonomy of strategic and technological imperatives', *International Journal of Production Research*, 40(6), 1357–85.

Heizer, J. and Render, B. (2009) *Operations Management, Flexible Version*, 9th edition, New Jersey: Prentice Hall.

Hill, T. (2000) *Manufacturing Strategy*, Basingstoke: Macmillan.

Holweg, M. and Pil, F. (2001) 'Successful build to order strategies: Start with the customer', *Sloan Management Review*, 43(1), 74–83.

Honeycutt, E.D., Siguaw, J.A. and Harper, S.C. (1993) 'The impact of flexible manufacturing on competitive strategy', *Industrial Management*, 35(6), 2–15.

Huckman, R.S. (2009) 'Are you having trouble keeping your operations focused?', *Harvard Business Review*, 87(9), 90–5.

Hutchison, G. and Holland, J. (1982) 'The economic value of flexible automation', *Journal of Manufacturing Systems*, 1(2), 215–27.

Industry Week (1998) 'The search for simplicity', 8 June 1998.

Keller, M. (1993) *Collision*, New York: Currency Doubleday.

Kulatilaka, N. (1984) 'Valuing the flexibility of flexible manufacturing systems', *IEEE Transactions on Engineering Management*, 35(4), 250–7.

Lampel, J. and Mintzberg, H. (1996) 'Customizing customization', *Sloan Management Review*, 38, 21–30.

Lei, D., Hitt, M.A. and Goldhar, J.D. (1996) 'Advanced manufacturing technology: Organizational design and strategic flexibility', *Organization Studies*, 17(3), 501–24.

Levitt, T. (1972) 'The industrialization of service', *Harvard Business Review*, 54(5), 63–74.

Lovelock, C.H. (1983) 'Classifying services to gain strategic marketing insights', *Journal of Marketing*, 47(3), 9–21.

MacCarthey, B., Brabazon, P.G. and Bramham, J. (2003) 'Fundamental modes of operation for mass customization', *International Journal of Production Economics*, 85, 289–304.

Monohan, G. and Smunt, T. (1984) 'The flexible manufacturing system investment decision', *Proceedings of ORSA/TIMS Conference*, November.

Pine, B.J. (1992) *Mass Customization: The New frontier in Business Competition*, Boston, MA: Harvard Business School Press.

Porter, M. (1980) *Competitive Strategy*, New York: Free Press.

Ridderstrale, J. and Nordstrom, K. (2000) *Funky Business*, London: FT Books.

Schmenner, R.W. (1986) 'How can services business survive and prosper?', *Sloan Management Review*, 27(3), 21–32.

Slack, N., Chambers, S. and Johnston, R. (2010) *Operations Management*, 6th edition, London: Prentice Hall.

Spring, M. and Boaden, R. (1997) 'One more time: How do you win orders? A critical reappraisal of the Hill manufacturing strategy framework', *International Journal of Operations and Production Management*, 17(8), 757–79.

Starr, M. and Biloski, A. (1984) 'The decision to adopt new technoplogy', *Omega*, 12(4), 353–61.

Ulrich, K.T. and Tung, K. (1991) 'Fundamentals of product modularity', *Working Paper No. 3335-91-MSA*, Sloan School of Management, MIT.

Willis, R. and Sullivan, K. (1984) 'CIMS in perspective', *Industrial Engineering*, February, pp. 28–36.

Woollard, F.G. (1954) *Principles of Mass and Flow Production*, London: Iliffe & Sons.

Zipkin, P. (2001) 'The limits of mass customization', *Sloan Management Review*, 42(3), 81–7.

MANAGING QUALITY

INTRODUCTION

In 2009 Toyota became the largest car manufacturer in the world, but since the 1980s it already had the enviable reputation of being the most productive. Its stellar reputation was built particularly on attention to the question of quality – an attribute which had allowed it to enter and then dominate markets around the world. Toyota models regularly topped league tables such as the J. D. Power Associates annual survey of quality in the USA – and the perception of high and consistent quality was shared by customers and dealers alike.

Yet in 2009 the company suffered a massive blow to its quality reputation, with millions of cars recalled for repair to several key systems, especially in the braking systems. Lawsuits proliferated and several cases of accidental death were argued to have been caused by faulty vehicles. Eventually – and after extensive negative press coverage – the company's Chairman, Akio Toyoda, was forced to issue a public apology in which he explained that the company could not train enough personnel to keep up with its rapid growth. He acknowledged that a misguided strategic focus at the company warped the 'order of Toyota's traditional priorities' so that the stress on product safety and quality first, and sales volume and cost second, became inverted as Toyota began rapidly expanding a decade ago. The overall cost to the company was estimated at $5.5bn but this did not include the serious damage to a reputation carefully built up over 70 years.

Cole, R. (2010) 'No big quality problems at Toyota?',
Harvard Business Review, 9 March 2010

In this chapter we will explore the theme of quality – what it is, why it is so important, and how we can manage it in our organizations. We will look at the ways in which thinking and practice about quality management have evolved, and at some frameworks for ensuring it becomes a key part of effective operations management. And we will explore another important issue – how can we manage continuous improvement of all aspects of quality?

Quality is not an option in most walks of life. For example, it would be unthinkable for airline pilots or hospital midwives to aim for anything less than perfection in what they do, and nonsense to think of only trying for an 'acceptable' level of failure – one plane crash in a 100 or one baby dropped per 500 deliveries! In similar fashion, no artist who is serious about his/her work would think of producing something that did not reflect their best endeavours and provide an object or artefact of lasting value.

Yet until recently these ideas of quality were not common in the world of business. Much of the early theory of manufacturing contained terms and concepts such as 'acceptable quality level' and an underlying philosophy which assumed mistakes would happen and that things would go wrong. This fed across into the development of services and became part of the underpinning assumptions about operations. Quality was seen as important but the belief was that with complex products and services being delivered via complicated processes there would inevitably be defects and problems which could not be predicted or prevented.[1] As a result, whole departments of specialists were recruited to manage the effects of having problems with quality as an endemic part of business life. This included inspectors whose job it was to catch defective products before they left the factory; customer support staff, processing complaints and warranty claims; and an army of people running around the business trying to repair or replace faulty items and sort out service glitches.

Needless to say, this kind of quality 'management' results in extra costs, and they may be considerable. It is not just the cost of the direct employees involved that we have to consider; it is also the disruption, the wasted effort producing something of poor quality in the first place, the risk to reputation and goodwill, the wasted time and effort in attracting customers who then become dissatisfied and tell their friends, etc. One of the key figures who shaped thinking about quality is Philip Crosby, who began working on these issues within the giant ITT Corporation. He tried to put some numbers to the real costs of quality

---

1   There is some truth in this at the most basic statistical level; in any population of events there will be an element of random variation but this level is very small – and even then action can be taken to ensure this does not adversely affect the perception of overall quality.

– and realized to his – and the company's – horror that these could account for as much as 40 per cent of sales revenue (Crosby, 1977). (For example, in 1984 when IBM first began looking at this problem they estimated that $2 billion of its $5 billion profits was due to improved quality – not having to fix errors.)

It would not be an exaggeration to say that there has been a revolution in thinking and practice around the theme of quality. Not only was there an urgent need to address this huge hidden cost, but there was also a great opportunity to deploy improved quality as a source of competitive advantage. In a whole series of industries – motorcycles and cars, consumer electronics, banking and insurance – the competitive landscape was reshaped by companies paying attention to systematic and significant improvements in quality. Commentators in the aerospace industry point out that achieving six sigma (a measure of very high-quality performance) is worth several points on Wall St., and that's why they are going for it.

As a result, quality has moved from being something about which firms have much choice – 'you can have it cheap or you can have quality' – to a position where it is a competitive imperative. In general, customers make their purchase decisions based on price and a set of non-price factors such as design, variety, speed of response, and customization. Quality sits high amongst these non-price factors and we can chart its evolution over the past 30 years from being a non-essential, to being a desirable feature, to being a necessary qualification to enter some markets.

Much of the early changes in thinking on quality took place in manufacturing but it soon became clear that the lessons applied equally in services. In many cases, quality is even more important, because service contains many tangible components and no-one values poorly cooked or served food or bedrooms which are not cleaned properly. But perceptions of service go beyond this to the overall experience – and the likelihood of returning. For example, it has been estimated that the potential value of securing a customer for life (through good service) for a purchase as trivial as a home-delivery pizza is of the order of $12,000 (Bentley 1999).

For the operations manager quality is of critical importance. Quality – as we shall see – is not the province of a specialist but the responsibility of everyone. It pervades all aspects of an organization's operations, and the development and maintenance of quality conscious-ness has become one of the key roles that strategic operations managers have to play.

WHAT IS QUALITY?

Before we explore how operations managers can influence quality performance it will be useful to reflect for a moment on what we mean by the word 'quality'. The New Elizabethan dictionary says it is 'the degree of excellence which a thing possesses', whilst John Ruskin, the nineteenth-century painter and art critic, makes a valuable additional point: 'quality is never an accident, it is always a result of intelligent effort'. Robert Pirsig suggests that quality is not a physical attribute, nor a mental concept, but something embodying both: 'even though Quality cannot be defined, you know what it is' (Pirsig, 1974, 29).

Joseph Juran spoke of quality as 'fitness for use' (Juran, 1985, 142). But the question is: for whose use? From this point of view, a better definition – certainly in terms of how markets perceive quality – is offered by Feigenbaum (1983, p. 7) who sees quality as:

the total composite product and service characteristics . . . through which the product or service in use will meet the expectations of the customer.

He adds further insight to our understanding of the definition of quality when he ties it to quality *control*:

> control must start with identification of customer quality requirements and end only when the product has been placed in the hands of a customer who remains satisfied.
>
> (p. 11)

This user-oriented approach is helpful in focusing attention on the customer rather than the producer, but it can be argued that it needs some modification. In particular, as Garvin (1988, p. 112) points out, it does not deal with two key problems:

- how to aggregate what may be widely varying individual perceptions of quality to provide something meaningful at the level of the market;
- how to identify the key product/service attributes which connote quality.

An alternative set of definitions emerge from considering the producer's side: these are concerned with establishing standards and measuring against them (Juran and Gryna, 1980). The *quality of design* represents the intentional quality which designers wish to see produced in order to meet their interpretations of the customer's needs. It is a multi-attribute definition but has the advantages of permitting measurement against each of these attributes to assess whether or not the intentional quality level has been achieved.

Associated with this is the *quality of conformance* which represents the degree to which the product or service, when delivered, conforms to the original design specifications. The extent to which this can be achieved will depend in turn on the various elements which went into creating the quality – people, processes, equipment, incoming raw materials quality, etc. This equates to Crosby's idea of quality as 'conformance to requirements' (Crosby, 1977).

So we need to see quality as something that doesn't simply happen, but as a business process linking needs and means – and this can be seen in Figure 8.1. Essentially, market needs are translated into a product/service strategy which in turn feeds through to the various players involved in the design of products and services – in order to provide a suitable specification. It is against this that quality can be measured in terms of conformance to that specification. On the process side (how we actually create and deliver our offering), quality will be affected by two things – the overall capability of the process (to hold tolerances, etc.), and the way in which quality is controlled within the process. The degree to which conformance to specification can be achieved will depend on these two factors.

Another way of looking at this is to see quality as the outcome of four interrelated sets of factors, as shown in Figure 8.2.

Much of this thinking developed around manufactured products, but the same principles can be applied to service design and delivery. Clearly, a key element of ensuring quality is to

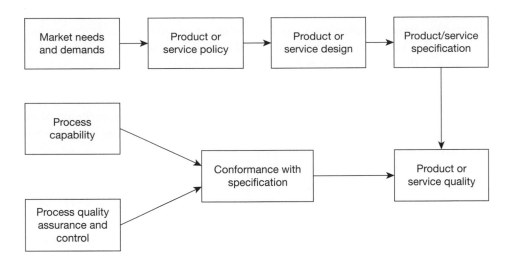

Figure 8.1 Quality in the design process

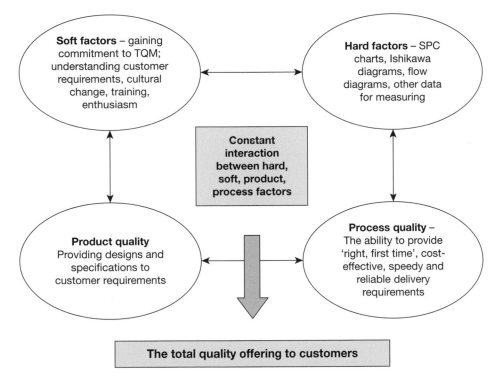

Figure 8.2 Understanding the total quality offering
Brown (2000, p. 119)

measure customers' responses to the product or service they have received. Understanding this provides strategic feedback as to the likely future success of the firm. At first it might seem simple to establish if customers are pleased or dissatisfied with their purchase – just ask them. With regard to products that have tangible characteristics, it is possible to ask customers about these and their degree of satisfaction with them.

In services it has been less straightforward. However, Parasuraman *et al.* (1985) developed the SERVQUAL model based on measuring the difference between a customer's expectation of a service and their perception of the actual experience. This has led them to identify five key characteristics which they claim apply across all services – tangibles, reliability, responsiveness, assurance, and empathy. Despite its general applicability, this approach is modified to reflect the specific characteristics of different service industries and can only be used with other forms of quality measurement techniques. The SERVQUAL model is shown in Figure 8.3.

Parasuraman *et al.* (1985) identified five gaps that can lead to service quality failures. These five gaps are:

1. Not understanding the needs of the customers;

2. Being unable to translate the needs of the customer into a service design that can address them;

Figure 8.3
The SERVQUAL model

(Parasuraman, Berry & Zeithaml 1985)

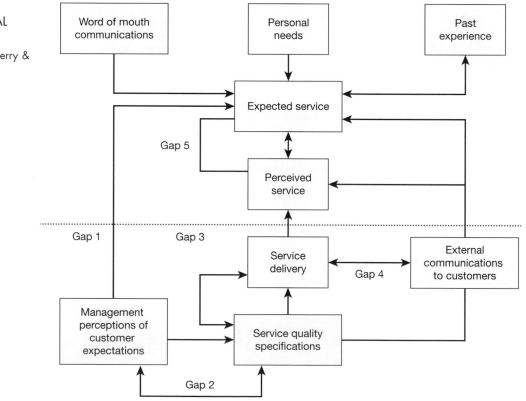

3. Being unable to translate the design into service expectations or standards that can be implemented;

4. Being unable to deliver the services in line with specifications; and

5. Creating expectations that cannot be met (gap between customer's expectations and actual delivery).

The task facing the organization is to ensure that these gaps are closed in order for the 'promise' of the offer to be on par with the actual delivery. Although the SERVQUAL model has been one of the most widely used research instruments in the operations field throughout the world, it is not without some controversy. The single biggest issue is in asking customers about their expectations and the difficulty of operationalizing this (Parasuraman, 1995).

Unfortunately, customer satisfaction measurement is more complex than simply asking questions. Completely satisfied customers may never repurchase because customer loyalty is not derived solely from satisfaction, but two other factors – the relative importance of the purchase to the customer and the ease of switching. From a strategic perspective it is customer loyalty that should be sought, not just satisfaction. Satisfied customers may purchase a competitor's product or service because the purchase is not significant to them and hence they do not mind which brand they use. Likewise, satisfied customers purchase a competitor's product or service when they cannot perceive any difference between them – in effect the product is a so-called 'commodity'. Firms therefore need to ensure that their product or service either is, or appears to be, a significant purchase and that their brand has features that no other brand has. From an operations perspective, making the product special and the brand differentiated derives from innovation (discussed in Chapter 4). The role of marketing is to ensure that this reality is also perceived by the customer.

CASE 8.1: THE ROADSIDE RESTAURANT CHAIN

Understanding customers is the key to making good products and delivering fine service. In the 1980s there were two major chains of roadside restaurants in the UK, and the CEO of one of them decided to conduct market research into why motorists stopped at one of his restaurants rather than his competitors. The CEO was very experienced in this industry. Indeed, 20 years earlier he had travelled to the United States to investigate the roadside dining concept and on his return had set up the very first operations of this kind.

Despite his experience, he had never conducted market research. Demand was such that units had been opened and traded successfully without such data. But given the increasing competition he decided the time was now right for more detailed information about his customers and their preferences.

Naturally enough the first question the researchers asked was 'Why have you stopped at this roadside restaurant?' The CEO was rather surprised to find that the principle reason given by 55 per cent of respondents was to use the washroom facilities. As he himself said – 'I had been in the industry for 20 years. I thought I was in the restaurant business, but it turned out I was in the toilet business'. As a result of this the operations strategy of the chain was changed. Up to that point washrooms had deliberately been placed at the back of the operation so that customers had to walk through the restaurant to get to them. The theory was that they would feel guilty just doing this, so would stay to buy something. After the market research, the chain decided that in all its new build units from that moment on, they would put the facilities near the front entrance – making it easier for people to use. Their theory was that this would make more people stop – and once stopped they would purchase something any way. Moreover the washrooms were built bigger and equipped with higher quality fittings. And along with this a procedure was introduced to check cleanliness more frequently than before.

Quality is more important than quantity.
One home run is much better than two doubles.

Steve Jobs

QUALITY AS A STRATEGIC ISSUE

Quality has risen to such a high place on the strategic agenda in large measure because of the explosion of competition in world trade. If we imagine a market square with various stalls trying to tempt customers to buy we can see this picture a little more clearly. When there are many stalls all offering the same thing then two factors will influence our choice to buy. One is, of course, price – but we are also swayed by what are called 'non-price' factors – perhaps the design of the product, perhaps the degree to which it can be tailored to our needs. And top of the list of non-price factors is likely to be quality. Unless there is no-one else to buy from we are likely to choose the stall which offers us good quality at a fair price.

The same is true in global markets – non-price factors play a hugely important role and quality has, in particular, reshaped the way in which global trade patterns operate. We saw some early examples of this back in the 1980s when industries like cameras, TV sets, music systems, cars, and motorcycles all become dominated by Japanese producers. This was not a pattern based on price competition (although the original Japanese versions of these products did have a reputation for being cheap but poor quality). Rather, it came about because manufacturers had developed ways of producing these items which combined both competitive pricing *and* consistently high quality. Faced with this kind of competition the rest of the world had nowhere to go – either it raised its own game to meet these new quality standards or it left the business.

For example, the major reason why quality became such a major issue for the 'Big Three' US car manufacturers in the 1980s was that it became abundantly clear that the Japanese plants' capabilities were vastly superior to their American competitors (Womack *et al.*, 1991). As Tom Peters (1997) succinctly stated, reflecting on the situation of the US auto industry at the beginning of the 1980s: 'Our cars were trash!' Back in 1994, *Business Week* (1994, p. 54) commented on the strategic importance of quality:

> Detroit, for instance, finally caught the quality wave in the 1980s and it's hard not to shudder at the thought of how the Big Three would be faring today if they were still turning out Chevy Citations instead of Saturns. And much of the rest of U.S. industry would be locked out of the game in today's global economy without the quality strides of the past few years.

This pattern was repeated across the whole spectrum of industry – first in manufacturing but with increasing speed in the field of services as well. Since most services do not have the luxury of patent or other protection the entry barriers to newcomers who can offer better levels of service – especially in the area of quality – are low. This intense competition has helped to redefine the term, *world-class*, when applied to quality. Kanter (1996) rightly argues that the term world-class has less to do with being *better* than competitors – the term merely denotes the ability to compete *at all* in global competition. It may well be necessary to speak of world-class quality capability as an order-qualifier in order to compete in markets (Hill, 1993). Significantly, it dominates thinking about entry into world markets by 'emerging' economies like India, China, and Brazil, where there is recognition that lasting competitive strength lies not in low labour costs (which provide a very shaky and footloose basis for economic growth) but rather in being able to compete on price *and* quality.

In recent years China has come to dominate the world of manufacturing, a position driven by huge labour-cost advantages. But with such rapid expansion have come growing concerns about safety and quality, culminating in some high-profile scandals. In 2007 the US toy manufacturer Mattel was forced to recall over 1.5 million toys which had been painted using a poisonous lead paint – and whilst the problem may have been due to a supplier to the Chinese manufacturer contracted by Mattel, the results were still a huge embarrassment for a country pledged to being a reliable exporter. Lida Industries was supplier of hundreds of thousands of Big Birds, Elmos, Dora the Explorers, and other figures made for the Fisher Price label, but faced strong criticism in the wake of the scandal; sadly the owner committed suicide in response to the pressure.

Chinese trade officials, recognizing the potential threat to their image as exporters, have come down heavily on those seen to be responsible for lapses in quality management. The head of the food and drug safety administration, Zheng Xiaoyu, was executed for accepting bribes in return for approving medicines that later proved to have deadly side-effects. But the problems have persisted with a more serious scandal in 2008 over contaminated milk powder which led to the deaths of six children and the hospitalization of nearly 1,000 more. It drew unwelcome attention again to the difficulties of rapid growth and economic expansion whilst trying to maintain high quality and safety standards.

One consequence of this is a change in the mindset of customers towards all of the things they consume – both products and services delivered by the private sector and increasingly around *public* services such as healthcare, education, and law and order. Expectations of good service are high and customers know that – as taxpayers – they can exert pressure to improve the levels of quality being offered. And the costs of failing to deliver may not simply be confined to money – in some cases they may literally be a matter of life and death.

The effect of this trend has been hugely beneficial for consumers – but it clearly places enormous pressures on those responsible for creating and delivering products and services. How can operations managers ensure not only that quality standards are up with the competitive frontier but also that they are maintained at this level – and continuously improved to create a competitive edge? That is the focus of this chapter – and we can begin to answer the questions by looking back at how current levels of 'world-class' quality management have developed.

LOOKING BACK

We have seen in previous chapters how the transition from craft to mass production through to the modern era has had a profound influence on operations management in both manufactured goods and in all kinds of services. This is very much the case with quality.

In the earliest days of manufacturing, quality was essentially built into the work of the craftsman. For example the notion of 'taking a pride in work' was a central pillar of the mediaeval guild system whereby concern for quality was trained into the hearts and minds of apprentices onwards. The Industrial Revolution destroyed much of this one-to-one identification with the product and led to a loss of the craft ethic to be gradually replaced by the factory system. Although quality was important, especially in the pioneering applications of new technologies evident in the bridges, machinery, and other products of that period, it was often in competition with the demands of high productivity for satisfying massively expanding demand.

In the latter part of the nineteenth century, the focus of attention in manufacturing shifted to the US, where the ideas of Taylor and Ford were of particular importance. In Taylor's model of the effective factory, quality was one of eight key functions identified as being of critical importance for shop foremen to manage, whilst in his influential book *The Control of Quality in Manufacturing*, published in 1922, Radford placed further emphasis on the task of inspection as a separate function (Radford, 1922; Taylor, 1947).

Taylor's model became the blueprint not only for the mass production factories of the 1920s and 1930s but also for many other types of business. Typically, emphasis was placed on inspection as the main control mechanism for quality, supporting a process of gradual refinement in product and process design which aimed to eliminate variation and error. Significantly, the majority of people were not involved; the task of managing quality fell to a handful of specialists.

In 1931, Walter Shewhart wrote a book based on his experience in the Bell Telephone Laboratories entitled *The Economic Control of Manufactured Products*. This study of methods for monitoring and measuring quality marked the emergence of the concept of *statistical quality control* as a sophisticated replacement for the simple inspection procedures of the 1920s (Shewhart, 1931). Members of his team, along with others including William Edwards Deming and Joseph Juran, helped establish the American Society for Quality Control. Within this forum, many of the key ideas underpinning quality management today were first articulated, but their impact was limited and little understanding of quality control principles extended beyond the immediate vicinity of the shop floor. They did find application in the wartime period when pressures on both output and quality forced significant improvements on a range of industrial sectors.

For most firms, the 1950s were a boom period – the era of 'you've never had it so good'. One consequence of this relatively easy market environment was that the stringencies of the war years were relaxed and there was a general slowdown in effort in both productivity growth and quality improvement practices.

In 1951 Juran published his *Quality Control Handbook* in which he highlighted not only the principles of quality control but also the potential economic benefits of a more thorough approach to preventing defects and managing quality on a company-wide basis (Juran, 1951). He suggested that failure costs were often avoidable, and the economic payoff from preventive measures to reduce or eliminate failures could be between $500 and $1000 per operator – what he referred to as the 'gold in the mine'.

A few years later, Armand Feigenbaum extended these ideas into the concept of 'total quality control', in which he drew attention to the fact that quality was not determined simply in manufacturing but began in the design of the product and extended throughout the entire factory (Feigenbaum, 1956). As he put it, 'the first principle to recognize is that quality is everybody's job'.

In the 1960s the concept of 'quality assurance' (QA) began to be promoted by the defence industry in response to pressure from the NATO defence ministries for some guarantees of quality and reliability. (An indication of the size of the problem can be gauged from the fact that in 1950 only 30 per cent of the US Navy's electronics devices were working properly at any given time.) Such approaches were based on the extensive application of statistical techniques to problems such as that of predicting the reliability and performance of equipment over time.

This link with the defence sector (and latterly, by association, with the aerospace industry) led to the formalizing of quality standards for products, including components and materials, supplied by subcontractors for military customers. In the US and the UK, the so-called 'military specifications' and 'defence standards' gave rise to the practice of formal assessment of suppliers, for purposes of accreditation as acceptable sources (see Chapter 5).

The combination of QA and the supplier assessment initiatives described above gave rise to the concept of supplier quality assurance (SQA). In order to ensure compliance with increasingly rigorous standards, the certification and checking of suppliers began to take place, where the onus was placed upon suppliers to provide evidence of their ability to maintain quality in products and processes. Such vendor appraisal was often tied to the award of important contracts, and possession of certification could also be used as a marketing tool to secure new business because it provided an indication of the status of a quality supplier. In keeping with the general tenor of quality management to date, however, SQA maintained the idea that quality was something 'outside' the process – as if it were the result of inspection (this time, with the customer wearing the 'white coat').

By the mid to late 1970s there were many SQA schemes in operation, all complex and often different for each major customer. As a result suppliers faced a major task in trying to ensure compliance and certification. Such congestion led to the need for some form of central register of approved schemes and some common agreement on the rules of good QA practice. There are now a number of national and international standards which relate to the whole area of quality assurance and require the establishment and codification of complete quality assurance systems, and achievement of certification (e.g. ISO 9000) has become a prerequisite for participation in many global markets.

THE EASTERN PROMISE: A NEW APPROACH TO QUALITY

There is no doubt that such procedural approaches made a contribution to improving quality levels in the West. However, they still represented a traditional view which saw quality as the province of specialists and primarily controlled through inspection at all stages. Something very different had been happening in the Far East. During the 1960s, and particularly the 1970s, it became clear that Japanese firms had not only managed to shake off their image of offering poor quality products but had actually managed to obtain significant competitive advantage through their improved performance in this field. In fact, their improved performance was the result of a long learning process which began in the aftermath of World War II.

In 1948 the Japanese Union of Scientists and Engineers (itself only formed two years earlier) formed a quality control research group, and invited Deming to give a series of seminars. These were extremely influential, especially in introducing some of the statistical approaches but also in encouraging a systematic approach to problem-solving. So successful was his visit that the Deming Prize for quality was initiated in 1951 in his honour. Pride in quality became a key norm in the post-war development of Japanese industry and state support was also present in the form of the Industrial Standardisation Law in 1949, which came out of the Ministry for International Trade and Industry (MITI) and attempted to improve the range of products being made and sold.

The early 1950s saw the growing trend towards SQC being applied across the organization, backed up by formal procedures and standardization. It is important to note that this trend was led by engineers and middle managers and was not necessarily seen as a key strategic development by senior management at the time. The concept of company wide quality control really emerged during the late 1950s as new mechanisms were developed and as the tools of statistical quality control were applied systematically across the piece. Once again, ideas that had originally developed in the West were influential here. Joseph Juran visited in 1954 and laid considerable emphasis on the responsibility which management had for quality planning and other organizational issues concerned with quality, while Armand Feigenbaum came two years later with his message about company wide quality control, taking his cue from Juran.

One lesson emerging from this experience was the need to involve those in the production process much more, to teach them *why* they had to guarantee quality as well as *what* they had to do. A key feature of this is the idea that operators are much more than simply interchangeable resources as they are represented in the Taylor/Ford model. As Kaoru Ishikawa, son of one of the founders of the Japanese quality movement, said:

> if Japanese workers . . . were obliged to work under the Taylor system, without encouragement of voluntary will and creative initiative, they would lose much of their interest in work itself . . . and do their work in a perfunctory manner.
>
> (Ishikawa, 1985, p. 24)

In many ways this is an obvious point – after all, the likely consequences of treating people as 'cogs in a machine' include:

- Uninterested operators;
- Increased defects in products;
- Drop in labour efficiency;
- No quality consciousness (why bother?);
- Increased absenteeism; and
- Increased labour turnover.

RELEARNING THE QUALITY LESSON IN THE WEST

A growing awareness (and in many cases impact on market shares) of the Japanese total quality model led to a renewed focus of interest and effort in the quality area and the beginnings of adoption of Japanese practices in the West. For example, Garvin (1988) reports that the Martin Corporation managed to supply a defect-free Pershing missile one month ahead of schedule in 1961, a remarkable achievement at a time when extensive inspection and testing was the norm and defects were accepted as being almost inevitable by final customers. Of particular significance was the fact that this had been achieved by focusing all employees on the common goal of 'zero defects'; as the company management reflected:

> the reason behind the lack of perfection was simply that perfection had not been expected.
>
> (Halpin, cited in Garvin, 1988)

This led them, and others, to experiment with ways of building worker involvement in programmes which were designed to promote higher quality consciousness and the desire to do things 'right first time'. The first Western quality circle (QC) was established in Lockheed in 1975 and others quickly followed. Firms quickly began to realize that there was no instant plug-in means of providing better quality – and many early QCs failed after early success.

Gradually firms recognized the need for more of a company wide approach which included operator involvement and a total system approach to quality management.

New tools helped this process, particularly the idea of statistical process control (SPC) which had been developed in the 1940s but which became easier to implement in total systems which stressed operator involvement. SPC, which was applied extensively in the early 1980s, not only improved the control of quality but, importantly, changed the location of responsibility. It brought control of the quality back to the point of manufacture, rather than placing it at the end of the process. Such approaches call for operator involvement, for top management commitment, for quality to be seen as a concept being applied to much more than just the product, and for the extension of problem-solving techniques beyond the quality area – in short, to company wide quality control or *total quality* management.

A summary of developments in quality is illustrated in Table 8.1.

Table 8.1 Major developments in quality

Emphasis	Major themes	Dates	Key figures
Inspection	Craft production	Prior to 1900s	
	Inspection	1900s	
	Standardized parts and gauging	1900s	
	Control charts and acceptance sampling	1920s	Walter Shewhart Harold Dodge Harry Romig
Statistical process control	Theory of SPC	1931	Walter Shewhart
	US experts visit Japan	1940s	W. Edwards Deming Joseph Juran Arnold Feigenbaum
Quality assurance	Cost of quality Total quality control	1950s	Joseph Juran Arnold Feigenbaum
	Quality-control circles in Japan	1950s	Kaoru Ishikawa Taiichi Ohno
	Reliability engineering Zero defects	1960s	
Total quality management	Robust design	1960s	Genichi Taguchi
	Quality function deployment	1970s	
	Design for manufacture/assembly	1980s	
	TQM in West	1980s–present	

Nicholas (1998, p. 20)

QUALITY TODAY

The picture today is very different to the mass production approach to quality. Quality has been reintegrated into the mainstream of operations thinking and concern for the development and maintenance of high standards runs throughout business, and increasingly in the public sector. It is seen as a national imperative, something which affects international competitiveness and is too important to be left to chance. (An indication of this can be seen in the number of government-backed programmes which have promoted the adoption of quality standards such as the ISO 9000 series –see below – which provide a measure of the overall quality of processes. These were characteristic of industrialized countries in the 1990s, but have now become widespread amongst 'emerging' economies as part of their strategic planning to enter world markets.)

Importantly, we have also moved on from the view that quality is the province (and problem) of a small group of specialists. These days quality is everyone's problem – and everyone can make a contribution to its development and maintenance. As we shall see, the notion of employee involvement in problem finding and solving is beginning to be recognized as a significant – and low cost – source of competitive advantage.

It will be useful to look at some of the key components of today's quality practice – at what is involved in building and maintaining quality in creating and delivering products and services of consistently high quality. Much is made of the term 'total quality management', but there is a risk that the term itself becomes meaningless. In essence, little has changed from the principles discovered (or perhaps rediscovered) in post-war Japan and later in the West: quality still comes from an approach which emphasizes everyone's involvement, from a view which integrates quality thinking and action into all operations, and from the pursuit of excellence. The target should always be an uncompromising 'zero defects', although every step towards this will be useful it is also important to reflect that 'best is the enemy of better'.

In putting this philosophy into action three areas are of interest: the *process* whereby quality is built into what we do; the *tools* and *techniques* which enable that to happen; and the *involvement* and *commitment* of everyone towards continuous improvement.

THE QUALITY PROCESS

At its heart, quality is the result of a sequence of activities embodied in a process within the business. The advantage of looking at it in this way is that it becomes possible to map the process and monitor and measure the outputs – and to use this information to identify where and how the process itself can be improved. This kind of thinking is central to the original statistical approaches developed in the early part of the century, but it can be applied on a broader scale to explore all the areas where quality is introduced, and to the influences on the process.

At the simplest level, we can consider a machine making a part: we know the desired output specification and can use this to compare what actually comes out of the process with what is supposed to. If there is a difference we know there is a problem affecting quality, and we can then apply tools and techniques to finding and rectifying the problem and eventually preventing its recurrence. This approach can be used on a single machine, on a series of machines, on the intangible processes which schedule those machines, on the various linked activities upstream and downstream of the machines, and so on. We can even look at the quality management process itself and how that might be improved.

Taking a process approach is a powerful start to improving quality and has the advantage of being generic – as long as we can define the process and specify inputs and outputs and relevant measures we can apply this approach. The argument then runs that if we can guarantee the process is OK then it follows that the quality coming out of that process will be OK. This kind of thinking underpins the many national and international standards around total quality management – such as ISO 9000. In this, organizations are required to define and document each process they employ and to show how quality assurance and improvement are built into it. If they do so then they have the framework for ensuring high and improving quality. (Of course it is possible to write elegant descriptions of processes and suitable procedures for monitoring and measurement which have nothing to do with the way things work in practice – but in principle such process-based standards are a powerful tool.)

BENCHMARKING IN QUALITY

An extension of the process idea is the use of benchmarking to compare performance on quality indicators – for example, defective parts per million – and the practices which different firms use to achieve such performance. This approach – which was originally developed in the Xerox Corporation – provides a powerful learning and development aid to quality improvement (Camp, 1989). Regular benchmarking can provide both the stimulus for improvement (because of the performance gap which has to be closed) and new ideas about things to try in terms of organizational tools, mechanisms, and practices.

Further development of these ideas of assessment and improvement comes in the form of integrated frameworks which provide definitions of 'ideal' quality organizations against which firms can benchmark themselves. Such models are sometimes associated with a prize – for example, the Deming prize in Japan – but their real value lies in offering a well-publicized target at which firms can aim in their quality improvement activities. In the US the Malcolm Baldrige Award provides such a framework, whilst in Europe the model originally developed by the European Foundation for Quality Management (EFQM) has found widespread application. Schemes of this kind – which were originally developed in the 1980s – have now diffused widely with, for example, winners of the European Quality Award increasingly featuring new entrant economies such as Poland and Turkey. Their impact has also spread to embrace smaller firms and different sectors, contributing to a general raising of interest and awareness in the theme of total quality management.[2]

---

2   For more details on benchmarking and examples see the websites www.nist.gov/baldrige/ and www.efqm.org.

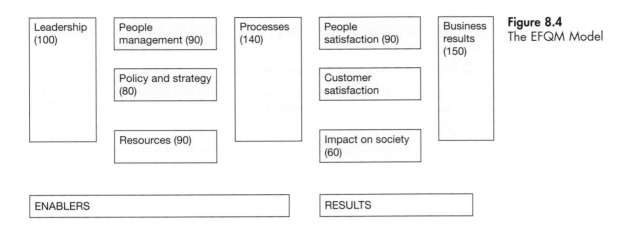

Figure 8.4
The EFQM Model

Importantly these models not only look at processes within the firm but increasingly at its interactions with the wider community. Equally, they are not simply concerned with aspects of product quality but also consider issues such as the quality of working life within the firm.

Figure 8.4 reproduces the model used in the EFQM approach, and shows the concern for both performance (essentially the 'results' measures) and practices which create that performance (the 'enablers' measures). Such models are used by firms for self-assessment or for feedback and guidance offered by a team of trained external and independent assessors. (The numbers represent the number of points which could be awarded in each category and so give an idea of relative importance.)

A limitation of benchmarking is that it focuses on measurable aspects of quality – but may miss other key features. In an influential paper Kano *et al.* (1996) set out a model of customer satisfaction and customer 'delight'. Their argument was that some features become expected – and the only thing which affects customer choice is when they are absent. A second set of features – qualifiers – are the minimum set needed to be seen as a player in the game. It is at this level that benchmarking tends to operate. But beyond that are features of products or services which have the capacity to surprise or delight – and which strongly affect decisions to purchase or consume.

For example, a train passenger is unlikely to be delighted by the train departing and arriving on time (the sort of thing that is benchmarked) because this is what is expected. The passenger might be delighted, however, to find that a complimentary newspaper or cup of coffee is included in the service.

OPENING THE QUALITY MANAGEMENT TOOLBOX

Although this chapter is primarily about the challenges quality management poses to strategic operations management, it is worth looking for a moment at the range of tools and techniques which can be deployed to help. In general, there are 'seven basic tools' of quality management:

1. *Pareto analysis*: this recognizes that it is often the case that 80 per cent of failures are due to 20 per cent of problems and therefore tries to find those 20 per cent and solve them first.

2. *Histograms*: used to represent this information in visual form.

3. *Cause and effect diagrams*: fishbone charts or Ishikawa diagrams which are used to identify the effect and work backwards, through symptoms to the root cause of the problem.

4. *Stratification*: identifying different levels of problems and symptoms using statistical techniques applied to each layer.

5. *Check sheets*: structured lists or frameworks of likely causes which can be worked through systematically. When new issues are found they are added to the list.

6. *Scatter diagrams*: used to plot variables against each other and help identify where there is a correlation or other pattern.

7. *Control charts*: which use SPC information to start the analytical process off, asking *why* these errors occur at this time.

Once a basic understanding of the problem and its contributing problems has been built up, other techniques for problem solving can be introduced. Since the search is on for as many different ways as possible of dealing with the problem, techniques which support creative problem-solving are especially helpful here. Brainstorming and other, related, techniques are often used. There are also many new and powerful tools associated with more advanced approaches linked to the wider questions of quality management – sometimes referred to as the *seven advanced tools* of quality management. These include affinity diagrams, relations diagrams, matrix diagrams, tree diagrams, arrow diagrams, matrix data analysis, and process decision progress charts. All of these take a system-wide perspective and provide ways of relating different elements in the quality process. A full description of these tools can be found in several sources (for example Oakland, 2003) and descriptions of some of them appear on the website that accompanies this book.

BEYOND TOOLS TO 'TOTAL' QUALITY MANAGEMENT

So far we have looked at the process aspects of quality and some of the tools which can enable its effective management. We now need to add the third essential ingredient – the active involvement of people in the process of quality control and improvement.

It is widely recognized that at the core of the original Japanese quality success was the idea of *company wide quality control* (CWQC) – a theme originally articulated by Feigenbaum (1956) in the mid-1950s. The basis of this concept is to be able to design, produce, and sell goods and services that satisfy the customer's requirements – and this takes us back to our initial definitions of quality. But CWQC recognizes that there are many dimensions to this, such as:

CASE: SIX SIGMA

One of the recent 'management revolutions' being widely applied is 'Six Sigma'. Although apparently a new concept this is, in fact, an approach built on well-founded total quality principles, applied within a disciplined company-wide framework. Pioneered by GE in the US, Six Sigma takes its name from a statistical term that measures how far a given process deviates from perfection. The central idea behind Six Sigma is that if you can measure how many 'defects' you have in a process, you can systematically figure out how to eliminate them and get as close to 'zero defects' as possible. To achieve Six Sigma quality, a process must produce no more than 3.4 defects per million opportunities. An 'opportunity' is defined as a chance for non-conformance, or not meeting the required specifications.

GE began moving towards a focus on quality in the late 1980s. A major employee involvement programme called 'Work-Out' established an approach which 'opened our culture to ideas from everyone, everywhere, decimated the bureaucracy and made boundaryless behaviour a reflexive, natural part of our culture, thereby creating the learning environment that led to Six Sigma. Now, Six Sigma, in turn, is embedding quality thinking – process thinking – across every level and in every operation of our Company around the globe'.

At its core, Six Sigma revolves around a few key concepts:

- *Critical to quality*: attributes most important to the customer.
- *Defect*: failing to deliver what the customer wants.
- *Process capability*: what your process can deliver.
- *Variation*: what the customer sees and feels.
- *Stable operations*: ensuring consistent, predictable processes to improve what the customer sees and feels.
- *Design for Six Sigma*: designing to meet customer needs and process capability.

GE website, www.ge.com/sixsigma/

Perhaps one of the key contributions to its success has been the highly disciplined approach taken to implementation and ongoing measurement. Taking a framework from the martial arts, Six Sigma involves a rigorous training and development process in which capability is measured in terms of grades, from beginner through to black belt.

A number of discussion forums have been set up where detailed information on tools, techniques, and case experiences can be found – see, for example, www.isixsigma.com or the American Society for Quality, www.sixsigmaforum.com

- Customer service;
- Quality of management;
- Quality of company;
- Quality of labour; and
- Quality of materials, techniques, equipment, etc.

Thus, quality becomes *total quality*, pervading everything both within the organization (all departments and functions) as well as the firm's supply network. The development from inspection under the mass-production era, which we saw earlier, to *total* quality management (TQM), reveals the increasing strategic importance of quality. The scope of each stage of development in quality is shown in Table 8.2.

TQM embraces the following points:

- *Top management commitment*: both in terms of 'setting an example' in their commitment to quality, particularly, in terms of their willingness to invest in training and other important features of TQM.

- *Continuous improvement*: Deming, Juran, Crosby and other quality 'gurus' may have slight differences in their actual approaches to quality. What becomes a common denominator, though, both for the 'quality gurus' and for firms involved in quality, is that quality is a 'moving target' and, therefore, a firm must have a strategic commitment to always improve performance (we discuss this in more depth in this chapter).

- *All aspects of the business*: the quality drive relates to all personnel within the firm and also outside: to all aspects of the supply chain.

Table 8.2 Stages of development in quality and related activities

Stage of development	Activities
Inspection	Salvaging, sorting, grading and corrective actions
Quality control	Quality manuals, product testing, basic quality planning, including statistics
Quality assurance	Third party approvals, advanced planning, systems audits, SPC
Company-wide QC	Quality measured in all areas of the firm and employee involvement in continuous improvement
TQM	Company-wide QC principles applied across the whole system and in pro-active fashion, emphasizing elements such as continuous improvement, involvement of suppliers and customers, and employee involvement and teamwork

Brown (1996)

- *Long-term commitment*: TQM is not a 'quick-fix' but, ideally, an everlasting approach to managing quality. As each stage developed – from inspection to TQM – the preceding stage was included as part of the next stage. TQM, therefore, *includes* company wide quality control, rather than ignoring it.

QUALITY FUNCTION DEPLOYMENT (QFD)

One of the problems in enabling TQM of this kind is in ensuring that the 'voice of the customer' (VOC) is heard throughout the organization. While those close to the customer – such as Marketing – may pick up clear messages, these need to be communicated to those elsewhere in the organization who are involved in design and delivery. This requirement has led to the development of several approaches which aim to integrate different perspectives around the challenge of delivering total quality. QFD represents one example which is widely used in practice.

While listening to customers has always been a good business practice, QFD formalizes the somewhat arbitrary practice of just listening to and then trying to meet some of the customers' needs by creating a ranking of the most important customer requirements. It also ensures these get heard within the firm by all the functions who need to.

It involves constructing a series of interconnecting matrixes – often called the 'house of quality' because the completed matrices resemble a house. An excellent description of how to build such a house is given in Hauser and Clausing (1988). Each segment of the matrix is important in assessing:

1. Customer requirements;
2. The actions over which a business has control; and
3. The relationship between these items.

A small team is formed to work on a new product opportunity or enhancement. A typical team can consist of members from the marketing, engineering, and production departments. In addition, customers are represented on the team. The team will explore a series of discussions with customers to determine needs and priorities. From this information, solutions will be identified to meet these needs.

Matrices convey information about the following issues:

- *Customer requirements* are identified and documented in the customer's own language.
- *Relative importance of each customer requirement*: not all customer requirements are of equal importance to the customer. Assigning a relative weight to each of them reflects the relative importance of the requirements.
- *Business parameters*: the business parameters that might be used to satisfy the customer requirements are listed across the ceiling of the house of quality. The parameters are written in the language of the business.

- *Relationship matrix*: relationships between the customer requirements and the business parameters are developed in the body of the matrix. The relationships are usually specified as 'strongly related', 'moderately related', 'weakly related', or 'not related', and the matrix is developed using a symbol for each.

- *Computed ranking of business parameters*: the results of fundamental computations integrating the information previously identified are presented in this area of the house of quality. The business parameters are ranked such that those with the highest score will have the greatest impact on the most important customer requirements and will address the greatest number of customer requirements.

- *Competitors' positions*: in a competitive market, realistic assessment of both the competition and your own capability is important.

- *Correlation between business parameters*: the purpose of this step is to define relationships between the technical requirements, especially those that may require a tradeoff in the final analysis.

A more complete description of QFD and some examples are on the website.

QUALITY CIRCLES (QCS)

A key factor in translating senior commitment to quality into 'front-line' operations comes from group-based activities which provide a focus for much of the powerful continuous improvement effort characteristic of TQM. Originally termed 'quality circles' (QCs), they represent a key link between the mechanics of quality tools and techniques and the behavioural components which make a living and developing quality system.

The origins of this approach lay in Japanese work in a number of different contexts – despite this variety there is considerable convergence around what makes for an effective QC and the core elements are simple. It involves a small group (between five and ten people) who gather regularly in the firm's time to examine problems and discuss solutions to quality problems. They are usually drawn from the same area of the business and participate voluntarily in the circle. The circle is usually chaired by a foreman or deputy and uses SQC methods and problem-solving aids as the basis of their problem solving activity. An important feature, often neglected in considering QCs, is that there is an element of personal development involved, through formal training but also through having the opportunity to exercise individual creativity in contributing to improvements in the area in which participants work.

The basic activity cycle of a QC goes from selection of a problem through analysis, solution generation, and presentation, to management and implementation by management. Once the problem is analysed and the root problem identified, ways of dealing with it can be identified. The valuable techniques here include brainstorming (in its many variants) and goal orientation. However, it is important that the structure and operation of the group supports suggestions from anyone (irrespective of levels in the organization, functional or craft skills background, etc.) and allows for high levels of creativity – even if some of the ideas appear wild and impractical at the time. The principles of brainstorming, especially regarding expert facilitation and enforcement of a 'no criticism' rule during idea-generation sessions, are important.

The circle does not have to confine itself to current problems – it can also involve itself in forecasting. Here the possible future problems resulting from each stage can be anticipated and explored, perhaps employing 'failure mode effects analysis' (described on the website). Finally, the group presents the solution to management who are expected to implement it. A key success factor in QC's survival and effectiveness is the willingness of management to be seen to be committed to the principles of TQM and to act on suggestions for improvement.

Small group activity of this kind is a powerful way of moving quality forward, but it is not the only vehicle for involvement. Many variants have emerged, ranging from large group/task force approaches to individual problem-solving approaches, and there is a need to match the selection of methods to the particular culture and operations of the firm. Another important aspect is the extent to which such groups are 'inline' as opposed to 'offline' (as the early QCs were); evidence suggests that strategic quality improvement only takes place when it becomes part of the day-to-day operations of the business.

CASE: QUALITY CIRCLES IN PRACTICE

Harry Boer and colleagues carried out extensive international survey research on the ways in which organizations configured and managed such activities and found wide variation (Boer *et al.*, 1999). In particular, there was a need to recognize prior and cultural influences in the selection of different approaches – for example, the long tradition of group working and devolution of responsibility in Scandinavian firms meant that such groupings could take a more 'inline' approach, carrying considerable responsibility for implementation as well as suggestion. This is in contrast to the Japanese model which is more of an 'offline' and indirect approach (Imai, 1987; Lillrank and Kano, 1990). Their survey involved over 1,000 organizations in a total of seven countries and provides a useful map of the takeup and experience with high involvement innovation. Some of the key findings were:

- Overall around 80 per cent of organizations were aware of the concept and its relevance, but its actual implementation, particularly in more developed forms (see Chapter 4) involved around half of the firms.
- The benefits directly attributable to these efforts included improvements in quality (16 per cent), productivity (15 per cent), delivery performance (16 per cent), lead-time reduction (15 per cent), and product-cost reduction (8 per cent).
- The bulk of efforts concentrated on shop-floor activities as opposed to other parts of the organization.

- Motives for making the journey down this road vary widely but cluster particularly around the themes of quality improvement, cost reduction, and productivity improvement.
- There was an average per capita rate of suggestions of 43 per year, of which around half were actually implemented.
- Almost all of these activities take place on an 'inline' basis – that is, as part of the normal working pattern rather than as a voluntary 'offline' activity. Most of this takes place in some form of group work, although around a third of the activity is on an individual basis.

CONTINUOUS IMPROVEMENT (CI)

The underlying principle of continuous improvement is clear and well expressed in a Japanese phrase – 'best is the enemy of better'. Rather than assuming that a single 'big hit' change will deal with the elimination of waste and the causes of defects, CI involves a long-term systematic attack on the problem. A metaphor for this is the gradual wearing down of stone through the continuous dripping of water on to it from above – it doesn't happen overnight but the cumulative effect is the same as a powerful drill. In the context of quality management CI has come to mean not only this process of continuous attack on problems but also the involvement of as many people a possible in the process. It could, perhaps, be more accurately called 'high involvement innovation' since it is about getting the majority of people in an organization to contribute at least at the level of regular incremental innovation.

There is, of course, no reason why people cannot participate in this process. After all, they are all equipped with sophisticated problem-finding and problem-solving capabilities – a point well expressed by one manager who commented that 'the beauty of it is that with every pair of hands you get a free brain!' Nor is there now a difficulty of lack of evidence – organized systems for engaging such commitment are commonplace now and have in fact been around in documented form since the nineteenth century (Schroeder and Robinson, 2004).

There are several cases on the website which show CI in action, and there are video interviews with operations managers in three different companies – a small instrumentation company, a large automotive components company, and a call centre – which explain some of the challenges in implementing this approach.

But making CI happen is easier said than done. Early attempts to emulate Japanese success in the West often led to disillusionment – firms set up problem-solving teams and invested heavily in training all their staff in relevant tools and techniques, only to find their programmes had run out of steam some six months later. These days it has become clear that introducing and embedding the new behaviour patterns which make up CI is something which takes time and effort, and there is no magic bullet which will achieve this overnight.

CASE STUDY

CASE 8.2: PRETTY IN PINK

Walking through the plant belonging to Ace Trucks (a major producer of forklift trucks) in Japan the first thing which strikes you is the colour scheme. In fact you would need to be blind not to notice it – amongst the usual rather dull greys and greens of machine tools and other equipment there are flashes of pink. Not just a quiet pastel tone, but a full-blooded, shocking pink which would do credit to even the most image-conscious flamingo. Closer inspection shows these flashes and splashes of pink are not random but associated with particular sections and parts of machines – and the eye-catching effect comes in part from the sheer number of pink-painted bits, distributed right across the factory floor and all over the different machines.

What is going on here is not a bizarre attempt to redecorate the factory or a failed piece of interior design. The effect of catching the eye is quite deliberate – the colour is there to draw attention to the machines and other equipment which have been modified. Every pink splash is the result of a *kaizen* project to improve some aspect of the equipment, much of it in support of the drive towards 'total productive maintenance' (TPM) in which every item of plant is available and ready for use 100 per cent of the time. This is a goal like 'zero defects' in total quality – certainly ambitious, possibly an impossibility in the statistical sense, but one which focuses the minds of everyone involved and leads to extensive and impressive problem-finding and solving. TPM programmes have accounted for year on year cost savings of 10 to 15 per cent in many Japanese firms and these savings are being ground out of a system which is already renowned for its lean characteristics.

Painting the improvements pink plays an important role in drawing attention to the underlying activity in this factory, in which systematic problem-finding and solving is part of 'the way we do things around here'. The visual cues remind everyone of the continuing search for new ideas and improvements, and often provide stimulus for other ideas or for places where the displayed pink idea can be transferred to. Closer inspection around the plant shows other forms of display – less visually striking but powerful nonetheless: charts and graphs of all shapes and sizes which focus attention on trends and problems as well as celebrating successful improvements; photographs and graphics which pose problems or offer suggested improvements in methods or working practices; and flipcharts and whiteboards covered with symbols and shapes of fish bones and other tools being used to drive the improvement process forward.

THE CI JOURNEY

Research on CI has been concerned with trying to understand the geography of this journey, and with trying to make up some basic maps which organizations can use to position themselves and guide their next steps. It also allows collecting and identifying useful resources which could be used to overcome the different kinds of obstacles which get in the way of moving down the CI road.

An example of such research is a model composed of five levels or stages of evolution of CI (Bessant, 2003). Each of these takes time to move through, and there is no guarantee that organizations will progress to the next level. Moving on means having to find ways of overcoming the particular obstacles associated with different stages.

At the first stage – level one – there is little, if any, CI activity going on, and when it does happen it is essentially random in nature and occasional in frequency. People do help to solve problems from time to time but there is no formal attempt to mobilize or build on this activity, and many organizations may actively restrict the opportunities for it to take place. The normal state is one in which CI is not looked for, not recognized, not supported – and often, not even noticed. Not surprisingly, there is little impact associated with this kind of change.

Level two involves setting up a formal process for finding and solving problems in a structured and systematic way – and training and encouraging people to use it. Supporting this will be some form of reward or recognition arrangement to motivate and encourage continued participation. Ideas will be managed through some form of system for processing and progressing as many as possible and handling those which cannot be implemented. Underpinning the whole setup will be an infrastructure of appropriate mechanisms (teams, task forces), facilitators, and some form of steering group to enable CI to take place and to monitor and adjust its operation over time. None of this can happen without top management support and commitment of resources to back that up.

Level two certainly contributes improvements but these may lack focus and are often concentrated at a local level, having minimal impact on the more strategic concerns of the organization. The danger is that, having established the habit of CI it may lack any clear target and begin to fall away. In order to maintain progress there is a need to move to the next level of CI – concerned with strategic focus and systematic improvement.

Level three involves coupling the CI habit to the strategic goals of the organization, such that all the various local-level improvement activities of teams and individuals can be aligned. In order to do this two key behaviours need to be added to the basic suite – those of strategy deployment, and those of monitoring and measuring. Strategy (or policy) deployment involves communicating the overall strategy of the organization and breaking it down into manageable objectives towards which CI activities in different areas can be targeted. Linked to this is the need to learn to monitor and measure the performance of a process and use this to drive the continuous improvement cycle.

Level three activity represents the point at which CI makes a significant impact on the bottom line – for example, in reducing throughput times, scrap rates, excess inventory, etc. It is particularly effective in conjunction with efforts to achieve external measurable standards (such as ISO 9000) where the disciplines of monitoring and measurement provide drivers for eliminating variation and tracking down root-cause problems. The majority of 'success stories' in CI can be found at this level – but it is not the end of the journey.

One of the limits of level three CI is that the direction of activity is still largely set by management and within prescribed limits. Activities may take place at different levels, from individuals through small groups to cross-functional teams, but they are still largely responsive and steered externally. The move to level four introduces a new element – that of 'empowerment' of individuals and groups to experiment and innovate on their own initiative.

Clearly this is not a step to be taken lightly, and there are many situations in which it would not be inappropriate – for example, where established procedures are safety critical. But the principle of 'internally directed' CI as opposed to externally steered activity is important, since it allows for the open-ended learning behaviour which we normally associate

Table 8.3 Stages in the evolution of CI capability

Stage of development	Typical characteristics
(1) 'Natural'/background CI	Problem-solving random No formal efforts or structure Occasional bursts punctuated by inactivity and non-participation Dominant mode of problem-solving is by specialists Short-term benefits No strategic impact
(2) Structured CI	Formal attempts to create and sustain CI Use of a formal problem-solving process Use of participation Training in basic CI tools Structured idea management system Recognition system Often parallel system to operations
(3) Goal-oriented CI	All of the above, plus formal deployment of strategic goals Monitoring and measurement of CI against these goals In-line system
(4) Proactive/empowered CI	All of the above, plus responsibility for mechanisms, timing, etc., devolved to problem-solving unit Internally-directed rather than externally-directed CI High levels of experimentation
(5) Full CI capability – the learning organization	CI as the dominant way of life Automatic capture and sharing of learning Everyone actively involved in innovation process Incremental and radical innovation

with professional research scientists and engineers. It requires a high degree of understanding of, and commitment to, the overall strategic objectives, together with training to a high level to enable effective experimentation.

Level five is a notional end-point for the journey – a condition where everyone is fully involved in experimenting and improving things, in sharing knowledge and in creating the complete learning organization. Table 8.3 illustrates the key elements in each stage.

LEARNING CONTINUOUS IMPROVEMENT

Moving along this journey is not a matter of time serving or even of resources – although without resources it is unlikely that things will get far, any more than a car without petrol can be expected to. But the essence of progress along the CI road is *learning* – acquiring, practising, and repeating behaviours until they become ingrained as 'the way we do things round here' – the culture of the organization.

The basic behaviour patterns or routines which have to be learned are outlined in Table 8.4.

Table 8.4 Behavioural patterns in continuous improvement

Ability	Constituent behaviours
'Getting the CI habit' – developing the ability to generate sustained involvement in CI	People make use of some formal problem-finding and -solving cycle People use appropriate simple tools and techniques to support CI People begin to use simple measurement to shape the improvement process People (as individuals and/or groups) initiate and carry through CI activities – they participate in the process Ideas are responded to in a clearly defined and timely fashion – either implemented or otherwise dealt with Managers support the CI process through allocation of time, money, space and other resources Managers recognize in formal (but not necessarily financial) ways the contribution of employees to CI Managers lead by example, becoming actively involved in design and implementation of CI Managers support experiment by not punishing mistakes but by encouraging learning from them
'Focusing CI' – generating and sustaining the ability to link CI activities to the strategic goals of the company	Individuals and groups use the organization's strategic goals and objectives to focus and prioritize improvements Everyone understands (i.e. is able to explain) what the company's or department's strategy, goals and objectives are Individuals and groups (e.g. departments, CI teams) assess their proposed changes (before embarking on initial investigation and before implementing a solution) against departmental or company objectives to ensure they are consistent with them Individuals and groups monitor/measure the results of their improvement activity and the impact it has on strategic or departmental objectives CI activities are an integral part of the individual or groups work, not a parallel activity
'Spreading the word' – generating the ability to move CI activity across organizational boundaries	People cooperate across internal divisions (e.g. cross-functional groups) in CI as well as working in their own areas People understand and share an holistic view (process understanding and ownership) People are oriented towards internal and external customers in their CI activity Specific CI projects with outside agencies – customers, suppliers, etc. – are taking place Relevant CI activities involve representatives from different organizational levels
'Continuous improvement of continuous improvement' – generating the ability to strategically manage the development of CI	The CI system is continually monitored and developed; a designated individual or group monitors the CI system and measures the incidence (i.e. frequency and location) of CI activity and the results of CI activity There is a cyclical planning process whereby the CI system is regularly reviewed and, if necessary, amended (single-loop learning) There is periodic review of the CI system in relation to the organization as a whole which may lead to a major regeneration (double-loop learning) Senior management make available sufficient resources (time, money, personnel) to support the ongoing development of the CI system Ongoing assessment ensures that the organization's structure and infrastructure and the CI system consistently support and reinforce each other The individual/group responsible for designing the CI system design it to fit within the current structure and infrastructure

continued . . .

Table 8.4 . . . *continued*

Ability	Constituent behaviours
	Individuals with responsibility for particular company processes/systems hold ongoing reviews to assess whether these processes/systems and the CI system remain compatible
	People with responsibility for the CI system ensure that when a major organizational change is planned its potential impact on the CI system is assessed and adjustments are made as necessary
'Walking the talk' – generating the ability to articulate and demonstrate CI values	The 'management style' reflects commitment to CI values
	When something goes wrong the natural reaction of people at all levels is to look for reasons why etc. rather than to blame individual(s)
	People at all levels demonstrate a shared belief in the value of small steps and that everyone can contribute, by themselves being actively involved in making and recognizing incremental improvements
'The learning organization' – generating the ability to learn through CI activity	Everyone learns from their experiences, both positive and negative
	Individuals seek out opportunities for learning/personal development (e.g. actively experiment, set their own learning objectives)
	Individuals and groups at all levels share (make available) their learning from all work experiences
	The organization articulates and consolidates (captures and shares) the learning of individuals and groups
	Managers accept and, where necessary, act on all the learning that takes place
	People and teams ensure that their learning is captured by making use of the mechanisms provided for doing so
	Designated individual(s) use organizational mechanisms to deploy the learning that is captured across the organization

Learning these behaviours begins with moving to a new level and then involves extensive broadening out and modifying within the level. There are plenty of problems to solve and bugs to iron out – but eventually there comes a point where a move to the next level is required. At this point the organization needs to take a step back and reconfigure its approach to CI – and doing this involves learning of a different kind.

In both cases learning is not only about practising behaviours – it is also about finding ways of overcoming blockages at particular points. But learning isn't easy, and many organizations don't learn at all. Others get blocked at particular points and never move on from there, which goes a long way to explain why so many CI programmes, despite early enthusiasm and commitment, eventually peter out.

MAINTAINING TOTAL QUALITY: THE LONG HAUL

CASE: TAKING THEIR EYE OFF THE BALL

On 20 April 2010, while drilling in the Gulf of Mexico, the BP-owned rig 'Deepwater Horizon' was rocked by an explosion which killed 11 crewmen in a fireball that could be seen 60 km away. The subsequent fire could not be extinguished and the well eventually sank, continuing to leak oil and contributing to one of the world's worst environmental disasters. Legal actions continue but estimates indicate that the cost to BP has so far been around $41 billion, (which is 2.5 times their entire profit for 2009). These provisions do not take account of the fines likely to be levied which have been estimated at up to $2,300 for every barrel of oil spilt – which may total close to $20 billion.

It is clear from the detailed research on the causes that BP and its operators were negligent in allowing pressures for output to override safety procedures which had been put in place. The National Commission on the BP Deepwater Horizon Oil Spill and Offshore Drilling found that 'The companies involved in the Gulf of Mexico oil spill made decisions to cut costs and save time that contributed to the disaster.'

This resonates with the Toyota story mentioned at the start of this chapter – again, a major company suffered huge losses and damage to its reputation through what was admitted to be a failure, not in its quality systems themselves, but in adhering to them. As Toyota President Akio Toyoda acknowledged in a public apology, a misguided strategic focus at the company warped the 'order of Toyota's traditional priorities' so that the stress on product safety and quality first, and sales volume and cost second, became inverted as Toyota began rapidly expanding a decade ago.

Sadly, these are not isolated events – there is an inherent pressure in operations management to skip or discount the attention to detail which effective quality management needs. The principles are simple to grasp – the real management challenge is to make sure they stay high on everyone's agenda.

The ideas behind total quality management are deceptively simple – the real challenge is in ensuring they become part of the underlying culture of the organization. Instilling such behaviour patterns is not easy and requires regular reinforcement through training, rehearsal, and leadership. There is a risk, in even well-developed quality systems (see the above box), of an initially good system drifting out of control. Amongst the rocks on which the idea of total quality management can run aground are:

- Over reliance on procedures so that people lose the sense of their meaning and quality management becomes bureaucratic form-filling.

- Managing quality within the process well, but failing to recognize that the process itself needs review and possible change (the basis of 'business process reengineering') (Hammer and Champy, 1993).

- Too much process change so there is no chance for a stable pattern to develop.

- Process changes causing dislocation, shifts in skills and working patterns, and even redundancies – all mean that people feel undervalued or insecure and lose their commitment to quality.

- Striking the wrong balance between innovation and maintaining stability – too much innovation and things go out of control, too little and there is a risk of stagnation.

LOOKING FORWARD

From the above discussion it is clear that even the most advanced firms still have a long way to go on their journey towards TQM. For this reason much of the future direction is likely to involve work towards integrating TQM into the daily life of the firm rather than seeing it as a special initiative or a fashion. There are also some specific areas in which we can see new challenges emerging for thinking about quality and how it can be built into strategic operations work.

One area is clearly in the kind of environment that is non-repetitive in nature. Much of the theory of quality comes from work with processes which are by their nature reproduced many times – for example, the operations in a mass-production factory. There is a sizable and growing part of economic activity which is not dealing with this kind of work but rather with one-off transactions or short-run work. Examples include most construction work, engineering prototypes, custom design, and delivery of services, etc. Here the challenge is one of capturing learning rapidly and transferring it to new environments through generic procedures and principles. Many professionals work on this kind of approach, but there has been little work on routinizing it such that it can underpin quality improvement in project-type businesses.

A second area for further development lies in the field of non-production environments. Most of the attention in TQM has been in the direct manufacturing area or in services at the point of delivery – for example, in customer care programmes. But many indirect activities support these – for example, R&D, finance, order processing, etc. – and the challenge is to take TQM principles into these environments. This will mean adapting tools, mechanisms, and structures and looking for ways to motivate and involve different groups. For example, the R&D challenge is partly one of engaging the interest and commitment of professionals who often believe that they already practice TQM and have no need to join in more formal approaches. The future is also likely to see much more emphasis on building quality in from the design of products and services.

Two trends have been mentioned in this chapter and are likely to play an increasingly important role shaping the quality agenda in the future. Safety very often emerges as an issue only when something has gone wrong, and the costs when that happens are often measured not in simple financial terms but in human and social pain. But ensuring safe operations is not an accident – it comes from taking a TQM approach and applying it consistently and sustainably. Significantly, there is considerable scope for cross-sector learning about where and how safety issues are experienced and managed so that we have a growing convergence around 'good practice'.

In a similar fashion, the question of 'sustainability' is increasingly on the radar screens of organizations in the public and private sector, and this translates to minimizing the negative aspects of creating and delivering the products and services which we are increasingly demanding. Whether it is about reducing carbon footprints, minimizing waste, reducing resource demands or controlling pollution, the challenge falls into the wide view of quality which we have been considering in this chapter. In the same way that quality has moved to become 'everybody's problem', so a growing employee involvement in delivering sustainability across the organization is likely to be increasingly important.

Finally, a major area for development lies in the concept of inter-organizational TQM. There is growing recognition of the need to think not just of operations within a business but in terms of the overall value stream. Improving performance of a system such as this can employ the principles of TQM but new tools and techniques need to be developed to help deal with some of the issues involved in developing the new relationships needed to underpin such work.

CASE 8.3: MARVELLOUS MOTORS

This Japanese firm is a major conglomerate with key interests in aerospace and motor vehicles: 80 per cent of sales now come from the automotive business and this is the prime source of growth for the company. However, the high value of the Yen and increasing global competition (especially from China) has meant that the company has had to place considerable attention on preserving a quality-led competitive position. They have responded to this crisis with the systematic deployment of continuous targeted improvements, with three core themes:

- Development of new, attractive products;
- Maintaining productivity levels; and
- Reconstruction of the company from within.

The long-term programme includes simultaneous attacks on quality improvement, cost reduction, employee motivation, and increased education and training. The specific 'stretch' targets are:

- Zero defects;
- Zero accidents;
- Zero breakdowns; and
- 20 per cent increase in labour productivity.

CASE STUDY

The pillars on which these are to be achieved are:

- *Jishu hozen* – voluntary operator inspection and maintenance;
- *Kaizen teian* – individual improvement activities;
- Education and training;
- Planned maintenance;
- Development management;
- Quality maintenance activities, including ISO 9000; and
- Tool/mould/die maintenance management aimed at zero defects and breakdowns.

They began by setting up separate taskforces to deal with each area, and developed a formal structure aimed at promoting TQM. In particular they emphasized 'total productive maintenance' (TPM) which targeted quality improvements around machine reliability and availability.

As with other Japanese companies, the three-year mid-term plan is the key mechanism for focusing and refocusing attention on continuous improvement. In this case the recent plans have involved three main themes over the past decade:

- TQM aimed at increasing productivity and quality;
- TPS (Toyota Production System) aimed at waste reduction; and
- TPM aimed at obtaining high machine efficiency and availability, and at increasing production rates through more reliable plant.

Visualization of this is important. The dominant image is one of 'equipment and operator upgrading'. There are story and display boards throughout the factory, including a master chart which is a giant Gantt chart tracking progress to date and plans for the future. Each work group meets daily and this take place around their own storyboard.

The implementation of TPM includes a number of components:

- Daily review and improvement cycle – i.e. a high frequency of small innovations;
- Small and regular inputs of training – a 'one point lesson system';
- Motivation events;
- Individual *kaizen teian* (small and simple to implement) activities;
- Small group *kaizen* (successors to quality circles);
- 5-S activities to ensure workplace cleanliness and order;
- Preventive maintenance analysis;
- Design for maintenance;
- Zero orientation – no tolerance for waste, defects, stoppages, etc. as the target;
- Step-by-step approach; and
- Voluntary participation and high commitment.

The implementation of TPM involves a five-year programme spanning two mid-term planning periods. Part one was designed to introduce the basic TPM mechanisms, and activities included awareness training and practice to embed the behavioural routines. Part two – the current phase – involves aiming for the Japanese Production Management Association's Special Award for TPM. Significantly the company is using very clear behaviour modelling approaches: articulating the desired behaviours and systematically reinforcing them to the point where they become routine.

Policy deployment is the link between these broad objectives and the specific improvement activities at shop-floor level. For each of the eight pillars of TPM there are specific targets which can be decomposed into improvement projects. For example, 'maintain your machine by yourself', 'increase efficiency of machine to the limit' or 'reduce start-up times'. These vague signposts are quantified and analysed in terms of how they can be achieved and the problems which would have to be solved to make that happen – using simple tools such as 5-whys and fishbone charts. Diagnosis is top down in terms of setting the actual numerical targets or the extent to which operators can maintain their own machines: a team of specialist engineers carries this out.

As with other plants, there is a step-by-step process for increasing capability in TPM, and this is linked to training inputs. For example:

Step 1 = clean up your machine.

Step 2 = learn to detect different sensitive points.

Step 3 = develop a procedure for lubrication and cleaning work.

Step 4 = total inspection and check of different key points.

Step 5 = autonomous inspection.

Step 6 = adjustment and ordering.

Step 7 = execution of this in self-management (unsupervised) mode.

The company places strong emphasis on mechanisms for embedding these behaviours in the culture so that they become the way things are done and taught to others. An important aspect of phase two – the current mid-term plan – is to find mechanisms for doing this. These include extensive use of training and development – for example, each employee receives ten hours initial training in TPM and then three hours per month additional training on the job. They are also allocated 30 minutes per day to carry out their individual maintenance and to learn and improve this.

In addition to this operator development and individual improvement there are also CI projects in particular areas on which groups work in team mode – for example, projects on sputterless welding or cleaning engine coolant, which involve consistently attacking problem areas over a period of weeks or months. Activities of this kind have led to, for example, major set-up-time reductions – the Komatsu 1,000 tonne presses take less than ten minutes to change and are changed four to five times per shift. Projects of this kind tend to take around three months.

There are around 30 groups working – ten to 15 in trim, 12 in body and assembly and six to eight in the press shop. Group leaders spend half their time with the groups, facilitating, training etc., and the remainder acting as a floating resource to cover sickness, holidays, etc.

The evolution of *kaizen* has been through early team activities going back 20 or more years. Individual *kaizen teian* ideas did not come through at first, so a campaign was launched with the theme of 'what makes your job easier?' – prior to that the focus was outside the individual operator's own job area. The evolution of suggestions can be seen in data collected by the Japanese Human Relations

Management Association, which suggests that on the site there is now 100 per cent participation of the 'eligible employees' (around 85 per cent of the total workforce). Of their suggestions around 88 per cent are implemented giving a saving of around 3.2 billion Yen.

At present they are receiving around 20 suggestions per employee per month. One of the difficulties raised by the generation of some 40,000 suggestions per month is how to process them; this is primarily the responsibility of the group leader. Many of the ideas are minor changes to standard operating procedures and foremen/team leaders are authorized to make these. Ideas are judged against four levels as below.

The importance of recognizing and rewarding the simple, low-level ideas was expressed by one manager: 'if we don't encourage fertile soil at the bottom, we'll never get the high-grade ideas later'. Motivation is also secured by strong top-level commitment. When the TPM programme was launched the first stage built on 5-S principles and involved cleaning up machinery and the plant. The plant director held a site briefing explaining his concerns and the ideas behind TPM and then led the setting up of a 'section chief's model line' which was a line cleaned up and improved by all the senior managers as a demonstration. Symbolically the plant director was the first to pick up a broom and begin the process. The line was followed by an 'assistant chief's model line', again to reinforce the commitment top down.

Table 8.5 Reward framework

Level	Reward	Volume
1. High level, considerable potential benefits and judged by senior management team	150,000Y upwards	Only 4–5 per year
2. Again reviewed by senior team	Medium – 10,000Y plus	20 per year
3. Basic, handled by team leader	300Y	
4. Minor – recognized to encourage continuous improvement activity	50Y	

SUMMARY

- Quality has moved from being an 'optional extra' – something you could have if you were prepared to pay for it – to an essential feature of the products and services which we consume. International competitiveness depends not only on price factors but also on non-price factors and quality is the first and most essential of these.

- Historically, quality was a part of what a craftsman would build into what he or she was making. Over time and through processes of industrialization a separation grew up, in which specialists concerned with design and control of quality took away direct responsibility from the individual. The key development over the past 40 years has been the gradual reintegration of the quality responsibility. These days quality is seen as being 'everyone's problem' not the province of specialists.

- A key challenge today for the strategic operations manager is to ensure that the design of such products and services – and the management of the operations which go into their creation and delivery – ensures quality. The framework for doing this involves a combination of strategy, tools, procedures, structures, and employee involvement and is conveniently grouped under the heading of 'total quality management'.

- There is a wide range of tools to support quality maintenance and improvement including basic and more advanced tools, as well as frameworks like quality function deployment (designed to bring customer input to the process) and systematic approaches such as Six Sigma.

- Central to TQM is employee engagement, and developing continuous improvement capability requires establishing and reinforcing a number of key behaviours in the organization, including those linked to finding and solving problems in a systematic fashion. This also requires extensive investment in training and in creating supporting structures for idea management, reward and recognition, and strategic alignment.

- In many ways the biggest challenge in TQM is not in the components but in their implementation. Evidence shows that although companies recognize the quality imperative they are not always able to respond – or if they do they have difficulties in sustaining such performance for the long haul.

KEY QUESTIONS

1. 'Quality is free' proclaimed the title of Philip Crosby's book in the 1970s. In what ways can investments in developing quality management in the business pay for themselves and make a difference to the overall bottom line of the company?

2. 'Total' quality management involves an integrated approach combining tools, strategy, structure, and involvement. What are the key components in a successful programme and how can strategic operations managers establish and sustain TQM in organizations?

3. What do you think are the main barriers to effective implementation of TQM – and how might they be overcome?

4. Quality management used to be a specialist function carried out by a specialist manager. Why has it become a mainstream task and a key part of the strategic operations manager's job? How can strategic operations managers contribute to creating businesses capable of competing on quality?

5. How might a well-designed TQM programme fail in the long-term – and what steps might you take, as an operations manager, to ensure that it stays alive and effective?

FURTHER READING

Asif, M. *et al.* (2009) 'Why quality management programs fail: A strategic and operations management perspective', *International Journal of Quality and Reliability Management*, 26(8), 778–94.

Avery, C. and Zabel, D. (1997) *The Quality Management Sourcebook*, London: Questia.

Bessant, J. (2003) *High Involvement Innovation*, Chichester: John Wiley and Sons.

Goetsch, D. and Davis, S. (2009) *Quality Management for Organizational Excellence: Introduction to Total Quality*, London: Pearson.

Imai, M. (1997) *Gemba Kaizen*, New York: McGraw Hill.

Schroeder, A. and Robinson, D. (2004) *Ideas Are Free: How the Idea Revolution Is Liberating People and Transforming Organizations*, New York: Berrett Koehler.

Vanichchinchai, A. and Igel, B. (2009) 'Total quality management and supply chain management: Similarities and differences', *The TQM Journal*, 21(3), 249–60.

REFERENCES

Abernathy, W. (1977) *The Productivity Dilemma: Roadblock to Innovation in the Automobile Industry*, Baltimore: Johns Hopkins University Press.

Asif, M. *et al.* (2009) 'Why quality management programs fail: A strategic and operations management perspective', *International Journal of Quality and Reliability Management*, 26(8), 778–94.

Avery, C. and Zabel, D. (1997) *The Quality Management Sourcebook*, London: Questia.

Bentley, J. (1999) *Fit for the Future*, Egham: Chartered Institute of Purchasing and Supply.

Bessant, J. (2003) *High Involvement Innovation*, Chichester: John Wiley and Sons.

Bessant, J., Caffyn, S. and Gallagher, M. (2001) 'An evolutionary model of continuous improvement behaviour', *Technovation*, 21(3), 67–77.

Boer, H., Berger, A., Chapman, R. and Gertsen, F. (1999) *CI Changes: From Suggestion Box to the Learning Organisation*, Aldershot: Ashgate.

Brown, S. (1996) *Strategic Manufacturing for Competitive Advantage*, Hemel Hempstead: Prentice Hall.

Brown, S. (2000) *Manufacturing the Future: Strategic Resonance for Enlightened Manufacturing*, London: Financial Times/Pearson Books.

Business Week (1994) 'Electric cars, will they work and who will buy them?' 30 May 1994.

Camp, R. (1989) *Benchmarking: The Search for Industry Best Practices that Lead to Superior Performance*, Milwaukee, WI: Quality Press.

Cole, R. (2010) 'No big quality problems at Toyota?', *Harvard Business Review*, 9 March 2010, http://blogs.hbr.org/

Crosby, P. (1977) *Quality is Free*, New York: McGraw-Hill.

Feigenbaum, A. (1956) 'Total quality control', *Harvard Business Review*, November, 34(6), 56.

Feigenbaum, J. (1983) *Total Quality Control*, 3rd edition, New York: McGraw-Hill.

Garvin, D. (1988) *Managing Quality*, New York: Free Press.

Goetsch, D. and Davis, S. (2009) *Quality Management for Organizational Excellence: Introduction to Total Quality*, London: Pearson.

Hammer, M. and Champy, J. (1993) *Re-engineering the Corporation*, New York: Harper Business.

Hauser, J. and Clausing, D. (1988) 'The house of quality', *Harvard Business Review* (May/June), 63–73.

Hill, T. (1993) *Manufacturing Strategy*, 2nd edition, London: Macmillan.

Imai, K. (1987) *Kaizen*, New York: Random House.

Imai, M. (1997) *Gemba Kaizen*, New York: McGraw Hill.

Ishikawa, K. (1985) *What is Total Quality Control?* Englewood Cliffs, NJ: Prentice-Hall.

Juran, J. (1951) *Quality Control Handbook*, New York: McGraw-Hill.

Juran, J. (1985) *Juran on Leadership for Quality*, New York: Free Press.

Juran, J. and Gryna, F. (1980) *Quality Planning and Analysis*, New York: McGraw Hill.

Kano, N., Saraku, N., Takahashi, F. and Tsuji, S. (1996) 'Attractive quality and "must-be" quality', in J. Hromi (ed.) *The Best on Quality* (pp. 165–186), Milwaukee: American Society for Quality Control.

Kanter, R. (1996) *World Class*, New York: Simon and Schuster.

Lillrank, P. and Kano, N. (1990) *Continuous Improvement: Quality Control Circles in Japanese Industry*, Ann Arbor: University of Michigan Press.

Oakland, J. (2003) *Total Quality Management*, 3rd edition, London: Elsevier.

Parasuraman, A., Zeithaml, V. and Berry, L. (1985) 'Measuring and monitoring service quality', *Journal of Marketing*, 49, 41–50.

Peters, T. (1997) *The Circle of Innovation*, London: Coronet.

Pirsig, R. (1974) *Zen and the Art of Motorcycle Maintenance*, New York: Bantam.

Radford, G. (1922) *The Control of Quality in Manufacturing*, New York: Ronald Press.

Schroeder, A. and Robinson, D. (2004) *Ideas Are Free: How the Idea Revolution Is Liberating People and Transforming Organizations*, New York: Berrett Koehler.

Shewhart, W. (1931) *The Economic Control of Manufactured Products*, New York: Van Nostrand Rheinhold.

Shiba, S., Graham, A. and Walden, D. (1993) *A New American TQ: Four Practical Revolutions in Management*, Portland, OR: Productivity Press.

Taylor, F. (1947) *The Principles of Scientific Management*, New York: Harper and Row (original published in 1911).

Tranfield, D., Smith, S., Whittle, S. and Foster, M. (1994) 'Strategies for managing the TQ agenda', *International Journal of Operations and Production Management*, 14(1), 75–88.

Vanichchinchai, A. and Igel, B. (2009) 'Total quality management and supply chain management: Similarities and differences', *The TQM Journal*, 21(3), 249–60.

Womack, J., Jones, D. and Roos, D. (1991) *The Machine that Changed the World*, New York: Rawson Associates.

CHAPTER 9

MANAGING INVENTORY, MRP, ERP, AND JIT

LEARNING OBJECTIVES

The purpose of this chapter is for you to:

*   Understand the strategic significance of managing inventory.

*   Gain insights into why tactical 'solutions' do not work.

*   Appreciate how MRP (materials requirement planning), MRPII (manufacturing resource planning), ERP (enterprise resource planning) and JIT (just-in-time) can be successful only if they are expertly managed both *internally* with outstanding operations in place as well as *externally* within networks (discussed in depth in Chapter 3).

INTRODUCTION

In this chapter we shall examine a range of areas linked to the topic of inventory management. Managing inventory successfully is a necessary ingredient to world-class practice in operations including lean processes (Holweg, 2007). From the outset it should be noted that:

> Managing inventory can be a huge task that includes areas of logistics, purchasing, and supply, involving the sourcing, developing, and nurturing of buyer–supplier relationships. Inventory management is a major strategic task for organizations.

The sheer costs of logistics alone can be enormous. As *Industry Week* noted:

> If you're thinking that it's gotten a lot more costly lately to transport and warehouse your manufactured products, you're exactly right. Total costs for business logistics in the

United States were up 10.4% in 2010, reaching $1.2 trillion. That total accounts for 8.3% of the U.S. gross domestic product.

Industry Week (2010) 'Recovery not reaching supply chain yet', 20 July 2011

Some firms have reverted from outsourcing to insourcing, and one of the main drivers for this has to do with inventory management.

> **Moving production overseas is an old story. Moving it back isn't, but that's what Stanley Furniture, an 85-year-old maker of home furnishings, is doing. The Virginia company will bring all of its remaining kid's line that is produced overseas back to the U.S.**
>
> **Although the company says its 2008 recall of 300 cribs made in Slovenia isn't the reason it's changing course (the product posed a hazard for babies), president Glenn Prillaman says the number of recalls throughout the industry has made consumers wary. And more control over the company's inventory, he adds, 'puts us in a better position.'**
>
> **Stanley may be part of a trend, as some companies find that the factors that made offshore production so attractive – cheap goods and labor – might no longer compensate for things like transportation costs, quality control, and intellectual property issues. GE CEO Jeff Immelt, who recently called for a reinvestment in U.S. manufacturing jobs, announced plans to move parts of its aviation components group back to the U.S., a strategy he calls 'insourcing.'**
>
> *Fortune International* **(2009) 'Back in the U.S.A. (Asia)', 28 September 2009, 160(5), p. 30**

We have stated throughout the text that it is important to think of manufacturing *and* services as a *total offering* to customers simply because wonderful services without excellent products will count for nothing; conversely, excellent products without good service is also not acceptable for customers (Ellram *et al.*, 2007). When problems occur in the interface between the two, the 'moment of truth' that we discussed in Chapter 1 becomes a major disappointment as shown in Case 9.1.

Managing inventory successfully is not about technical solutions; rather, a key factor to bear in mind with inventory management is that much of it is service-related – it has to do with managing relationships throughout the supply network (which we explored in Chapter 3) and this is fully linked to service operations.

THE PROBLEM: THE TACTICAL 'SOLUTION' TO MANAGING INVENTORY

Many Western firms have tended to view inventory management as a 'tactical' activity – this same 'tactical' attitude has also been applied to operations management in general.

CASE 9.1: TOYS 'R' US.COM

'eToys SUCKS!!!' one customer shouts on a thread dubbed 'Online Shopping Hell.' Another rants, 'I doubt I will ever shop again online for Christmas. It is not worth the wait, lies, ill-informed customer service reps, and the hassle and stress.'

No brand did more to infuriate shoppers than toysrus.com. It kicked off the season with a big ad campaign that lured thousands to the site – traffic jumped more than 300 per cent. But midway through the holidays, the company announced it could not guarantee delivery by Christmas day. . . . When Shaun Lawson learned his orders wouldn't arrive on time, he e-mailed the company to cancel. He received a form e-mail from toysrus.com telling him orders could only be canceled within 30 minutes of the time they were placed. After several more attempts and a slew of form e-mail responses, an apoplectic Lawson fired off an e-mail he was sure the company couldn't ignore: 'Your form letter is grossly insulting. Cancel the —ing order (yes, that means do not ship) and never bother me again.' He posted his rant on a Website so 'others have an opportunity to learn from my mistake.' Toys 'R' Us' response came a few days later: 'Dear Shaun Lawson: Thank you for contacting toysrus.com. Our records indicate that your order was shipped . . . and is in route to you!'

Fortune (2000a) 'The Nightmare Before Christmas', 24 January 2000

Consequently, purchasing and supply management has been performed, in the main (until recently), at lower levels of the organization and has been relegated to a reactive function – again, much like operations itself. In the West this has meant that purchasing has been seen as a 'buying function' responding to production and service level requirements – after they have been, in turn, determined by marketing. This mentality has changed to some degree as *Industry Week* pointed out in their article 'Now it's a job for the CEO'.

CASE: 'NOW IT'S A JOB FOR THE CEO'

There was a time when top-ranking executives in manufacturing tended to distance themselves from such operational details as supply-chain management or information sharing with upstream and downstream partners in the 'value chain' – that continuum of activities that ultimately delivers something of value to an end customer. In the past, company presidents and CEOs were more inclined to fret about internal politics and bottom-line earnings than plunge into the various intercompany relationships that can either elevate or undermine the ultimate success of a business.

But, like last month's stock price, that's history.

Today, in many firms, executives at the highest corporate levels are driving the development of value-chain strategies to enhance interactions with business partners. They've seen, for example, what innovative business models have done for leading companies like Dell Computer Corp. and Cisco Systems Inc., shrinking inventory costs and accelerating the cash-to-cash cycle.

In adopting elements of the so-called virtual corporation – often through outsourcing – they are trying to leverage the efficiencies of their value-chain partners. And they are beginning to understand that all of this requires a higher level of collaboration and information sharing if they expect to improve not only the performance of their own companies but also the overall performance of the value chains in which they participate. To varying degrees that's true whether their companies are 'chain starters' that supply raw materials and components, midchain suppliers, finished-product manufacturers, distributors, or direct marketers.

Executives in each of those segments – including 1,309 who lead finished-product firms – were among the more than 2,000 respondents to an INDUSTRY WEEK survey designed to assess the impact of effective value-chain strategies and identify major obstacles to optimizing the performance of a value chain.

Among the major findings of the extensive research project, conducted in association with Ernst & Young, the New York-based management consulting firm, were these:

- Nearly one-third of the survey participants (31.2%) said that, in their companies, the CEO or president is 'most responsible' for value-chain-improvement initiatives. Another 33.6% indicated that responsibility rested at the vice-president level.

- More than half of the executives said that their firms have adopted – or are in the process of developing – formal value-chain strategies. Of the 36.7% who now have formal strategies in place, a heavy majority believe their efforts have been at least 'somewhat effective' – although only 26.1% think the strategies have been 'highly effective.'

- Only 13.3% of the respondents rate the overall performance of the primary value chain that they participate in as 'very good' or 'excellent' – indicating that there is considerable room for improvement.

- Companies that have adopted formal strategies – and especially those with highly effective strategies – tend to be more successful in growing top-line revenues.

- Intercompany pressures on pricing issues are the most common stumbling block to value-chain optimization. Fully 44.2% of the executives cited pricing issues as a 'major' barrier, while 39.7% blamed poor communication.

A strategic imperative

Considering the level of executive involvement, value-chain management has clearly become 'a strategic imperative' in most companies, observes Robert Neubert, Ernst & Young's national director of automotive and industrial products services. 'It is not something that is being left to the purchasing department. It has reached the highest levels in the corporation,' he says. 'People see it as a key element of strategy.'

In smaller companies – those with revenues of less than $100 million – the president or CEO is most likely to bear the primary responsibility for value-chain improvement, the IW survey found, while large companies more frequently assign vice presidents the leading role.

Industry Week (2000) 'Now It's A Job For the CEO', 20 March 2000, p. 22

Taking a very pragmatic viewpoint, *Industry Week* offer some ways to reduce inventory:

12 WAYS TO REDUCE INVENTORIES

Inventory takes on a lot of different identities within a manufacturing company, depending on who's doing the looking. An accountant sees inventory as an asset, a controller sees it as a liability, a production supervisor considers it a safety net, while a materials manager finds it a tightrope. One common aspect to inventory, though, is that everybody agrees that holding it can be costly. The following are a dozen ways to reduce inventory, suggested by supply chain consulting firm Cornerstone Solutions:

1. Reduce demand variability
2. Improve forecast accuracy
3. Re-examine service levels
4. Address capacity issues
5. Reduce order sizes
6. Reduce manufacturing lot sizes
7. Reduce supplier lead times
8. Reduce manufacturing lead times
9. Improve supply reliability
10 Reconfigure the supply chain
11. Reduce the number of items
12. Eliminate questionable practices

Industry Week (2008a) '12 ways to reduce inventories', 12 September 2008, 257(9), p. 60

Technology can help but isn't enough, although we shall discuss some of the software applications used in inventory later in this chapter. A growing area of interest in inventory technology is *radio frequency identification* (RFID).

> Although radio frequency identification (RFID) has been around for decades, it mostly sat on the technological bench until retail giant Wal-Mart Stores Inc. began to mandate that its key suppliers would adopt and implement these chips on every pallet shipped to Wal-Mart's Dallas, Texas-based distribution centers (DCs), with the eventual goal of having RFID deployed in every Wal-Mart DC and retail store. . . . Reducing out-of stocks and keeping the shelves replenished is the be-all and end-all of retail. . . . Preliminary analysis at the university's RFID Research Center indicates that an automated, RFID-enabled inventory system in

test stores improved accuracy by 13%. . . . 'Inventory accuracy, which determines important processes such as ordering and replenishment, is often poor, with inaccuracy rates sometimes as high as 65%,' points out Bill Hardgrave, director of the RFID Research Center. In contrast, the 13% improvement at the test stores indicates that RFID 'can significantly reduce unnecessary inventory.' The value of such reductions for major retailers and their suppliers can be measured, he claims, 'in millions of dollars.'

Industry Week (2008b) 'Wal-Mart lays down the law on RFID', (cover story) 4 May 2008, 257(5), pp. 72–4

However, the degree to which a strategic view is really embraced by firms using RFID is still unclear. Inventory management has been a strategic problem and challenge for firms over decades, as we shall now see.

LOOKING BACK

The perceived management wisdom between the 1950s and 1980s was that a firm should try to vertically integrate as much as possible. So, looking at Figure 9.1, the former desired aspiration was that, wherever possible, a firm would own all of the 'supply chain', or network.

We use the term 'chain' here because it is commonly used but, as we saw in Chapter 3, firms typically operate within networks, which are often complex, rather than within linear 'chains'.

The reasons for the strategy of vertical integrations were complex but included the following factors:

- The need for control (including costs, assurance of delivery, and perceptions of quality) within the supply chain;
- The possibility of diversification of business activities within the firm's business portfolio; and
- There was a commonly held belief that the 'bigger we are the better we are' and that owning activities – including entire firms – within the supply chain could then be shown on the balance sheet as an asset.

The rationale behind this strategy was captured in the *Harvard Business Review*:

Ever since the birth of the modern industrial corporation in the 1920s, manufacturing strategy has been built on three foundations: the vertical integration of supply and production activities to control the cost and maintain the predictability of raw materials and other inputs; disciplined research to create superior products; and a dominant market position to provide economies of scale. With these in place, manufacturers could be assured of a durable cost advantage, steady revenue growth, and substantial scale barriers to competition. The usual reward was double-digit margins and returns on capital.

(Wise and Baumgartner, 1999, p. 133)

What became clear over time, however, was that this strategy had major flaws. This was brought to light in the 1980s when Western firms began to understand how Japanese companies managed buyer–supplier relationships. As Brown (1996, p. 224) commented:

Nowhere has the contrast between Western and Japanese manufacturing been more evident than in materials – or inventory – management. This area has also been one of the great areas of organizational learning by the West in terms of how it has tried to emulate some of the Japanese practices which have underpinned Japan's success in key industries.

However, buyer–supplier relationships still pose problems for many firms that are reluctant to commit to transparency in the relationship (New, 2010).

The major shift in thinking since the 1980s has been to move away from the idea of inventory as an asset (which can be shown on a balance sheet as part of the firm's 'worth')

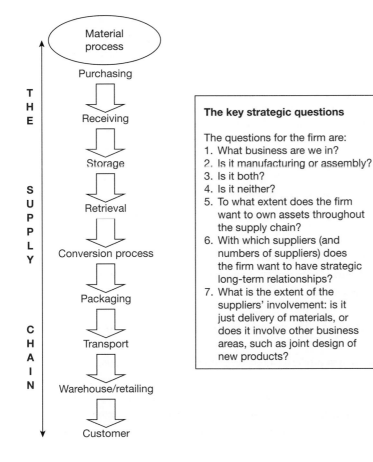

Figure 9.1
Questions within the 'supply chain'
Brown (2000)

to the idea that inventory can instead become a huge liability for the firm. If inventory is managed poorly this will weaken competitive capabilities in terms of delays, increased costs, reduced output, and poor responsiveness to market requirements.

THE POOR SOLUTION: THE ECONOMIC ORDER QUANTITY (EOQ) 'FIX'

As can be seen from the Toys 'R' Us case earlier, having stock-outs, or zero-inventory, is not acceptable for customers. However, there is a tension here because holding too much inventory can also cause major problems for firms. All operations have to hold some level of inventories (although the less held in the shortest time is typically the best for all within the supply chain).

TRADITIONAL REASONS FOR HOLDING INVENTORY

- To act as a buffer between different operations.
- To allow for mismatches between supply and demand rates.
- To allow for demands which are larger than expected.
- To allow for deliveries which are delayed or too small.
- To avoid delays in passing products to customers.
- To take advantage of price discounts.
- To buy items when the price is low and expected to rise.
- To make full loads and reduce transport costs.
- To provide cover for emergencies.

Adapted from Waters, 2003, p. 7

Many of the reasons for holding inventories, however, are no more than excuses, either for bad in-house performance or for poor buyer–supplier relationships. Similarly, work-in-process and finished goods inventories tend to act as covers or 'buffers' for possible operations and inventory management failures. If finished goods inventories are held in order to 'supply the product quickly to the consumer', then action should be taken to ensure that speed is improved within the in-house process, rather than keeping large quantities of finished goods, 'just in case', due to the current process being incapable of rapid response. In addition, keeping a finished goods inventory in high-tech markets is dangerous, due to rapid product/component obsolescence. Admittedly, there are industries that are seasonal or extremely erratic and where the threat of obsolescence is low, in which case holding raw materials and finished stock makes some sense. However, this approach makes little sense in many industries.

Figure 9.2 A telling example of finished goods inventory in the car industry
Courtesy of Professor Mickey Howard, University of Exeter.

One of the problems in the car industry is in levels of finished goods, as can be seen in Figure 9.2.

As we shall see in our discussion on 'just-in-time', there are major challenges that need to be addressed in managing inventory, including those associated with holding inventory and with stock-outs (see boxes below).

POTENTIAL PROBLEMS WITH HOLDING INVENTORIES

- Storage costs.
- Interest is tied up and there is therefore a loss on capital.
- Stock becomes obsolete.
- Less money is available for the business.
- Prices fall on held items.
- Stock deteriorates, is stolen or gets damaged.

THE PROBLEMS ASSOCIATED WITH STOCK-OUT

- Failure to satisfy customer demands.
- Costly emergency procedures to rectify situations.
- Higher replenishment costs for stock replacement.

Stock-outs can be a huge problem, leaving customer frustrated and annoyed. Even the most dedicated of customers may be tempted to switch if stock-outs occur.

CASE: 'LOW INVENTORY ANGERS JOHN DEERE CUSTOMERS'

Jay Armstrong just broke a 50-year family tradition at his Kansas farm: He bought his first major piece of equipment that's not a John Deere brand. The Italian-made corn harvesting combine attachment Armstrong ordered from Dragotec USA will arrive in May. The same $59,000 part from Deere wouldn't have been delivered until August. 'I used to be blind to all colors but [Deere's] green and yellow,' he says. 'My color blindness is now gone.'

In recent years, Deere has been focusing on becoming a build-to-order company. That bolstered prices and profit because keeping smaller stockpiles on hand reduces the amount of materials and working capital a company needs. But production cuts and the tightest inventories in the industry have led to a shortage of Deere equipment as the farm economy is strengthening. And that's pushing customers such as Armstrong toward competitors.

Deere shrank its inventory 28% in the 12 months ended on Jan. 31. As a percentage of sales in the most recent reported 12 months, Deere's inventory was just 12.3%, the lowest among 15 farm and construction equipment makers, including Agco and Caterpillar. Fewer products have big implications for the company's dealers. 'It means I am losing market share,' says Larry Southard, co-owner of a central Iowa dealership that gets 90% of its sales from Deere gear. He figures his dealership's sales would be up to 20% higher this year if it had enough inventory to meet customer demand and products were shipped more quickly. 'I suspect we can lose at least half a dozen deals a month,' Southard says.

One reason: 'A farmer who recently has ordered a tractor for crops such as corn and soybeans, which are harvested starting in September, may not be able to get the equipment until December or January', he says.

Ken Golden, a spokesman for Moline (Ill.)-based Deere, says the manufacturer's 'intense focus' on managing inventory has improved its financial performance and has allowed it to design better products for customers. Deere's sharp-penciled ways certainly helped temper the hit to its profits during the recession, when sales declined for some equipment makers. Deere's 52% decline in trailing 12-month profit was smaller than Agco's 65% drop and Caterpillar's 75% plunge. 'Deere is likely a little ahead [in managing its stocks],' says UBS analyst Henry Kirn, because it has 'focused on taking inventories out of the channel and becoming leaner over time.'

Deere Chief Financial Officer James M. Field said on a Feb. 18 conference call that the company had been too pessimistic about the effect of the global recession on North American farmers. In November, Deere predicted its net sales would decline about 1% in the year ahead after dropping 19% in the 12 months ended Oct. 31. Deere expected production tonnage to decrease 3%. In February the company revised its outlook upward, forecasting sales to increase up to 8% in 2010 as gains in farm cash receipts rise far more than expected.

Deere's Golden says the company is boosting production to match the improved orders. Still, Kansas farmer Armstrong says bad feelings may linger as a result of the company's inventory squeeze. 'Deere's business plan of trying to control the supply vs. selling a product and providing a service is going to come back and haunt them,' he says.

The bottom line: Inventory management is crucial in a slump. But maximizing profit without forgoing future sales is difficult as business strengthens.

Business Week (2010) 'Low Inventory Angers John Deere Customers', 26 April 2010

However, carrying inventory can result in enormous costs. These costs include the option of ordering large quantities infrequently, thereby keeping order costs down and increasing bulk discounts, or ordering small quantities frequently, to keep storage costs down and improve cash flow. The 'solution' to this problem was seen to be in the economic order quantity (EOQ), which *de facto* is the order size that minimizes both total stock holding and ordering costs.

However, it should be noted that the EOQ is based on weak assumptions, including the idea that demand is constant, there is little uncertainty, only order and storage costs are relevant, and orders are placed for only single items. Furthermore, the EOQ only identifies how much to order, not when to place the order. Two approaches to this may be adopted: the continuous review system or periodic review system. Under the continuous review system, the order is placed when the stock held is at a pre-designated reorder point. The reorder point is determined by calculating the average use of stock over time compared with the expected lead time between the order being placed and materials being delivered. So, there are major problems with the EOQ formula.

PROBLEMS OF THE EOQ FORMULA

The EOQ formula is based on the following assumptions:

1. All costs are known and do not vary – demand for an item is also similarly known and will not vary.

2. As a result of point one, both the unit cost of an item and the reorder costs are fixed and do not change according to quantity.

3. There is only one delivery for each order – this is fine on an as-required basis for JIT but under the EOQ approach this 'one delivery' means that the buyer will incur stock-holding costs until the materials are actually required and then decline over a period of time. The delivery will not necessarily act as a driving force to speed up its use and even if it did it might merely encourage forcing a material onto a work area before it is required. This will create a bottleneck and act to increase work in process.

From Brown, 1996

The EOQ formula glosses over important issues including:

1. *The ordering cost*: in the EOQ formula, this is seen to be constant, regardless of: (a) the distance in placing the order; (b) the mode of communication (phone, fax, EDI) and the time spent in placing the order; and (c) the salary cost of the particular person(s) who placed the order.

2. *The cost of stock-holding*: trying to determine this value is – for all practical purposes – impossible. Waters (2003) suggests that 'The usual period for calculating stock costs is a year, so a holding cost might be expressed as, say, £10 a unit a year.'

Another approach is to charge a percentage (25 per cent for example) against the actual cost of a bought item. A $100 item, therefore, will have a storage charge of $25. The problem with this is that holding an item for any period – particularly if the item is a high-tech component, will run the risk of obsolescence, which makes the unit itself redundant. Moreover, trying to work out a 'standard time' that an item might be expected to be in stock is, at best pseudo-scientific, and at worst becomes a means of providing an overhead cost on a unit component in order to fund another major overhead cost – warehousing. The EOQ approach is alien to just-in-time management which, as we shall see, seeks to 'pull' the exact number of materials or components to a particular work station only when it is required and not before. The EOQ formula encourages buffer stock and endorses a 'just-in-case' mentality rather than a just-in-time approach.

Usually a buffer stock is added to cope with uncertainties, such as higher than average usage or delayed stock delivery. Under the periodic review system, there is no fixed order size, as order are placed routinely at fixed time intervals, with order size being determined by comparing planned stock levels and actual stock levels. For instance, most pubs and bars have an identified 'par stock' level and make reorders of this once or twice a week. In practice there are many combinations of these two basic approaches to inventory management, including base-stock, optional replenishment, and visual systems.

It should be clear, then, that the EOQ 'solution' is not really a solution at all. What this approach perhaps shows is that academics and practitioners alike are fond of seeking 'answers' to what are often complex, dynamic variables. The impact of managing inventory is summarized by Lee and Schniederjans (1994, p. 323):

Implementing a new inventory system takes more than a commitment from the inventory manager. It takes a commitment from the entire organization, from purchasing to shipping and from top management to the workers of the at the shop floor level of the organization.

A good starting point for an inventory manager intent on managing inventory in a strategic manner is to assess the range of inventories in an 'ABC' analysis.

ABC ANALYSIS

An ABC analysis is a surprisingly accurate, although simplistic, approach to managing inventory. It is based on the reality that components within the organization's total inventory range have various values or costs. ABC analysis can be undertaken in two ways. First, it can done by focusing on a particular product and analysing its costs; second, it can be undertaken by looking *across* the complete range of products within the firm (this is done where there is a large range of products) and analysing costs of components across the range.

In ABC analysis, the basic rule is: if we were to dismantle a finished product into a list of parts or 'bill of materials' (which we shall discuss later) and lay out all of the components and then group them in terms of cost, we would find that around 20 per cent of the *number of components* account for 80 per cent of *the costs of the product*. This 'rule of thumb' is not fixed, of course; it might well be that say, 17 per cent of the components account for 76 per cent of costs, for example. ABC analysis is important because it helps to focus on the key issues in inventory management. The Class A components are those that need to be managed within strategic buyer–supplier relationships that will be discussed in this chapter and which we explored in Chapter 3.

A basic ABC analysis is shown in Figure 9.3.

Once we have undertaken ABC analysis we can then manage inventory by using powerful systems. Some of the most important in recent times have included MRP, MRPII, and ERP and we will deal with these in turn.

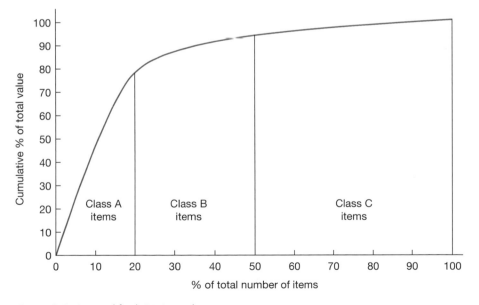

Figure 9.3 A simplified ABC analysis

THE EMERGENCE OF MATERIAL REQUIREMENT PLANNING (MRP), MANUFACTURING, RESOURCE PLANNING (MRPII) AND ENTERPRISE RESOURCE PLANNING (ERP)

Materials requirements planning (MRP) came about with the recognition that in high-volume manufacturing environments, assumptions that underpinned materials management in the craft era did not apply in the mass-production era. The inventory control systems of the earlier era treated demand as if it were *independent*, that is to say externally generated directly by the customer and as a consequence generally smoother due to the aggregation of demand over time. Whilst demand from one customer may be 'lumpy', demand from many customers may create relatively uniform demand.

Such independent demand is still relevant today to many kinds of operations, especially those mass retailing directly to the public such as supermarkets, restaurants, department stores, and so on. Indeed, 44 per cent of the inventory held in the US economy is wholesale and retail merchandise (Krajewski and Ritzman, 2010). However, this notion of relatively uniform and continuous demand is not likely to apply within organizations as far as demand for parts or components is concerned. In this context, demand is *dependent*. This means demand is 'lumpy' because demand for components varies over time according to the output being produced. Such demand does not aggregate to smooth demand, but is determined by schedule of activity planned, and independent demand-based reordering systems look at historic usage and ignore future plans.

MRP was developed and refined by Joseph Orlicky at IBM and by Oliver Wight, a consultant, in the 1960s and 1970s (Orlicky, 1975). It replaced reorder point systems by deriving dependent demand for parts and raw materials from production schedules and determining order points based on delivery lead times and production needs. A materials requirements plan is derived from the master production schedule (MPS), inventory records, and the product structure. The product structure refers to a diagram, engineering drawing or list of materials and their quantities, usually called a 'bill of materials' (BOM), needed to produce one item of output (see 'the scope of management activities in MRP' box). The structure is often shown as a hierarchy of levels or 'parts explosion'. For instance, the end product (level zero) may be made up of assemblies (level one), each of which is made up of sub-assemblies (level two), each of which may be made up of component parts (level three).

MRP systems are often in the form of commercial software. Such commercialization has led to different terminology for similar aspects of the system although there are some common terms in use. Generally, all MRP systems would involve the management of the following:

THE SCOPE OF MANAGEMENT ACTIVITIES IN MRP

- *Gross requirements*: the total quantity of material needed to produce planned output in a given period.
- *Available inventory*: actual stock available for use in any given time period.
- *Allocated inventory*: stock not available as part of the plan since it has been allocated to another use, such as spares.
- *Safety stock*: stock not available for the plan as it exists to cope with uncertainty.
- *Net requirements*: the quantity of material needed to meet scheduled demand.
- *Scheduled receipts*: inventory already ordered and expected to be received from suppliers which can be assumed to be in stock for planning period.
- *Planned ordered receipts*: quantity of material planned to be received to meet net requirements or greater than net requirements if required by order size limitations.
- *Planned ordered releases*: the quantity of output planned for a given time period to satisfy planned ordered receipts.

In essence, MRP is very simple. It seeks answers to the following questions:

KEY QUESTIONS IN MANAGING MRP

1. How many products are to be made?
2. When do these products need to be made?
3. What is the finished product composition in terms of materials and components?
4. What are the numbers and types of components and materials currently in stock?

A figure is determined (by subtracting the answer to question 4 from the answer to question 3) to then ask:

5. How many items have to be ordered from suppliers?
6. What is the lead time for suppliers and, consequently, when do orders have to be placed?

Once these questions have been answered, the 'number crunching' begins on a component basis. The basic calculations are shown in Figure 9.4.

		1	2	3	4	5
Gross requirements			50		150	
Scheduled receipts			100		50	
Stock on hand (inventory balance)		100	150	150	50	50
Planned order release		100		50		
Lead time = 1 week						

Time period (weekly)

Figure 9.4 The basic MRP calculation

Note: Some systems make a difference between 'scheduled receipts' and 'planned receipts', which is not listed above. For the sake of simplicity, the above example assumes that a 'planned order release' requested in one period becomes the 'scheduled receipt' in the next, because the lead time is one week. Brown (1996)

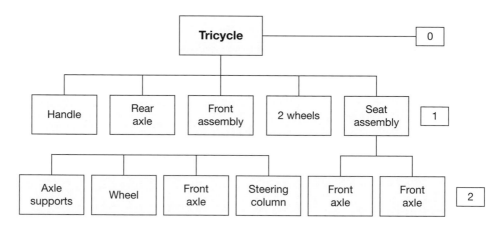

Figure 9.5 A simple parts explosion

Another feature of the MRP system is the 'parts explosion', whereby a finished product is 'exploded' into 'levels' of components so that it becomes clear which components are dependant upon others. For example, in Figure 9.5 it is clear that some parts of the tricycle are level one only, whereas others are level two. This is important in tracing components in terms of where they 'line up' across the range of the firm's products.

Using these data, these computerized systems typically produce a materials requirements plan, priority reports, performance reports, and action notices, which draw management attention to exceptions. In fact, one of the requirements of successful MRP is that it should be an integrated, cross-functional process. Oliver Wight listed 20 key points – which he called the ABCD checklist – against which firms could rate their level of adoption of MRP. It was clear that this was meant to encourage close liaison between operations, marketing, and financial functions.

THE ABCD CHECKLIST

1. Company has a formal monthly Sales and Operations planning process chaired by the Managing Director.
2. Company has a Business Planning process that is fully integrated with its operating system.
3. All functions within the company use a common set of numbers to drive the business.
4. There is a single database that drives all material and capacity planning.
5. System supports daily planning buckets and may be run daily (i.e. MPS, MRP, and CRP).
6. Company has the appropriate levels of data accuracy to support business excellence: (a) stock records (98 to 100 per cent); (b) bills of materials (98 to 100 per cent); and (c) routings at (98 to 100 per cent).
7. The master production schedule is realistic in that there are no plans to produce that have dates in the past and that there are no overloads against critical resources.
8. Valid material plans exist for all components and ingredients of master schedule items.
9. Valid capacity plans exist for all work centres.
10. Company is committed to schedule achievement. It achieves: (a) on time in full delivery to customers (98 to 100 per cent); (b) factory schedules on time (98 to 100 per cent); and (c) vendor schedules on time (98 to 100 per cent).
11. Forecasts are updated at least monthly and customer order promising is directly related to the master schedule.
12. New product introductions and engineering changes are managed effectively within the common system.
13. Company has a programme to reduce lead times, batch quantities, and inventory to gain competitive advantage. Results are visible.
14. Company has sufficient level of user understanding to support business excellence: (a) initial education of 80 per cent of all employees; and (b) a structured ongoing education programme.
15. Company is working in partnership with its vendors through use of vendor scheduling and associated techniques.
16. Company is working in partnership with its customers through closer linkage and shares information.
17. Company monitors that it is improving its level of customer service and increasing inventory turns.
18. Company uses performance measurements as the mechanism for monitoring and improving all business processes.

19. Company uses such measurements to continually monitor and improve its competitive position in the marketplace.

20. Company is committed to continuous improvement to maintain competitive advantage.

A *Class 'D'* user is typically one where either MRP is not operated or, if it is, no-one believes the MRP figures. Frequently the store man will have a manual record that anyone will refer to if they want to find out what is really in stock. Manual records and schedules are a dead give-away to poor data accuracy and a Class 'D' level of performance. Even if all the MRPII bits were in place, the lack of accurate data would render the output worthless. A Class 'D' user uses the MRP package as a (very expensive) typewriter!

A *Class 'C'* user may have a pretty good MRP system as was common in the 1950s and 1960s. The system will launch orders and progress chasers will expedite them according to which customers shout the loudest. They can never be better than Class 'C' because they do not attempt to manage the MRP according to the resources available. The lack of a managed master schedule and integrated capacity planning are class 'C' indicators.

A *Class 'B'* user will have capacity resource management in place via a sales and operations plan and a managed master scheduling process but the failure to properly control all the elements of ERP/MRPII will typically be shown up by the necessity to have secondary priority information to get the 'hot' jobs through production.

A *Class 'A'* user will score 18 or more on the check sheet and will need neither shortage sheets nor progress chasers. Instead, production control and monitoring will typically be carried out using the output from the planning system. The 98 per cent or better on-time delivery to customers will soon become an accepted part of the company's culture. A missed shipment or even a stock error will become a major cause for concern instead of just a way of life.

BPIC, The Manufacturing Planning Resource, www. BPIC.co.uk

MRP, however, is not a magic solution. Oliver Wight thought that less than 10 per cent of companies were what he termed 'Class A' users – firms scored at least 18 or more from the ABCD checklist. Cerveny and Scott (1989) identified that 40 per cent of the firms they surveyed had adopted it, but only 67 per cent regarded it as a success.

MRP also requires high data integrity; that is, the accuracy of the data must be high and consistent. Since inventory level data is traditionally poor and quoted lead times from suppliers even worse, the general failure of MRP should not surprise us. The precision was also inherently poor – a lead-time for delivery of a component, for example, might typically

MRP OPERATES BEST UNDER FOUR CONDITIONS

1. High volume, line processes.
2. Product structure is complex and there are many levels of bills of materials.
3. Production is carried out relatively large batch sizes.
4. There is limited volatility. Bottlenecks, rush jobs, high scrap rates and unreliable suppliers create volatile conditions unsuited for the MRP system.

be quoted and entered into the database as, say, 14 weeks. The suggestion that anyone can predict what materials will be needed in 14 weeks' time, and the excessively loose unit of a week for a delivery promise, are both problematic.

FROM MRP TO MRPII

MRP evolved into MRPII which, in essence, *included* MRP and added other management ingredients such as tooling, routing procedures, capacity availability, and man-hours requirements. MRP is therefore a sub-set of MRPII, as shown in Figure 9.6.

Often plant managers will refer to MRP when, in fact, the system they have is MRPII – the terms have become almost interchangeable. When executed properly, MRPII can make a powerful contribution to materials planning and capacity management. However, both MRP and MRPII have been severely criticized, as Luscombe (1994, p. 123) observes:

> One article referred to 'disillusionment with existing MRPII-based production planning tools' another stated that MRP II implementation methodologies 'belong to a different era' whilst a third offered reasons why 'so many large-scale MRP II systems failed'.

But, as Luscombe (ibid.) also suggests:

> Those who abandon MRPII in search of some form of instant-response, shop floor-driven system are likely to be disappointed, as they ignore the realities of manufacturing as reflected in both MRPII and leading Japanese production systems.

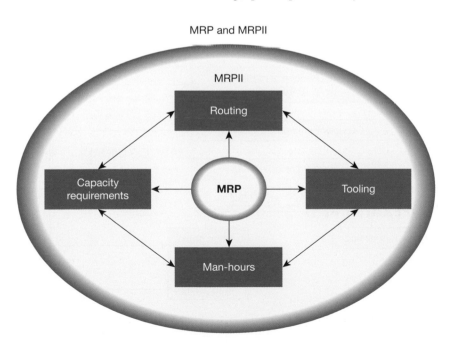

MRP and MRPII

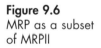

Figure 9.6
MRP as a subset
of MRPII

The real problem is that often managers expect an instant solution to poor management of inventory. They suspect that software alone, via MRP/MRPII, will solve these problems. The lack of strategic importance given to materials management by senior managers becomes a key reason for failure. But when there is a strategic and holistic approach to managing inventory, the following 'closed loop' system becomes a reality as shown in Figure 9.7.

In addition, MRP should facilitate better relationships with suppliers because, in theory, all lead times are known and therefore unreasonable delivery requirements are not made on suppliers. Admittedly, shorter lead-times are preferable, especially when MRP is used alongside JIT, but that has more to do with an ongoing pursuit of improvement in delivery performance via relationships with suppliers, than as a reflection on MRPII itself.

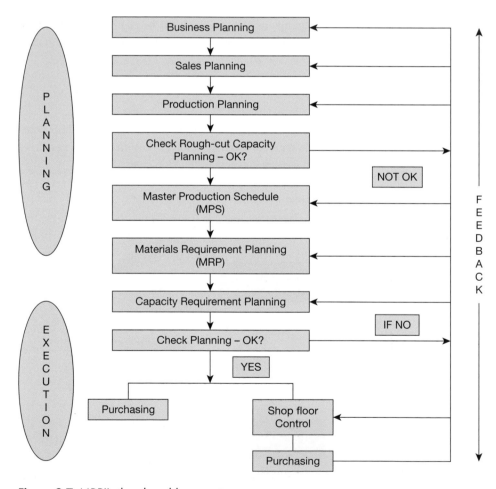

Figure 9.7 MRPII: the closed loop system

RESOLVING PROBLEMS ASSOCIATED WITH MRP

There is nothing to stop MRP being used as the *planning system* and then for the tools and techniques of JIT, which we will discuss later in this chapter, to be used to actually 'pull' the materials only when needed. At any rate, there must be some sort of 'master plan' for a given time period because inventory cannot appear out of nowhere. MRP/MRPII can, therefore, be used as an exhaustive management tool whereby numbers of products and, consequently, sub-components can be determined and tracked throughout the process. MRP should not be used to 'push' components or materials onto a work-station before they are required. Advocates of JIT (and critics of MRP) have stated that MRP is inclined to do this (Plenert and Best, 1986) – but, again, this has more to do with management's failure in terms of using MRP, rather than the system itself. MRP can provide a discipline so that key areas such as master production schedules, bill of materials, lead times with suppliers and other data integrity is reliable, accurate, relevant, and known to all parties, which is essential to any well-run management information system.

MRP encourages an holistic approach within the firm itself. As Waters (2003, p. 279) states:

> The introduction of MRP needs considerable changes to an organisation and these require commitment from all areas.

The MRP system can also serve to highlight business performance problems with delivery speed and reliability. As Schmenner (1990, p. 487) suggests:

> Not only can an MRP system detail what should be ordered and when, but also it can indicate how and when late items will affect other aspects of production. It can signal . . . how tardiness will alter the existing production schedule.

Since delivery speed and reliability are crucial in many markets it is clear that MRP can play an important role in achieving these market requirements. MRP can also become a powerful ally to just-in-time management. As Karmarker (1989, p. 125) states:

> MRPII . . . initiates production of various components, releases orders, and offsets inventory reductions. MRPII grasps the final product by its parts, orders their delivery to operators, keeps track of inventory positions in all stages of production and determines what is needed to add to existing inventories. What more could JIT ask?

The answer to this question is twofold:

1. Much better internal quality control systems to enable JIT to become a reality; and
2. A strategic vision with suppliers: a vision of shared destiny between them rather than the buyer *versus* supplier relationship that pervades in much of Western manufacturing.

The linkages within MRP are shown in Figure 9.8.

MRP became an important step in the evolution toward the strategic management of inventory, as shown in Figure 9.9.

Figure 9.8
Linkages within
the MRP system

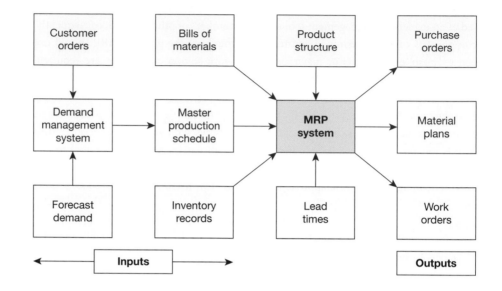

Figure 9.9
The development
of the strategic
importance
of inventory
management

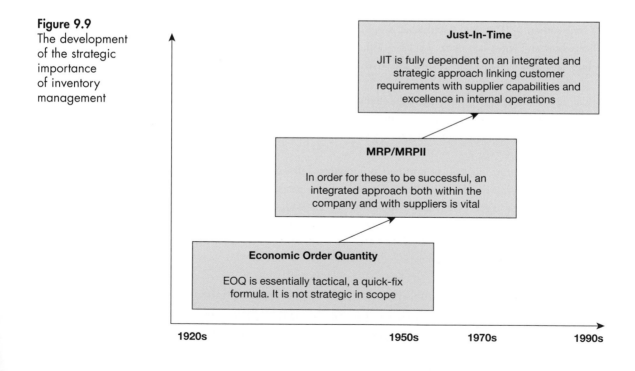

ENTERPRISE RESOURCE PLANNING (ERP)

Enterprise resource planning (ERP) systems go beyond MRP and MRPII to integrate internal and external business processes. Although ERP systems have become popular, implementing ERP is time-consuming and costly. Like all software 'solutions', ERP has its advocates and critics alike. The basic flow of the system is shown in Figure 9.16.

ERP has gained in popularity over MRP to some extent although MRP and MRPII remain in use. The benefits of using ERP can include:

- Greater visibility of what is happening in all parts of the business;
- Process-based changes can help to make all parts of the business more efficient;
- A better 'sense of control' of operations – this in turn enhances continuous improvement and quality;
- The development of better communication with customers, suppliers, and other business partners; and
- The potential for integrating whole supply chains including suppliers' suppliers and customers' customers.

CASE: THE CHALLENGES IN IMPLEMENTING ERP

In early 2007, Chesterfield-based Stainless Steel Fasteners Ltd – a subsidiary of engineering conglomerate IMI, and a world leader in the manufacture of high integrity special fastener products – recognized it had to replace its ageing ERP system. Lacking a Customer Relationship Management capability, and relying on spreadsheets for master scheduling, it was clear that the system was no longer fit for purpose.

But what to replace it with? The days are long gone when an ERP system, on its own, offered competitive advantage. For the typical manufacturer, having an ERP system is these days simply part of the price of doing business – rather like having a phone system, for instance.

But that doesn't mean that the choice of an ERP system is an unimportant, low-key decision. Far from it. ERP systems are costly, complex to implement, and can hamper and hinder the business if not selected and implemented with care. In short, choosing an ERP system is very much a case 'marry in haste, repent at leisure.'

'ERP systems need to be flexible enough to allow the business to maximise growth, and in the desired timeframe,' stresses John Hammann, industry principal for manufacturing at SAP UK. 'They shouldn't be an inhibitor, or a brake.'

And in truth, of course, many firms already know this. That's why so much very evident care is taken over the process, and why attendance at events such as ERP Connect 2011 is so popular.

But there's another, less well-understood reason for taking care over the choice of an ERP system – and it's got nothing to do with cost, technology, size of vendor or any of the other common selection criteria.

And it's this: competitive edge. Every manufacturing business, in short, has one or more competitive differentiators that allows them to stand out from the pack. But all too frequently these competitive differentiators fail to feature prominently enough in the selection process, being lost among lengthy checklists of looked-for features that are in fact far less important to the business.

The result? A system that holds the business back, damaging competitiveness, and running the risk of losing customers, margin and sales growth. Indeed, go back a few years, and with vendors desperate for a sale at any price, stories abounded of companies being pushed towards unsuitable systems.

Back in 2000, for instance, analyst firm META Group damningly concluded that the average ERP implementation took 23 months, cost $15 million, and rewarded the business with a negative net present value of $1.5 million. That's right: a negative ROI.

No longer. Vendors, to their credit, have woken up to the problem, and are no longer so prone to over-promising and under-delivering. The result? Much greater clarity about a given system's true strengths – enabling manufacturers to home in on what a prospective system can truly deliver in terms of enhancing their competitive edge, allowing them to firmly focus on leveraging it to the full.

'We encourage potential customers to go through a "discovery phase": where is the business being hurt – and what do they want to do about that?,' says Steve Farr, product manager at Microsoft, whose AX and NAV-badged ERP systems have proved popular with mid-sized manufacturers. 'These days, it's very much the strategic business issues that drive the sale.'

Engineered-to-order manufacturers, for example, or distinctively project-based businesses, won't derive much benefit from an ERP system that is largely aimed at repetitive consumer products manufacturing businesses.

In the latter, bills of material and routings are largely static, and competitive issues revolve around slick scheduling, pull-based replenishment, and the supply chain. In the former, it's the ability to link costs and manpower to specific projects that matters, coupled to bills of material and routings that may well be project-specific one-offs.

'"Fit" is vital,' says Antony Bourne, global sales director at IFS. 'We specialise in the engineering-to-order and contract manufacturing markets, with an ERP system finely-tuned to the needs of manufacturers in those markets.'

Infor, meanwhile, claims process industry expertise, through its System 21 Aurora ERP system – one of several such systems offered by the firm.

Back at Stainless Steel Fasteners, the eventual choice of ERP system came from the recognition that the business's competitive edge lay in balancing complex product configurations – some twenty million variants are theoretically capable of being ordered – with superior inventory management and strong customer relationship management.

And as a result, EFACS E/8, from Exel Computer Systems, has enabled Stainless Steel Fasteners to drive down both inventory levels and purchase prices, notes managing director Stephen Wilkinson.

'Having access to historical information, at a customer, order and stock level, is important if we are to be able to make the best strategic and tactical decisions,' he says. 'We deal with materials with varying degrees of availability and fluctuating prices – and by having a historical record of who tends to buy what, and when, we can time our buying to take advantage of particularly favourable conditions.'

TheManufacturer.com (2011) 'Can ERP Boost Your Business's Competitive Edge?', Zone: IT in manufacturing, April 2011

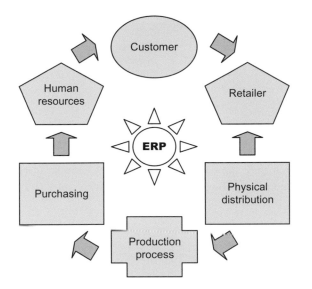

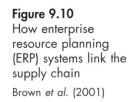

Figure 9.10
How enterprise resource planning (ERP) systems link the supply chain

Brown *et al.* (2001)

However, the downsides to ERP can include the following:

- It is very expensive;
- It can very difficult customize;
- Implementation may pose major organizational changes in the company; and
- Commitment to implementation can be a protracted and almost never-ending saga.

The basic problem with MRP and ERP is that they can be a 'push' system of inventory management. This means that there can be a danger of ordering materials and then 'pushing' them through the system before an operator is ready. The danger of a 'push' system is shown in the Figure 9.11.

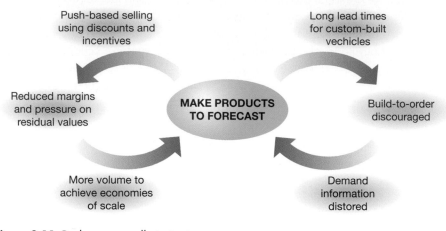

The Destructive Cycles of Make-to-Forecast

In the first cycle, the company must rely on larger economies of scale to compensate for the use of push-based selling. In the second, the company loses sight of real customer requirements because it is selling too many products from stock

Figure 9.11 Push versus pull strategies
Holweg and Pil (2001)

An alternative approach based on a 'pull' approach was developed by some Japanese companies in the 1950s – most famously by Toyota. It is called 'just-in-time' (JIT) management.

JUST IN TIME (JIT) MANAGEMENT

JIT is more holistic in nature than earlier systems of inventory management and MRP. It is not solely concerned with capacity, materials, and inventory, but also includes aspects of quality management, such as continuous improvement and total quality control. TQM is a vital pre-requisite in order for JIT to be successful in manufacturing plants. Just-in-time management is, therefore, not simply an inventory reduction exercise. In fact, just simply reducing stocks will, in the first instance, *create* major problems. As Shingo in Zipkin (1991, p. 44) explain:

> Stock reduction should not become an end in itself, however, since cutting stock blindly may cause delivery delays . . . Rather the conditions that produce or necessitate stock must be corrected so that stock can be reduced in a rational fashion.

Just-in-time is a complete shift away from traditional Western manufacturing. Hutchins (1999, p. 11) describes how:

JIT is part of a fundamentally different approach to management which when fully developed will help to create a totally new industrial culture.

JIT includes elements of production scheduling and inventory management. This approach identified for the first time that tradeoffs were not an essential aspect of operations. JIT is linked to capacity management. For example, Toyota creates a fixed monthly production schedule each month. The production level will change each month but what Toyota is doing by adhering to the monthly production schedule is to manage the uncertainty of capacity by making the production 'fixed' for a given month. This schedule is then communicated to Toyota's suppliers. This then means that capacity has become synchronized between Toyota and its suppliers so that deliveries can be planned with a great deal of certainty in relation to manufacturing operations.

JIT enables improvements to be made to costs, delivery times, and quality. Perhaps the most fascinating aspect of JIT, in retrospect, is that it was developed entirely without computers (although latterly much computerization has been incorporated into it). At a time when managers in the West were fixated with the computer programs in MRP, missing the absurdity of relying on data such as '14 weeks lead time', the Japanese were dealing with immediate requirements – making a virtue out of living from hand to mouth and employing common sense, not rocket science.

JIT production was conceived by Taiichi Ohno, the former head of production at Toyota, in the 1980s. World-class JIT streamlines production, exposes problems and bottlenecks, and attacks waste. As we saw in Chapter 8 (on quality), Suzaki (1987) quotes Jujio Cho of Toyota who identifies seven types of waste.

SEVEN CATEGORIES OF WASTE

1. OVERPRODUCTION

- More than customer needs.
- Out of sequence.
- The wrong part.
- Early or late.

2. WAITING

- By people.
- By products.
- By machines (bottlenecks).
- By customer.

3. TRANSPORTATION

- Not value added.
- Effort and cost.
- Inventory.
- No control, no ownership.

4. THE PROCESS ITSELF

- Basic raw material.
- Basic process.
- Value eng, value analysis.
- Make/buy.
- Why do it at all?
- Process choice.

5. STOCK ON HAND

- Buffer against variability.
- Store excess parts.
- WIP deadens responsiveness.
- Money tied up.

6. MOTION

- Process choice.
- Efficiency of task.

- Maintain operator flow.
- Maintain work flow.
- Improve the method first, *then* inject capital.

7. DEFECTIVE GOODS

- Cost of scrap.
- Creates inventory (just in case!).
- Cost of rectification.
- Causes poor delivery performance.

JIT operations do not employ safety stocks, therefore, as they are seen as wasteful. At the heart of the system is the *kanban*, the Japanese word for card. In practice, *kanban* can take many forms – cards, magnetic strips, electronic communications, plastic containers, and so on. They are the means for communicating to, from, and within work centres. Information about the part is written on the *kanban*, including reference number, storage area, and associated work centres. These days, much of this information is now in the form of a barcode. In a JIT system, parts can only be used, moved or produced if accompanied by a *kanban*. Movement of parts is further simplified by bins or containers of fixed size, designed to hold a specific, and relatively small number of units of the same part. Different parts are never put into the same containers. In a typical production situation, an operator at a workstation has one or more *kanban*. When one is empty, this then becomes the authorization to obtain a replacement level of inventory for the *kanban* from either the storage area or next workstation. The arrival of an empty *kanban* at a workstation is authorization for that operator to produce sufficient parts to refill it. Thus, production is activity generated by demand from the next operator down the line ('downstream'), which is why it is a 'pull' system.

MRP and JIT systems are not mutually exclusive. Many operations operate a hybrid of these two in an attempt to take advantage of the best elements of both. MRP/MRPII will be used to plan materials; JIT will then 'pull' materials as required.

Another element of the Japanese approach to manufacturing has been to dampen the impact of variations in the production schedule, by producing relatively small quantities of the same mix of products. Operations schedules are planned on a daily basis to achieve monthly planned output. The adoption of uniform plant loading may have the impact of increasing the frequency of machine setups, however, as the plant switches from producing one output to another. Hence the Japanese, notably Shigeo Shingo in Toyota, spent many years seeking to achieve 'single digit' setup – the ability to change a machine tool from one setup to another in less than ten minutes.

By the late 1970s, a Toyota team of press operators was able to change over an 800-ton press, from one part to another, in less than ten minutes, compared with six hours for the same activity (i.e. the same two parts) in a US car plant. They achieved this simply by differentiating between external setup, which can be carried out whilst the machine is running, and internal setup, which requires the machine to be stopped. External setup may include transfers of dies or moulds from a storage area to the machine and preheating the machine or its component up to operating temperature. Setup time may also be reduced by standardizing the setup function of the machine, conveyors, and cranes to move dies, eliminating unnecessary adjustments, synchronizing operator tasks, and automating some of the procedures such as feed and position work, if possible. Furthermore, in Japanese factories changeover teams would go into the factory at weekends, when production was shut down, to practice set-ups. This same approach can be observed during Formula 1 races when the pit team changes tyres. They can change all four wheels, and put large volumes of fuel into the tank, in under ten seconds, whereas the average motorist can take up to half an hour to change one wheel.

CASE: THE APPLICATION OF JIT

On-demand manufacturing

More manufacturers are cutting costs by producing only what they know will sell.

When surgical device maker Conmed decided in 2007 to streamline production, executives explored the usual options. The Utica (N.Y.) company could ship more manufacturing to China. Or it could invest in automation.

Conmed chose a third path instead: It completely overhauled its production. Long assembly lines at its 600-worker Utica plant have given way to compact U-shaped workstations. Piles of plastic boxes stuffed with enough parts to last weeks have been replaced by just a few bins containing the exact number of parts needed.

No longer do workers furiously crank out products that languish in warehouses. Instead they build only as many as customers need at the time. Conmed calculates that every 90 seconds hospitals worldwide use one of its disposable devices for inserting and removing fluids around joints during orthoscopic surgery. So that's precisely how long it takes for a new one to roll off its assembly line. A growing number of products, such as instruments for cutting bone, are assembled only after hospitals place orders. 'The goal is to link our operations as closely as possible to the ultimate buyer of the product,' says David A. Johnson, vice-president for global operations.

Lean manufacturing – producing goods with minimal waste of time, materials, and money – was pioneered by Japanese companies such as Toyota Motor decades ago. Now a growing number of U.S. businesses are trying a more extreme form of lean. Besides making factories superefficient, they are gearing output to current demand rather than three- to six-month forecasts. 'We're seeing a precipitous rise in companies adopting a religious commitment to producing only what they know will sell,' says William A. Schwartz, managing director for business development at TBM Consulting in Durham, N.C., which shapes make-to-demand strategies for producers of chemicals, building materials, and packaged foods.

In capital-starved times, companies can ill afford to tie up cash by letting parts and finished goods lie idle in inventory. And these days, even if companies place orders, there's no guarantee they'll get the financing to complete the purchase. In most past recessions, notes Richard Seaman, CEO of Seaman Corp., a Wooster (Ohio) maker of heavy fabrics for industry and construction, companies could generally predict demand for the next month with an accuracy within 5%. 'In the past four or five months,' he says, 'there has been a sea change.' Converting to very lean manufacturing helped the company adjust to the new environment. It used to fill large orders in six weeks. Now some fabrics are out the door 48 hours after an order is placed.

Tying everyone in

The next challenge is getting a clearer picture of what's happening on the customer's end. Celestica, the $7.7 billion contract manufacturer of electronics gear, is rolling out a system it calls Liveshare. Within two years, the company hopes Liveshare will let all of Celestica's customers, global factory network, and 4,000 suppliers share real-time data on demand, production, inventories, and shipping for every product. Some suppliers already use Liveshare, but the plan is to include major electronics buyers as well.

Say a purchase manager for Best Buy needs supplies of a hot video game console assembled by Celestica. Today, most buyers would use phone, fax, and e-mail to assess how quickly Celestica could deliver. But a buyer checking Celestica's online database would see up-to-the-minute diagrams showing how many consoles are rolling off production lines. And Celestica could peer into Best Buy's inventory and sales data to estimate how many consoles the chain needed. 'What a tremendous breakthrough this would be,' says CEO Craig Muhlhauser.

Not all goods can or should be built to order. Some 80% of Conmed's $742 million in 2008 sales came from disposables sold by the millions to hospitals, where demand is fairly steady. For mass-produced items, it bases hourly output targets on forecasts updated every few months. Before, mass quantities of goods sat in warehouses until they were sold.

At Conmed's Utica plant, the assembly area for fluid-injection devices once consumed 3,300 square feet and had $93,000 worth of parts on hand. Now it covers one-fifth that space and stocks just $6,000 worth of parts. Output per worker is up 21%. Do the improvements yield savings superior to what could be had in China? Wages there, though vastly lower, are largely offset by the costs of long lead times, inventory pileup, quality problems, and unforeseen delays. 'If more U.S. companies deploy these production methods,' says Johnson, 'we can compete with anybody.'

Business Week (2009) 'Lean and mean gets extreme',
23 March 2009, (4124), 60–2

THE CHALLENGES OF JIT

Just-in-time is a very simple idea which has been extraordinarily difficult for many companies to implement. Zipkin's (1991, p. 40) statement is pertinent here:

a storm of confusion swirls around JIT. Ask any two managers who have worked with it just what JIT is and does, and you are likely to hear wildly different answers. Some managers credit JIT with giving new life to their companies; others denounce it as a sham.

The essence of JIT is that the exact number of components will arrive at a work station *exactly at the time required* and in JIT, the *supply* of materials will exactly match the *demand* of materials both in terms of quantity and time.

Although JIT management approaches emanated from Japan it is clear that the techniques have been transferred – with varying degree of success – to the West. For many companies, JIT will present a massive challenge to the way in which the firm operates its business. These factors will include both internal and external factors: the internal factors will include an obsession with quality – 'getting it right first time' because JIT cannot tolerate rework and scrap since only the exact amount of materials will be 'pulled' to satisfy the component requirements for a particular work station. The internal challenges of JIT are shown in Table 9.1.

One of the main factors in JIT is in the elimination of waste resulting in measurable benefits, not always centred on costs: areas such as flexibility, rapid response to customer requirements, innovation, and delivery speed and reliability.

In world-class operations there should not be idle time, waiting, or buffers – the Japanese terms for these are:

Muda: waste.
Mura: inconsistency by machines or workers.
Muri: excessive demands upon workers or machines.

Table 9.1 The effect of JIT on operations

	Traditional manufacturing	JIT/Enlightened approaches
Quality	'Acceptable' levels of rejects and rework – an inevitability that failures will occur. A specialist function	'Right first time, every time' constant, ongoing pursuit of process improvement. Everybody responsible for ensuring quality
Inventory	An asset, part of the balance sheet and, therefore, part of the value of the firm; buffers necessary to keep production running	A liability, masking the operational performance by hiding a number of problems.
Batch sizes	An economic order can be determined to show the balance between set-up time and production runs	Batch sizes must be as small as possible, aiming toward a batch size of one
Materials ordering	Determined by the economic order quantity	Supply exactly meets demand – no more no less, in terms of quantity; delivery is exactly when required, not before and not after
Bottlenecks	Inevitable – shows that machine utilization is high	No queues – production is at the rate which prevents delays and queues
Workforce	A cost which can be reduced by introducing more automation	A valuable asset, able to problem-solve, who should be supported by managers

Brown (1996)

When there is little 'buffer' inventory, the three factors *muda*, *mura*, and *muri* become prominent. Conversely, these three factors are disguised by holding amounts of inventory. Holding inventory – at any stage – can serve to 'cover' poor operational performance and reducing inventory will, in the first instance, cause these problems to surface which will then focus the firm in having to make improvements in production/operations areas, as shown in Figure 9.12.

Interestingly, when these problems appear the *strategic* importance is revealed. Instead of a 'quick fix', tactical approach – buying more stock to cover problems – the firm must take strategic measures: continuous and ongoing improvements in-house to reduce stock levels, coupled with strategic alliances with suppliers to enhance delivery, innovations, and reduce total costs.

We hinted at the differences between 'push' and 'pull' earlier in the chapter. The challenges and benefits of this transition to JIT are shown in Figure 9.13.

As well as the internal requirements for JIT there are also external factors: a major failure of some Western companies in terms of implementing JIT is their inability to forge long-term, strategic partnerships with their suppliers. We discussed this in depth in Chapter 3, but a note is also pertinent here in our discussion on Just in Time.

You will recall how, earlier in this chapter, we stated that the former perceived wisdom within management was for the firm to own as much of the supply chain as possible for the reasons that we listed. Over time this perception changed, although this did not mean that there were mutually beneficial strategic relationships in place between buyers and suppliers within the supply network. Indeed, Porter (1980) had pitched the buyer–supplier relationship in, largely, adversarial terms – the buyer, for example, should pursue the 'threat of backward integration' and 'use of tapered integration' (p. 125) according to Porter. Over time this has changed, although there many firms who remain routed in this approach. However, over time buyer–supplier relationships had changed, as Turnbull *et al.* (1993, p. 51) commented:

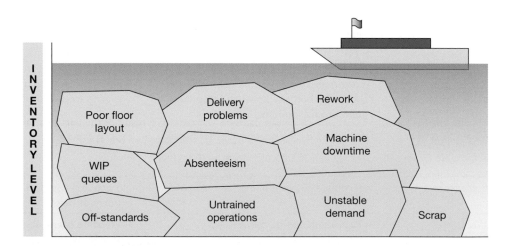

Figure 9.12 The challenge of JIT on operations

	PUSH				PULL
	Make-to-Forecast (MTF)	Locate-to-Order (LTO)	Amend-to-Order	Hybrid Build-to-Order	True Build-to-Order (BTO)
Goals	■ Produce standard products from long-term demand forecasts ■ Manage stock reactively to allow for efficient production	■ Use MTF, but increase stock visibility (through the internet, for example) to enhance customer choice	■ Provide custom orders when specifications or product in system can be easily amended	■ Rely on forecasting for high-volume, stable products, and build low-volume products to order	■ Build products only after the customer orders them ■ Make customer needs visible to all parts of the value chain
Benefits	■ Efficient production ■ Local optimization of factory operations	■ Higher chance of finding right product in stock ■ Inexpensive to implement	■ Higher degree of custom-built vehicles in production	■ Stable base production ■ Relatively short order-to-delivery times on average ■ Less inventory ■ Less discounting	■ No stock apart from showroom and demonstrators ■ No discounting
Weaknesses	■ High levels of finished stock in market ■ MTF requires alternative product specifications and discounting to sell aging stock ■ Customer orders compete with forecast: for capacity MTF loses sight of real customer demand ■ MTF loses sight of real customer demand	■ High stock levels remain ■ Discounting still required ■ Custom orders still compete with forecast for capacity ■ Extra cost to transfer product to location close to customer	■ Customer orders built only when they fit ■ Unsold orders are built anyway ■ High temptation to revert to MTF if demand drops	■ Stock is still in market ■ Still requires discounting to cope with forecast error ■ Danger of reverting to pure MTF when demand shifts	■ System is sensitive to short-term demand fluctuations, so will not work without proactive demand management ■ Active revenue management required to maximize profit

Figure 9.13
Key factors in push versus pull strategies
Holweg and Pil (2001)

In Japan, the actual contract between motor manufacturer and supplier is based on co-operation, a full exchange of information, a commitment to improve quality, and a recognition . . . that prices can (and will) be reduced each year . . . bargaining is not simply focused on price per se but on how to reach the target price while maintaining a reasonable level of profit for the supplier.

Clearly, the partnership is not based on complacency and ease, as a result of the partnership deal having been made. Rather, demands are made on the supplier but these are made achievable as a result of the Japanese (and other world-class) buyers helping the supplier to improve its business in terms of lower cost and faster delivery. The partnership approach is summarized by Schonberger and Knod (2001, p. 291):

In the partnership approach, the idea is not to change suppliers. The rule is: Stay with one, in order that it may stay on the learning curve, get to know the customer's real requirements, and perhaps participate with the customer on product and process improvements.

CASE: PRESSURES ON JOINT BUYER–SUPPLIER EFFORTS TO REDUCE WASTE

Toyota's cost-cutting program – dubbed CCC21, or Construction of Cost Competitiveness for the 21st Century – has been a remarkable success by any measure. With just one year to go, the plan is on track to save the auto maker some $10 billion over its five-year time frame. Not only is CCC21 sourcing components more cheaply but Toyota has also improved the parts' quality . . . [the] CCC21 team disassembled the horns made by a Japanese supplier and found ways to eliminate six of 28 components, resulting in a 40% saving. No part has been too mundane to escape the Watanabe squad's notice. His favorite example: interior assist grips above each door. There once were 35 different grips. Now, *Toyota*'s entire 90-model lineup uses just three basic styles. *Toyota* gearheads call this process kawaita zokin wo shiboru, or 'wringing drops from a dry towel.'

Business Week (2005) 'A 'China price' for Toyota',
21 February 2005, (3921), 50–1

In order for buyer–supplier relationships to be strong there has to be considerable trust shown between both parties.

THREE TYPES OF TRUST

Sako (1992) suggests that three types of trust need to be in place:

Contractual trust: which is the adherence to formal, legal promises
Competence trust: that either side is capable to provide what has been promised
Goodwill trust: which borders on 'ethics': trusting that appropriate behaviour will ensue

The ability to form such partnerships, essential to successful JIT, is a major challenge and calls for the very best of management expertise. It is clear that, sometimes, this expertise is not in place and this has been evident for decades. Back in 1994, *Business Week* noted how:

GM's relations with its suppliers remain the worst in Detroit. . . . An electronics supplier tells of a $30 part he developed jointly with GM. He says that after he slashed the price to $15, the GM purchasing agent demanded more cuts, citing a $9 bid from a Chinese company that had never made the part in question . . . One parts maker that does $600 million in business with car makers says it is focusing its efforts on selling to GM's rivals'.

(p. 26)

In 2000, *Fortune* provided insights into how buyer–supplier relationships within the car industry had not improved across many companies:

> The relationship between an auto-parts company and its customer, the automaker, is like the relationship between a masochist and a sadist. Really. The parts maker slashes margins to the bone to get a contract in which the difference between a winning bid and a losing one may be one-thousandth of a cent. Then the real pain begins. The manufacturer demands that the parts maker meet rigorous schedules, adjust to wide fluctuations in production, and cut prices by several percent every year that a contract runs. If a part turns out to be defective, the parts maker may have to share in the manufacturer's added warranty costs – or perhaps pay damages from a class-action lawsuit.
>
> (2000b, p. 265)

The *Financial Times* commented on how buyer–supplier relationships were far from perfect in retail services, with appalling behaviour taking place:

> From September 2001, the report says, they operated a programme called – almost comically – Project Slow It Down. Payments to suppliers were systematically delayed or reduced, suppliers were denied access to computer records of accounts payable and were deceived about why they were not being paid.
>
> (2003, p. 19)

Even though JIT was pioneered within the car industry, there are still problems in place. One of these relates to the time taken for a car to be transferred from customer order to delivery to the customer. The problem is captured in Figure 9.14.

Another challenge with JIT is that even when there are mutually beneficial relationships in place, with both parties striving to continuously improve their operations, such relationships within the same industry may encounter unforeseen problems (Sako, 2004). These can have a devastating effect upon JIT, which although vastly superior to the 'just-in-case', buying in bulk, scenario under traditional mass production, is a very fragile, almost delicate phenomenon.

Clearly, the management of inventory has developed over time from a largely tactical activity to a senior-level strategic position within firms. Changes from EOQ to MRP and JIT have shown profound developments over time. JIT is more than inventory management because it represents a fundamental change in how firms product good by utilizing a 'pull' system that we discussed earlier. With the development of outsourcing and the growth of buyer–supplier relationships, keeping track of inventory can be a huge challenge.

Boeing says it can't supply a full list of subcontractors that are working on the project, but industry analysts estimate that their numbers are greater than the 900-plus that contributed to the 777, which began construction in 1990. Boeing spokesperson Loretta Gunter confirms that the processes used to construct the

Figure 9.14
Ongoing problems
with JIT

Courtesy of Professor
M. Howard, University
of Exeter, and Professor
Graves, University of
Bath

The problem

The 3DayCar programme shows it takes on average 40 days to fulfil an order in the UK,
but *only 1.5* are actually spent building the vehicle

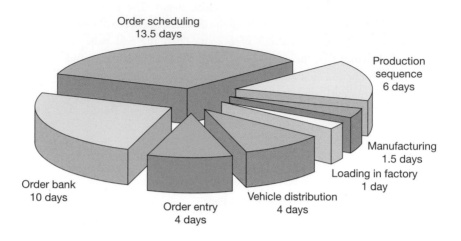

two planes are markedly different. 'We have fewer first-tier subcontractors on
the 787 than we did on the 777 because each is providing bigger components,'
she says. 'Likewise, many of them are contracting out bigger jobs to their subs.'

Boeing's new manufacturing template has captured the imagination of the
aerospace industry. Recently officials from Airbus told analysts that the company
will up its outsourcing to become more competitive.

Fortune (2007) 'How many small businesses does it
take to build a jet?', July/August 2007, pp. 42–5

WHEN JIT GOES WRONG

Although JIT can be a very powerful way of managing operations – and this has direct
impact on managing inventory – when JIT goes wrong it can be disastrous.

CASE: THE DOWNSIDE OF JUST-IN-TIME INVENTORY

U.S. companies such as Boeing have learned to boost profits with tight inventories. Now, with 130 plants
closed in Japan, they're learning the risks. In a control center above a wide-body jet plant in Everett, Wash.,
a group of Boeing staffers is poring over data from suppliers in Japan – making sure the company has enough
parts to build its 787 Dreamliner in the U.S.

It's a long list. Japanese manufacturers helped design and now produce 35 percent of the 787, 20 percent of the 777, and 15 percent of the 767. What they build can't be duplicated anywhere else, and Boeing can't call in a new supplier to make one piece if it runs short. So far, the jetmaker says it has enough inventory to keep running for a few weeks.

Thirty years ago, Japan taught U.S. companies to boost profit by keeping inventory lean. Now it's teaching them the risks. Mitsubishi Heavy Industries builds the 787's wing; no one else can do that job. General Motors decided on Mar. 17 to close its Shreveport (La.) Chevrolet Colorado and GMC Canyon pickup plant for a week because it lacked components. Deere is delaying deliveries of excavators and mining equipment. And Honda Motor suspended orders from U.S. dealers for Japan-built Honda and Acura models that would be sold in May.

'Instead of months' worth of inventory, there are now days and even hours of inventory,' says Jim Lawton, head of supply management solutions at consultant Dun & Bradstreet and a former procurement chief for Hewlett-Packard. 'If supply is disrupted as in this situation, there's nowhere to get product.'

Beginning in the 1980s, to compete with Japanese manufacturers, U.S. companies became reliant on single suppliers for key parts. It was cheaper to buy in bulk from one outfit than to split orders. Now quake damage has interrupted 25 percent of the world's silicon production because of the shutdown of plants owned by Shin-Etsu Chemical and MEMC Electronic Materials, says IHS iSuppli, an El Segundo (Calif.)-based researcher. The earthquake forced more than 130 plants, mostly in auto and electronics, to close as of Mar. 22, according to data compiled by Bloomberg. Some of the affected factories make items sold directly to consumers; others are sold to manufacturers.

At Dell the world's third-largest personal computer maker, managers are concerned that the supply of optical disk drives and batteries from Japan may be interrupted, according to a person familiar with the matter. Power failures at plants that make silicon wafers could also cause shortages in the computer-chip market in six to 10 weeks, said the source, who asked not to be identified discussing matters involving suppliers. In a statement, Dell said it doesn't 'see any significant immediate supply-chain disruption.'

From a command center in Boeing's Everett factory, engineers can see aircraft production from a window and a 40-foot screen that displays live video from supplier operations, weather reports, and global news. Translators are on hand around the clock. Chicago-based Boeing, which has bought parts from Japan since the end of World War II, found damage at several sites, according to Boeing Japan President Mike Denton, who is working with officials there to get them running. The leading edge of the 787's wings are built at Spirit AeroSystems Holdings in Tulsa and shipped to Mitsubishi Heavy in Nagoya, where the full wings are assembled, then flown to Everett. Boeing and Mitsubishi Heavy use special autoclave ovens to bake composite-plastic sections of the plane and wing skins. Boeing is three years late and billions of dollars over budget on the 787.

Only about 10 percent of companies have detailed plans to deal with supply disruptions, says Lawton, who calls logistics the fastest-growing piece of Dun & Bradstreet's business. Shortages may crop up in other countries as companies seek alternative sources, he adds. Despite the risks, companies won't abandon just-in-time inventory because the cost savings are too great, says James Womack, founder of the Lean Enterprise Institute in Cambridge, Mass. 'Once they grasp the situation and they've got a plan, I would predict they are able to restore a remarkable amount of production very quickly,' he says. 'Never sell Japan short.'

The bottom line: *Japan taught U.S. companies the value of just-in-time supply chains; the crisis has exposed the downsides.*

Business Week (2011) 'Supply chains', 24 March 2011, www.businessweek.com/magazine/content/11_14/b4222017701856.htm

SOME FINAL THOUGHTS ON JUST-IN-TIME

Just-in-time, although a necessary requirement in many industries today, is undoubtedly a delicate, rather fragile system and when things go wrong this can be hugely problematic. Problems include suppliers – and this may not be down to operations management. It may be as a result of poor weather, or Tsunami conditions, which can wreck entire supply chains – as well as the havoc it brings to physical buildings. Also, we have to note that, in an era of sustainability and 'green operations', JIT with its daily high frequency deliveries of the *same type of inventories* in order to minimize stock-holding, may well be challenged because if its lack of sustainability. Pollution and traffic gridlock can often be evident when suppliers have to deliver to very tightly defined delivery schedules. It may well be, therefore, that JIT will have to radically change if the JIT system is to survive, because the business world mentality is very different in the twenty-first century compared with the 1980s and 1990s.

CASE 9.2: THE VIRTUES OF VERTICAL INTEGRATION

Crown Equipment Corp. seems on first impression to be a company that time forgot. Tucked away in the small Ohio town of New Bremen (population: 2,909) that prides itself on its 19th century streetscape, the company has leveraged vertically integrated *manufacturing* facilities to produce products for the mature material-handling *industry*. Yet with its passionate attention to the products it makes and uncommon attention to the needs of the people who use them, the company represents at least one aspect of U.S. *manufacturing's* future: the ability to design, manufacture, distribute and service innovative, high-tech products in mature segments for which buyers are willing to pay a little bit more.

Consider Crown's achievements: the privately held company entered the material-handling *industry* late, in the early 1950s. The last North American entrant to the lift-truck *manufacturing* market, the company thrived amid a consolidating *industry*, rising to become the fifth-largest lift-truck company in the world and capturing the top spot in the electric lift-truck segment. It's now a $1 billion company.

Its financial success is complemented by its innovation and design accomplishments, represented by a substantial list of design awards – including an international award that ranks Crown ahead of such design stalwarts as Audi, Jaguar and Porsche.

Company executives insist that no grand *strategy* or implementation of the latest management trend drives their success. They contend that what might be considered their 'management *strategies*' are simply work processes that work for them, given the company's mission. Take the vertically integrated manufacturing '*strategy*,' for example. The fact that Crown plants produce 85% of the parts in its products came about not because of 'some big strategic thing that we want to be vertically integrated and by golly that's what we're going to do,' says Senior Vice President Don Luebrecht. He notes that executives rarely even employ the term 'vertical integration.' Rather, the company's bias toward in-house *manufacturing* evolves from a 'product-focused, product passionate' mindset, says Mike Gallagher, vice president, Crown Design Center. Vertical integration gives the company 'the ability to cook more of ourselves and this passion into the product,' enabling them to build a product that is more central to the Crown brand.

CASE STUDY

Crown's FC4000 series sit-down counterbalanced electric lift truck, a recent Industrial Design Excellence Award (IDEA) winner, was developed along with a three-wheel model. Having in-house manufacturing, design and engineering helped the company leverage its product development investment over the two products.

Figure 9.15 Crown's FC4000 series sit-down counterbalanced electric lift truck, a recent Industrial Design Excellence Award (IDEA) winner, was developed along with a three-wheel model. Having in-house manufacturing, design and engineering helped the company leverage its product development investment over the two products.

Both men are quick to point out that they and other executives at the company are not adamantly opposed to outsourcing *manufacturing* and other functions. 'We do tend to review these things, and revisit them to make sure we're still competitive,' says Luebrecht.

Most often though, says Gallagher, 'It would be harder to achieve the brand promise with everyone else's supplied content.' Both executives stress that the company's focus on meeting the forklift operator's needs and their emphasis on ergonomics and safety has set Crown apart from its competitors. But it's also created the type of *manufacturing* challenges that few or no outside vendors address. He explains that the company's breakthrough product, Crown's first counterbalance truck introduced in the '70s, is a good example. In developing the lift, the first in the *industry* to combine a multi-function control handle with a side-stance operator position, Crown could have found suppliers to contribute components to the control device but no supplier had the technology to build it. Says Luebrecht, 'That first multi-function handle was an incredible mechanical and electronic combination of things. That combination of things just wasn't around in those days.'

Ultimately, says Luebrecht, the company's intense customer and product focus inspires designers, engineers and production employees at the company to be 'more willing to be challenged and find new ways of solving problems – to sweat the details of each component – than somebody else who is one or two times removed from that feeling. I think at times we've found ways of doing things that weren't impossible in other ways, but [most companies] wouldn't have had the patience or taken the time to get there.'

CASE STUDY

Tight integration between the design and production also accelerates product innovation, say company executives. They note that once they've solved technological or ergonomic challenges for one product, they can quickly adapt the innovation to other products. When the company started development of its three-wheel sit-down counterbalance lift track, the design team all had in mind the future development of a four-wheel model. This allowed them to consider design challenges associated with both applications and essentially address them for both models at the same time.

One question that remains to be answered is whether low-cost, overseas manufacturers will redefine competition in the electric lift-truck *industry* and render the vertical *manufacturing* approach obsolete, as it has in so many other industries. The executives readily admit they are very aware of the possibility, noting that they do not only compete on price: 'We're at the higher end of the price continuum,' notes Joe Ritter, director of marketing. They also allow that they've been somewhat insulated from low-cost competition from overseas: 'The electric lift truck *industry* has not been impacted over the years nearly the way the internal combustion *industry* has with offshore products,' says Ritter. He notes that while low-cost, overseas manufacturers tend to be good at mass *manufacturing*, 'electric lift trucks tend to be more specialized. Our products are not cookie cutter and that's a different challenge for manufacturers, and those challenges have not created opportunities for those other countries in the electric lift truck *industry*.'

No one can say for sure, but many speculate that U.S. manufacturers will survive by producing highly specialized products that do not compete on price, but rather better meet customer needs and provide better customer service. Who knows? Maybe this smallish company, steeped in history and practicing what many think is an outmoded vertical *manufacturing strategy*, just might represent U.S. *manufacturing's* future.

Industry Week (2003) 'The virtues of vertical integration', September 2003, pp. 50–2

SUMMARY

- For many years, inventory management was one of the major contrasts between the Japanese and Western approaches to manufacturing, although there is evidence that many Western firms are improving in the area of inventory management.

- Inventories can, if badly managed, serve as a means of covering problems both in terms of in-house operations and poor supplier performance.

- 'Quick-fix' purchasing formulas (such as EOQ) do not provide any strategic advantage for the firm.

- The firm must concentrate on improving operations performance in order to avoid a 'just in case' approach. In this way inventory costs will decrease and, just as important, the firm's capabilities in terms of delivery reliability, rapid response and flexibility will be greatly enhanced.

- Material requirement planning (MRP), manufacturing resource planning (MRPII), and enterprise resource planning (ERP), can be powerful means of controlling inventory. However, MRP should not be used to 'push' materials through the production system; rather, MRP is a management planning system whereby all components can be planned in advance for a particular time period.

- Just in time (JIT) is part of world-class, strategic manufacturing. However, JIT is not simply about inventory reduction; it is a complete shift from traditional 'push' approaches based around production of large batches (made to stock). Instead, a 'pull' system based upon 'make to order' for customers becomes the focus of production.

- A vital feature of JIT is the buyer–supplier relationship. The 'traditional' buyer *versus* supplier approach makes little sense: instead, the manufacturing firm must concentrate on focusing on key suppliers and forming strategic partnerships with them.

KEY QUESTIONS

1. Why has inventory management emerged as a strategic factor?
2. What is the main difference between a push and pull system?
3. What internal and external capabilities need to be in place for successful JIT?
4. What are the shortcomings of the EOQ 'solution'?
5. Why is ABC analysis of value in relation to buyer–supplier relationships?
6. What role does operations strategy have to play in the example given in Case 9.2?

WEB LINKS

Some of the dangers linked with JIT: www.businessweek.com/magazine/content/11_14/b4222017701856.htm

FURTHER READING

Economist (2006) 'Manufacturing complexity', 17 June 2006, 379(8482), 6–9.

Ellram L.M., Tate, W.L. and Billington, C. (2007) 'Services supply management: The next frontier for improved organizational performance', *California Management Review*, 49(4), 44–66.

Holweg, M. (2007) 'The genealogy of lean production', *Journal of Operations Management*, 25(2), 420–37.

Lincoln, J., Ahmadjian, C. and Mason, E. (1998) 'Organizational learning and purchase-supply relations in Japan', *California Management Review*, 40(3), 241–64.

Sako, M. (2004) 'Supplier development at Honda, Nissan and Toyota: Comparative case studies of organizational capability enhancement', *Industrial and Corporate Change*, 13(2), 281–308.

REFERENCES

Brown S. (1996) *Strategic Manufacturing for Competitive Advantage*, Hemel Hempstead: Prentice Hall.

Brown, S. (2000) *Manufacturing the Future: Strategic Resonance for Enlightened Manufacturing*, London: Financial Times/Pearson Books.

Brown, S., Cousins, P., Blackmon, K. and Maylor, H. (2001) *Operations Management: Policy, Practice and Performance Management*, Oxford: Butterworth Heinemann.

Business Week (2004) 'Hardball is still GM's game', 8 August 1994, (3384), 26.

Business Week (2005) 'A "China price" for Toyota', 21 February 2005, (3921), 50–1.

Business Week (2009) 'Lean and mean gets extreme', 23 March 2009, (4124), 60–2

Business Week (2010) 'Low inventory angers John Deere customers', 26 April 2010, (4176), 29–30.

Business Week (2011) 'Supply chains', 24 March 2011, www.businessweek.com/magazine/content/11_14/b4222017701856.htm

Cerveny, R.P. and Scott, L.W. (1989) 'A survey of MRP implementation', *Production and Inventory Management*, 30(3), 177–81.

Economist (2006) 'Manufacturing complexity', 17 June 2006, 379(8482), 6–9.

Ellram, L.M., Tate, W.L., and Billington, C. (2007) 'Services supply management: The next frontier for improved organizational performance', *California Management Review*, 49(4), 44–66.

Financial Times (2003) 'Kmart probe finds ex-execs behaviour allegedly "grossly derelict"', 29 January 2003, p. 12.

Fortune (2000a) 'The Nightmare Before Christmas', 24 January 2000, 141(2), 24–5.

Fortune (2000b) 'Stepping on the gas believe it! The world's largest auto-parts company is racing to join the new economy', 15 May 2000, 141(10), 265–74.

Fortune (2007) 'How many small businesses does it take to build a jet?', July/August 2007, pp. 42–5.

Fortune International (2009) 'Back in the U.S.A. (Asia)', 28 September 2009, 160(5), p. 30.

Goldratt, E.M and Cox, J. (1986) *The Goal*, New York: North River Press.

Harrison, A. (1992) *Just-in-time Manufacturing in Perspective*, Hemel Hempstead: Prentice Hall.

Holweg, M. (2007) 'The genealogy of lean production', *Journal of Operations Management*, 25(2), 420–37.

Holweg, M. and Pil, F.K. (2001) 'Successful build-to-order strategies start with the customer', *Sloan Management Journal*, 43(1), 74–83.

Hutchins, D. (1999) *Just in Time*, 2nd edition, London: Gower Books.

Industry Week (2000) 'Now it's a job for the CEO', 20 March 2000, 249(6), 22.

Industry Week (2003) 'The virtues of vertical integration', September 2003, 252(9), 50–2.

Industry Week (2004) 'Census of manufacturers shows challenges, reality and, yes, even optimism', 1 January 2004, 253(1), 20–7.

Industry Week (2008a) '12 ways to reduce inventories', September 2008, 257(9), p. 60.

Industry Week (2008b) 'Wal-Mart lays down the law on RFID', (cover story) May 2008, 257(5), pp. 72–4.

Industry Week (2011) 'Recovery not reaching supply chain yet', 20 July 2011, 260(7), 44.

Karmarker, U. (1989) 'Getting control of just in time', *Harvard Business Review*, September/October, 67(5), 122–31.

Krajewski, L. Ritzman, L. (2010) *Operations Management: Strategy and Analysis*, New Jersey: Prentice Hall.

Lee, S. and Schniederjans, M. (1994) *Operations Management*, Boston, MA: Houghton Mifflin.

Lincoln, J. Ahmadjian, C. and Mason, E. (1998) 'Organizational learning and purchase-supply relations in Japan', *California Management Review*, 40(3), 241–64.

Luscombe, R. (1994) 'Getting better all the time', in *Proceedings of BPICS Conference*, Birmingham.

New, S. (2010) 'The transparent supply chain', *Harvard Business Review*, 88(10), 76–82.

Orlicky, J. (1975) *Material Requirements Planning*, New York: McGraw Hill.

Plenert, G. and Best, T.D. (1986) 'MRP, JIT, and OPT? What's "best"?', *Production and Inventory Management*, 27(3), 22–30.

Porter, M. (1980) *Competitive Strategy*, New York: Free Press.

Sako, M. (1992) *Prices Quality and Trust: Inter-firm Relations in Britain and Japan*, Cambridge: Cambridge University Press.

Sako, M. (2004) 'Supplier development at Honda, Nissan and Toyota: Comparative case studies of organizational capability enhancement', *Industrial and Corporate Change*, 13(2), 281–308.

Schmenner, R. (1990) *Production/Operations Management*, New York: Macmillan.

Schonberger, R. and Knod, E. (2001) *Operations Management: Improving Customer Service*, New York: Irwin.

Suzaki, K. (1987) *The new manufacturing challenge: Technqiues for continuous improvement*, New York: Free Press.

TheManufacturer.com (2011) 'Can ERP boost your business's competitive edge?', Zone: IT in manufacturing, April 2011.

Turnbull, P., Delbridge, R., Oliver, N. and Wilkinson, B. (1993) 'Winners and losers: The "tiering" of component suppliers in the UK automotive industry', *Journal of General Management*, 19, 48–63.

Waters, D. (2003) *Operations Management: Producing Goods and Sevices*, Harlow: Addison Wesley.

Wise, R. and Baumgartner, P. (1999) 'Go downstream: The new profit imperative in manufacturing', *Harvard Business Review*, 77(5), 133–42.

Womack, J., Jones, D and Roos, D. (1990) *The Machine That Changed the World*, New York: Rawson Associates.

Zipkin, P. (1991) 'Does manufacturing need a JIT revolution?', *Harvard Business Review*, January–February, 69(1), 40–50.

CHAPTER 10

CAPACITY AND SCHEDULING MANAGEMENT

LEARNING OBJECTIVES

The purpose of this chapter is for you to:

- Understand the strategic importance of capacity.

- Be able to utilize specific approaches to managing scheduling.

INTRODUCTION

Managing capacity is a central feature of strategic operations management. In some ways managing and understanding capacity is twinned with 'process choice' that we discussed in Chapter 7, because understanding both areas can then enable the firm to make informed decisions about what it can and cannot do in the market.

> Understanding capacity is vital because by doing so managers can make strategic decisions about the business, including:
>
> - Whether to take on new commitments and business opportunities;
> - Whether to divest; and
> - Whether or not to increase manufacturing and service capacity levels to deal with changing customer demands.

EXAMPLES OF STRATEGIC CAPACITY

Strategic capacity involves a number of decisions that deal with the relatively long-term positioning of the organization. For example, in manufacturing firms new plants will be allocated and built; or existing plants will be reduced or expanded to meet specific capacity needs in local markets. Many retailers stake out a strategic position in setting up new outlets. In doing so, they create what Porter (1980) describes as an 'exit barrier'. This is where an organization of any type announces that it is in business for the foreseeable future. This has been very evident in recent times in many firms' expansion activities in China and the Far East.

> **Guangqi Honda Automobile, a Honda automobile production and sales joint venture in China, has announced plans to expand its annual production capacity from the current 360,000 units to 480,000 units in China.**
>
> **Guangqi Honda's current overall production capacity of 360,000 units includes 240,000 units at the HuangPu plant and 120,000 units at the ZengCheng plant. The company has decided to double the annual capacity of the ZengCheng plant to 240,000 units by the later half of 2011.**
>
> **To expand its production capacity, the ZengCheng plant will add new equipment. In addition, Guangqi Honda aims to enhance the plant's standing as an environmentally-responsible plant through various improvements including further advancement of the complete wastewater recycling system, which was introduced to this plant in 2006.**
>
> **The total investment for this expansion is expected to be approximately RMB930 million. Guangqi Honda's total employment is expected to be increased from the current 6,800 to 8,000 associates.**
>
> **Combining Guangqi Honda's capacity expansion and the addition of Dongfeng Honda's second plant, scheduled to begin operations in the later half of 2012 with annual production capacity of 60,000 units, Honda's overall annual automobile production capacity in China will be expanded from the current 650,000 units to 830,000 units by the later half of 2012.**
>
> *Datamonitor* (2010) 'Honda to expand automobile
> production capacity in China', 26 May 2010

In high-tech market segments, the need to respond quickly to ever changing demands is critical. This capability has to be part of the operations remit to make sure that the right quantities and speed of delivery are poised and ready to be utilized – and such capabilities have to be part of operations strategy that we discussed in Chapter 2. See the following for an example of such rapid change.

> **The global consumer electronics market (including OEM and retail sales) was valued at approximately $681bn in 2009, a decrease of 1.7% over 2008. Growing at a CAGR of 8.4% during 2005–10, Business Insights anticipates that the size of the global consumer electronics market will remain flat at $681bn in 2010. This flat growth owes to the weakness in the global economy.**
>
> **The fastest-growing products of 2010 will be LED and OLED displays, Ethernet-enabled TVs and receivers, eBook readers, and 3D TVs. Cloud computing and virtualization emerging as the new growth engines.**

Against the backdrop of the global recession, cost competitiveness, technological innovations and emerging markets are the key drivers of the industry's transformational growth. The emergence of South Korean giants – Samsung and LG – as market leaders is commoditizing the industry.

The fall-out of this fierce competition is that companies such as Sony are struggling to retain a foothold in the industry, while other Japanese rivals are diversifying into new growth areas such as environment, energy and infrastructure in order to survive. On the other end of the spectrum there is Apple, which is able to earn huge profits by leveraging on its disruptive innovations, reinforcing the necessity of innovation.

Even in the core hardware industry, technology companies are shifting to services and software in response to the declining margins. Several small M&A deals are facilitating this transition to emerging technologies such as smartphones and specialized software such as business analytics.

Business Insights (2010) 'The top 10 consumer
electronics manufacturers', 21 September 2010

Adding capacity allows firms to position plants and service outlets in key areas around the world. In some cases location may be influenced by industry trends (e.g. in order to develop a fluid labour pool in a certain geographical area). For example, before its merger with Hewlett-Packard, Compaq invested $90 million in order to double its capacity at its Singapore manufacturing plant. In addition, the firm injected a further $11 million into its manufacturing plant in Scotland to enhance the manufacturing capabilities there. These additions to capacity formed part of Compaq's pronounced plan to become the world's leading PC manufacturer. The question of whether this has been actually realized after its merger with Hewlett-Packard remains unanswered.

As we have noted earlier – organizations have to be flexible even with strategic capacity decisions because times and demands change rapidly. For example, Dell Computers doubled the size of its manufacturing plant in Ireland as part of its long term strategic positioning in Europe but then closed the plant.

Capacity expansion can often be targeted within specific countries as illustrated in the example of Pepsi-Cola:

What the Chinese want now are more bottles of Mountain Dew. At least that is the hope of PepsiCo, which says it plans to spend $150 million to expand bottling capacity by a third. That will mean 100 million more cases of Pepsi, 7 Up, and the caffeine-charged Mountain Dew. While the company's annual sales in China have grown at around 10 percent in recent years, it still has only about half the penetration of rival Coca-Cola. PepsiCo executives say they are determined to increase their beverage presence in China, despite the threat of severe acute respiratory syndrome (SARS).

Business Week, 2003

These examples clearly show the strategic intents of those companies that utilize capacity in order to achieve aims of growth and expansion into existing or entirely new areas.

CAPACITY DEFINED AND MEASURED

> ### CAPACITY CAN BE DEFINED AS . . .
>
> The potential output of a system that may be produced in a specified time, determined by the size, scale and configuration of the system's transformation inputs.

At all stages of any process, limitations are placed on capacity. A machine has a maximum output per hour, a truck has a maximum load, a production line has a limit to its speed of operation, an aeroplane has a certain number of seats for passengers, a computer processes a specified number of bytes per second, and so on.

Capacity is therefore normally measured by considering how much can be processed in any given time period. This is commonly the case in materials processing operations, many information processing operations and some customer processing operations (CPOs). For example, a car plant is designed to produce a certain number of cars per shift; the work pattern of an insurance company worker is designed to process a certain number of claims per hour; and fast-food stores expect to be able to serve a certain number of customers in a defined time period (typically at a rate of one every 90 seconds).

Waters (2001) suggests that there is a difference between 'designed capacity', defined as 'the maximum output of a process under ideal conditions', and 'effective capacity', defined as 'maximum output that can be realistically expected under normal conditions'. He explains that effective capacity is usually less than designed capacity, due to set up times, breakdowns, stoppages, maintenance, and so on. Whilst this is true in many cases, especially in materials processing operations, there are instances in which effective capacity may be greater than designed capacity. For example, there are many mass transit systems around the world, such as the London Underground and metropolitan railways in the Far East, where more passengers routinely travel than the system was designed for. Likewise, under normal conditions it might be thought a hotel could sell its rooms only once in a twenty-four hour period but some hotels, those at airports for instance, routinely sell their rooms more than once per day. Overbooking in any setting can be an issue as in the case of one of the author's experience with two airlines in Case 10.1 (extracts from two letters from one of the authors).

CASE STUDY

CASE 10.1: OVERBOOKING AND POOR CAPACITY MANAGEMENT IN THE AIRLINE INDUSTRY – THE CASE OF THE ANGRY PASSENGER

Letter 1

XXX Airlines,
Customer Care Department,

16 June 20XX.

Dear sir/madam,

It is with much regret that I am writing to you to convey our disappointment with the lack of customer care and poor quality of service that we encountered in our last flight from Gatwick to Newark. The facts are as follows:

1. We booked a flight with XXX from Gatwick to Newark on the morning of 29 March. This booking was for 2 adults (my wife and I) and our baby daughter and we had specified that we needed a bassinette for our baby.

2. When we checked in, we were told that that the bassinette would not be offered because we had 'requested' but not 'booked' it – I am at a loss as to what this really means and the distinction between the two terms is meaningless.

3. What became annoying was the dismissive attitude, with comments from your staff that included 'you're not the only family with children' (we didn't assume that we were!) and 'all seat allocations are made on a first come-first served basis'. If this is the case then the question is: what is the point of requesting a bassinette (which in turn demands allocations to specific seating areas on the plane that can house this unit) if this is overridden with a first come-first served basis, regardless of need?

4. More annoyingly, was that we were informed that seats had already been allocated to families with children who had booked in earlier. However, as we later discovered on the plane, when we walked round the body of the plane, this was clearly a lie.

5. When asked why our request had not been honoured, I also had to endure standard nonsense statements about how all airlines overbook. I am a Professor of Business Management with a very good knowledge of the airline industry, and I really do not need to be lectured on the industry.

6. Finally, at the departure gate we were told that we were 'lucky' because the airline had managed to persuade a couple of other passengers to change seats.

To summarize, the issues are as follows:

(a) We had ordered a bassinette, which was evident from the on-screen data, but were then told we had not.

(b) We were, frankly, misled and lied to about seat allocations having been given to other families in the two rows of seats where bassinettes can be located. This was clearly not the case.

I have travelled with XXX on many occasions. However, the nature of the response to this letter will determine the extent to which I, my family, and colleagues will continue to book with you.

We look forward to hearing from you.

Yours sincerely,

To the Airline's credit, there was a response dated 1 July, which included the following: 'Because we value you as a customer, I will forward a tangible token of goodwill under separate cover.'

However, by November, no such 'tangible token' had been offered. Consequently, another letter was sent.

XXXX Airlines,
Customer Care Department,

5 November 20XX

Dear

You may recall that I wrote to you on 16 June and that you responded to my concerns about poor service quality that my family and I were exposed to on the Gatwick/Newark flight in your letter, dated 1 July 20XX.

I appreciate the fact that you responded and in your letter you stated:

'Because we value you as a customer, I will forward a tangible token of goodwill under separate cover'.

As of today, nothing has been forthcoming. This is highly disappointing given the tone and content of your letter.

I trust you will respond by return and I look forward to hearing from you.

Yours sincerely,

A week later, a $50 gift voucher to be redeemed within the airline's shop was sent.

Letter 2

XXXX Airways,
Customer Relations Department
PO Box

12 March 20XX

Dear sir/madam,

I am writing to you to convey my huge disappointment in the poor service quality offered by XXXX on our recent flights to Athens. The facts are as follows:

Flying to Athens 4 March

1. We booked a flight with XXXX from Heathrow to Athens, for 4 March, returning on 8 March. This booking was for 2 adults (my wife and I) and our baby daughter and we had specified that we needed a bassinette for our baby. The reservation for the bassinette was confirmed.
2. When we checked in, we were told, initially, that we would not be able to sit together and the plan was that I would be in row 20 and my wife and child would be in row 27.
3. We were then told that XXXX would be able to accommodate us in row 27, where the bassinette would be.
4. When we boarded the plane we found to our annoyance, that our seat allocations in row 27 were not where the bassinette would be! It took about 15 minutes of fuss, arguments and conflict in order to move seats.
5. To (your) credit we were, finally, moved to the Business Class area and the bassinette was brought on board.
6. The net result to our flight was that we had to endure considerable and unnecessary stress in order to have what had been agreed. It gets worse. . .

Flying to Heathrow 8 March

1. Again, we confirmed that we needed a bassinette for our return flight on 8 March.
2. When we boarded the plane we found that, again, there was a problem. This time there was no bassinette on the plane and we were told, wrongly I believe, that the 757 could not accommodate a bassinette (even though our seats were in front of what was, clearly, a bassinette holder).
3. Your flight attendant, (name provided) showed a great deal of empathy and tried to diffuse the problem.
4. However, again after a great deal of fuss we were moved to Business Class but this time there was no bassinette and my wife was left carrying our child for the full 4-hours flight!

Clearly, the above is unacceptable. We were promised that a bassinette would be available for both flights; we endured a great deal of fuss and stress, which was avoidable and we were left with a poor sense of service quality from XXXX. The fact that we were moved to Business Class did not solve the problem. Indeed, on the return flight we would have preferred to have been in economy class with a bassinette, as clearly agreed, booked, confirmed and paid for!

I have travelled with XXXX on many occasions. However, the nature of the response to this letter will determine the extent to which I, my family, and colleagues will continue to book with you.

We look forward to hearing from you.

Yours sincerely,

On 17 March the following standard reply was provided. It had no address on it and no details of the person who sent the letter:

17 March 20XX

Dear

Thank you for completing our comment card on your flight from Athens.

I understand your disappointment, and I am sorry we could not arrange for you to have the bassinet seat for your child, which you had asked for. We try and make your time in the air as relaxed and comfortable as possible, but I'm afraid we cannot positively guarantee a particular seat to anyone. I do hope you will choose to fly with us again soon.

Yours sincerely
Customer Relations

CASE STUDY

KEY QUESTIONS FROM CASE 10.1

1. Why do airlines typically overbook and what does this say about how they manage capacity in relation to customer expectations?
2. Given the nature of the replies from both of these airlines, which would you choose to fly with and why?

Waters (2001) suggests that 'actual output will normally be lower than effective capacity'. This will certainly be the case if capacity is not managed well. As we shall see, managing capacity is a challenging task, because matching output with effective capacity is very difficult. However, by distinguishing between designed capacity and effective capacity, we can establish the difference between 'utilization' and 'efficiency'. Utilization is the ratio of actual output to designed capacity; whilst efficiency is the ratio of output to effective capacity. In some operations, management focuses very much on utilization. For example, key performance measures in many capacity constrained services, such as hotels, airlines, and theatres, are *utilization measures*, namely room occupancy, passenger load, and seat occupancy. In other operations, especially those adopting high-volume production processes, the focus is often focused upon efficiency measures.

THE IMPORTANCE OF CAPACITY MANAGEMENT

Strategic capacity management – knowing the *maximum* as well as the *attainable* inputs and output capabilities within a period of time – enables the firm to make vital strategic decisions. One of these is to reject potential opportunities. Hill (2000) describes how many firms suffer from the 'can't say no syndrome'. By that he means that, sometimes, firms embark on growth and expansion and take on business for which they have neither the capability nor the capacity to satisfy customers.

In this book, we argue that the aim of operations management is to deliver an offer (often a combination of aspects of both products and services) to the consumer at the time they need it, to an appropriate quality standard, and at a price they are prepared to pay. The role of capacity planning and scheduling management in making this aim possible is to ensure the products and services are available when needed by the consumer. This is achieved by managing processes as efficiently as possible.

The management of capacity focuses on two aspects of the operation.

1. Transformation inputs and their organization into processes. Transformation inputs are those resources used to process the final output. They comprise both hard systems such as plant, machinery, and technology, and the so-called soft systems, which are essentially work processes and human resources. Capacity planning is largely focused on the effective and efficient utilization of these transformation inputs. In operations management terms, at the operations level, this is typically and variously referred to as: capacity planning, aggregate planning, or master scheduling. For separate processes within an operation, capacity management includes activities such as production control, loading or activity scheduling.

2. Ensuring the transformation inputs are utilized efficiently depends on the flow of inputs through the system. This requires the adoption of an appropriate strategy for inventory management. As we saw in Chapter 9, such strategies include inventory management, material requirement planning/manufacturing and resource planning (MRP/MRPII), and just-in-time (JIT) production.

INPUTS AND OUTPUTS OF CAPACITY

We need to make a distinction between outputs and inputs of capacity. They are linked, of course, but we need to focus on each because inputs can act as *constraints* to outputs. One of the key constraints that need to be managed in capacity are bottleneck problems.

Schmenner and Swink's (1998) 'law of bottlenecks' states that productivity is improved if the rate of flow is consistent throughout the whole process. Applying this to manufacturing in job shops has lead to the emergence of a number of rules:

- Throughput is governed by the capacity of the bottleneck;
- Balance material flow rather keep all resources fully occupied;
- Inventory will accumulate at the bottleneck;
- Any decrease in the output of a bottleneck, will be a decrease in the output of the whole system; and
- Any increase in the output of a non-bottleneck will not increase the output of the system as a whole.

Managing bottlenecks is an important feature of scheduling. One solution to this comes from Goldratt and Cox (1986) who speak of 'optimized production technology' (OPT). OPT is, essentially, based around software, aimed at locating and dealing with possible bottlenecks in the system. There are ten principles to OPT.

THE TEN PRINCIPLES OF OPTIMIZED PRODUCTION TECHNOLOGY

1. Balance flow, not capacity.
2. The level of utilization of a non-bottleneck is determined by some other constraint in the system, not by its own capacity.
3. The utilization and activation of a resource are not the same thing.
4. An hour lost at a bottleneck is an hour lost forever out of the entire system.
5. An hour saved at a non-bottleneck is a mirage.
6. Bottlenecks govern throughput as well as inventory in the system.
7. The transfer batch may not, and at times should not, equal the process batch.
8. The process batch should be variable, not fixed.
9. Lead times are the result of the schedule and cannot be predetermined.
10. Schedules should be established by looking at all constraints simultaneously.

THE CAPACITY CHALLENGE

From an internal, resource-management point of view, the first challenge of capacity planning is to maximize utilization and, if this is constrained by process capability, to maximize efficiency. However, there is not much point in producing output if it cannot be sold. The second major challenge of capacity management is therefore fundamentally about matching the productive output of the operation with market demand. These challenges interact. Fluctuating demand increases the challenge of utilization and managing capacity efficiently.

There are two principal variables that need to be managed. These are the total demand for the product/service offering and the range of different product/service offerings being made available to consumers. The former defines the size of the productive capacity of the operation; the latter defines the scope of this capacity. Both of these may change over time. These can be considered as the 4Vs.

> ## THE 4VS OF CAPACITY
>
> *Volume*: total demand for output.
>
> *Variety*: range of output.
>
> *Variation*: change in total demand.
>
> *Variability*: change in demand for each type of output.

In addition to the 4Vs, there are two other factors that impact on capacity management that may increase its complexity. These are the predictability of demand and the 'perishability' of the output. In markets where there is high variation and variability, the complexity of capacity management can be reduced if there is a high degree of certainty about what demand will be. Some firms manage this by 'fixing' the amount that will be produced in a particular period of time, thus creating certainty. This will be made possible by having a master production schedule within a 'time bucket' – a week or month – in which output will be determined and information will then be provided to both suppliers and customers. Likewise, variation and variability are less problematic if the product is non-perishable, since a long shelf-life may enable stocks to be built up as a buffer against variability, even though this may add to costs. These key aspects of capacity planning are summarized in table 10.1.

Back in 1967, Thompson wrote: 'the ideal operation is one in which a single kind of product is produced at a continuous rate and as if inputs flowed continuously at a steady rate and with specified quality', or, in other words, a continuous flow process. In this 'ideal' operation, capacity management is simple – volume is stable, there is no variety (and hence no variability or variation).

Continuous flow processes tend to produce outputs, like petroleum, that are commodities with relatively long shelf-lives for which demand is reasonably predictable over the medium term. A key point to note is that variation, variability, and predictability are inherent features of market forces, whilst perishability is an inherent feature of the output. Firms may try to

Table 10.1 Factors affecting complexity of capacity management

Capacity factors	Straightforward	Complex
Variety	Low	High
Variation	Low	High
Variability	Low	High
Predictability	High	Low
Perishability	Low	High

smooth demand and make their markets more predictable, by for example, introducing a reservation system, but they can only do so if consumers are prepared to accept such influence. Likewise, firms often seek to make their product less perishable to facilitate smoothing production capacity, but their ability to do so is constrained by the physical properties of the output. Variety, on the other hand, is a strategic choice that firms make in relation to the scale and scope of their operations. In the very early days of manufacturing it was recognized that variety added costs, which is one reason that Henry Ford only wanted to make black cars. This is the law of variability, which states 'the greater the random variability, either demanded of the process or inherent in the process itself or the items processed, the less productive the process is' (Schmenner and Swink, 1998).

So far this discussion of capacity has focused on aggregate demand. We know, however, that many operations are made up of complex processes that can be divided into sub-systems. The 4Vs, predictability, and perishability also affect the utilization and efficient performance of each sub-system. Hence capacity and scheduling management becomes more complex the greater the number of different sub-systems and the greater the flexibility of their use.

CAPACITY IN SERVICES

It is in the nature of some services, specifically customer-processing operations, that scale economies are limited because in some cases the firm's physical assets have to be located where the customer is. Thus, whilst manufacturers may be highly selective as to the countries in which they locate their plants, from which to ship their products elsewhere, service firms often need a physical presence wherever they identify sufficient demand for their services. For example, of more than two million hotel rooms operated by the world's major hotel chains, 89 per cent are in just 1,200 locations, typically capital cities, gateway cities (with an international or national airport), and major industrial centres.

Multi-unit operations

A key strategic issue for firms in managing capacity is the extent to which they own and operate their own assets. This is a particularly important issue for firms which need to utilize a large number of assets, specifically buildings. Such firms tend to be in the consumer service companies which operate 'chains' of hotels, restaurants, and retail outlets. In this instance, the property itself and its location are essential elements of the operations strategy. For instance, in the hotel industry Conrad Hilton is famous for identifying the three keys to success in the business – 'location, location, location'.

Such chains have specific characteristics and face particular operational challenges. Firstly, production is geographically dispersed across many units because these are sited close to their market. Secondly, most of these units are small. By definition they cannot be centralized into one large unit in order to achieve economies of scale. Thirdly, production is local. Whilst some back-of-house activity or operation may be centralized, all front-of-house delivery is carried out at the point of contact with the consumer. Fourth, each outlet will be operated within the brand standards established by the chain. Just as manufacturers use brands to assure consumers of the quality of the product wherever it may be bought and consumed, service chains also use branding to assure consumers of the conformity of service in whatever outlet they visit.

Localized, small-scale operations of multiple units present both a challenge and an opportunity (Jones, 1999). The three major challenges are: growing quickly, finding the right sites, and ensuring each outlet satisfies its local market whilst conforming to brand standards. Amongst consumer service firms, rapid growth is desirable for two main reasons. First, new service concepts are easily copied by competitors. Unlike new products, which may be patent protected, it is very difficult to define a service concept and to legally protect this from commercial exploitation by others. In most cases, all consumer service firms can do is copyright the brand name they adopt, and some firms, such as McDonald's, are highly proactive in protecting their brand. Second, sites are difficult to find and rapid growth is desirable to get these before the competition does.

But rapid growth is difficult because the firm may lack the capital and cash flow needed to fund this. Property construction or acquisition is highly capital intensive. A relatively simple new-build 100 room hotel may cost 6 million Euros and a roadside restaurant with 80 covers in the region of 900,000 Euros (Jones, 1999). Many firms, therefore, have adopted franchising as a means by which they can grow rapidly. However, there is evidence to suggest that the higher the investment cost, the higher the risk (Brickley and Dark, 1987). As a result of this, single franchisees (so-called 'Mom and Pop' operators) may be replaced by corporate franchisees. For instance, the British company Whitbread is a corporate franchisee of US-based Marriott Hotels, owning and operating a number of hotels under the Marriott flag throughout the UK.

Franchising has three main advantages. Firstly, the franchisee typically 'owns' and develops the unit. Hence they provide the funding to enable rapid expansion. Secondly, the franchisee is typically local to the community, region or country that the franchisor is expanding into. This local knowledge greatly assists with regards the findings of a suitable site for the outlet. Thirdly, this same local knowledge should also ensure that operations are managed effectively – both in terms of serving local customers as well as operating within the local labour market.

Operations management in multi-unit firms

The third issue faced by multi-unit chains is to ensure each unit is operated effectively and efficiently. In chains which own and operate outlets directly, the operations function has total control over performance in each of the units, usually through the 'area manager' role. How this is specifically achieved depends on a number of dimensions. These dimensions are:

- *Job scope*: this is the range of tasks and responsibilities at area management level;
- *Organizational congruence*: this is the extent to which all managerial levels within the firm share a common vision and work together towards a common purpose;
- *Geographic density*: this is the number of units in an area relative to the size of the area; and
- *Unit conformity*: this is the extent to which units within an area are identical or not.

When Sasser *et al.*, (1978) first proposed the concept of the service firm life-cycle, they drew heavily on the growth of fast food and restaurant chains in the US. Such chains demonstrated characteristics of high market penetration, strongly branded identical units, tightly and narrowly defined job descriptions for area managers, tightly specified standards of performance, effective organization-wide systems and strong organizational cultures. The archetype of this kind of multi-site business is McDonald's. At that time, it can be inferred that area manager effectiveness required relatively narrow, tightly defined job scope, a high degree of organizational congruence, high geographic density, and high unit conformity.

But there is growing evidence from the US that chains are abandoning these established traditions of multi-site management. For instance, at a conference in 1993 the CEO of PepsiCo outlined how he was refashioning the management of Pizza Hut, KFC, and Taco Bell by increasing dramatically (from 12 to 24) the span of control of area managers, empowering managers and employees, flattening the hierarchy, and investing in information technology.

It does not appear that the orientation towards a strategic role for the area manager versus an operational role is sector specific. In one UK study (Goss-Turner and Jones, 2000), the *job scope* of area managers appeared to vary greatly – from those who clearly had a narrowly defined operational role as a line manager, with tasks focused around unit inspection and control, to those with a broad range of responsibilities for developing the business. Indications were that there are two alternative business strategies adopted by firms. The first focuses on achieving high levels of profit through tight control of operating units. The second is more concerned with sales growth and market share through a strategic service vision related to customer service, hence a differentiation strategy. It would appear that multi-unit managers from firms in the first category have a narrower job scope. Again this is not necessarily sector specific. Although the hotel area managers in this study tended to have a narrower job scope than restaurants or pubs, this appears to be a reflection of their strategy, rather than related to the relative complexity of the business at unit level.

An alternative explanation may not be the strategy adopted by the firm but the attitude of the firm to operating in a mature marketplace. Certainly hotels and pubs are mature businesses in some countries, notably the UK, with some kinds of restaurants less so. Baden-

Fuller and Stopford (1994) suggest that two alternative mindsets apply in this context. 'Mature businesses' perceive the industry as stable, believe profitability derives from giving stakeholders less value, regard themselves victims of external economic forces, strive for market share, and seek economies of scale. 'Dynamic businesses', however, seek new ways of operating, give better service to customers, believe profit derives from their own ability to control events, see market share as the reward for creating value not the means of achieving it, and use innovation to compete. There is some evidence that firms like Taco Bell in the US have adopted this dynamic perspective.

Such a shift may have implications for *organizational congruence*. New ways of thinking and operating take a while to develop within firms. This concept of congruence is largely concerned with organizational systems or culture. In one study (Goss-Turner and Jones, 2000) that examined contrasts between the UK and the US, formal systems were most evident in those firms operating UK corporate franchises of international brands originating in the US. On the other hand, one firm stood out as a firm in which cultural norms rather than formal systems dominated. It appears that rather than having both strong systems *and* culture, as is the case with the US archetypes, most firms were strong in one but weaker in the other. The relative lack of strong cultures may relate to the British approach to business, a lack of clear identity in businesses that were franchises of concepts (in restaurants), a very strong tradition of management (in pubs), and few firms operating single concepts. The relative lack of strong systems, especially integrated IT support, may be due to the age of the infrastructure and lack of new-build units in the UK compared with the US. Most firms in the study were investing in IT to address this issue.

Business units may vary in a number of different ways – sales volume, sales revenue, operating capacity, number of employees, and so on. There tends to be a close fit between these factors: the larger the physical capacity of the unit the larger its sales revenue. In firms which have units that vary in size, there is a tendency to adapt the size of an area to reflect this. However, there is no evidence of any formal method, such as a formula or statistical analysis, used to determine the size of areas. According to Goss-Turner and Jones (2000) firms with the highest level of *unit conformity* are those which have grown through new-build or greenfield site development. But most UK chain hospitality businesses, unlike the US, have a relatively old property portfolio, especially in the pub and hotel sectors, which significantly reduces unit conformity.

Reflecting the diverse range of operations within firms, many UK hospitality chains have developed brands, notably in the hotel and pub sectors. Hence there is potential tradeoff in these large firms between geographic density and unit conformity. Areas may be organized with high density but low conformity, or low density and high conformity.

Based on their work (Goss-Turner and Jones, 2000), firms have a *strategic* choice as to how they should organize the operation function in multi-unit chains. There are four types of area manager.

The archetype

Area management in the archetypal multi-site service firm conforms to the McDonald's model – strongly branded identical units, tightly and narrowly defined tasks for area managers, tightly specified standards of performance for units, and an emphasis on operational control over units. The job scope of this type of multi-unit manager is relatively narrow and there is a high degree of organizational congruence, with a focus on operational performance. Firms would like to have high geographic density, as they believe their area managers should be in the units as much as possible.

The entrepreneur

Entrepreneurial area managers are responsible for a single concept, also tightly branded, but are expected to develop the potential of each unit as a business. It is possible in this context for control to be exerted over and by the area manager entirely through cultural norms. Organizational congruence also tends to be culturally driven. Such managers therefore have a wide job scope, applying a range of skills to operating units to reflect local and regional influences.

Multi-brand manager

The area manager in the multi-brand context has more than one concept to manage but does so by applying almost identical 'rules of the game' to them all – namely tight cost controls, standards conformance, and revenue growth. Job scope remains quite narrow, but because the manager is responsible for more than one brand or type of operation, there is more flexibility. In this context achieving high levels of organizational congruence may be difficult. Typically geographic density is high as the rationale for defining an area is based on this.

The business manager

The 'business manager' is responsible for more than one brand and applies creative solutions to each of their units within the context of overarching policy guidelines and marketing strategies. Such managers, like their firms, need to be dynamic. They coach and influence their unit managers, rather than control them. Geographic density is not too great an issue for them as they do not believe they have to spend a lot of time in each unit.

Goss-Turner and Jones (2000) suggest that individual managers could not easily move from one firm to another with different characteristics. For instance, area managers used to operating with high geographic density might dislike managing a large area with long drive-times, those used to tight control over a single brand may be challenged by more strategic responsibility for a number of brands, and those used to a clearly defined job may find a lack of definition and emphasis on cultural norms disquieting. This appears to be confirmed by industry practice, which is for most firms to appoint area managers from within.

Franchisor–franchisee relationships

In firms that have adopted franchising as their approach to growth, the firm still requires units to be operated effectively and efficiently. They want units to be profitable as franchise fees are often based on a proportion of profits, whilst they also want to ensure brand standards are maintained. Rather than have area managers, such firms have franchise managers. Whilst the role these managers play is essentially the same, the means by which they do it is quite different. Franchise managers have to operate in the context of the legal franchise agreement agreed between the firm and its franchisees.

Franchise contracts have many similarities whatever market they may be applied to and whatever country they operate in. The franchisee agrees to operate the business according to policies and procedures laid down by the franchise 'system'. Such a system typically stipulates the products to be sold, inventory items, opening hours, plant maintenance, staffing levels, insurance cover, accounting procedures, and auditing processes. In return the franchisor provides national brand marketing, along with a range of managerial assistance such as help with site selection and development, training, standard operating manuals, and financing. The franchise fees for the right to operate the system and have access to assistance are usually in the form of royalties, such as a percentage of sales. In addition, franchisees are usually required to purchase their raw materials from the franchisor or designated suppliers. The contract will also have clauses in relation to the termination of the agreement by either party. The franchisor typically may terminate the contract if the franchisee operates the unit outside the parameters of the stipulated 'system' and terms of the contract, and there will be constraints on the franchisee in terms of opening a competing business.

In the popular press, the relationship between franchisor and franchisee is often portrayed as coercive – big business controlling and coercing the little guy. For instance, in his book *Fast Food Nation*, Eric Schlosser (2001) talks about conflicts between franchisor and franchisee as 'commonplace', franchisees being 'afraid to criticize their chains' for fear of reprisals or termination of contract, and firms anxious to expand 'encroaching' on the territories of their franchisees (p. 99). This relationship tends to be further supported by the approach adopted by multi-unit forms to monitor and regulate quality in their operations (owner or franchised). The typical approach is to have a mystery shopper scheme, whereby each unit is visited on a random basis by an incognito quality inspector posing as a typical consumer.

In reality, the relationship between the two parties is much more complex than this and firms have a *strategic* choice with regards to how they work with their franchisees. Hunt and Nevin (1974) argued that the franchise relationship is a specific type of distribution channel and that as such power in the relationship may be exercised by the franchisor in five ways: by *coercive* sources (typically enshrined in the contract), and by four *non-coercive* sources, namely reward, expertise, legitimacy, and identification (or referent power). *Reward*-based power derives from one party being able to reward the other to their mutual benefit. A relationship based on *expertise* derives from one party sharing its expertise with the other. *Legitimate* power is based on the one party accepting the right of the other party to exert power over it, whereas *identification* means 'a feeling of oneness' or desire for it between the two parties. Hunt and Nevin (1974) showed that those franchisors that used non-coercive approaches had franchisees that were more satisfied than those who were contracted to coercive franchisors.

It is suggested that the non-coercive style and resultant higher levels of franchisee satisfaction lead to considerable benefits. First, franchisees will have higher morale. Second, cooperation between the two parties will be better. Together this should lead to both better business performance and a higher level of compliance with system requirements. Furthermore, the non-coercive approach will reduce the likelihood of legal action by either party with regard to terminating the contract, filing law-suits, or taking out class actions.

CAPACITY AND SCHEDULING IN MASS SERVICES

During the mass-production era, service operations began to be addressed, initially from the viewpoint that they were becoming more like manufacturing. This view was articulated by Ted Levitt of the Harvard Business School who wrote two seminal articles in 1972 and 1976: 'The production-lining of service' and 'The industrialisation of service', respectively. The success of hamburger fast-food chains, notably McDonald's, in the late 1950s, partly derived from appearing to offer a reasonably wide range of products at different prices, made from a small stock of 'components' and using a small number of processes. So from the same food items (meat pattie, bun, salad items, and sauce), based on identical processes (grilling, toasting, assembly, and wrapping) the basic hamburger could be turned into a cheeseburger by adding a slice of cheese, a Big Mac by including two patties instead of one, and so on. Meanwhile, in manufacturing, many operations adopted various forms of mass customization, as we saw in Chapter 7. However, others required variety reduction programmes in order to remove redundant processes and duplicated components.

In contrast to Levitt's perspective, Sasser *et al.* (1978) suggested some different and new ideas about services. These new ideas originated from their analysis of services as being intangible, heterogeneous, perishable, and 'simultaneous'. Services are 'perishable' in the sense that those not consumed today cannot be stored until tomorrow. As Sasser *at al.* put it: 'a hotel room unused today cannot be sold twice tomorrow'. This perishability derives from the fact that the production and consumption of many services are simultaneous: 'production' only occurs when a consumer arrives to use the service facilities. Such facilities may also have a fixed capacity that derives from the physical infrastructure that delivers the service offer. For instance, aircraft or cinemas have a defined number of seats, hotels a certain number of bedrooms, and schools an optimum class size. Due to the perishability of the service offer, and fixed capacity, there is greater emphasis in services capacity management on managing demand. Hence, from the 1980s onwards there has been a growing synergy between the operations and marketing functions of organizations, especially those delivering services.

These developments lead to a paradox. On the one hand, a growing number of authors and researchers were actively developing theories and models based on the idea that services and manufacture were different. On the other hand, a growing number of practitioners and operations managers were using similar ideas and methods irrespective of whether they were engaged in goods production or service delivery. The reason for this confusion is clear. Often the examples of industrialized services cited in the literature were not pure customer processing operations (CPOs), but had strong elements of materials processing as with fast food, or information processing as with automatic teller machines. Hence it is not surprising that they could be managed like batch production operations. While those that were closer to being true CPOs continued to be operated as job shops like they had always done, albeit with better utilization than before due to better forecasting and priority management.

The adoption of yield management in hotels is a good example of this. In discussing 'priority management' Westbrook (1994) identifies that it is a key element of batch production operations so that organizations 'pursue certain kinds of order to fill capacity . . . and choose which customer orders are to have priority'. A hotel is a particular kind of batch production operation in that it produces a number of rooms available for sale every 24 hours. Its output is therefore highly perishable. Yield management is an approach to priority management which comprises a range of systems and procedures designed to maximize sales of a product or service under more-or-less fixed supply conditions, where the revenue producing ability diminishes with time. The following case illustrates this.

CASE STUDY

CASE 10.2: HOTEL YIELD MANAGEMENT

The Portsmouth hotel is part of an international chain. It has 160 rooms and is located on the south coast of England. The General Manager's performance and that of his hotel are evaluated by the company on the basis of profitability, sales revenue, customer satisfaction, and employee satisfaction. Thus, yield management is the key tool for delivering revenue and contributing to profitability. The General Manager emphasizes the role that strategic decisions have in the yield management system. On an annual basis, a business plan is drawn up that sets sales targets for seven market segments ('premium', corporate, conference, leisure, promotions, tours/groups, and 'special company'). These targets derive from an analysis of the hotel's previous performance, analysis of achieved rate per segment, a competitor analysis, and an environmental analysis. This leads to the setting of rates for these segments, designed with the overall aim of increasing the overall average rate performance.

In 1996, a key decision was made to lower the rack rate significantly, adjust sales mix, and reduce the number of special companies (those with specially negotiated, discounted rates) from 200 down to just 20. This has led to an increase of £4 in the average room-rate achieved, even though the rack rate is £10 lower. The aim is to establish what the manager calls a 'fair price' (or price–value relationship) thereby attracting the right volume of business and negating the need to negotiate price.

The business plan is reviewed on a quarterly basis by the full management team. Rooms performance is specifically reviewed by a group comprising the general manager, sales manager, reservations manager, front-office manager, and financial controller. This group also convenes weekly for a sales strategy meeting. The routine agenda for this weekly event is based around a review of the previous week's performance (rooms sold, occupancy rate, actual revenue, average rate achieved, lost potential sales from declines/denials); a competitor review (five hotels regarded as direct competition are telephoned twice per day to establish room availability and rack-rate offered); a 35-day occupancy forecast by market segment; a monthly financial forecast; and a three-month forecast of occupancy. The meeting analyses the reasons for any deviation from the plan and proposes action to ensure future plans are achieved. Special events, such as (in the case of this hotel) the Whitbread Round the World Race, are also considered and responses to these considered.

These annual, quarterly, and weekly planning meetings enable the reservations manager, who is largely responsible for managing the yield management system, to take appropriate action on a daily basis. Over 80 per cent of the hotel's reservations are taken in the reservations office in the hotel, comprising the manager and two full-time reservationists. Each day, the yield management system presents a report showing the current level of bookings for the next seven-day period by each 'rate category'. These categories are related to, but not identical to, the seven market segments. A is the rack rate, and B to H are different levels of discount on this rate. It is possible for a 'special company' to pay a significantly discounted rack rate, but still be categorized as A, due to the volume of business they provide the hotel. The system also provides a breakdown of what would be 'acceptable' lengths of stay that could be accepted by each of seven rate categories, A to H.

In response to an enquiry, the reservationist establishes the rate category and desired length of stay. If the hotel is near capacity, lower rate categories, such as D to H, are likely to be blocked out, so the reservationist will identify that this rate is unavailable and offer occupancy at whichever category rate is the minimum available. The reservationist may also turn away business at these lower rates if the requested length of stay spans a period during which higher rates are forecast to be achievable. The system can be overridden by anyone taking a booking. A detailed record is kept of these denials (due to the hotel being fully booked or a length-of-stay mismatch) and declines (due to customers not accepting the rate offered). These are regarded as 'lost sales opportunities' and are analyzed at the weekly meeting against the actual occupancy achieved. Such sales may be acceptably 'lost' if the hotel was fully booked or the enquiry was made some time in advance. Recent denials and recent declines (in the previous week) are reviewed if the hotel did not achieve full occupancy. The daily demand forecast can be adjusted by the reservations manager in the light of adjustments to the overbooking policy and policy decisions made at the weekly review meetings. The system is also has a sub-system that enables decisions to be made about conference or group bookings. Based on demand forecasts, the sub-system predicts the sales mix and identifies the potential level of displacement of rack rate. On this basis it advises what rate to propose for the conference.

The core team engaged in yield management is the reservations manager and two reservationists. In terms of strategic decision making, the reservations manager has strong support and encouragement from the general manager, as well as effective cooperation with other members of the hotel's management team. Operationally, the reservations manager liaises with the front office manager and her team, especially with regards to the 10 to 15 per cent of reservations taken through the front office. There is a clear distinction between the level of knowledge and skill displayed by the reservationists compared with the receptionists. The reservations manager undertook a two-week induction course based on simulation exercises before taking up his post, but believes that it took him a further six months to really understand the system. He has personally supervized the training of the reservationists, who have also taken months to become fully competent. The receptionists, on the other hand, have had a minimum level of training. A high proportion of their 'reservations' are actually 'walk-ins' on nights when rooms are available. Given the emphasis on keeping 'lost sales' to a minimum, the reservations manager always follows up a reservation taken by a receptionist that has overridden the system (usually by accepting a lower-rate category).

The yield management team is not directly incentivized. The hotel's management team have a bonus based on their performance, whilst employees are able to collect points towards household goods and other consumables based on their individual performance. However, this company's emphasis on employee satisfaction and the prevalent corporate culture, creates an environment in which good performance is recognized and praised by the general manager down. The technology that supports yield management is based around a central reservations system that enables bookings to be made in the central sales office, or in each individual property. This system advises reservationists on room availability and rate (as described above) and records all the relevant data for a booking to be made. A number of sub-systems use this data to facilitate yield management. These comprise a demand forecasting system, a decline/denial model, guest history database, group demand forecasting system and a travel agency commission system. The chain also has a hotel information system that supports accounts, guest check-in and check-out, audit, and payroll.

STRATEGIES FOR MANAGING CAPACITY

Over time it became clear that there were two basic strategies that operations could adopt when managing capacity. Starr (1978) proposed an 'aggregate planning model' which led to two strategies: either 'vary W [the workforce] so that P [production] matches the demand as closely as possible' or 'do not vary the work force, thereby keeping P constant over time'. This is illustrated in Figure 10.1. Sasser *et al.* (1978) observe that these same strategies may be applied to service operations. Under a chase demand strategy the emphasis is placed on matching output to demand and hence there is a need to forecast demand. In the level capacity strategy the emphasis is on maximizing utilization.

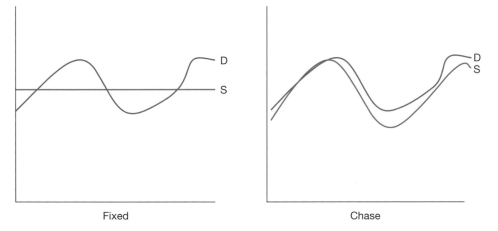

Figure 10.1 Fixed capacity and chase demand

Managers are faced with decisions about matching demand with supply in capacity and these are for both short-term and longer, more strategic, decisions on capacity. The three types of capacity (see Figure 10.2) are:

- *Lead*: adding capacity in advance of demand growth;
- *Lag*: adding capacity after demand growth; and
- *Average*: trying to maintain average capacity.

The first of these, 'lead' capacity, can be a sign of aggressive growth from an organization whereby it will 'stake out a position' geographically and actively create demand. Japanese transplants have been hugely successful at doing this, and some types of pharmaceutical and biotechnology capacity management is handled in this way. 'Lead' capacity can be viewed as a 'risk-seeking' strategy.

The second, 'lag' capacity, is a more reactive, risk-averse approach whereby an organization responds to specific demands. It is, nonetheless, a powerful approach. For example, the tragedy of the Aids epidemic has caused some pharmaceutical companies to increase capacity in response to this tragic phenomenon.

The third type, 'averaging' capacity, is typically used within service organizations to smooth out the relationship between demand and supply. As we have mentioned earlier, some services cannot store capacity and so the key task is to match demand with supply so that capacity requirements are met on both sides.

Further strategies that are used across organizations to manage fluctuations in demand and supply are:

- Providing the same level of supply, no matter what the demand level. This strategy may be called *demand smoothing* in service operations, or *level production* in manufacturing operations.

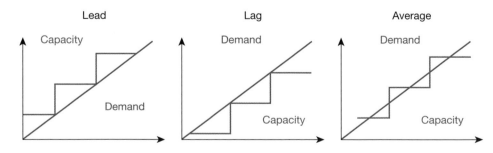

Figure 10.2 Three strategies in managing capacity

- Exactly matching the level of supply to the level of demand. This strategy is usually called *chase demand*.
- Adjusting demand to better match supply. This strategy is called *demand management*.

'Level capacity' strategies (see Figure 10.3) are used by organizations to match demand and supply, to produce and store outputs in advance of demand. These strategies rely on building inventory. Other types of operations – such as service operations – have only limited recourse to inventory-building strategies. In many service organizations mismatches between supply and demand will result in queues.

'Chase' strategies (see Figure 10.4) are used by organizations to adjust their activity levels to reflect the fluctuations in demand.

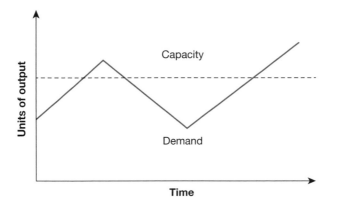

Figure 10.3 A level capacity strategy

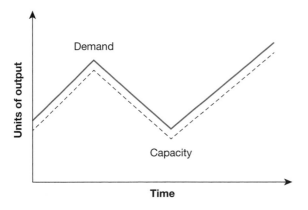

Figure 10.4 A chase capacity strategy

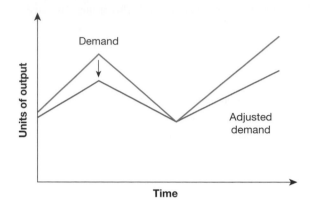

Figure 10.5 A comparison of the three types of capacity management policies

'Demand management' strategies (see Figure 10.5) are used by organizations to try and change demand in order to smooth high and low periods.

According to Shore (1973) the 'essence of aggregate planning is to devise a strategy by which fluctuations in demand can be economically absorbed'. In this sense, this approach to capacity management is largely concerned with managing volume and reducing or controlling the impact of variation through improved predictability. The focus is therefore on forecasting.

The two stages of aggregate planning are firstly to add together all productive output to arrive at a total level of production (the equivalent of what we have called 'volume') and secondly to predict or forecast the fluctuations in this output (what we have called 'variation'). De facto, therefore, this approach eliminates, or rather ignores, variety and variability.

Once a strategy or aggregate plan has been drawn up, it has to be put into practice. In manufacturing, especially where high-volume batch or line processes are in place, this is usually through a master production schedule. Such a schedule includes information about promised delivery dates, resources and materials needed, assembly capacity, set-up costs, and inventory. The particular approach will depend on the competitive priorities of the organization. Those with a make-to-stock strategy schedule production of output or end items, those with a make-to-order strategy schedule inputs or purchase items, and those with an assemble-to-order strategy schedule assemblies to capitalize on making common components for various output items.

Although volume, variety, variation, and variability are derived from finished output, they feed back through each stage in the production process. Likewise, prediction about finished output leads to prediction about each stage of the process, while there may be perishability of components at each stage of the process. The 'make or buy?' approach to capacity management reduces variety with regard to inputs and in-process activity by shifting production to suppliers. Often the final stage of the process is the assembly of components. Hence the 'make or buy?' decision identifies the extent to which a process should also include the 'manufacture' of these components. By outsourcing the production of some or all of component production, the variety of sub-processes within the operation is reduced, and just as capacity may be more easily managed if the variety of output is reduced, so it is if the variety of process is reduced.

The profound implication of outsourcing for capacity planning is the shift from a process that is controlled within the operation to one that requires coordination with suppliers. The growth of so-called 'supply chain management' during the 1980s (although as we saw in Chapter 3 it is perhaps better to think in terms of networks, rather than chains) indicates the extent to which this was increasingly identified as a key aspect of operations management. Operations have always been faced with the challenge of deciding whether or not to use raw materials or processed materials supplied by intermediaries. Even the archetypal job shopper, the blacksmith, did not smelt his own ore to produce iron. The key difference in managing capacity that was adopted was the idea of a strategic approach to outsourcing, from which supply chain management emerged. Decisions about whether to make or buy therefore shifted from consideration about individual items on a piecemeal basis, to decisions about whole groups of components and whole sets of processes.

THE CAPACITY/SCHEDULING INTERFACE

We have deliberately spent much of this chapter discussing types of capacity. Capacity has clear strategic consequences but it is also linked to day-to-day scheduling. In essence the link between capacity and scheduling is one of timing, as can be seen in Figure 10.6.

SCHEDULING METHODS

Given that operations scheduling is so important for utilization and efficiency, order sequencing, or as Westbrook (1994) terms it 'priority management', is essential. From the

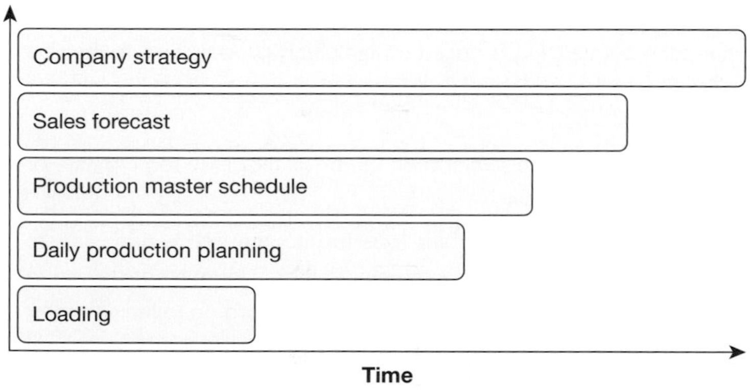

Figure 10.6 Links between long-term capacity and daily scheduling

craft era onwards, order sequencing has been determined using a range of criteria. Informal scheduling methods include those in the box below.

EXAMPLES OF INFORMAL SCHEDULING METHODS

- Giving priority to the best customer. For instance, hotel clients (often large companies) that provide a high number of bed nights are not only given a discounted room rate but also 'last room' availability.
- Prioritizing emergency cases. This applies particularly in medical circumstances, such as accident and emergency departments, which often have a 'triage' system.
- Giving in to pressure from the most demanding customer.

Other 'good ideas' of scheduling based on systematic order sequencing can include those in the box below.

EXAMPLES OF SYSTEMATIC ORDER SEQUENCING SCHEDULING METHODS

- *First come, first served*: this is the fairest system, and is often applied where people are processed through the operation.
- *Earliest due date.*
- *Shortest or longest total processing time*: this is based on the idea of getting jobs that take the least, or most, time out of the way.
- *Least slack time*: this sequencing is based on matching process time to the due date so that the finished output can be shipped to the customer as quickly as possible.
- *Least changeover cost*: jobs are selected on the basis that they require little or no machine set-up or changeover.
- *Shortest first/last operation first*: enables jobs to become active and aims to make good utilization of plant. The problem is that it can create work in process and bottlenecks at later stages. Loading jobs according to their shortest last operation attempts to ensure that jobs are not held up at the point where most cost has been accrued (i.e. at the last stage). Once again, though, this can cause bottlenecks at earlier stages of the overall process.

- *Critical ratio*: this is determined by dividing the time to due date by the process time. Less than one means that the job will finish after the promised delivery date. In this situation, steps can be taken to reduce process time through employee overtime and so on. Orders are sequenced by the lowest critical ratio.

Scheduling is an art and not just a science brought about by software calculations. What operations managers must do is to understand the strategic consequences of scheduling so that customers are satisfied, at the same time as making the best use of limited resources. No software solution provides a 'perfect answer' to this tension because there will always be tradeoffs in making a judgement on 'what gets scheduled first' – either in terms of one customer over another; or one process over another. This calls for knowledgeable operations managers who can see beyond 'solutions' and who can make wise scheduling decisions based on sound business skills when scheduling takes place.

CASE 10.3: FINANCIAL SERVICES

The provision of financial services such as banking, mortgages, and insurance have been transformed in recent years by the increase in power of desktop computing and the development of the information superhighway. Many 'virtual' firms have entered the market, without the physical retail infrastructure of their predecessors. These firms have radically transformed this sector.

They have been able to handle significantly higher volumes of business through access to sophisticated databases. Customers making a telephone enquiry need only cite their postcode (or zip code) for detailed information about the enquirer to be revealed to the telesales operator. This also reduces the transaction time through accelerated data entry.

But the same databases may also hold considerably more information. Insurance companies are now able to 'customize' individual home insurance policies based on postcode data which identifies the level of crime and hence risk for any given area, along with the detailed information provided by the customer as to the content of their properties. Again standardized data entry enables swift data entry, along with highly individual policy production.

Claim processing has also become very much more flexible and responsive to customer needs, while at the same time reducing costs. Claims settlements has traditionally comprised two stages – an assessment of the damage sustained, usually determined in the field by a loss adjuster, and processing of the associated paperwork and issuance of the cheque, usually centrally processed in batches back-of-house. Today it is possible for loss adjusters to be equipped with technology that enables them to respond to claims immediately, travel to the claimant, assess the claim, process the documentation and issue the cheque, all within three hours of the accident occurring. This combination of mobile computing

CASE STUDY

CASE STUDY

and telephony also enables the adjuster to liaise with other service providers that the claimant may need, such as in the case of a car accident a towing vehicle, medical treatment, and overnight accommodation. This form of provision adds considerable value, customizes the experience, and is relatively cheap to provide with the right kind of technological support.

The same information that enables insurance policies or mortgages to be customized, also enables these firms to engage in more effective marketing of other products or services to the point where the concept of one-to-one marketing has emerged. Information about the age, sex, residence, and particularly spending habits of the customer, identify key lifestyle changes that may trigger new sales opportunities for financial services firms. For instance, the regular purchase of airline flights might signal the opportunity to sell travel insurance or travellers' cheques.

SUMMARY

- Capacity management is based on understanding the specific characteristics of volume, variety, variation, variability, predictability, and perishability.
- There are two main strategies available for managing capacity – level capacity or chase demand.
- Early operations management approaches to capacity were based on order sequencing, scheduling activities, and process control. Materials management was based around economic order quantities, standardized components, and inventory control.
- It is erroneous to assume that because some approaches to capacity planning were developed early in the twentieth century they are no longer relevant to today. There are many operations, businesses, and even sectors that continue to need and indeed use these methods.
- Such operations are often small-scale, owner-operated in sectors with some technology that has remained largely unchanged.
- There are some 'good rules of scheduling' that can be used as a guide.
- It is always vital to remember that there is no such thing as a perfect solution when scheduling and the process has to be based on sound business reasons and not driven purely by software calculations.

KEY QUESTIONS

1. How well do firms really understand the 4Vs of their business and the concepts of perishability and predictability?
2. How should firms go about making the choice between improving their existing approach to capacity and scheduling management or radically changing their process to reconfigure the notion of capacity?
3. Why is it strategically important to understand global capacity and industry capacity?

4. Apply any five approaches to scheduling to an organization of your choice – what were the challenges you faced in doing so?

5. 'There are no prefect solutions in scheduling.' Why is this the case and what can be done to help manage scheduling strategically?

FURTHER READING

Buxey, G. (2005) 'Aggregate planning for seasonal demand: Reconciling theory with practice', *International Journal of Operations and Production Management*, 25(11), 1083–100.

White, D.L., Froehle, C.M. and Klassen, K. (2011) 'The effect of integrated scheduling and capacity policies on clinical efficiency', *Production and Operations Management*, 20(3), 442–55.

REFERENCES

Baden-Fuller, C. and Stopford, J. (1994) *Rejuvenating the Mature Business*, London: Routledge.

Brickley, J.A. and Dark, F.H. (1987) 'The choice of organisational form: The case of franchising', *Journal of Financial Economics*, 18, 401–21.

Brown, S. (1996), *Strategic Manufacturing for Competitive Advantage*, Hemel Hempstead: Prentice Hall.

Business Insights (2010) 'The top 10 consumer electronics manufacturers', 21 September 2010, 34–6.

Business Week (2003) 'Mountain Dew wants some street cred', 6 September 2003, (4277), 24–7.

Buxey, G. (2005) 'Aggregate planning for seasonal demand: Reconciling theory with practice', *International Journal of Operations and Production Management*, 25(11), 1083–100.

Datamonitor (2010) 'Honda to expand automobile production capacity in China', 26 May 2010.

Fortune (2002) 'Fast food, slow service', 30 September 2002, 146(6), 38.

Goldratt, E.M and Cox, J. (1986) *The Goal*, New York: North River Press.

Goss-Turner, S. and Jones, P. (2000) 'Multi-unit management in service operations: Alternative approaches in the UK hospitality industry', *Tourism and Hospitality Research: The Surrey Quarterly Review*, 2(1), 51–66.

Hill, T. (2000) *Manufacturing Strategy*, Basingstoke: Macmillan.

Hunt, S.B. and Nevin, J.R. (1974) 'Power in a channel of distribution: Sources and consequences', *Journal of Marketing Research*, 11, 186–93.

Jones, P. (1999) 'Multi-unit management in the hospitality industry: A late twentieth century phenomenon', *International Journal of Contemporary Hospitality Management*, 12(3), 155–64.

Levitt, T. (1972) 'Production-lining service', *Harvard Business Review*, 50(5), 41–52.

Levitt, T. (1976) 'The industrialisation of service', *Harvard Business Review*, September/October, 54(5), 63–74.

Porter, M. (1980) *Competitive Strategy*, New York: Free Press.

Sasser, W.E., Olsen, M. and Wyckoff, D.D. (1978) *The Management of Service Operations*, Boston, MA: Allyn & Bacon.

Schlosser, E. (2001) *Fast Food Nation*, London: The Penguin Press.

Schmenner, R. (1990) *Production/Operations Management*, New York: Macmillan.

Schmenner, R.W. and Swink, M. (1998) 'On theory in operations management', *Journal of Operations Management*, 17, 97–113.

Schonberger, R. (1986) *World Class Manufacturing*, New York: Free Press.

Shore, B. (1973) *Operations Management*, New York: McGraw-Hill.

Starr, M.K. (1978) *Operations Management*, Englewood Cliffs: Prentice-Hall.

Suzaki, K. (1987) *The New Manufacturing Challenge: Technqiues for Continuous Improvement*, New York: Free Press.

Thompson, J.D. (1967) *Organisations in Action*, New York: McGraw-Hill.

Waters, D. (2001) *Operations Management*: *Producing Goods and Services*, Harlow: Addison Wesley.

Westbrook, R. (1994) 'Priority management: New theory for operations management', *International Journal of Operations and Production Management*, 14(6), 4–24.

White, D.L., Froehle, C.M. and Klassen, K. (2011) 'The effect of integrated scheduling and capacity policies on clinical efficiency', *Production and Operations Management*, 20(3), 442–55.

CHAPTER 11

MANAGING SERVICE OPERATIONS

INTRODUCTION

We mentioned in Chapter 1 how important it is for operations and marketing personnel to work closely together in order to ensure success. In service environments the relationship between these two functions is critical and, without it, the service offer will either fail or be weakened. What, though, is a service? It's not quite as straightforward as we might think, as the following confirms:

> Despite more than 25 years of study, scholars do not agree on what a service is. . . . The problem is trying in a few words to describe 75% of the economic activity of developed nations.
>
> (Haywood-Farmer and Nollet, 1991, p. 5)

DEFINING SERVICES

The concept of service has been defined in different ways. Grönroos (2001, p. 7) defines the service concept as:

an activity or series of activities of a more or less intangible nature that normally, but not necessarily, take place in the interaction between the customer and service employees and/or physical resources or goods and/or systems of the service provider, which are provided as solutions to customer problems.

Edvardsson *et al.* (2005, p. 107) add to our understanding by suggesting that the three core dimensions in this definition are:

- Activities;
- Interactions (which we could say are what separate services from physical products); and
- Solutions to customer problems.

Others have provided insights into the nature of services. For example, Johnston and Clark (2001) define the service concept as:

- *Service operation*: the way in which the service is delivered;
- *Service experience*: the customer's direct experience of the service;
- *Service outcome*: the benefits and results of the service for the customer; and
- *Value of the service*: the benefits for the customer.

So the key elements here are operation, experience, outcome, and value. These elements are important for managers to bear in mind when managing service operations.

Further, a very insightful definition of a service comes from Fitzsimmons and Fitzsimmons (2007, p. 5):

A Service is a Time-perishable, Intangible Experience Performed for a Customer Acting in the Role of a Co-producer.

So the key factors here are that services tend to be:

- Time perishable (but not all aspects of the service will be);
- An intangible experience; and
- Co-produced between the provider and recipient of the service.

This aspect of co-production is something that we will explore further in this chapter, because it provides important clues as to how service operations management has changed over time.

Before then, we present a case that shows some of the dangers with service operations. Without being too dismissive, some service operations have a low barrier to entry (Porter, 1980). This means that competitors are able to enter industries with relative ease and compete aggressively. Also, the other danger for services is that many aspects of services are easy to copy. This is a big danger in retail, as Case 11.1 shows.

CASE 11.1: CHINESE RETAILERS HIJACK THE IKEA EXPERIENCE

Nestled in a sleepy southern district of Kunming city in southwest China, is a 10,000 square meter, four-story building that could make Swedish furniture giant Ikea uneasy.

11 Furniture, as the store is known, copies Ikea's blue and yellow color scheme, mock-up rooms, miniature pencils, signage and even its rocking chair designs. Its cafeteria-style restaurant, complete with minimalist wooden tables, has a familiar look, although the menu features Chinese-style braised minced pork and eggs instead of Ikea's Swedish meatballs and salmon.

This knock-off Ikea store is emblematic of a new wave of piracy sweeping through China. Increasingly sophisticated counterfeiters no longer just pump out fake luxury handbags, DVDs and sports shoes but replicate the look, feel and service of successful Western retail concepts – in essence, pirating the entire brand experience.

'This is a new phenomenon,' said Adam Xu, retail analyst with Booz&Co. 'Typically there are a lot of fake products, now we see more fakes in the service aspect in terms of (faking) the retail formats.'

Brands are much more than a logo on a handbag or some half-eaten pipfruit on a computer.

Many of the most successful consumer companies have invested millions in promoting and building brands which encapsulate ideals, values and aspirations, creating valuable and loyal customer bases that sometimes border on cults.

Last month, an American blogger set off a media storm after she posted pictures of an elaborate fake Apple Store in Kunming, selling genuine if unauthorized iPhones, Macbooks and other widely popular Apple products.

Desirable brands

The presence of the fake stores in Kunming highlights China's seemingly insatiable appetite for western brands in some consumer segments that have not been tapped, particularly in smaller cities far from the affluent eastern seaboard.

'What these fake stores indicate is that there is demand for the types of products and concepts that these brands sell,' said Hong Kong-based Torsten Stocker, a China retail analyst with Monitor Group.

The problem for companies that have been faked is that even if the fake stores sell genuine products, the brands have no control over how customers experience their brands.

Zhang Yunping, 22, a customer service representative at 11 Furniture, is used to the questions about Ikea.

'If two people are wearing the same clothes, you are bound to say that one copied the other,' Zhang said, shrugging her shoulders. 'Customers have told me we look like Ikea. But for me that's not my problem. I just look after customers' welfare. Things like copyrights, that is for the big bosses to manage,' she said.

11 Furniture's owner could not be reached for comment.

Ikea said it has teams working at both the country and global level to handle intellectual property protection issues. 'Ikea as one of the biggest home furnishing companies in the world, protecting Ikea's intellectual property rights is crucial,' Ikea China said in a statement to Reuters.

At 11 Furniture – its Chinese name 'Shi Yi Jia Ju' sounds very much like Ikea's Chinese name 'Yi Jia Jia Ju' – furniture is made to order, not flat-packed as it is at Ikea.

Customers also notice other differences. Ikea has nine stores in China, most of them in the wealthier coastal and southern cities. Xiao Lee, a Kunming resident who was shopping at 11 Furniture for a bedroom wardrobe with her husband, had visited Ikea stores in Beijing and Shanghai.

'I thought of shipping their products from the real Ikea store by cargo, but I thought that would be too troublesome so I came here,' Lee said.

'At the real Ikea, the layout is much neater and the decorations are laid out properly, you really can't compare them,' she said.

Loving Mickey, courting Nike

Sometimes telling the difference between fake and real is not so easy.

'My favorite character is Mickey Mouse,' said Ling Xiao, a six-year-old girl walking out of a Disney Store along Kunming's popular pedestrian-only shopping street Zhengyi Road.

Ling Xiao and her mother shop at the Disney store about once a month and they have been going there for the past few years to browse for Mickey Mouse handbags and accessories.

'It should be real; it has been here a long time. I prefer coming to this store because it sells a big variety of toys,' said Ling Xiao's mother, who declined to be named. Apart from Disney products, the store sells poorly made Angry Bird soft toys of dubious origin.

A Walt Disney spokeswoman said there are over 6,000 points of sale for Disney branded goods in China. Disney confirmed the store is legitimate, declining to elaborate further.

Outside a Nike store on the same retail strip, Han Zhimei, a 17-year-old student, looks longingly at a 'Help Wanted' sign posted in the store's window.

'I feel their stores have a spirit of teamwork and I really like the Nike brand,' said Han, who sports a trendy asymmetrical haircut. Han stopped by to apply for a job at Nike.

When asked how she knows the store is a legitimate reseller and that the goods are real, she pauses before answering. 'Well, it's a Nike store, so the things in there should be real. I think people will be honest about these things and we should have brand loyalty,' Han said.

On Zhengyi Road alone, there are four Nike stores, all claiming to be legitimate. A check with Nike's store locator brought up three stores in that street, meaning at least one is fake.

A Nike spokesman said the issue of unlicensed stores was part of the broader challenge of combating counterfeiting in China. 'We take the protection of our brand very seriously and have a variety of protocols in place,' he said. The jumble of real and fake stores in lower tier cities across China makes it hard for companies such as Apple, Disney, Nike and more so Ikea, which are closely identified with their outlets, to exert control over their brand image.

Companies such as Starbucks Corp have long battled copycats in China, but the shift to imitations of the likes of Ikea presents a new set of challenges.

'The store is a key element of the brand, so faking it, in particular in a way that consumers don't recognize as a fake, is impacting the brand image and reputation,' said Stocker.

Apple, which had its brand valued at more than $150 billion earlier this year, declined to comment.

Who protects your IPR?

For those setting up the fake, unauthorized or pirated goods stores, the attraction is obvious.

'We don't need to advertise, everyone has heard of Disney,' said Dong, a 23-year-old store supervisor at a Walt Disney retail store a stone's throw from where Ling Xiao and her mother were shopping.

That brand recognition has far outstripped the ability of companies to expand fast enough to tap demand exploding in inland China.

Sportswear brands such as Nike, Adidas and Li Ning, which have been in China for many years, are the leading fashion choice for those residing in less wealthy cities like Kunming, said a Boston Consulting Group report last month.

As the world's second-largest economy races forward, the number of middle-class affluent households is expected to hit 130 million by 2020 from 50 million in 2010, BCG said. These factors are fueling the race for brands like Nike and Adidas to open stores in less wealthy Chinese cities. Ikea has said it will open an average of one to two stores a year in China. 'Many foreign brands are already aware of the importance of lower tier cities but they are trying to figure out a way to go to market in these cities,' said Xu of Booz&Co.

In some cases, beating them to the punch are the Chinese pirates who, once established, may be hard for foreign companies to get shut. Chinese law prohibits firms from copying the 'look and feel' of other companies' stores, but foreign companies must register their trademarks with China and enforcement is often spotty.

The United States and other Western countries have often complained China is woefully behind in its effort to stamp out intellectual property (IP) theft.

'Foreign companies often expect the Chinese government to handle their enforcement for them and though they sometimes will, they also sometimes will not,' said Dan Harris, a lawyer with Harris & Moure and co-author of China Law Blog.

'The problems often arise from the fact that the damages are often quite low and the Chinese courts do not have a lot of power to make sure their own judgments are enforced,' Harris said.

Back at 11 Furniture, it is apparent that copying Ikea's ideas may not be enough to win over all consumers.

Examining cushion covers at 11 Furniture, Ms. Zhang, a woman in her fifties, sniffs derisively.

'The designs don't look like typical Chinese designs. It's not what everyday Chinese people would use,' Zhang said, pointing to a checkered cushion cover. 'It looks too fancy.'

Reuters (2011) 'Who protects your IPR? Chinese retailers hijack the Ikea experience', 1 August 2011, www.reuters.com/article/2011/ 08/01/us-china-brand-piracy-idUSTRE77017720110801

KEY QUESTION FOR CASE 11.1

With reference to Case 11.1, what can IKEA (and other firms) do when faced by competitors that simply copy their model of service operations?

PERCENTAGE OF WORKERS IN THE SERVICE SECTOR: 1960 TO 2005

There can be no doubt that there has been a remarkable rise in the number of people employed in a range of sectors related to services. We might think this to be the case with, for example, the UK and US economies. However, the growth in the number of service sector employees has been worldwide, including countries that we might associate with manufacturing, for example Germany and Japan. This growth in services was noted as far back as 1972 when Levitt stated that 'we're all in services now' (1972, p. 72).

Grönroos claims that 'every business is a service business' (2000, p. 5) and that 'the product . . . becomes just one element in the total, ongoing service offering' (ibid). We shall develop the importance of *combining* products with services in the next section. Before then, here are some examples of the importance of the service sector across the world. Table 11.1 shows the dramatic rise in the percentage of workers in the service sector since 1960.

Clearly, the rise of the service economy is worldwide. Today, over 75 per cent of US employment is in services. Further statistics from the service sector can be gained from the following US Department of Labor website: www.bls.gov.

Some would suggest that a great deal of innovation resides within service sectors. As Möller *et al.* (2008, p. 34) state:

Table 11.1 Percentages of workers in the service sector

Percentage of workers in the service sector

Country	1960	1965	1970	1975	1980	1985	1990	1995	2000	2005
United States	58.1	59.5	62.3	66.4	67.1	70.0	72.0	74.1	76.2	78.6
United Kingdom	49.2	51.3	53.6	58.3	61.2	64.1	66.7	71.4	73.9	77.0[a]
The Netherlands	50.7	52.5	56.1	60.9	65.1	68.3	69.5	73.4	75.2	76.5[b]
Canada	54.7	57.8	62.6	65.8	67.9	70.6	72.4	74.8	74.9	76.0
Australia	n/a	54.6	57.3	61.5	64.9	68.4	70.5	73.1	73.9	75.8
Sweden	44.6	46.5	53.9	57.7	62.9	66.1	67.9	71.5	73.4	75.6[a]
France	40.7	43.9	48.0	51.9	56.3	61.4	65.6	70.0	72.9	73.4[a]
Japan	41.9	44.8	47.4	52.0	54.8	57.0	59.2	61.4	64.3	68.6
Germany	40.2	41.8	43.8	n/a	52.8	51.6	45.0	60.8	64.3	67.4[a]
Italy	33.4	36.5	40.1	44.0	47.7	55.3	58.6	62.2	64.9	65.5[a]

Notes:
a Most recent year is 2004.
b Most recent year is 2002.
Source: U.S. Bureau of Labor Statistics www.bls.gov (02 October 2006), U.S. Department of Labor Statistics, Comparative Civilian Labor Force Statistics, Ten Countries, Table 6 in Civilian Employment Approximating U.S. Concepts by Economic Sector.

We are in the midst of a service-driven business revolution. Innovative service providers such as Google, MySQL, and Skype strive to promote service co-production with customers, as services become the key value drivers for companies. This is evident in the current list of Fortune 500 companies, in which the share of revenue derived from services has increased considerably over the past few decades. This service-driven revolution has powered an economic boom in which the majority of economic activity consists of services.

However, like manufacturing, some services are in danger of being outsourced and offshored as Youngdahl, *et al.* (2010, pp. 798–9) explain:

Offshoring of service processes and knowledge-based activity has redrawn the operations management landscape in first decade of the twenty-first century. . . .

These processes span routine back-office functions and call centers (business process offshoring, BPO) to focused research support functions (knowledge process offshoring, KPO). McKinsey, the global consulting company, estimated that the total addressable market for offshore services would reach close to $300 billion by 2010 [. . .] More recently, Gartner Research reported that by 2012, revenues of $239 billion were expected in the area of BPO alone.

Clearly, this trend represents a threat to some companies and, when many companies have their operations outsourced, this has implications for the economic wellbeing of entire nations. This is because, as indicated in Figure 11.1, the contribution from services to global economies is considerable.

Figure 11.1
Contribution of
services industries
to global GDP

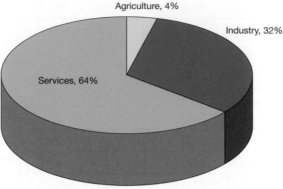

Source:
The World Factbook 2007, Central Intelligence Agency, https://www.cia.gov/library/
publications/the-world-factbook/fields/2012.html, accessed January 2008.

Figure 11.2
Anticipated growth
in wage and salary
employment in
selected industries,
2008–2018

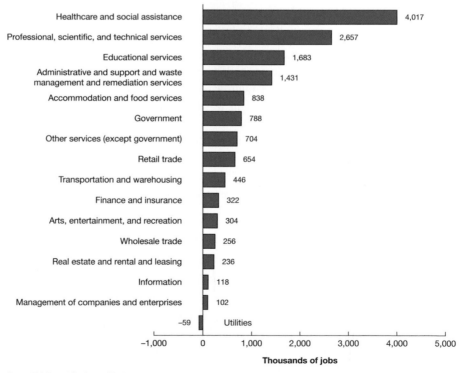

Numeric change in wage and salary employment in service-providing
industries, 2008–18 (projected)

Source: BLS National Employment Matrix

Figure 11.3 An indication of the range of service sectors
Hoffman *et al.* (2009)

As can be seen from Figure 11.2, the anticipated growth in services is set to continue with the increase growth in a number of key sectors likely to be huge.

As we see in Figure 11.3, the range of service sectors is wide and each particular segment demands that segment-specific operations capabilities are in place to serve the needs of customers, clients, and other key stakeholders.

THE EXPERIENCE ECONOMY

An important development related to services has been the emergence of what is termed the *experience economy*. This concept has developed from the recognition that customers do not buy 'a product' or 'a service' but, instead, purchase 'experiences' that include goods and services within an integrated offer. As Pullman and Gross (2004, p. 553) explain:

> An experience occurs when a customer has any sensation or knowledge acquisition resulting from some level of interaction with different elements of a context created by a service provider. Successful experiences are those that the customer finds unique,

memorable and sustainable over time, would want to repeat and build upon, and enthusiastically promotes via word of mouth.

Many articles and texts make sweeping distinctions between manufacturing and service operations. As we shall see later in this chapter, we argue that this is not always helpful when trying to manage operations. What provides better insight is in viewing manufacturing and service operations as collaborative activities in providing goods and services to customers. Perhaps a more relevant distinction is to differentiate between those operations that process materials and those that process customers. It needs to be remembered that materials do not think or act for themselves, whereas customers can and do. Service companies that forget this and start to treat their customers as if they were materials will not survive in the long term, even if they provide excellent value.

In Chapter 2 we saw the vital importance of an operations strategy. We argued that operations strategy includes both manufacturing and services activities and that these need to be integrated in a combined, holistic manner. However, we have identified that these sectors may well process different things, which we have categorized as materials, customers, and information. This may have implications for the specific implementation of strategy, but not for operations management principles or issues per se. Comparing manufacturing and service industries can be useful but in an operations management context we suggest that some of the divisions between them are over stated.

For example, in its review of 75 years of management thinking, the *Harvard Business Review*, in 1997, traced the operations management thread from 'production' in 1922, with such functions as 'inventory control' mechanization, etc. to 'growing attention of service management' in the mid-1970s, 'lean manufacturing' in the late 1980s, and 'supply chain management' in the mid 1990s. By the end of their story, the generic term for the area of business upon which we are focusing is 'adding value' (Ross, 1997).

Similarly, Gilmore and Pine (1997) traced the developments of operations over time and concluded that the consumer will increasingly think in terms of 'experiences' rather than a manufacturing or service offering as shown in Figure 11.4.

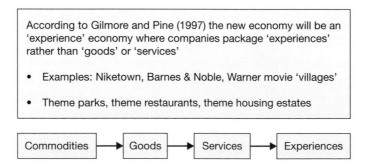

Figure 11.4 Changes from 'commodities' to 'experiences'

Similarly, the renowned management academic, C.K. Prahalad, stated in 2002 that:

> People talk about the convergence of technologies. I think the most fundamental convergence is between the role of producer and the role of consumer. . . . The consumer goes from being a very passive person to being a very active co-creator of products, services and value. . . . Companies spent the 20th century managing efficiencies. They must spend the 21st century managing experiences.
>
> (Quoted in *Financial Times*, 2002, p. 14)

However, another challenge for service operations managers – in addition to the threat brought about by the low barriers to entry and the ability of competitors to copy existing operations – is that, on occasion, some aspects of a service offer can be annihilated with the emergence of new technology. For example, it was only a few years ago that Borders, the famous bookstore, was hailed as a model of service experience. The reason for this was that the stores had developed from merely selling books to, instead, offering an enjoyable experience where customers could take time, relax, and buy coffee while deciding on what books and other goods they would purchase. However, the emergence of the Kindle has annihilated this business model for Borders who have now gone out of business.

CASE 11.2: BORDERS

Borders Closing Signals Change In Bookselling Industry

NEW YORK – What happens when a pioneer like Borders goes out of business?

Depends on who you ask.

A day after the bankrupt chain said it would seek court approval to sell off its assets and shutter its remaining 399 stores, everyone from publishers to consumers is assessing what it would mean if the

CASE STUDY

company that started the big-box bookseller concept vanished. The move could have a wide-ranging – and different – impact on everyone from authors to consumers to competitors at a time when the industry is desperately trying to adapt to a new generation of readers who'd rather browse on an electronic book or tablet computer than turn the page of a paperback.

The biggest changes could come to the book publishing industry: As Borders stores disappear, the bookselling landscape could rapidly change, forcing authors to look for other places to market their work.

Jennifer Romanello, executive director of publicity at Grand Central Publishing in New York who stopped sending authors to most Borders for book signings after they declared bankruptcy in February, says she already looks for alternative places to promote their work.

'It's one less outlet to use in promoting our authors,' she said. 'There are still other things out there; we see if there's an independent bookstore nearby. But the number of bookstores has been contracting, not expanding, so we're selective where we send out authors.'

That ultimately could lead to more business for Barnes & Noble, a 705-store chain and one of Borders' main competitors. In fact, while Barnes & Noble revenue could be hurt initially as shoppers flock to Borders' liquidation sales, Barclays Capital analyst Alan Rifkin predicts ultimately the chain could gain $220 million to $330 million in revenue, or about 10% to 15% of Borders' annual revenue if the chain closes.

Still, Rifkin said even though Barnes & Noble has more aggressively and successfully pursued the e-book space than Borders did – with Barnes & Noble's Nook e-reader and e-bookstore – it still faces the same stiff competition from online retailers.

'As the demand for physical books continues to decline, the need for big-box physical bookstores will likely continue to decline as well,' he wrote in a client note.

That sentiment is being echoed by analysts and consumers alike who say the demise of Borders could close a chapter for bricks-and-mortar stores and open a new one for digital reading. To be sure, brick-and-mortar stores have not gone the way of the dinosaur, but some say it's only a matter of time.

Adrian Sierra, 36, a real estate agent from Westchester, N.Y., for instance, walked out of a Borders store in Penn Station in New York without a shopping bag filled with books. He was, however, carrying his iPad.

'I'll miss them,' he says, but, 'I'm not going to buy another paperback in my life. There's no reason to anymore.'

A growing number of customers like Sierra are the reason that Borders' liquidation will most likely accelerate sales of e-books, said Forrester media analyst James McQuivey. He predicts e-book sales will nearly triple by 2015 to $2.18 billion, with the number of e-readers jumping from 10.3 million at the end of 2010 to 29.4 million by 2015.

'People who read a lot are not just going to suddenly read less just because 400 stores close,' he said. 'With Borders out of the picture, people might think "If I'm not comfortable with digital shopping, browsing or buying, I might as well get comfortable with it."'

Simba Information senior trade analyst Michael Norris disagrees, saying that if Borders goes out of business, it might actually decrease sales of e-books since there are fewer places for people who buy e-books to browse and research new titles physically before they buy electronically.

'Bookstores are a tremendous vehicle for e-book discovery,' he said. 'We've often tried to quantify the exact number of consumers who "mooch" off of bookstores, who browse at a store and leave to order a book they find off their Kindle or iPad. It's hard to quantify – but we know it happens.'

Morningstar analyst Peter Wahlstrom said consumers who so-call 'mooch' will likely adapt. 'Individuals that are pure physical book readers will find another outlet, be it independent bookstores or the Targets or the Costcos,' he said.

There are indeed many other places to go to find out about books. Still, some consumers who love browsing Borders' bookshelves say it will be hard for them to adjust if the chain closes.

'That whole thing about stumbling across a book, or stumbling across a stranger who recommends a book – the serendipitous aspect of your literary journey in life – is evaporating as these stores evaporate,' said Rachel Simon, author of the New York Times best seller 'The Story of Beautiful Girl,' who says she visits her local Borders several times a week.

Started in 1971, Borders once operated 1,249 Borders and Waldenbooks book stores at its peak in 2003. But it failed to adapt quickly to the changing industry and lost book, music and video sales to the Internet and other competition. It filed for bankruptcy protection in February and has since shuttered stores and laid off thousands of employees.

Borders' attempt to stay in business unraveled quickly last week, after a $215 million 'white knight' bid by private-equity firm Najafi Cos. dissolved under objections from creditors and lenders who argued the chain would be worth more if it liquidated immediately. On Thursday, Borders is expected to ask the U.S. Bankruptcy Court of the Southern District of New York at a scheduled hearing to allow it to sell off all of its assets. If the judge approves the move, liquidation sales could start as soon as Friday; the company could go out of business by the end of September.

USA Today (2011) 20 July 2011

REVISITING THE INPUT–OUTPUT MODEL FOR SERVICE OPERATIONS

We saw in Chapter 1 how an input–output model can help as a starting point for mapping operations. As we stated then, and we emphasize again now, this model can become very complicated due to the roles of various inputs – for example, a supplier may subsequently become a customer. Also, a supplier may become a competitor depending on the complexity of the supply network that we discussed in Chapter 3. The basic model has been challenged by some who see customers as an *input* rather than an *output* of the input–output model, and this has come about by the notion of the 'customer as a co-creator' (which was referred to in Chapters 3 and 9 when we discussed the nature of buyer–supplier relationships).

Vargo and Lusch (2004, p. 3) suggest that the 'customer is always a co-creator', in services and 'with service processes, the customer provides significant inputs into the production process' (Sampson and Froehle, 2006, p. 331). This view is important within the emerging *service dominant logic* of service operations. The idea of the customer as co-producer is evident at Dell Computers, see box below.

> Michael Dell predicts that customer relationships will 'continue to be more intimate.' He even speaks of 'co-creation of products and services,' a radical notion from a giant manufacturer. 'I'm sure there's a lot of things that I can't even imagine, but our customers can imagine,' Dell says, still sounding very bloggish. 'A company this size is not going to be about a couple of people coming up with ideas. It's going to be about millions of people and harnessing the power of those ideas.'
>
> *Business Week* (2007a) 'Dell learns to listen',
> 29 Oct. 2007, pp. 118–20

So, operations and marketing personnel need to have a unified view to have any hope of providing world-class offerings to customers. Not surprisingly, this view is shared by some marketers referring to service dominant logic, and the following clearly shows the importance for operations:

> In S-D logic, service is defined as the application of specialized competences (operant resources – knowledge and skills), through deeds, processes, and performances for the benefit of another entity or the entity itself. It is important to note that S-D logic uses the singular term, 'service,' which reflects the process of doing something beneficial for and in conjunction with some entity.
>
> (Vargo and Lusch, 2008, p. 26)

Although this notion is becoming increasingly popular in services, it is not entirely new. Back in 1986 Normann observed how:

> the customer is often more than just a customer – he is a participant in the production of the service. A haircut, the cashing of a cheque, education – none of these can conceivably be produced without the participation of the consumer. Thus the service company not only has to get in contact with the consumers and to interact with them socially; it is also necessary to 'manage' them as part of the production force.
>
> (p. 7)

The service dominant logic therefore changes the input–output model, as shown in Figure 11.5.

The goods-dominant logic focused on tangible resources, whereas this model talks about services as the driver of operations. This in turn has led to a change of terminology as Lusch and Vargo (2006a, p. 286) show in Table 11.2.

Also, as Cova and Salle (2008, p. 271) state, this is more than just a change of words for their own sake:

> S-D logic moves the orientation of marketing from a 'market to' philosophy where customers are promoted to, targeted, and captured, to a 'market with' philosophy where the customer and supply chain partners are collaborators in the entire marketing process

(Lusch & Vargo, 2006a) being thus totally in tune with postmodern trends (Cova & Salle, 2008) and the CCT – Consumer Culture Theory – tradition (Arnould, 2006). Lusch & Vargo (2006b) proposed an S-D logic lexicon in order to break free from the confines and words of goods-dominant logic. . . .

S-D logic also recognizes that customers as well as suppliers are resource integrators, consistent with the concept of co-creation of value. S-D logic not only brings the customer

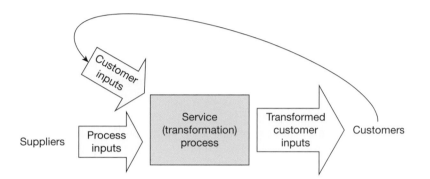

Figure 11.5 Modifying the input–output model for service operations

Table 11.2 Service dominant terminology

A tentative S-D logic lexicon

Goods-dominant logic concepts	*Transitional concepts*	*Service-dominant logic concepts*
Goods	Services	Service
Products	Offerings	Experiences
Feature/attribute	Benefit	Solution
Value-added	Co-production	Co-creation of value
Profit maximization	Financial engineering	Financial feedback/learning
Price	Value delivery	Value proposition
Equilibrium system	Dynamic systems	Complex adaptive systems
Supply chain	Value chain	Value-creation network/constellation
Promotion	Integrated marketing communications	Dialogue
To market	Market to	Market with
Product orientation	Market orientation	Service orientation

Source: page 286 in Lusch & Vargo (2006b).

into the process of co-creation of value, but organizations' partners throughout the value network as well. Consequently, S-D logic recognizes that each entity should collaborate with other entities and integrate resources with them.

In addition, Payne *et al.* (2008, p. 85) describe how:

> The value co-creation process involves the supplier creating superior value propositions, with customers determining value when a good or service is consumed. Superior value propositions, that are relevant to the supplier's target customers, should result in greater opportunities for co-creation and result in benefits (or 'value') being received by the supplier by way of revenues, profits, referrals, etc. By successfully managing value co-creation and exchange, companies can seek to maximize the lifetime value of desirable customer segments.

We saw in Chapter 1 how *Servitization* has become important for many firms. The two key reasons for this are:

1. Many 'manufacturing' firms make very little profit on the products alone because margins are very thin.
2. Customers increasingly want complete 'solutions', and so the 'offer' from the provider has to go beyond the mere transfer of a product to include the provision of help, support, knowhow, experience, and a range of service aspects.

Manufacturing companies adopting service logic will increasingly provide not only services as part of their total product-based offerings but also service concepts as the basis for their business. Therefore, with new competitors and changing customer strategies, industrial companies will need to understand how to manage the co-creation of their offerings together with buyers, and to restructure their existing buyer relationships. This dramatically impacts the involvement of the customer or buyer, from a largely passive role into much more of a co-value creator with the supplier:

> The emergent 'service-dominant' logic challenges the view of buyers as passive consumers and includes buyers in the value creation process by asserting that the customer is always a co-creator of value . . . In this perspective, goods are merely 'intermediate products that are used by other operant resources (customers) as appliances in value creation processes.
>
> (Vargo and Lusch, 2004, p. 7)

Furthermore:

> Consumers act as resource integrators . . . when they use their competence, tools, raw materials, and sometimes professional services to produce maintenance services, entertainment, meals, etc. for themselves.
>
> (Xie *et al.*, 2008, p. 109)

Cova and Salle (2008, p. 271) offer a simple but insightful model of how this works in Figure 11.6. As can be seen, the supplier and customer networks become combined, integrated entities rather than opposing parties as has often been the case. Instead of confrontation, both 'sides' work jointly in the provision of solutions which is what customers often need.

We saw in Chapter 2 how important strategy is to manufacturing operations and the same is true for services, although, of course, the two elements often merge in many ways. To that end, authors have come up with models of service strategy that we saw in Chapter 2. One of these comes from Goldstein *et al.* (2002, p. 126), as shown in Figure 11.7.

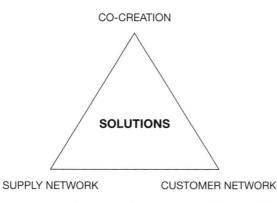

Figure 11.6 The co-production process between buyer and supplier in services

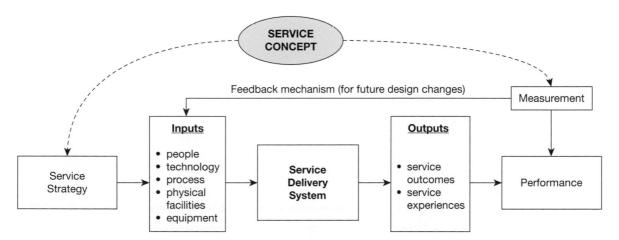

Figure 11.7 The service strategy concept

THE 'MOMENT OF TRUTH' IN SERVICES

Once customers and suppliers engage in a transaction – both in consumer and business (B2B) settings – organizations must ensure that resources go into producing the services so that 'the moment of truth' (Normann, 1991) that takes place in this contact, is positive. Part of the problem, though, is that many senior-level managers are fond of the rhetoric of providing customer services but the disconnect between strategy and operations in delivering this is as large within service settings as it is within manufacturing firms, as we discussed in Chapter 2. This was nicely summarized by Hemp (2001, p. 51):

> It's easy for senior executives to hold forth about the importance of getting close to customers, anticipating their needs, exceeding their expectations. But how many of them have ever been out there on the front lines, experiencing firsthand what this actually feels like? What might they discover if they tried to find out – particularly at a company known for its obsessive commitment to customer service? Certainly, they would learn a lot from observing the operation at close range. But they would also glean useful insights from being part of the operation, from standing in the shoes and getting inside the heads of employees trying to satisfy demanding customers.

However, some CEOs and other senior-level managers do see the importance, as CEO A.G. Lafley at Procter & Gamble observes below.

> **I stressed the need for all of us to focus on two consumer 'moments of truth.' The first moment is when the consumer makes the decision to buy a product. P&G had to ensure that it won at this first moment of truth. The second moment is when the consumer uses the product. At that moment, they have to be satisfied and experience quality and value. This ensures they will buy the product again and become loyal consumers.**
>
> AMR Research (2008) 'A conversation with
> Procter & Gamble CEO A.G. Lafley',
> 18 April 2008

The importance of a positive 'moment of truth' cannot be over-emphasized. As we saw in Chapter 9 with regard to Toys 'R' Us online, if things go wrong, irate customers are more than prepared to post their experience on the Internet as a warning to others. The moment of truth often becomes *moments* of truth, where the customer evaluates the experience at key touch-points. This can include when a customer wants to end the relationship with an organization. Again, when this goes wrong, the customer can make their unhappiness very well known. Key issues to bear in mind are:

- Very satisfied customers are six times more likely to repurchase (Heskett *et al.*, 1994);
- A focus on service quality means retaining customers 50 per cent longer (Zemke, 1997);

- A 5 per cent increase in customer loyalty delivers a 25 to 85 per cent growth in profits (Reicheld, 1996); and

- Very high levels of service quality and customer satisfaction are needed to prevent defections (65 per cent of customers who leave are 'satisfied') (Reicheld, 1996).

However, the following link provides an example of someone trying to cancel their AOL account. When it goes wrong the result is that it was picked up by the Today Show on NBC and consequently millions of viewers became aware of problems with AOL: www.youtube. com/watch?v=xmpDSBAh6RY. As you can see from this video, the moment of truth takes place not just at the *initial* point of contact between the provider and the recipient of the service – each experience within the overall encounter becomes a 'moment of truth'.

The 'moment of truth' can come in stages. Lovelock *et al.* (2009, p. 9) describe how these stages take place within a restaurant setting, as shown in the box below.

MOMENTS OF TRUTH IN A RESTAURANT

Act 1: Introductory scenes.

Act 2: Delivery of core product:

- Cocktails, seating, order food and wine, wine service.
- Potential fail points: Menu information complete? Menu intelligible? Everything on the menu actually available?
- Mistakes in transmitting information a common cause of quality failure – for example, bad handwriting and poor verbal communication.
- Customers may not only evaluate the quality of food and drink, but how promptly it is served, serving staff attitudes, or style of service.

Act 3: The drama concludes:

- Check presented, customer pays, takes keys/coat and leaves.
- Customer expectations: accurate, intelligible and prompt bill, payment handled politely, guests are thanked for their patronage.

As Voss and Zomerdijk (2007, p. 6) rightly point out:

> Every touch point a customer has with an organisation is an experience, no matter how mundane the product or service being delivered.

Again, the importance of positive experiences at each stage of the service provision is vitally important – we saw this, of course, with the AOL example above. As Chase and Dasu (2001, p. 81) suggest:

Most service providers believe that the beginning and end of an encounter – the so-called service bookends – are equally weighted in the eyes of the customer. They're dead wrong. The end is far more important because it's what remains in the customer's recollections. Sure, it's important to achieve a base level of satisfactory performance at the beginning, but a company is better off with a relatively weak start and a modest upswing at the end than with a boffo start and a so-so ending.

Some companies are now relentless in their pursuit of making customer satisfaction very positive via outstanding service operations. Dell is one such example.

> **Dell's worst problem had been that customers were having too many of the wrong conversations with too many service technicians in too many countries. 'It was a real mess,' confesses Dick Hunter, former head of manufacturing and now head of customer service. Dell's DNA of cost-cutting 'got in the way,' Hunter says. 'In order to become very efficient, I think we became ineffective.'**
>
> **Hunter has increased service spending 35%, cut outsourcing partners from 14 to 6 (and is headed to 3), and retrained staff to take on more problems and responsibility (higher-end techs can scrap their phone scripts; techs in other countries learn empathy). Crucially, Hunter also stopped counting the 'handle time' per call that rushed representatives and motivated them to transfer customers so they would be someone else's problem. At Dell's worst, more than 7,000 of the 400,000 customers calling each week suffered transfers more than seven times. Today, the transfer rate has fallen from 45% to 18%. Now Hunter tracks the minutes per resolution of a problem, which runs in the 40s. His favorite acronym mantra (among many) is RI1: resolve in one call. (Apple claims it resolves 90% of problems in one call.) He is also experimenting with outreach e-mails and chatty phone calls to 5,000 selected New Yorkers before problems strike, trying to replace the brother-in-law as their trusted adviser.**
>
> **Business Week (2007a) 'Dell learns to listen',**
> **29 October 2007, 118–120**

Again, the role of operations strategy is important here because these outcomes will not come about by mere chance. Instead, there has to be strategic intent on the part of the service provider as Goldstein *et al.* (2002, p. 122) note:

> Regardless of how the service organization defines their service and how customers perceive the service, a delivered service should function seamlessly for customers to perceive it correctly (i.e. as designed). Customers have a preconceived notion of what a service is, even if they have not experienced it previously . . . In other words, customers have an image of the service concept regardless of whether it has been defined by word-of-mouth or other sources of information or from real service experiences.

Chase and Dasu (2001, p. 81) provide an example of how cruises offer a range of events in order to make the whole experience positive throughout the trip, as shown in Table 11.3.

Table 11.3 Why cruises work

Modern cruise lines apply many of the operating principles suggested by behavioural science.

Principle	What Cruise Lines Do
Finish strong	End each day on a high note with raffles, contests, shows, and so on. End the cruise with the captain's dinner. Pass out keepsakes or bottles of wine upon reaching home port.
Segment the pleasure	Pack many events into one short vacation.
Create rituals	Offer captain's dinner and midnight buffets.

Chase and Dasu (2001, p. 81)

Not surprisingly, Disney theme parks pay an enormous amount of attention within their service operations strategy to ensure that customers have positive experiences, as shown in the box below.

CASE: THE DISNEY EXPERIENCE

Each cast member is responsible for how customers, within a few metres of them, are feeling about their experience and enhancing it if they can.

Every one of the thousands of park trees in Disney has an understudy so it can be replaced overnight if it becomes sick or damaged.

They promise snow, and snow it does, on time each night, in the right place. Disney Imagineers have created clusters of tiny bubbles to look and act like snowflakes.

There are hidden networks of tunnels under Disney World in Orlando, with store rooms and control centres. An underground railway moves cast members and costumes around the park, unseen.

Professor R. Johnston, Warwick Business School

UNFORTUNATE 'DIFFERENTIATION' IN SERVICES

It is clear that service operations have to be fully geared to make sure that all aspects of the service offer, meet, and (where possible) exceed customer expectations. Unfortunately, sometimes this can go wrong – even with the very best of intentions. Ultimately, the success of differentiation is determined by customers and not by the provider, however well intended the offer may be, as can be seen in Case 11.3.

CASE 11.3: FAILED DIFFERENTIATION AT SILVERJET

- *Super service*: no carts clog the aisles. All food and drink is delivered by hand – a first for the industry. Silverjet hired its attendants primarily from hotels and restaurants.

- *Boys, keep out*: aeroplane lavatories are usually unisex, but Silverjet added a dedicated women's bathroom, an idea the CEO got from an outspoken female passenger at Heathrow.

- *Bending down*: a standard Boeing 767 has more than 200 seats. Silverjet has 100, which recline into six-foot three-inch beds. Cost: $2,200 for a round trip.

- *Eco-aware air*: with a fee of roughly $20 on every ticket, Silverjet is the first airline to completely offset the 124 tons of carbon dioxide released by each transatlantic flight.

- *Time savings*: At London's Luton airport, passengers arrive at a private Silverjet terminal as little as 30 minutes before takeoff. The company has its own dedicated security process.

Fortune (2007) 'Upgrading the business-class jet', 15 October 2007

Unfortunately, in spite of being heralded for its great service offering to its customers, Silverjet no longer exits. Ultimately its customers decided that the premium fee to fly with Silverjet did not justify the differentiation on offer and Silverjet went out of business.

ARE MANUFACTURING AND SERVICE OPERATIONS SO DIFFERENT?

Since the first edition of this text in 2000 we have always made the case for manufacturing and services to be seen as complementary – and not contradictory – aspects of operations and, indeed, business. The two sectors are often seen as mutually exclusive or, at best, overlapping with varying degrees of similarities. We suggest that the distinctions are not so clear cut as might be first thought. This is endorsed by Normann (2001, p. 114) who argues that the traditional distinction between goods and services is misleading:

> Services are activities (including the use of hard products) that make new relationships and new configurations of elements possible. . . . Viewing the economy as a web of activities and actors linked in co-productive value creation gives us another . . . more creative view of the nature of 'offerings'. Offerings are artifacts designed to more effectively enable and organize value co-production.

Some of the distinctions are not quite as pronounced as they may first appear. For example, in the box below we can see the typical statements concerning service industries and their contrast to manufacturing operations.

PERCEIVED DIFFERENCE BETWEEN MANUFACTURING AND SERVICES

- The product is intangible.
- Services cannot be kept in stock.
- Services vary and cannot be mass produced.
- There is high customer contact.
- Customers participate in the service.
- Facilities are located near to customers.
- Services are labour intensive.
- Quality is difficult to measure.
- Quality depends largely on the server.

We shall now take each of these in turn and explore them.

Services are intangible?

Is this necessarily the case? Increasingly, service organizations speak in terms of 'products' for their customers. This is very clear across a range of financial services where the term *product* is used and where the 'intangible' becomes 'tangible'. For example, customers choosing a mortgage can think in terms of a range of *products* including fixed versus variable rates; the duration of the loan; and comparisons between various interest rates tied to a particular offer. Vacations or holiday *packages* are within the realms of services, yet holiday organizations speak in terms of 'products'. Similarly, time-share organizations will make the intangible more identifiably tangible when they speak in terms of purchasing and accumulating a number of points to obtain a particular holiday or time away. Airlines that offer 'air miles' for their customers offer the same approach. In education, universities are able to offer a range of 'products', or different modes of attendance for a particular degree. An MBA, for example, may be offered via distance learning; as a one-year intensive programme; as a two/three-year part-time course; or through a sporadically attended, intensive modular design over various times. Being able to offer a range of products means that although a professional service is being provided, the potential students on the course can choose a particular offer over another because certain, identifiable, tangibles have been put in place – duration of course, modes of attendance etc.

Although the transaction that takes place – for example, advice in a doctor's surgery – is intangible, that does not mean that the whole experience is, likewise, intangible and it is vital to pay attention to the physical aspect of the service. In the US, in a doctor's surgery we pay for a doctor's advice. However, if there is paint peeling off the wall, or the waiting area is dirty or the carpet is worn, we will pay attention to these physical aspects – and tell others too. It's for this reason that world-class service providers pay much attention to the physical aspect of the service:

Disney spends considerable time, thought, and money designing the optimal environment for the experiences it provides to customers. One example is the diligence of the Main Street painters at both the Magic Kingdom and Disneyland. Their only responsibility, all year long, is to start at one end of Main Street and paint all the buildings and other structures until they get to the other end, and then start all over again. Each painted rail is completely stripped down to the metal and repainted five times a year. The servicescape supporting the feeling of a fantasy experience for visitors requires a clean, freshly painted park, and the customer who finds the painting chipped or soiled will define the quality of the experience in a less favorable way.

(Ford *et al.* 2001, p. 42)

Often the physical aspect of the service can make an enormous difference, which is why so much attention is now being paid to what is termed the *Servicescape*, an example of which is shown in Figure 11.8.

Nike Town

■ **Store atmosphere** created through design, colour and layout-interior and exterior

■ **Experiential marketing:** creating an experience where the hoped-for result is an emotional connection to a person, brand, product or idea

■ Retail outlets like Nike Town are designed to create a **customer experience,** not for sales

Figure 11.8 Nike as an example of servicescape

Wilson, A. *et al.* (2008)

The contribution of the physical aspect of the service is vital in all types of service. It will have a profound influence upon the psychological reaction to the service offer, as can be seen in Table 11.4.

Services cannot be kept in stock?

In 'tangible' services (such as restaurants, fast-food chains, and car repair outlets) the supporting element of the service – supplies – is clear and will be kept in stock. In service retail outlets, the goods have to be available for the customer. In professional services – a solicitor, a doctor, or a consultant, for example – it becomes clear that delivery of the services depend on the intellectual capital, experience, and 'know-how'. That being the case, we can speak in terms of a body of knowledge or know-how being accumulated over time and 'stored' in readiness. This may be through a particular individual specializing in one area or by a group of professionals who can offer a variety of professional services. Likewise, there are some products that cannot be kept in stock for long – most obviously perishable food products. But other markets which are subject to rapid, short-term changes in demand, such as the pop-music industry, also make it inadvisable to hold stock for too long. Whilst the physical shelf-life of a CD may be many years, the sellable shelf-life will only be as long as the music is popular.

Services vary and cannot be mass-produced?

Again, such an assertion depends on where and how we view the service. As a generic term, fast-food restaurants would come under a 'service' as opposed to 'manufacturing'. Clearly, where there is a considerably high tangible feature or input as part of the service provision, we can say that the product can be produced in volume and is not a truly unique event at the point of service delivery. All fast food is mass-produced to some degree. In Russia, eye surgery on cataracts has been 'production-lined'. In the field of education, the provision of distance learning has standardized the student experience to a significant degree. The issue of volume and variety is an important one for manufacturing and services, as discussed in Chapter 7.

There is high customer contact?

Technology has made a great deal of difference in tempering this statement. Clearly, in many financial transactions there may be little or no customer/client contact. Also, if you take a long-distance flight you will discover that even in a 'customer care' service, the actual amount of contact between customer and provider may be minimal. One of the authors estimated that in an eight-hour flight from the US to the UK no more than two minutes was spent in contact with staff. That is not a criticism of the service – in fact when a passenger wants to use the flight to sleep, the very last thing that he/she wants is to be disturbed by a service offering that the passenger does not want!

Table 11.4 Importance of the physical element within services

Receptor*	Environmental stimuli	Impact upon environment users	For example see
Visual	Colour	Moods and emotional states	Ornstein (1990)
	Colour	Health/physiology	Bellizzi et al. (1983)
	Colour	Taste perception	Tom et al. (1987)
	Colour	Temperature perception	Hayne (1981)
	Colour	Spatial demarcation and direction of in-store movement	Razzano (1986)
	Lighting/brightness	User satisfaction	Lewison (1994)
	Lighting/brightness	Attraction to/handling of goods	Areni and Kim (1994)
	Lighting/brightness	Task performance	Butler and Biner (1987)
	Lighting/brightness	Image perception	Smith (1989)
	Lighting/brightness	Metamerism	Green (1986)
	Lighting/brightness	Direction of in-store movement	Cobb (1988)
	Lighting/brightness	Visual privacy	Gifford (1987)
	Natural light/windows	Psychology and mood	Heerwagen (1990)
	Pattern	Direction of in-store movement	Proctor (1990)
	Shapes	Symbolic association/psychological connotations	Proctor (1990)
	Spatial arrangement	Interaction with others and reaction to space limitations	Martin and Pranter (1989)
	Spatial arrangement	Ergonomics and productivity	Barron (1991)
	Spatial arrangement	Efficient flow of in store movement	Newman (2002)
	Spatial arrangement	Mood/emotional response i.e. pleasure	Spies et al. (1997)
	Spatial density/space availability	Avoidance behaviour/stress	Mehrabian and Russell (1974)
	Clearly demarcated zones	Identity reinforcement/dominance of territory holder	Russell and Ward (1982)
	Personal space	Visual and aural privacy – stress and performance	Wineman (1982)
Aural	Music	Speed of movement	Milliman (1986)
	Music	Emotional response	Gordon (1990)
	Sound/noise	Perceived duration of shopping trip	Yalch and Spangenberg (1988)
	Sound/noise	Arousal, task performance	Wineman (1982)
	Background noise	Acoustic privacy	Wineman (1982)

continued . . .

Table 11.4 . . . *continued*

Receptor*	Environmental stimuli	Impact upon environment users	For example see
Tactile	Temperature	Performance, interaction with others	Gifford (1987)
	Comfort – hard and soft furnishings	Speed of movement/time spent in area	McGoldrick and Greenland (1994)
	Contrasting fabrics	Tactile quality associations/evaluation	Solomon *et al.* (2002)
Olfactory	Pollutants/air quality	Aggression/irritation/fatigue	Evans *et al.* (1982)
	Negative ions	Performance	Baron (1987)
	Scents and odours	Mood/behaviour	Russell and Ward (1982)
	Scents and odours	Perceived service quality	McDonnell (1998)
	Scents and odours	Stimulating purchase	Bainbridge (1998)
	Scents and odours	Learning and memory recall	Smith *et al.* (1992)
Taste	Food/drink samples	Arousal	Mehrabian and Russell (1974)

Note: *cues may impact upon several senses at the same time; some elements could therefore be included under other sensory receptors
Table I. Environmental cues and their impact upon the environment user
Greenland and McGoldrick (2005)

In manufacturing environments, while it may be true to say that within the manufacturing end of the supply chain it is unlikely that the customer comes into contact with the manufacturing plant itself, this is not always the case. In a job-shop environment, for example (see Chapter 7), there may be joint design and strong customer links with the supplier. Conversely, in services there will not always be high customer contact. Financial services are a point in case. Often customers do not engage in contact with other persons during the provision of the service. Indeed, there may be occasions when the customer does not need or require such contact – obtaining funds from a cash machine involves little contact and it is wholly appropriate for this to be so. Even in professional services, there may not be a great deal of customer involvement (although the client will be billed for hours spent by the professional).

Customers participate in the service?

As we have noted, this is not necessarily the case, or if there is 'participation' it may be to a very small degree. This is noticeable where automation helps to speed up the process and, by implication, to reduce the amount of time required by the customer in the service transaction.

Facilities are located near to customers?

This used to be a critical distinction between manufacturing and services. In the past we could have said, with a high level of confidence, that manufacturing plants are located close to suppliers for ease of transportation; in contrast, services are located near to customers. This distinction between manufacturing and services is still valid in some cases. Large retail organizations will, typically, be located close to a large town or be close enough to a city to attract customers. Here, a key factor is capacity for customers, especially in determining the size and ease for customers in car-parking facilities. However, the increase in technology in many service operations has often reduced the need for facilities to be physically close because much of the transaction can be automated via computer, telephone, or other types of technology, as is the case with insurance, hotel reservations, or banking services. The Internet will play a central role in such decoupling, as the success of Amazon.com demonstrates in books and other products in its retailing operations.

Services are labour intensive?

We need to focus on specific service sectors in order to evaluate the application of the statement. In high volume manufacturing it is true to say that direct labour costs are relatively small – typically less than 10 per cent in industries such as automobiles and markets within 'high tech'. In manufacturing, the largest cost will tend to centre on materials or inventory management. In services, though, if there is a large tangible element to the overall provision of the service (for example, fast foods) then labour will similarly form a small part of the overall costs. Increasingly, technology in services has helped to reduce the extent of labour involvement in the transaction process and, therefore, labour costs are reduced to suit.

Quality is difficult to measure and depends on the server?

One of the myths surrounding service provision is that quality is impossible to measure. Certainly, measuring quality within manufacturing plants might be seen as easier in that the product can be measured in terms of weight, height, overall dimensions, and so on. But such measurement is only part of the overall evaluation of quality (see Chapter 8) and it is sufficient to say here that there has been a major shift in recent years concerning quality, particularly in professional services. In services, time is an important dimension in measuring quality – speed and reliability of response are measurable and quantifiable. Such measures are used in the fire service – the frequency of timely responses within specified standards to fire alarms, for example. The same type of measure is used in responses from ambulance crews to emergencies. In health care, measurements such as patient waiting lists for operations, or the time spent waiting in accident and emergency units, or patient throughput times and other time-related measures, are used as part of the quality assurance procedures. However, speed of response times may not be sufficient, as we can see in the box below.

In professional services, quality has become an important issue. For example, the Law Society in the UK takes a much more involved role than it used to regarding the provision

---

CASE: DON'T TAKE CALLS, MAKE CONTACT

A large U.S. auto insurance company had a long-standing rule that when a customer called to cancel a policy, it would honor the request immediately in order to heighten efficiency. Recently, though, the company launched a pilot program to gather information from departing customers. Skillful, gentle questioning let the company not only identify the reasons for cancellation, which is very valuable marketing information, but also retain 17 per cent of those customers who had called to cancel. Of course, the average discussion time increased, but the agents generated a significant amount of additional revenue. The company has since abandoned its speed-at-any-cost policy.

Arussi (2002) 'Don't take calls, make contact',
Harvard Business Review, 80(1), 16–18

---

of the service quality by solicitors. This is due in part to the fact that clients are far more likely to take action against their solicitors than used to be the case, and that their ability to do so is due to a far greater understanding and awareness of critical issues surrounding service quality in professional services.

In consumer services, within retail outlets or various types of franchises, firms will utilize 'mystery shoppers' to gain feedback and thus measure the performance of the server. Sometimes such feedback can be quite negative, as exemplified below.

CASE: FAST FOOD, SLOW SERVICE

A McDonald's memo accusing franchisees of service shortcomings has McDonaldland grimacing. In the three-page document obtained by *Fortune*, which was recently sent to McDonald's franchisees in the Raleigh region, vice president Marty Ranft cites 'alarming research' showing how bad service has gotten. 'Mystery shoppers' hired by the company to make unannounced visits found that restaurants were meeting speed-of-service standards only 46 per cent of the time, with three of every ten customers waiting more than four minutes for their meals – an eternity in the fast-food business. It also cited complaints of 'rude service, slow service, unprofessional employees, and inaccurate service.' The letter is a stunning admission. For years, CEO Jack Greenberg insisted that his pricey 'Made for you' food-preparation system would spur lackluster sales. 'They're finally admitting that service is a big problem,' says Dick Adams, a franchisee consultant based in San Diego. Perhaps a bigger problem is the stock: It just hit a seven-year low.

Fortune (2002) 'Fast food, slow service', 30 September 2002

In healthcare quality is everything but, sometimes, this is notable by its problems.

CASE: HEALTH CARE FOR US KIDS FALLS SHORT

Some of the more startling discoveries:

- Sixty-nine percent of 3- to 6-year-olds did not have their height and weight measured at annual checkups, and only 15% of adolescents were weighed and measured, even though one-third of American children are overweight or obese.

- Fifty-four percent of children diagnosed with asthma did not get recommended treatment.

- Sixty-two percent of children were not screened for anemia in the first two years of life, although the test is recommended for all babies.

- Only 38 percent of children received the proper care for acute diarrhea, one of the main causes of hospitalizations in children under age 5.

The researchers blamed much of the care deficit on insurers, whom they said pressure doctors to spend only 10 minutes on a regular checkup, leaving them little time to run all the recommended tests. In addition, pediatricians are trained to deal with acute illnesses rather than preventive care because their residential training is all in hospitals, where they don't do regular checkups, just serious illnesses. 'Until now, most people assumed that quality was not a problem for children,' says Elizabeth McGlynn, associate director of Rand Health and a co-author of the study. 'This new study tells us that's not true.'

Business Week (2007b) 'Health care for U.S. kids falls short',
11 October 2007, www.businessweek.com/stories/2007-10-11/
health-care-for-u-dot-s-dot-kids-falls-shortbusinessweek-
business-news-stock-market-and-financial-advice

What we need to bear in mind is that, today, patients are prepared to go to other countries for their healthcare in a process that is termed 'medical tourism'. So healthcare providers should be aware that their patients are no longer geographically 'locked in' as they have been in the past but are prepared to travel considerable distances.

Health care has long seemed one of the most local of all industries. Yet beneath the bandages, globalization is thriving. The outsourcing of record keeping and the reading of X-rays is already a multi-billion-dollar business. The recruitment of doctors and nurses from the developing world by rich countries is also common, if controversial. The next growth area for the industry is the flow of patients in the other direction – known as 'medical tourism' – which is on the threshold of a dramatic boom.

Economist (2008) 'Importing competition',
16 August 2008, 388(8593), 12

KEY TIPS TO MANAGING SERVICES

Services are many and varied in nature and it is always difficult to prescribe a 'one size fits all' approach. However, some good insights come from Frei (2008).

DIAGNOSING SERVICE DESIGN

The success or failure of a service business comes down to whether it gets four things right or wrong – and whether it balances them effectively. Here are some questions that will sharpen managers' thinking along each dimension and help companies gauge how well their service models are integrated.

1. The Offering

- Which service attributes (convenience? friendliness?) does the firm target for excellence?
- Which ones does it compromise in order to achieve excellence in other areas?
- How do its service attributes match up with targeted customers' priorities?

2. The Funding Mechanism

- Are customers paying as palatably as possible?
- Can operational benefits be reaped from service features?
- Are there longer-term benefits to current service features?
- Are customers happily choosing to perform work (without the lure of a discount) or just trying to avoid more-miserable alternatives?

3. The Employee Management System

- What makes employees reasonably able to produce excellence?
- What makes them reasonably motivated to produce excellence?
- Have jobs been designed realistically, given employee selection, training, and motivation challenges?

4. The Customer Management System

- Which customers are you incorporating into your operations?
- What is their job design?
- What have you done to ensure they have the skills to do the job?
- What have you done to ensure they want to do the job?
- How will you manage any gaps in their performance?

The Whole Service Model

- Are the decisions you make in one dimension supported by those you've made in the others?
- Does the service model create long-term value for customers, employees, and shareholders?
- How well do extensions to your core business fit with your existing service model?
- Are you trying to be all things to all people – or specific things to specific people?

Frei, F.X. (2008) 'The four things a service business must get right',
Harvard Business Review, 86(4), 70–80

In the 2008 *Harvard Business Review* article, Frei suggests that there are four key things that need to be in place if services are to be useful to the customer. However, as important as these are, there is often little guidance as to how service operations managers can help to ensure that services are well managed. In the next section we offer some specific tools that might help in this challenging task.

MANAGING SERVICES OPERATIONS

One of the challenges of managing services operations is that there can be a perception that 'a service is a service' and that all services are the same. Clearly they are not and, without being overly prescriptive, we offer a number of ways in which services need to be managed. We call these *key tips to managing services*.

Key tip 1: where possible, make the 'intangible' nature of the service as tangible as possible.

It is important for service providers to get away from vague propositions to customers and move towards much more clearly defined offerings instead. This can come from being much clearer about the nature of the service offering, whether it's healthcare, by specifying 'health packages' for patients that define very clearly what the health service will – and will not – do; or in consulting, where the scope, timing, and specification of the consulting project are made very clear before it has begun, and so on.

Also, as pointed out, it is always important to *pay attention to the physical aspect of the service*. We have noted that we pay for intangible advice in many professional settings. However, it is important for the professional service to pay attention to the physical aspect of the service offering, because the customer, or client, or patient, or another stakeholder *will* pay attention to the physical nature of the service offering. Of course, not all services are the same and the degree to which the physical aspect plays a vital part will depend on the context, as shown in Figure 11.9.

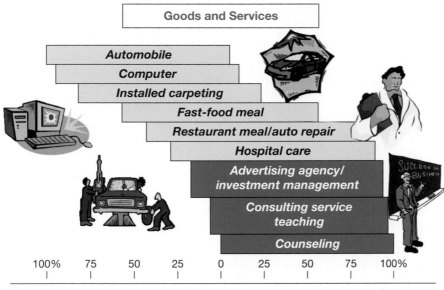

Figure 11.9 A goods–services continuum model

Key tip 2: focus, focus, focus!

Service providers need to be clear about specific needs within services industries and market segments. For example, Figure 11.10 shows the wide range of businesses that comes under the term, 'services'. How these are managed depends upon the context in which they operate.

Zeithaml (1981) suggests that an important way of seeing the service offer from the customer's point of view is in the degree of ease of evaluation. She also suggests that there are differences between 'search' and 'experience' attributes in the customer's selection of a service as shown in Figure 11.11.

The need for focus is evident in the airline industry and this is captured in the following box.

The airline industry is very competitive, with a number of mergers taking place resulting in fewer and larger service providers. This does not always mean better service for the customer, of course, and as we saw with Silverjet earlier in the chapter, some airlines go out of business in spite of the best intentions of offering some sort of differentiation to their customers.

Another way of using focus in managing services is in determining the amount of time that the customer will take in the service process as shown in Table 11.5.

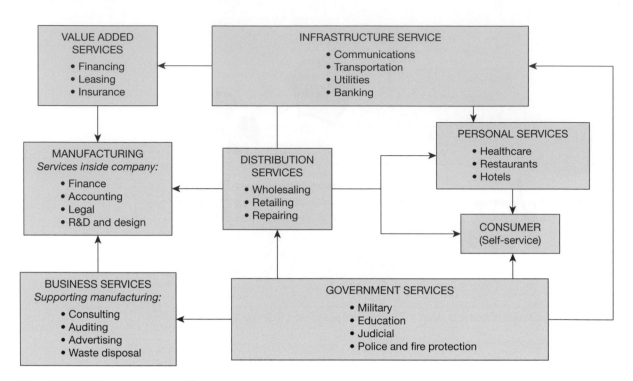

Figure 11.10 Various contexts of service operation settings

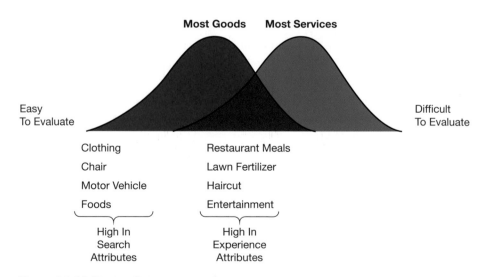

Figure 11.11 Types of customer evaluation

Zeithaml (1981)

FULL-SERVICE AIRLINES ARE 'BASKET CASES'

Q: Is there anything full-service airlines can do to restore their health?

A: No. They're *basket* cases. They're incredibly high-cost, very inefficient, and they're locked into businesses where yields are in inexorable decline. These are stupid businesses for the amount of capital tied up in them. They never make any money.

Q: Everyone is worried about *business* travel. What percent of *business*-class travelers do you think has permanently disappeared?

A: On short-haul travel around Europe, in the next four or five years, probably 100 percent of [how we define] *business* class in Europe – drinking champagne at 6 in the morning and eating inedible crappy food that you paid $500 for.

If you look around the States on short-haul – one-, two-, and three-hour flights – even in first class you still don't get fed. I think the whole thing will migrate to an economy product. In five years on short-haul, no one will be fed – maybe drinks and peanuts, but that will be about it. The age of quaffing champagne in the morning is just gone.

Business Week (2002) 'Full-service airlines are "basket cases"'
9 December 2002

Table 11.5 Classifications of physical service environments

Time spent in facility	Utilitarian	Purpose of consumption	Hedonic
Minutes	Dry-cleaner Post office Taxi	Coffee shop Lecture theatre Hairdresser	Games arcade Sauna Play park
Hours	Hospital outpatients Supermarket Lawyer	Bar Airport/aircraft Museum	Shopping centre Casino Theatre
Days	School Hospital Training centre	Health spa Caravan park Hotel	Cruise liner Theme park Coach tour

Wilson *et al.* (2008)

Key tip 3: manage services by mapping processes

Undoubtedly, the origins of this come from manufacturing in the earliest generation of work study. However, the application to services is vitally important and relevant within services.

In the past, at best, the perception of process mapping/work study was that it created a manager/worker divide; at worst, the perception was that it created scenes exemplified in *Schindler's List* in the scene where the Nazi general asks one of the workers to make a hinge; he then uses a stop watch, calculates the number of hinges the worker should have made versus what had actually been made . . . and then attempts to shoot the worker! For generations the image of work study and process mapping, which is an integral part of work study, was poor – and the process was best avoided. Over time, though, this image changed and in Adler's (1993) observation on the former GM/Toyota NUMMI project, he states that:

> NUMMI's intensely Taylorist procedures appear to encourage rather than discourage organizational learning and, therefore, continuous improvement.
>
> (p. 101)

And concludes that:

> time-and-motion discipline . . . need not lead to rigidity and alienation. NUMMI points the way beyond Taylor-as-villain to the design of a truly learning-orientated bureaucracy.
>
> (p. 102)

Process mapping is undertaken in method study via a process called SREDIM (see box below).

THE SREDIM MODEL

Select: work to be studied.

Record: all relevant facts.

Examine: the facts critically.

Develop: the most practical and efficient method of doing the job.

Install: the new method as standard.

Maintain: by regular checks.

Processes are recorded via a range of approaches (stop watches aren't normally used today) and information is then fed back. In more enlightened service operations environments, no 'finger pointing' takes place and continuous improvement (CI) groups that we mentioned in Chapter 8, will undertake brainstorming in order to develop better ways of managing a service operation. Typically, a range of ratios are examined including productivity and efficiency ratios:

Productivity = Output/Input

Efficiency = Actual output/'Expected' or 'standard' output

The five symbols used in method study can serve as a simple, yet powerful, approach to measuring current processes, in terms of time and other factors in order to make improvements.

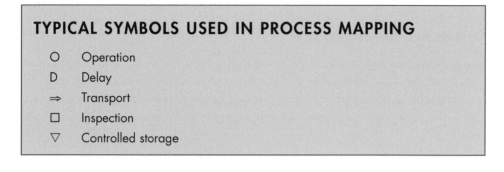

TYPICAL SYMBOLS USED IN PROCESS MAPPING

O   Operation

D   Delay

⇒   Transport

☐   Inspection

▽   Controlled storage

THE SERVICE MANAGEMENT SYSTEM

Normann (2000) provides a useful model that identifies five important aspects of the service management system, which is shown in Figure 11.12.

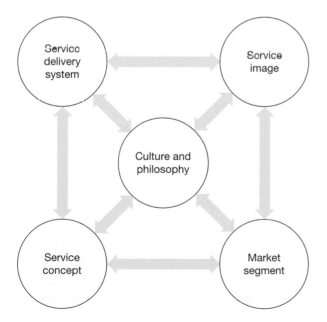

Figure 11.12 Normann's service system

We'll discuss the five aspects in turn.

Market segment

The market segment is important because it describes the particular types of client at whom the service management system is targeted. It defines where the organization chooses to be – as well as where it chooses *not* to be.

Culture and philosophy

Normann suggests that the core of the service management system is the company's culture and philosophy. This describes the overall values and principles guiding the organization, including values about human dignity and worth. This is of paramount importance for some companies (The Body Shop being a prime example) and forms part of their mission statements.

Service image

The image is vitally important because within services, customers typically participate in the production of a service as well as its consumption. As a result, the physical environment in which the service is produced has important effects. This includes:

- The *external environment*, including location, premises, ease of access, ambience; and
- The *internal environment*, including atmosphere and structure within which the service personnel operate.

Thus, the service image becomes part of the information system for influencing clients and customers alike.

The service concept

The *service concept* is the specification that describes the benefits offered by the service. This becomes a key element in the customer's perception of the 'moment of truth', when the service provider and customer actually meet. The service concept can include a complex set of values – physical, psychological, and emotional – and these affect both what the company does and how it is perceived by its customers and clients. The service concept also describes the way in which the organization would like its employees and stakeholders to perceive its service offering.

The service concept includes the *service package* within the offer and includes both the physical and tangible elements of the service offering and its intellectual/intangible elements. The total service package – the bundle of goods and services (Heskett *et al.*, 1990) – includes:

- *Physical items*: the physical good that is changing hands, if any (often called facilitating goods in services);
- *Sensual benefits*: aspects that can be experienced through the sensory system (explicit intangibles); and
- *Psychological benefits*: emotional or other aspects (implicit intangibles).

The service delivery system

The service delivery system is the way in which the service concept and service package are actually delivered to the consumer. This process may include customer participation in the manner in which the offer is designed and delivered to customers, including personnel, clients, technology, and physical support. The service delivery system is dictated by and defined by the service concept.

THE ICEBERG PRINCIPLE

In Chapter 1, when defining operations management, we emphasized how important it was to see operations as an activity that takes place across an entire organization and within a range of businesses linked together by a network. Often, some of these operations are not visible and might not be encountered directly by the customer or client. However, they are vitally important. Behind the scenes (in services this is often called 'back-office' operations) there will be a number of operations that will need to be in place. In services, the difference between the point of contact and all of the support activities has been likened to an 'iceberg' (Normann, 2000) as shown in Figure 11.13.

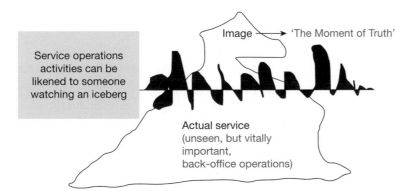

Figure 11.13 The iceberg principle in service operations

Managers must therefore make sure that necessary resources are provided 'below the surface' of the iceberg, because these are critical in providing excellent service to customers. Such activities can include planning bed space and buying in capital equipment for healthcare; and a range of technological, back-room operations that take place in many financial services. These operations are not seen, but they are strategically important for operations.

As we have seen, then, services play an enormously important role in economies across the world. We should not think in terms of manufacturing *versus* services but must see the importance of both in providing an overall offer to the customer. Many firms have embraced servitization as a means of providing benefits to customers. Increasingly, the customer is seen as an input, rather than an output in the input–output model, and many organizations think in terms of *creating with* rather than *creating for* their customers. There are a number of things that can done to manage services successfully – and the ability to do can provide powerful strategic benefits.

SUMMARY

- The percentage of workers in the service sector has grown considerably since the 1960s and the contribution of services industries to global GDP is also vitally important across nations.
- The need to focus is vitally important in managing services in order to move away from notions of 'a service is a service'. Services need specific approaches and infrastructure for particular segments and industries.
- Old models of manufacturing *versus* services in operations management make little sense in an era where customers buy 'an offer' which includes experiences.
- We are increasingly involved in an experience economy where bundles of products and services need to be in place in order to create customer satisfaction.
- The input–output model has been challenged by *service dominant logic* that sees the customer as an *input*, whereby marketing works *with and not just for* the customer.
- It is important to keep the 'moment of truth' as positive as possible throughout the customer experience – and not just at the beginning with the initial contact.
- Services can be difficult to manage but we offer some 'key tips' to managing them.
- Process mapping can play a vital role in service operations.

KEY QUESTIONS

1. To what extent are there major differences between manufacturing and service operations?
2. Why are services so important to the global economy?
3. What are the threats that many service organizations face in terms of competition?
4. Why is focus so important when managing services?
5. How would you apply the Iceberg principle to each of the following: a bank; a hotel; a restaurant?

WEB REFERENCES

This deals with the demise of Borders: www.usatoday.com/money/industries/retail/2011-07-20-Borders-Effect_n.htm

This provides insights into the changes to Service Economies on a global basis: www.bls.gov (US Department of Labor

This is an excellent short video that shows the problems associated with poor customer service – a customer wants to cancel his account with AOL and encounters many problems: www.youtube.com/watch?v=xmpDSBAh6RY

FURTHER READING

Brandt, J.R. (2008) 'Customer service from hell', *Industry Week*, 257(5), 88.

Chase, R. and Dasu, S. (2001) 'Want to perfect your company's service?', *Harvard Business Review*, 79(6), 79–84.

Ford, R. Heaton, C. and Brown, S.W. (2001) 'Delivering excellent services', *California Management Review*, 44(1), 39–56.

Frei, F.X. (2008) 'The four things a service business must get right', *Harvard Business Review*, 86(4), 70–80.

Hemp, P. (2002) 'My week as a room service waiter at the Ritz', *Harvard Business Review*, 80(6), 4–11.

Karmarkar, U. (2004) 'Will you survive the services revolution?', *Harvard Business Review*, 82(6), 101–7.

Möller, K., Rajala, R. and Westerlund, M. (2008) 'Service innovation myopia? A new recipe for client–provider value creation', *California Management Review*, 50(3,) 31–48.

Swank, C.K. (2003) 'The lean service machine', *Harvard Business Review*, 81(10), 123–9.

Womack, J.P. and Jones, D.T. (2005) 'Lean consumption', *Harvard Business Review*, 83(3), 58–68.

Zeithaml, V.A., Rust, R.T. and Lemon, K.N. (2001) 'The customer pyramid', *California Management Review*, 43(4) 118–42.

REFERENCES

Adler, P. (1993) 'Time and motion regained', *Harvard Business Review*, 71(1), 97–108.

AMR Research (2008) 'A conversation with Procter & Gamble CEO A.G. Lafley', 18 April 2008.

Arnould, E. (2006) 'Consumer culture theory: Retrospect and prospect', *Advances in Consumer Research – European Conference Proceedings*. 7, 605–7.

Arussy, L. (2002) 'Don't take calls, make contact', *Harvard Business Review*, 80(1), 16–18.

Bitner, M.J. (1992) 'Servicescapes: The impact of physical surroundings on customers and employees', *Journal of Marketing*, 56(2), 57–71.

Brandt, J.R. (2008) 'Customer service from hell', *Industry Week*, 257(5), 88.

Business Week (2002) 'Full-service airlines are "basket cases"', 9 December 2002, www.businessweek.com/stories/2002–09–11/full-service-airlines-are-basket-cases

Business Week (2007a) 'Dell learns to listen', 29 October 2007, 118–20.

Business Week (2007b) 'Health care for U.S. kids falls short', 11 October 2007.

Chase, R. and Dasu, S. (2001) 'Want to perfect your company's service?', *Harvard Business Review*, 79(6), 79–84.

Cova, B and Salle, R. (2008) 'Marketing solutions in accordance with the S-Dlogic: Co-creating value with customer network actors', *Industrial Marketing Management*, 37, 270–7.

Economist (2008) 'Importing competition', 16 August 2008, 388(8593), 12.

Edvardsson, B. Gustafsson, A. and Roos, I. (2005) 'Service portraits in service research: A critical review', *International Journal of Service Industry Management*, 16(1), 107–21.

Edvardsson, B., Holmlund, M. and Strandvik, T. (2008) 'Initiation of business relationships in service-dominant settings', *Industrial Marketing Management*, 37, 339–50.

Financial Times (2002) 'An interview with C.K. Prahalad', 13 December, p. 14.

Fitzsimmons, J.A. and Fitzsimmons, M.J. (2007) *Service Management*, 6th edition, New York: McGraw-Hill.

Ford, R., Heaton, C. and Brown, S.W. (2001) 'Delivering excellent services', *California Management Review*, 44(1), 39–56.

Fortune (2002) 'Fast food, slow service', 30 September 2002, 146(6), 38.

Fortune (2007) 'Upgrading the business-class jet', 15 October 2007, 156(7), 32–3.

Frei, F.X. (2008) 'The four things a service business must get right', *Harvard Business Review*, 86(4), 70–80.

Gilmore, J.H. and Pine, J. (1997) 'Beyond goods and services', *Strategy and Leadership*, 25(3), 10–18.

Goldstein, S., Johnston, R., Duffy, J. and Rao, J. (2002) 'The service concept: The missing link in service design research?', *Journal of Operations Management*, 20, 121–34.

Greenland, S. and McGoldrick, P. (1995) 'Atmospherics within retail service environments', *European Journal of Marketing* 29(5), 56–8.

Grönroos, C. (2000) *Service Management and Marketing*, Chichester: Wiley.

Grönroos, C. (2001) *Service Management and Marketing: A Customer Relationship Management Approach*, 2nd edition, New York: Wiley.

Haywood-Farmer, J. and Nollet, J. (1991) *Services Plus: Effective Service Management*, Boucherville, QC: Morin.

Hemp, P. (2002) 'My week as a room service waiter at the Ritz', *Harvard Business Review*, 80(6), 4–11.

Heskett, J.L., Jones, T.O., Loveman, G.W., Sasser Jr., W.E. and Schlesinger, L.A. (1994) 'Putting the service-profit chain to work', *Harvard Business Review*, 72(2), 164–70.

Heskett, J., Sasser, E. and Hart, C.W. (1990) *Service Breakthroughs*, New York: Free Press.

Hoffman, J., Colorado Bateson, J., Wood, E. and Kenyon, A. (2009) *Services Marketing*, Andover: Cengage Learning EMEA.

Johnston, R. and Clark, G. (2001) *Service Operations Management*, Harlow: Prentice-Hall.

Karmarkar, U. (2004) 'Will you survive the services revolution?', *Harvard Business Review*, 82(6), 101–7.

Levitt, T. (1972) 'Production-line approach to service', *Harvard Business Review*, 5(5), 41–52.

Lovelock, C.H., Wirtz, J. and Chew, P. (2009) *Essentials of Services Marketing*, Eaglescliff, NJ: Prentice Hall.

Lusch, R.F. and Vargo, S.L. (2006a) 'The service-dominant logic of marketing: Reactions, reflections, and refinements', *Marketing Theory*, 6(3), 281–8.

Lusch, R.F. and Vargo, S.L. (2006b) *The Service-dominant Logic of Marketing: Dialog, Debate, and Directions*, Armonk, NY: M.E. Sharpe.

Möller, K., Rajala, R. and Westerlund, M. (2008) 'Service innovation myopia? A new recipe for client–provider value creation', *California Management Review*, 50(3,) 31–48.

Normann, R. (1986) *Service Management: Strategy and Leadership in Service Businesses*, New York: John Wiley.

Normann, R. (1991) *Service Management: Strategy and Leadership in Service Business*, 2nd edition, Chichester: Wiley.

Normann, R. (2000), *Service Management; Strategy and Leadership in Service Business*, 3rd edition, Chichester: Wiley.

Normann, R. (2001). *Reframing Business: When the Map Changes the Landscape*, Chichester: Wiley.

Payne A., Storbacka, K. and Frow, P. (2008) 'Managing the co-creation of value', *Journal of the Academy of Marketing Science*, 36, 83–96.

Porter, M. (1980) *Competitive Strategy*, New York: Free Press.

Pullman, M. and Gross, M. (2004) 'Ability of experience design elements to elicit emotions and loyalty behaviors', *Decision Sciences Journal*, 35(3), 551–78.

Reicheld, F.F. (1996) 'The satisfaction trap', *Harvard Business Review*, 74(2), 58–9.

Reuters (2011) 'Who protects your IPR? Chinese retailers hijack the Ikea experience', 1 August 2011, www.reuters.com/article/2011/08/01/us-china-brand-piracy-idUSTRE77017720110801

Ritzer, G. (1993) *The McDonaldization of Society*, Thousand Oaks, CA: Pine Forge Press.

Ritzer, G. (2005) *Enchanting a Disenchanted World: Revolutionizing the Means of Consumption*, Second Edition, Thousand Oaks, CA: Pine Forge Press.

Ross, J.A. (1997) 'Why not a customer advisory board?', *Harvard Business Review*, 75(1), 12.

Sampson, S.E. and Froehle, C.M. (2006) 'Foundations and implications of a proposed unified services theory', *Production and Operations Management*, 15(2), 329–43.

Schmenner, R. (2004) 'Service businesses and productivity', *Decision Sciences*, 35(3), 333–47.

USA Today (2011) 'Borders closing signals change in bookselling industry', 20 July 2011, www.usatoday.com/money/industries/retail/2011-07-20-Borders-Effect_n.htm

Swank, C.K. (2003) 'The lean service machine', *Harvard Business Review*, 81(10), 123–9.

Vargo, S.L. and Lusch, R.F. (2004) 'Evolving to a new dominant logic for marketing', *Journal of Marketing*, 68, 1–27.

Vargo, S.L. and Lusch, R.F (2008) 'Why "service"?', *Journal of the Academy of Marketing Science*, 36, 25–38.

Voss C. and Zomerdijk L. (2007) 'Innovation in experiential services: An empirical view', appeared as Chapter 4 in *Innovation in Services*, DTI Occasional Paper No. 9, published by the Department of Trade and Industry.

Wilson, A.M., Zeithaml, V., Bitner, M. and Gremler, D. (2008) *Services marketing: 1st European edition*, Maidenhead: McGraw Hill.

Wise, R. and Baumgartner, P. (1999) 'Go downstream: The new profit imperative in manufacturing', *Harvard Business Review*, 77(5), 133–41.

Womack, J.P. and Jones, D.T. (2005) 'Lean consumption', *Harvard Business Review*, 83(3), 58–68.

Xie, C., Bagozzi, R. and Troye, S. (2008) 'Trying to prosume: Toward a theory of consumers as co-creators of value', *Journal of the Academy of Marketing Science*, 36, 109–22.

Youngdahl, W., Kannan, R. and Dash, K.C. (2010) 'Service offshoring: The evolution of offshore operations', *International Journal of Operations and Production Management*, 30(8), 798–820.

Zeithaml, V. (1981) 'How consumer evaluation processes differ between goods and services', in J.H. Donelly and W.R. George, *Marketing of Services* Chicago: American Marketing Association.

Zeithaml, V.A., Rust, R.T. and Lemon, K.N. (2001) 'The customer pyramid', *California Management Review*, 43(4), 118–42.

Zemke R. (1997) *Service Recovery: Fixing Broken Customers*, New York: Productivity Press.

Part 4

THE FUTURE

CHAPTER 12

THE FUTURE OF OPERATIONS MANAGEMENT

The future has already arrived. It's just not evenly distributed yet.

William Gibson

LEARNING OBJECTIVES

The purpose of this chapter is to:

- Develop your thinking about where current trends might lead.

- Show how international developments are changing and how operations managers might influence them.

- Connect you with many avenues to explore in forming your own view of the future, to inform you, and to help you choose your options.

In this, our final chapter, we pick up on some of the themes and trends that we have discussed throughout this book and suggest some ways in which they may develop in the near future. The picture we create is, of course, just our view; our purpose is to provoke some discussion and thinking about what might be around the corner. One of our objectives is to spot where, as William Gibson (1999) puts it 'the future has already arrived'.

We shall explore some key trends and then bring them together in a final discussion on the implications for strategic operations managers.

WHAT CAN WE LOOK FORWARD TO?

A service ethic

If we put together the implications of the increased consumption by human beings (Chapter 5), the supply chain complexity at a global level (Chapter 3), the demands and threats associated with sustainability and responsibility (Chapter 5), and the need for constantly improving quality (Chapter 8), we can envisage that the future of operations management will be fundamentally concerned with heightened, global competition and a corresponding need to provide customer service and satisfaction. This may have been seen in the past as the responsibility of sales, marketing, and after-sales service departments. In the future we may expect it to be reflected in the role of operations management.

Two of the challenges involved in achieving this will be how to deal with the impacts of the technologies and fashions that create product churn, and how to respond to the gradual disappearance of resources that are necessary to give an organization operational choices. Given the pressure of customer choice, a service ethic is a necessary part of operations management in the future, as we have explored in several places in this book. This effect is sometimes called the 'voice of the customer' (see Griffin and Hauser, 1993; and Schmenner and Tatikonda, 2005). This concept is associated with Quality Function Deployment, the Baldridge Award, and Joseph Juran (see Chapter 8, and also http://zomobo.com/Voice-of-the-customer).

Of course, where a customer does not really have choice (either prior to a purchase due to monopoly etc., or afterwards, due to switching costs) we should not expect companies to provide it (in other words, we are assuming that efforts aimed at providing customer satisfaction are related to competition, not altruism). The situation described in Case 12.1 is a rather alarming example of this.

The scenario in Case 12.1 is perhaps not the future for operations management that a firm would wish their customers to perceive, although it may make commercial sense where customers have limited choice (the futurologist was doubtless speaking off-message as far as his employer was concerned). It does however reflect a well-known and established problem encountered by operations managers which we might expect to get even more challenging in future: the need to keep present operations performing while constantly gearing up for delivering the promise of amazing new customer offers.

For some industries, this 'future' has already arrived: for others it is looming. Sometimes it can simply be teething problems (in manufacturing, design, delivery etc.). At other times, it may come close to the grim scenario described by the futurologist in Case 12.1, perhaps resulting in business failure for all but the monopolies. The futurologist's point was that companies with massive market power can afford to ignore customer dissatisfaction. This is perhaps a dangerous assumption. There is an ancient Greek proverb: 'Those whom the Gods wish to destroy they first make mad.' Microsoft's cofounder, Bill Gates, is said to have modified this in the 1990s to 'Those whom the Gods wish to destroy they first give 30 years of success.'

> ## CASE 12.1: TECHNOLOGICAL ARROGANCE VERSUS SERVICE
>
> About ten years ago, two of the authors of this book attended a conference in London at which a 'futurologist', employed by a large firm that provided telecommunications and internet services, made a presentation about the future, focusing especially on his industry. The talk included all sorts of exciting possibilities coming up (some of which still appear, a decade later, as technological fairy tales).
>
> After the presentation, the speaker was challenged by a question from the floor. The questioner pointed out that, while all the future wonders about which the speaker had eulogized were indeed marvellous, the reality was that his organization's present provision of telecommunications and intranet services to private customers (exploiting a very strong market position) was the cause of widespread and frequently expressed dissatisfaction. Stories of poor service, incomprehensible responses from call centres, and technical failures, were regularly aired, earning the organization a very bad reputation for customer service.
>
> Placing the promised marvels in the context of the problematic, actual situation, the questioner asked the speaker whether society should look forward to a constantly dreadful present, in terms of customer service, accompanied by a promised future full of glittering wonders. Sensing a taunt, and to the astonishment of the audience, the speaker agreed that this would indeed be the case and that the questioner 'had better get used to it!'

In helping to avoid failure, the clear challenge for operations managers is to achieve a very prompt process implementation for new products and services (or technologies), coupled with excellent customer after-sales service, without the luxury of plenty of time to get to market or sustained, steady-state operating conditions. These were features of mass production and were aligned to benign, immature consumer markets and early twentieth-century world geography. As we saw in Chapter 5, with Colin Chapman's concept of lean design – still reflected in each modern Formula 1 Grand Prix – tomorrow's products or services may differ profoundly from those we knew yesterday and it is dangerous to assume that proficiency in current techniques will help with managing the future.

So, our first conclusion about the future is that the operations manager who hopes that it will be business as usual – perhaps like the world for which they were trained – is in for a shock. The way to avoid the shock is to learn and innovate, in a real, practical way, constantly.

A SUSTAINABLE FUTURE

We have dealt with the topics of sustainability and responsibility, and their implications for operations managers, at length in Chapter 5 and shall not repeat them here. Their importance for considering the future is great, however, and it is worth following several sustainability-orientated organizations and websites dedicated to the future. These include:

- Forum for the Future: www.forumforthefuture.org/our-work/hub/sustainable-business
- The Natural Step: www.naturalstep.org
- John Elkington: www.johnelkington.com

Sites such as these both inform and point the way to future practices, without resorting to doomsday scenarios or naïve passion about nature. We may confidently expect many of the themes described in Chapter 5 to continue and the problems caused to become exacerbated. The detailed implications for operations management will emerge over time and it is important to keep well informed. Some of the future trends have 'already arrived' at a practical level, including 'remanufacturing' or refurbishment rather than disposal, and renting rather than buying.

Tackling product churn

As we noted in Chapter 5, product churn feeds conspicuous consumption through the forces and vagaries of technology and fashion, to the long-term benefit of the manufacturer or service provider and the transient delight of the consumer. The result has emerged as a 'throwaway' culture, which now appears to be unsustainable. While this can be addressed through design for recyclability, reverse logistics, and sound recycling (industrial and personal), the concept of product churn will always run counter to the imperative of reducing consumption in order to achieve one-planet living.

We cannot expect product churning to cease although shortages and costs of materials can be expected to lead businesses to find other ways of achieving it. (Remember that product churn helps to increase sales and can secure customer loyalty, so despite the negative aspects of over-consumption, businesses will always see it as a desirable activity.) What is required of operations managers, therefore, is some innovative way of achieving it. Perhaps the simple answer is to throw less away and reuse as much as possible.

Remanufacturing

Remanufacturing could be said to be a feature of a more sustainable future that is already with us. It entails dismantling a product and then rebuilding it for a further useful life, refurbishing and reusing as many components as possible. This relatively simple idea has generated much interest and a great deal of work has been done in the UK at the Centre for Remanufacture and Reuse (www.remanufacturing.org.uk/).

An excellent account of the concept, including many examples of current practice, was provided in 2006 by researchers Casper Gray and Martin Charter, who reported that:

> Remanufacture is currently practised in numerous industry sectors, [including] automotive and aerospace; the imaging industry is also involved in remanufacture e.g.

copiers and ink cartridges. Through remanufacture Caterpillar and Xerox have generated ongoing revenue opportunities from 2nd, 3rd, 'nth' life products. Xerox [claim] that their products can have up to 7 lives i.e. 7 [sequential] revenue streams!

(Gray and Charter, 2006)

Figure 12.1 shows how Xerox achieved this.

The remanufacturing process starts with the business model which leases machines to customers rather than selling them. Xerox takes old machines back from customers after 5 years or more, depending on the number of copies the machine has taken.

Gray and Charter, 2006

Gray and Chapman also report that

> Machines at Xerox are designed for disassembly and contain fewer parts because of this. Parts are also designed for durability over multiple product lifecycles. As a result each new generation of Xerox products offers increasing functionality while conserving energy and materials, and requiring fewer hazardous substances throughout the product lifecycle.

Other companies actively engaged in remanufacture include Caterpillar, Milliken Carpets, Perkins Engines, Flextronics, Hanover, Siemens, and the US Military (with BAE Systems).

So, remanufacturing (coupled with reverse logistics – see Chapter 5 – and, of course, everyday recycling) can provide a significant way of reducing the impact of products in the

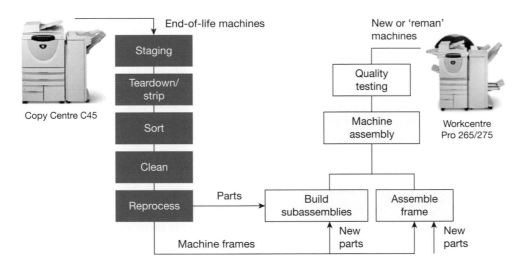

Figure 12.1 An overview of Xerox's remanufacturing process
Gray and Charter 2006

future; it may even be able to assuage the problems of unsustainability caused by product churn. In addition, it would appear to be a good way of reducing costs.

Rental not buying

We saw in Chapter 3 that Henry Ford initially insisted on owning everything he needed for manufacturing his cars and that he was safe in doing so in the benign consumer markets of the mass-production era. We also saw that this principle was reversed over the ensuing century. Ways of doing this include subcontracting and outsourcing. As we saw in the Xerox example, another way of increasing flexibility may lie in rental, rather than ownership. This might reduce the risks of capital equipment becoming obsolete or falling into disrepair, while at the same time improving sustainability when combined with remanufacture.

For sales organizations in equipment manufacturing this is a marketing option; for an operations manager – in any sector – it is a possible sourcing policy. The economics of this will be the deciding factor. For example, if the utilization of a piece of complex equipment is low or its maintenance is specialized, it may be preferable to rent, perhaps on a 'power-by-hour' basis (the concept originated by Rolls-Royce in the 1950s for aero engine rental) where the user pays only for the actual usage or output of the equipment. As we saw in Figure 12.1, this practice is well established in the provision of imaging capability. Other factors in the decision to rent or buy (working in favour or against the rental option) may include the need to own critical, high-specificity resources, unattractive rental offers from providers, and product churn leading to existing equipment impacting negatively on competitiveness.

As maintenance and complexity are reduced, rental appears to make less sense. This is especially so for relatively simple appliances. For example, to rent a 32" screen LCD television in the UK costs over £400 per year, with a minimum contract of 17 months; the same set would cost less than £350 to buy and probably not require any maintenance. There are, however, companies providing television rental services to hotels, where the need for maintenance and repair may be significant. The strategy of outsourcing IT, meanwhile, can be seen as a form of rental, including such features as regular upgrades of equipment.

An interesting rental approach was taken by British Telecom (BT) in the mid-1990s when it had one of the largest commercial fleets of small vehicles in the UK. The company struck a deal with the supplier of engine oil whereby the oil was rented rather than bought, and returned to the supplier after a specified distance. The supplier reconditioned the oil for reuse. Similar systems are operated by suppliers of chemicals used in industrial cleaning equipment for high specification products.

Naturally lean

As we have seen, the twentieth-century drive for efficiency in production and services operations management can be traced back to Frederick Taylor's work at the close of the nineteenth century (labelled by Louis Brandeis as 'scientific management'). As a result, much of its dominant paradigm (Henry Ford's 'mass production') could be said to be efficient but perhaps unnatural for human beings in terms of working conditions. Even the serried ranks of mill workers in the industrial revolution, over a century before, were not separated and made to work in the isolated style of early mass-production lines.

The century of labour unrest perhaps reflected a rejection of the crude deskilling that was built into the paradigm from its origins in the nascent US industrial combine (where it was a necessary factor, see Chandler, 1964). A theme running through the just-in-time systems that developed in post-World War II Japan, much copied in the West, was a reversal of this – bringing operators closer together, encouraging their involvement in problem solving, and removing the wasteful inventory stacks and conveyor belts that typified mass production.

The removal of waste – or *muda* – that we saw in earlier chapters, is at the heart of lean thinking (Colin Chapman's 'lightness' – Chapter 5). Following this enables an operations manager to design, develop, run, and constantly improve more competitive and less resource-hungry production or service systems. As we saw in Chapter 5, one feature of the future that we can confidently predict is a constant drive to use less and less of every resource. As well as addressing the need for competitive cost reduction, as labour rates increase quickly with economic prosperity in developing countries (see the section on China, below), this approach also contains potential for sustainable operations, in terms of materials and resource usage, as we saw in Chapter 5.

Leanness is intrinsically linked to innovation. This includes incremental and radical forms (see Chapter 5) and, when it is shared between customers (or clients) and suppliers in supply chains, open innovation (Chapter 3 and Chapter 5).

Operations managers and strategists in the future, therefore, may be expected to face the need for constant process innovation, to seek ways of reducing resource usage – even further than has been achieved in the last two decades – to stay competitive and to create businesses that can be sustained. Part of this challenge will be internal to the organization – how operations are conducted, and financed. Part of it, however, will be external, requiring a global perspective that has so far only occurred in a limited form. Managers would undoubtedly say they already face these challenges; our response would be, expect an acceleration in the pace of change. However, as we saw in Chapter 5, if it leads to planned obsolescence and product churn, it will either be at odds with sustainability or require some different service paradigm.

Technology

Since its invention in 1975, the microprocessor and its derivatives have steadily changed manufacturing technology. The evolution of new applications shows every sign of continuing, perhaps exponentially (i.e. as one new application makes several others possible). The products that emerge from such manufacturing processes have themselves changed what is possible in service operations. Information technology, the platform for communications and data management, has changed both. The development of wireless technologies and the advent of nanotechnology, Internet protocol, and satellite-based communications, have made possible the global business world we recognize today. As we shall see below, this is very much a case of the future arriving in some places first – what is surprising is how quickly emerging economies catch up, and perhaps overtake, others. The technologies currently under development will clearly impact operations management, sometimes in ways that we cannot imagine.

For the operations manager, the specific applications and technologies available will depend upon their business – perhaps. The concept of technology transfer is well established and process innovation has always included applying an idea that works well elsewhere – perhaps in an entirely different sector – to one's own operations.

There is not space here to dwell on specific technologies but there are some good sources on knowledge to explore. For example, www.manufuture.org/manufacturing is full of great ideas and information on developments. In addressing this imperative – to be aware of emerging technologies – there is really no substitute for reading, browsing, and following the conference presentations in engineering and science – in addition, of course, to experimenting.

A GLOBAL FUTURE

The emerging geographic logic

In April 2011, the news media in the UK were excited to report that the British brand 'MG' was to reappear, with two new models, built in the south Birmingham 'Longbridge' plant, idle for five years since its closure after the collapse of the last British-owned car producer MG-Rover in 2005. (The brand, originally 'Morris Garages', was founded in 1924.)

The company, including the emotive sporting marque, MG, had been bought by the Chinese firm Nanjing, and later incorporated into the Shanghai Automotive Industry Corporation (SAIC). Six thousand jobs went in 2005; 400 were created in 2011. Before this, SAIC had already invested £5m in a design studio and technical centre at Longbridge and their designers and engineers had been working on the new models since the demise of Rover.

The important point for us is not to bemoan the demise of UK manufacturing but to note the fact that the two new models, while developed in Longbridge, were to be assembled from parts manufactured in China and shipped to the UK. The irony of this is that the strategy was the same as the one used by UK automotive manufacturers in building cars in developing countries some 50 years before. Vehicle component kits, known as CKD ('completely knocked down'), were shipped from the UK to parts of the world where skills were lacking, so that supervized operators could assemble products easily. The same activity was popular later in the electronics industry, where components would be shipped to low-labour-cost countries for assembly in so-called 'screwdriver plants'. Here we are seeing a strategy from the past that appears to be a part of the future, whenever a thriving country begins to work with an emerging – or possibly re-emerging – one.

As the new MG models were being readied, Japan suffered the horrific disaster of the Tohoku earthquake, the tsunami, and consequent nuclear calamity at Fukushima. One of the less immediate effects of this was that Japanese automotive assemblers in the UK suspended production, as parts made in Japan became unavailable. The published lists of parts affected naturally included only high value-added items – airflow sensors and electronic components, computerized engine-management systems, batteries, and petrol–electric hybrid engines. All three major Japanese car assemblers claim to source 80 to 90 per cent of their components for the UK plants within Europe.

CKD assembly, following the geographical logic of added value, leads to disaggregated production – components of systems produced anywhere in the world brought together anywhere else for assembly. It can be used for specific purposes: for example, Volkswagen's entry into Malaysia in 2010 employed CKD to gain local production status while avoiding the country's very high import tariffs on component supply, a tactic employed previous by Mercedes-Benz and BMW. The physical nature of this, and its risks, is already with us; it is the political dimension that needs to be considered for the future. The information technology that allows this to happen has been around for some time.

In his 2001 book, *The New Barbarian Manifesto: How to Survive the Information Age*, Ian Angell predicted that advances in technology and transportation would soon mean that countries would have major problems in finding work for their 'unemployed and unemployable citizens'. One of the effects of this, Angell claimed, would be that countries would seek to attract companies to set up operations in their territories by offering inducements such as tax holidays and infrastructural investments (such as secure and fully serviced gated residential areas for employees, appropriate catering, etc.) These 'barbarian' companies (the term is not necessarily pejorative, having been coined by the Greeks to mean anyone who was not Greek; Angell takes his cue from Nietzsche's use of the term) would move from location to location as better inducements were offered. Initially, one could see this applying to headquarters and other office functions – easily relocated quickly as economic (or political) situations change. Increasingly, however, it seems production and other less mobile facilities may need to be treated in this way – see the case of China, below.

Angell's manifesto is daunting – as he says, it 'foretells an age of doom and gloom for the many [and] a message of salvation for the few'. SAIC did not choose to build an unremarkable small car at Longbridge because of low labour rates in the UK; they realized the potential benefits of resurrecting a romantic automotive brand in its home country with unemployment at a 17-year high (9 per cent nationally and almost 10 per cent in the West Midlands – the second highest in the country), and forming an English-speaking bridgehead in Europe – just as the Americans did a century earlier, and the Japanese in the 1980s. For the 400 or so new workers, this may indeed be seen as salvation.

China

Intra-regional developments

If we can assume that competition in future will have little regard for the geographical logic of the past (i.e. national boundaries, free-trade areas, logistics costs, and perhaps even labour rates) then we need to know what to expect as each new player emerges in order to plan investments in operations, and think through ways of working. For example, how long can low labour-rates support a new competitor before social pressures occlude them and new predators emerge?

China provides an excellent case for us to explore in order to understand how regions form and change in economic development (to borrow Gibson's aphorism, 'major parts of the future have already arrived'). This might give us some idea of possible developments in the future elsewhere. China is the latest country to go through the familiar pattern of economic growth based on low labour-costs, followed by increases in those costs, skills shortages, increased consumption, and strengthened currency. This has happened in smaller countries (Singapore, Hong Kong) and also to bigger players, such as Malaysia and Japan. Each of these, very different, Asian territories has experienced difficulties along the way but remains a successful world player. The question is whether China can do the same, bearing in mind the pros and cons of its massive scale and its centrally-planned economy.

As great amounts of foreign direct investment flowed into China from 1980 onwards the east coast of the country saw significant development and growth. The principal incentive for this were low labour costs, the potential for in-country demand for products (with a population of 1.3 billion, expected to become more affluent) and a base from which foreign firms could supply to the other developing countries in Asia. Few Westerners understood China, however, and there were some famous failures (see Studwell, 2002 for an excellent history of the development of modern China).

Chinese labour rates began to grow, and they continued to do so in the first decade of this century (a rise of 70 per cent between 2004 and 2009). See Figure 12.2.

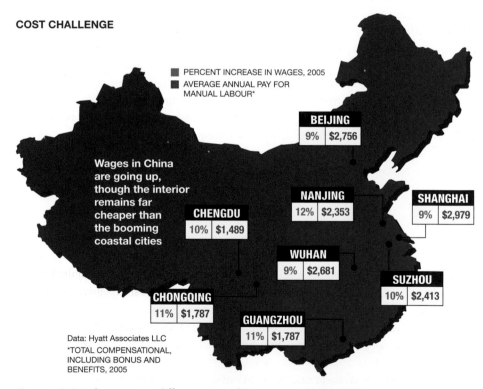

COST CHALLENGE

PERCENT INCREASE IN WAGES, 2005
AVERAGE ANNUAL PAY FOR MANUAL LABOUR*

Wages in China are going up, though the interior remains far cheaper than the booming coastal cities

BEIJING 9% $2,756

NANJING 12% $2,353

SHANGHAI 9% $2,979

CHENGDU 10% $1,489

WUHAN 9% $2,681

SUZHOU 10% $2,413

CHONGQING 11% $1,787

GUANGZHOU 11% $1,787

Data: Hyatt Associates LLC
*TOTAL COMPENSATIONAL, INCLUDING BONUS AND BENEFITS, 2005

Figure 12.2 Labour costs: differences and increases, 2005–2006
Businessweek, 27 March 2006, www.businessweek.com/magazine/content/06_13/b3977049.htm

Table 12.1 Labour costs in Asia

Country	Wage Overheads in Emerging Asia		
	Avg. minimum annual salary (worker, Intl. dollar)	Avg. mandatory welfare (% against salary)	Total labour cost (Intl. dollar)
Bangladesh	798	n/a	798
Cambodia	672	n/a	672
China	1,500	50	2,250
India	857	10	943
Indonesia	1,027	6	1,089
Laos	1,057	9.5	1,157
Malaysia	4,735	23	5,284
Mongolia	2,004	n/a	2,004
Myanmar	401	n/a	401
Nepal	1,889	n/a	1,889
Pakistan	984	7	1,052
Philippines	2,053	9.4	2,246
Sri Lanka	1,619	n/a	1,619
Thailand	2,293	6.9	2,451
Vietnam	1,002	15	1,152

See http://forums.imf.org/showthread.php?t+125 for a simple explanation. The International Dollar is the IMF Purchasing Power Parity (PPP) unit.
China Briefing January 2011/IMF World Economic Outlook Database, October 2010

The boom led to an increase in the working population, from 764 million in 2006 to 780 million in 2009, with manufacturing employment growing from 98 million in 2007 to 99 million in 2008. Higher wages bring higher consumption: average annual disposable incomes increased by 10.2 per cent annually during this period (Credit Suisse 2010/2011).

The increases were significantly affected by regulations in 2008, which introduced a minimum wage and a 'welfare' charge – a percentage that employers were required to add to the salary. This led to China's labour becoming amongst the most expensive in Asia (see Table 12.1).

It is expected that China's next five-year plan will see mechanisms put in place to double these salaries by 2015, to boost domestic consumption and reduce the reliance on exports as the currency hardens. Some estimates are that this will raise the typical worker's salary to US$3,000, plus 50 per cent welfare charge – a total minimum salary of US$4,500. Skilled workers' salaries will be far higher, making China's average labour costs second only to Malaysia in East Asia (*China Briefing*, 2011). At the world's largest contract electronics manufacturer, Shenzen-based Foxconn, salaries for migrant workers, the mainstay of the company's China workforce, rose 30 to 40 per cent in 2010 and were expected to increase by another 20 to 30 per cent annually until at least 2013 (Credit Suisse, 2011).

With the increase in wage costs comes a reduction in price competitiveness, perhaps moderated through process innovation. This means the near future might see the relocation of manufacturing of lower added-value products from China to elsewhere. Typically these will be low labour-cost countries (see note on China's investment in Africa, below) but there may also be more of the CKD activity we saw at MG, above: retention of the higher technology products for home producers accompanied by low added-value activities conducted remotely (note that Sweden's Volvo Cars was bought in 2010 by the Chinese low-end high-volume automotive company, Geely, based in Hangzhou, with support from the Chinese government).

In China's case, this development has been accompanied by a growing shortage of skilled workers. This is being addressed through the development of higher education – China now has more graduates employed than any other country (6.4 million in 2010) and twice the number in the US. Learning English is now compulsory in schools (in 2010 around 10 million Chinese people spoke English: less than 1 per cent of the population).

Other resultant factors include inflation (at 6.5 per cent p.a. in July 2011, having risen steadily since it was zero in 2009) – expected to fuel demands for further increased wages in the increasingly affluent East, and a strengthening currency, making imports more affordable.

So, the intra-regional geography may be expected to include the move of manufacturing (by foreign and Chinese producers) from China to other Asian countries (perhaps Thailand, Vietnam, the Philippines, etc.) but also to other parts of the world – for example to Mexico, with low-cost labour, stable political economy, and membership of the North American Free Trade Agreement, or even to 'old world' activity, such as at the MG plant or Volvo.

In-country developments

The growing affluence in the East of China has already led to an in-country geographical dislocation – labour costs are significantly lower in central and western China. See Table 12.2.

In 2006, this factor, coupled with lower costs of land in such regions (Table 12.3) spurred the Chinese government to launch a 'Go Inland' campaign to encourage the spread of employment into the provinces and rural areas (for an interesting explanation of this and related factors, see www.smartchinasourcing.com/china-competitiveness/operational-costs-of-business-in-chinas-inland-c.html).

This may lead to foreign direct investment drying up in eastern China in the near future, with existing activities being relocated, and a slowing of the demographic shift that has seen people move from rural to urban areas in large numbers for over 20 years. Foxconn (whose products include Apple, Nokia, Sony, Dell, and H-P) is said to be moving 200,000 production jobs from its plants in Shenzhen (just inland from Hong Kong), to new inland sites including Chengdu, Chongqui, Zhenzhou, and one in Vietnam (*Financial Times*, 2011a; 2011b; *Industry Week*, 2011). There is a downside to such a move, however: it can raise shipping costs for exporters who decide to move hundreds of miles from China's eastern ports (Chengdu is over 2,000 km from Shanghai and Shenzhen). See Table 12.4.

Table 12.2 Differential labour rates and welfare contribution: East China versus Central areas

Minimum Salary (RMB per employee per month)			Minimum Employer Welfare Contribution (% of monthly salary per employee per month)			
				City	Low	High
1st Tier Cities (East, South)	Guangzhou	1,300	1st Tier Cities (East, South)	Guangzhou	33.45	48.45
	Beijing	1,160		Beijing	44.30	44.30
	Shanghai	1,120		Shanghai	44.00	44.00
	Shenzhen	1,100		Shenzhen	30.60	30.60
2nd Tier Cities (East)	Ningbo	1,100	2nd Tier Cities (East)	Nanjing	40.00	44.00
	Nanjing	960		Hangzhou	37.00	41.00
	Hangzhou	960		Ningbo	33.00	40.00
2nd Tier Inland Cities	Wuhan	900	2nd Tier Inland Cities	Wuhan	37.70	41.70
	Chongqing	870		Chongqing	31.00	39.00
	Taiyuan	850		Taiyuan	39.45	39.45
	Changsha	850		Changsha	35.10	42.10
	Chengdu	850		Chengdu	35.72	41.72
	Zhengzhou	800		Zhengzhou	40.50	42.5
	Lanzhou	760				
	Xi'an	760				
	Hefei	720		Hefei	35.2	50.2
	Nanchang	720		Nanchang	37.2	41.2

Source: China Briefing 7 March 2011

Source: Analysis & Compilation of Social Insurance Policy & Legal Benefits of China, 2010 Edition, Expo Group, Shanghai Foreign Service Co. Ltd.

Table 12.3 Differential factory rental costs: East China versus Central areas

Standard Factory Rental Cost, Q4 2010 Southern east coast cities versus inland cities (RMB per square meter per month)

1st Tier Cities (East, South)	Guangzhou	19.4
	Shanghai	24.7
	Shenzhen	26.9
2nd Tier Cities (East)	Nanjing	11.7
	Hangzhou	11.9
	Ningbo	12.2
2nd Tier Inland Cities	Wuhan	13.3
	Chongqing	12.8
	Chengdu	13.6
	Xi'an	15.8

Sources: CBRE; China Briefing

Table 12.4 Differential transportation costs: East China versus Central areas

Transportation Costs, Rail to Nearby Port (RMB/standard container)

	Origin	To Shanghai	To Shenzhen	Lowest Cost
2nd Tier Cities (East)	Nanjing	2,900		2,900
	Hangzhou	2,600		2,600
	Ningbo	3,000		3,000
2nd Tier Inland Cities	Wuhan	3,198	4,650	3,198
	Chongqing	6,200	6,090	6,090
	Taiyuan	5,017	7,030	5,017
	Changsha	4,332	3,825	3,825
	Chengdu	6,518	7,262	6,518
	Zhengzhou	3,917	5,868	3,917
	Hefei	2,874	4,643	2,874
	Nanchang	3,570	3,570	3,570

Source: Shanghai Shengchang Logistics Co.

We can expect China to take the traditional path in the near future – moving up the value-adding chain, with higher skilled, better educated workers producing higher specification products (R&D expenditure and investments in higher education have been increasing for some time) while component production and lower value-adding operations are 'off-shored' (see Chapter 3). As China buys foreign brands, the MG model may be repeated, keeping the international networks healthy and the control of technology at home. This model has been used for over a century (first by imperial Europe and then by the mass-production-oriented US and most recently by 'Japan Inc.') – it is simply China's turn. Early Chinese players included the white-goods producer Haier which is headquartered in Qingdao but has run operating facilities in the Philippines, Indonesia, and Malaysia since the mid-1990s. We should expect to see aggressive acquisition strategies: in 2005, Haier was narrowly beaten by Whirlpool in a bid to buy white goods giant Maytag in the US.

In August 2011 Terry Gou, Chairman and CEO of Foxconn, announced plans to increase the company's robot population from 10,000 to 300,000 by 2013 (compared with an established workforce of around 1 million). He said he wanted to cut rising labour costs and improve efficiency by using the machines for simple and routine tasks such as spraying, welding, and assembling, moving his employees 'higher up the value chain beyond basic manufacturing work'. In a subsequent company statement Mr Gou added that the move towards automation was aimed at shifting 'workers from more routine tasks to more value-added positions in manufacturing such as research and development, innovation and other areas that are equally important to the success of our operations' (Xinhua, 2011; *Financial Times*, 2011c).

The advantage that China has in this expansion is a massive domestic market: 'China Inc.' can turn its attention inwards when it needs to, for economic balancing (reducing reliance on exports and demand for imports).

India

Five thousand kilometres west of Shanghai, the world's other giant, India, is going through very similar development and again it has the benefit of an underdeveloped home market, perhaps tempered with more significant social problems (half the population lives in poverty). Consumption in India is still low: 0.51 planets in 2007, while China increased from 1.00 planets to 1.24 between 2005 and 2007 (WWF, 2010; see Chapter 5). The world's largest democracy struggles with its climate but has built impressive modern infrastructure in the last few years – especially airports. And again, its industrial combines are strong, with Tata owning several UK companies, including Jaguar, Landrover and Aston Martin, as well as producing its own extraordinary, home-grown 'Nano' – famously on sale in India for 'one Lakh' or 100,000 Rupees (about €1,500). The two-cylinder 624 cc Nano, with claimed CO_2e emissions of 101 g/km (see Case 5.4) is a great example of the sort of competition that is on the way. What is to stop Tata exporting the small car to markets where it would sell for perhaps 20 per cent of the price of its competitors' offerings? And what would be the impact on the components suppliers and retailers serving those competitors?

We can expect developments in India to be similar to those we have observed in China in the near future. Perhaps the global networking will be similar (both have long histories in this respect). Given their different political structures, it will be interesting to see whether (and how quickly) the internal factors we have seen in China are replicated in India.

BRINGING IT TOGETHER: IMPLICATIONS FOR OPERATIONS MANAGERS

These trends clearly contain some major new challenges for operations managers.

Skills

In addition to the skills and knowledge required to run a successful operation, in the future those responsible for production and the delivery of services will need an awareness and familiarity with external factors that has not previously been expected of them. These include geography, foreign political and economic developments, and the externalities of logistics and demographics. These weighty subjects have been handled by specialists in some organizations for many years – and operations managers will always need to rely on such colleagues. However, the new geographic logic will pose complex and perhaps novel choices for location of facilities, planning production costs, and sourcing of components and materials – issues for operations strategy. This will need an information system that informs operations strategists and managers, on a timely basis, of developments and forecasts that may affect their decisions. For some, perhaps especially in large organizations, this may not be new. Its increased importance and rate of change, however, will be key for all.

Coping with innovation, sustainability and product churn

We saw the concept of 'product churn' earlier and in Chapter 5, where it was characterized as a problem for sustainability. The pressure on consumers to buy a new product and dispose of the old one (or perhaps recycle it) has brought problems for operations management; new designs and products are presented by development departments just when operations managers had the system stabilized for the current version, and so on. The increase in pressure to be competitive and lean in use of resources will mean that process innovation (including matters relating to the physical location of facilities and sources of supply) may experience 'churn'. For operations managers, this would mean constantly changing (rather than just tuning) their systems, sometimes to the extent of radical changes in ways of working and managing. Once again, this future has already arrived for some operations managers but we can expect the pace of change to surprise everyone. Other pressures such as increased scarcity of resources or energy costs may militate against product churn, or perhaps increase the introduction of remanufacture and recycling.

Nine billion one-planet lifestyles

It is generally agreed that Earth's human population will reach 9 billion in the next 30 years or so. The implications of this can be addressed from several standpoints. As Alan Knight points out, the challenge for mankind is to produce a decent lifestyle for everyone on Earth, and one that can be sustained. This means working and living at close to the one-planet level in each region (see Chapter 5). For those countries above the three-planets consumption level (20 countries in 2007, including the usual suspects but also some surprises in most parts of the world) or perhaps even above two planets (a further 20), this will surely be a painful process and one that cannot be addressed through belt tightening (see Figure 12.3). The increased appetite for consumption shows us that the new members of the African and Asian populations will want to have all that the West has built up: but it has to be produced in entirely different ways and in new locations.

No direction 'home'

European operations managers have been going abroad to live and work for centuries. North Americans did likewise in the twentieth century and the Japanese for the last three decades. Now it is the turn of the Chinese. In addition to European specifics such as Volvo and MG, Chinese general overseas investment is massive. In Africa, for example, estimates vary between $80 and $100 billion so far (Schiere and Rugamba, 2011).

For the countries receiving such Chinese ex-patriots, the agenda is complex. In the 1980s, the UK press (and academia) was awash with stories of British workers adapting to Japanese ways as firms such as Nissan, Honda, Toyota, Sony, and Panasonic built plants there. (The American influx 70 years earlier could be said to have begun the influence of the US on Europe that still exists.) Western managers will clearly need to understand the Confucian concepts of *ying* and *yang*, so firmly built into the Chinese commercial custom of *Guanxi*, just as Europeans had to understand American production ideas half a century

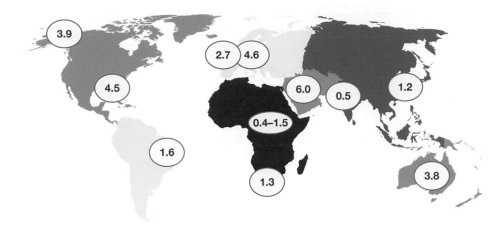

Figure 12.3
Some examples of national consumption levels. Developed from the WWF (2010) 2008 data: the figures indicate the number of planets that would be required if the human race consumed at the national rate.

before. It will be interesting to see whether social trends will follow, in the way that jazz, rock 'n' roll and the bikini did!

All this was foreseen, of course, by the visionary Kenichi Ohmae in his 1995 book *The End of the Nation State: The Rise of Regional Economies*. The macro issues addressed by Ohmae are now the day-to-day realities for operations managers, and the implications they bear may be expected to increase.

Whether you consider this picture of the future an opportunity or a problem – a glass half full or half empty – will depend upon your view of life and possibly the stage you are at in your career. Other future trends should be considered too – we have not touched on technology here, for example, and the profound implications of cultural adaptation – and the tendency of the human race to self-destruct periodically should never be underestimated (although as we have seen many times, warfare is often paradoxically beneficial for operations management and innovation).

We can end on the positive observation that people will always want things – products and services – provided to and for them, and this will require strategists and managers to work out how to do it. The task will become more complex and tougher but it will always represent a noble engagement and a satisfying activity.

SUMMARY

In the future, we may expect:

- Organizations to face the need to satisfy customer demands without a 'steady state' operating system, at the same time as embracing new technologies and gearing up for new market offerings (the promises of their marketing colleagues) which may need to be produced in entirely different ways, in different locations, and at dramatically lower cost.

- The drive for leanness to continue, both for competitiveness in cost terms but also for constant reductions in resources usage and waste.
- Sustainability, especially in the context of carbon emissions and increasingly scarce resources, to grow as a strategic driver.
- A new geographic logic: operations managers may not be able to identify any specific territory as exclusively 'home'.
- Process innovation in 'churn'. Constant need to tune and change operations technology and ways of working.
- Operations managers with much broader skill-sets, including knowledge and awareness of global geography, understanding of cultural differences, and economic and political trends.
- 'The future' to continue to arrive in some parts of the world earlier than in others.

KEY QUESTIONS

1. What new skills need to be developed in operations managers for the future and what are the implications for human resources strategies?
2. How might the regional economies of the world change in the next ten years and what are the implications for operations managers?
3. How might 'churn' in process innovation differ in its implications from product churn?
4. Is the answer to the future challenges increased globalization or networked individual national entities?
5. With which other organizational functions must operations management work to address future challenges, and in what ways?

FURTHER READING

Angell, I.O. (2001) *The New Barbarian Manifesto: How to Survive the Information Age*, London: Kogan Page.

Diamond, J. (2005) *Collapse: How Societies Choose to Fail or Survive*, London: Penguin.

Forum for the Future, www.forumforthefuture.org

Gladwell, M. (2000) *The Tipping Point: How Little Things Can Make a Big Difference*, London: Abacus Books.

Knight, A., www.singleplanetliving.com

Natural Step, www.naturalstep.org

Ohmae, K. (1995) *The End of the Nation State: The Rise of Regional Economies*, New York: McKinsey and Co. (Paperback edition, 1996, New York: Free Press).

Sachs, J.D. (2008) *Commonwealth: Economics for a Crowded Planet*, London: Penguin.

REFERENCES

Angell, I.O. (2001) *The New Barbarian Manifesto: How to Survive the Information Age*, London: Kogan Page.

Chandler, A. (Ed.) (1964) *Giant Enterprise: Ford, General Motors and the Automobile Industry*, New York: Harcourt Brace and World.

China Briefing (2011) www.china-briefing.com/en/

Credit Suisse (2010/2011) *Credit Suisse Economics Research*, New York: US Economics Digest, www.credit-suisse.com/researchandanalytics

Diamond, J. (2005) *Collapse: How Societies Choose to Fail or Survive*, London: Penguin.

Financial Times (2011a) 'China's computer makers march inland', 23 May 2011, www.ft.com/cms/s/2/433041d0–8568–11e0–ae32–00144feabdc0.html#axzz20nqwsAlm

Financial Times (2011b) 'China labour costs push jobs back to US', 6 October 2011, www.ft.com/cms/s/0/e5b774ca-f037–11e0–96d2–00144feab49a.html#axzz20nqwsAlm

Financial Times (2011c) 'Foxconn looks to a robotic future', 1 August 2011, www.ft.com/cms/s/2/e5d9866e-bc25–11e0–80e0–00144feabdc0.html#axzz20nqwsAlm

Gibson, W. (1999) 'Talk of the Nation', interview with *NPR*, 30 November 1999: 'The Science in Science Fiction'.

Gladwell, M. (2000) *The Tipping Point: How Little Things Can Make a Big Difference*, London: Abacus Books.

Gray, C. and Charter, M. (2006) *Remanufacturing and Product Design: Designing for the 7th Generation*, The Centre for Sustainable Design, University College for the Creative Arts, Farnham, UK, www.cfsd.org.uk/Remanufacturing per cent20and per cent20Product per cent20Design.pdf

Griffin, A. and Hauser, J (1993) 'The voice of the customer', *Marketing Science*, 12(1), 1–27.

Industry Week (2011) 'China tops U.S. in manufacturing', 14 March 14 2011, www.industryweek.com/articles

Knight, A., www.singleplanetliving.com

Ohmae, K. (1995) *The End of the Nation State: The Rise of Regional Economies*, New York: McKinsey and Co. (Paperback edition, 1996, New York: Free Press).

Sachs, J.D. (2008) *Commonwealth: Economics for a Crowded Planet*, London: Penguin.

Schiere, R. and Rugamba, A. (2011) *Chinese Infrastructure Investments and African Integration*, African Development Bank Working Paper Series No. 127, May 2011, www.afdb.org/fileadmin/uploads/afdb/Documents/Publications/WPS%20No%20127%20Chinese%20Infrastructure%20Investments%20.pdf

Schmenner, R.W and Tatikonda, M.V. (2005) 'Manufacturing process flexibility revisited', *International Journal of Operations and Production Management*, 25(12), 1183–9.

Studwell, J. (2002) *The China Dream: The Quest for the Last Great Untapped Market on Earth*, New York: Atlantic Monthly Press.

WWF (2010) *Living Planet Report 2012: Biodiversity, Biocapacity and Development*, Gland, Switzerland: WWF International, www.panda.org

Xinhua (2011) 'Foxconn to replace workers with 1 million robots in 3 years', 30 July 2011, http://news.xinhuanet.com/english2010/china/2011–07/30/c_131018764.htm

INDEX